The Art of Society
1900 – 1945

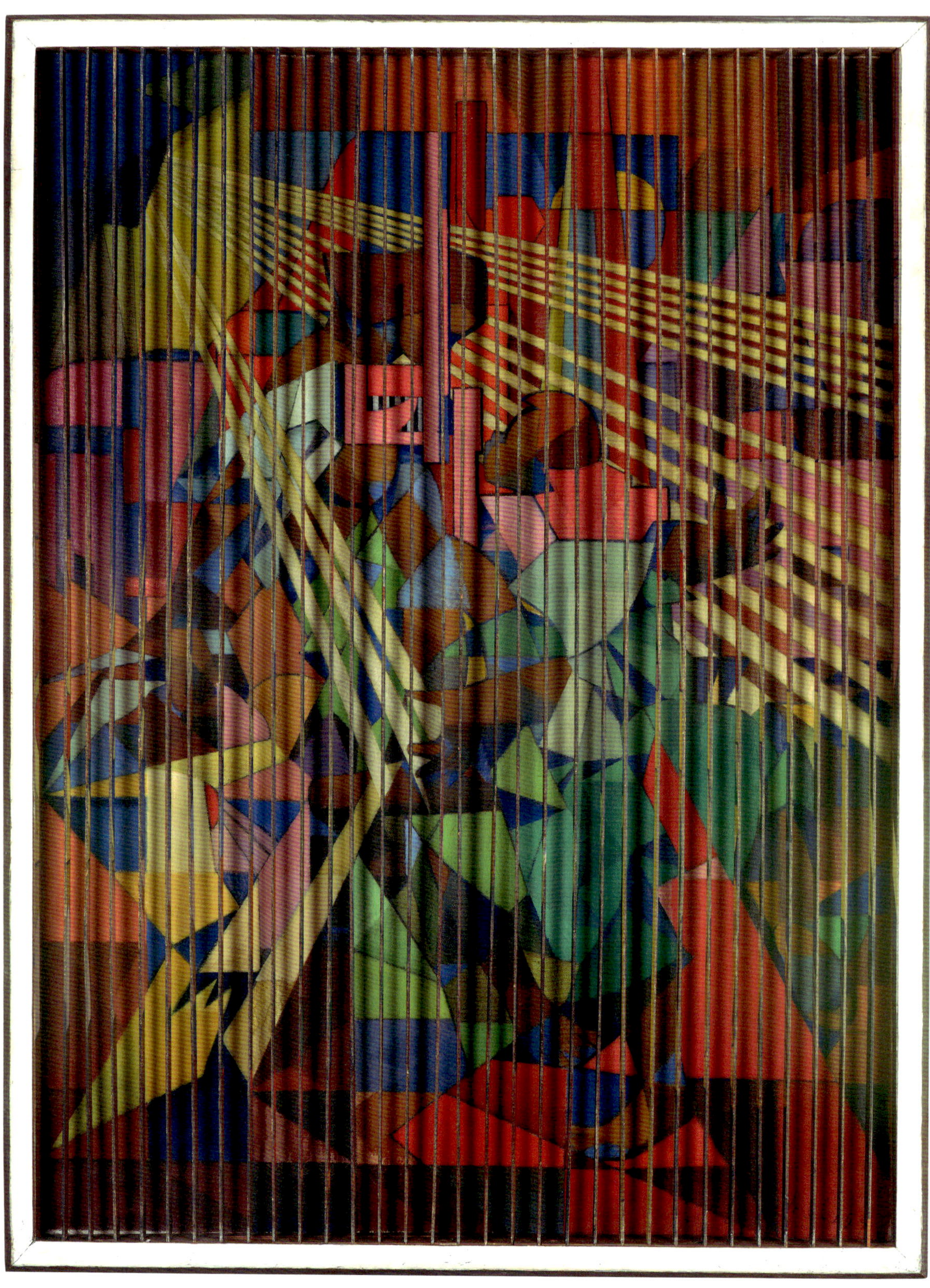

Moriz Melzer, *Blessing*, 1917/1922
Oil on wood, 136 × 103 cm
Gift to the Nationalgalerie, Berlin (West) from Kurt Reutti, Berlin, from the estate of the artist, 1966

The Art of Society 1900–1945

The Nationalgalerie Collection

For the Nationalgalerie, Staatliche Museen zu Berlin,
edited by Dieter Scholz, Irina Hiebert Grun and Joachim Jäger

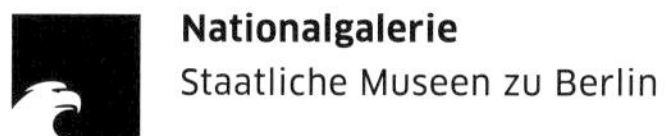

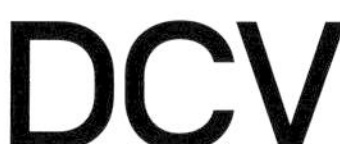

Contents

Foreword **6**

The Art of Society **9**

Life and Reform **22**
Longing for What? 28
Images from the Modern Psyche: Edvard Munch's Frieze 34

Freedom of Expression **40**
Who Were the Female Models for the Brücke Artists? 46
Rosa Schapire, More Than a "Passive" Brücke Member 56
How Is the Brücke Connected to Germany's Colonial History? 60

Slivers of the City **66**
What Is "Modernity"? 70
At the Centre of the Metropolis: Potsdamer Platz 82
Ernst Ludwig Kirchner and Max Liebermann 88
Hannah Höch's Epochal Image of the Weimar Republic 94

The Powers of Der Sturm **100**
Rediscovered Identity: Erich Mühsam 106
Women Artists at the Sturm Gallery 110

Trauma and Destruction **118**
Where Did the First World War Take Place? 124
Who Were the *Pillars of Society*? 130

Politics and Propaganda **136**
Heinrich Vogeler Produced a New Form: The *Komplexbild* 140
Women in Need. The Struggle to Legalize Abortion 148

Modes of Abstraction **152**
Creativity and Child's Play at the Bauhaus 156
Envoy of the Metaphysical: Hilma af Klint 170

The Architecture of Progress **174**
A Railway Station with Three Bridges: Social Analysis in Painting 178
The Great Metaphysician – What's Wrong with It? 182

Dream Worlds **186**
"Oscillation" and "Action Painting" 194
The Nonconformist Surrealist Leonor Fini 200

Sharp Looks **206**
The New Feminine Self-Image 220
Who Is *Sonja*? 224

Exile **230**
What Is “Degenerate Art”? 234
A Discomforting Portrait by Max Beckmann 240

Faces of the Day **244**
The Sculptor Renée Sintenis 248
Sculpture and the Human Being: *Prometheus* and *Zwitter* 254

War and Annihilation **258**
Alice Lex-Nerlinger: *Field-Grey Yields Dividends* 262
Why Are Paintings Altered Retroactively? 270

Selected Bibliography **278**
List of Names **282**
Photo Credits and Copyrights **284**
Acknowledgements **286**
Imprint **288**

Foreword

The presentation of the collection to mark the reopening of the Neue Nationalgalerie is titled *The Art of Society* to point out the museum holdings' close association with contemporaneous events. Berlin has always been at the centre of Germany's political and historical affairs, which explains the collection's strong focus on social processes. Going beyond a mere history of aesthetics, the works from the period 1900 to 1945 impressively illustrate the connection between art and society. The paintings and sculptures mirror the German Empire, colonial history, the First World War, the Weimar Republic's "Golden Twenties", and the ostracism of the avant-garde under National Socialism, as well as the effects of the Second World War and the Holocaust. With the partition of Germany, the collection was divided, subsequently being shaped under two competing political systems until 1990. Only since reunification has it been possible to view the works with their divergent perspectives on art and society together – and solely in Berlin in this constellation.

The exhibition does not trace a linear chronology of art movements in the first half of the 20th century. Instead, it seeks to emphasize the simulaneity between various avant-garde tendencies. The open floor plan of Mies van der Rohe's architecture does not prescribe a fixed course through the exhibition, offering visitors a variety of perspectives on the erratic transition of art styles, including Expressionism, Cubism, Surrealism, Dada and New Objectivity. The exhibition sections focus on social themes, such as the big city, the German *Lebensreform* (life and reform) movement, politics and propaganda, exile, and war.

Embedded historically in the respective social conditions, the collection, however, also has its limitations. Its national and Eurocentric profile has resulted in holdings stemming primarily from Germany and created mainly by men. This composition has inevitably produced a narrower view of society. To provide a critical impetus addressing these gaps, works by internationally active women artists have been included via loans: Hilma af Klint from Sweden, Irma Stern from South Africa, Nadezhda Udaltsova from Russia and Tarsila do Amaral from Brazil.

The exhibition queries and discusses images of society prevailing at the collection's time of origin and draws an arc to the present day. Who is part of a society and who is not? These questions underlie the exhibition's didactic objectives, with a special space dedicated to this topic located in its midst. Its intention is to open new perceptions on art and society. Experts on post-colonialism and feminism have been invited to comment on individual works in the Nationalgalerie collection presentation.

Two film projection spaces integrated into the exhibition provide a contemporary critique of modernism. Julian Rosefeldt's *Deep Gold* (2013–14) immerses visitors in the intoxicating atmosphere of nightclubs in 1920s Berlin, while Javier Téllez's 2011 film, *Rotations (Prometheus and Zwitter)* explores the role of outsider art and its instrumentalization by the National Socialist regime.

In addition to major works from the collection, the exhibition also features rarely displayed art, including Wilhelm Lembruck's *Torso der Knienden* (1911–13, *Kneeling Woman*). Severely damaged in 1989, the sculpture is being shown for the first time following a complicated restoration funded by the Hermann Reemtsma Stiftung and carried out by Wolfgang Maßmann and Nina Wegel. Two spectacular new acquisitions also enhance the collection: Auguste Herbin's *Porträt Erich Mühsam* (1907, Portrait of Erich Mühsam), initially on permanent loan, and Sascha Wiederhold's painting *Bogenschützen* (1928, Archers), purchased with funds provided by the Ernst von Siemens Kunststiftung. Surrealist works from the Ulla and Heiner Pietzsch Collection, which have been on permanent loan to the Nationalgalerie since 2010, represent a significant enrichment. The exhibition testifies once again to the generous support of the collector couple, who have enjoyed close ties with the Nationalgalerie for decades.

Our special thanks go to all lenders who have supported this exhibition. We would like to mention the international institutions that through loans of their works have made it possible to furnish examples of global interrelationships: especially the Pinacoteca do Estado de São Paulo, the Hilma af Klint Foundation, the Irma Stern Trust Collection and the Tretyakov Gallery. We express our thanks to Maike Steinkamp, who advanced our curatorial work with valuable suggestions. Judith Boegner and Veronika Deinzel, in collaboration with Jessica Aimufua and Josephine Apraku, designed the outreach space and its associated tools, thus broadening our view of society through polyphony. We extend our gratitude to exhibition coordinator Katharina Wippermann and conservators Hana Streicher, Ina Hausmann and Ella Dudew, who contributed significantly to the success of the exhibition project. Holzer Kobler Architekten and 2xGoldstein, in collaboration with David Chipperfield Architects, have designed the exhibition architecture and graphics that allow the newly restored spaces of the Mies architecture to sustain their aesthetic. We owe our appreciation to Moira Barrett, James Bell and Wendy Wallis for their careful translations into English. Johanna Yeats took on the image editing, for which we sincerely thank her. We are indebted to graphic designer Felix Walser of the Book Book studio for the exceptional look of this catalogue, whose publishing by the DCV Verlag, headed by Uta Grosenick, has been based on an excellent partnership.

Joachim Jäger, Irina Hiebert Grun, Dieter Scholz

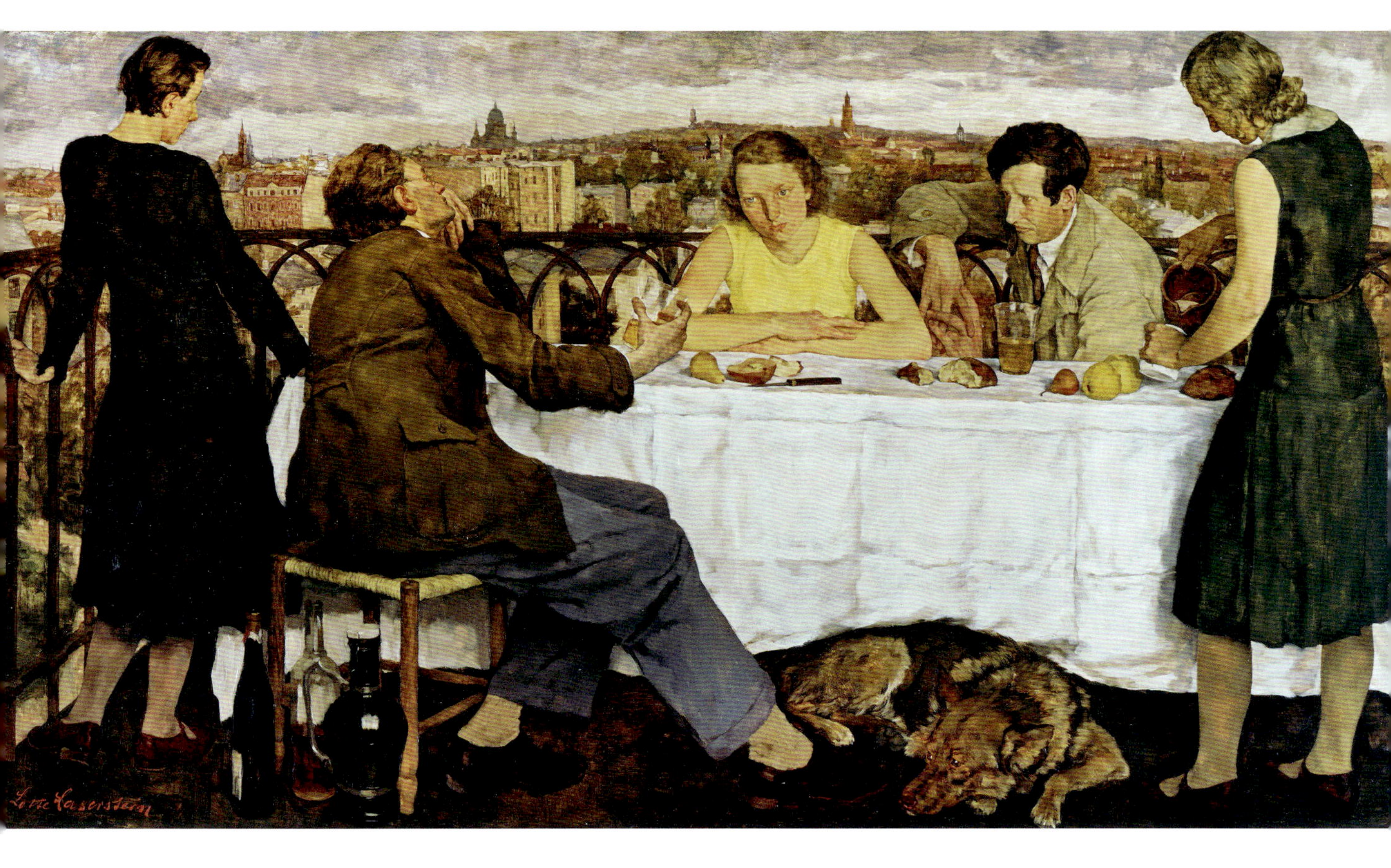

Lotte Laserstein, *Evening Over Potsdam,* 1930
Oil on canvas, 110 × 205 cm
Acquired in 2010 from a private collection, Great Britain, with support from the Bundesrepublik Deutschland, the Stiftung Deutsche Klassenlotterie Berlin, the Kulturstiftung der Länder, the Ernst von Siemens Kunststiftung and others

The Art of Society

Dieter Scholz

The Neue Nationalgalerie's presentation of its collection, with works from 1900 to 1945, focuses on *Die Kunst der Gesellschaft* (The Art of Society). Societal issues played a pivotal role in this period encompassing the German Empire and its colonies, colonial genocide, the Weimar Republic, National Socialism, two world wars and the civilizational rupture of the Holocaust. A striking number of the works at the Nationalgalerie reveal a connection to these issues.

The exhibition and catalogue explore the interplay between art and society during this period in 13 sections. Two paintings by Lotte Laserstein and Sascha Wiederhold form the prelude. They were created almost concurrently, yet they represent two different options for art. The large-format painting *Abend über Potsdam* (Evening Over Potsdam, fig. p. 8) from 1930 is considered to be Lotte Laserstein's magnum opus. She was one of the first women to study at the Berlin Academy of Arts, where she was awarded a gold medal in 1925. She had her first solo exhibition in 1930 at the renowned Galerie Gurlitt in Berlin.

Laserstein's work has only begun to be appreciated again in recent years. Her long obscurity had in part to do with the struggle for visibility that women are still waging.[1] Women were long denied access to art academies, even if this no longer applied to Laserstein. Women artists have been and continue to be underrepresented. The proportion of their works remains low in the Nationalgalerie as well. This state of affairs, however, was not the only reason for decades of oblivion in Laserstein's case. Her realistic style was overshadowed by the artistic avant-gardes. The painting *Abend über Potsdam,* like the painter's other works, is indebted to a realism that runs as a common thread through modern art alongside these avant-gardes but has received considerably less attention. Although Laserstein's work undoubtedly evokes atmospheric echoes of the New Objectivity movement, her painting style is neither objectifyingly cool nor markedly socially critical.

Laserstein's *Abend über Potsdam* is, to some extent, a counterproposal to a mural by Anton von Werner, a history painter of the German Empire. His work was painted in 1899 for the dining room of newspaper publisher Rudolf Mosse's villa on Leipziger Platz in Berlin. *Das Gastmahl der Familie Mosse* (The Mosse Family Banquet, fig. p. 11) depicts a lively repast against a rural backdrop. The family and their circle of friends are costumed in the style of 16th and 17th century Spanish and Dutch fashions. The painter draws on imagery familiar in Old Masters' paintings. When compared with Anton von Werner's historicist pomp, the modernism of Lotte Laserstein's work becomes particularly apparent.

The clear readability of Laserstein's image makes it tempting to attribute it the immediacy of a photographic snapshot. However, her representation of reality is carefully constructed while also exhibiting art historical references. The set table with its white tablecloth, rendered parallel to the picture plane, inevitably recalls Leonardo da Vinci's famous portrayal of *The Last Supper*, located in the refectory of the Dominican Church of Santa Maria delle Grazie in Milan (1494–98). In that depiction, Jesus is shown at the centre of the gathering.

Laserstein has radically secularized the scene, placing a young woman in Jesus' position. In addition, this woman is wearing a yellow dress. Judas, who betrayed Jesus for money, is often traditionally portrayed in art in a yellow robe (although not in Leonardo's fresco). Furthermore, Jews in many countries and regions of Europe have since the Middle Ages repeatedly been obliged to wear a particularly shaped yellow cloth badge prominently on their chests. The National Socialists picked up on that practice, instituting the compulsory identifying symbol of the stigmatizing yellow Star of David in 1941. This ostracizing measure initiated the everyday persecution, deportation and systematic murder of some six million people at concentration and extermination camps.

It is not known whether Laserstein consciously chose the colour. The yellow could also supplant the sun missing in the image – which, however, would then also pertain to the state of society. "Through this irritating, even unsettling effect, *Abend über Potsdam* can hardly be considered a romantic, atmospheric picture, but rather a sophisticated visualization of the mood of a generation that later would be called the 'lost' one", remarks Anna-Carola Krausse, author of the Laserstein catalogue raisonné. She observes, "Together and yet alone, literally sitting at the edge of the abyss and separated from the rest of the world by a deep chasm, the young people await the things that are to come."[2]

The "Golden" Twenties

Lotte Laserstein created her most impressive works at the end of the 1920s. She masterly portrayed the people of her time, often in specifically modern contexts (such as women in front of a motorcycle or on a tennis court). The artist drew the sum of these individuals into her multi-figure painting *Abend über Potsdam*. Set before a topographically accurate cityscape of Potsdam, just outside Berlin, five people linger in a foreboding melancholy. With the onset of the Great Depression in 1929, the Weimar Republic's Golden Twenties have come to an end; the evening meal has been consumed, the table is almost bare, the future uncertain. Laserstein's painting shares in this social experience of insecurity. The dark clouds presage the advent of bleak times. The rise of National Socialism soon put an end to Laserstein's budding career. As a Jew, the artist found herself compelled to immigrate

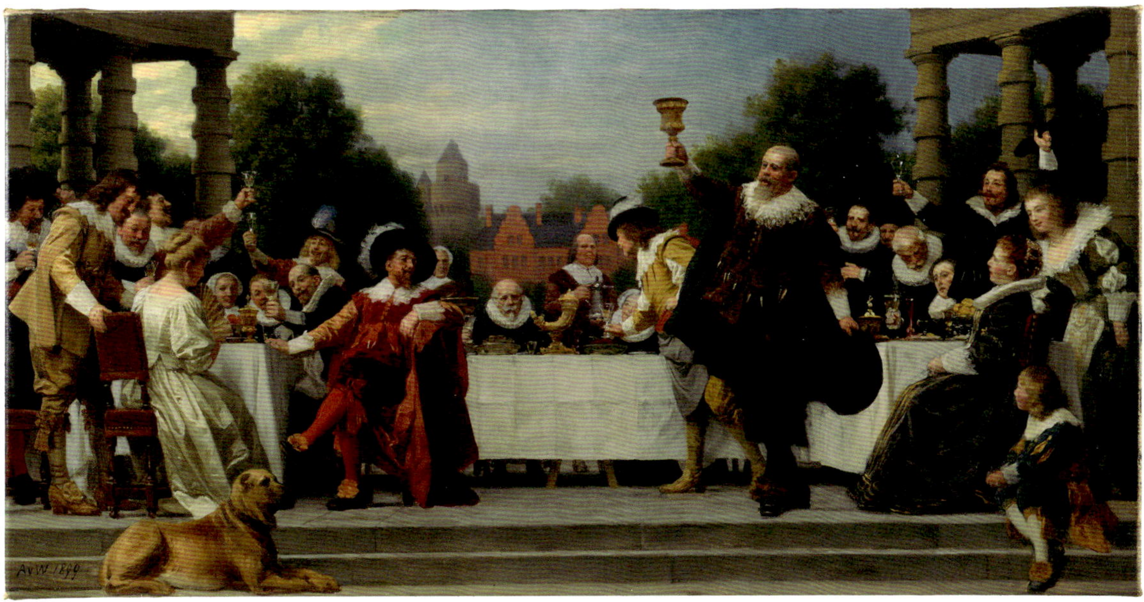

Anton von Werner, *The Mosse Family Banquet*, 1899
Oil on canvas, 44.7 × 89 × 3 cm
(oil sketch for the mural destroyed in 1945)
Jüdisches Museum Berlin, formerly in the Rudolf Mosse Collection; confiscated in 1934; restituted in 2016

to Sweden in 1937, where she lived until her death in 1993. These life circumstances also explain the artist's prolonged obscurity. With knowledge of the subsequent course of events, *Abend über Potsdam* becomes a visionary farewell to an entire world.

To some degree, Laserstein chose a traditional approach to the painting. She first sketched the figures on an actual terrace, and also painted the city panorama on location. The painting's detailed final appearance was then realized during numerous sessions with her models in the studio. Even if the work seems true to life, it nonetheless depicts an imagined or fictional reality. In a different sense, this is also true of Sascha Wiederhold's 1928 painting *Bogenschützen* (Archers, fig. pp. 20–21). In its assortment of swirling forms and patterns, and its intense colours, the painting initially conveys a stunning visual effect. The image seems abstract, yet anyone willing to make the effort can discover four drawn bows loaded with arrows. Some of the circles are recognizable as hands, with the arms, heads and bodies of the archers and their horses also discernible. A large animal writhes on the ground, obviously wounded and bleeding.

Wiederhold has transformed the pictorial idea of the archers into an exuberant ornamental composition suggesting a cosmic *theatrum mundi* (world stage), in which life and death are linked to the eternal cycle of the stars. The large-scale work may have served as a backdrop for a costume party, a theatre curtain, or a stage set. Indications of such use emerge in the artist's biography. Sascha Wiederhold was born Ernst Walther Wiederhold in 1904 in Münster, Westphalia. In 1924 he went to Berlin, where he commenced studies with Cesar Klein, who instructed the studio class for decorative painting and stage design at the Vereinigte Staatsschulen für Kunst und Handwerk (United State Schools for Fine and Applied Arts). Some of Wiederhold's titles reveal his enthusiasm for theatre arts, while others indicate his fondness for all things Russian. The Cyrillic letter "C", with which Wiederhold signed all his works, derives from a more personal variant of his first name, *Cascha*, and corresponds to the Latin "S".

As early as July 1925, Wiederhold was granted a solo exhibition at Herwarth Walden's gallery Der Sturm. Some aspects of *Bogenschützen* seem to have been inspired by various artworks displayed in *Der Sturm* magazine and gallery.[3] The abundance of colour and form, as well as the image's representational subject, could also be a distant response to Wassily Kandinsky's 1909 *Bild mit Bogenschützen* (Picture with an Archer), which the latter included as a hand-coloured woodcut in the deluxe and museum edition of the *Der Blaue Reiter Almanac* in 1912. Wiederhold merges aspects of theatre-related works from Russia, France and Italy with elements of Futurism, Orphism, Art Deco and Russian folklore in a completely original way to create a novel and unusual blend in his five-square-metre painting. The glow of the colours, intensity of the patterns and rhythm of the forms all exude the spirit of the 1920s. Like the recent television series *Babylon Berlin*,[4] the painting demonstrates this epoch's aesthetic radiance and how profoundly it resonates in our time – also with regard to sociopolitical parallels.

The elegance and sophistication of Wiederhold's painting is due in part to the use of imitation gold leaf. The material lends a shimmering lustre to the work, which was painted in oil on two different-sized sheets of paper and mounted on canvas. The gilt recalls medieval sacral imagery. Wiederhold's work similarly enriches the world with a transcendent festive realm, offering the opportunity to be more colourful, more multiform, and more dazzling. Yet horror also lurks in this depiction. It is, after all, about the killing that occurs during a hunt.

In real life, Wiederhold was precluded from working as an artist soon after this painting was created in 1928, especially as

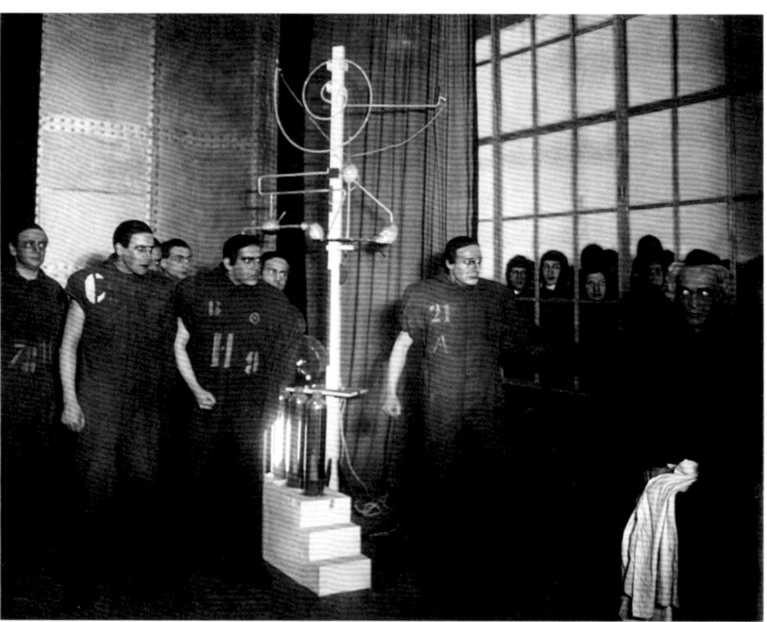

Friedrich Kiesler, Laboratory scene with robots in the play *W. U. R.* by Karel Čapek at the Theater am Kurfürstendamm, Berlin, 1923

a modern artist. After losing his ability to make a living under National Socialism as of 1933, Wiederhold ceased his artistic activities and worked as a bookseller. Unlike many artists who tried to come to terms with the National Socialist regime, Wiederhold abandoned his career as a painter. Consequently, there has been little if any consideration of his work. His artistic oeuvre can only be traced from 1924 to 1930, after which just a few drawings from 1946 are known. Only four large-format paintings are extant, with each one extremely rare and precious. The artist's most important work is considered to be *Bogenschützen*, which, as a new acquisition to the collection, can now be viewed for the first time at the Neue Nationalgalerie.

Classical Modernism

The works of Lotte Laserstein and Sascha Wiederhold are outstanding examples of what German art history terms Classical Modernism. In the visual arts, this designation refers to the period ranging approximately from 1900 to 1945, and especially to those movements that strove for formal innovation. In contrast to what has long been assumed by art historians, there has not been a continuous succession of styles, but rather a "simultaneity of the non-simultaneous",[5] in other words, a temporal overlap of various new currents with older modes of representation. And this pluralism of styles can sometimes even be found in the work of one and the same person. For instance, Pablo Picasso, when he began producing neoclassical drawings in alternation with Cubist ones in 1914–15, or Rudolf Belling, who declared in 1922: "Whether representational or non-representational, I allow myself everything."[6] This diversity of simultaneously employable expressive means not only derived from European precedents but was also nourished by non-European cultures. Decades later, such pluralism would be considered characteristic of *postmodernism*, although this combinatory richness could already be observed in Classical Modernism.

Another distinctive example of modernism is Rudolf Belling's *Skulptur 23* (Sculpture 23, fig. p. 81), whose title incorporates its date of origin. The head, reduced to basic geometric forms, recalls Oskar Schlemmer's Bauhaus logo from 1922 (fig. p. 157). It has to do with rational organization. An inspiration was perhaps a 1920 play by Karel Čapek, *R. U. R. – Rossumovi Univerzální Roboti* (Rossum's Universal Robots), whose German version, *W. U. R.* (*Werstands Universal Robots*) opened in the spring of 1923 at the Theater am Kurfürstendamm in Berlin (fig. p. 12). The plot involves the production of artificial humans in an industrial civilization in 1932. It is a vision of a world to come. The word *robot*, used for the first time in the play to describe such beings, quickly entered everyday language, pointing far into the future at that time. *Skulptur 23* has also been characterized as a machine being and has a mechanically movable eyelid.

From a formal standpoint, and in terms of its social relevance, Belling's sculpture is an example of the avant-gardes' love of experimentation, which, especially during the 1910s and 1920s, led to entirely new pictorial compositions. The term *avant-garde*, as applied to the small artistic movements interested in radical innovation and originality, stemmed from French military terminology for an army's front line of troops. These artistic groups, which often deliberately emerged with programmatic manifestos in hand, decisively shaped European art history during the first half of the 20th century and were extremely influential.

In 1925 El Lissitzky and Hans Arp published a volume entitled *Die Kunstismen* (*The Isms of Art*, fig. p. 15). The book's cover, whose typography was designed by Lissitzky, reveals the diversity of artistic tendencies designated by the suffix *ism*. These new isms did not by any means all get along with one another, but they did all see themselves as particular manifestations of modern art. The compilation also included – undogmatically and wryly – the categories of *Metaphysics* and *Film*, although these did not qualify linguistically as *isms*. The compilation on the *Isms of Art* is, on the one hand, testimony to a lively and, at the time of its publication, still ongoing development, and on the other, already a review of a decade of artistic experimentation. It was, in the words of El Lissitzky, a "last parade of all the isms from 1914–24".[7]

It was not long before the avant-gardes were being persecuted and all art classified as *modern* was defamed. In a speech Adolf Hitler held at the opening of the *Great German Art Exhibition* in the newly constructed Haus der Deutschen Kunst (House of German Art) which opened to the public on 19 July 1937, he proclaimed: "Until National Socialism came to power, there had been a so-called 'modern' art in Germany, that is – as the term intrinsically implies – a different art style almost every year. National Socialist Germany, however, wants a 'German art' again, and it, like all of a people's creative values, should and will be an eternal one."[8] By this time, German art museums had been complying with the new regime's agenda for four years. As director of the Nationalgalerie in Berlin, Eberhard Hanfstaengl banished the pieces assumed to be particularly controversial to storage in 1933 but dared to continue showing moderately modern works at the former Kronprinzen-Palais. This building on Berlin's prestigious boulevard Unter den Linden had served as the Nationalgalerie's branch for contemporary art since 1919. It was where art that still seemed unusual to the public at the time was shown and elucidated. The venue was closed in 1937 by the National Socialist regime, which abhorred modern art. After Hanfstaengl refused to participate in the "Degenerate Art" campaign's confiscations, he was "put on leave" and removed from his post.[9] Nonetheless, even though the National Socialists countered artistic and social diversity with the process of *Gleichschaltung* (political alignment), Classical Modernism did not cease in 1933. Those productively engaged in it carried on, provided they were not murdered during the Holocaust. And they continued to work, albeit partially in hiding, without income or means to exhibit their works – or in exile outside of Germany.

El Lissitzky, *The Isms of Art*, 1925, cover of the publication co-edited with Hans Arp.

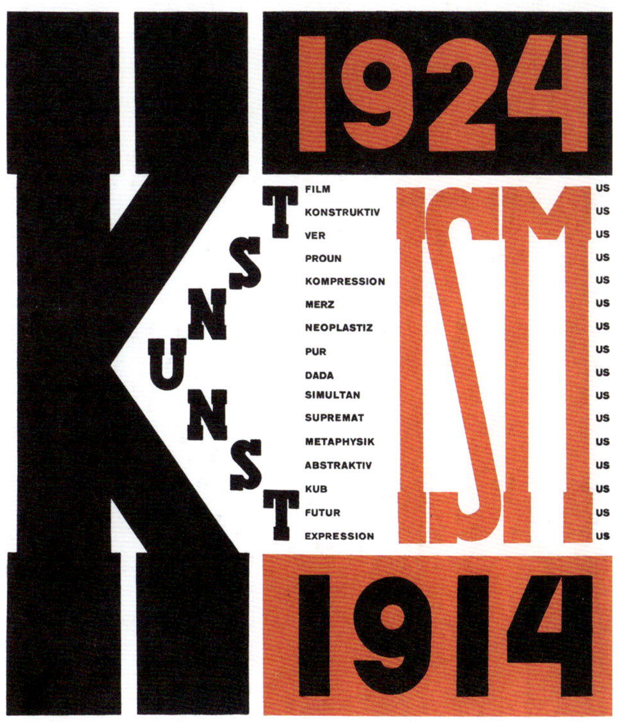

"The Nationalgalerie seems to me to be the right place."
The Nationalgalerie and the former Kronprinzen-Palais, which Hanfstaengl's predecessor Ludwig Justi conceptualized as a "gallery of the living",[10] had just a few years earlier, during the Weimar Republic, been considered the appropriate place for preserving outstanding new works of modern art. The esteem the museum enjoyed is illustrated by the history of a particular painting, reproduced on the cover of this book. The image shows a fervent orator in a white shirt and blue suit, his arm outstretched in a passionate gesture (fig. p. 143). He points upwards with his index finger. The crowd in the hall consists of workers, listening intently to the agitator's every word. He has only his voice to fill the large hall. His body language reveals his determination, with his head jutting forward, eyes wide, brow furrowed, lips parted, and hand clenched into a fist.

Who is the speaker? The painting provides only one clue. Visible in its upper left corner is the inscription *Felixmüller*. This is the artist name used by painter Conrad Felix Müller. He wrote in thick letters on the back of the painting (here in translation): "Conrad Felixmüller April–May 1920 No 209 Otto Rühle speaks". It clarifies the orator's identity. Otto Rühle was originally a teacher, and from 1912 to 1918, a member of the Reichstag, serving until 1916 as a member of the Social Democratic Party of Germany (SPD).

When the SPD voted in the parliament to approve war bonds to finance the First World War, Rühle dissented and left the party's parliamentary fraction. Subsequently, he participated in founding the Spartacist League and shortly after the Communist Party of Germany (KPD), and in April 1920 the Communist Workers' Party of Germany (KAPD). However, he was expelled from both parties for opposing the recognition of Moscow's leadership role and seeking to establish a decentralized, local governing body based on the soviet, or council model. Rühle was familiar with this organizational form from his time as co-chairman of the Vereinigte Revolutionäre Arbeiter- und Soldatenrat (United Revolutionary Workers' and Soldiers' Council) of Greater Dresden during the 1918 November Revolution. Painter Felixmüller later recounted his impression of Otto Rühle:

"With heart and soul, I accompanied the storm of the revolution and was borne by hopes for peace – *Nie wieder Krieg* [No More War] – and socialism accompanied by the emancipation of the working class (I was its son). At that time, Otto Rühle was an energetic, eloquent leader. The masses thronged to hear him; he spoke captivatingly and was confident of his following. While his wife was still alive, he lived in nearby Hellerau [outside Dresden]. We soon became friends, leading to his being my model for this painting, many drawings and two lithographs. I made my actual studies for the painting during assemblies while he spoke: his mouth, a mass of muscles in the booming barrage of words, his whole body extended to the pointing fingertip, with his balled fist ready to thrust forward. The painting shows a gathering at the Dresden Kristallsäle, a dance hall in the workers' and industrial quarter in the outlying district of Friedrichstadt. The faces in the foreground were party members, willing to follow Rühle. The hall was packed to the galleries. An image from the days of revolution – 1920."[11]

A few years after completing the painting, Felixmüller wrote a programmatic text, "Über Kunst" (About Art), published in 1925 in the book *Künstlerbekenntnisse* (Artists' Statements). He declared: "Art is a historical matter, for it is the expression of human society, with the aesthetic moment being of secondary importance – even more so in today's moment of economic disruption and spiritual collapse. Need and misery focus thoughts and feelings in real terms, and their interpretation is factual, curt and pointed. Economic, political, religious and techno-scientific ideas constantly influence the character of our art, giving it a seal of disintegration or newness, revolution or romantic rapture. Its attitude towards life and humanity is critical, analytical and rational. Its substance is drawn from the day's thoughts and events, and it is partial in every decisive case. Humankind is consciously placed at the focus of art; in art, humanity is no longer an unaccountable and boundless phenomenon, but rather one full of social responsibility."[12]

Felixmüller's art sets itself apart from the abstraction of his contemporaries, but this does not mean that the "aesthetic moment" is really of "secondary importance" to him, as he wrote. On the contrary, the painter carefully positioned his painting's central figure to create a diagonally ascending movement from his fist to his lips to his outstretched index finger. In the manner of the Old Testament prophets, Felixmüller's agitator points over the heads of the crowd to a higher goal. The gallery set diagonally into the picture also enhances this dynamic. Belching smokestacks visible through a window allude to factory work, and a cloth along the edge of the stage hints at a red flag. This symbolic colour is echoed in the lips and red-rimmed eyes of the speaker, who is engrossed in his mission. He sees a better world and wants to show the way into this future.

The portrayal of Otto Rühle's speech in Dresden in 1920 is a painting and therefore unique. Yet this rendition is also a replica because only a fragment of the original has survived (fig. p. 143). Conrad Felixmüller attached great importance to his painting and wanted to ensure that it was preserved for posterity at a prominent location. On 4 September 1929 he wrote to Ludwig Justi, the director of the Nationalgalerie, that the work was "the only first-hand artistic record of the revolution created during the revolution [...] Numerous collectors have a lively interest in this picture – but I have always withheld this work and wish to see it in a public space, in keeping with its contemporary historical and artistic significance. The Nationalgalerie seems to me to be the right place."[13]

For Felixmüller, this painting was particularly authentic because it artistically documented German history. The Nationalgalerie, however, did not purchase the work, and it remained in the possession of the artist, who cut it into pieces in 1933 out of a well-founded fear of the newly powerful National Socialists. Felixmüller hid the central fragment showing the head of the orator Otto Rühle. Shortly after the Second World War, he repainted the image in 1946 based on photographs. His son Titus donated the second version to the Nationalgalerie in the eastern part of Berlin in 1977. The Felixmüller heirs gave the original fragment from 1920 to the reunified Nationalgalerie in 2019. Both works are brought together in the Neue Nationalgalerie.

The painting has now arrived at the destination Felixmüller once desired. If the purchase had occurred in 1929, this likely would not be the case. For the painting of agitator Otto Rühle would, like some five hundred other works at the Nationalgalerie, probably have been sold or destroyed in the course of confiscations carried out during the National Socialist Degenerate Art campaign in 1937.[14] An artist such as Felixmüller was persecuted under National Socialism not only because of his political orientation but also because of his art, which was considered "modern".

The Art of Society

The *art of society* is any art created within a society, even though only some of that art is handed down to subsequent generations. Not all of it survives. Many works of art have fallen victim to war and destruction throughout history. And what does exist today has also been determined by process of selection. These decisions take place at the Nationalgalerie, among other art institutions because it is there that decisions are made on behalf of society about which art should be collected, preserved, researched, exhibited and imparted. The Nationalgalerie is an enduring art repository, as well as a public place of education and encounter.

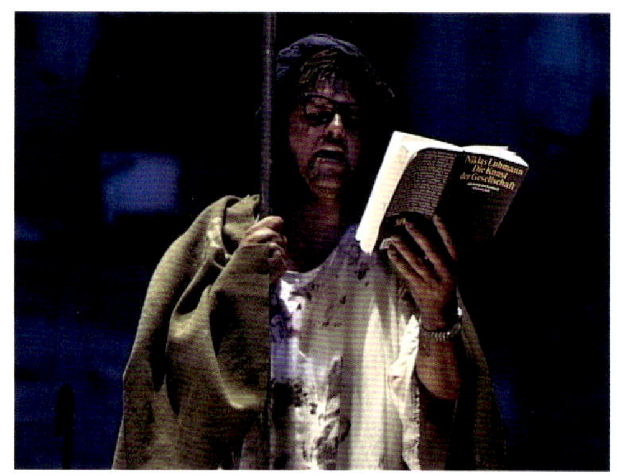

Christoph Schlingensief, *Atta Atta – Art Has Broken Out*, Volksbühne am Rosa-Luxemburg-Platz, Berlin, 2003

Very generally defined, *society* is considered to be the "totality of people living together under certain political, economic and social conditions".[15] This refers to the populations of the current nation-states. However, living under certain conditions does not mean that all people live under the same economic and social conditions. And it is not only since the advent of globalization and digitization that there has been talk of a "world society".[16] The title of the exhibition, *The Art of Society*, with its double meaning, can also be understood as the artistry of coexisting in the world.

In art, a particular historical period reflects its past and present. However, through art and the discourse about art, society also constantly envisions its future. For Felixmüller, art was, as cited earlier, "a historical matter, for it is the expression of human society". He was convinced that "economic, political, religious and techno-scientific ideas constantly influence the character of our art". Yet art creates something of its own in response. And unlike religion, politics, science and law, art is able to demonstrate that "modern society and, from its perspective, the world can be described only in polycontextural terms", according to sociologist Niklas Luhmann.[17]

In his book *Die Kunst der Gesellschaft* (in translation as *Art as a Social System*), Luhmann conceives art as something that goes beyond simply describing prevailing conditions and participating in social experiences. The art of society can be described as a space of possibility that stands in contrast to existing reality: "The work of art, then, establishes a reality of its own that differs from ordinary reality. And yet, despite the work's perceptibility, despite its undeniable reality, it simultaneously constitutes another reality, the meaning of which is imaginary or fictional."[18]

This passage was recited by film, theatre and action artist Christoph Schlingensief in his play *Atta Atta – Die Kunst ist ausgebrochen* (Atta Atta – Art Has Broken Out) at the Volksbühne theatre at Rosa-Luxemburg-Platz in Berlin in 2003 (fig. p. 18). In the scene, he was wrapped in a felt cape, in a nod to Joseph Beuys. The former altar boy Schlingensief intoned the text like a Catholic litany, thus likening the book *Die Kunst der Gesellschaft* to a holy scripture. However, he did this in the guise of a theatrical production, that is, of an ostensible reality. Luhmann himself suspects that "art tests arrangements that are at once fictional and real in order to show society, from a position within society, that things could be done differently".[19]

1 See *Kampf um Sichtbarkeit. Künstlerinnen der Nationalgalerie vor 1919*, Yvette Deseyve and Ralph Gleis, eds., exh. cat., Nationalgalerie – Staatliche Museen zu Berlin (Berlin, 2019).
2 Anna-Carola Krausse, *Lotte Laserstein (1898–1993). Leben und Werk* (Berlin, 2006), p. 162.
3 The boldly coloured concentric circles allude to Robert Delaunay (97th *Sturm* exhibition, May 1921) and the jagged patterns to the weavings from the Hablik-Lindemann workshop (141st *Sturm* exhibition, May 1925). Similarities to the circles on the figures' joints can be found in Alexandra Exter's *Kostüm des Kriegs* (*Der Sturm* 15, no. 2, June 1924, p. 89) and Mikhail Larionov's *Bühnenfigur "Pfau"*, or peacock stage figure (*Der Sturm* 17, no. 3, June 1926, p. 39). A decoration by Wiederhold is shown in that same special theatre edition of *Der Sturm*, immediately following the *Pfau* (p. 40). Wiederhold was probably also aware of the Leon Bakst's costume ornamentation and of Fortunato Depero's and Gino Severini's visual language.
4 The television premiere of the crime series *Babylon Berlin*, directed by Tom Tykwer, Achim von Borries and Henk Handloegten, was broadcast on the Sky 1 private television channel in fall 2017.
5 This turn of phrase is attributed to philosopher Ernst Bloch, although it is not found in his book *Erbschaft dieser Zeit* (1935, *Heritage of Our Times*, 2009) but later in historical scholarship; see Reinhart Koselleck, "Das achtzehnte Jahrhundert als Beginn der Neuzeit", in *Epochenschwellen und Epochenbewusstsein*, Reinhart Herzog and Reinhart Koselleck, eds. (Munich, 1987), pp. 268–82, here pp. 280 and 273.
6 Rudolf Belling, "Skulptur und Raum", in *Kunstchronik und Kunstmarkt* 6 (10 November 1922), pp. 105–07; see Dieter Scholz and Christina Thomson (eds.), *Rudolf Belling. Skulpturen und Architekturen*, exh. cat., Neue Galerie im Hamburger Bahnhof – Museum für Gegenwart – Berlin (Munich 2017), pp. 11–13.
7 El Lissitzky, letter to his mother dated 30 March 1924, quoted from Alois Martin Müller, *Letzte Truppenschau*, insert to *Die Kunstismen*, El Lissitzky and Hans Arp, eds. (Erlenbach-Zurich/Munich/Leipzig, 1925, reprint CH-Baden, 1990).
8 Adolf Hitler, *Programmatische Kulturrede des Führers*, in *Völkischer Beobachter* 50, no. 200, 19 July 1937, quoted from Adolf Hitler, *Reden zur Kunst- und Kulturpolitik 1933–1939*, edited and annotated by Robert Eikmeyer, with an introduction by Boris Groys (Frankfurt am Main, 2004), pp. 123–43, here p. 129.
9 See Paul Ortwin Rave, *Kunstdiktatur im Dritten Reich* [1949], Uwe M. Schneede, ed. (Berlin, undated [1987]), p. 97; Jörn Grabowski, *Eberhard Hanfstaengl als Direktor der Nationalgalerie. Zu ausgewählten Aspekten seiner Tätigkeit zwischen 1933 und 1937*, in *Jahrbuch Preußischer Kulturbesitz* 33 (1996), pp. 327–42.
10 See Dieter Scholz, *Die Nationalgalerie und die Moderne*, in *Die Sammlung der Nationalgalerie. 1900–1945. Moderne Zeiten. Die Dokumentation einer Ausstellung*, Udo Kittelmann, Joachim Jäger and Dieter Scholz, eds. (Berlin, 2014), pp. 59–107, here p. 72.
11 *Conrad Felixmüller. Legenden 1912–1976*, G. H. Herzog, ed. (Tübingen, 1977), p. 46.
12 Conrad Felixmüller, "Über Kunst", in *Künstlerbekenntnisse. Briefe, Tagebuchblätter, Betrachtungen heutiger Künstler*, compiled and edited by Paul Westheim (Berlin, undated [1925]), pp. 313–14.
13 Conrad Felixmüller to Ludwig Justi, 4 September 1929, Staatliche Museen zu Berlin, Zentralarchiv, SMB-ZA, I/NG 931, Bl. 633.
14 See *Kunst in Deutschland 1905–1937. Die verlorene Sammlung der Nationalgalerie im ehemaligen Kronprinzen-Palais. Dokumentation.* Selected and compiled by Annegret Janda and Jörn Grabowski (Berlin, 1992). See also the database of the research centre "Entartete Kunst" at Freie Universität Berlin: http://www.geschkult.fu-berlin.de/e/db_entart_kunst/datenbank/index.html
15 This is the succinct definition provided by the Duden dictionary editorial staff: https://www.duden.de/rechtschreibung/Gesellschaft (accessed 07 June 2021).
16 Niklas Luhmann, "Die Weltgesellschaft", in *Archiv für Rechts- und Sozialphilosophie* 57, no. 1 (1971), pp. 1–35; Theresa Wobbe, *Weltgesellschaft* (Bielefeld, 2000); Silvio Vietta, *Die Weltgesellschaft. Wie die abendländische Rationalität die Welt erobert und verändert hat* (Baden-Baden, 2016).
17 Niklas Luhmann, *Art as a Social System,* translated by Eva M. Knodt (Stanford, USA, 2000), p. 306.
18 Luhmann, *Art as a Social System*, p. 142.
19 Luhmann, *Art as a Social System*, p. 313.

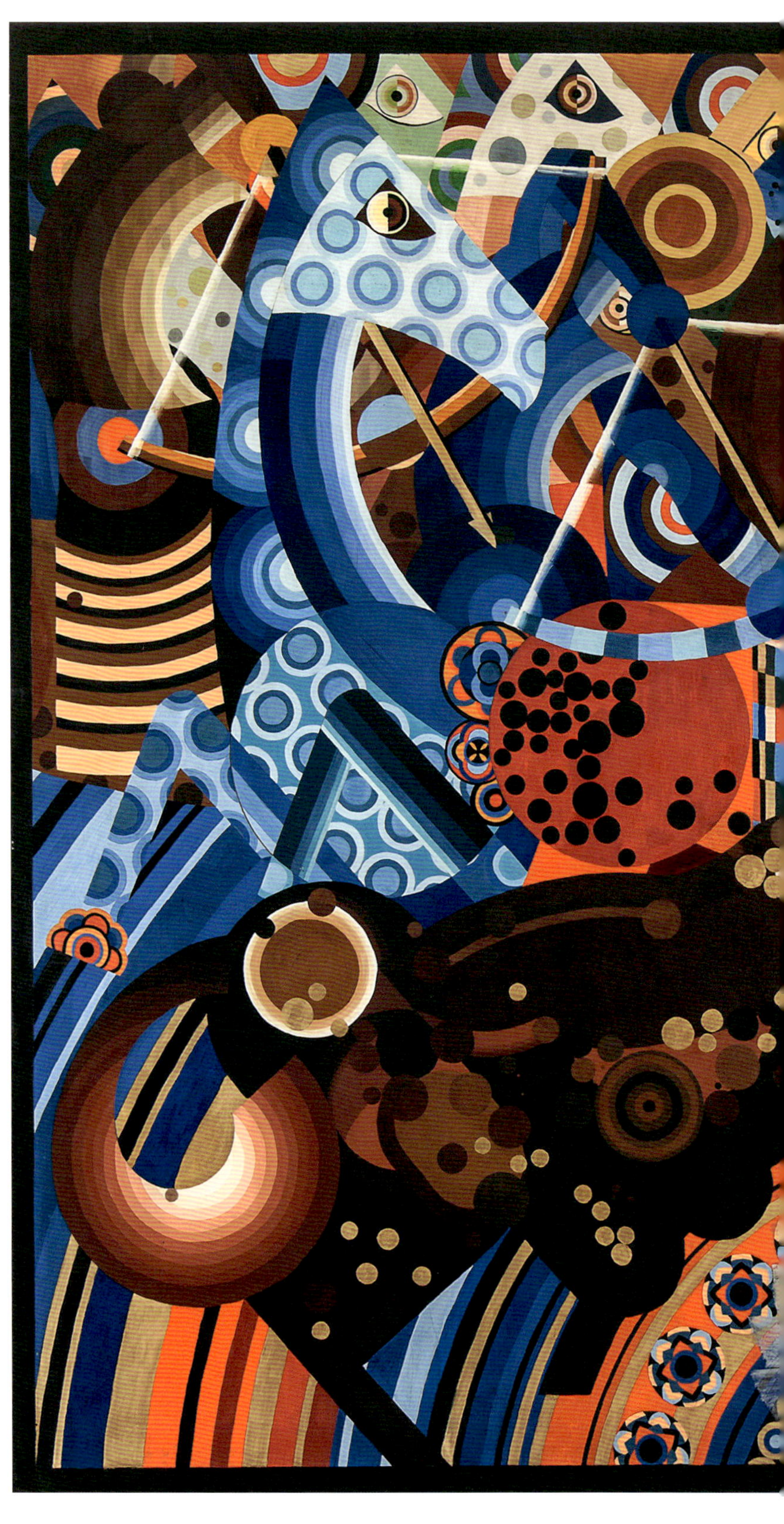

Sascha Wiederhold, *Archers*, 1928
Oil on cardboard and canvas, 204 × 240 cm
Acquired in 2021 by the Ernst von Siemens Kunststiftung

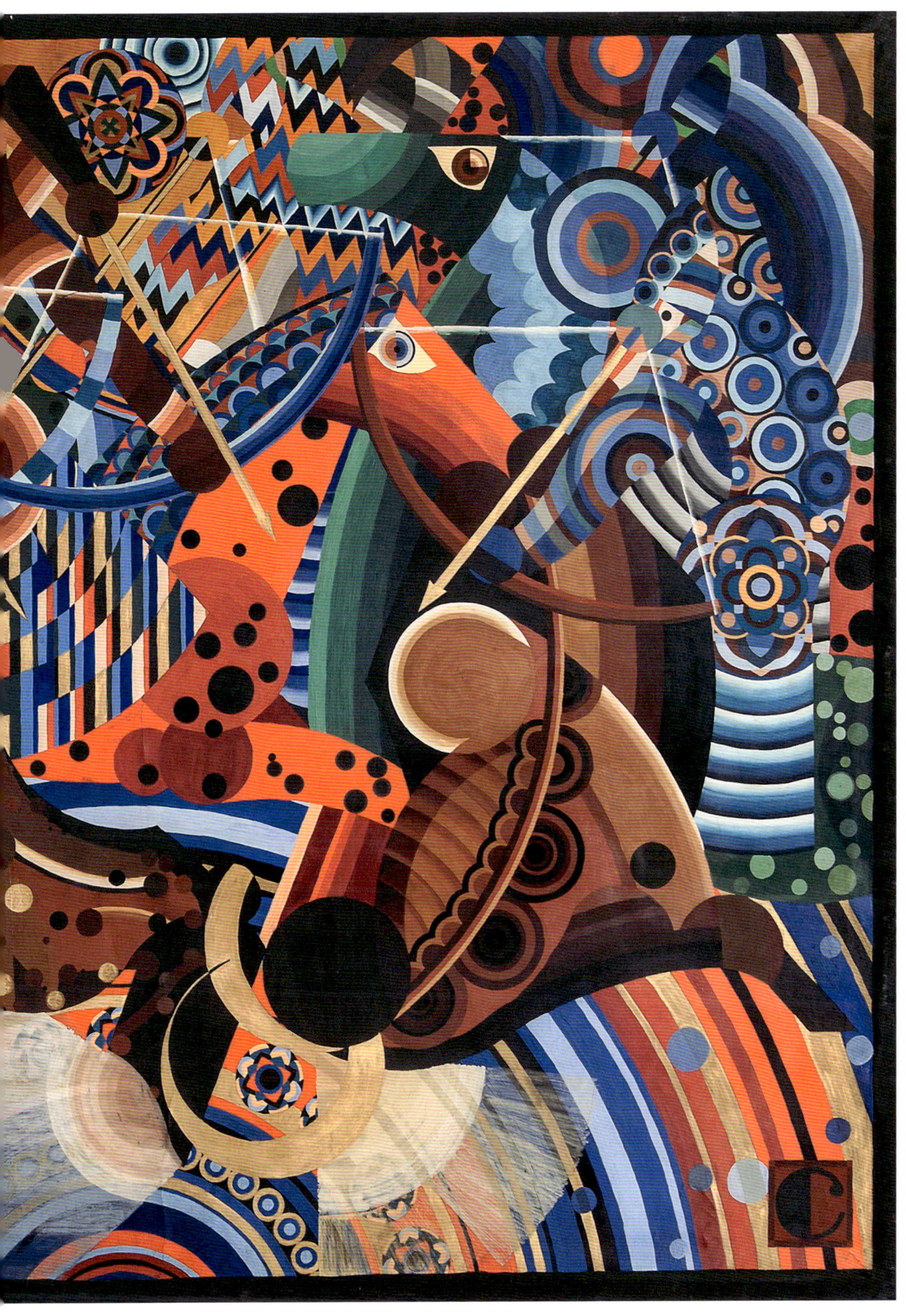

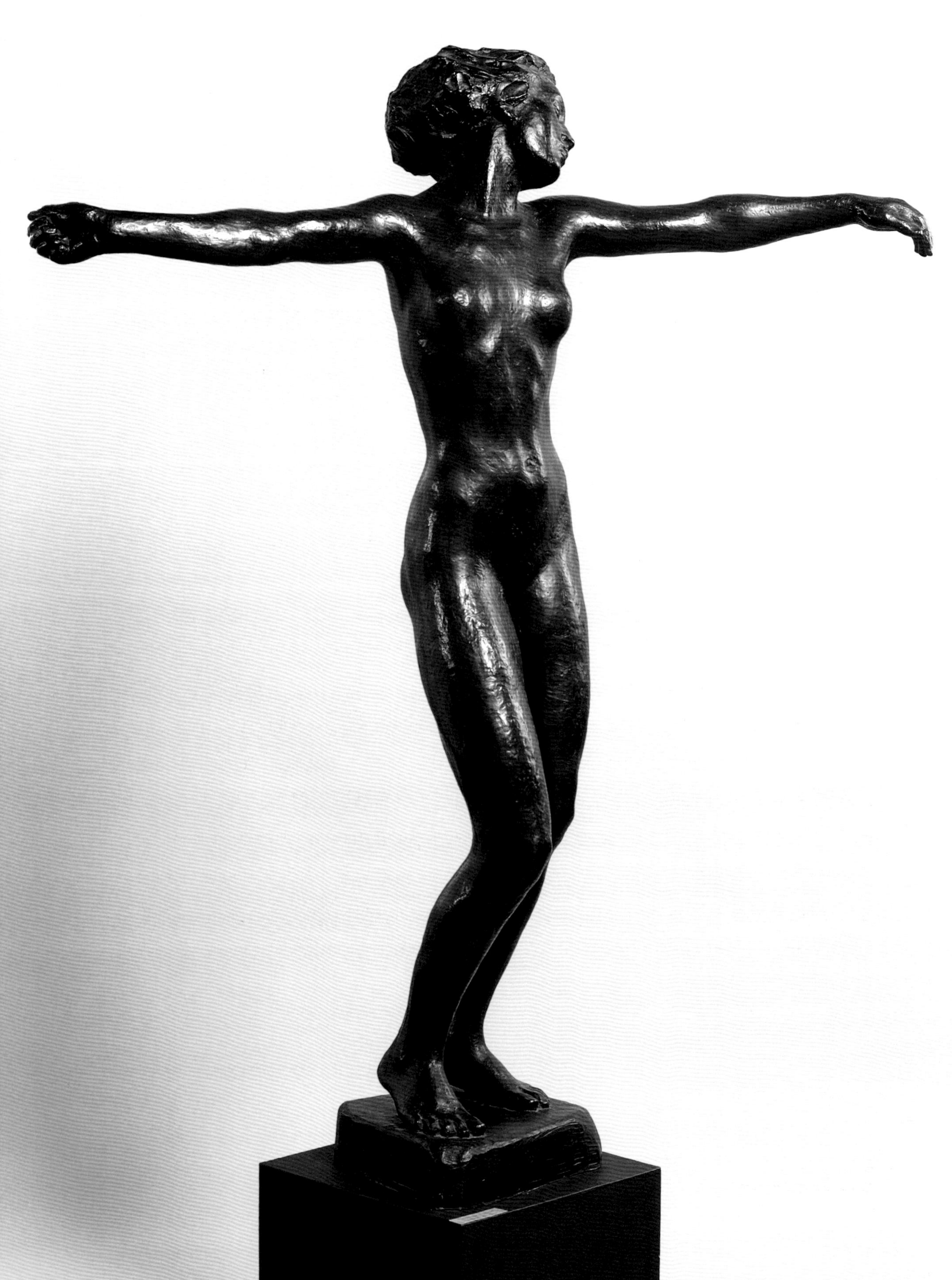

Life and Reform

Many images from the start of the 20th century evoke a desire for a cultural awakening to diffuse the social stagnation of the German Empire under Kaiser Wilhelm II, whose rule continued until the end of the First World War. A wide variety of reform movements began to take hold. Germany's youth, in particular, longed for a return to nature to offset urban life and industrialization. Rebellions against narrow bourgeois conventions found expression, such as the nudist lifestyle propagated by *Freikörperkultur*. A vision of a new society, of a life lived more freely, was unfolding. Women, too, were beginning to stand up for their rights.

Imagery of youth and beauty was appropriated from the Art Nouveau style – known as Jugendstil in German-speaking countries – that had been popular since before 1900. But its playful exaggeration of forms now gave way to an emphasis on large surfaces and distinct contours. Elementary themes of existence were added to the subject matter, for example, a mother with an infant at her breast depicted in the work of Paula Modersohn-Becker. Edvard Munch created a series of paintings showing young men and women gathered at the beach on Midsummer's Eve. But like all good things, this party comes to an end, and only melancholy remains.

Georg Kolbe, *Dancer*, 1911–12 (cast 1912)
Bronze, 54 × 127 × 88 cm
Acquired in 1912 from the artist

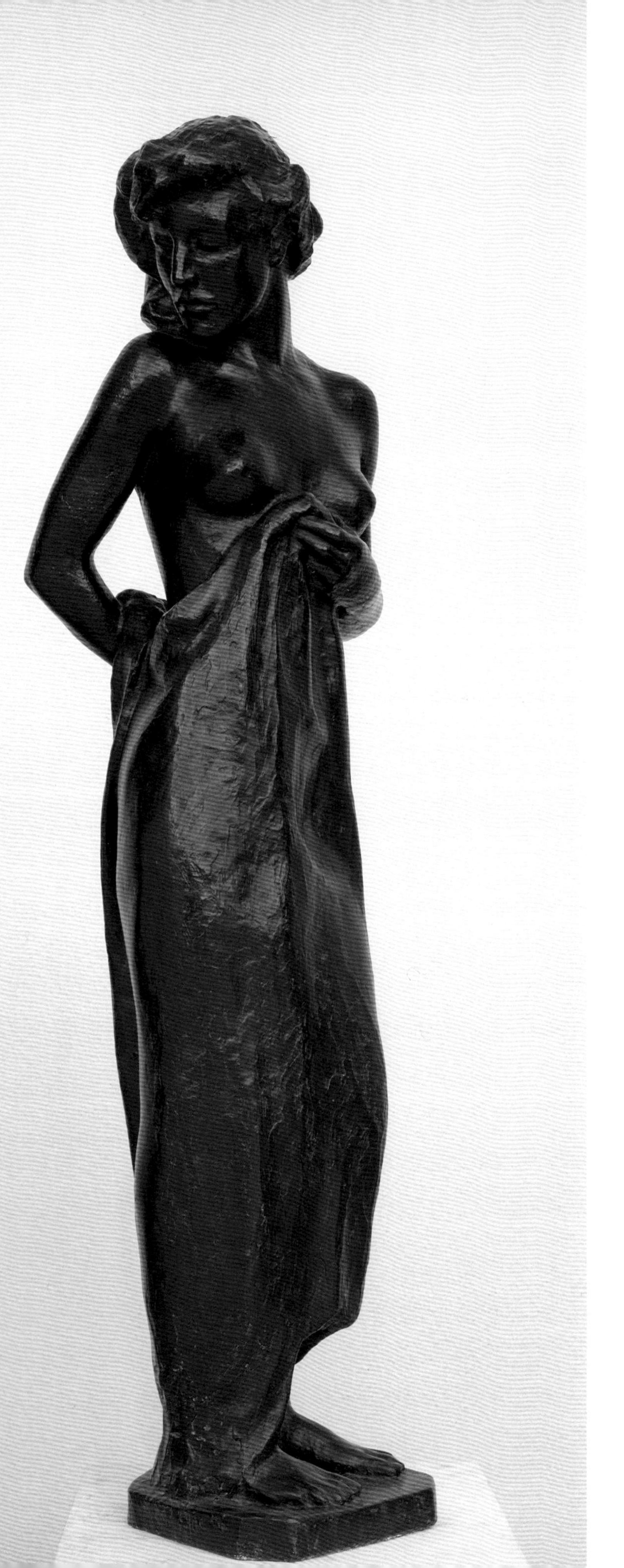

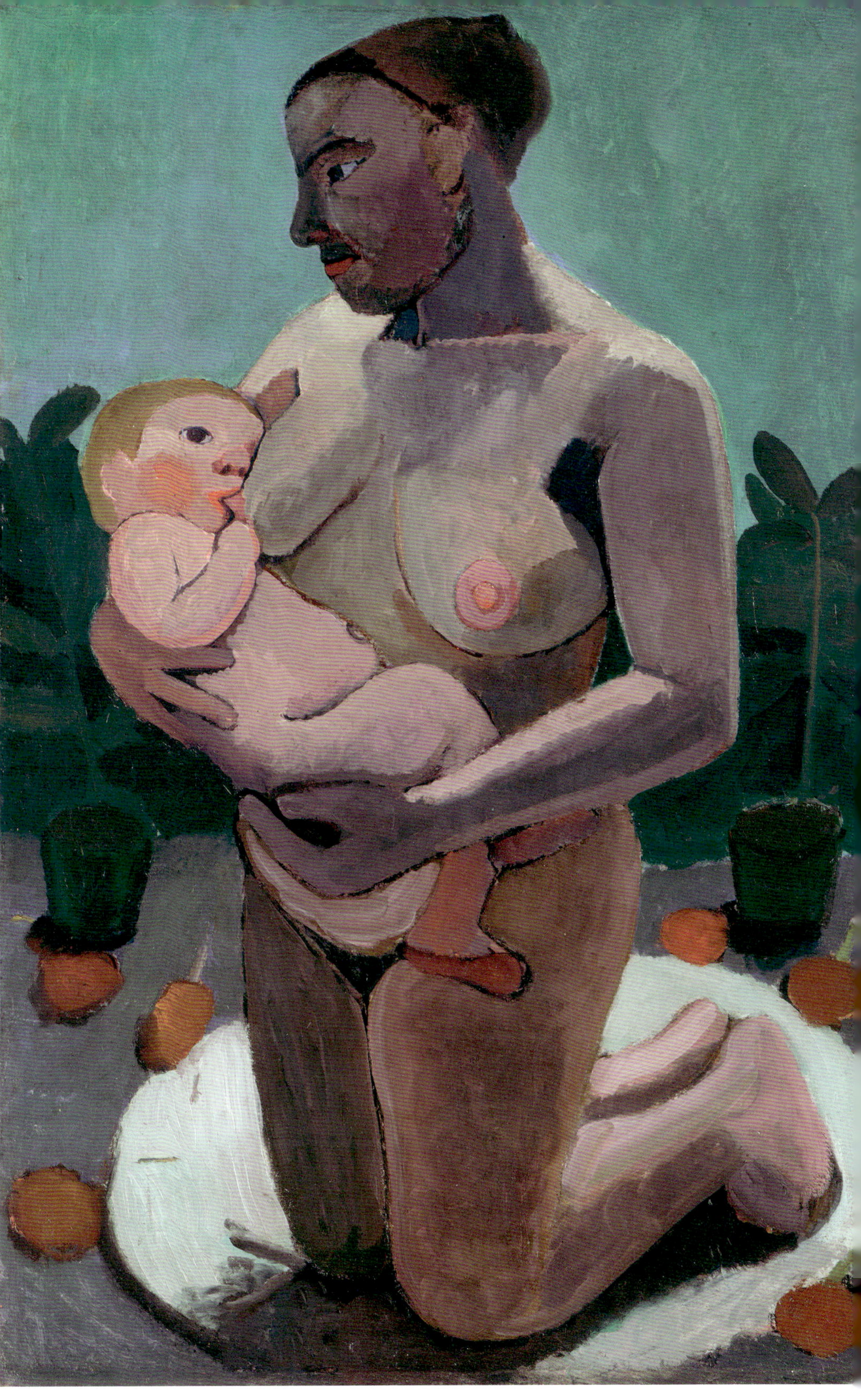

↗ Paula Modersohn-Becker, *Kneeling Mother with Child at Her Breast,* 1906
Oil and tempera on canvas, 113 × 74 cm
Acquired in 1985 from Dr Ludwig Roselius, Hamburg, with special funds from the Stiftung Preußischer Kulturbesitz for the Nationalgalerie, Berlin (West)

← Georg Kolbe, *The Bather,* c. 1910
Bronze, 145 × 43 × 37 cm
Acquired in 1957 for the Nationalgalerie, Berlin (West)

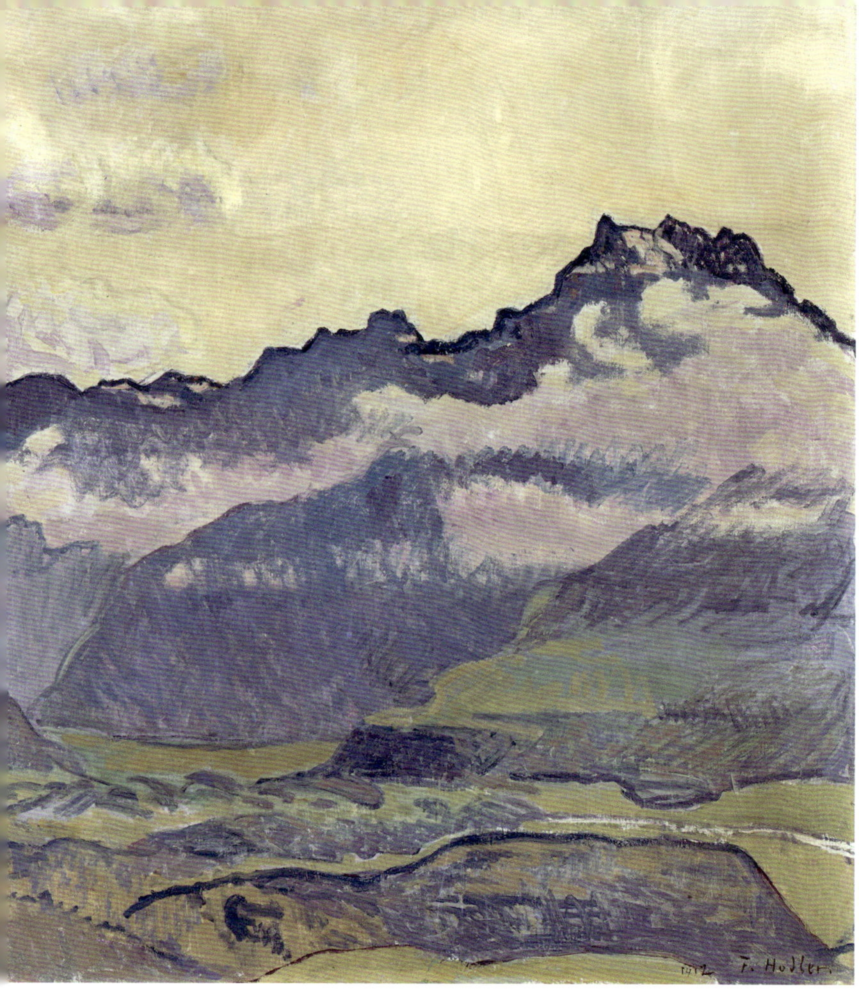

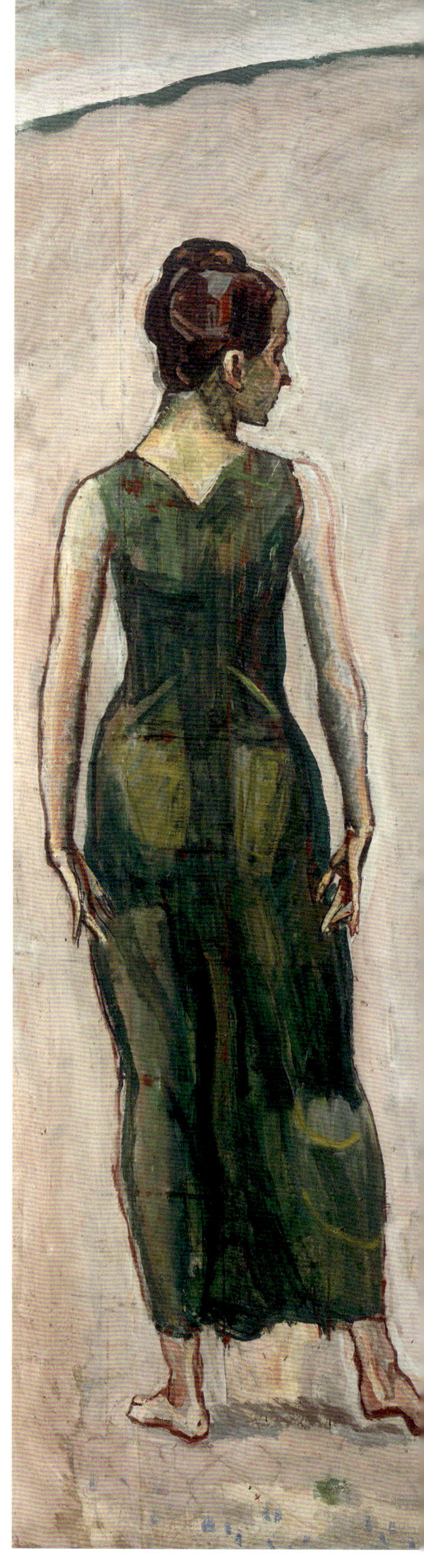

↑ Ferdinand Hodler, *Dents-du-Midi*, 1912
Oil on canvas, 76.5 × 70.5 cm
Loan from the Ernst von Siemens Kunststiftung since 1991

↗ Ferdinand Hodler, *Young Man Admired by Woman II*, c. 1904
Oil on canvas, 206 × 244 cm
Loan from the Gottfried Keller-Stiftung and the Kunsthaus Zürich to the Nationalgalerie, Berlin (West) since 1983

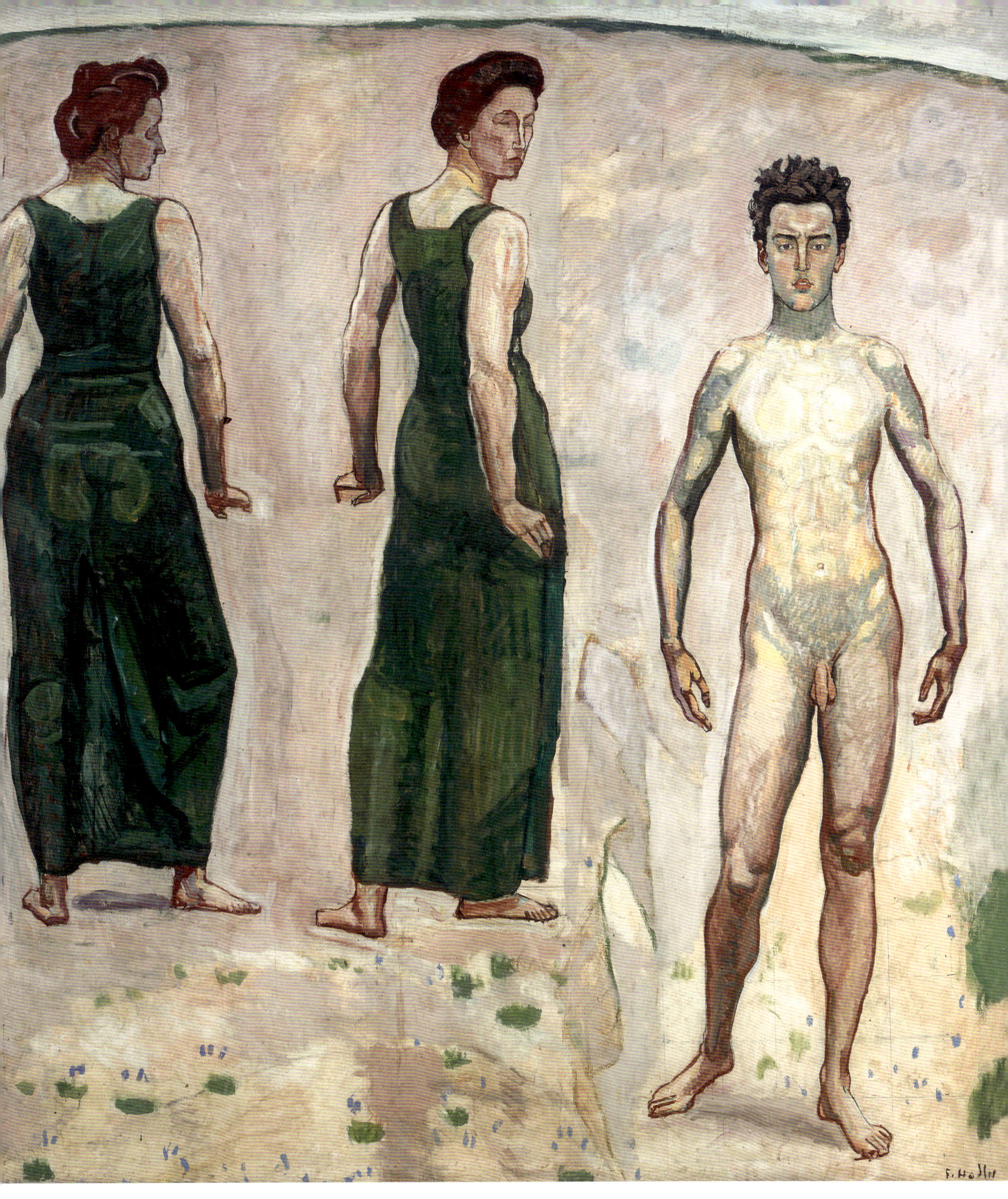

Longing for What?

People on shorelines and riverbanks were a popular motif in visual art at the start of the 20th century. These idyllic scenes appear to tell of a passage into another world. Their figures seem to be longing for something, but longing for what?

Often, it was the past. A certain sense of nostalgia was in the air. The architecture of the time was full of structural references to Romanesque, Gothic, Renaissance and Baroque buildings. The zeitgeist can be characterized by the title of Ludwig von Hofmann's 1893 painting *Das verlorene Paradies* (Paradise Lost).

Isolated individuals can also be found in a painting by the young Georg Kolbe. *Die Goldene Insel* (The Golden Island) shows three couples on a rocky shore in the shadows taking in a radiant white-gold island lit up by the sun. Kolbe's working title in 1898 was *Das Land unseres Sehnens* (The Land of Our Longing). The island in the painting does not appear to represent an earthly destination that people are striving to reach but rather a symbol of that which remains eternally outside our grasp.

The pose of a standing woman seen from behind is adopted from the stranded mythological hero Ulysses. He longs to return home in Arnold Böcklin's 1882 painting *Odysseus und Kalypso* (Ulysses and Calypso), on which Kolbe's work was based. Böcklin also painted five versions of the highly influential *Die Toteninsel* (The Island of the Dead) between 1880 and 1886, which inspired Wenzel Hablik. But the latter's visual imagination led him to turn the painting on its head: instead of death and yesteryear, he painted a life-affirming futuristic vision. In his 1917 painting *Meereszauber* (The Wonder of the Sea), Hablik pushed Böcklin's cypresses to either side of the frame to make way for a floating crystalline construction. However, this ethereal airborne palace seems to be an entirely normal facet of the bathers' reality.

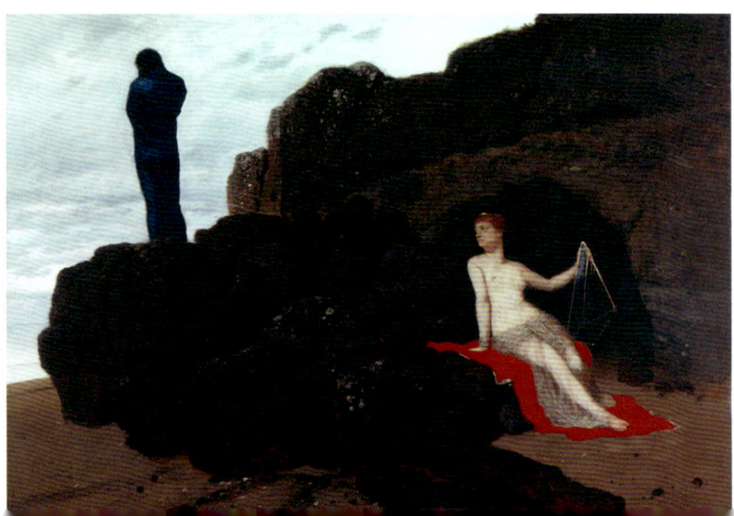

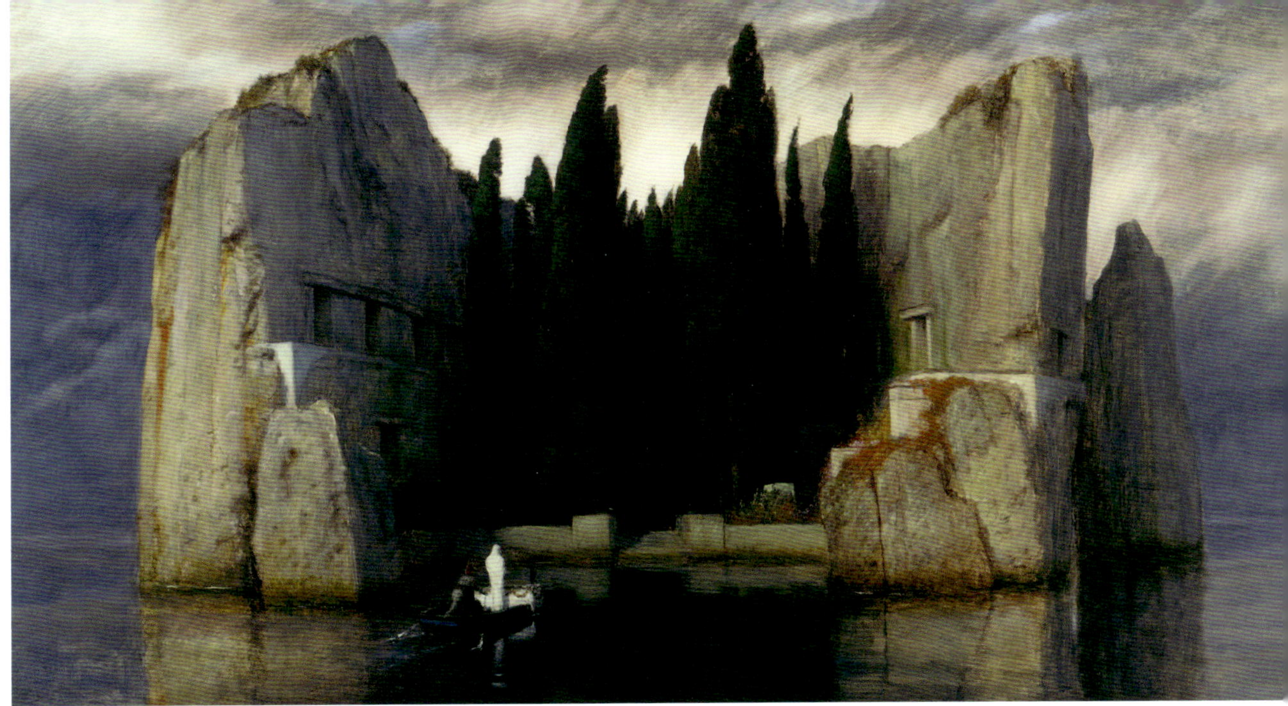

Crystal had been an important motif in Hablik's work since 1902. He used it to "confront the conscience with something that illustrated the idea of a collective struggle to transform the world", as he wrote in 1906. Hablik was not alone in this pursuit, which can be traced back to the romantic literary works of Novalis as well as Hablik's visionary contemporary Paul Scheerbart. Architect Bruno Taut went so far as to construct a Glashaus (Glass House) for the 1914 Deutsche Werkbund exhibition in Cologne. Along with Taut and other architects, Hablik founded the collective Die gläserne Kette (The Glass Chain) in 1919–20, which was more concerned with visionary architecture than actually constructing edifices.

In 1921 Hablik painted his *Cyklus utopische Architekturen. Flugzeugtürme, Silos, Künstlerwohnungen* (Cycle of Utopian Architectures. Aeroplane Towers, Silos, Artist Apartments). The cypresses are now crystalline trees and the island castle is a plant-shaped residential tower. The journey from Böcklin's Symbolism to Hablik's Expressionism shows that even while certain imagery remained comparable, a shift in the social mindset held the power to completely transform an artwork's message. The sense of longing had turned away from the past and towards a better future. In 1923 Hablik described his crystalline domes as "emblems of world peace".

Dieter Scholz

↑ Arnold Böcklin, *The Island of the Dead*, 1883
← Arnold Böcklin, *Ulysses and Calypso*, 1882
→ Bruno Taut, *Glass House*, Deutscher Werkbund exhibition, Cologne, 1914

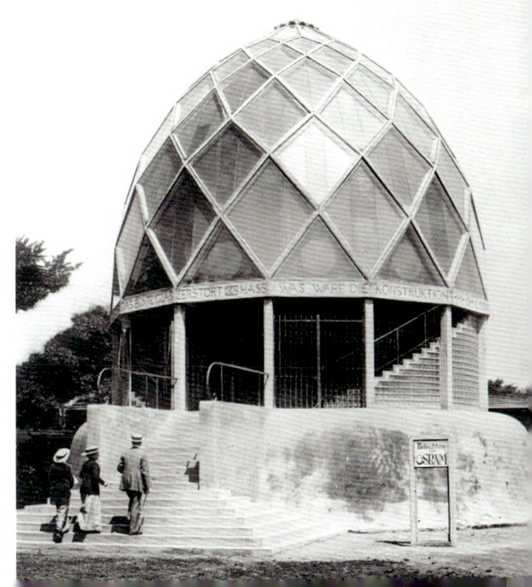

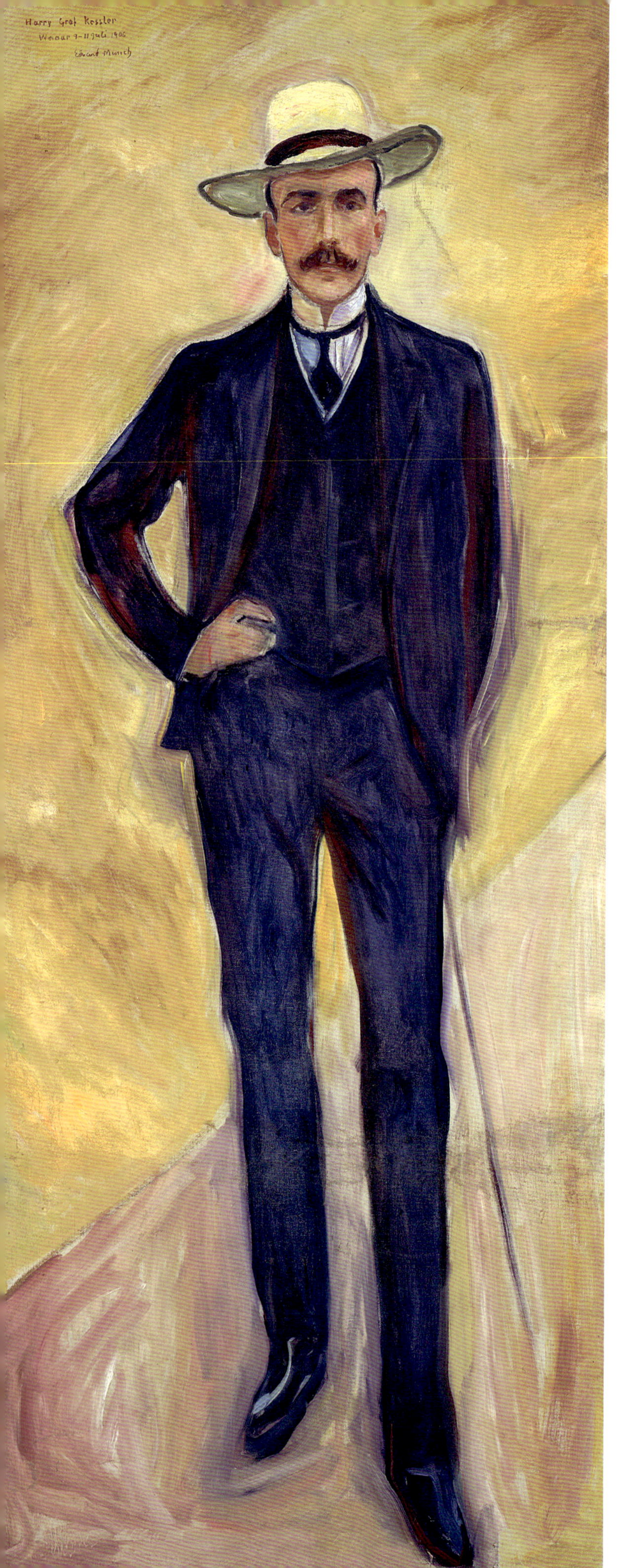
Harry Graf Kessler
Weimar 9–11 Juli 1906
Edvard Munch

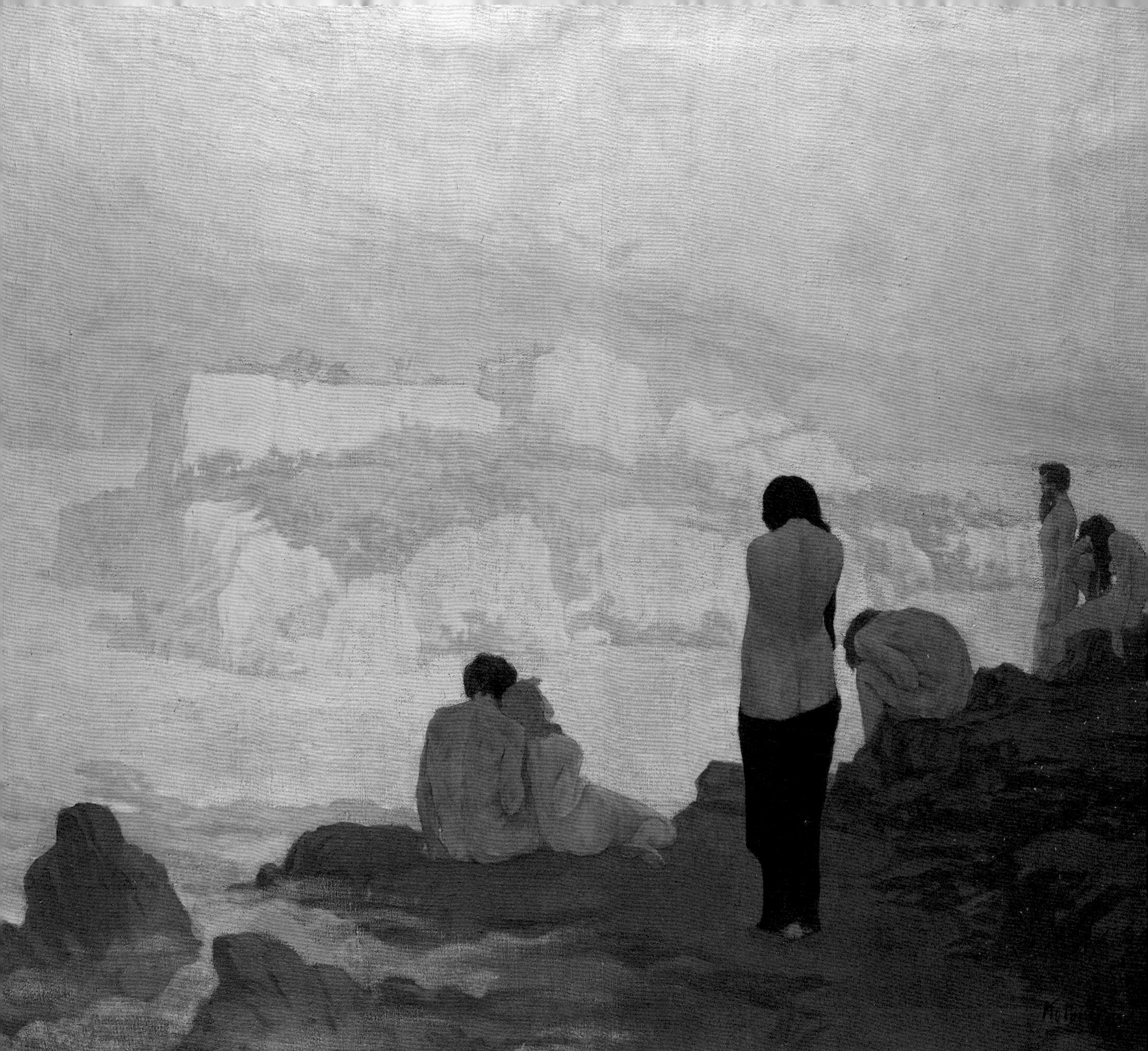

↑ Georg Kolbe, *The Golden Island*, 1898
Oil on canvas, 106.5 × 120.3 cm
Acquired in 1935

← Edvard Munch, *Count Harry Kessler*, 1906
Oil on canvas, 200 × 84 cm
Acquired in 1950 by the Land Berlin for the
Galerie des 20. Jahrhunderts, Berlin (West)

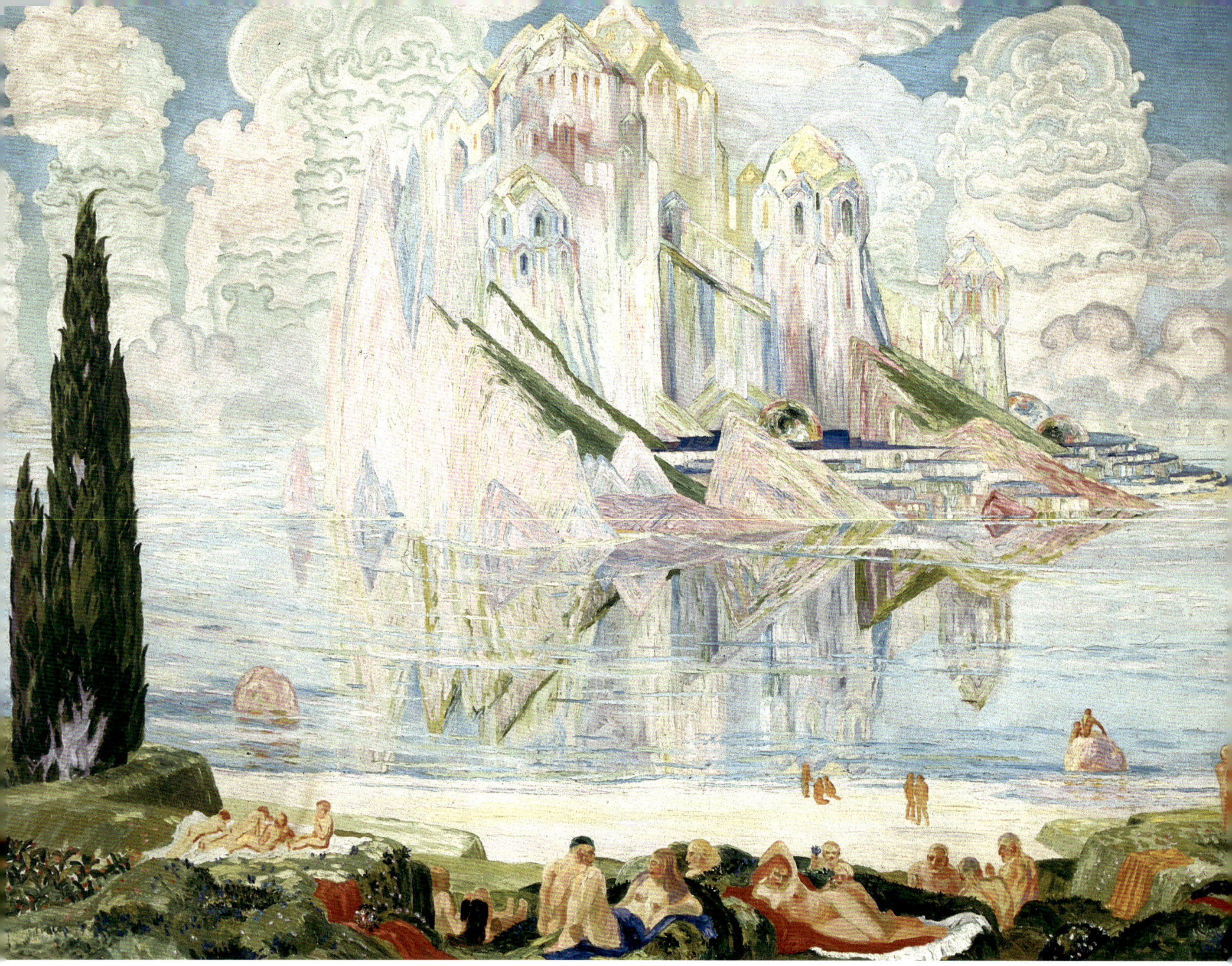

↑ Wenzel Hablik, *The Wonder of the Sea*, 1917
Oil on canvas, 150.5 × 241 cm
Loan from the Wenzel-Hablik-Stiftung, Itzehoe

→ Wenzel Hablik, Cycle of *Utopian Architecture. Aeroplane Towers, Silos, Artist Apartments*, 1921
Oil on canvas, 94 × 189.5 cm
Loan from the Wenzel-Hablik-Stiftung, Itzehoe

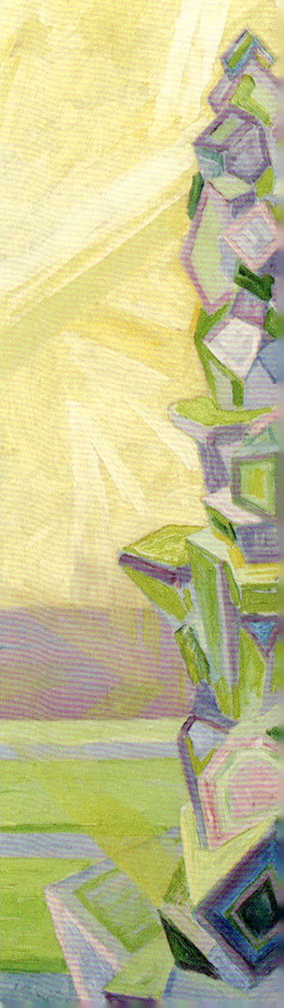

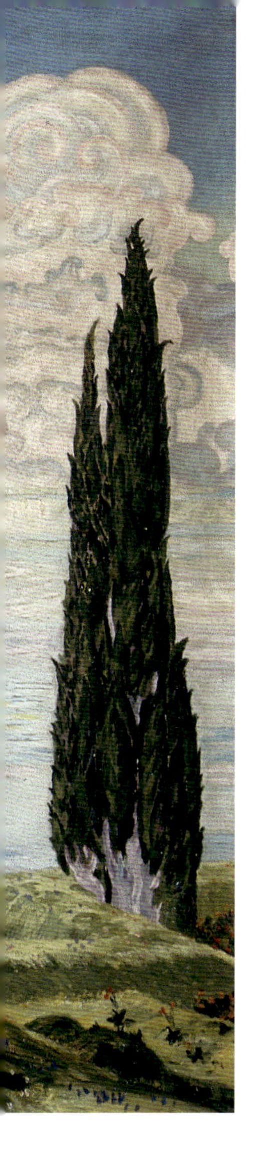

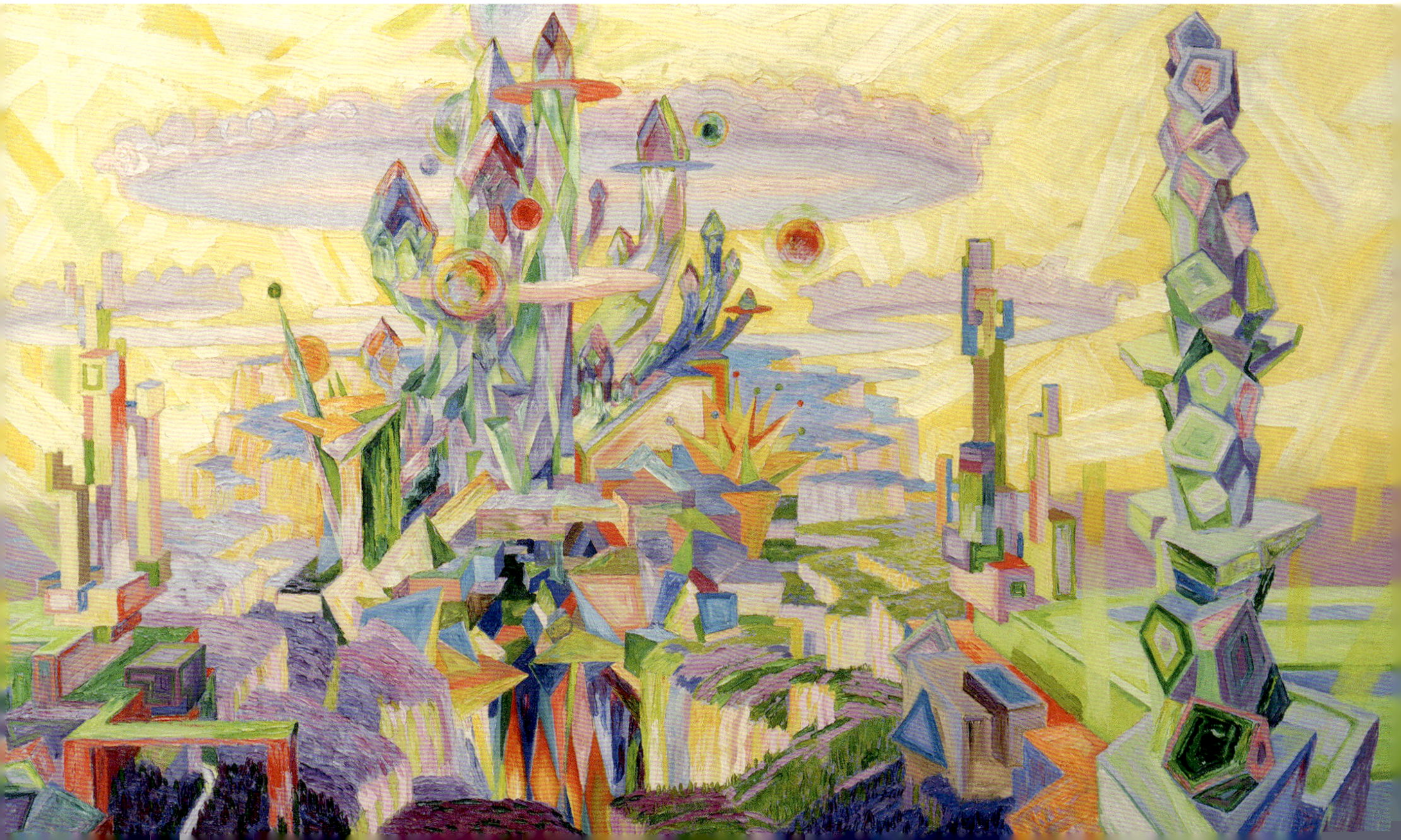

Images from the Modern Psyche: Edvard Munch's Frieze

At the turn of the century, Norwegian painter Edvard Munch was already known in Germany. The "unfinished and raw" nature of his paintings was perceived as so provocative that an exhibition of his work at the Verein Berliner Künstler in 1892 closed after only a few days. But he also had loyal followers, such as the cosmopolite Count Harry Kessler, who worked as a museum director in Weimar from 1903 to 1906. Munch painted several portraits of him during this period.

In Berlin, the theatre director Max Reinhardt contacted Munch to commission a set design for Henrik Ibsen's drama *Gespenster* (*Ghosts*). It was performed shortly after the Norwegian poet's death in 1906 when the Kammerspiele opened as a second stage of the Deutsches Theater. Munch was also asked to create a frieze for a hall on the upper level of the Kammerspiele, a space that was not completed until 1907 due to construction delays.

For some time, Munch had been developing variable arrangements for his paintings, the style of which his contemporaries referred to as "psychic naturalism". He titled them *Fries. Darstellung einer Reihe von Lebensbildern* (Frieze: Representations of Life) for the Berlin Secession in 1902, while in 1904 he presented them as *Motive aus dem modernen Seelenleben* (Images from the Modern Psyche) in Christiania (now Oslo). It was not until much later, in 1918, that he chose the overarching title *Lebensfries* (The Frieze of Life) for these paintings.

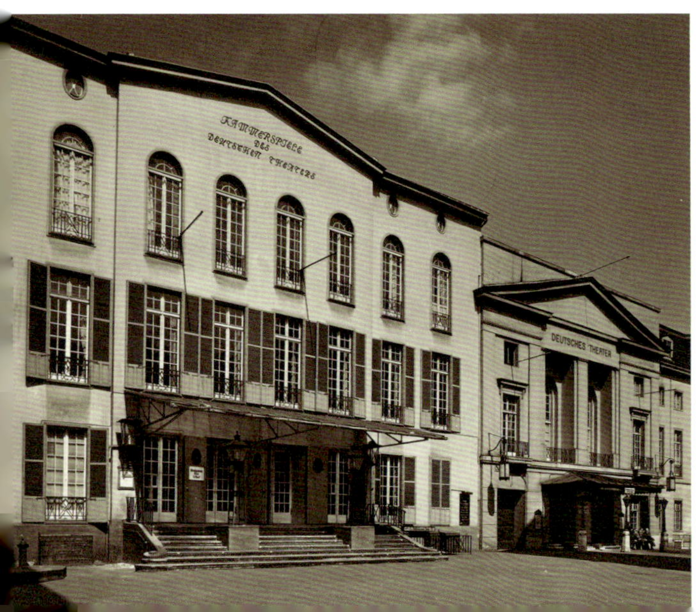

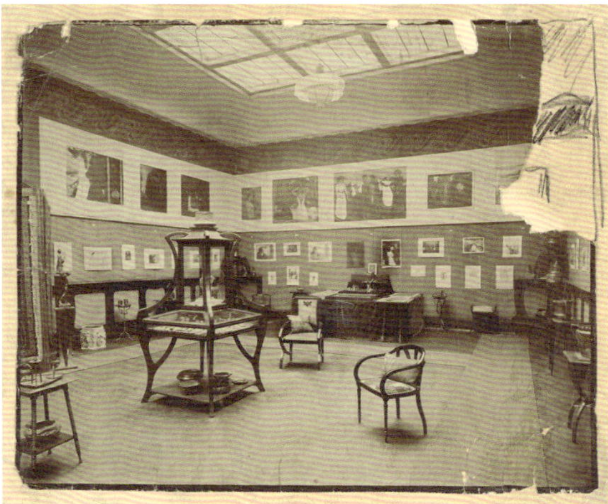

Munch's frieze for Max Reinhardt consisted of twelve paintings, nine of which are now part of the Nationalgalerie collection. Unlike other frieze arrangements, it was created for a specific location: a Kammerspiele foyer above the oval entrance hall leading to balcony and loge seats. The works were shown there until 1912 and could be seen directly under the 4.70 m high ceiling of the rectangular space. Before it opened to the public, Munch explained the works to painter Emil Nolde and Gustav Schiefler, an art collector and Hamburg's district court director. On 29 December 1907, the latter wrote, "Munch interpreted the images for us. They show the daily lives of coastal Norwegians: girls gather at the beach, talking, until young fellows from the neighbourhood arrive on the scene in rowboats. They dance and play parlour games together. At last, the boys leave, and the girls scatter, but one stays behind to sit on the beach in her red dress, deep in melancholic thought." The story takes place at Åsgårdstrand, where Munch's studio house with a view of the Oslofjord was located.

Like Ibsen's dramas, Munch's paintings are about a modern articulation of timeless themes. This is also true of the frieze, whose shapes and figures were never filled in with identifying details because they were designed to be hung high up on the wall. Munch used brittle, chalky casein tempera paints and unprimed, raw canvasses that absorbed the paint to create a mural painting aesthetic. It's no coincidence that the rough ground and the matte colouration have much in common with frescoes of the past.

Dieter Scholz

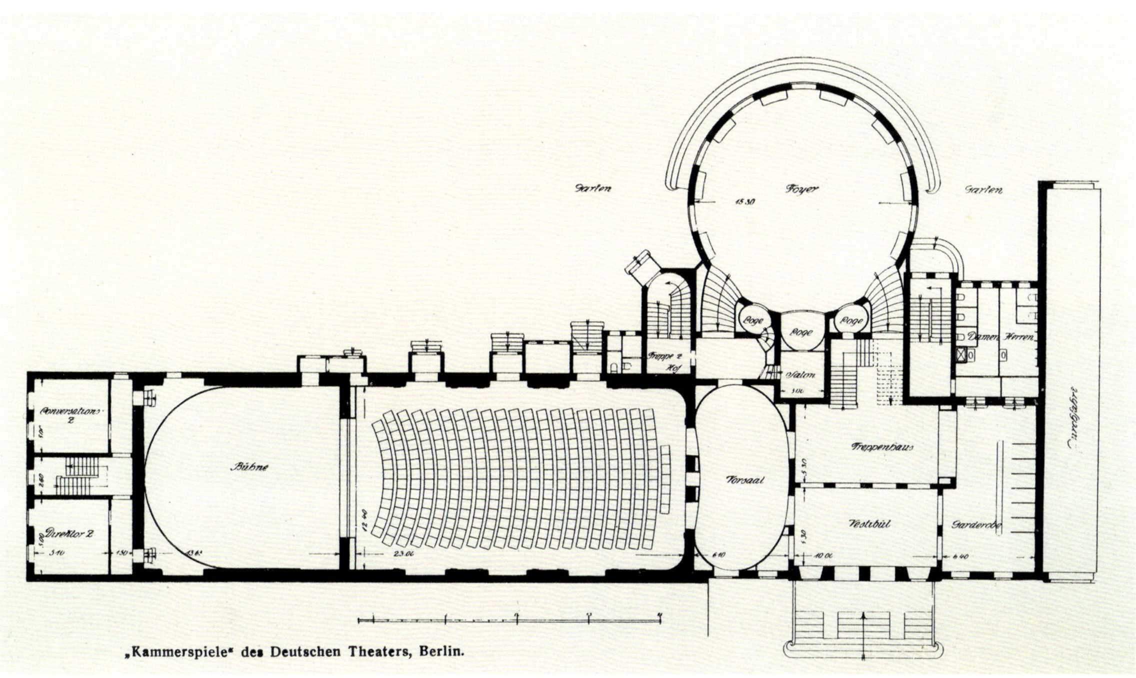

↑ Floor plan of the Kammerspiele in Berlin, *Der Baumeister*, no. 10, August 1912, p. 129
← Kammerspiele of the Deutsches Theater, Berlin, 1905–06
← Edvard Munch exhibition at the Kunsthalle P. H. Beyer & Sohn, Leipzig, 1903

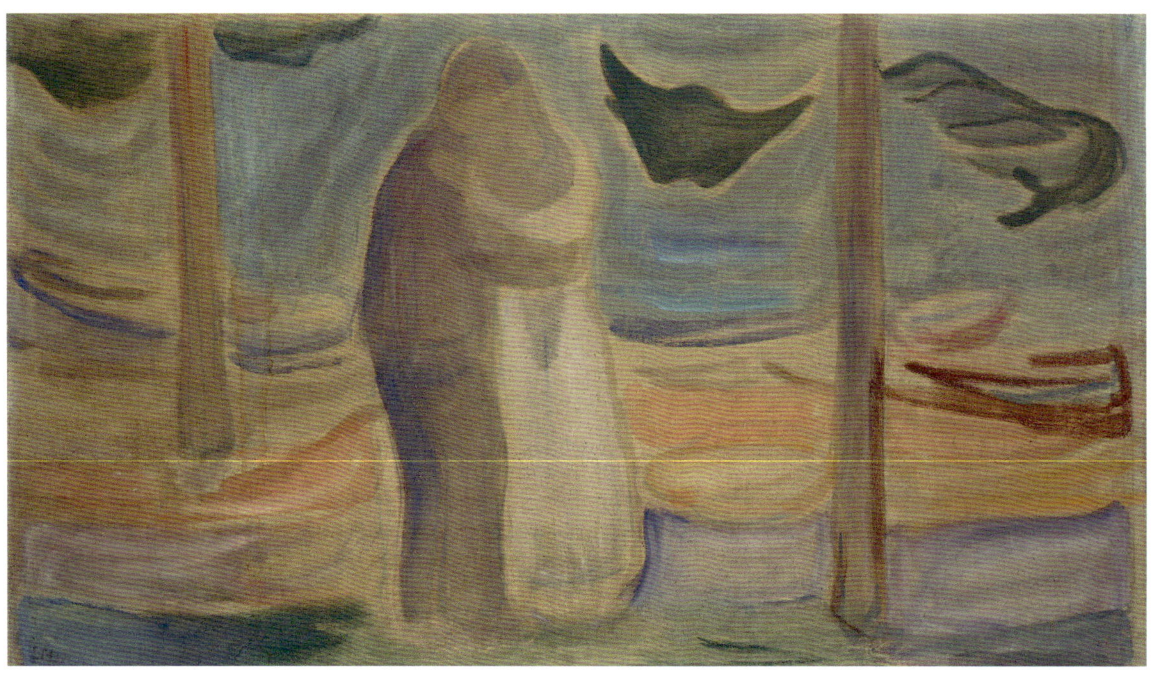

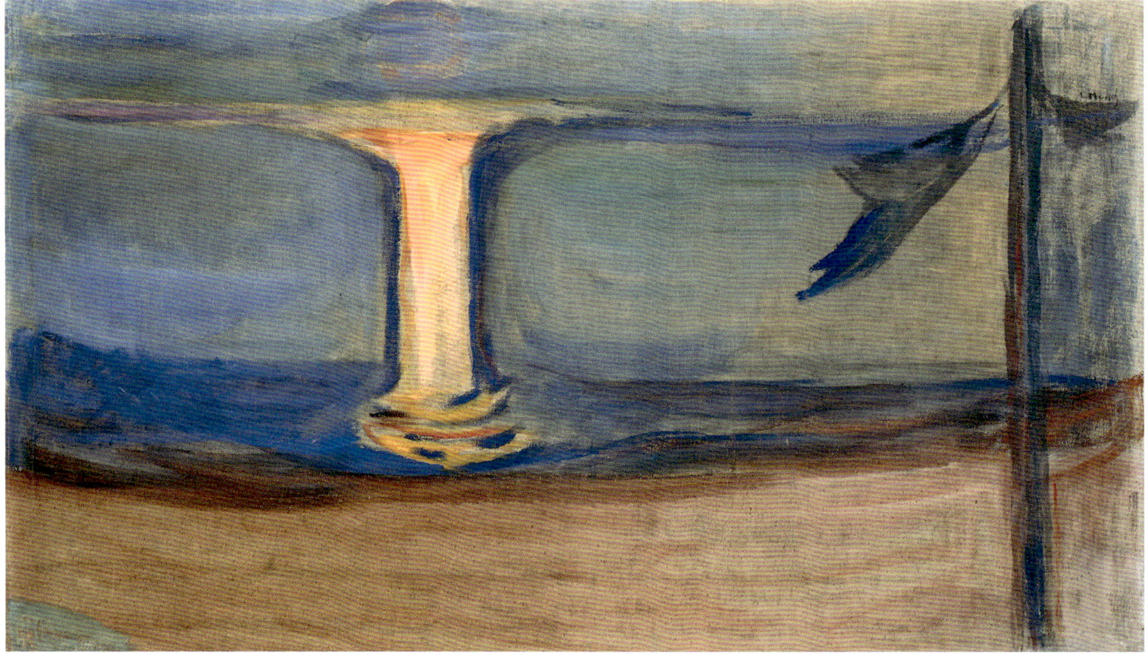

Edvard Munch, *Frieze* for the theatre of Max Reinhardt in Berlin, 1906–07

Aasgaard Beach; Two Young Women; Summer Night; Couple on the Beach; Trees by the Sea; Desire; Two Young Women with Sunflower; Young Women Picking Fruit
Acquired in 1966 from Galerie Beyeler, Basel, by the Land Berlin with funds from the Deutsche Gesellschaft für bildende Kunst and the Deutsche Klassenlotterie for the Galerie des 20. Jahrhunderts, Berlin (West)

Melancholy
Acquired in 1930; exhibited at the Kronprinzen-Palais until 1936; confiscated in 1937 as "degenerate"; appropriated by Hermann Göring in 1940; afterwards in a private collection in Oslo; reacquired in 1997 with support from the Ernst von Siemens Kunststiftung and the Kulturstiftung der Länder

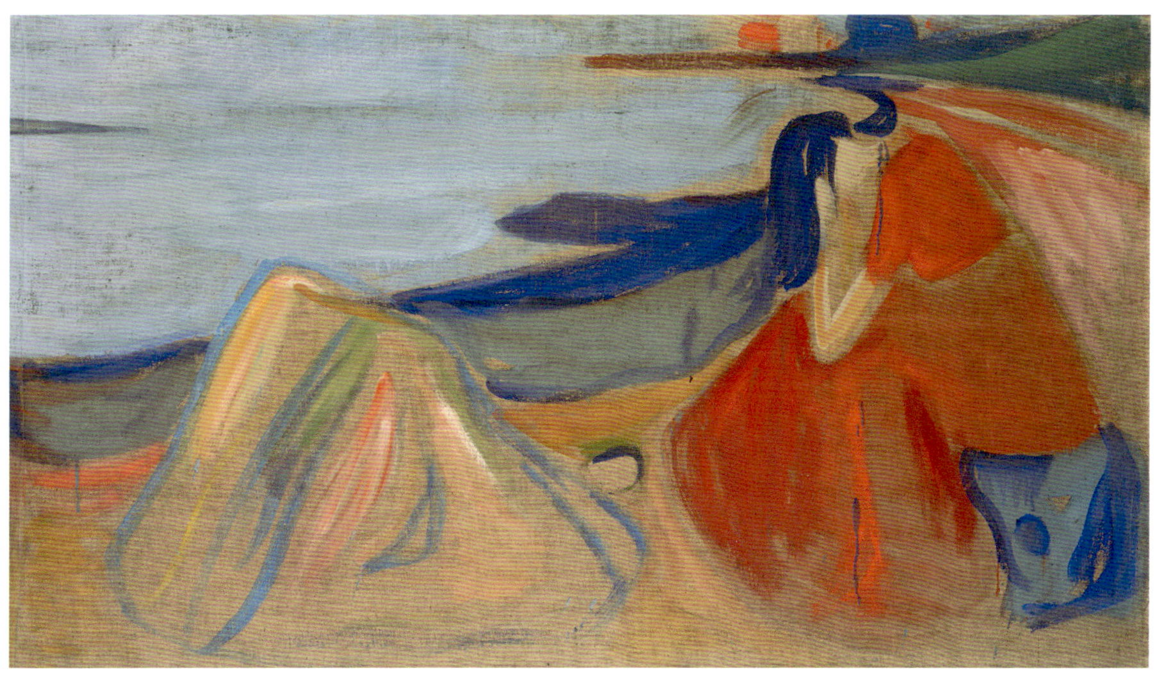

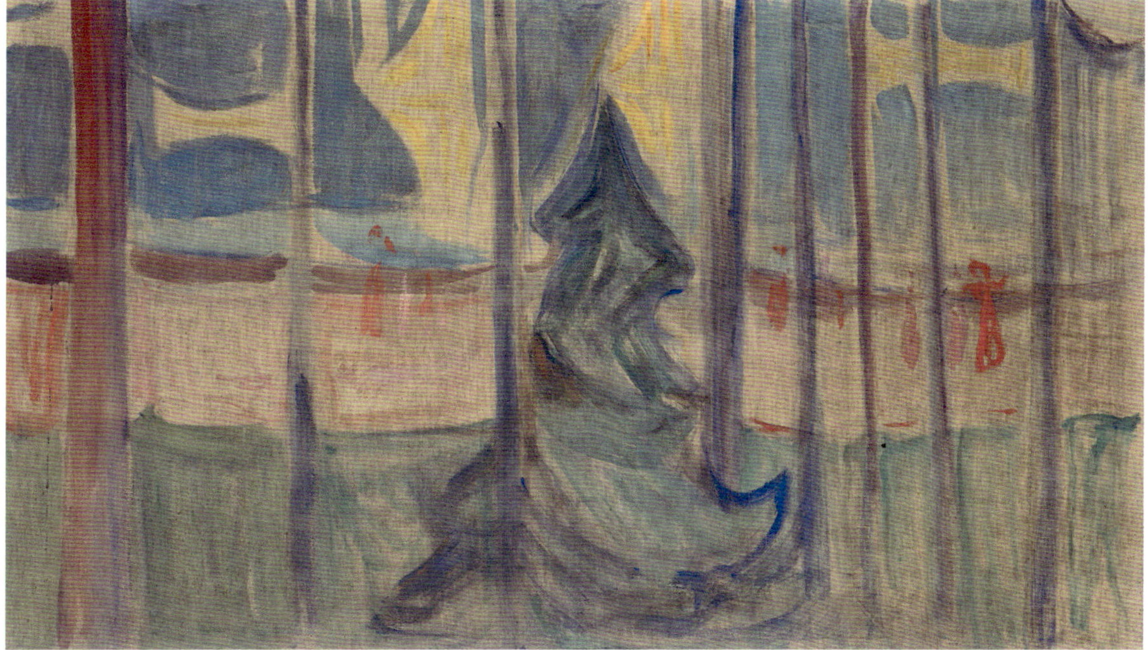

↖ *Couple on the Beach*, 1906–07
Tempera on canvas, 90 × 155 cm

↖ *Aasgaard Beach*, 1906–07
Tempera on canvas, 91 × 157.5 cm

↑ *Melancholy*, 1906–07
Tempera on canvas, 87 × 156 cm

↑ *Trees by the Sea*, 1906–07
Tempera on canvas, 91 × 157.5 cm

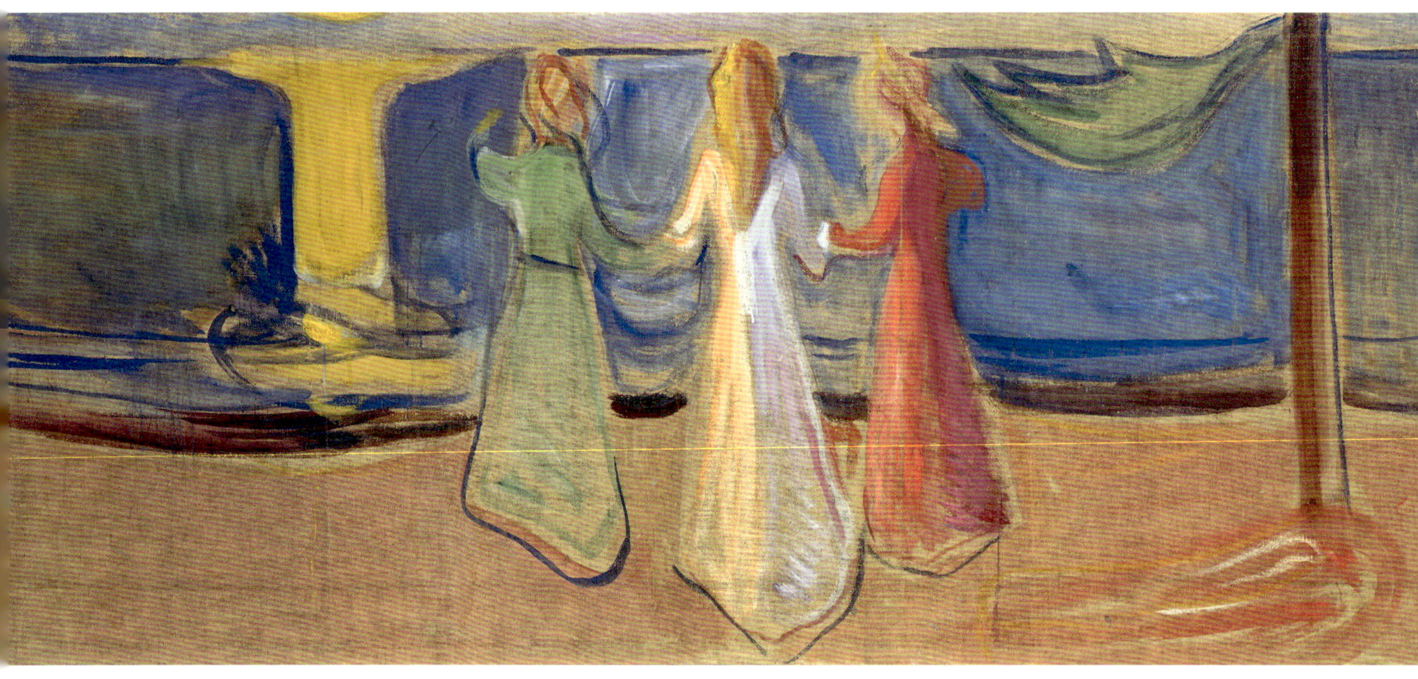

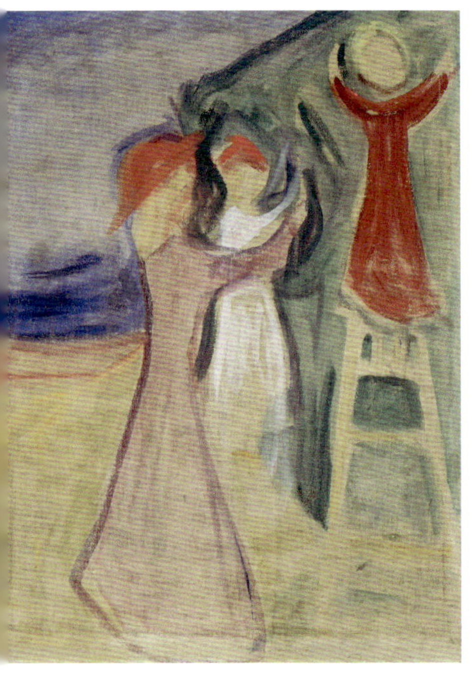

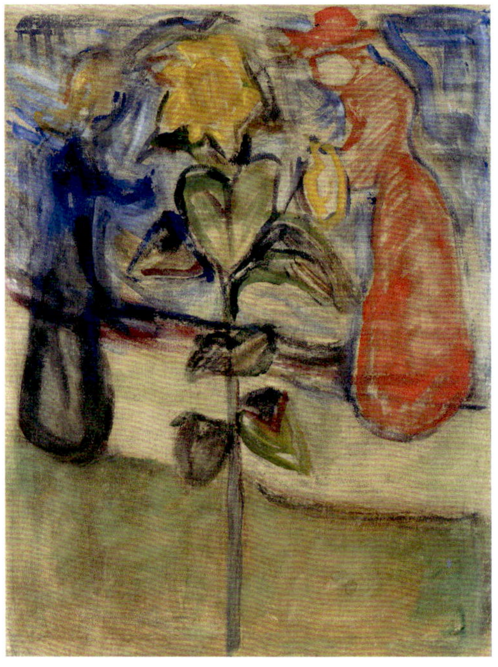

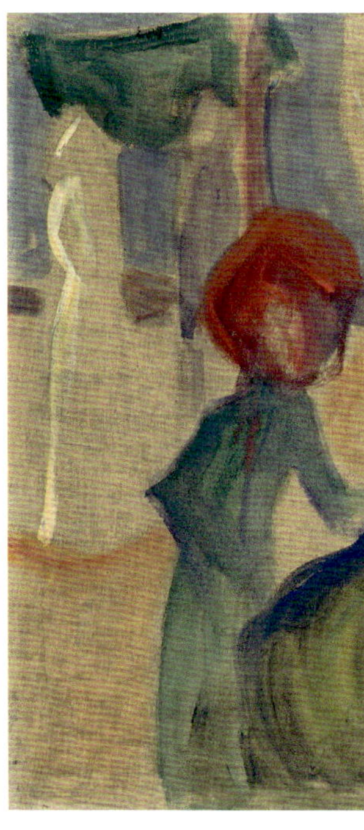

↑ *Desire*, 1906–07
Tempera on canvas, 91 × 252 cm

↖ *Young Women Picking Fruit*, 1906–07
Tempera on canvas, 89.5 × 70 cm

↗ *Two Young Women with Sunflower*, 1906–07
Tempera on canvas, 89.5 × 70 cm

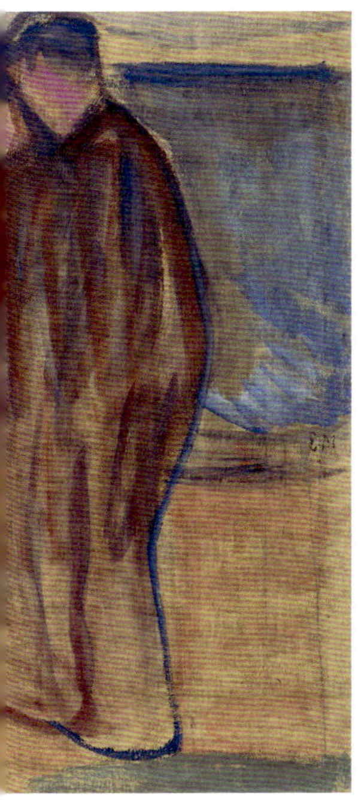

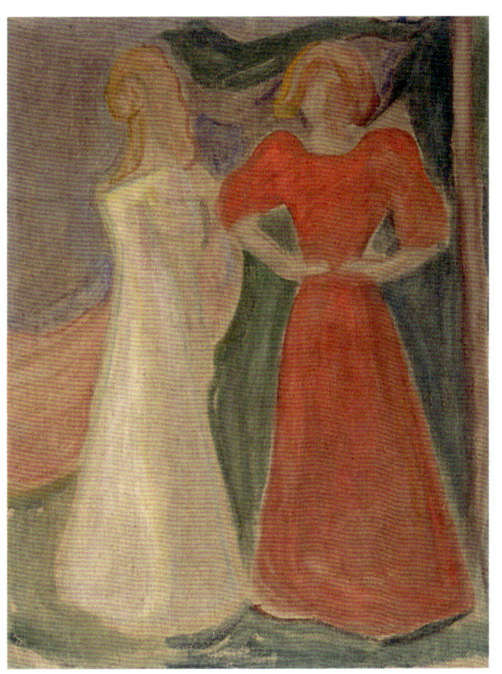

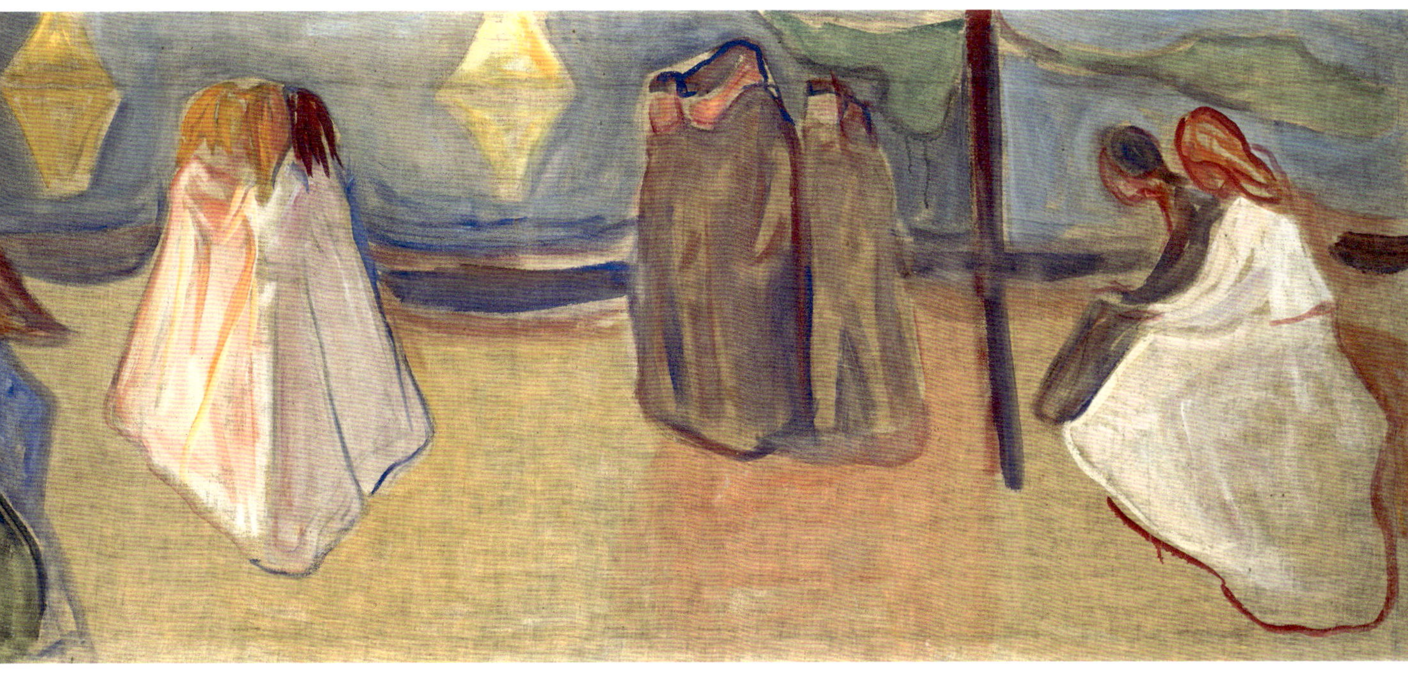

↗ *Two Young Women*, 1906–07
Tempera on canvas, 90 × 70 cm

↑ *Summer Night*, 1906–07
Tempera on canvas, 91 × 252 cm

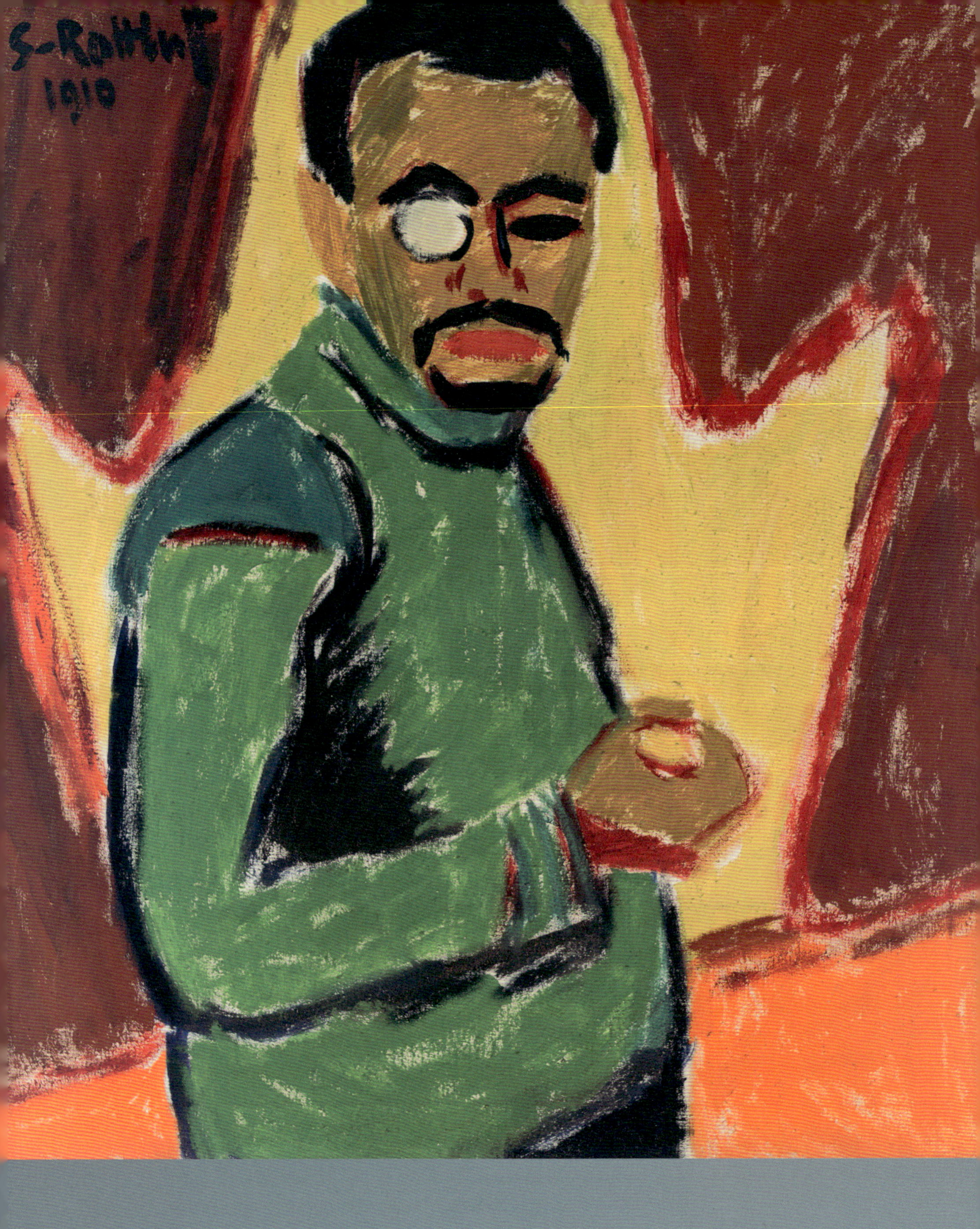
1910

Freedom of Expression

In the first two decades of the 20th century, Expressionism mirrored a social transformation that was turning away from the *impressions* reality made on the senses and towards a new emphasis on the significance of the individual. Now painting was looking to become an *expression* of inner experiences that intended to exaggerate formal representation. This was achieved with the help of strong contours, luminous colours, broad brushstrokes, an absence of detail and unusual perspectives.

Expressionism was a European phenomenon. The term was originally used for emerging French painting but soon came to be associated only with new German art, particularly the works created by the artists groups Brücke (Bridge) and Der Blaue Reiter (The Blue Rider). The painters of the Brücke group, founded in 1905, were interested in overcoming the academic *Gedankenkunst* (cerebral art) and instead creating immediate emotions through the use of intense colours and simplified forms. Their inspiration also came from non-European sources: The early years of the Brücke saw the artists draw from Japonism; later, they were inspired by African and South Pacific sculptures.

Karl Schmidt-Rottluff, *Self-Portrait with Monocle*, 1910
Oil on canvas, 84 × 76.5 cm
Gift to the Nationalgalerie, Berlin (West) from Maria Möller-Garny, Cologne, in memory of Ferdinand Möller, 1961

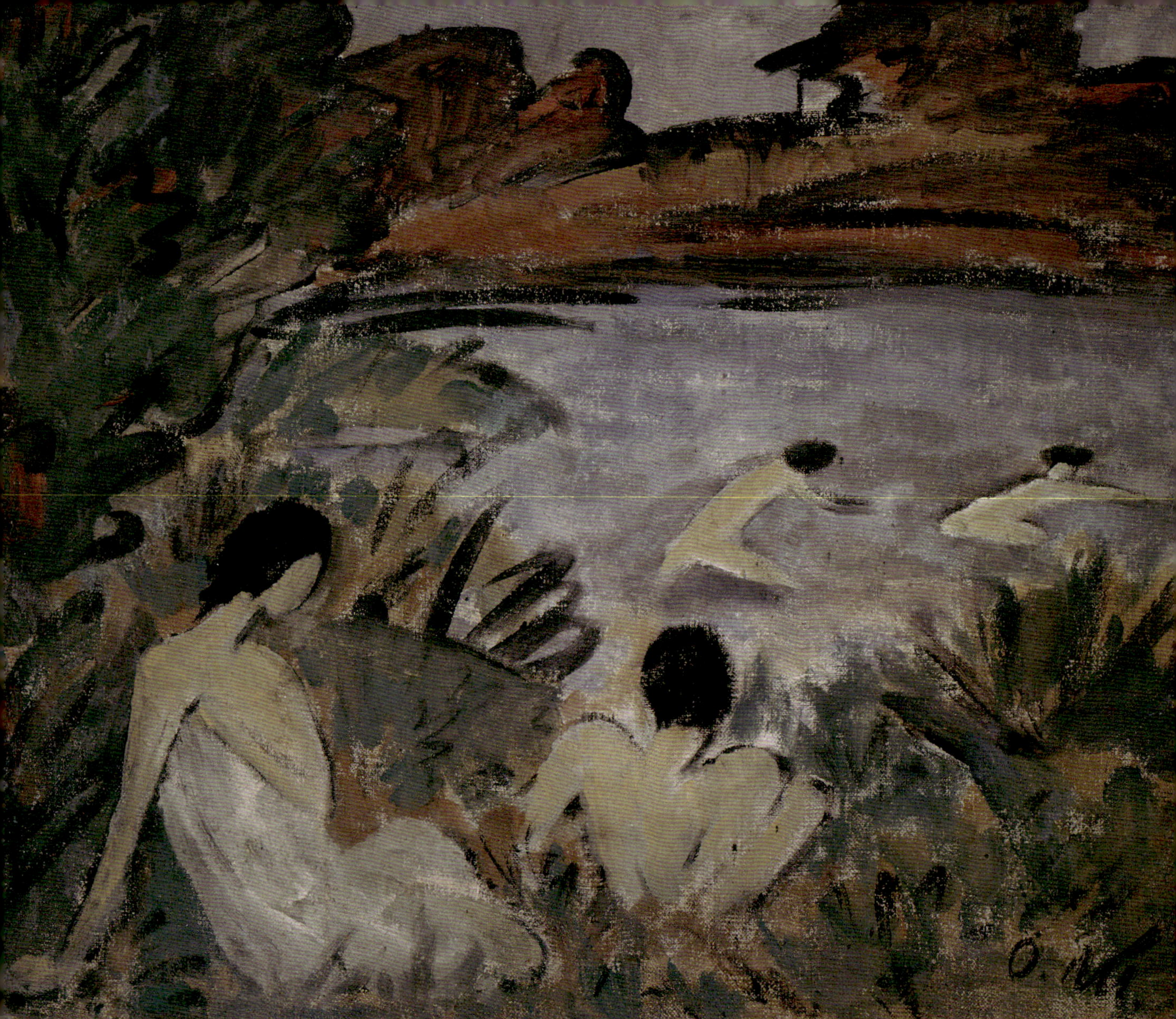

↑ Otto Mueller, *Summer Day*, c. 1922
Distemper on canvas, 80 × 98 cm
Acquired in 1922 in exchange at the Galerie Goldschmidt & Wallerstein, Berlin; confiscated in 1937 as "degenerate" and sold; reacquired in 1958 for the Nationalgalerie, Berlin (West)

→ Otto Mueller, *Bathers in the Thicket of Reeds*, c. 1924
Distemper on burlap, 92 × 79 cm
Acquired in 1955 by the Land Berlin for the Galerie des 20. Jahrhunderts, Berlin (West)

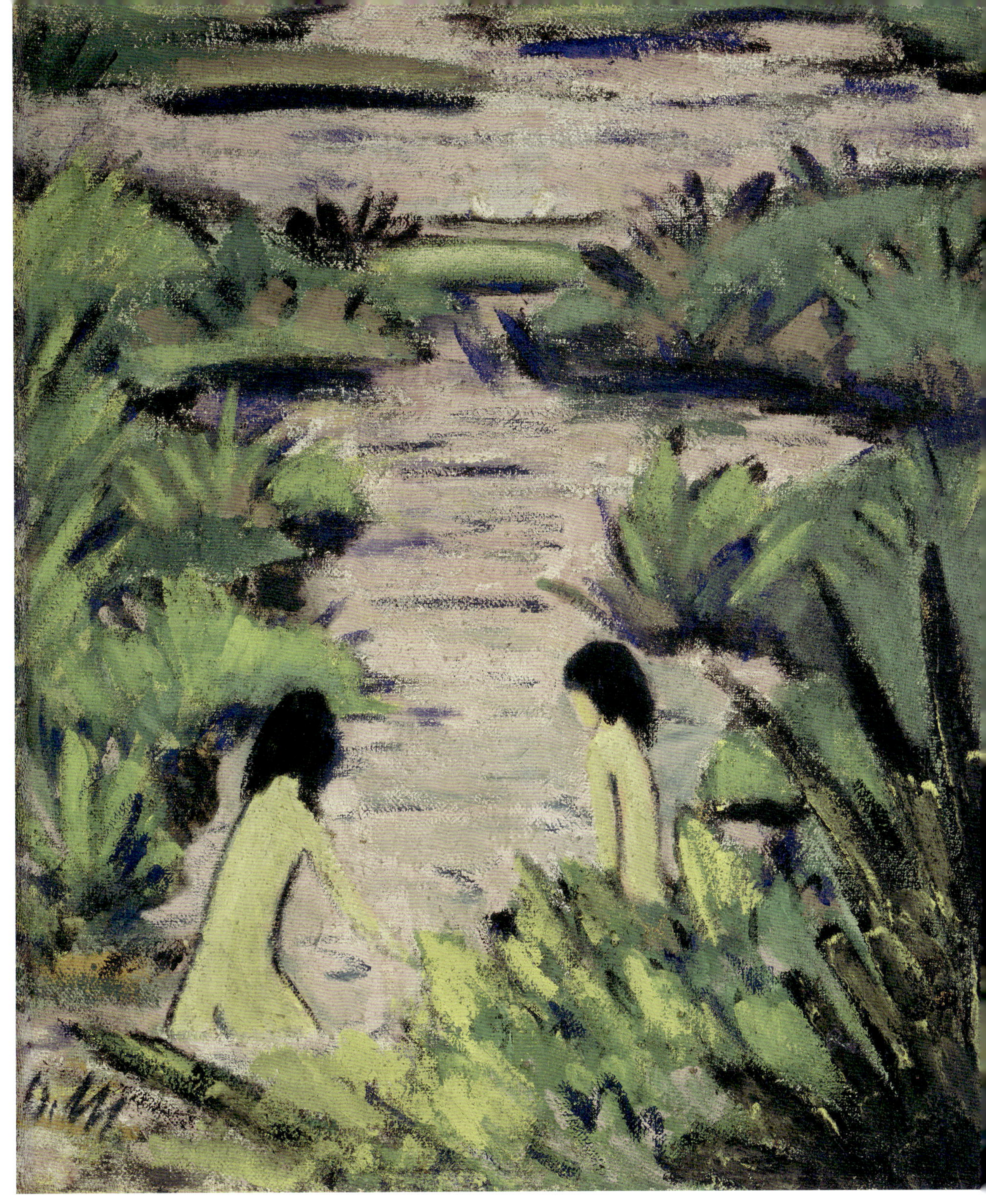

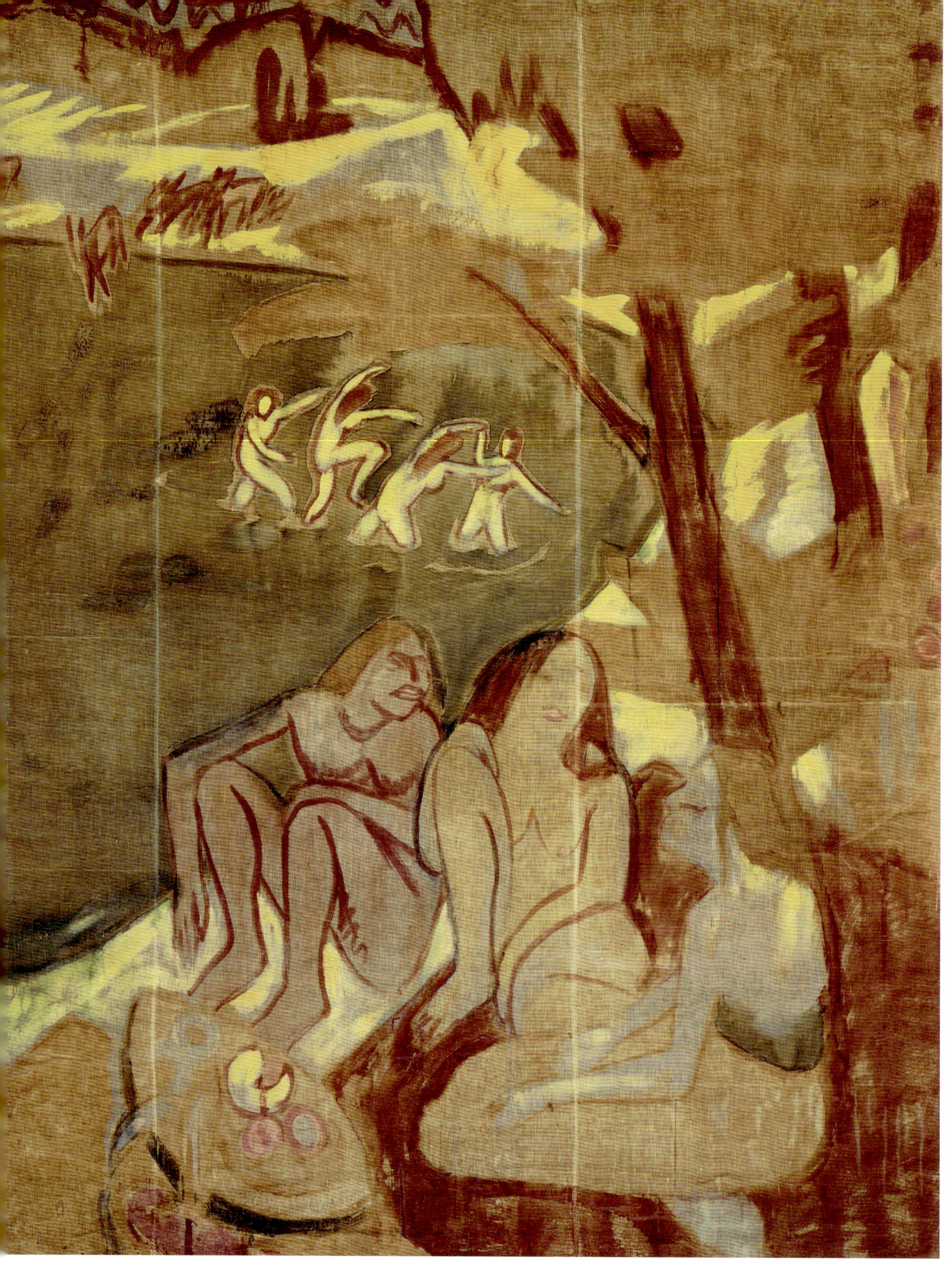

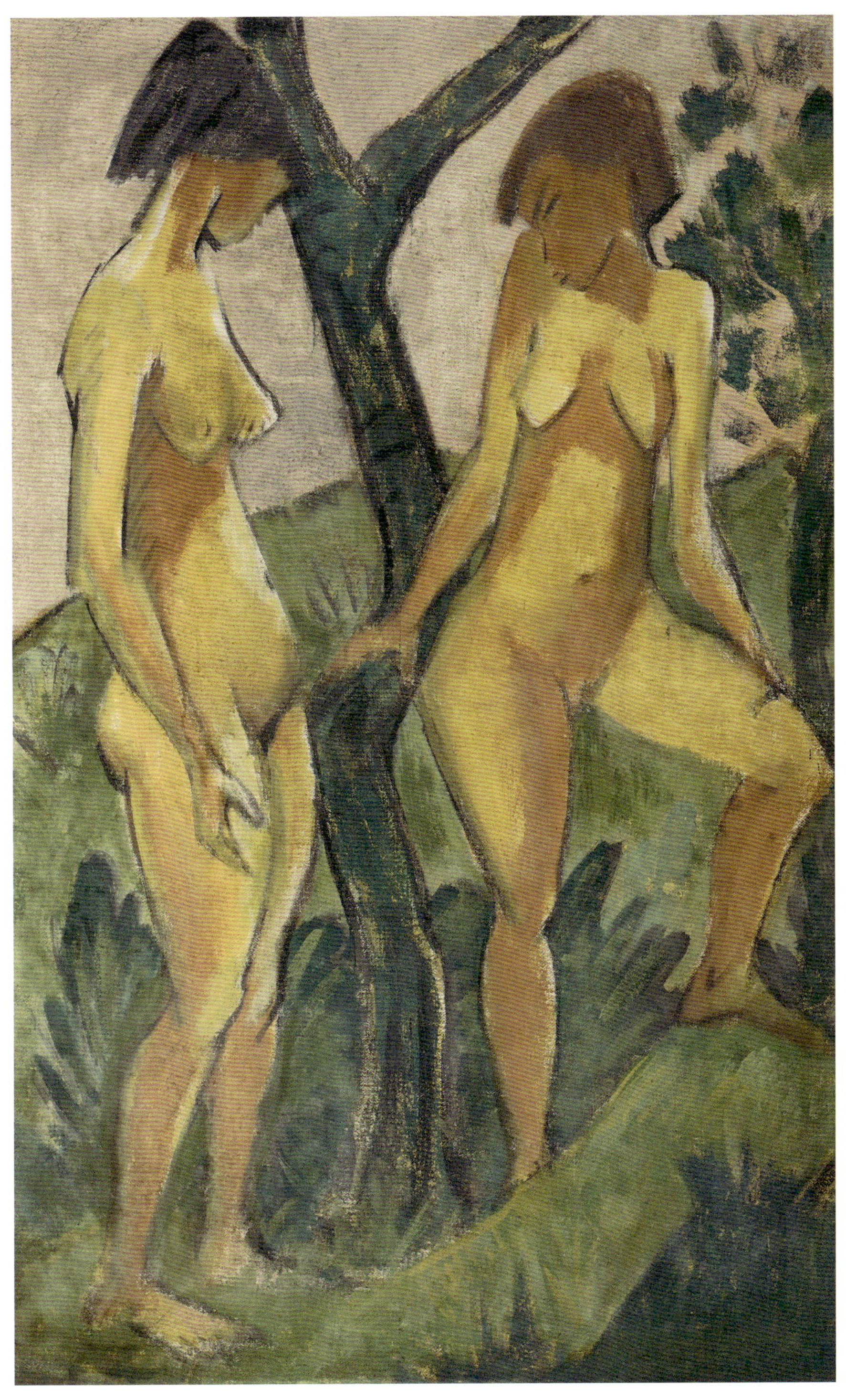

↗ Otto Mueller, *Two Girls,* c. 1927
Distemper on burlap, 175 × 111 cm
Acquired in 1953 by the Land Berlin for the
Galerie des 20. Jahrhunderts, Berlin (West)

↖ Max Pechstein, *On the Lakeshore,* 1912
Fabric paint on calico, 257 × 204 cm
Acquired in 1961 from the Eduard Plietzsch
Collection, Berlin/Cologne, by the Land Berlin
for the Galerie des 20. Jahrhunderts, Berlin (West)

Who Were the Female Models for the Brücke Artists?

The architecture students Ernst Ludwig Kirchner, Erich Heckel, Karl Schmidt-Rottluff and Fritz Bleyl formed the artist collective Brücke in Dresden in 1905. They were later joined by Max Pechstein and Otto Mueller. At first, they hired professional models to pose nude for their work. To achieve a more natural and spontaneous aesthetic, they introduced a "fifteen-minute rule" that required the models to frequently change their positions. Soon, the painters began painting female acquaintances, partners, and girls from their immediate environment to save money. They, too, were depicted nude.

Who were the female nude models for the Brücke artists? One of Heckel's paintings shows two naked women playing a board game in Kirchner's studio. Completed in 1910, the painting is titled *Die beiden Schwestern* (The Two Sisters), but recent research refutes this implied familial connection. The figures shown are named Dodo and Fränzi, and they were not related. Doris Große (Dodo) was Kirchner's 26-year-old partner at the time; she worked as a sales clerk and later became a milliner. However, Lina Franziska Fehrmann (Fränzi), whose mother managed a store that sold hats and cleaning supplies, was still a child, only nine at the time. Fränzi frequented the artists' studios and accompanied them on trips to the Moritzburg lakes north of Dresden.

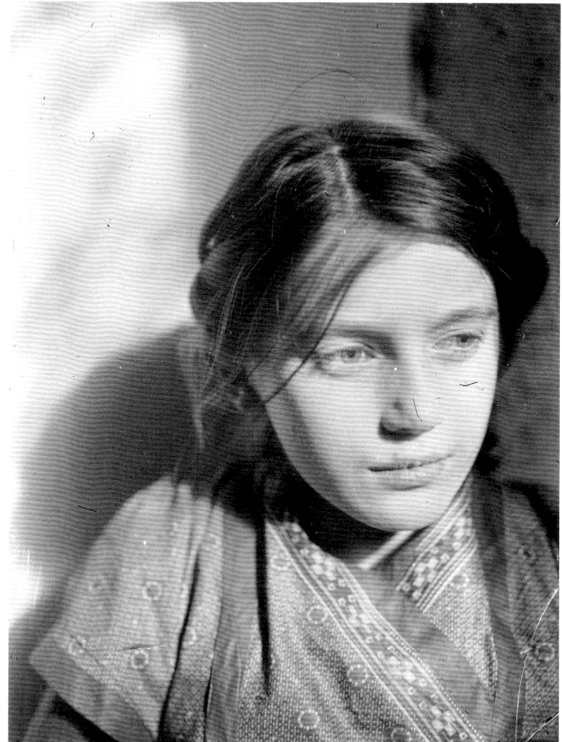

↗ Dodo Große and Ernst Ludwig Kirchner, c. 1910
→ Ernst Ludwig Kirchner, Photo of Fränzi Fehrmann, 1910

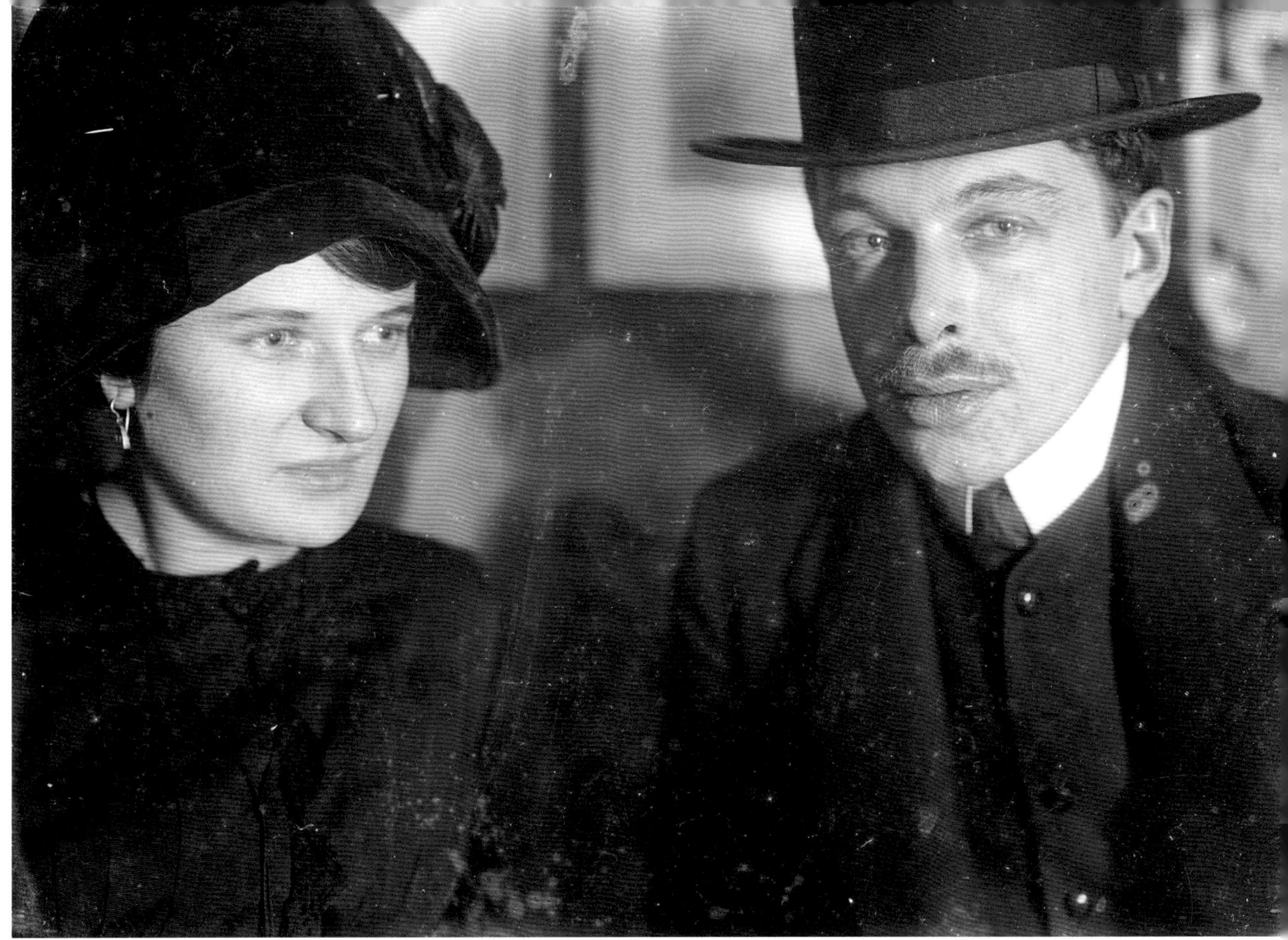

Max Pechstein met the 15-year-old model Charlotte Kaprolat (Lotte) at sculptor Georg Kolbe's Berlin studio in the winter of 1908–09. He married her shortly after her 18th birthday in the spring of 1911. That summer, he painted her portrait and titled it *Am Strand von Nidden* (On the Beach at Nidden).

Kirchner also painted several likenesses of his partner Erna Schilling in *Badende am Strand (Fehmarn)* [Bathers at the Beach (Fehmarn)]. She was 28 years old when they met in Berlin in 1912. The two lived together until he died in 1938 without having married. Paintings produced by Otto Mueller, such as *Zwei Mädchen* (Two Girls) from 1925–28, also showed different nude women reminiscent of his later wife, Maria Mayerhofer (Maschka). The couple lived together from 1899 until 1919.

All these works suggest an intimacy with those portrayed. If the sitters were still minors, this intimacy becomes problematic, as is the case with Fränzi, who was only nine years old. Seen in the light of the sexual abuse of children, these images become questionable. Lingering suspicions tinge the images and their creators, making them controversial. But questions about possible sexual misconduct or abuse by the painters involving their underage nude models can no longer be clarified from today's perspective.

Dieter Scholz

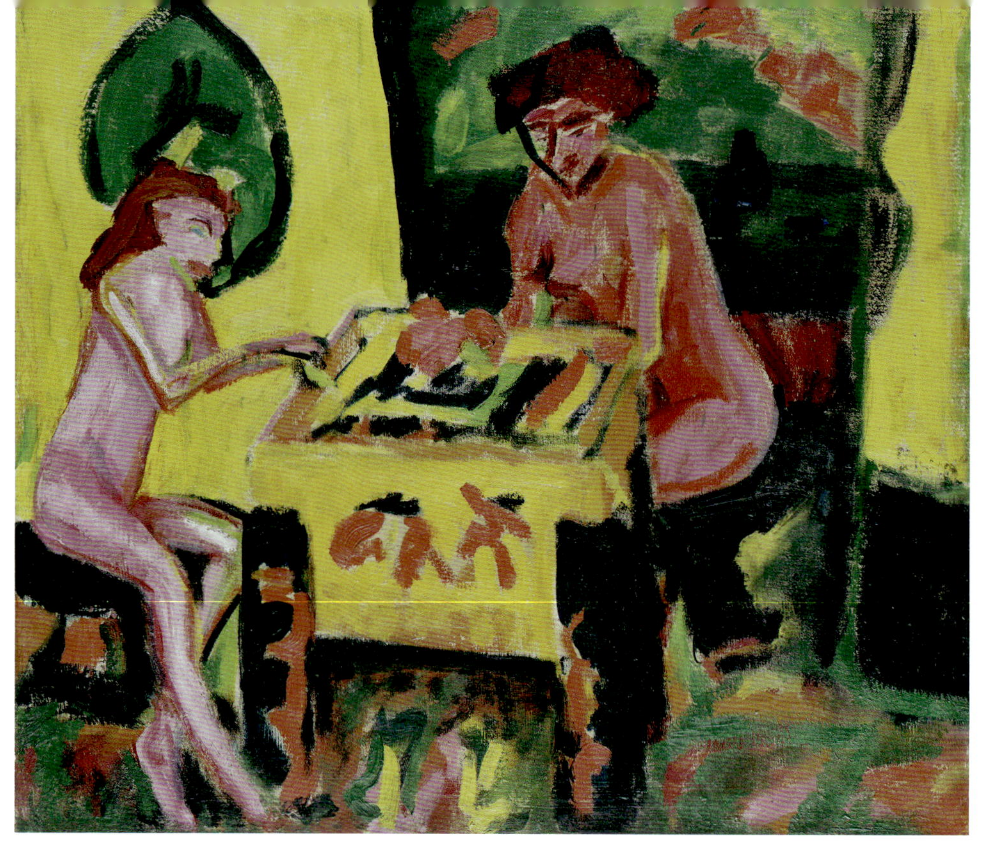

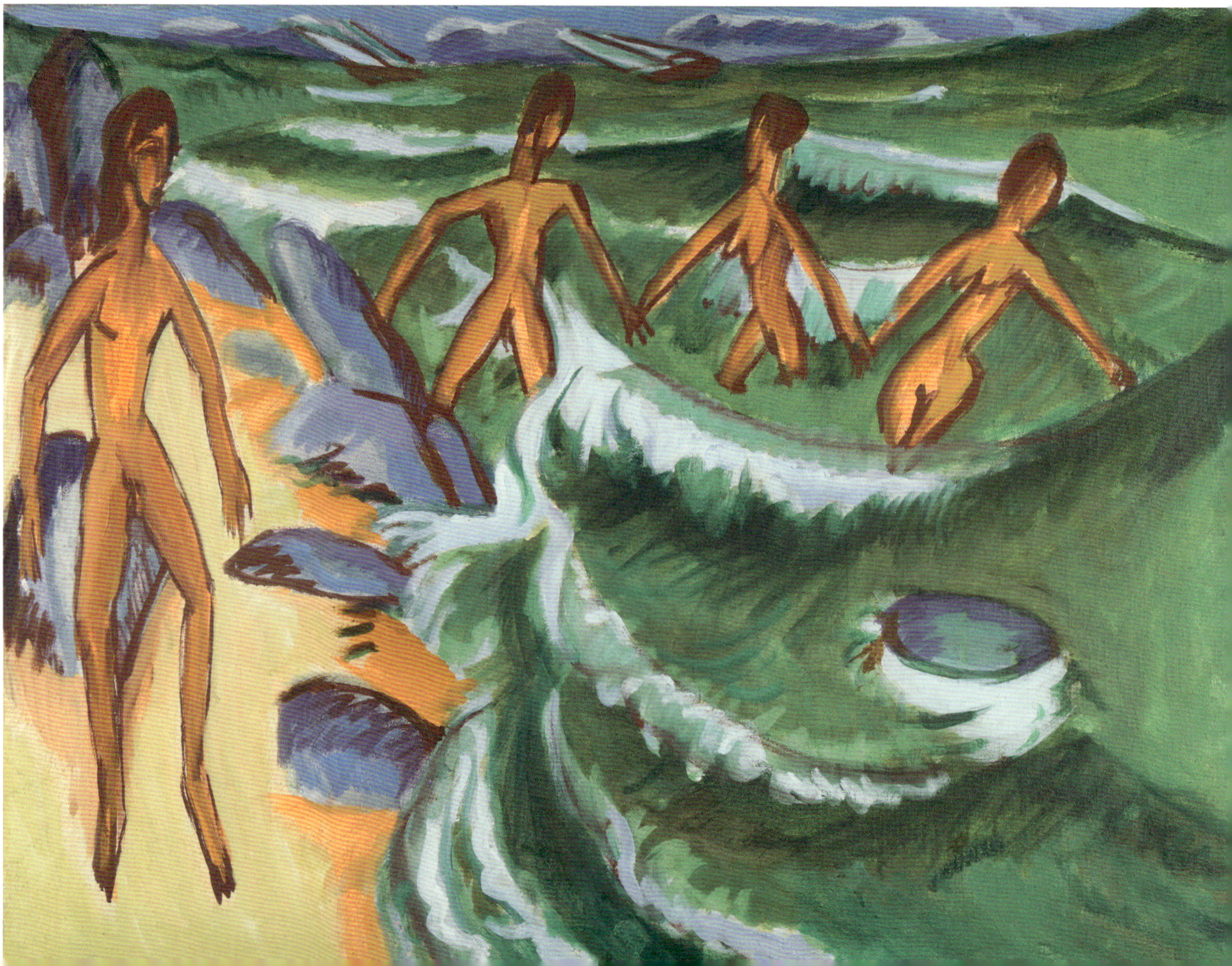

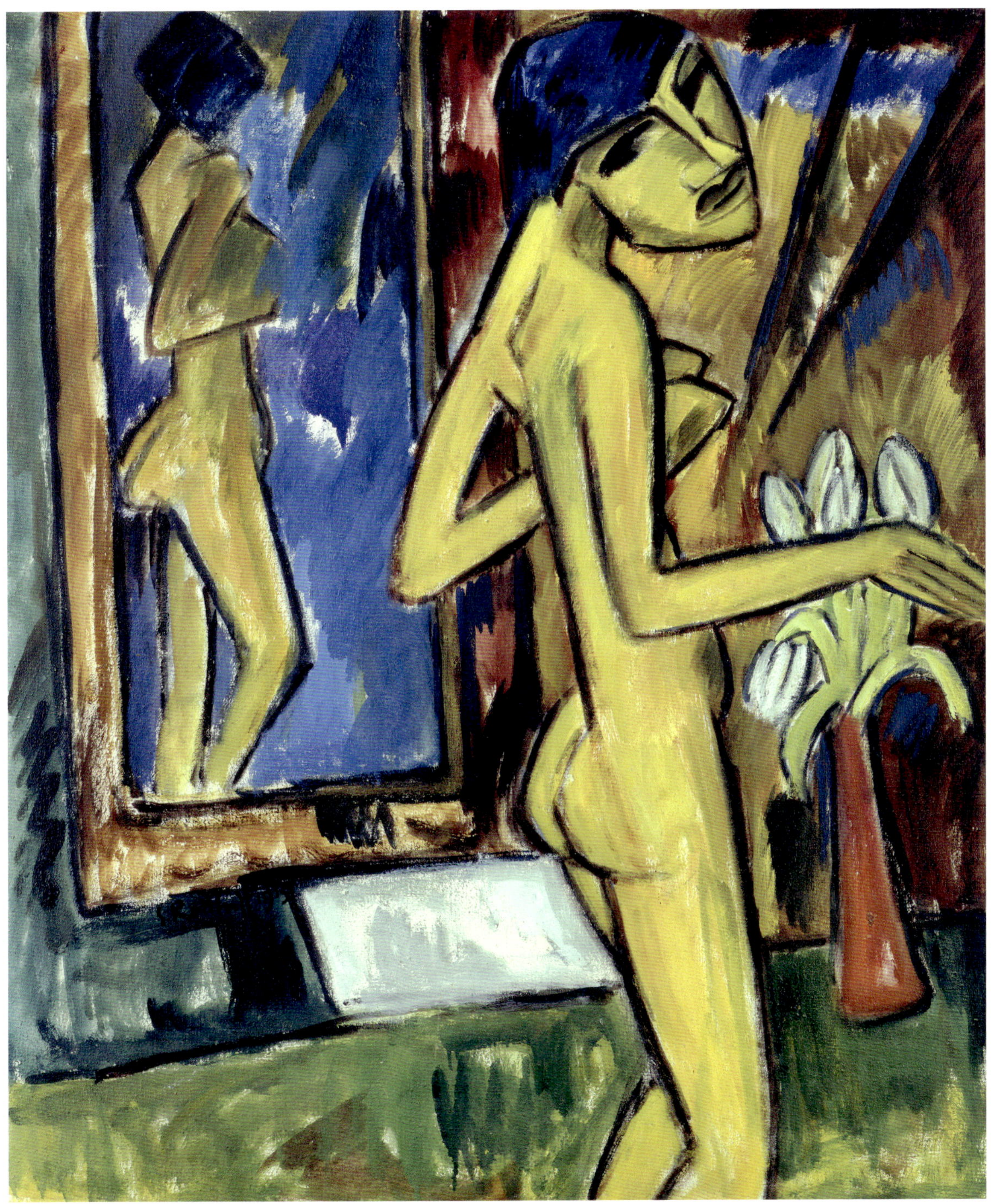

↑ Karl Schmidt-Rottluff, *Girl in Front of a Mirror*, 1915
Oil on canvas, 101 × 87 cm
Acquired in 1954 from the artist by the Land Berlin for the Galerie des 20. Jahrhunderts, Berlin (West)

↖ Erich Heckel, *The Two Sisters*, 1910
Oil on canvas, 69.5 × 79.5 cm
Acquired in 1949 by the Land Berlin for the Galerie des 20. Jahrhunderts, Berlin (West)

← Ernst Ludwig Kirchner, *Bathers at the Beach (Fehmarn)*, 1913
Oil on canvas, 76 × 100 cm
Acquired in 1955 by the Land Berlin for the Galerie des 20. Jahrhunderts, Berlin (West)

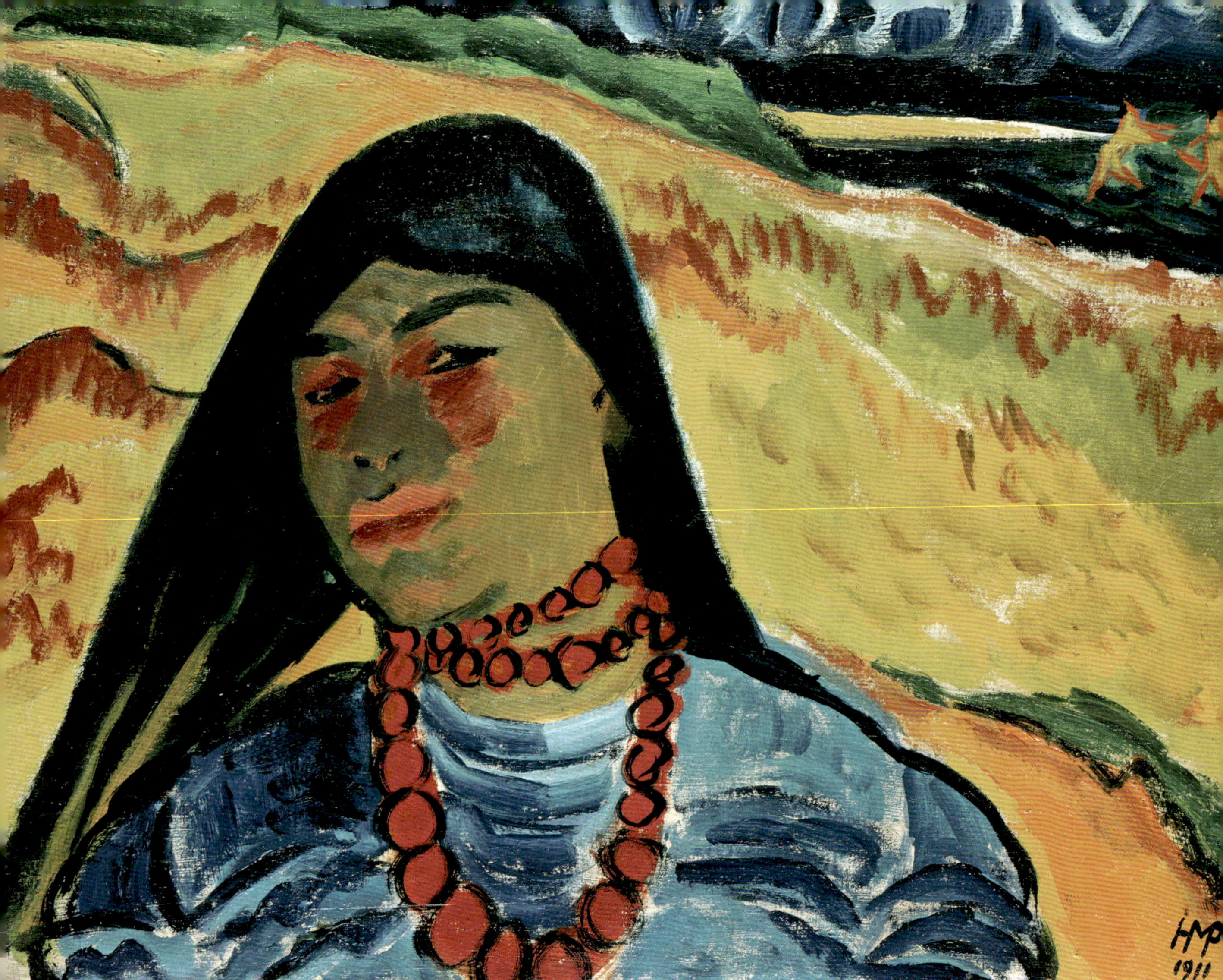

↑ Max Pechstein, *On the Beach at Nidden*, 1911
Oil on canvas, 50 × 65 cm
Acquired in 1959 for the Nationalgalerie, Berlin (West)

→ Max Pechstein, *Seated Girl*, 1910
Oil on canvas, 80 × 70 cm
Acquired in 1948 from the artist for the Galerie des 20. Jahrhunderts; gift from the Magistrat von Groß-Berlin to the Nationalgalerie, Berlin (East), 1951

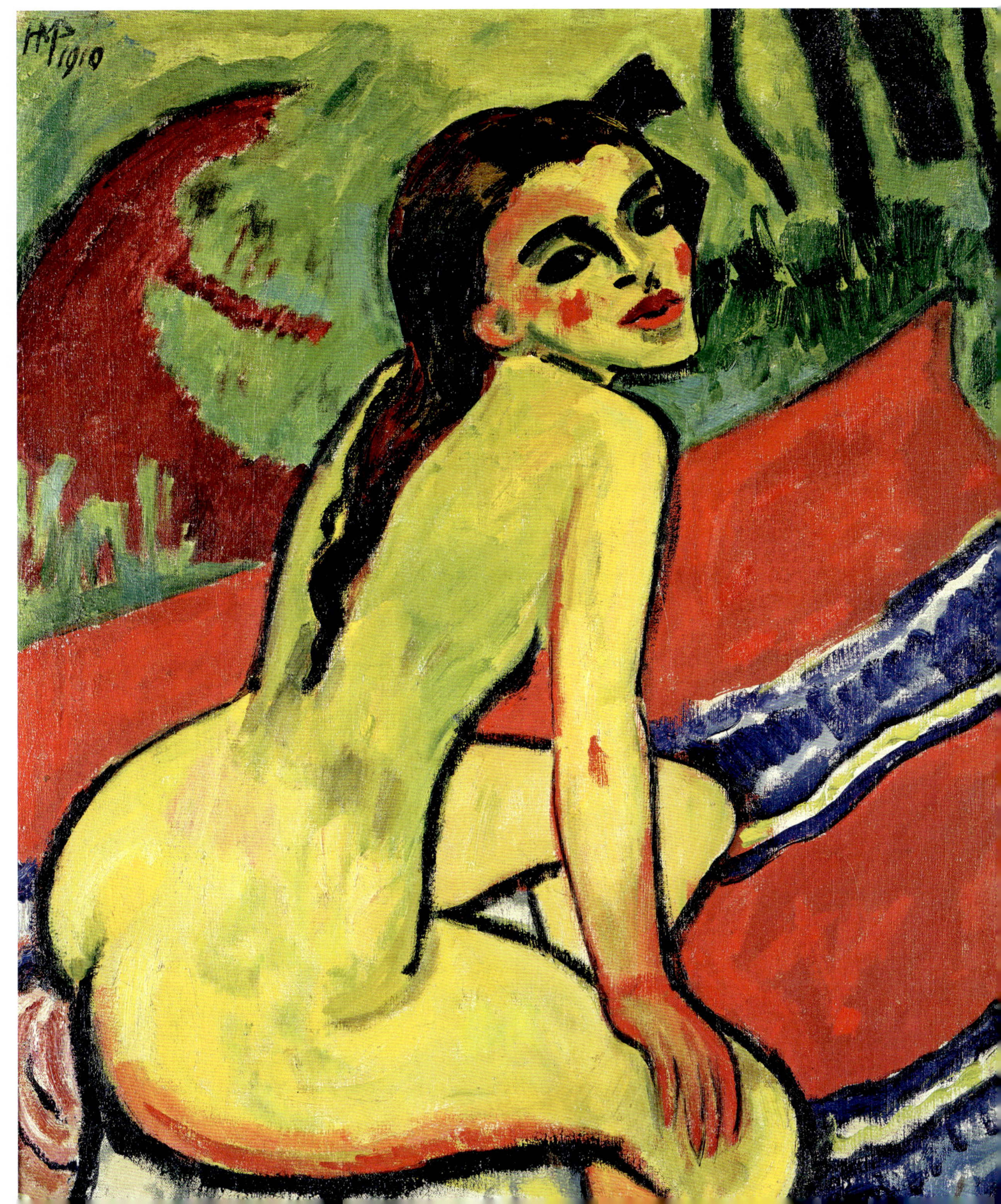

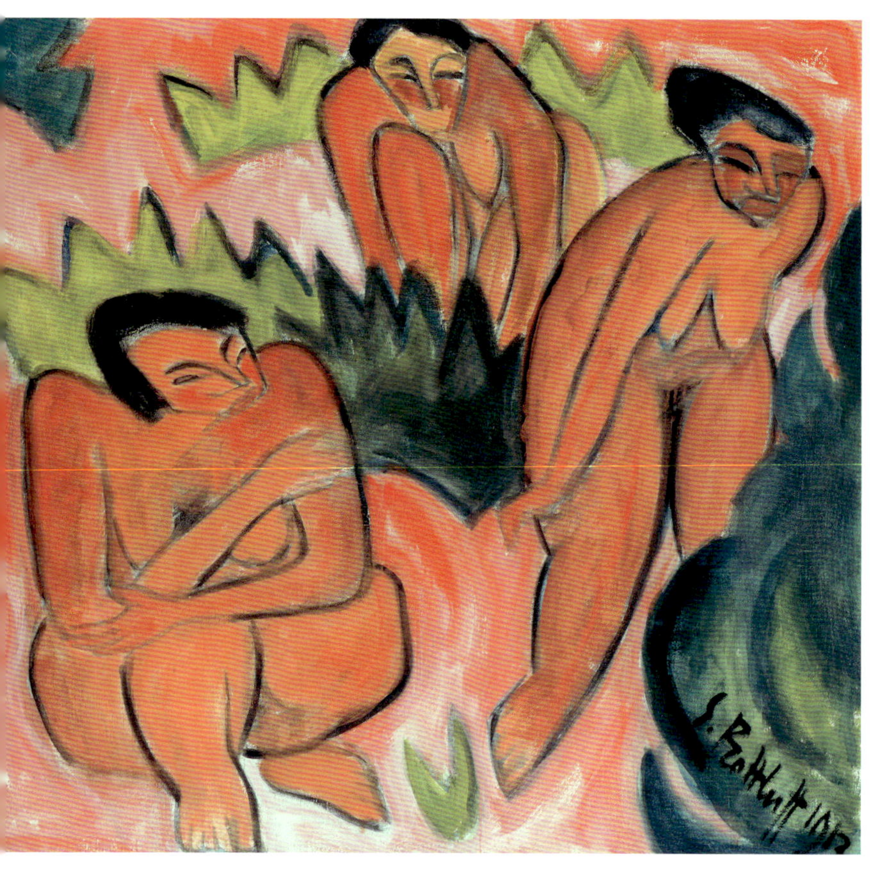

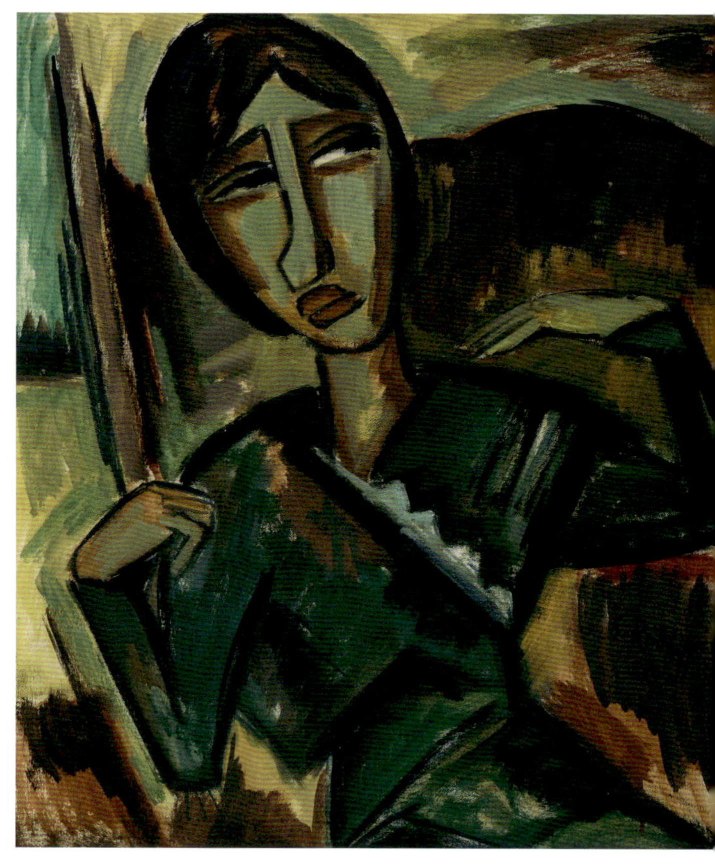

↑ Karl Schmidt-Rottluff, *Three Nudes (Picture of Dunes at Nidden)*, 1913, oil on canvas, 98 × 106.5 cm
Acquired in 1949 by the Land Berlin for the Galerie des 20. Jahrhunderts, Berlin (West)

→ Karl Schmidt-Rottluff, *Green Girl*, 1915
Oil on canvas, 85 × 76 cm
Acquired in 1969 for the Nationalgalerie, Berlin (East)

↗ Otto Mueller, *Young Girl in Front of Male Heads*, 1928
Distemper on burlap, 130 × 75 cm
Acquired in 1959 from the Galerie Ketterer, Stuttgart, for the Nationalgalerie, Berlin (West)

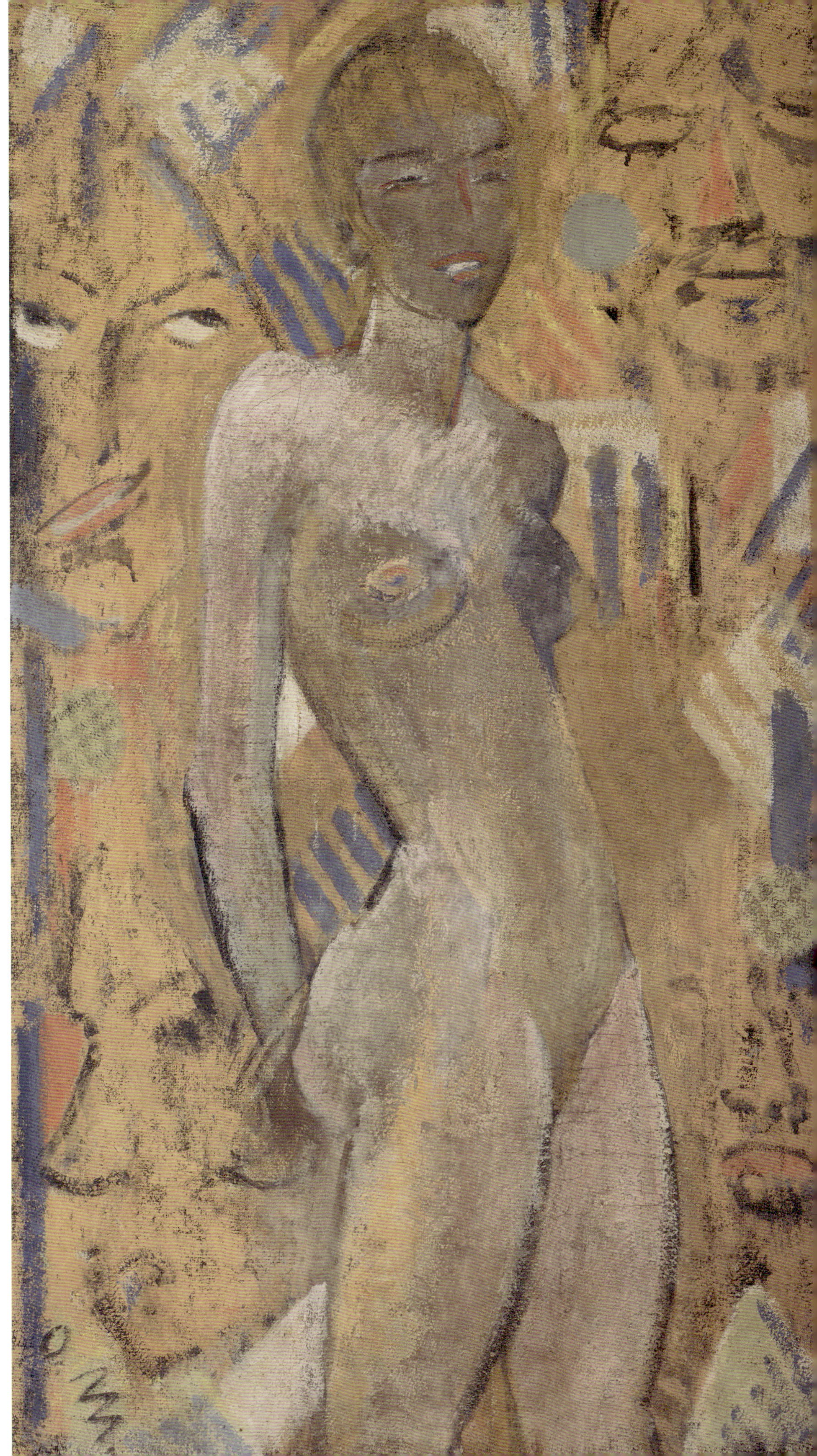

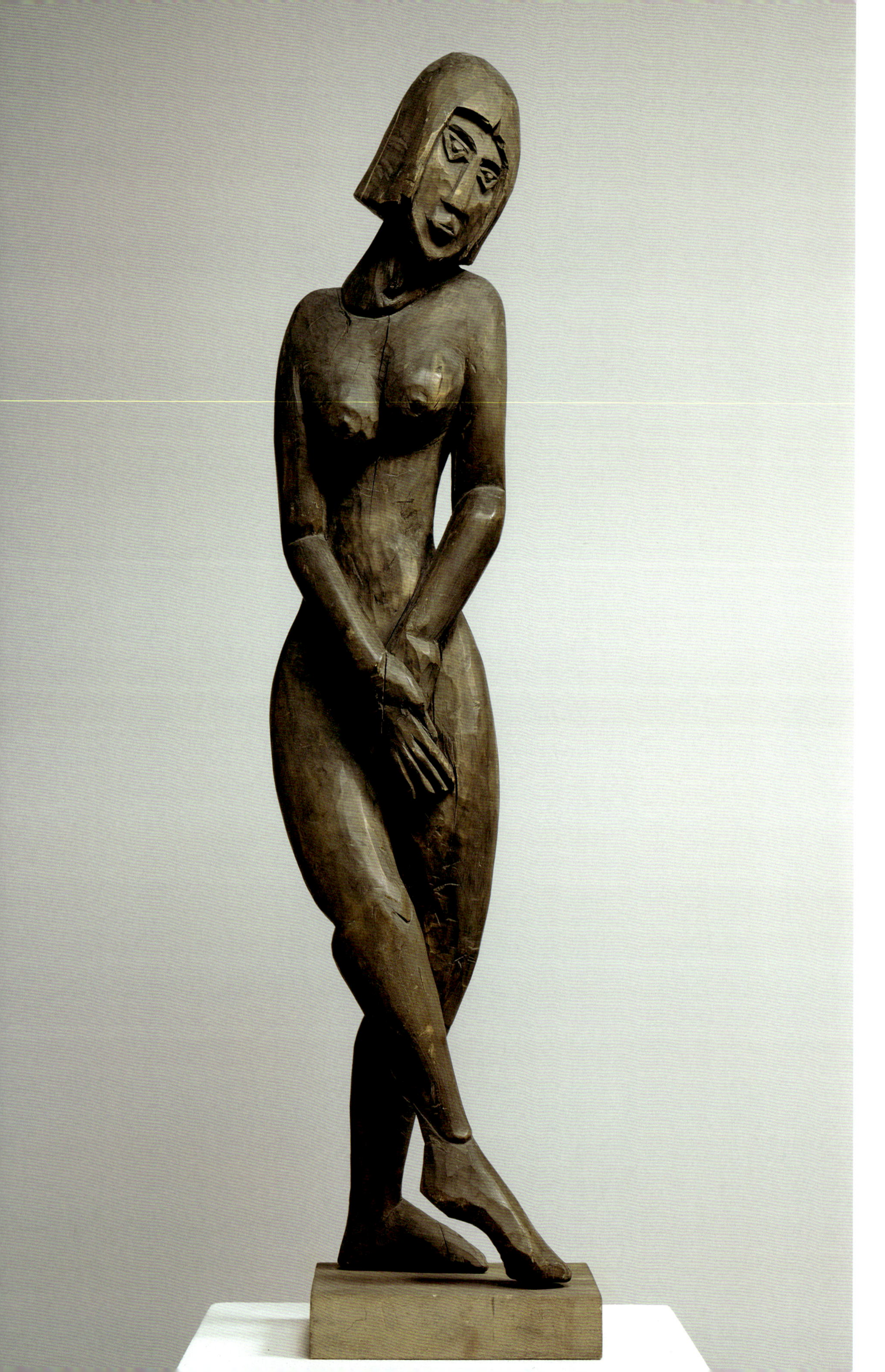

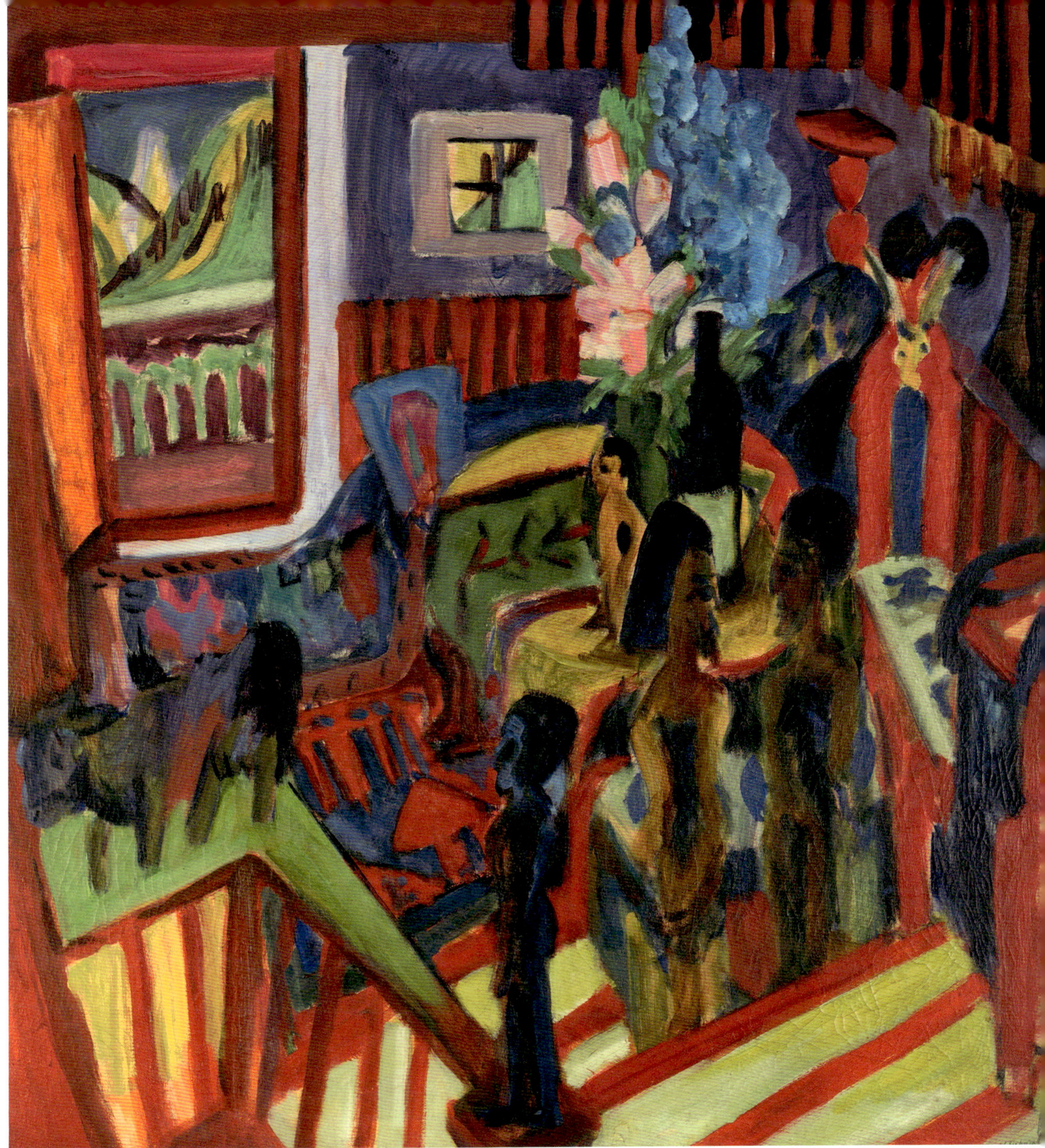

↑ Ernst Ludwig Kirchner, *Studio Corner*, 1919–20
Oil on canvas, 126 × 121 cm
Acquired in 1923 in exchange; confiscated in 1937 as "degenerate"; given to the art dealer Ferdinand Möller in exchange; retained in 1948 while on loan in Halle (Saale); returned to the Nationalgalerie, Berlin (East) in 1953; restituted to the heirs of Ferdinand Möller in 1995; reacquired in 1997

← Ernst Ludwig Kirchner, *Standing Woman*, 1912
Alder, 98 × 23 × 18 cm
Gift from Sabine Lepsius from the estate of her brother Botho Graef, Jena, 1931

Rosa Shapire, More Than a "Passive" Brücke Member

Who was Rosa Schapire? Her portrait was created in late August 1920 in Northern Germany's "Holstein Switzerland", where the second generation Expressionist Walter Grammatté and his wife Sonia spent their holidays. Gramatté depicted Shapire elegantly clothed, sitting in an armchair in a classic thinker's pose. She was 46 years old at the time, but her white hair, pronounced bone structure and serious expression in the painting make her appear older and gaunter than she actually would have been. The questioning, critical look in her dark and deep-set eyes reveals the painter's great respect for this art connoisseur. Shapire was a patron of Gramatté and many other artists. She published an essay about his work in the magazine *Cicerone* and remained one of his closest confidantes throughout his life.

Born in Eastern Galicia in 1874, the art historian completed her dissertation in Heidelberg in 1904 and soon became an eminent patron of the arts. Her unmarried and self-employed status made her an exception in the Expressionist milieu. She did not serve as a muse but was an active and independent figure on equal footing with the artists. She was more than a "passive" Brücke member, and aside from a yearly financial contribution she published her own texts, arranged possibilities for exhibitions and recruited new patrons and buyers for the Brücke artists. Postcards from Erich Heckel, Ernst Ludwig Kirchner and Max Pechstein are testaments to the committed exchanges Schapire maintained with them. She was particularly close to Karl Schmidt-Rottluff. In 1924 she created an inventory of his graphic prints still used as a standard reference. The artist, in turn, decorated a room in her apartment entirely with furniture and accessories he had designed.

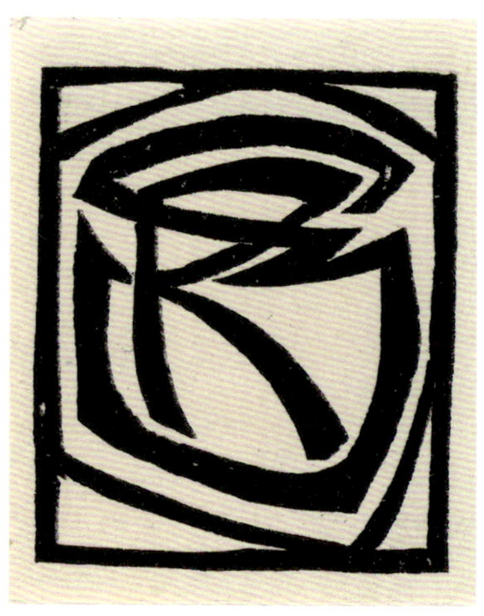

Dr phil. Rosa Schapire

Schapire gradually built up her collection of Expressionist art, which included many pieces that had been given or even dedicated to her as tokens of gratitude for her efforts on the artists' behalf. Nevertheless, she also supported the expansion of public art collections as a founding member of the Frauenbund zur Förderung deutscher bildender Kunst (1916–21), a women's league in Hamburg dedicated to the advancement of German art. This association of upper-class women with an inclination towards feminism was particularly invested in purchasing Expressionist works to be able to present them to German museums.

Under the National Socialist regime, Schapire worked for the Jüdischer Kulturbund (Jewish Cultural Association) in Hamburg before emigrating to Great Britain shortly before the Second World War. She was only able to save her Schmidt-Rottluff collection and her artist postcards when she fled. Her library and the works of art she had been forced to leave behind were seized and auctioned off by the Gestapo in 1941. Stored at the port of Hamburg, the furniture designed by Schmidt-Rottluff was destroyed in an air raid in 1943. Schapire continued doing art historical work in exile, under contract as a freelancer for the Tate Gallery in London, but until she died in 1954 she also had to work as a translator to make ends meet.

Irina Hiebert Grun

↑ Karl Schmidt-Rottluff, Business card for Rosa Schapire, 1912
← Karl Schmidt-Rottluff, Bookplate for Rosa Schapire, 1909
→ Ernst Ludwig Kirchner, Membership card for passive members of the Brücke, issued to Rosa Schapire, 1908

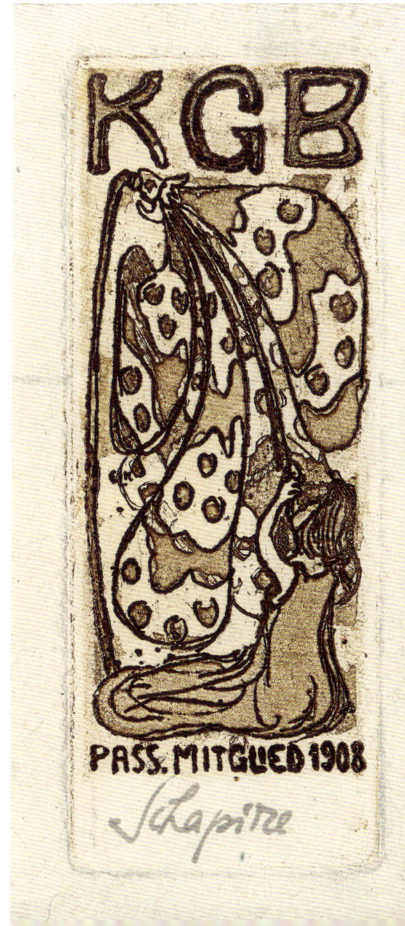

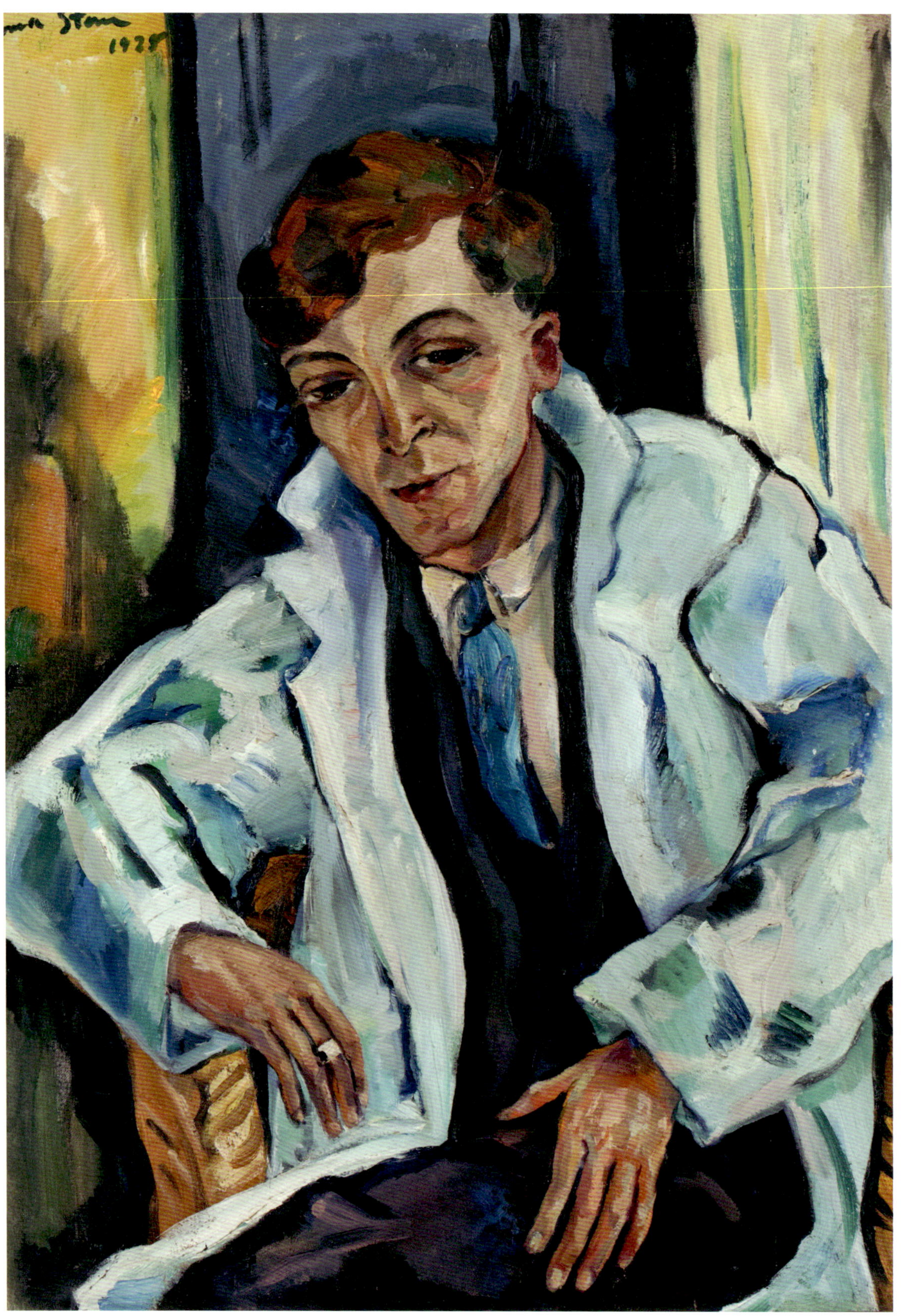

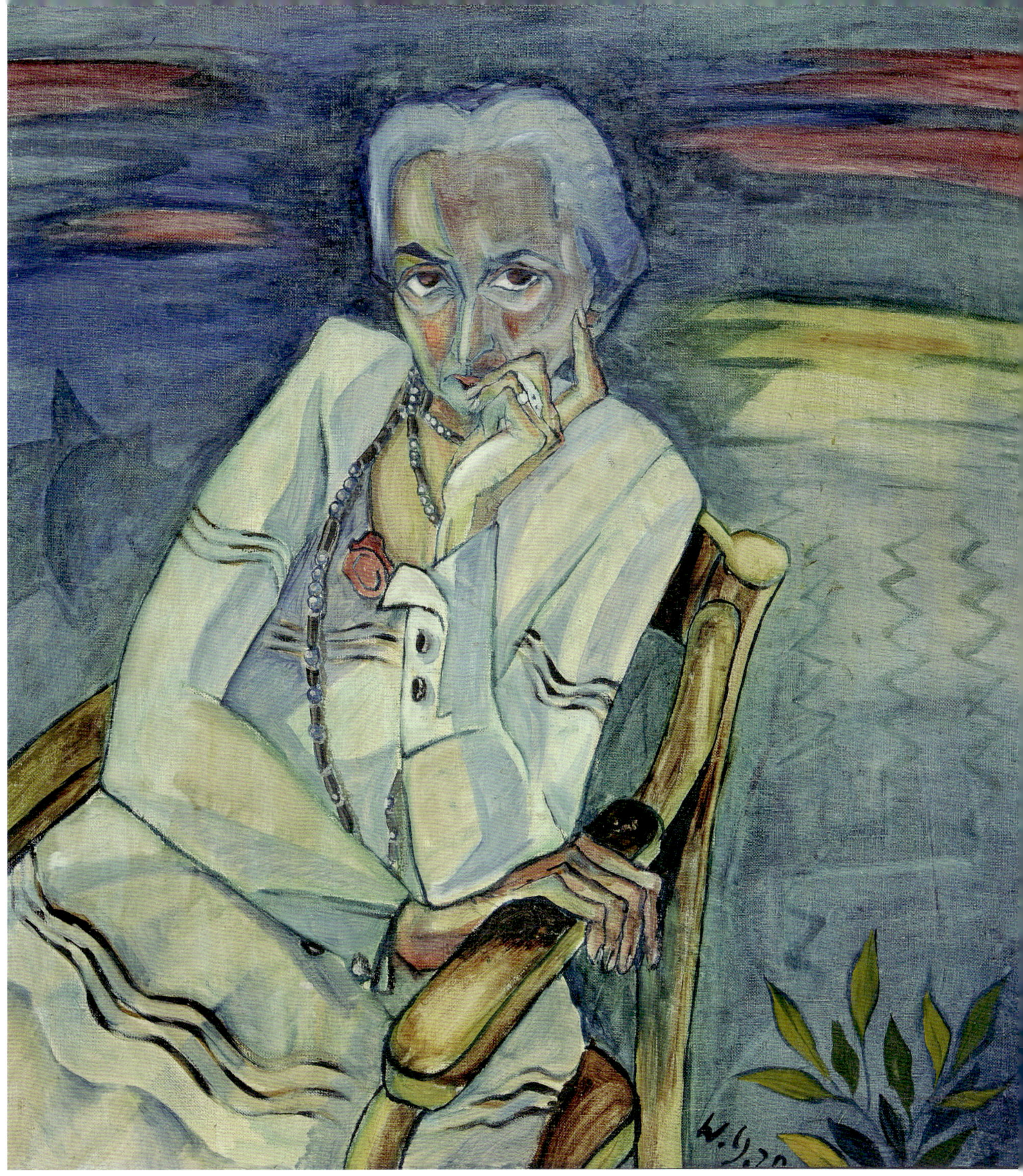

↑ Walter Gramatté, *Portrait of Rosa Schapire*, 1920
Oil on canvas, 74.7 × 67.5 cm
Gift to the Nationalgalerie, Berlin (East) from the estate of Sonia Eckhardt-Gramatté and Dr Ferdinand Eckhardt, Canada, 1966

← Irma Stern, *Portrait Lancelot Hogben*, 1925
Oil on canvas, 94 × 69 cm
Courtesy of the Trustees of the Irma Stern Collection, Cape Town

How Is the Brücke Connected to Germany's Colonial History?

The Brücke artists were all born around 1880, except Emil Nolde, who was born in 1867. They grew up at a time when the German Empire became the third largest colonial power in the world. In competition with Spain, Portugal, the Netherlands, Great Britain and France, Germany laid claim to territories in Africa and the South Pacific. In the winter of 1884–85, the "Congo Conference" took place in Berlin, where the colonial powers divided African regions among themselves.

The German colonies were referred to as "protectorates". They were based on German merchants' trading posts, which were guaranteed military protection. For the colonized peoples, German rule manifested itself in everyday oppression and the economic exploitation of people and resources, as well as brutal acts of war and even genocide. The violent aspects of colonial politics received little coverage in the German press. Instead, the German perception of life in the colonies was shaped by imported goods from overseas. Products such as tea, rice, cocoa powder and spices could be purchased in "colonial goods stores" in Germany. People from non-Western cultures were exhibited in circus-like *Völkerschauen* – human zoos. Their ritual and everyday objects were on view in ethnological museums.

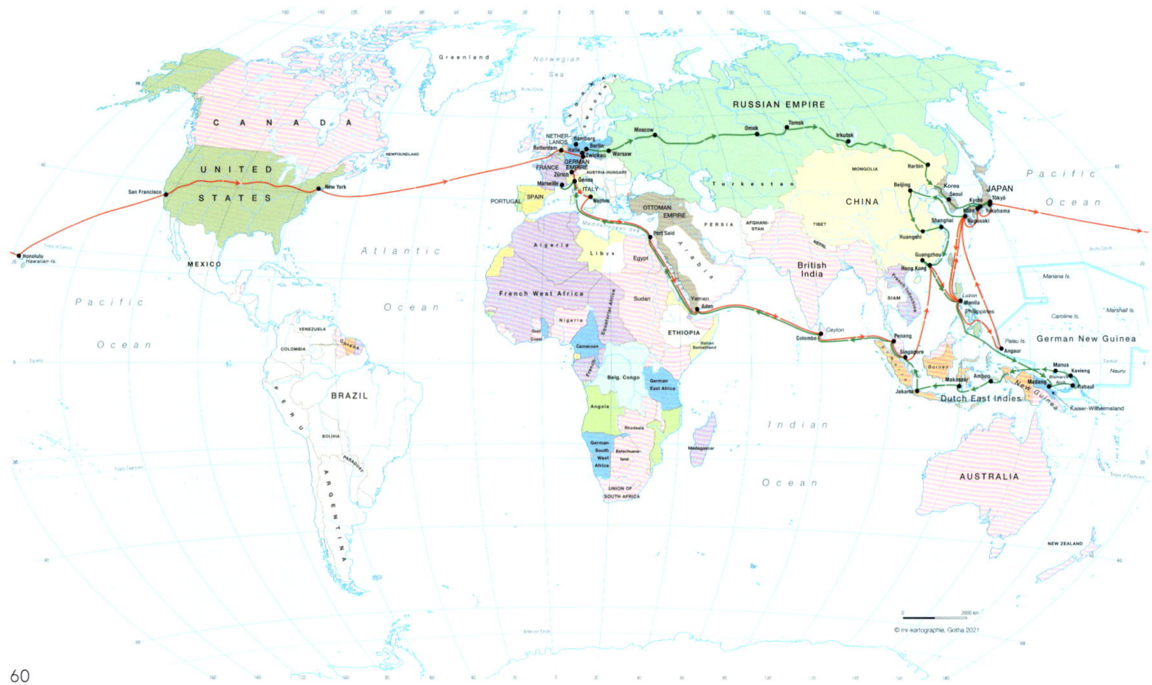

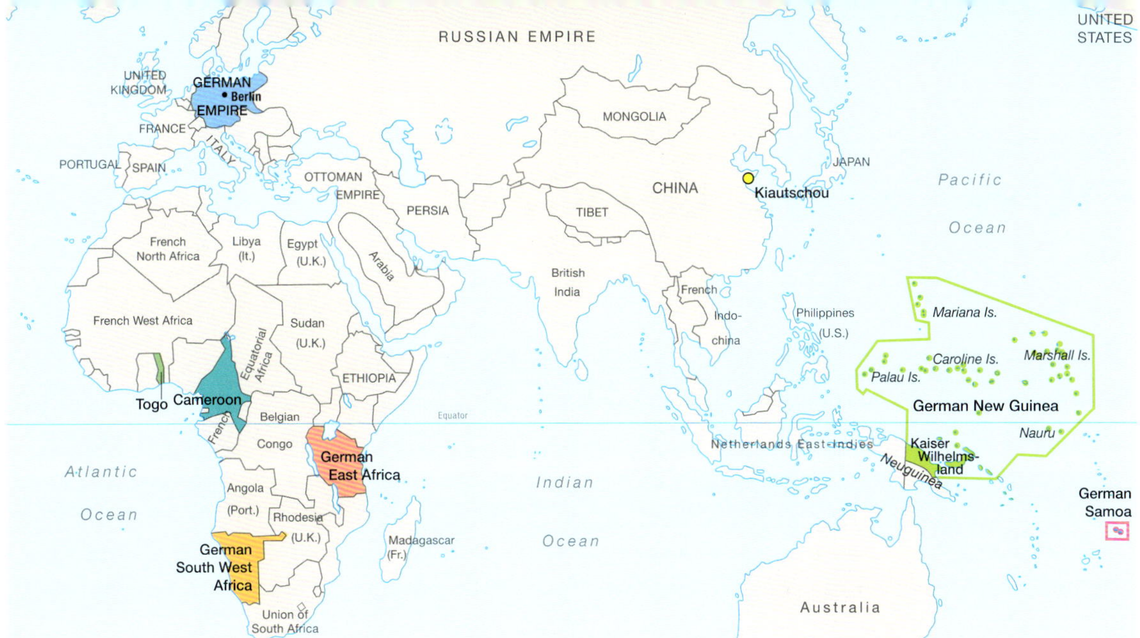

The acquisitions of many objects in European museums must today be considered unlawful because they were based on dishonest trading practices, plundering or the theft of cultural heritage. These objects nevertheless had a significant impact on European art. The Brücke artists were particularly fascinated by them. By 1909 these artists had begun visiting the ethnological collections in Dresden, Berlin and Hamburg. They were enthralled by sculptures from Cameroon and bronzes from Benin and works from Mexico's Indigenous Pueblo culture. African culture found its way into the work of the Brücke artists because Erich Heckel's brother Manfred, an engineer in German East Africa (present-day Tanzania), brought back art objects from his travels. Many Brücke paintings are clearly influenced by the figural carvings on meeting house beams from the Palau Islands. The artists adopted their strikingly simplified forms.

Paul Gauguin's works in Tahiti and the Marquesas Islands greatly impacted the Brücke artists' notion of an "earthly paradise". Emil Nolde and Max Pechstein both spent time in the South Pacific in 1913–14, following Gauguin's example. Nolde painted *Papua-Jünglinge* (Papuan Boys) while privately taking part in the "Medical-demographic German New Guinea Expedition" supported by the German Empire's colonial office. The wider setting in which this painting came about was informed by ostensibly scientifically legitimized "racial studies", which assumed the existence of "primitive" levels of civilization. Many of the watercolours Nolde painted during this expedition reference ethnographic photography by combining frontal and profile views of his subjects. A reflection of this approach is evident in the painting *Papua-Jünglinge*.

Dieter Scholz

↑ Colonies of the German Empire in 1914
← Route of the "Medical-demographic German New Guinea Expedition" in which Emil and Ada Nolde took part in 1913–14 in green, and Max Pechstein's itinerary from 1914 in red
→ Ada Nolde on Manus Island, 23 April 1914

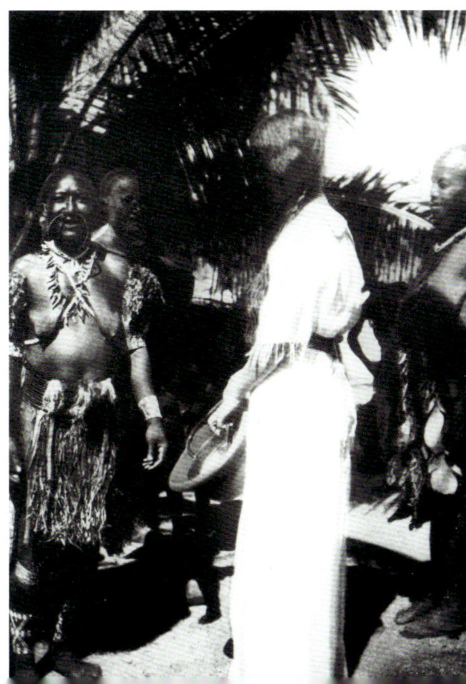

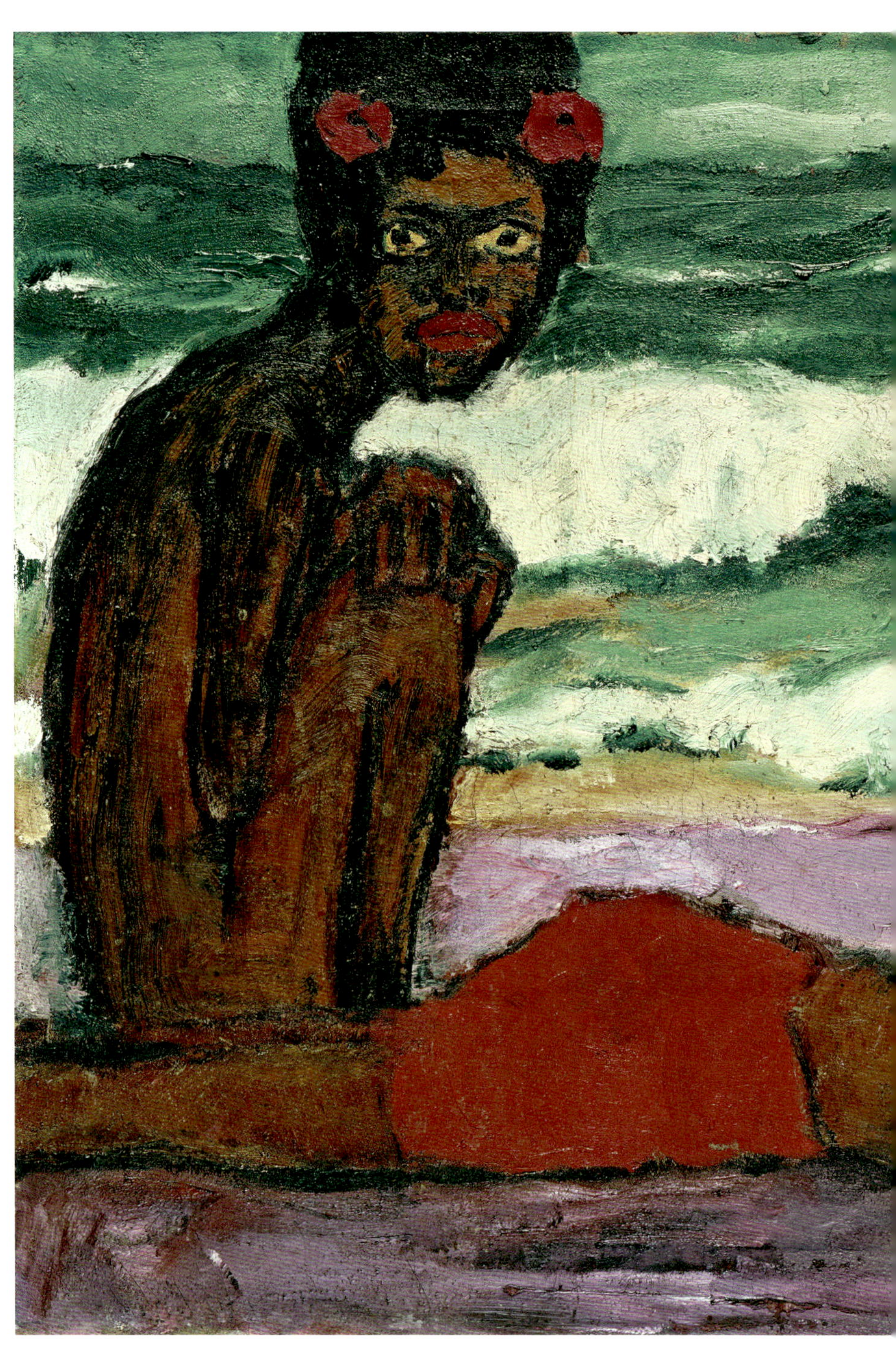

Emil Nolde, *Papuan Boys*, 1914
Oil on canvas, 70 × 103.5 cm
Owned by the Kunstsammlungen der Stadt Königsberg i. Pr. (now Kaliningrad) in 1930; confiscated as "degenerate" in 1937, brought to Güstrow by Bernhard A. Böhmer where it was seized in 1947 and given to the Nationalgalerie, Berlin (East) in 1949; gift from the Magistrat von Groß-Berlin to the Nationalgalerie, Berlin (East) in 1951

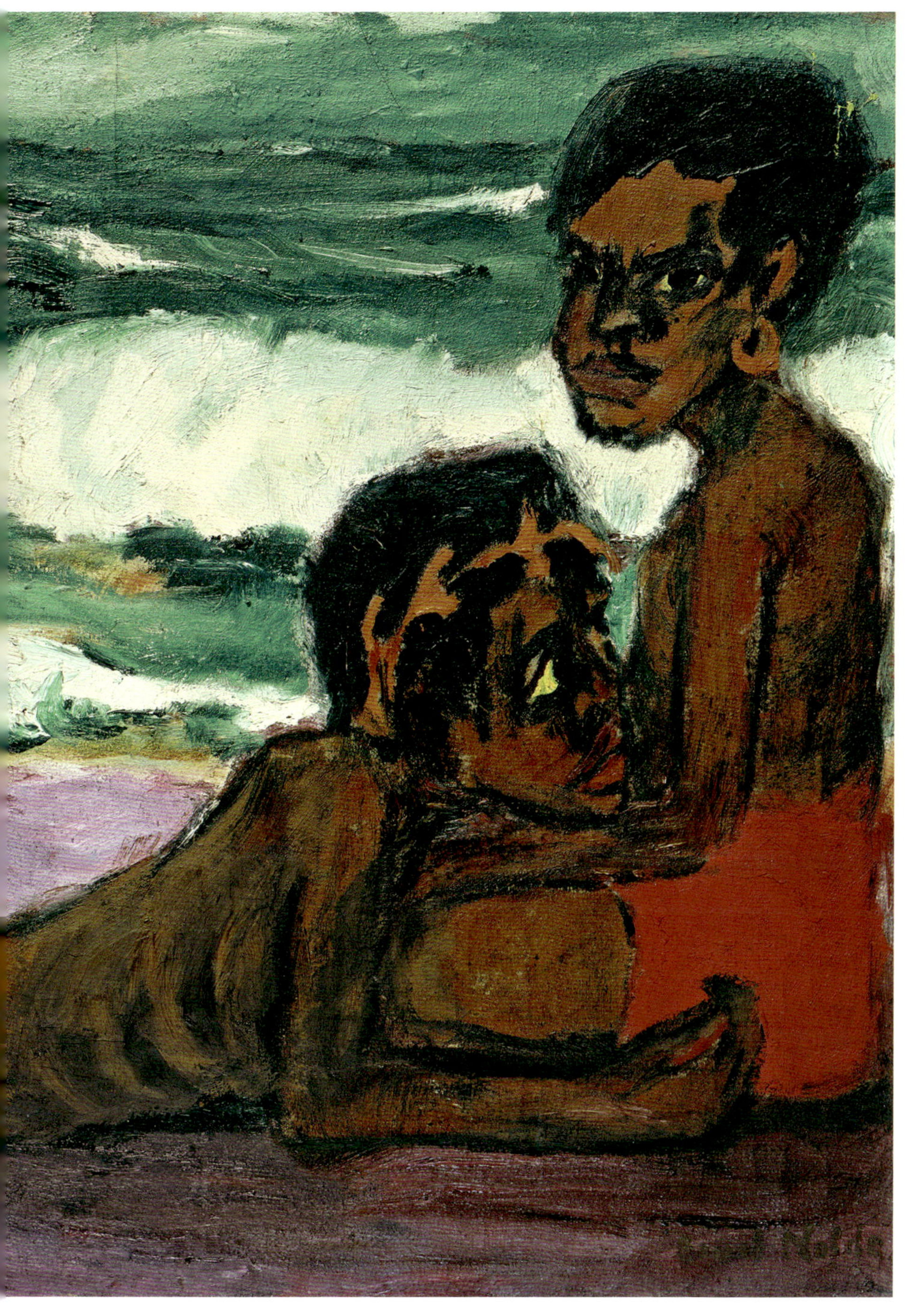

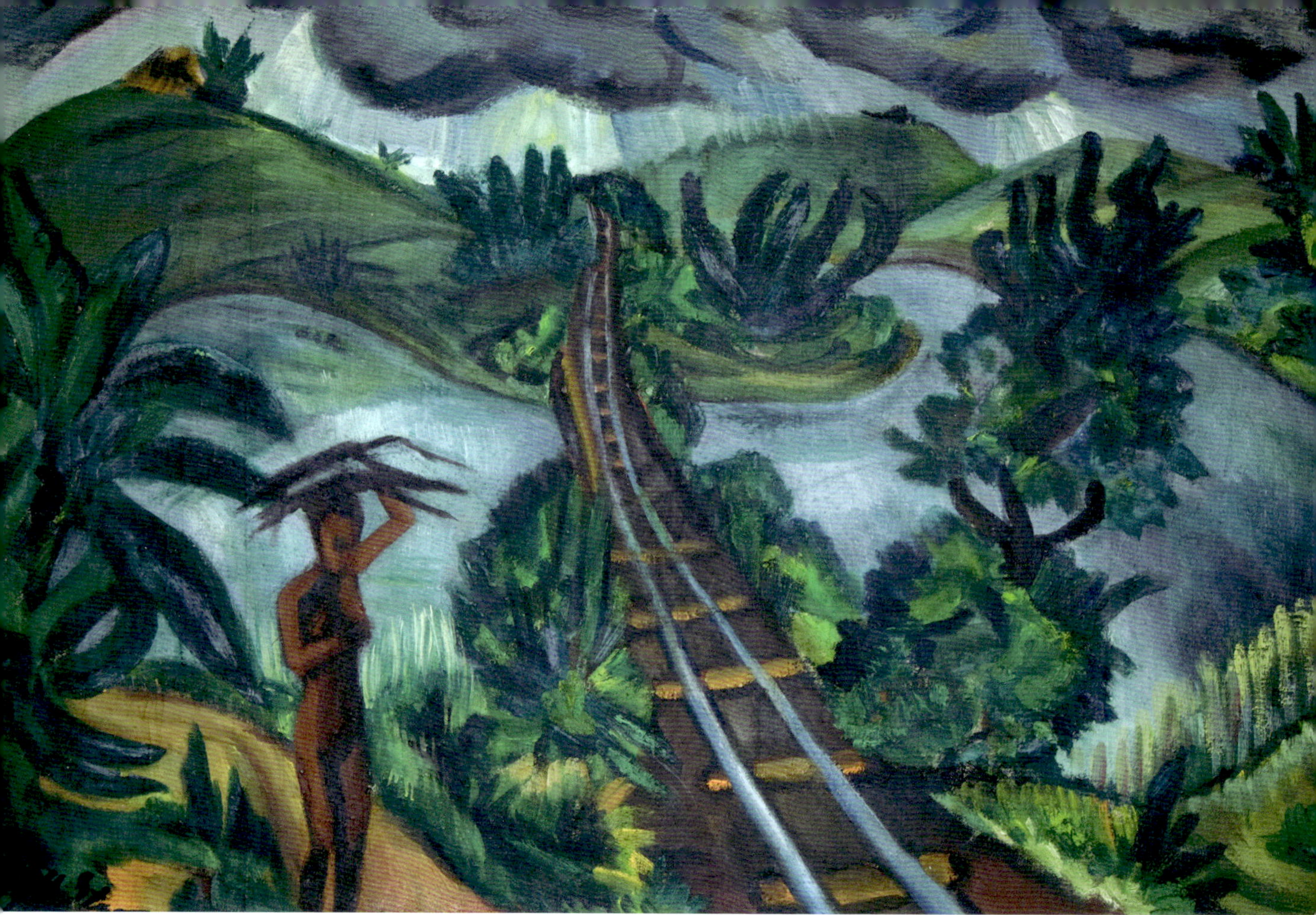

↑ Irma Stern, *Umgababa*, 1922
Oil on canvas, 60.5 × 91 cm
Courtesy of the Trustees of the Irma Stern Collection, Cape Town

→ Walter Spies, *Village Street*, 1928
Oil on canvas, 75 × 47 cm
Loan from a private collection since 2019

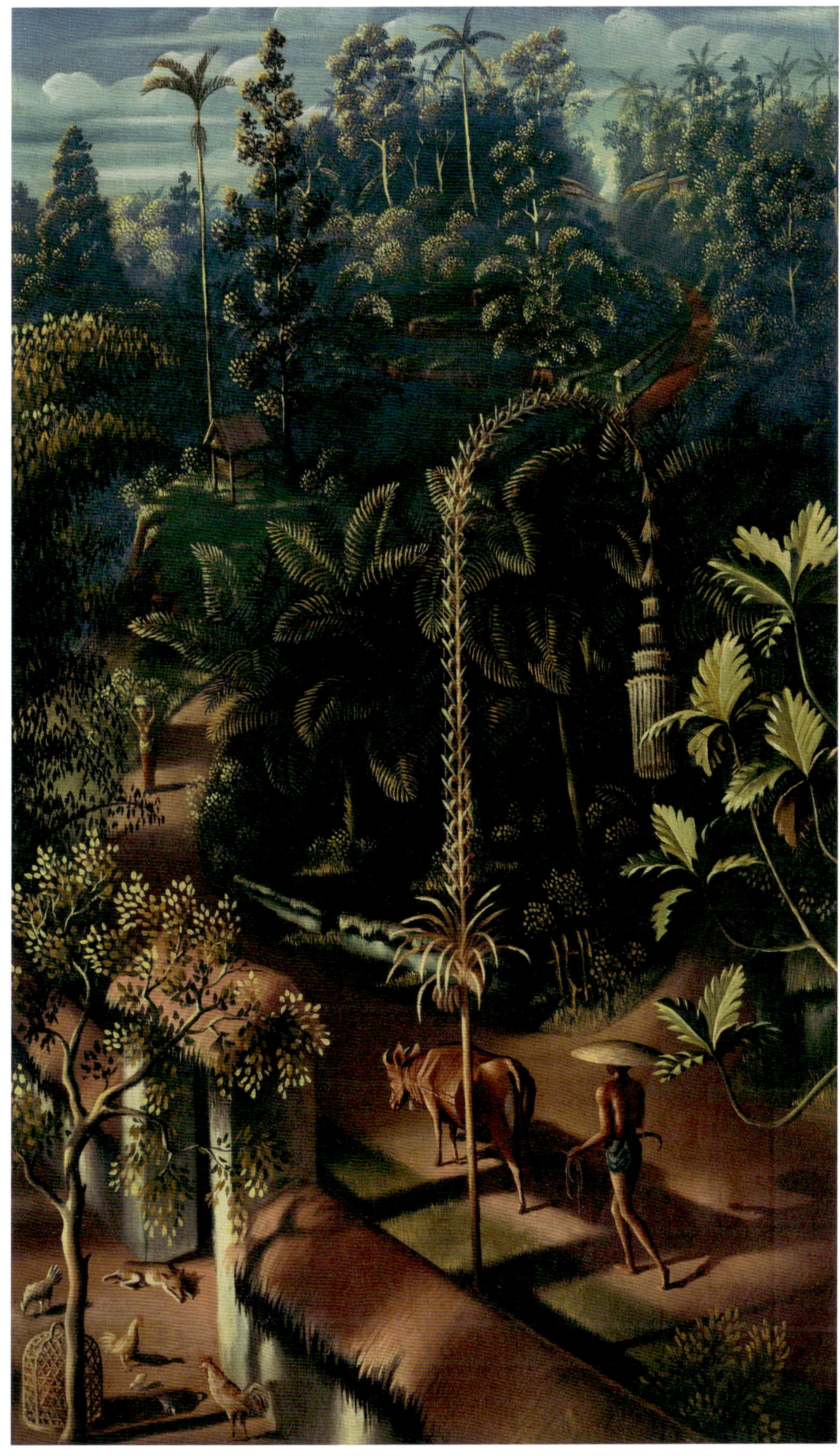

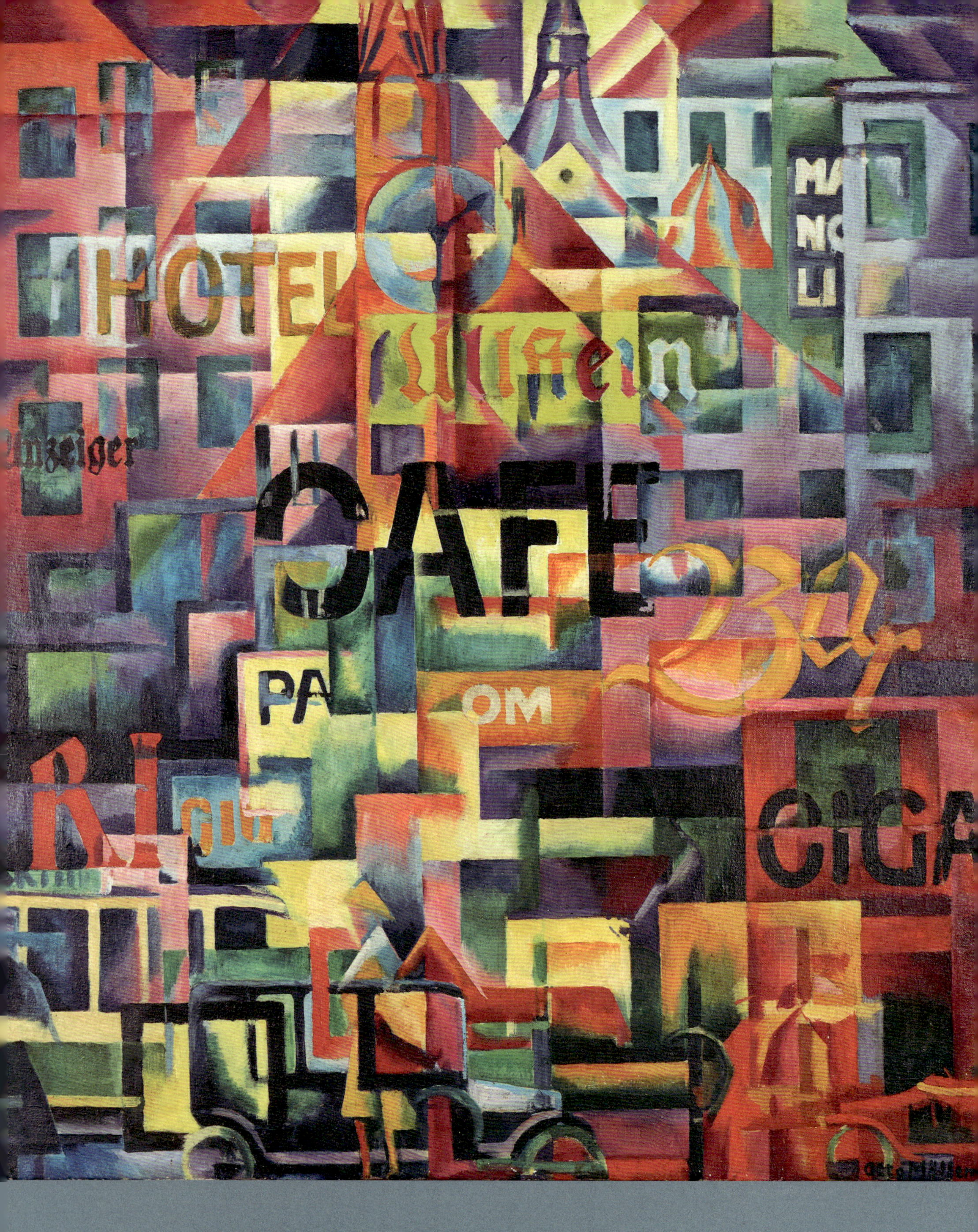
HOTEL
CAFE
PA
OM
CIGA

Slivers of the City

The city has always been a centre of crystallization for society. Cities expanded rapidly during the age of industrialization, becoming catalysts of cultural development like never before. An overabundance of stimuli, diversity and dynamic change in the urban environment frequently leads to a fragmented sense of perception, making it impossible to grasp the whole. The eye is only offered isolated perspectives, fragments, slivers.

Berlin and Paris are metropolises in which such transformations in the 1910s each took on distinctive pictorial shapes. Although the forms in Ernst Ludwig Kirchner's Expressionist Berlin street scenes are distorted, his subject matter is nevertheless still recognizable. By contrast, they must first be sought out and reassembled in Pablo Picasso's Cubist works, produced while the artist was living in Paris. Different perspectives are combined in a single image. Dada artist Hannah Höch ultimately allowed the cohesion of the image itself to shatter. New interpretations of the montage principle no longer dealt with manual craftsmanship, but instead aligned themselves with industrial production on the assembly line. Individual images were combined using the montage technique, much like in the successful and innovative medium of film. Each image stands on its own and yet is part of a larger context – like people in a big city.

Otto Möller, *City*, 1921
Oil on canvas, 91.3 × 81.5 cm
Acquired in 1961 from the artist for the Nationalgalerie, Berlin (West)

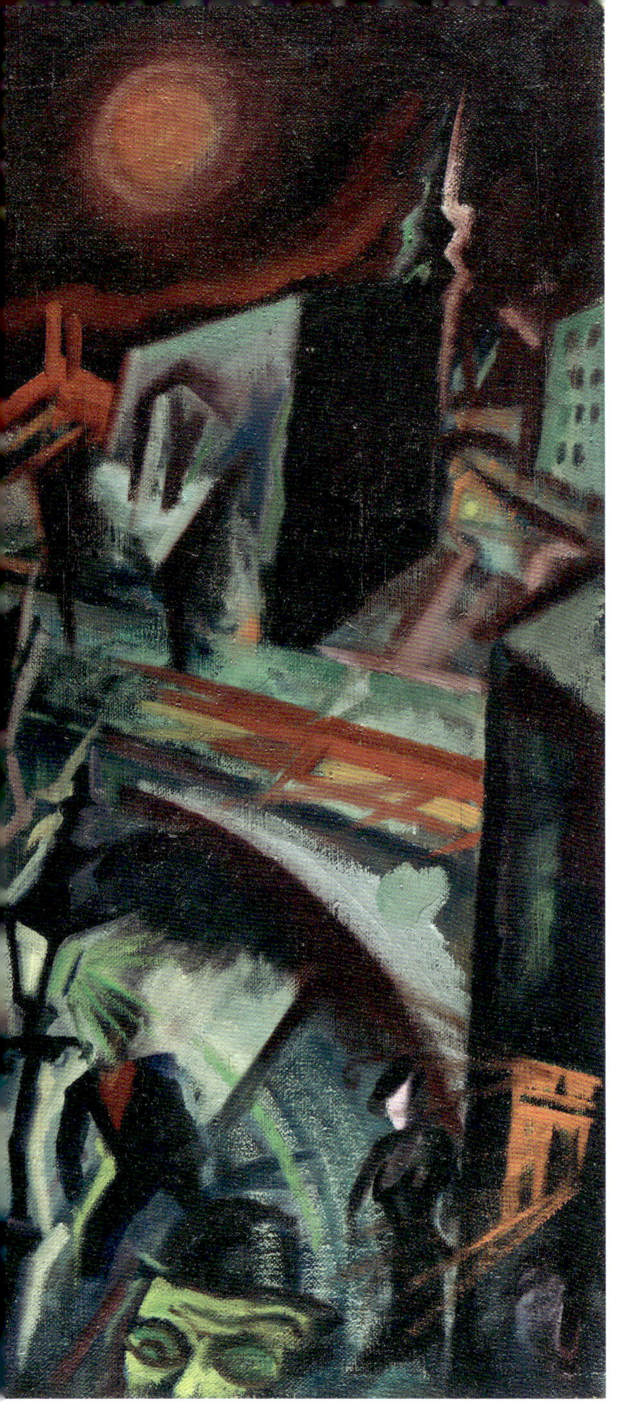

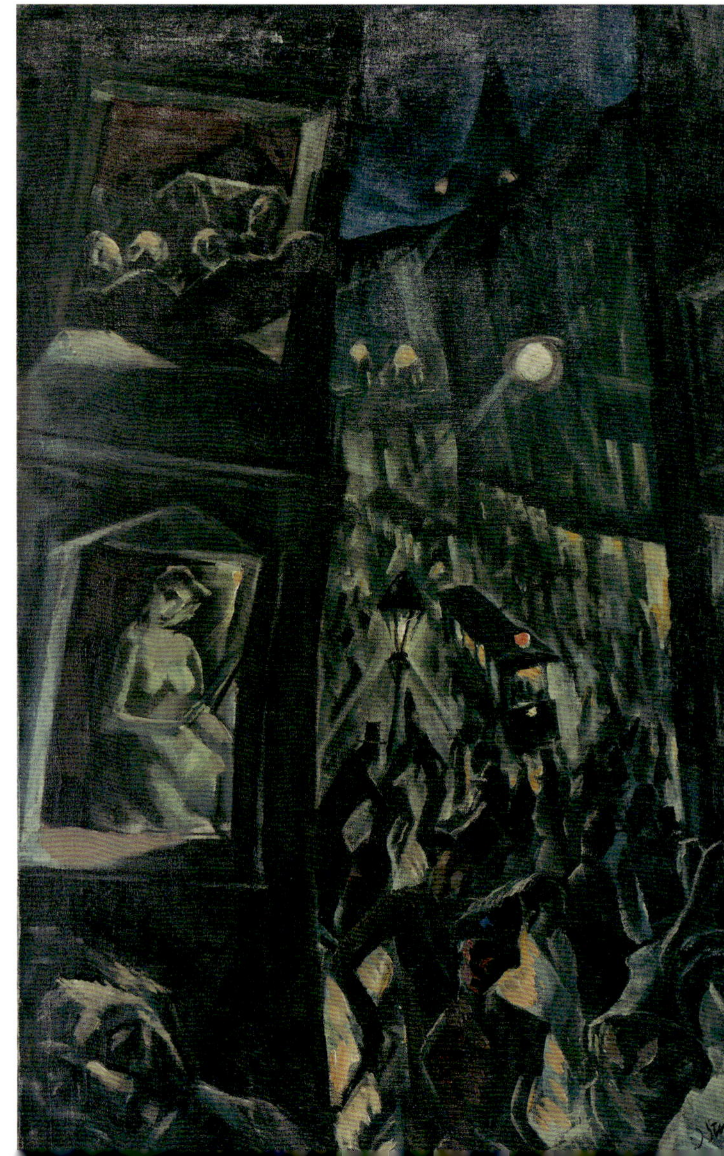

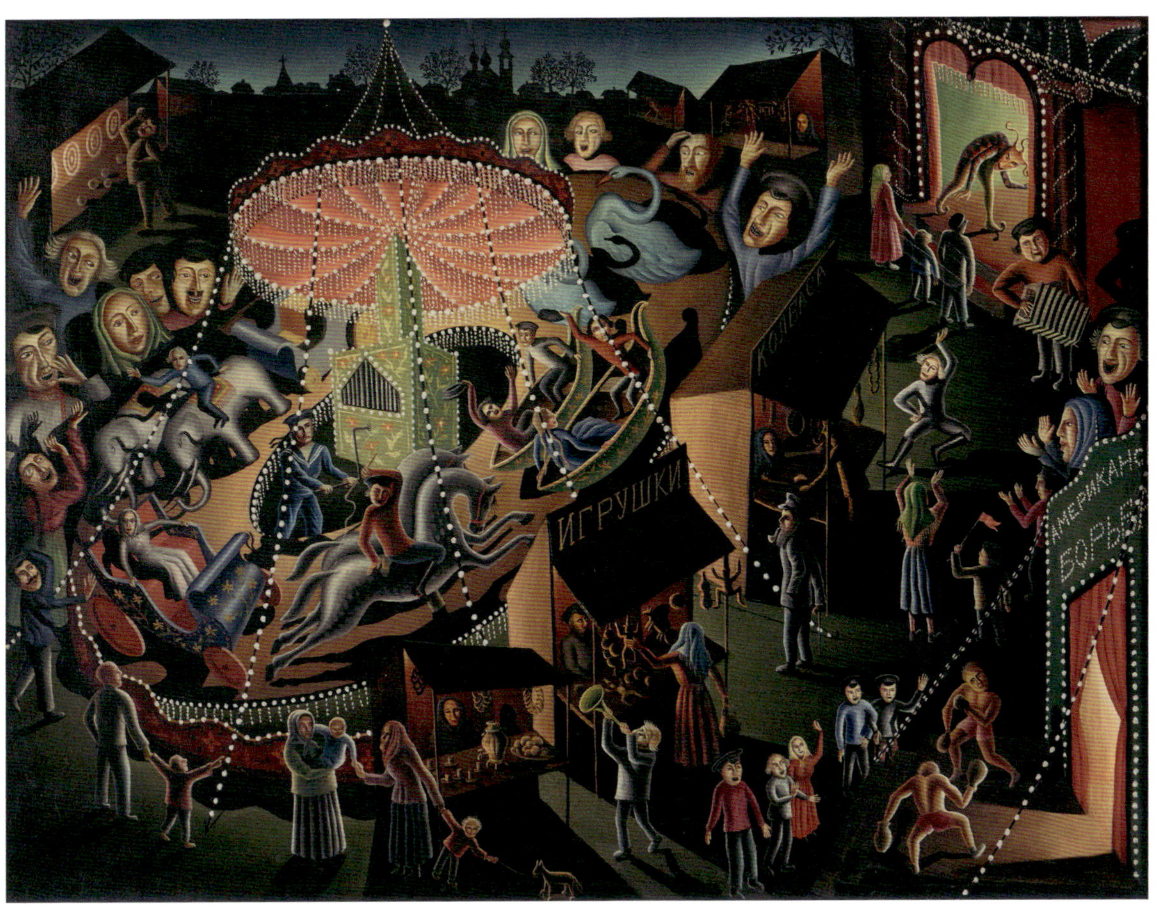

↑ Walter Spies, *The Carousel*, 1922
Oil on canvas, 80 × 105 cm
Loan from a private collection since 2018

↖ George Grosz, *Nocturne (Berlin-Südende)*, 1915
Oil on canvas, 74.5 × 36.2 cm
Acquired in 1964 by the Land Berlin for the Galerie des 20. Jahrhunderts, Berlin (West)

← Jakob Steinhardt, *The City*, 1913
Oil on canvas, 61 × 40 cm
Acquired in 1961 from the artist, Jerusalem, for the Nationalgalerie, Berlin (West)

What Is "Modernity"?

Western thought is heavily influenced by the concept of "modernity". But what is modernity? In many European countries, the term refers to the radical new beginning that marked the end of the Middle Ages and was heralded by the invention of letterpress printing in Europe, the rise of science, and the first global conquests. In Germany, modernity is most often used to describe a rupture with the past triggered by industrialization around 1900. The achievements of this modernity went beyond the numerous inventions and innovations that affected peoples' daily lives, bringing radical change to how and where they lived and got around. Modernity is also credited with major movements for equality and freedom, such as democracy, women's emancipation, and an open-minded lifestyle shaped by urban culture. But the history of modernity also stands for violence and oppression. The conquests of other countries beginning around 1500 and the establishment of colonies are deep injustices from today's perspective. Global trade conducted by the West also led to widespread exclusion and inequities. In hindsight, from today's perspective, it becomes particularly evident that modernity's newfound freedoms only applied to some people.

The tendency to declare Western lifestyles and attitudes associated with modernity as universal ideals and to forcefully implement them in other countries and cultures has been criticized from many sides. The simplistic, linear model of history that underlies a concept of modernity reliant on technological or social innovation is equally questionable. Art history, for example, is not the series of successive movements it was long assumed to be. Instead, it is a mercurial back and forth between different styles and forms of expression – such as Expressionism, Cubism, or Dada – that includes references to previous naturalistic and realistic currents in art.

Many congruent and opposing movements in art and society developed in Asia, Latin America, and Africa parallel to Western "modernism/modernity". More recent cultural history therefore tends to speak of a complex process of global exchange. New terms such as "multiple modernities/multiple modernisms", "transmodernity/transmodernism", or "ex-centristic modernity" have been developed to highlight the diversity of regional developments and cultural dialogue. Particularly works of art from 1900 to 1945, representative of the styles and movements known under the umbrella term "Classical Modernism", would not have been possible without global interdependence. New schools of thought choose to avoid one-sided descriptors like "original" and "imitation" while emphasizing an open concept of hybrid cultures instead.

Joachim Jäger

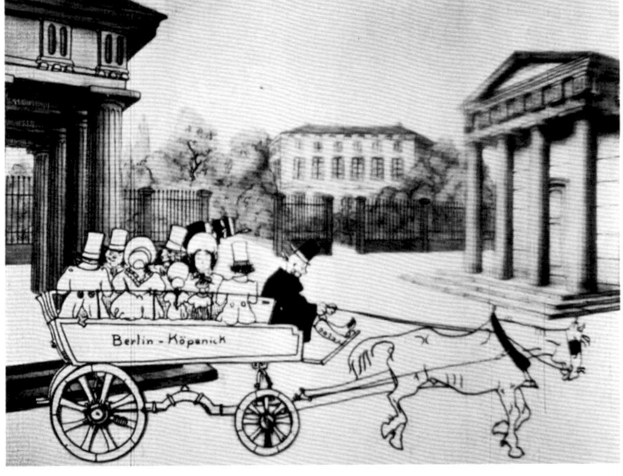

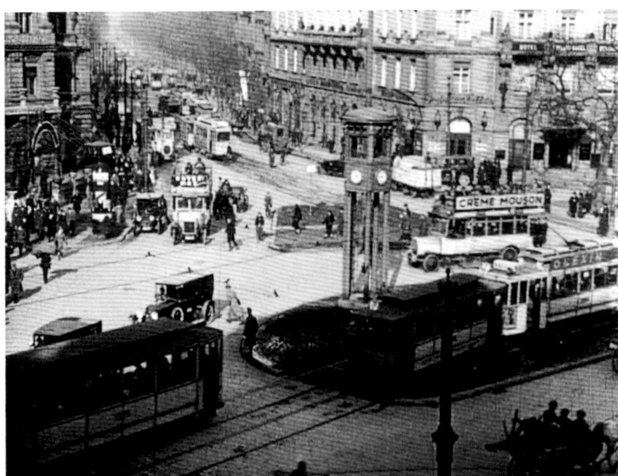

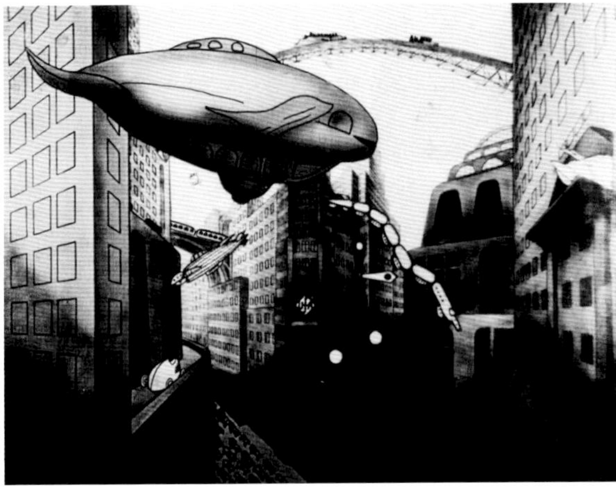

Adolf Trotz, *City of Millions*, 1925
Film (stills from the sequence "The Potsdamer Platz yesterday – today – tomorrow"), b/w, 80 min.

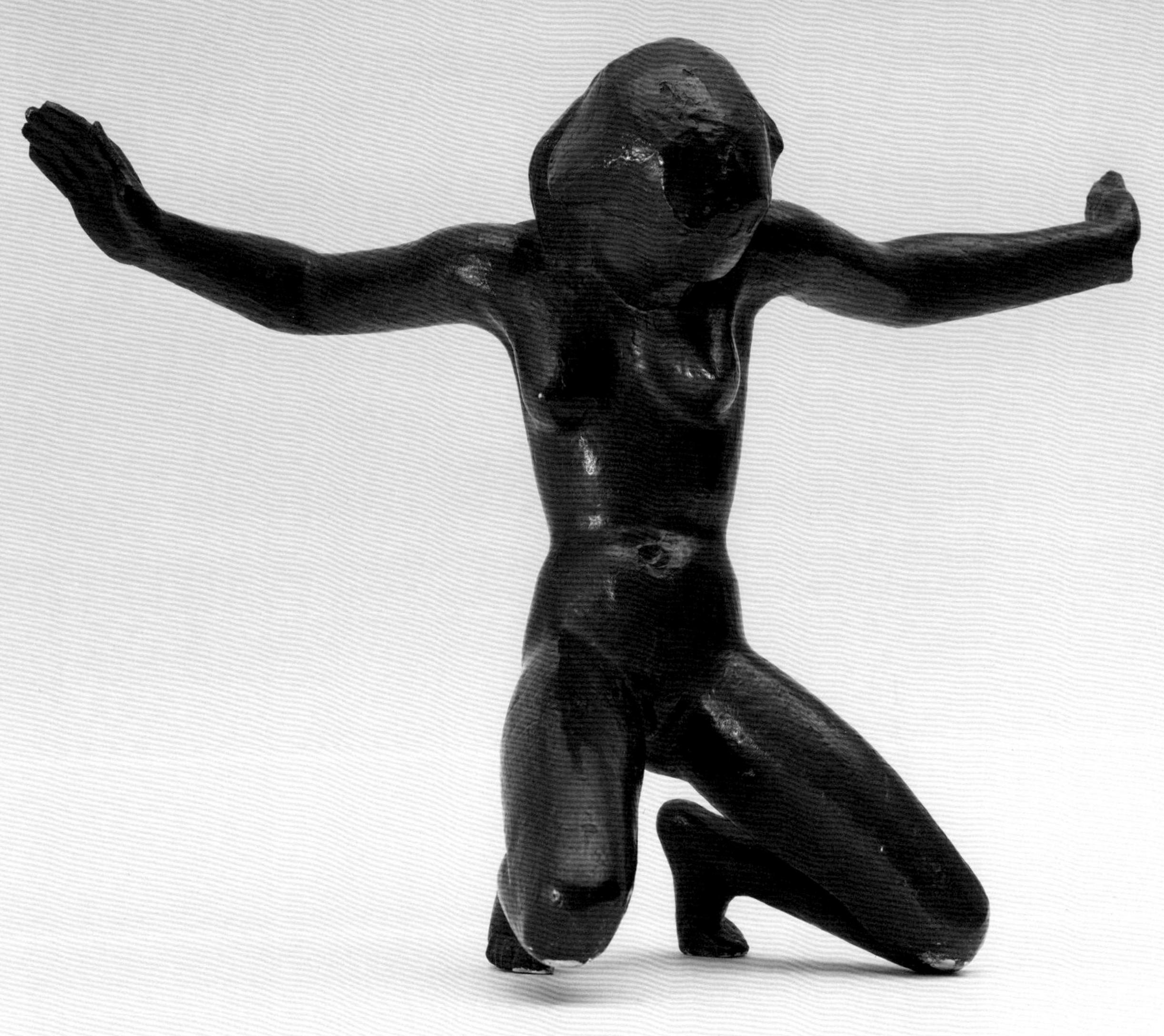

↑ Georg Kolbe, *Lamentation*, 1921 (cast 1921)
Bronze, 40 × 56 × 28 cm
Acquired in 1921 from the artist

→ Rudolf Belling, *Nature Group*, 1918
Painted plaster, 75 × 28 × 20 cm
Acquired in 1952 by the Land Berlin for the Galerie des 20. Jahrhunderts, Berlin (West)

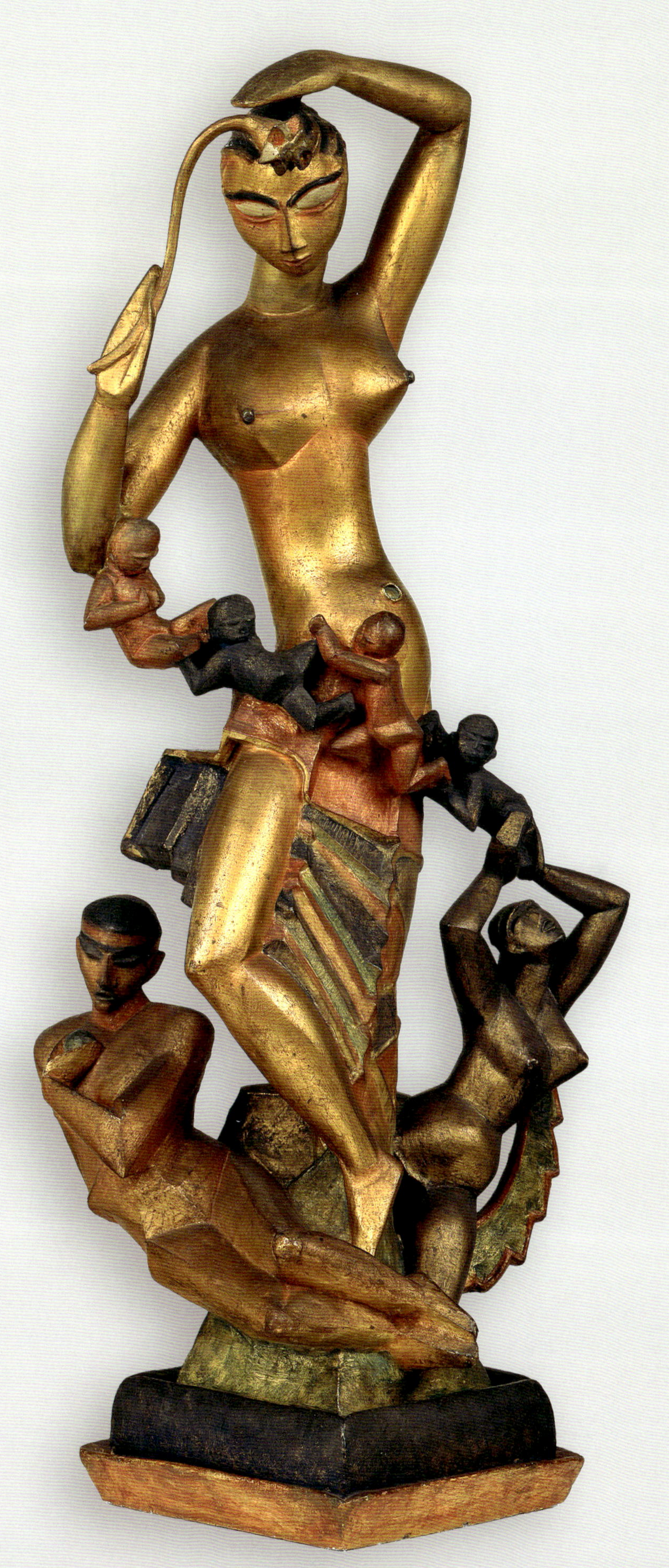

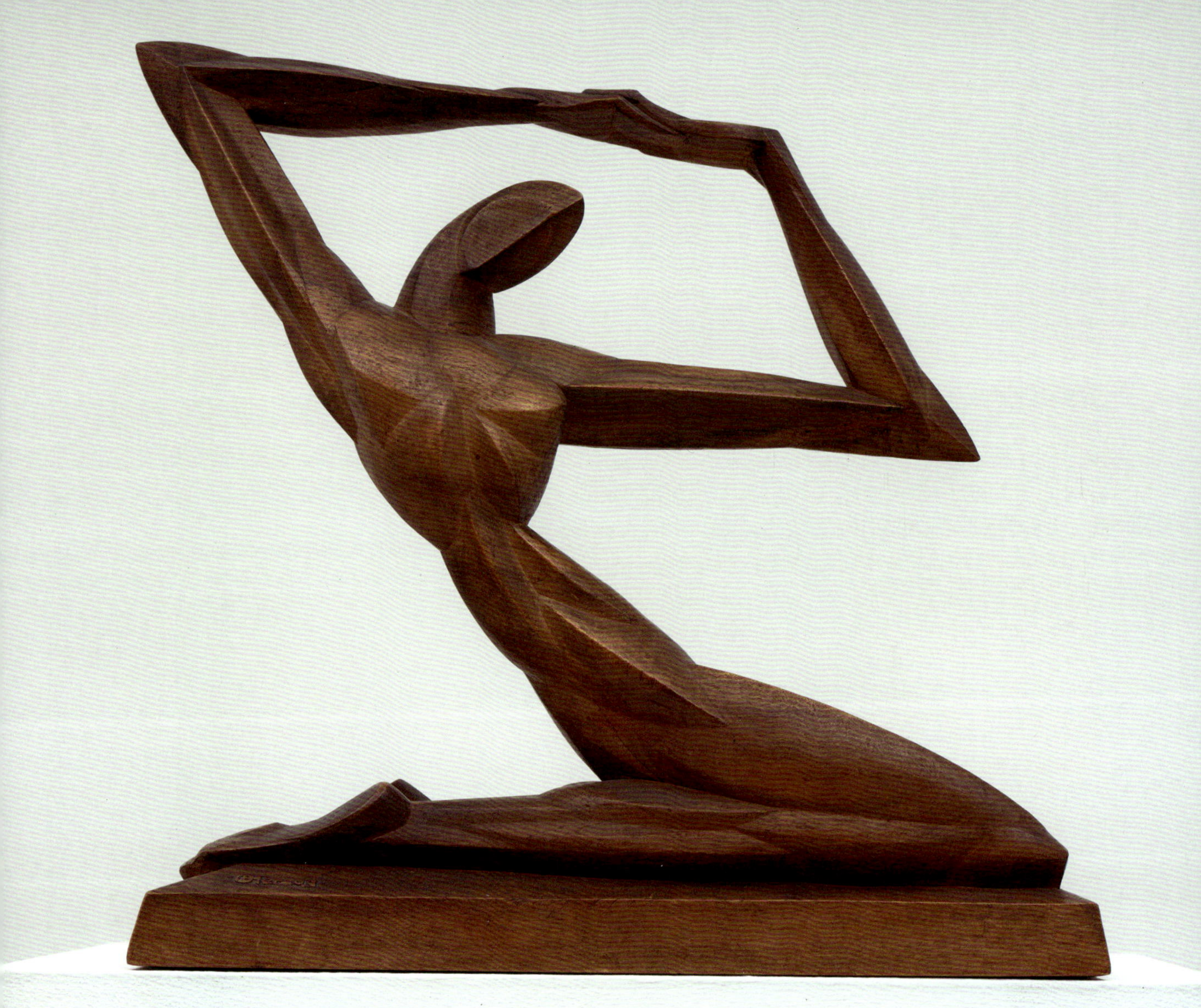

↑ Oswald Herzog, *Consecration*, 1920
Wood, 48.5 × 49.5 × 15.5 cm
Acquired in 1961 for the Nationalgalerie, Berlin (West)

→ Rudolf Belling, *Triad*, 1919 (wood 1924)
Birchwood, 91 × 77 × 77 cm
Acquired in 1924 from the artist; exhibited at the Kronprinzen-Palais until 1933; confiscated in 1937 as "degenerate" and brought to Munich; on consignment to Bernhard A. Böhmer, Güstrow in 1939 where it was seized in 1947 and returned to the Nationalgalerie, Berlin (East) in 1949

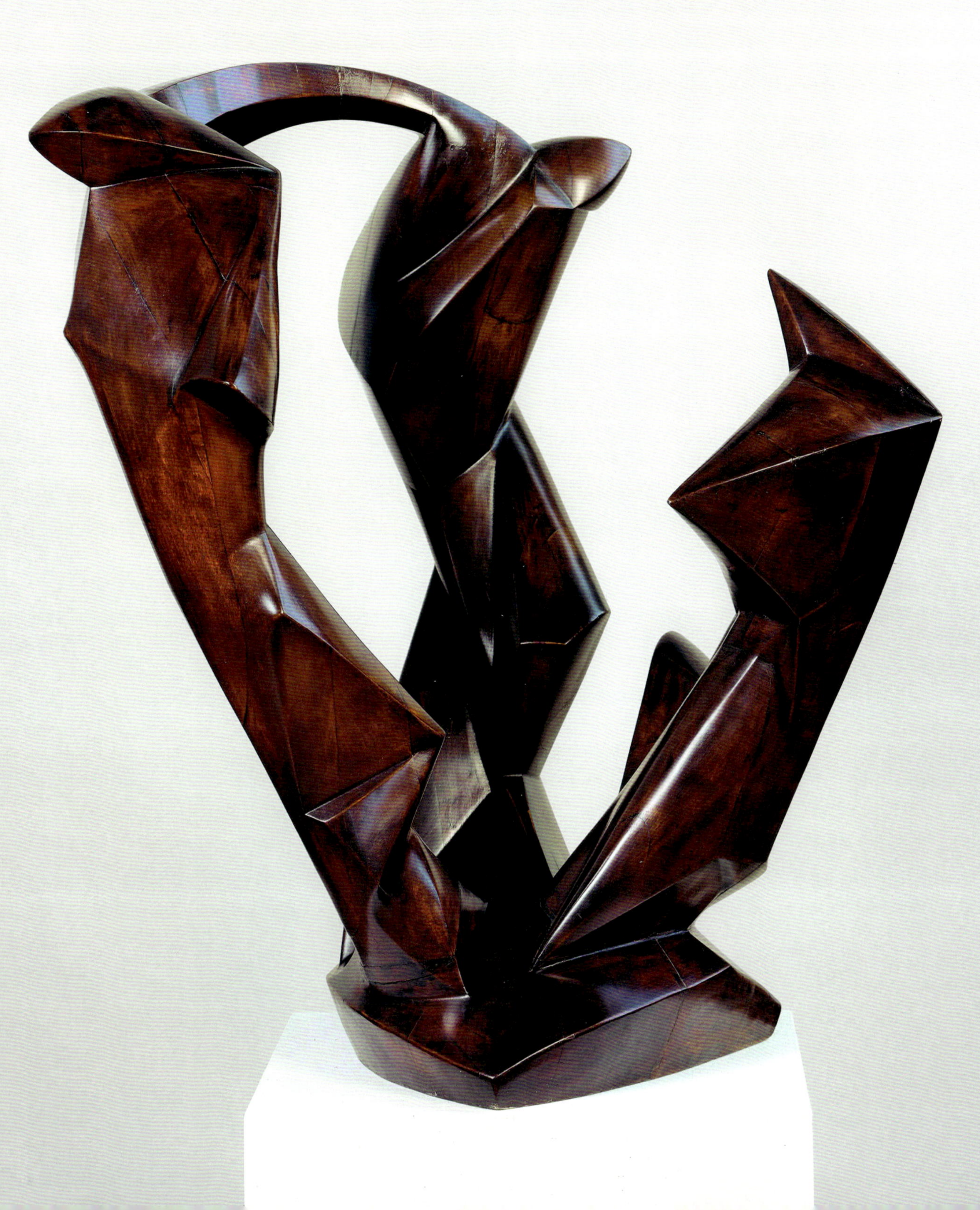

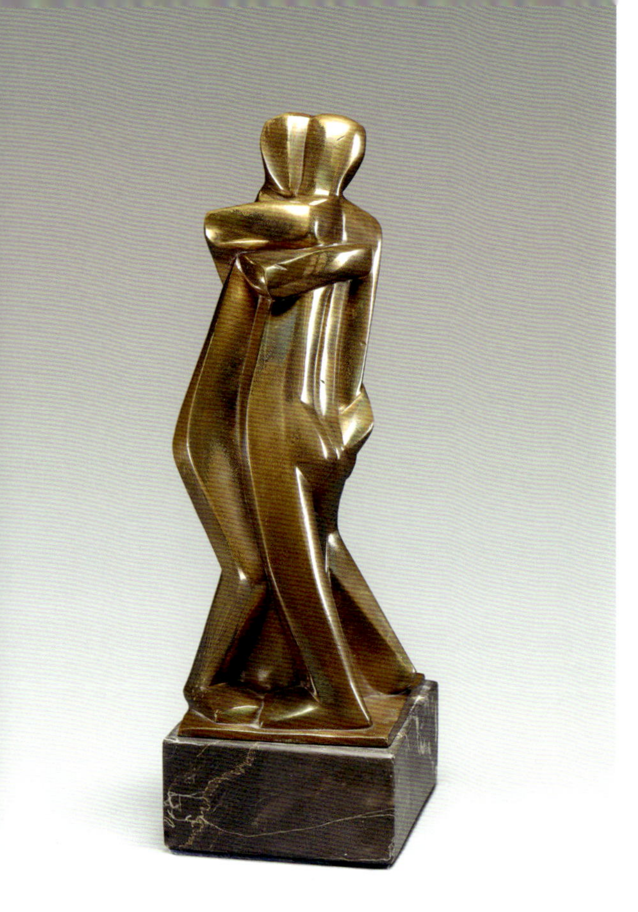

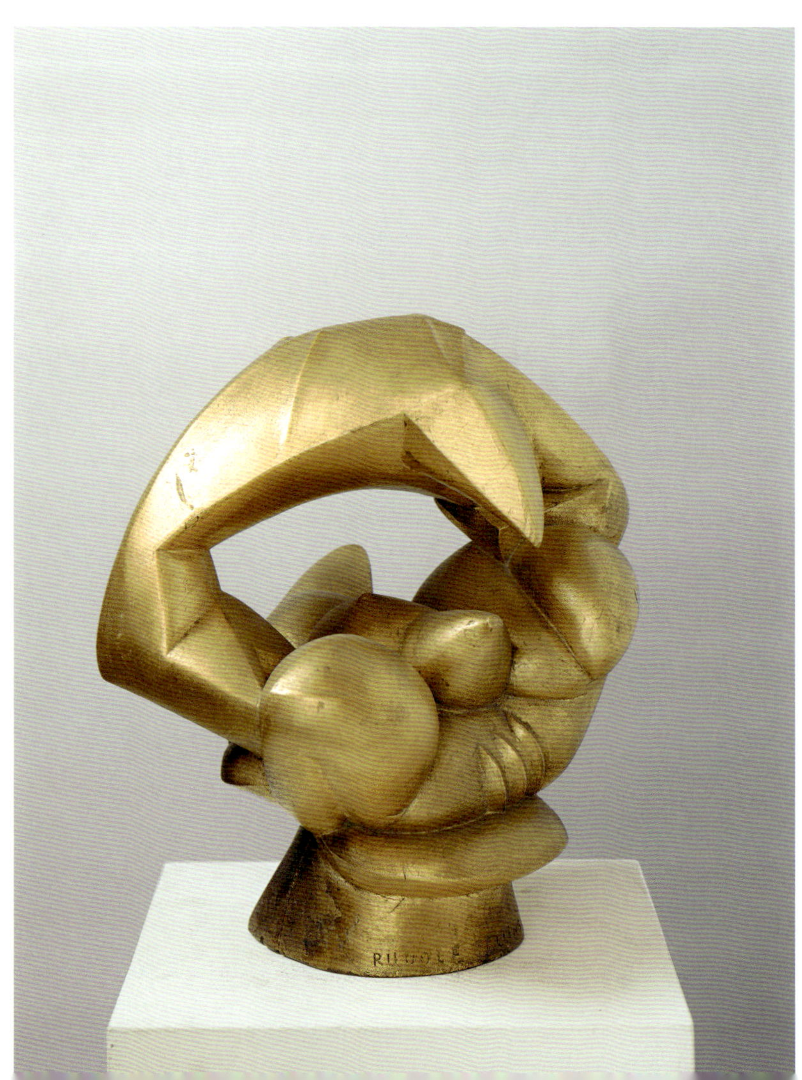

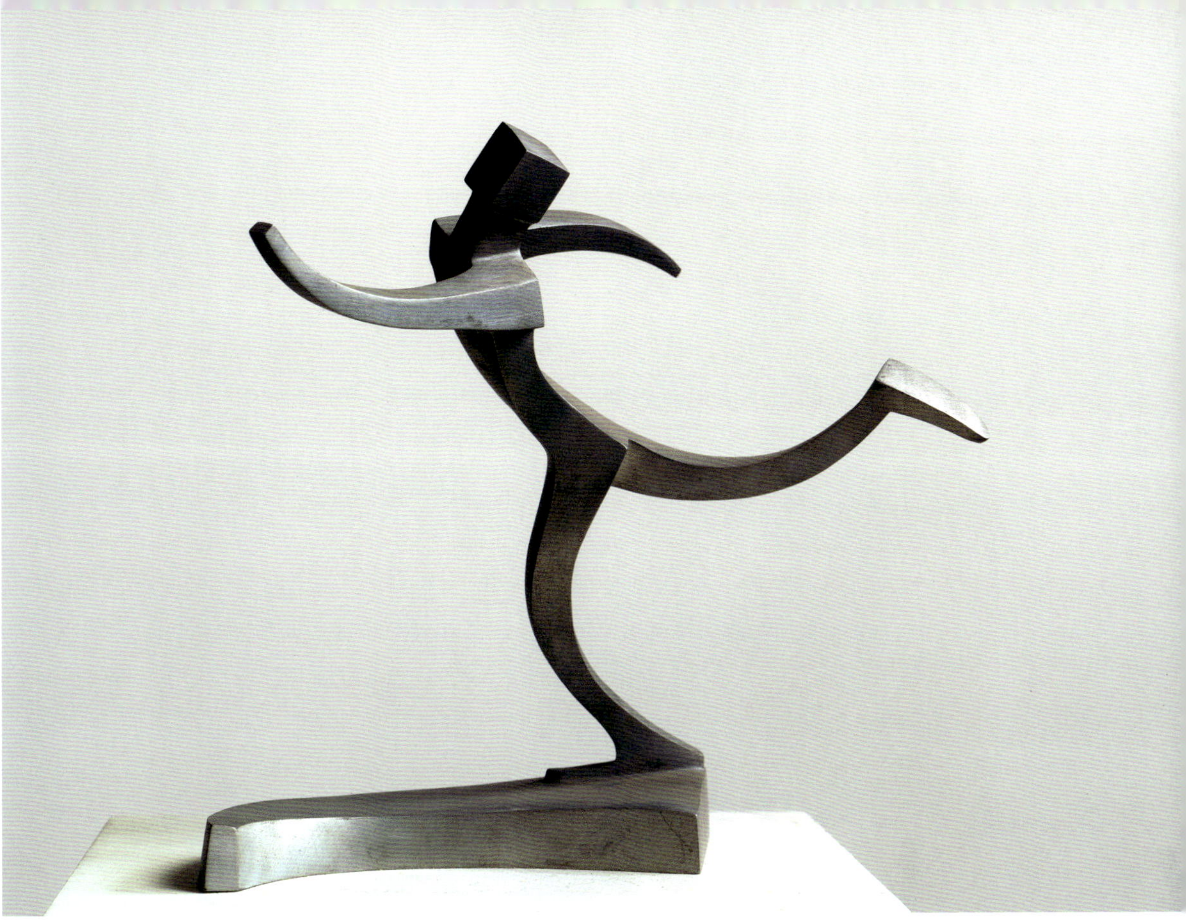

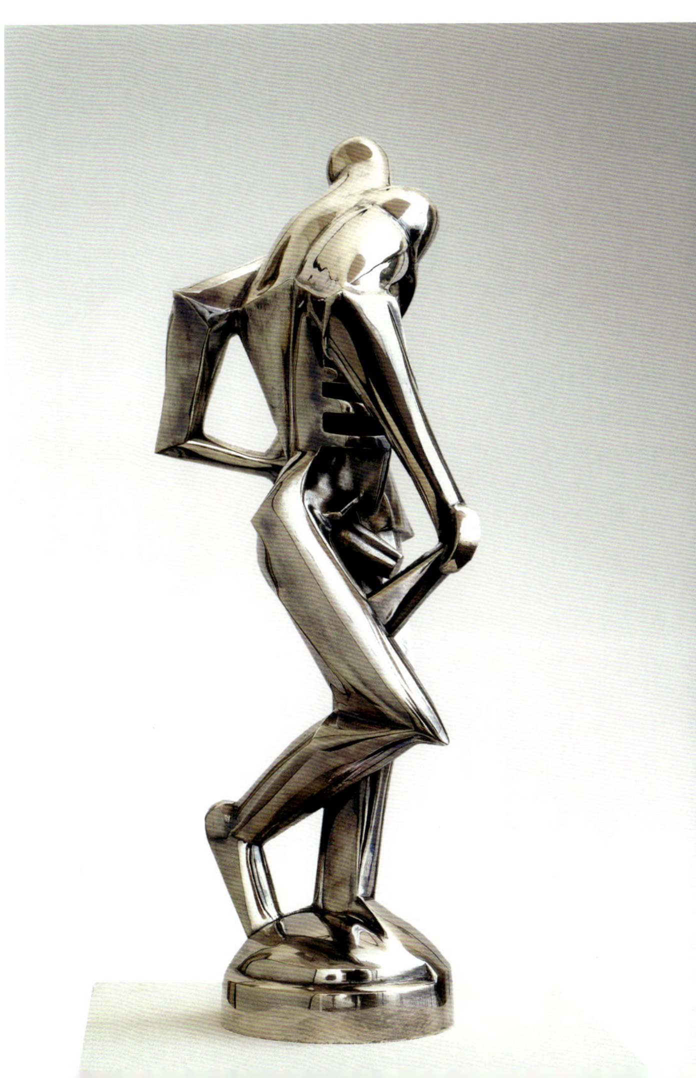

↖ Marg Moll, *Dancing Couple*, c. 1928
Brass, 33.5 × 14.5 × 16 cm
Acquired in 2016

↗ William Wauer, *Ice Skater*, 1918 (cast 1950)
Aluminium, 25.5 × 26 × 15 cm
Acquired in 1950 by the Land Berlin for the Galerie des 20. Jahrhunderts, Berlin (West)

← Rudolf Belling, *Eroticism*, 1920
Gold leaf on wood, 32.4 × 30.5 × 24 cm
Acquired in 1981 with funds from the Stiftung Renée Sintenis for the Nationalgalerie, Berlin (West)

→ Rudolf Belling, *Organic Forms (Striding Man)*, 1921
Silver-plated bronze, 54 × 21 × 18 cm
Gift from the artist's heirs to the Freunde der Nationalgalerie, 2004

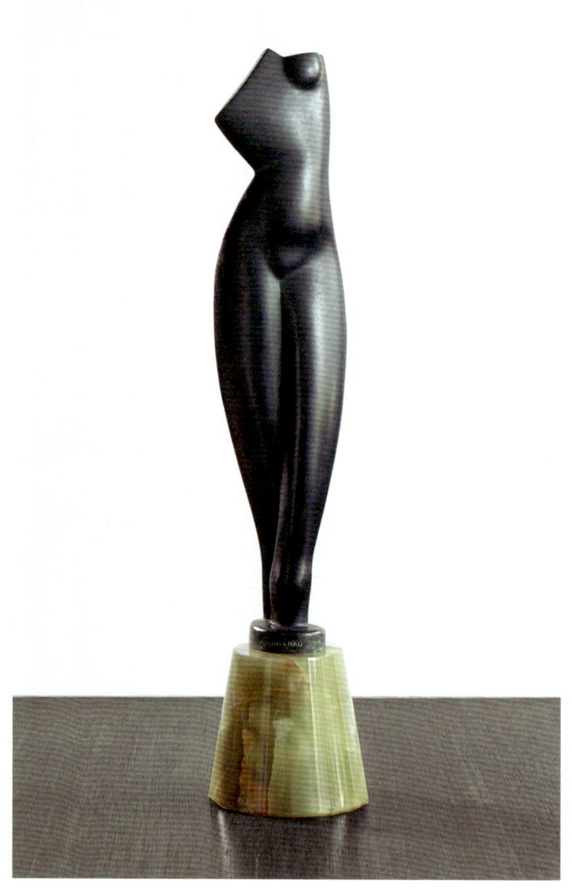

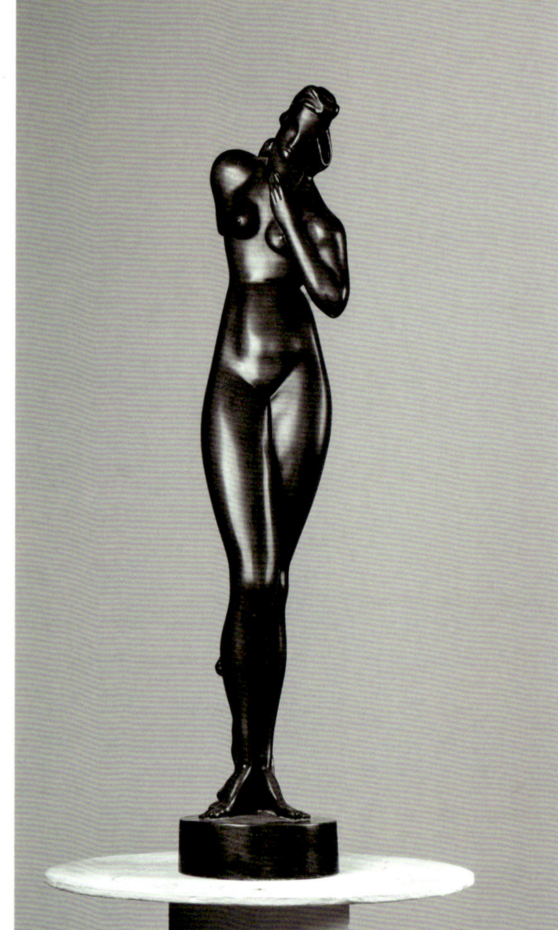

↗ Alexander Archipenko, *Flat Torso*, 1914 (cast, late 1950s)
Bronze, 48 × 10.5 × 10.5 cm (base included)
Acquired in 1965 from the Galerie Grosshennig, Düsseldorf, by the Land Berlin for the Galerie des 20. Jahrhunderts, Berlin (West)

→ Alexander Archipenko, *Woman Standing*, 1921
Bronze, 67.5 × 14.5 × 15 cm
Acquired in 1977 from the Handelsorganisation (HO) Cottbusser Börse, Cottbus, for the Nationalgalerie, Berlin (East)

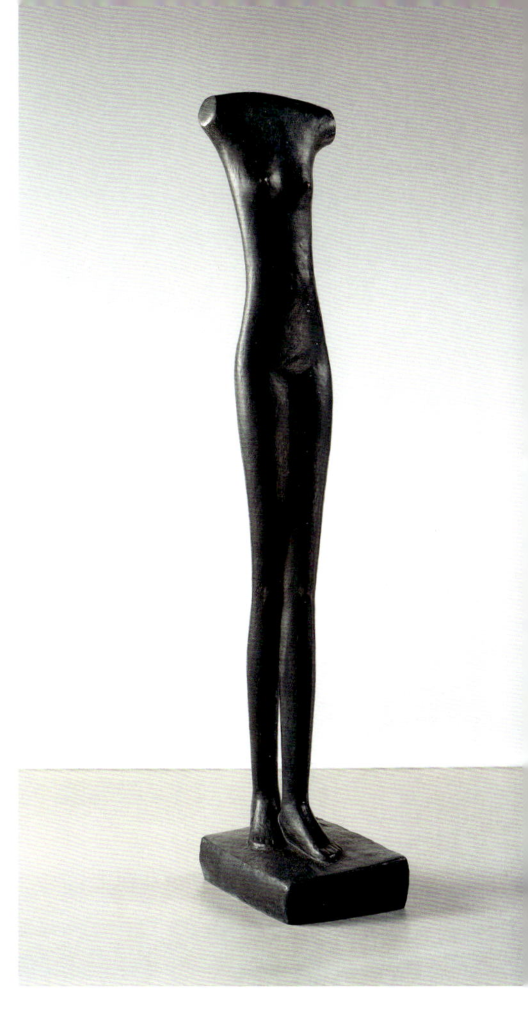

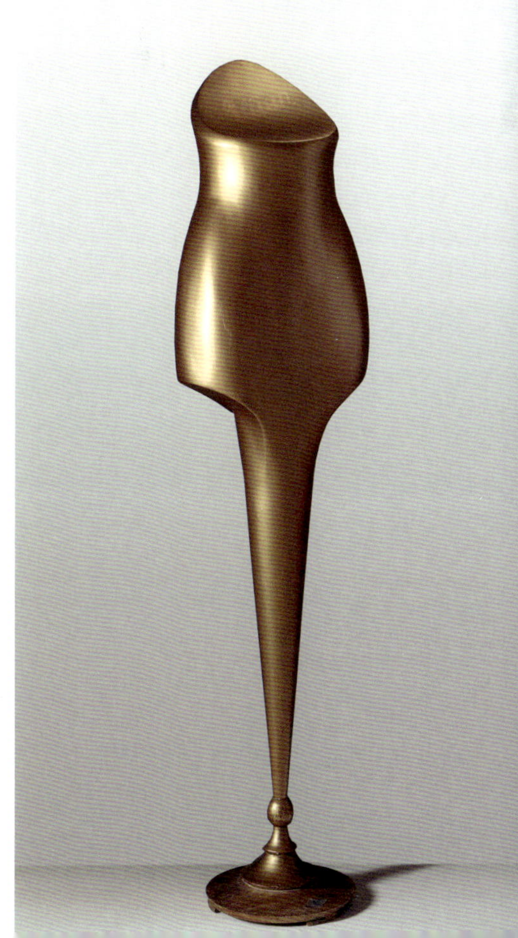

↗ Alberto Giacometti, *The Striding Woman*, 1932
Bronze, 149 × 24 × 38.2 cm
Gift from the Ulla and Heiner Pietzsch Collection to the Land Berlin, 2010

→ Rudolf Belling, *Fashion Sculpture, Model D (Skirt Sculpture "Lillian")*, c. 1923
Nitrocellulose paint on papier mâché and wood, metal, 139 × 35 × 25 cm (base included)
Acquired in 2016 by the Freunde der Nationalgalerie

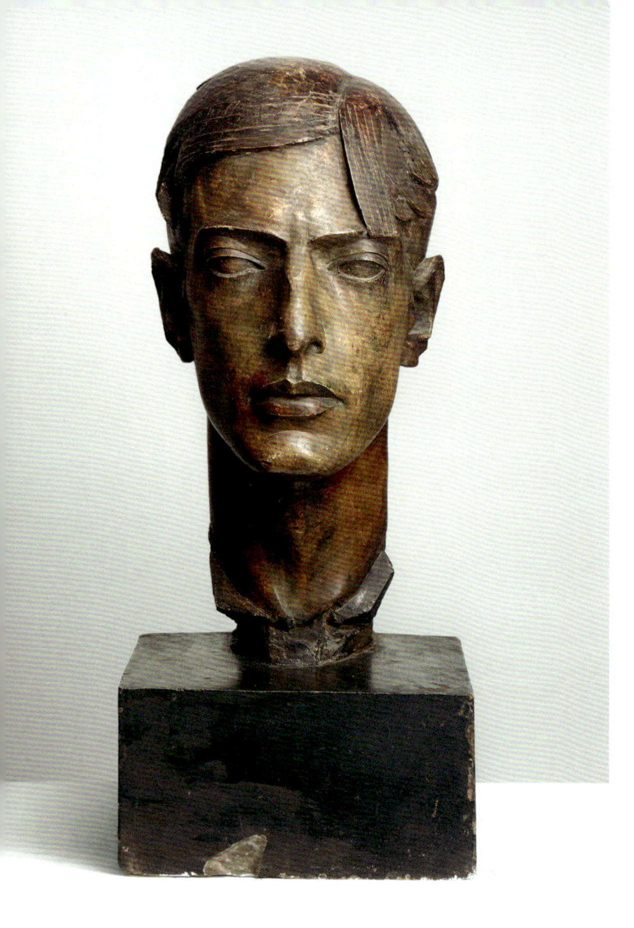
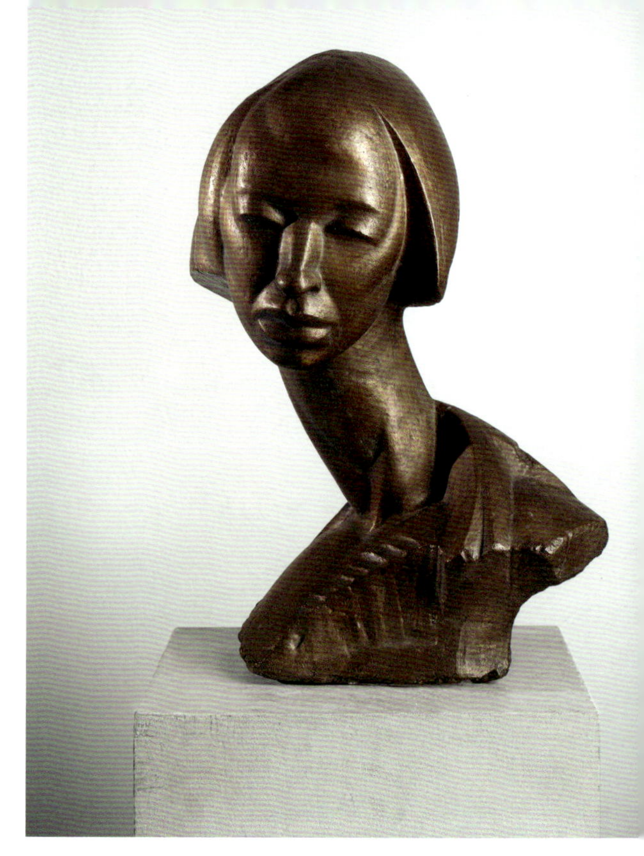
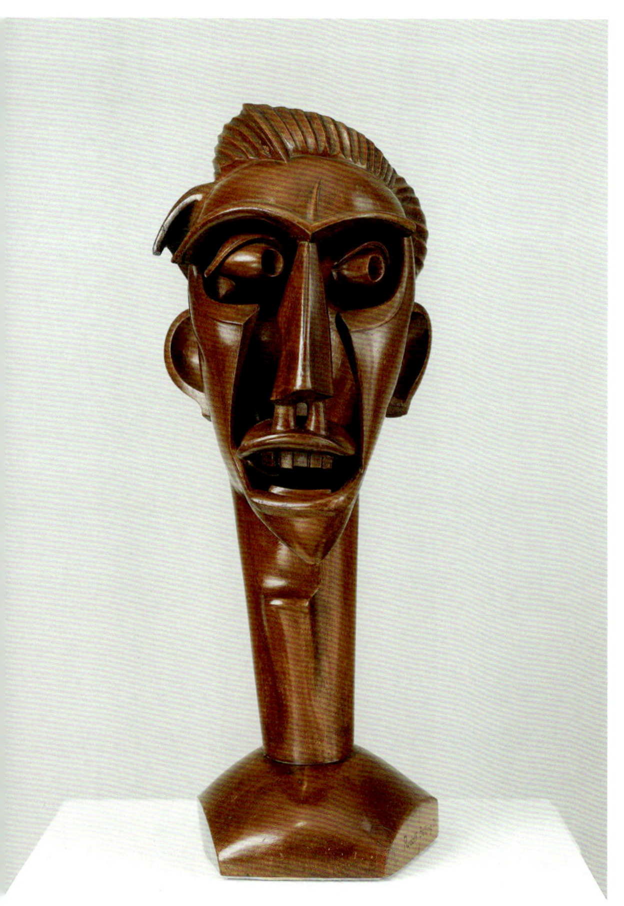
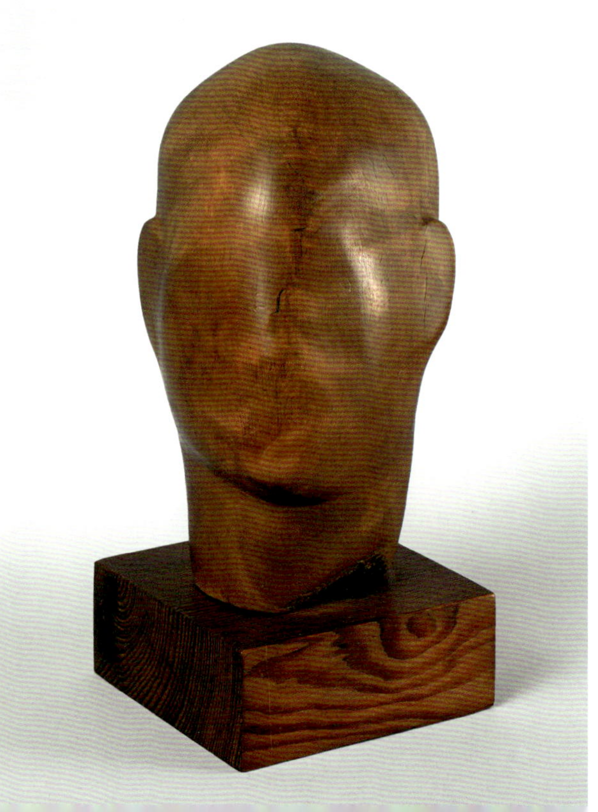

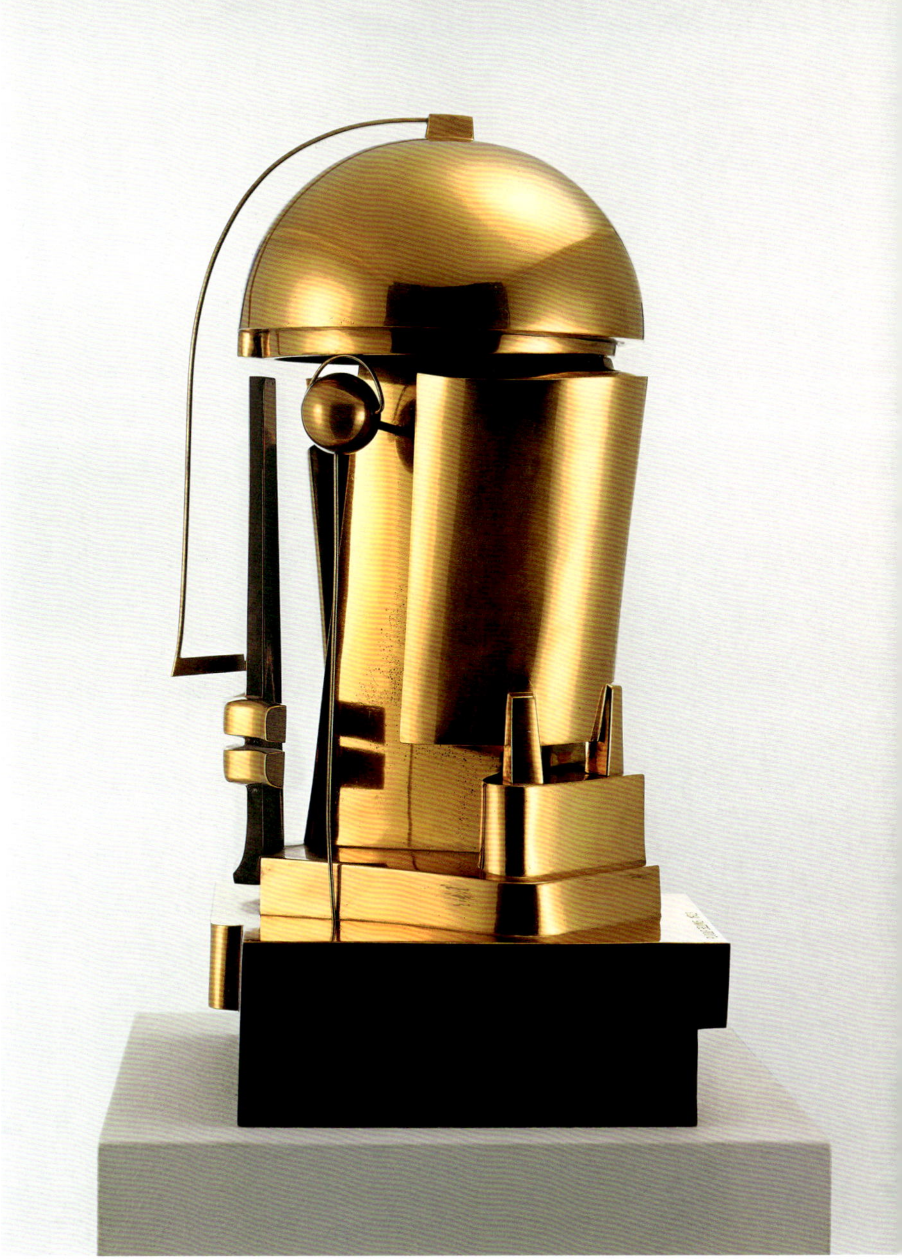

↗ Rudolf Belling, *Sculpture 23*, 1923 (cast 1966)
Brass, 41.5 × 21.5 × 24.5 cm
Acquired in 1973 for the Nationalgalerie, Berlin (West)

↖ Igor von Jakimov, *Bust of the Art Historian Ludwig Thormaehlen*, 1919
Stained plaster, 45 × 23 × 30 cm
Gift to the Nationalgalerie, Berlin (West) from Louise Jakimov, the artist's widow, Fribourg, Switzerland, 1967

↑ Will Lammert, *Portrait of the Dancer Ruth Tobi*, 1919 (cast 1988)
Bronze, 57 × 39 × 28 cm
Acquired in 1989 from the estate of the artist by Staatlicher Kunsthandel der DDR, Galerie Schönhof, Görlitz, for the Nationalgalerie, Berlin (East)

← Rudolf Belling, *Mahagony Head*, 1921
Mahogony, 52.5 × 21 × 21 cm
Acquired in 2004 by the Freunde der Nationalgalerie

← Ewald Mataré, *Male Head*, c. 1926
Birch wood, 21 × 12.8 × 15 cm
Acquired in 1984 from the Galerie Hella Nebelung, Düsseldorf, with funds from the estate Renée Sintenis for the Nationalgalerie, Berlin (West)

At the Centre of the Metropolis: Potsdamer Platz

Two prostitutes stand at the centre of the metropolis in Potsdamer Platz. Ernst Ludwig Kirchner finished the nocturnal scene in Berlin in 1914, following the outbreak of the First World War. It is the largest and most important painting in the series of street scenes the artist produced between 1913 and 1915.

Kirchner, a founding member of the artist group Brücke, moved from Dresden to Berlin in 1911, where he made the modern city his subject matter. Potsdamer Platz was the busiest square in Europe at the time. The visually overlapping, perspectively distorted and dynamized architectural backdrop shows Haus Vaterland, known as Café Piccadilly before the war, on the left, the Potsdamer Bahnhof train station in the middle, and the Bierhaus Siechen (a beer hall later known as the Pschorrhaus) that is cropped on the right side of the composition. A site of bustling business life during the day, Potsdamer Platz became a place of big-city entertainment at night. In spontaneous pencil sketches, Kirchner captured showgoers attending cabaret and vaudeville and streetwalkers, which he later combined and developed into the painting's composition.

Standing on an oval traffic island, the prostitutes (known at the time in German as "Kokotten" – coquettes) symbolize an individual's isolation and alienation within mass society. One of the two prostitutes wears a Prussian blue dress, the other a garment of mourning. Her gaze is directed outside the painting

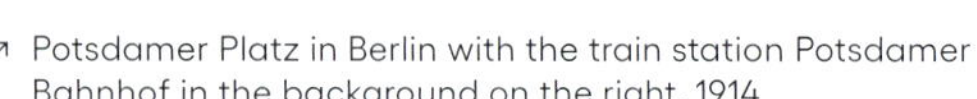

↗ Potsdamer Platz in Berlin with the train station Potsdamer Bahnhof in the background on the right, 1914
→ Ernst Ludwig Kirchner, *Women on Potsdamer Platz*, 1914
→ Ernst Ludwig Kirchner, *Women on Potsdamer Platz*, 1914

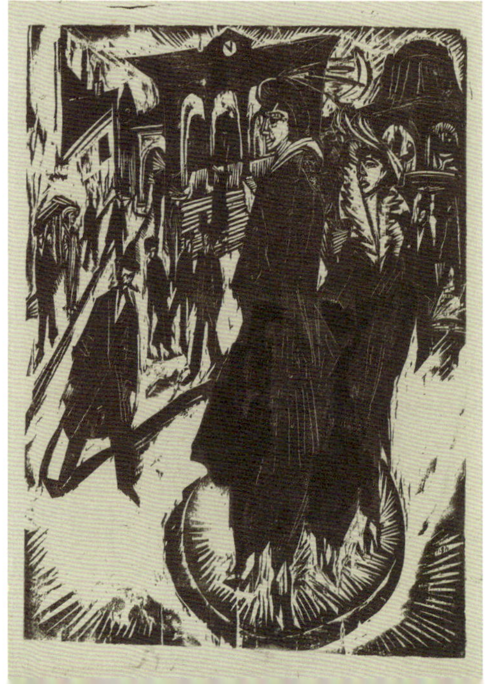

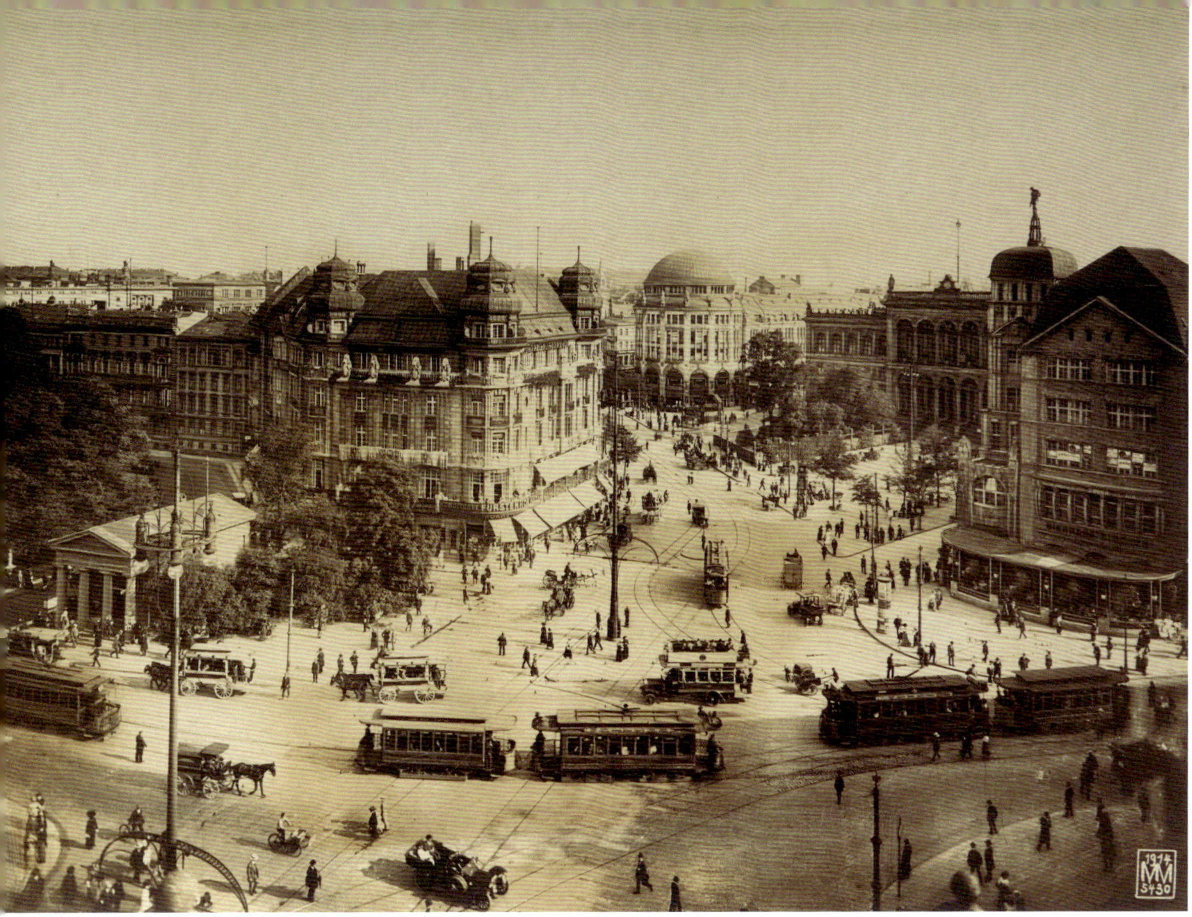

towards a cemetery located in front of the train station. It had been closed since 1909. Kirchner added her lace veil after the war began. It refers to the occasional prostitution practised by war widows who found themselves in economic straits. However, the veil also serves as a disguise because street prostitution was prohibited in imperial Berlin.

Kirchner's lifelong partner Erna Schilling posed for the veiled figure; her elder sister Gerda for the second woman. Both worked as dancers in a nightclub. Like his friend, the author Alfred Döblin, Kirchner viewed the prostitute as symbolic of modern life: alone and aimless in her relationships. Their clientele, the men lurking around the women, cannot overcome the gulf between themselves and the objects of their desire. But a sexual encounter is implied by the acute angles of the male strides and the sidewalk shaped like a ship's bow – a symbol of virility – pushing its way toward the female-occupied rondel, or circular space, set amidst the greenery of the nocturnal street. Kirchner's choice of colour recalls the green of absinthe, an alcoholic drink, also called "the green fairy".

The intensity of the colours increases the drama and stands for social exhaustion and disintegration. Only a short time later, in November 1916, Kirchner wrote: "Right now I'm just like the streetwalkers I painted. Whisked away, gone the next moment. I try, nevertheless, […] to create an image of the times out of the confusion – that is my task."

Johanna Yeats

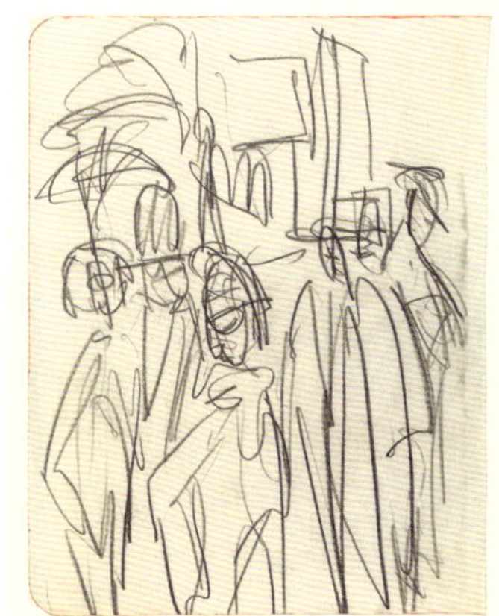

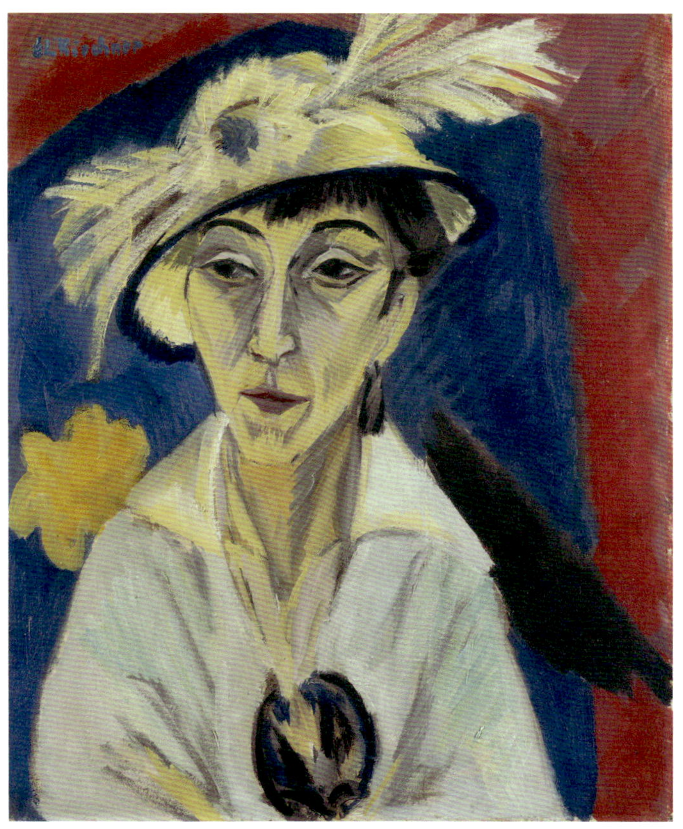

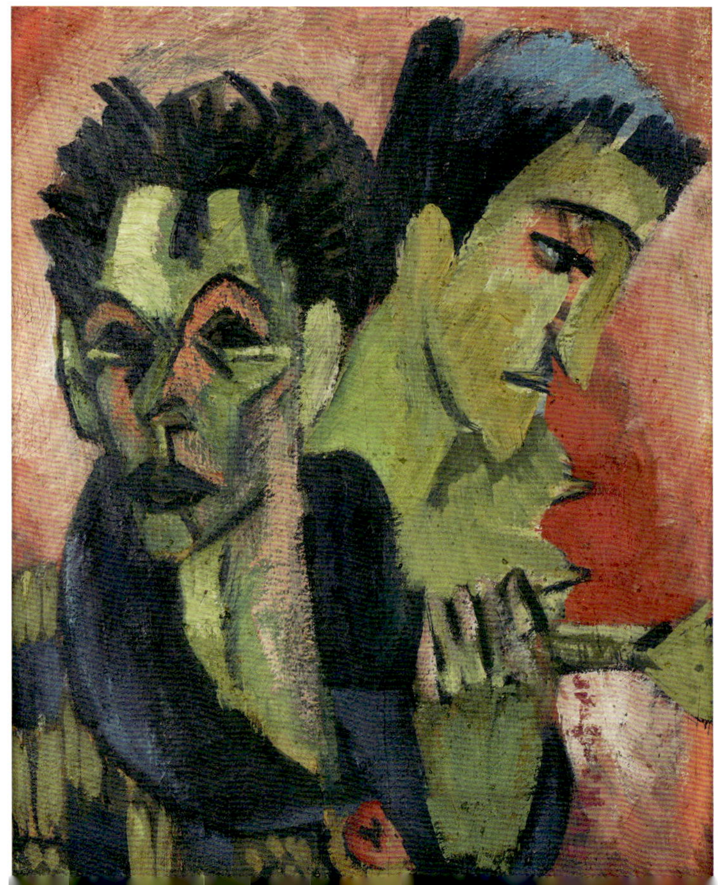

↑ Ernst Ludwig Kirchner, *Portrait of Erna Schilling*, 1913, oil on canvas, 71.5 × 60.5 cm
Acquired in 1989 by the Freunde der Nationalgalerie and the Bundesrepublik Deutschland from the estate of Karlheinz Gabler, Frankfurt am Main, for the Nationalgalerie, Berlin (West)

→ Ernst Ludwig Kirchner, *Self-Portrait with a Girl*, 1914–15, oil on canvas, 60 × 49 cm
Acquired in 1949 from the Galerie Gerd Rosen, Berlin, by the Land Berlin for the Galerie des 20. Jahrhunderts, Berlin (West)

↗ Ernst Ludwig Kirchner, *Potsdamer Platz*, 1914
Oil on canvas, 200 × 150 cm
Acquired in 1999 with support from the Bundesrepublik Deutschland, the Kulturstiftung der Länder, the Ernst von Siemens Kunststiftung, the Kultur-Stiftung der Deutschen Bank and others

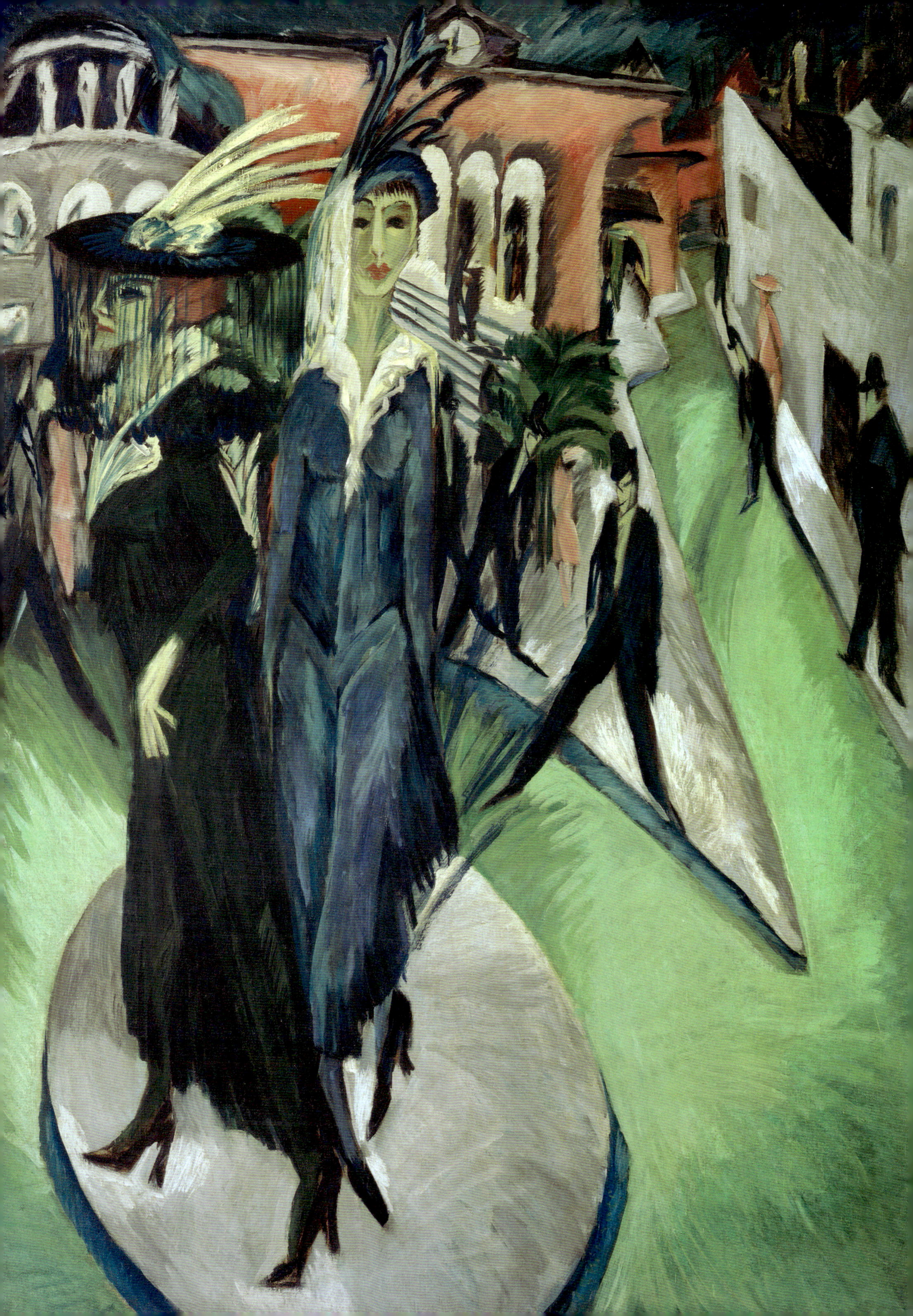

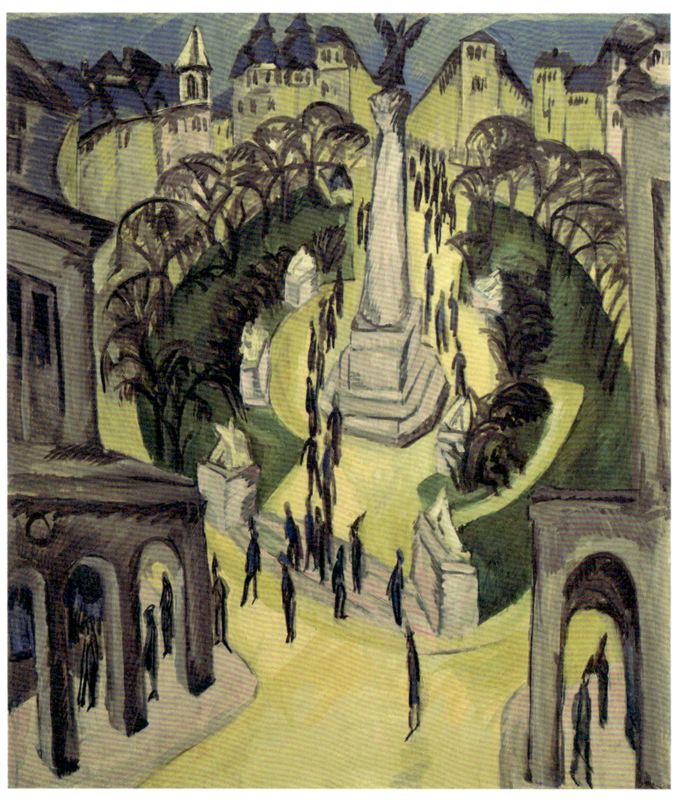

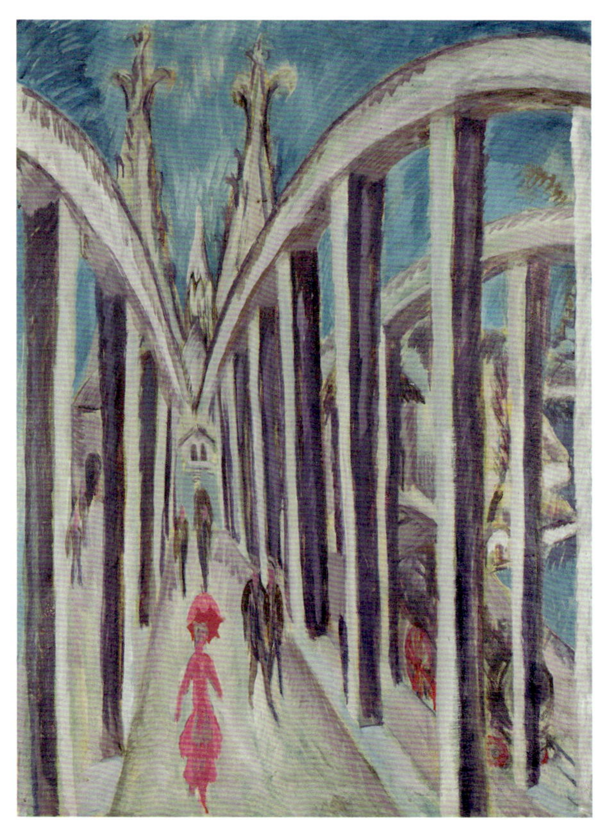

↑ Ernst Ludwig Kirchner, *Belle-Alliance-Platz in Berlin*, 1914, tempera on canvas, 96 × 85 cm
Acquired in 1955 from the Galerie Grosshennig, Düsseldorf, by the Land Berlin with funds from the Deutsche Klassenlotterie for the Galerie des 20. Jahrhunderts, Berlin (West)

→ Ernst Ludwig Kirchner, *Bridge over the Rhine in Cologne*, 1914, oil on canvas, 120.5 × 91 cm
Acquired in 1920 from the artist

↗ Ernst Ludwig Kirchner, *Max Liebermann*, 1926
Oil on canvas, 80 × 70 cm
Acquired in 2014 by the Freunde der Nationalgalerie with funds from the Manuela Müller bequest

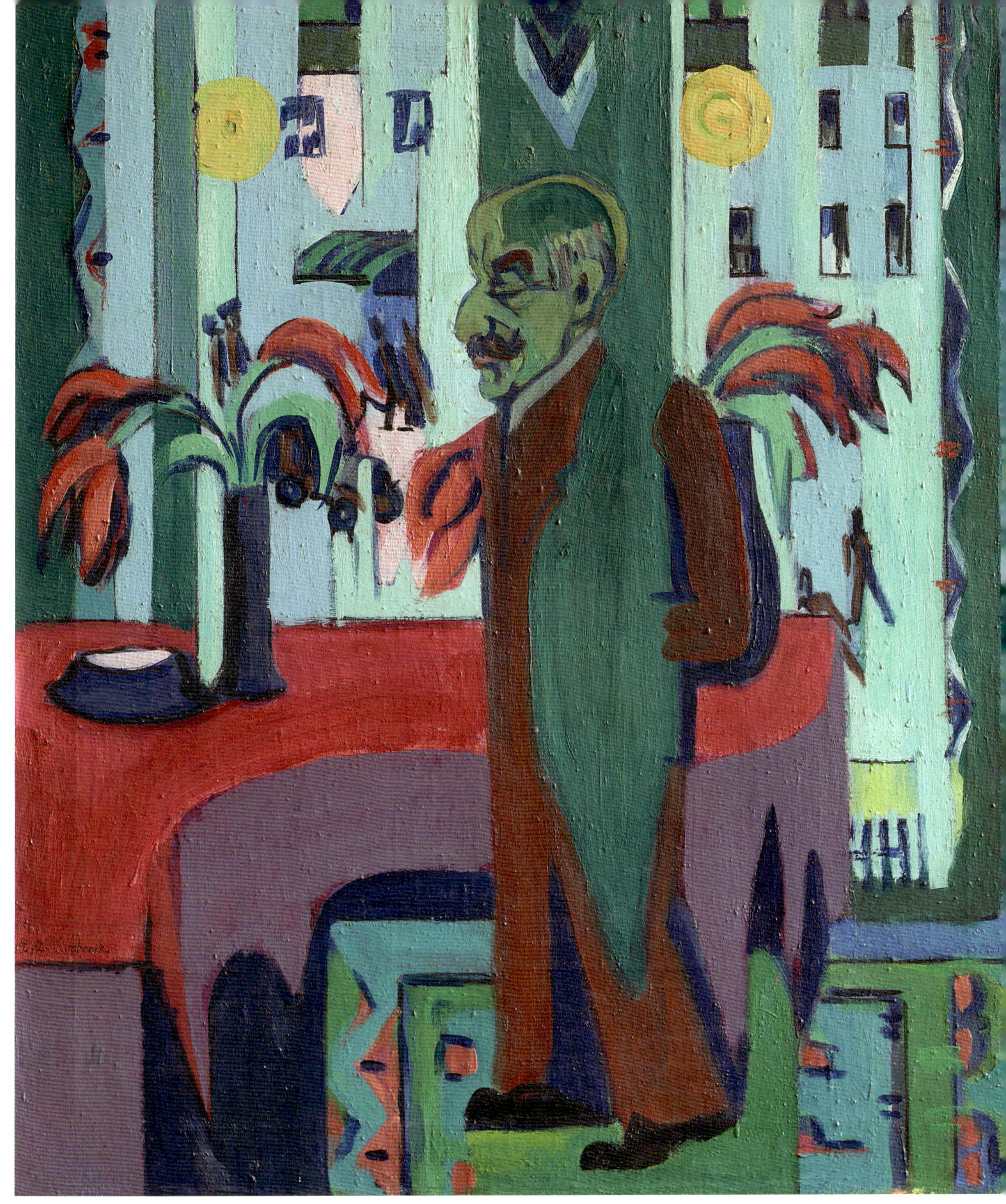

Ernst Ludwig Kirchner and Max Liebermann

Ernst Ludwig Kirchner and Max Liebermann each embody an epoch. Liebermann is considered the most important Impressionist painter in Germany, while Kirchner stands just as prominently for Expressionism. On 5 March 1926, Kirchner paid a visit to Liebermann's home on Pariser Platz. The 78-year-old host, who came from the Jewish upper middle class, was a well-known personality in Berlin society and was still in office as president of the Preußische Akademie der Künste (Prussian Academy of Arts). Kirchner, aged 45, had been living in a Swiss farmhouse since 1918. Liebermann supported the younger artist, whom he had invited to partake in exhibitions at the academy. During the visit or shortly after, Kirchner made two drawings: a portrait of Liebermann in profile and a compositional sketch.

When the painting *Max Liebermann in seinem Atelier* (Max Liebermann in His Studio) entered the Nationalgalerie collection in 2014, its previous title was called into question because it is not the house's attic studio that is depicted, but rather the music room in the living space below it. The painting shows Liebermann standing before a piano, enraptured in otherworldly concentration. The German word for the musical instrument – *Flügel* (wings) – may have prompted Kirchner to place a bouquet of tulips in the scene, making it appear as if Liebermann had grown wings. And this discreet reference to his presumed impending death (even though Liebermann would live until 1935) is further emphasized by the fact that his eyes seem closed. Several details augment the effect: the colour of Liebermann's face is mustard green, arrows fall towards his head,

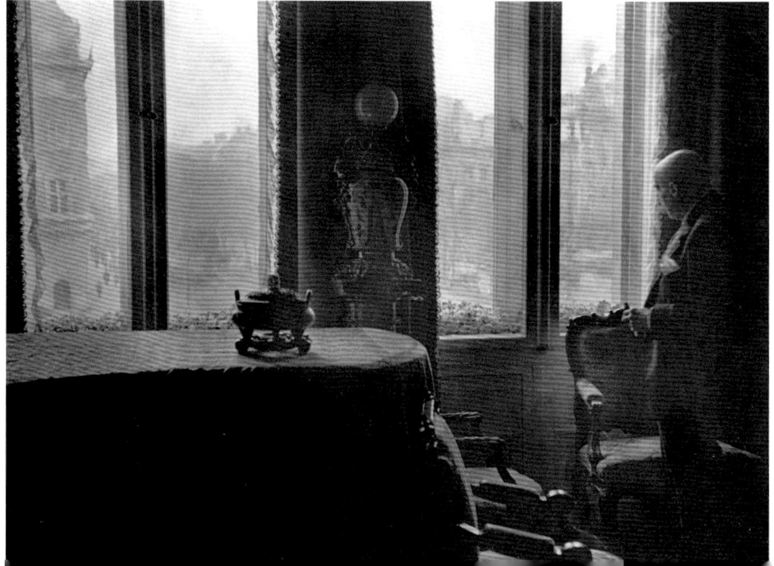

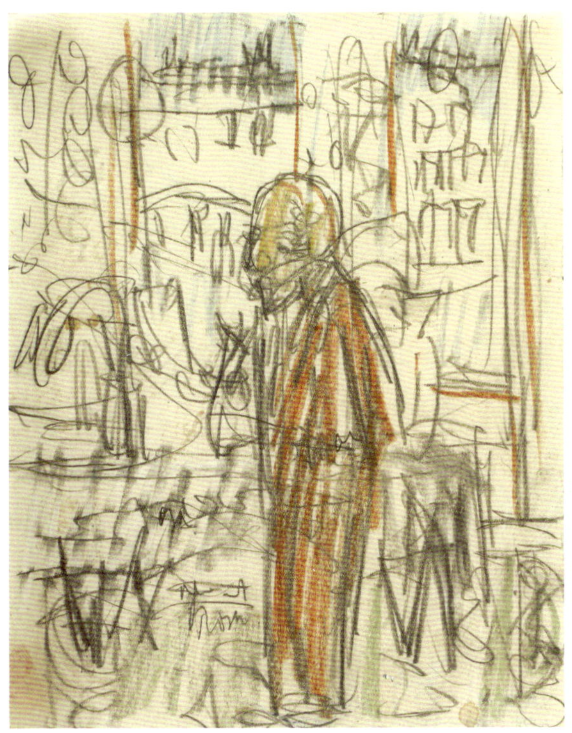

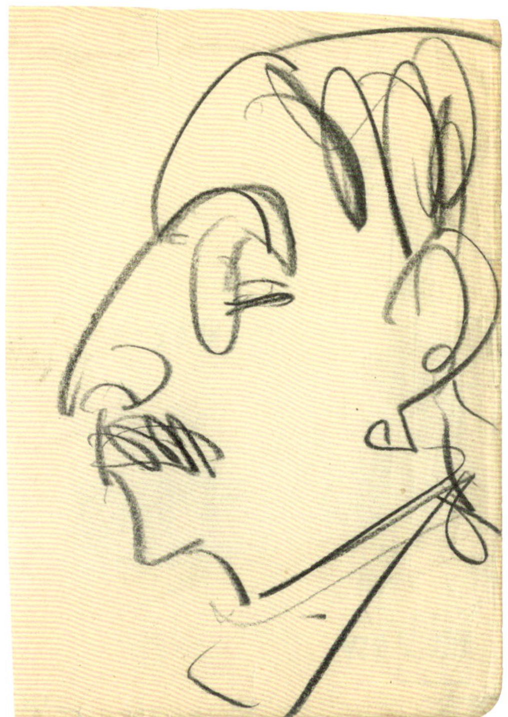

the house jacket he wears over his suit partially obliterates his figure, the plants bow their heads, the dusk of evening can be seen outside, and the streetlights are already lit.

Kirchner, who had carpets woven based on his own designs, placed Liebermann, a fellow painter, on a Persian rug that can be interpreted as an abstract representation of the Garden of Eden. And he posed the figure before window curtains that oddly recall a canvas tacked into a frame. As a result, Liebermann simultaneously stands on, before and in Kirchner's pictorial imagery. Kirchner's abbreviated hieroglyphics for striding figures can be seen in the view out the windows, recalling his urban scenes of Berlin. The striped marquee of the Hotel Adlon is recognizable, as is the Akademie der Künste building, which Liebermann heads. The view is from Liebermann's music room, whose walls were hung with works by Claude Monet, Édouard Manet, Edgar Degas and Paul Cézanne. But Kirchner consciously left out the Impressionist art and he directs our view to the modern metropolis instead.

The fact that Kirchner dedicated a painting to Liebermann attests to the artist's respect for him. At the same time, it is a thoroughly ambivalent portrayal of a fading artistic age – a colourful death mask, exaggerated like a caricature. It may also illuminate Kirchner's secret resentment, because he likely wished to play a role in the art world as significant as the one Liebermann occupied.

Dieter Scholz

↑ Ernst Ludwig Kirchner, *Preliminary sketch for Max Liebermann*, 1926
↗ Ernst Ludwig Kirchner, *Male Head – Portrait of Max Liebermann*, 1926
← Max Liebermann in his music room with a view of Pariser Platz, 1931

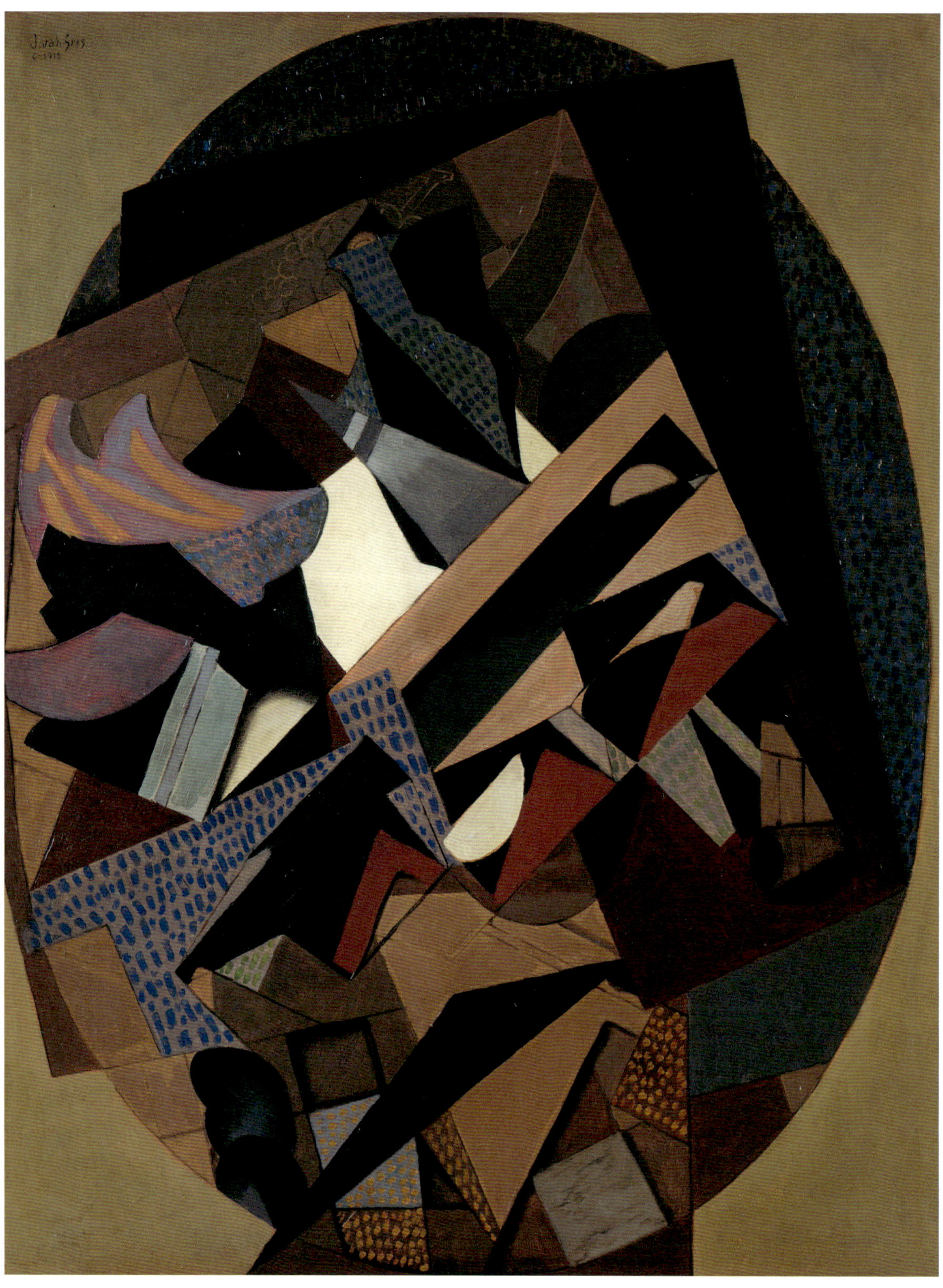

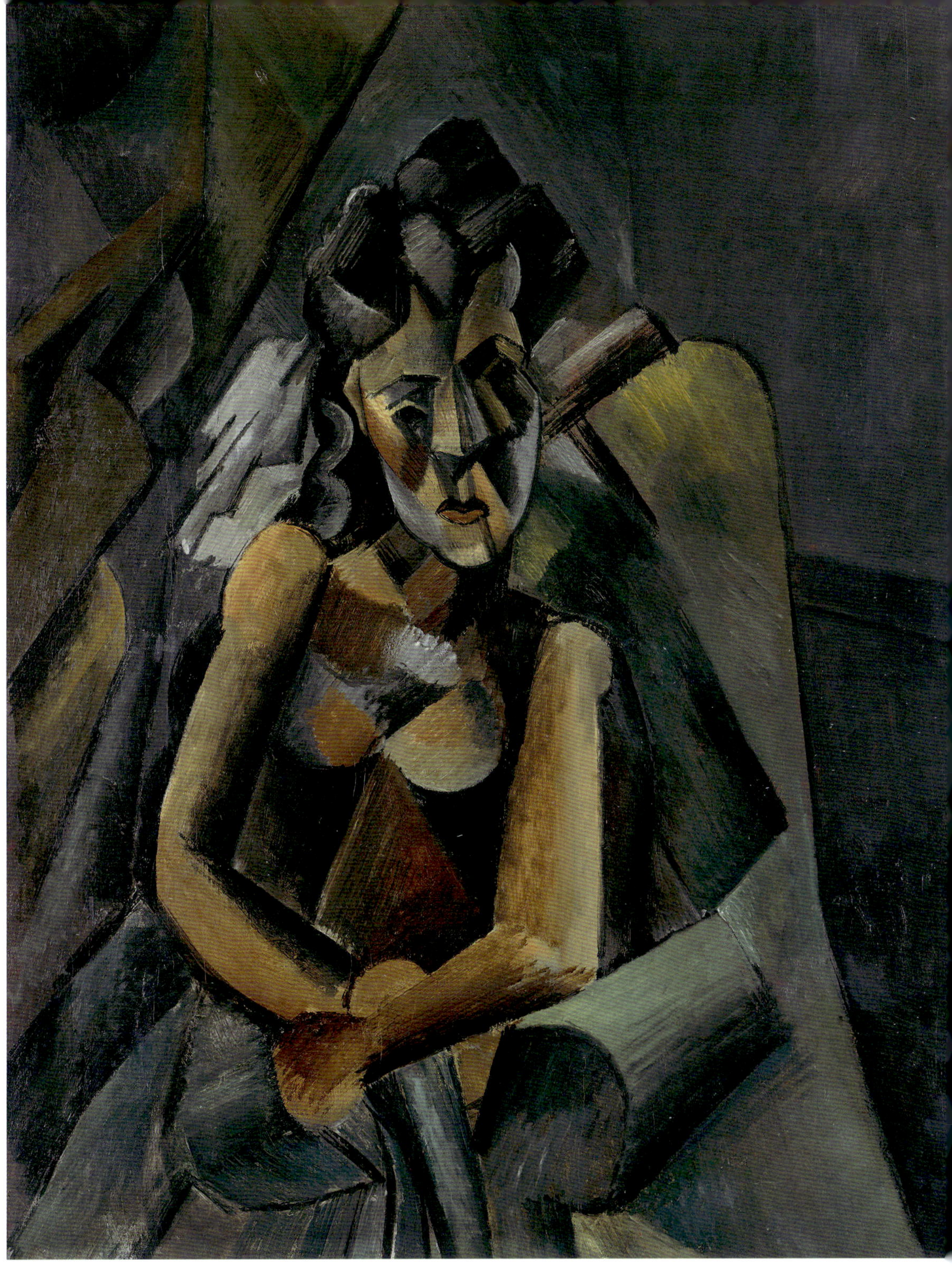

↗ Pablo Picasso, *Woman Sitting in an Armchair*, 1909
Oil on canvas, 100 × 80 cm
Acquired in 1980 for the Nationalgalerie, Berlin (West)

↖ Juan Gris, *Still Life*, 1915
Oil on canvas, 116 × 90 cm
Acquired in 1968 from the Galerie Grosshennig, Düsseldorf, by the Deutsche Gesellschaft für bildende Kunst with funds from the Deutsche Klassenlotterie for the Nationalgalerie, Berlin (West)

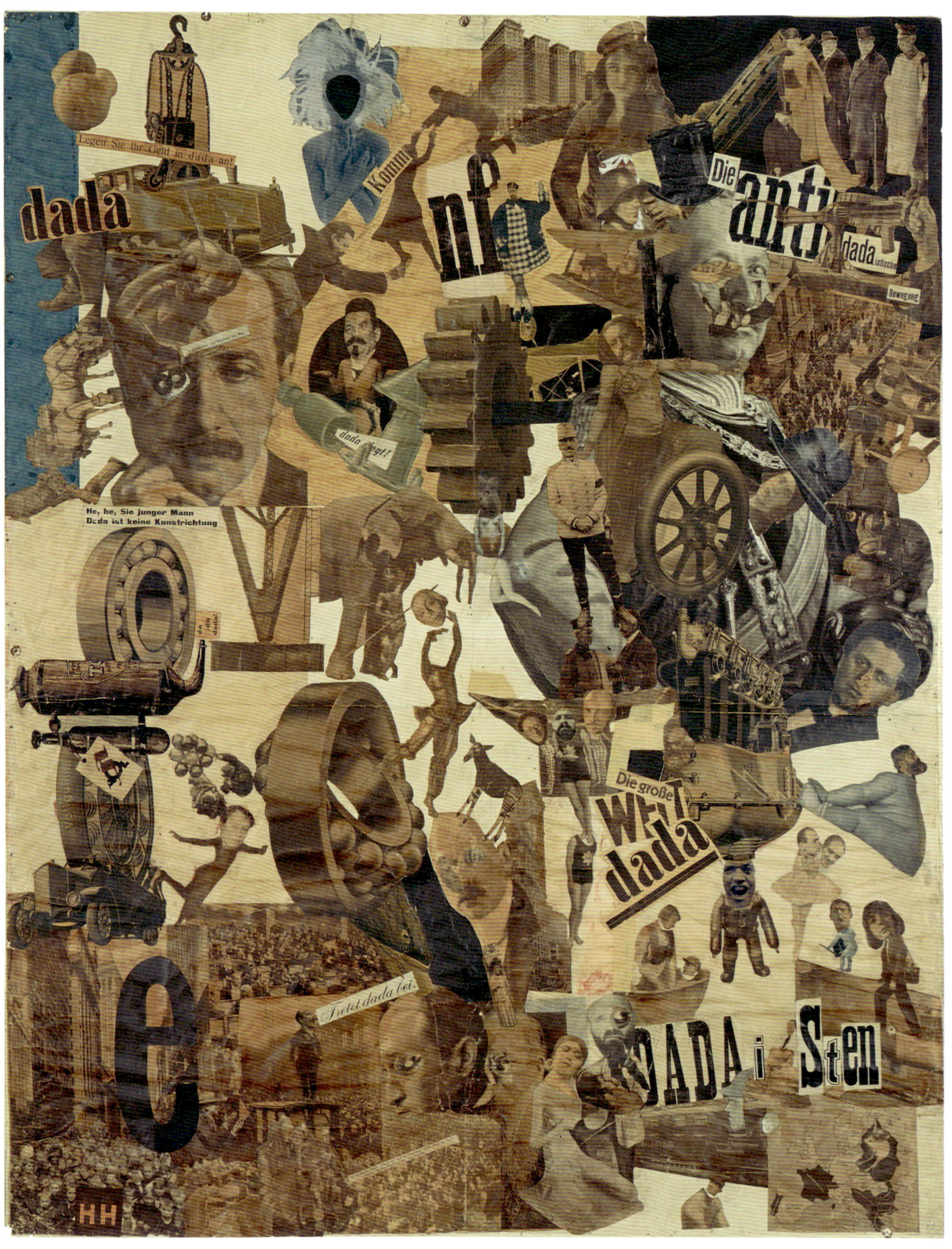
Legen Sie Ihr Geld in dada an!
dada
Komm
Die anti
dada
Bewegung
He, he, Sie junger Mann
Dada ist keine Kunstrichtung
Die große
dada
Tretet dada bei.
DADA i Sten
HH

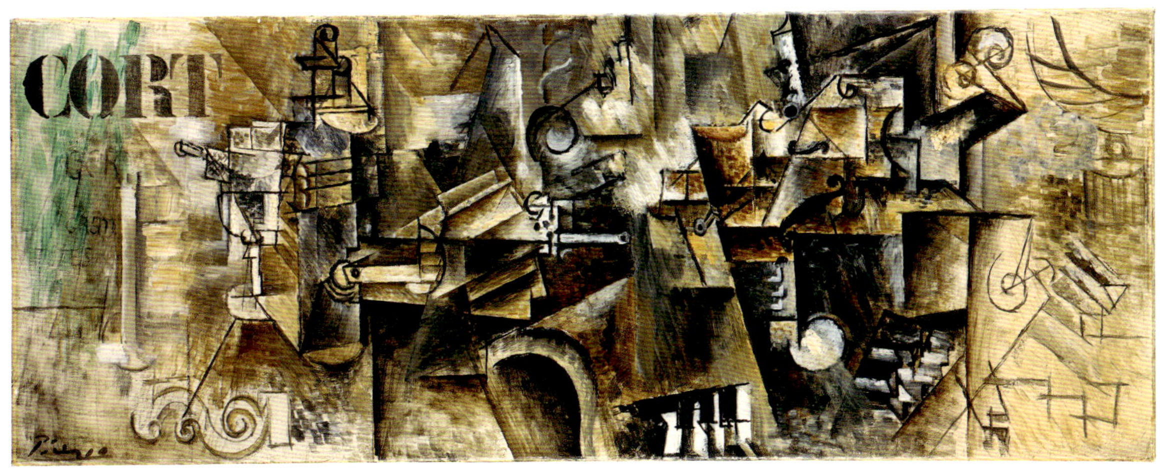

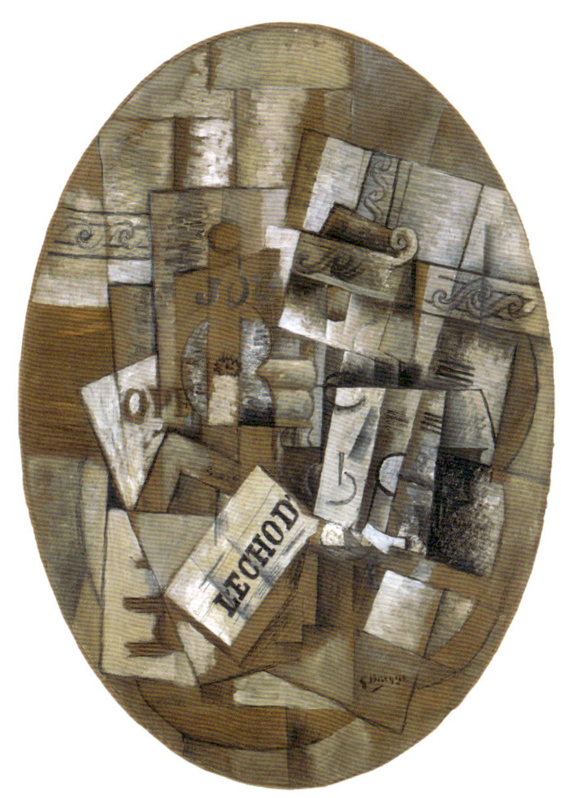

↑ Pablo Picasso, *Still Life on a Piano,* 1911–12
Oil and charcoal on canvas, 50 × 130 cm
Acquired in 2000 from Heinz Berggruen with support from the Bundesregierung and the Land Berlin

→ Georges Braque, *Still Life with Glass and Newspaper*, 1913
Chalk, charcoal and oil on canvas, 98.7 × 72.5 cm
Acquired in 2000 from Heinz Berggruen with support from the Bundesregierung and the Land Berlin

← Hannah Höch, *Cut with the Kitchen Knife Dada through the Last Weimar Beer-Belly Cultural Epoch in Germany*, 1919, paper on cardboard, collage, 114 × 90 cm
Acquired in 1961 from the Galerie Meta Nierendorf, Berlin, with funds from the Badische Anilin- und Sodafabriken (BASF), Ludwigshafen, for the Nationalgalerie, Berlin (West)

Hannah Höch's Epochal Image of the Weimar Republic

"He, he, Sie junger Mann, Dada ist keine Kunstrichtung" (Hey you, young man, Dada is not an art movement) is a saying on the large photomontage, which Hannah Höch created in summer 1920 for the *Erste Internationale Dada-Messe* (First International Dada Fair) in Berlin. But what exactly is Dada – and who was the young man? Perhaps he was the then 40-year-old physicist Albert Einstein, who seems to be wondering about these words. Or were the words put in his mouth? Is he voicing them, or is the artist addressing a male viewer of her image?

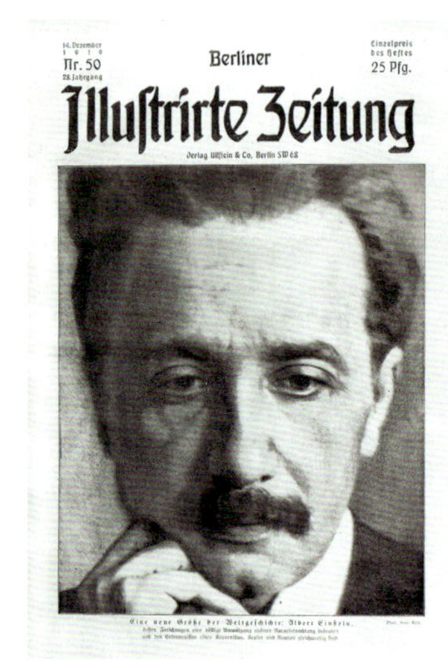
14. Dezember 1919
Nr. 50
28. Jahrgang
Berliner
Einzelpreis des Heftes
25 Pfg.
Illustrirte Zeitung
Verlag Ullstein & Co, Berlin SW 68

Eine neue Größe der Weltgeschichte: Albert Einstein,

The photo of Einstein came from the cover page of the *Berliner Illustrirte Zeitung* (Berlin Illustrated Newspaper). At that time, the physicist had already become a celebrity through his General Theory of Relativity. The knowledge that matter, space and time are not independent of each other but stand in a permanently changing interrelationship was also met with great fascination in artistic circles. A fixed point no longer exists; everything is in motion in a dynamic process.

Hannah Höch converted this insight into a structure. In her work, visual elements seem to turn and move wildly around at will: wheels and ball bearings, dancers, wrestlers, figure-skating movements. And with even atoms now no longer being indivisible, individuals, too, are broken down and recombined into new configurations. In the process, gender divisions became blurred, for instance, when the head of General Field Marshall Paul von Hindenburg, well-known from the First World War, is transplanted onto the body of the dancer Sent M'Ahesa, so that the hybrid creature is caressing the abdicated Kaiser Wilhelm II.

The German Empire was a thing of the past. The demonstrations and street battles of the November Revolution in 1918 were over, as were the National Assembly sessions, which drew up the democratic constitution in Weimar in 1919, and the failed Kapp Putsch attempt in March 1920. All of these political and

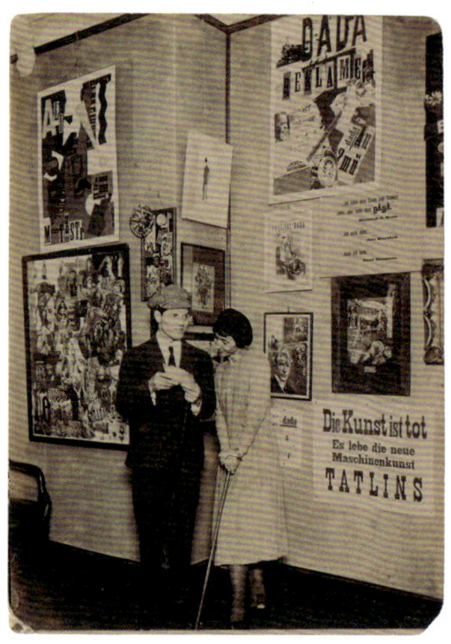

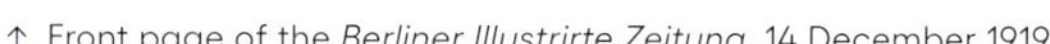

↑ Front page of the *Berliner Illustrirte Zeitung*, 14 December 1919
→ Raoul Hausmann and Hannah Höch at the First International Dada Fair next to Höch's collage *Cut with the Kitchen Knife Dada through the Last Weimar Beer-Belly Culture Epoch in Germany*, 1920
↗ Hannah Höch's Ullstein publishing house ID, 1916
→ Hannah Höch, Sketch identifying individual figures in *Cut with the Kitchen Knife Dada through the Last Weimar Beer-Belly Culture Epoch in Germany*, 1961

social events reappear in Höch's photomontage. It is an epochal image of the nascent Weimar Republic, a dynamic kaleidoscope. Hannah Höch emphasized two opposing groups: "the anti-Dada movement" made up of armed military forces faithful to the former Kaiser and the "Dadaists" – including Raoul Hausmann, Johannes Baader, George Grosz, John Heartfield, Walter Mehring and Höch herself – whose weapons were wit and fury.

Hannah Höch had worked as a drafting artist since 1916 in the editorial office for handicrafts and needlework at the Ullstein Verlag, where the *Berliner Illustrirte Zeitung* was published. She cut out the photographs she used in her collages from this and other magazines, as art historians Jula Dech and Hanne Bergius have shown in detail. At the bottom of Höch's photomontage is a map of Europe showing the countries where women had the right to vote. The artist pasted her face on the edge of the map. And her initials "HH" sound like laughter when spoken in German. The list of works for the *Erste Internationale Dada-Messe* ultimately includes an entry for catalogue number "20 Hannchen Höch: *Schnitt mit dem Küchenmesser Dada durch die letzte weimarer Bierbauchkulturepoche Deutschlands*" (Cut with the Kitchen Knife Dada through the Last Weimar Beer-Belly Cultural Epoch of Germany). The title provides an answer to what Dada intended to be: Dada was the knife used to dissect society.

Dieter Scholz

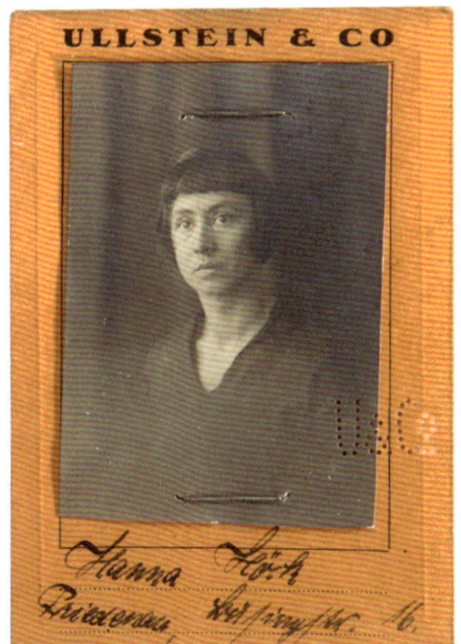

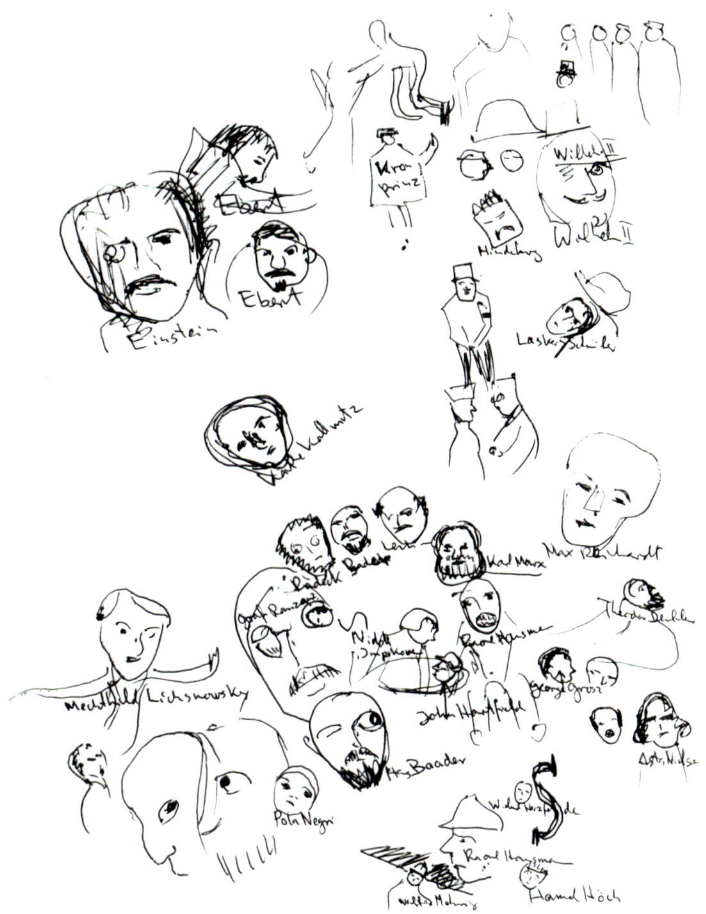

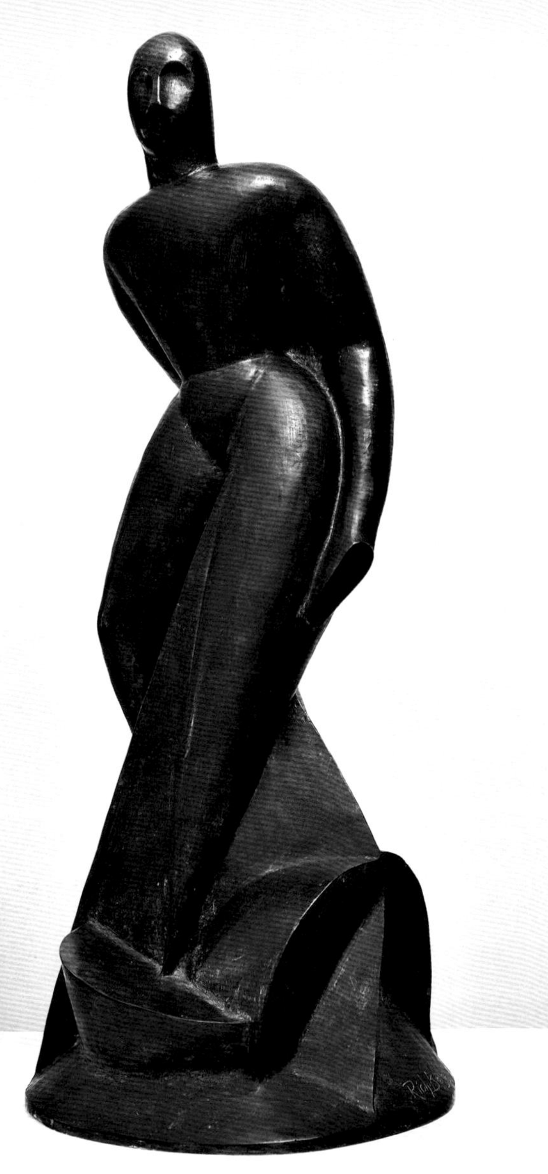

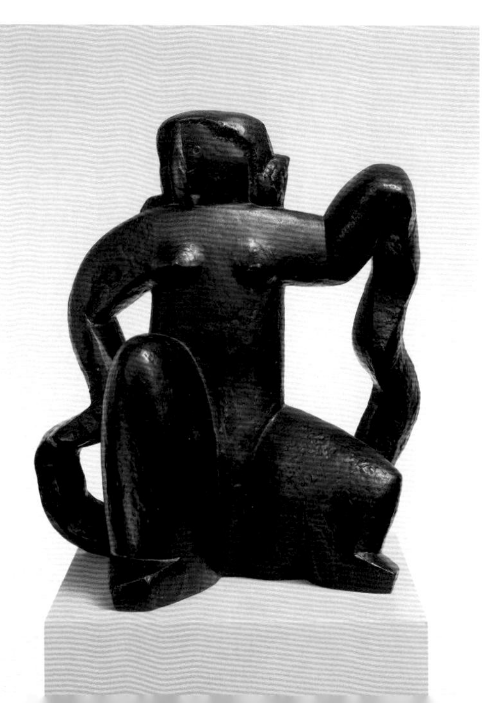

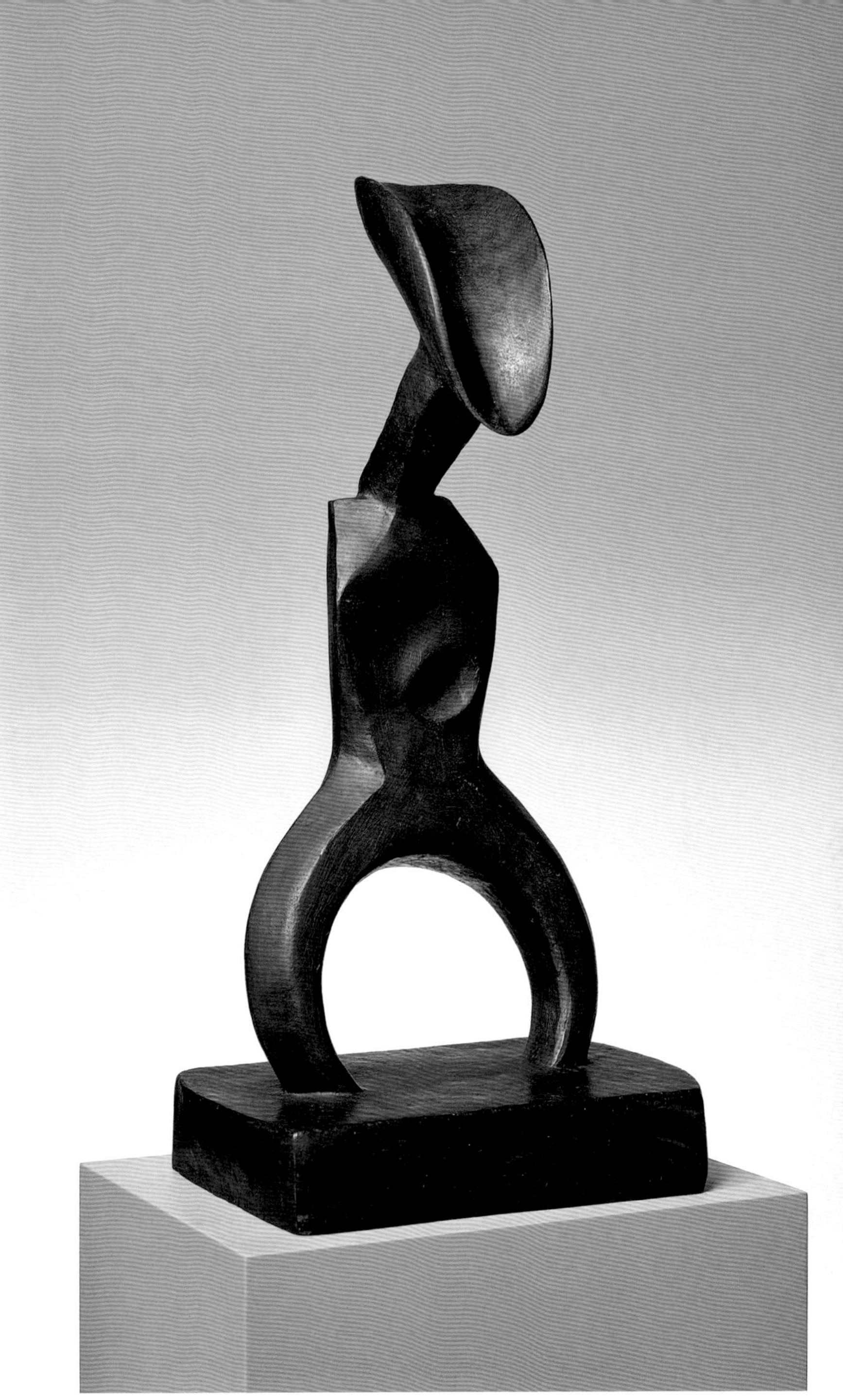

↗ Max Ernst, *Young Man with Fluttering Heart*, 1944 (cast 1953)
Bronze, c. 65 × 34 × 22 cm
Gift from the Ulla and Heiner Pietzsch Collection to the Land Berlin, 2010

↖ Richard Horn, *Departure*, 1919 (cast 1982)
Bronze, 97 × 39 × 40 cm
Acquired in 1982 from the artist for the Nationalgalerie, Berlin (East)

← Henri Laurens, *The Banderole*, 1931
Bronze, 36.5 × 33 × 26 cm
Loan from the Ulla and Heiner Pietzsch Collection

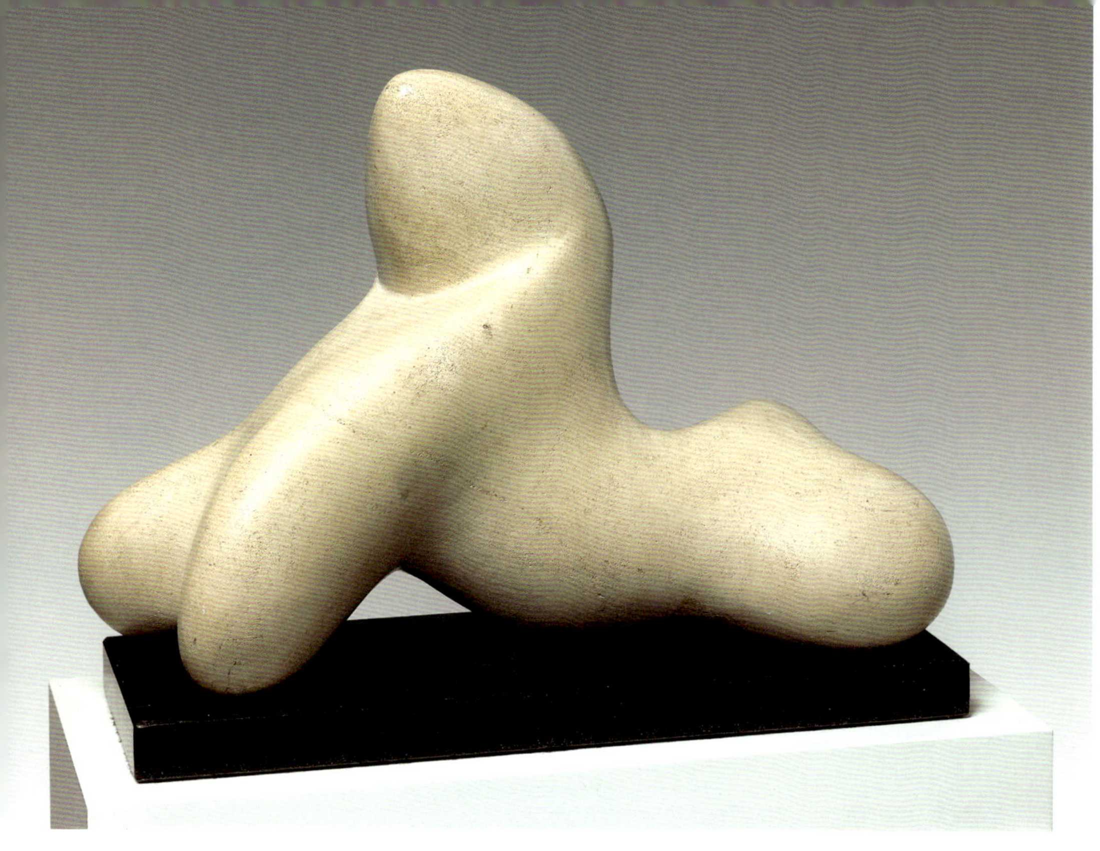

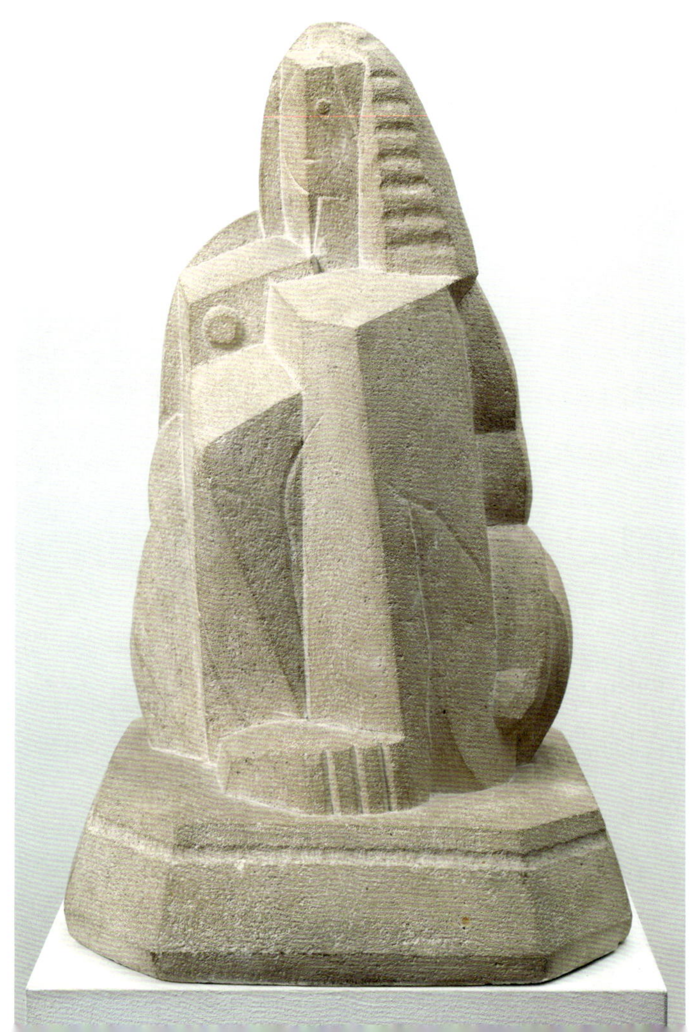

↑ Hans Arp, *Sitting*, 1937
Limestone, 29.5 × 44.5 × 18 cm
Gift from the Ulla and Heiner Pietzsch Collection to the Land Berlin, 2010

→ Henri Laurens, *Crouching Woman*, 1922
Limestone, 53 × 33 × 29.5 cm
Acquired in 1966 from the Galerie Michael Hertz, Bremen, by the Land Berlin for the Galerie des 20. Jahrhunderts, Berlin (West)

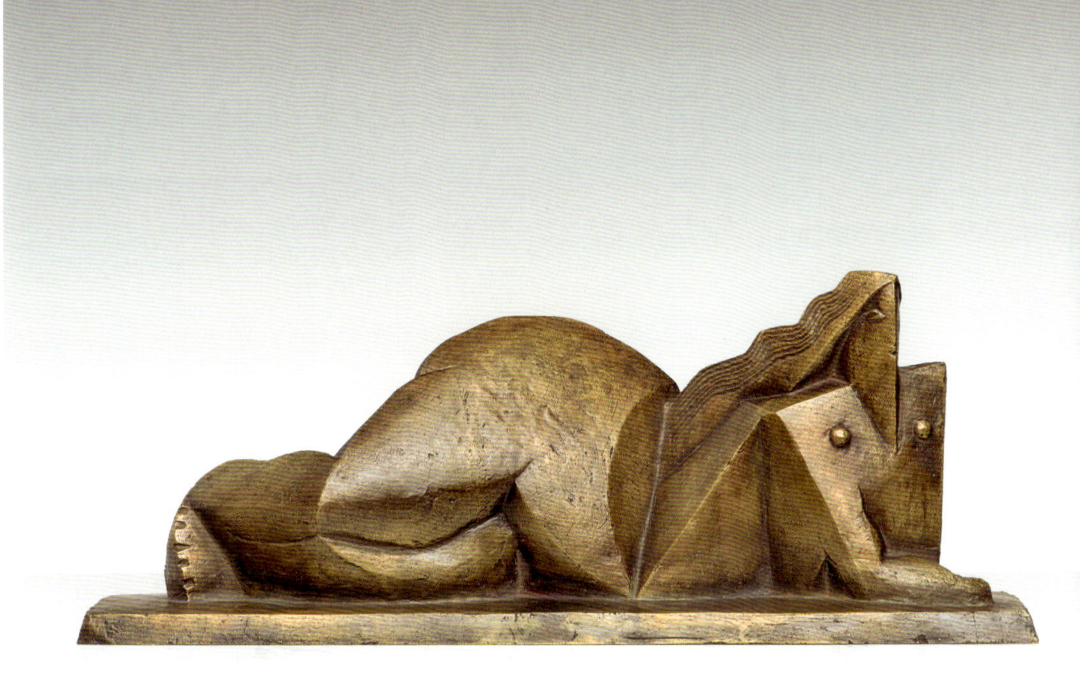

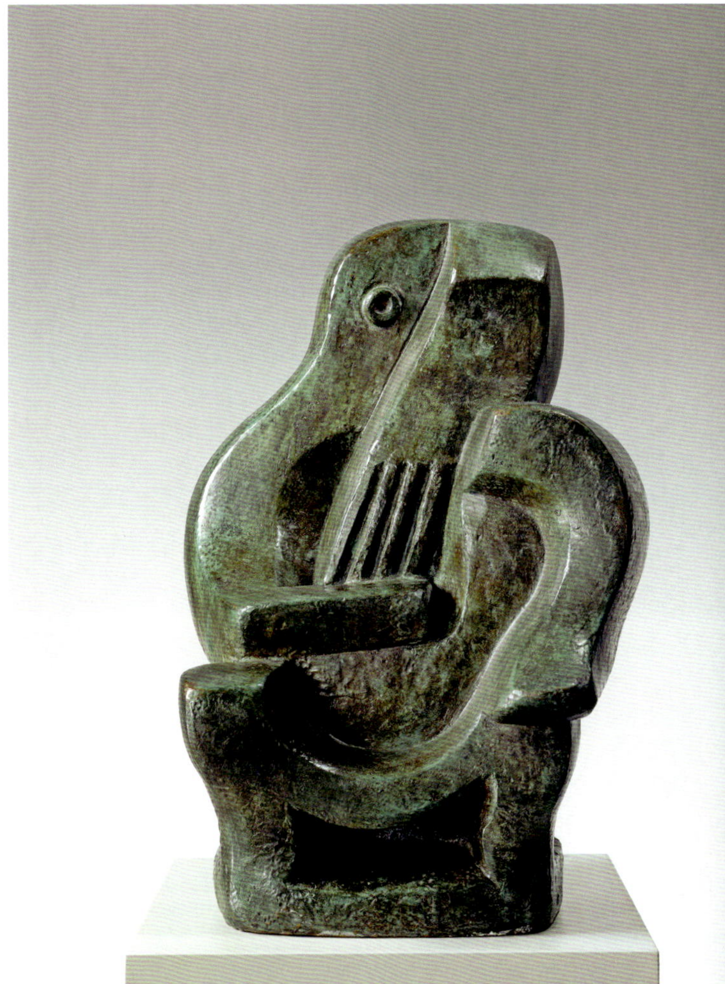

↑ Henri Laurens, *Recumbent Woman*, 1921
Bronze, 11.3 × 30.8 × 9.2 cm
Acquired in 1952 from the Galerie Springer, Berlin, by the Land Berlin for the Galerie des 20. Jahrhunderts, Berlin (West)

→ Jacques Lipchitz, *Sitting Man with Guitar*, 1922
Bronze, 38 × 26 × 28 cm
Gift from the Ulla and Heiner Pietzsch Collection to the Land Berlin, 2010

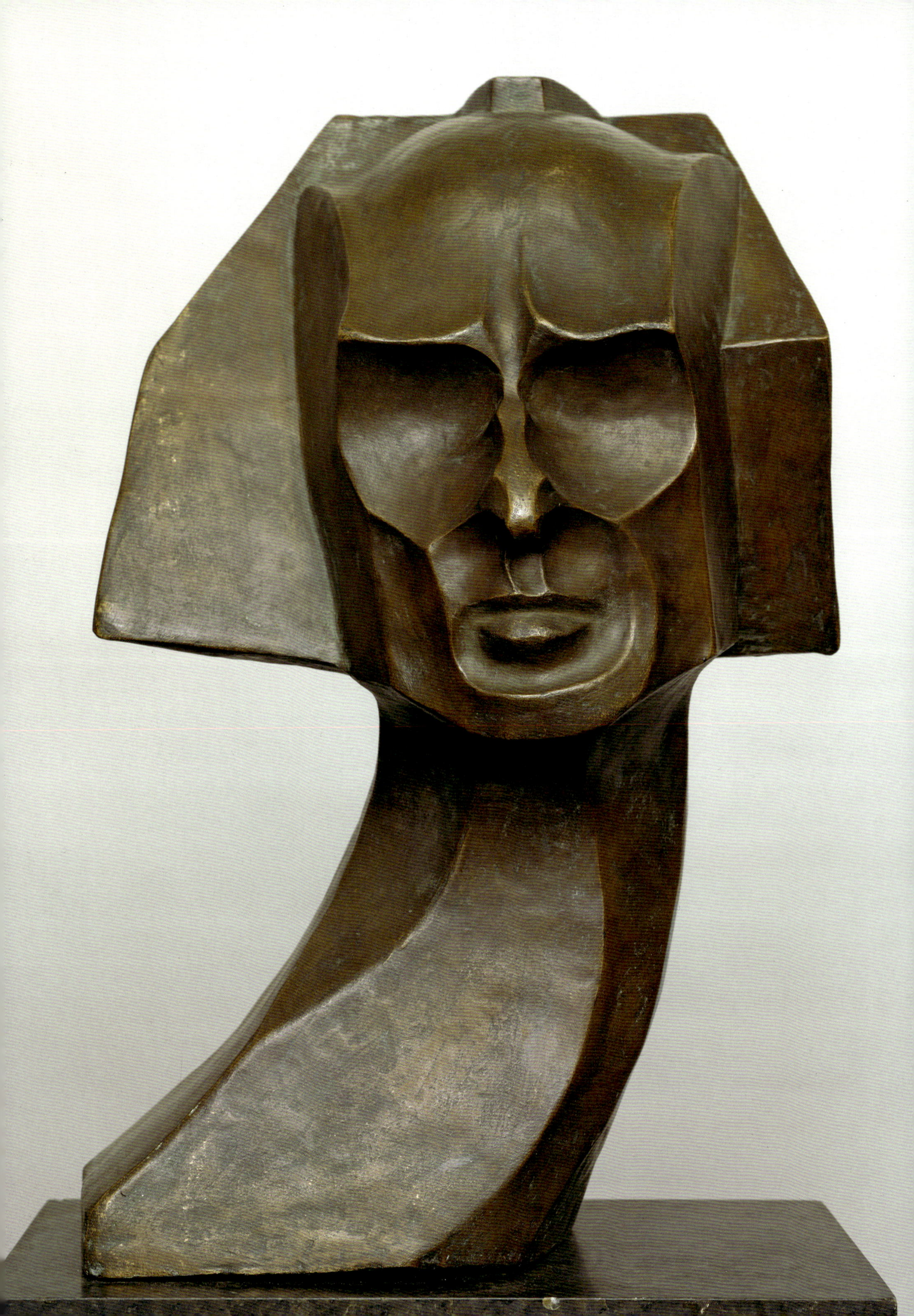

The Powers of Der Sturm

In 1910 a centre for the artistic avant-garde originated in Berlin under the name Der Sturm (The Storm). Herwarth Walden – a musician, writer, gallerist and publisher – was its founder. He initially published a magazine, then opened a gallery, later an art school, a bookshop and the Sturm-Bühne (Expressionist theatre). Aspiring forces from the visual arts, literature, music, theatre, and architecture encountered one another there.

In the Sturm gallery's first exhibition, side by side with works by Oskar Kokoschka and the painters Max Pechstein and Ernst Ludwig Kirchner from the artist group Brücke, works by the Munich group Der Blaue Reiter – including the artists Wassily Kandinsky, Franz Marc, August Macke and Gabriele Münter – were also shown in Berlin for the first time. Although Der Sturm was primarily associated with Expressionism, Walden also offered a platform to many other revolutionary art movements, such as Constructivism. Financial problems led to the gallery's closure in 1929, although Walden continued to publish the magazine *Der Sturm* until 1932. A short time later, Walden, who came from a Jewish family, moved to the Soviet Union as he was a member of the Communist Party. In 1941 Walden fell victim to Stalin's reign of terror and died in a Soviet prison.

William Wauer, *Herwarth Walden*, 1917 (cast 1964)
Bronze, 62 × 40.5 × 34 cm (base included)
Acquired in 1964 from Edmund Kesting, Birkenwerder,
for the Nationalgalerie, Berlin (East)

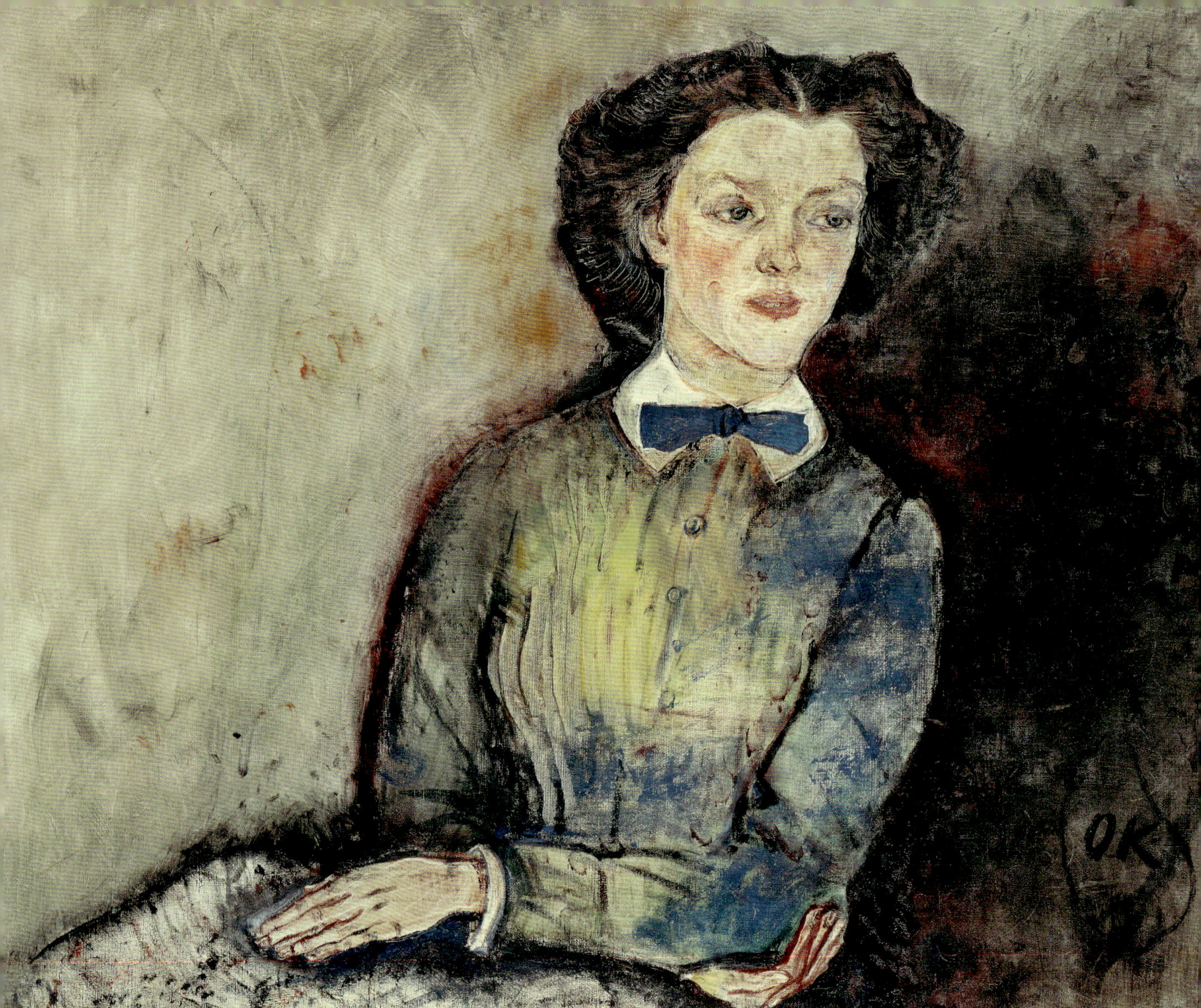

↑ Oskar Kokoschka, *Portrait of Bessie Bruce*, 1910
Oil on canvas, 72 × 91 cm
Acquired in 1926 from the Galerie Paul Cassirer, Berlin; considered a war loss after removal from storage c. 1946; reacquired for the Nationalgalerie, Berlin (West) in 1971 from a private collection, New York

→ Robert Delaunay, *Portrait of Herwarth Walden*, 1923
Distemper on canvas, 100 × 81 cm
Acquired in 1964 by the Land Berlin with funds from the Deutsche Klassenlotterie for the Nationalgalerie, Berlin (West)

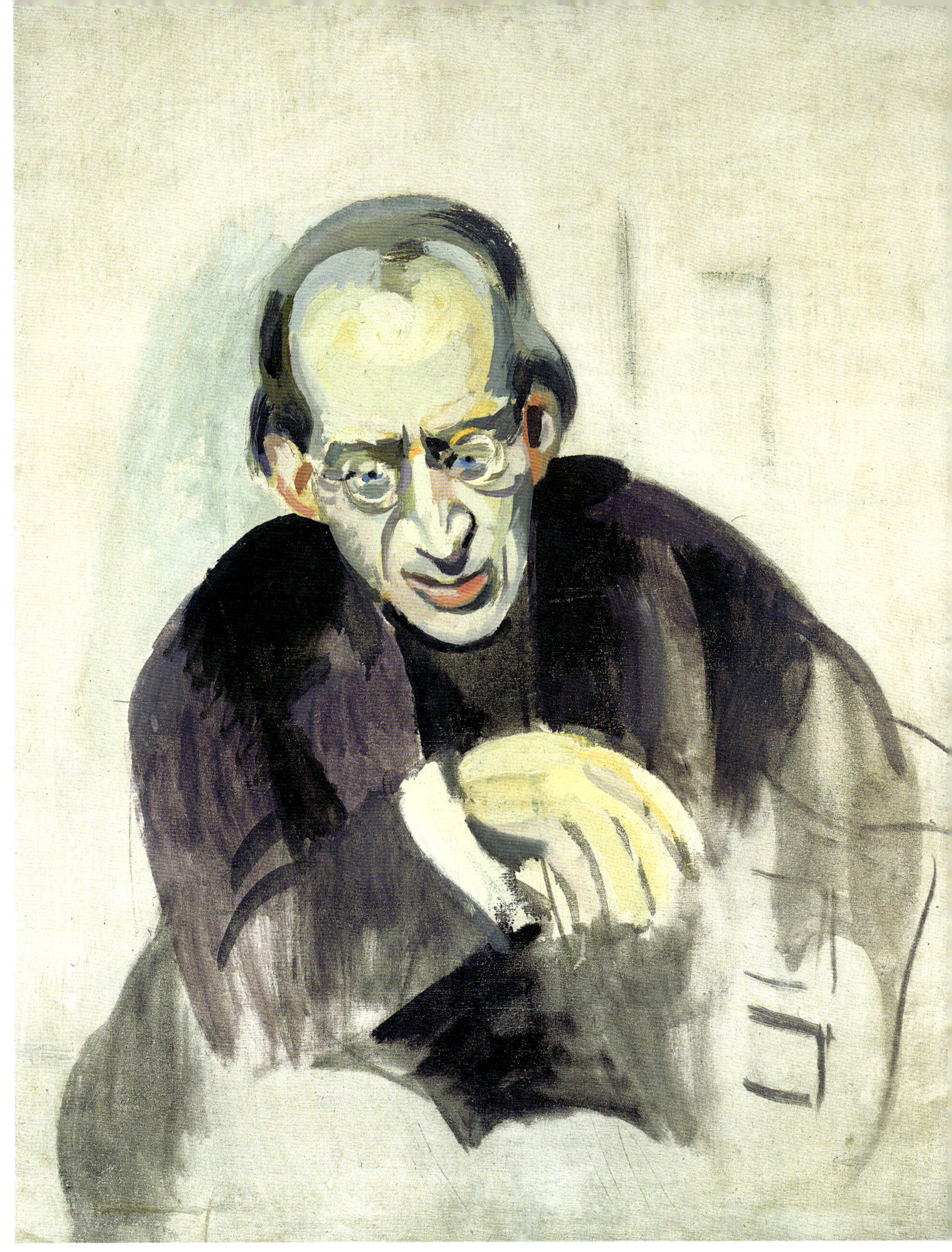

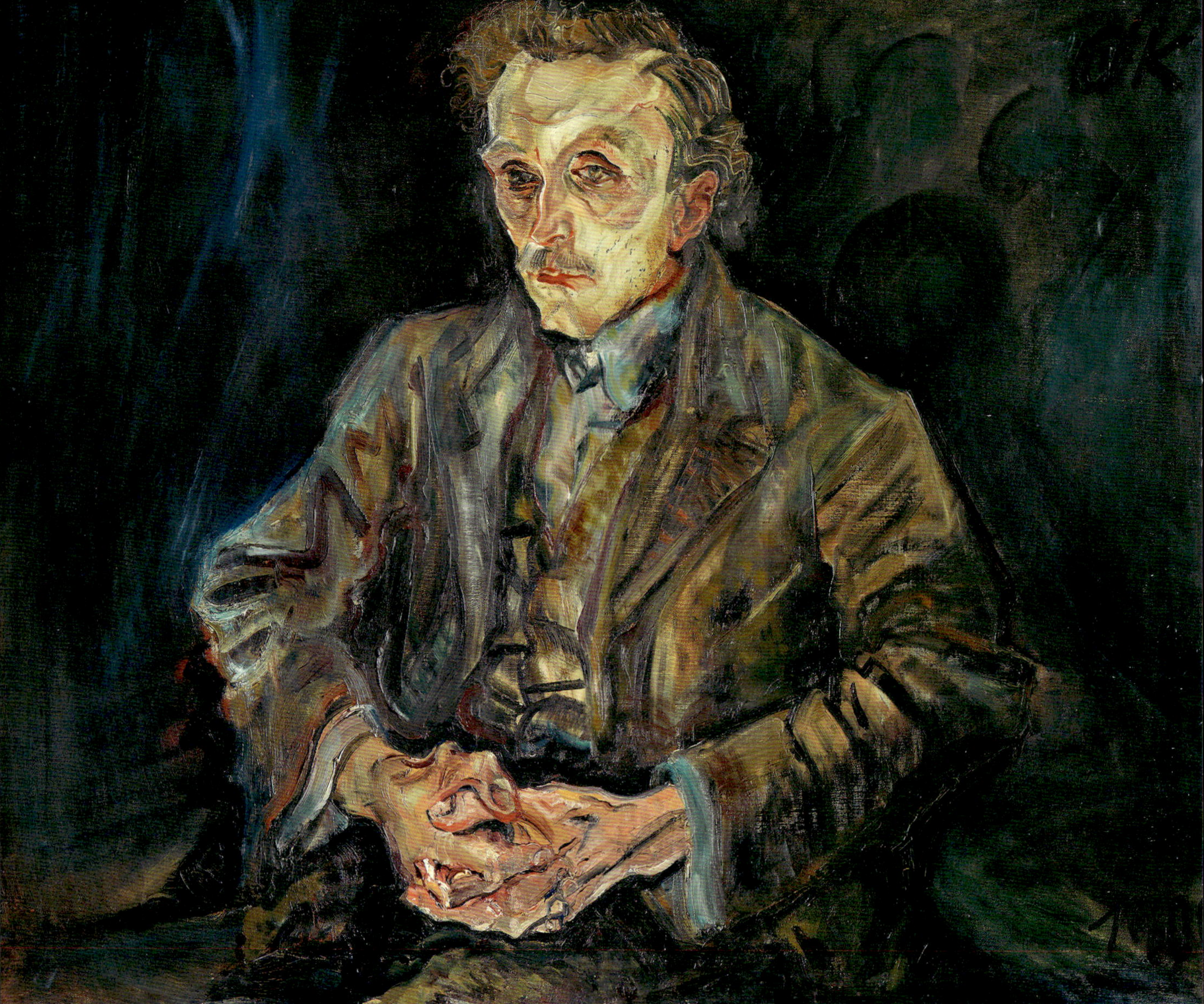

↑ Oskar Kokoschka, *The Austrian Architect Adolf Loos*, 1909
Oil on canvas, 74 × 91 cm
Acquired in 1925 from the Galerie Ernst Arnold, Dresden

→ Auguste Herbin, *Portrait of Erich Mühsam*, 1907
Oil on canvas, 92 × 73 cm
Loan from the Indivision Lahumière, Paris, since 2020

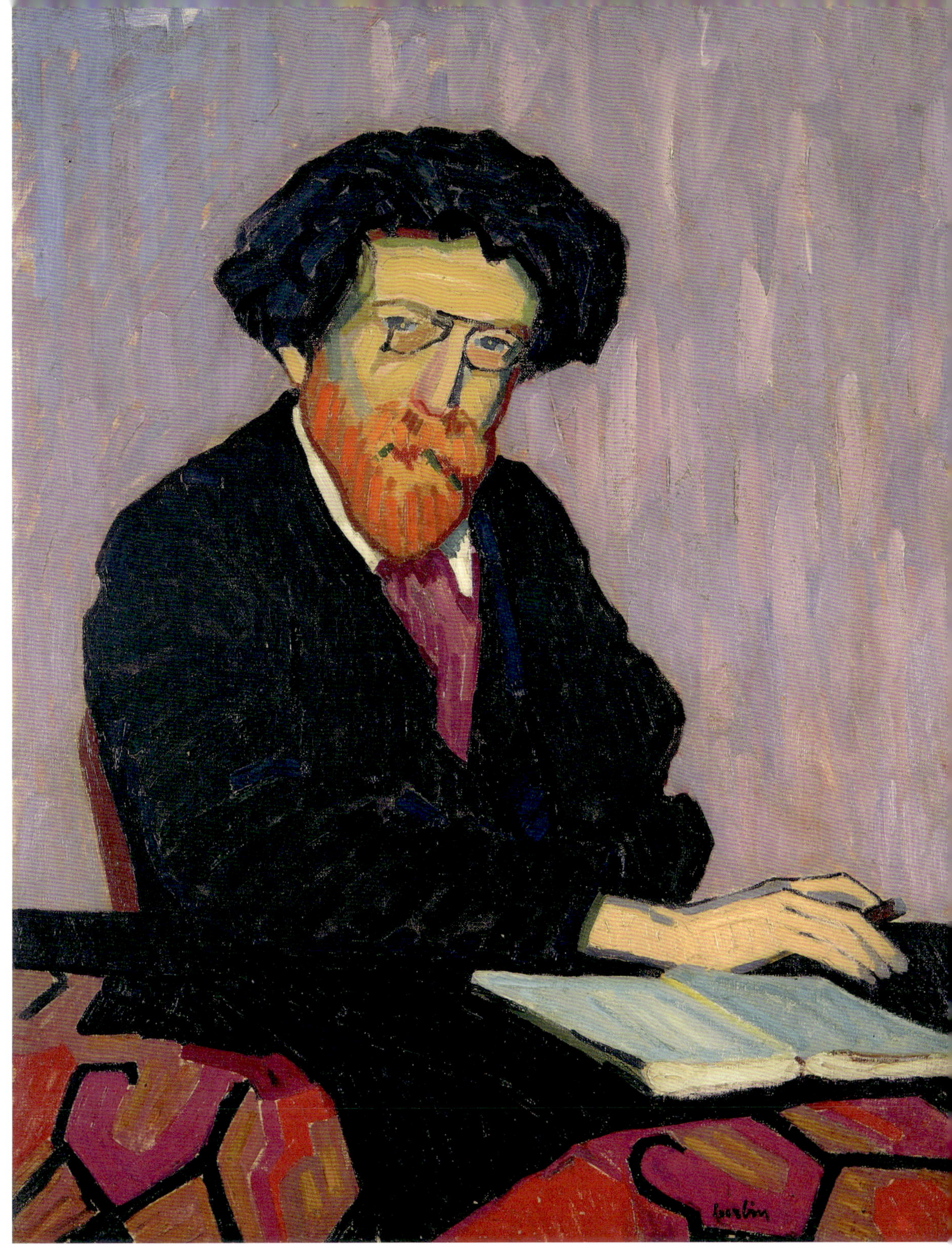

Rediscovered Identity: Erich Mühsam

Who is the man with the fiery red beard? In 2012, French artist Auguste Herbin's 1907 painting was still catalogued under the misspelled title *Kurt Musham*, and no further information about the sitter was known. However, art historian Peter Kropmanns' research led to the rediscovery of the sitter's identity. We now know with certainty who is depicted in the portrait. It is "the most tender anarchist in the world", "the lyrical anarchist", as the *Berliner Tageblatt* (a Berlin daily newspaper) described Erich Kurt Mühsam in 1908.

Mühsam, whose interests included both literature and politics, was initially involved with the *Neue Gemeinschaft* in Friedrichshagen near Berlin. This circle experimented with lifestyles that went beyond the norms of conventional bourgeois society. Herwarth Walden, Else Lasker-Schüler and Johannes Holzmann also belonged to this circle. Like Mühsam, they published in *Kampf*, an anarchist magazine. Mühsam's hopes for a social revolution rested equally on the "lumpenproletariat" (the proletarian subclass) and a "Bohemia, that shows the way forward to a new culture", as he wrote in 1906. The following year, Mühsam travelled to the bohemian capital, to Paris.

At the Café du Dôme, a meeting place for German artists, Mühsam met Wilhelm Uhde, who was active in publishing, ran an art dealer's business in Paris, and also supported the painter

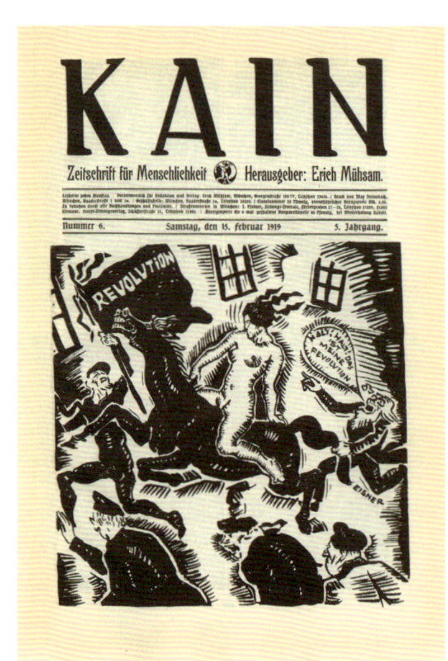
KAIN

Zeitschrift für Menschlichkeit Herausgeber: Erich Mühsam.

Nummer 6. Samstag, den 15. Februar 1919 5. Jahrgang.

↗ Richard Seewald, *Revolution*, cover page, *Revolution*, vol. 1, no. 1, October 1913
↗ Herbert Anger, *Revolution*, cover page, *Die Aktion*, vol. 9, no. 45/46, November 1919
→ H. Pessati, *Revolution*, cover page, *Kain*, vol. 5, no. 6, February 1919

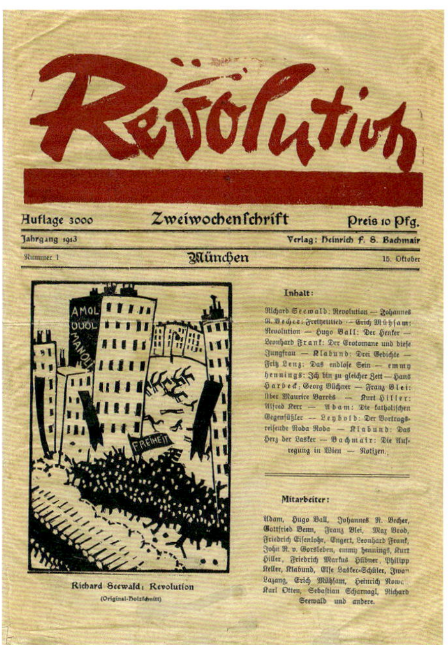

Revolution

Auflage 3000 | Zweiwochenschrift | Preis 10 Pfg.

Jahrgang 1913 | Verlag: Heinrich F. S. Bachmair

Nummer 1 | München | 15. Oktober

Richard Seewald: Revolution
(Original-Holzschnitt)

Inhalt:

Richard Seewald: Revolution — Johannes R. Becher: Freiheitslied — Erich Mühsam: Revolution — Hugo Ball: Der Henker — Leonhard Frank: Der Erotomane und diese Jungfrau — Klabund: Drei Gedichte — Fritz Lenz: Das endlose Sein — emmy hennings: Ich bin zu gleicher Zeit — Hans Harbeck: Georg Büchner — Franz Blei: Über Maurice Barrès — Kurt Hiller: Alfred Kerr — Adam: Die katholischen Gegensätzler — Leybold: Der Vortragsreisende Roda Roda — Klabund: Das Herz der Lasker — Bachmair: Die Aufregung in Wien — Notizen.

Mitarbeiter:

Adam, Hugo Ball, Johannes R. Becher, Gottfried Benn, Franz Blei, Max Brod, Friedrich Eisenlohr, Engert, Leonhard Frank, John R. v. Gorsleben, emmy hennings, Kurt Hiller, Friedrich Markus Hübner, Philipp Keller, Klabund, Else Lasker-Schüler, Iwan Lazang, Erich Mühsam, Heinrich Nowak, Karl Otten, Sebastian Scharnagl, Richard Seewald und andere.

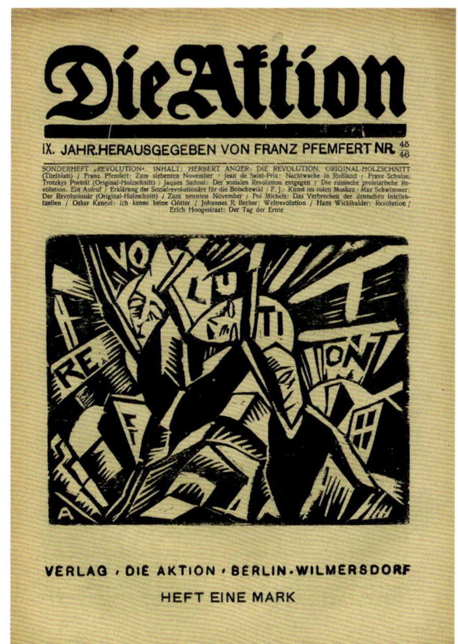

Die Aktion

IX. JAHR. HERAUSGEGEBEN VON FRANZ PFEMFERT NR. 45/46

SONDERHEFT „REVOLUTION“. INHALT: HERBERT ANGER: DIE REVOLUTION. ORIGINAL-HOLZSCHNITT (Titelblatt) / Franz Pfemfert: Zum siebenten November / Jean de Saint-Prix: Nachtwache in Rußland / Franz Schulze: Trotzkys Porträt (Original-Holzschnitt) / Jaques Sadoul: Der sozialen Revolution entgegen / Die russische proletarische Revolution. Ein Aufruf / Erklärung der Sozialrevolutionäre für die Bolschewiki / F. J.: Kunst im roten Moskau / Max Schwimmer: Der Revolutionär (Original-Holzschnitt) / Zum neunten November / Pol Michels: Das Verbrechen der deutschen Intellektuellen / Oskar Kanehl: Ich kenne keine Götter / Johannes R. Becher: Weltrevolution / Hans Wickihalder: Revolution / Erich Hoogestraat: Der Tag der Ernte

VERLAG · DIE AKTION · BERLIN-WILMERSDORF
HEFT EINE MARK

Auguste Herbin. The portrait of the 29-year-old writer was painted in his studio in 1907. Calm and self-confident, Mühsam peers at us through his glasses. There is a cigar in his hand and a book on the table. The embers of his revolutionary spirit seem to pass over into the colours of the painting. The poet's black mane and orangish-red full beard, his violet ascot, and black coat are presented in striking contrast. The light violet wall and an unevenly patterned tablecloth add resonance to the space.

The painter Auguste Herbin was still at the start of his career in 1907. He had his first solo exhibition in Berlin that same year. Herbin was represented with several works at the Sturm gallery opening in 1912, and later with a solo exhibition there in 1919. At the same time, in April 1919 in Munich, the anarchist Mühsam had just co-authored the proclamation of the Bavarian Soviet Republic together with Gustav Landauer. Mühsam spent five years in prison in connection with this act. Afterwards, he returned to Berlin, where he took up publishing again. The National Socialists murdered Mühsam at the Oranienburg concentration camp in 1934.

Herbin and Mühsam's biographies intersect in the portrait – for both men politics held great importance, in addition to the arts. Herbin joined the Communist Party in France in 1920 and remained a member until 1948. Together with Georges Vantongerloo, he founded *Abstraction-Création* in 1931, an artist group in which Hans Arp, Robert Delaunay and Otto Freundlich were also members for a time. In the series of publications produced by the group, the then-current issue from 1933 proclaimed that it stood "under the sign of a total opposition to any form of oppression". Mühsam's life stood under the same sign.

Dieter Scholz

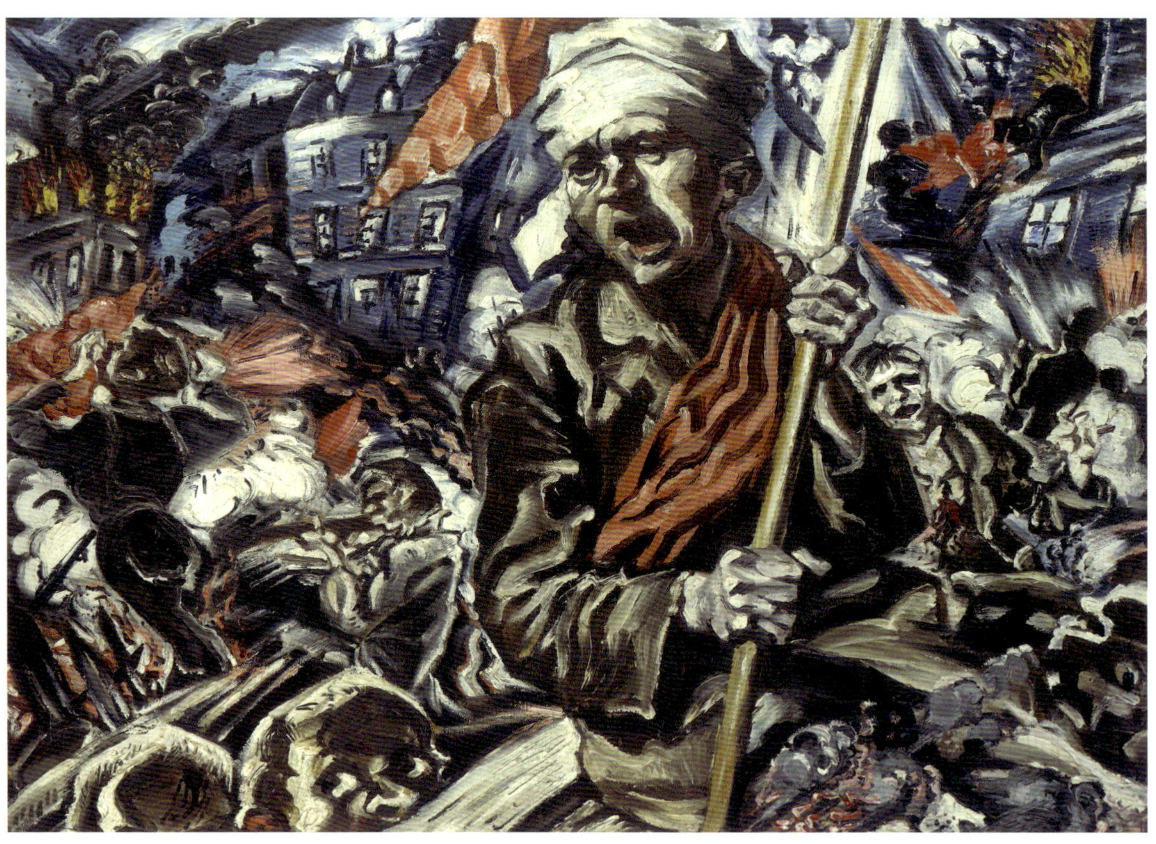

↑ Ludwig Meidner, *Revolution (Fighting on the Barricades)*
→ Verso: *Apocalyptic Landscape*, 1912–13
Oil on canvas, 80 × 116 cm
Acquired in 1961 from the Galerie Grosshennig, Düsseldorf, for the Nationalgalerie, Berlin (West)

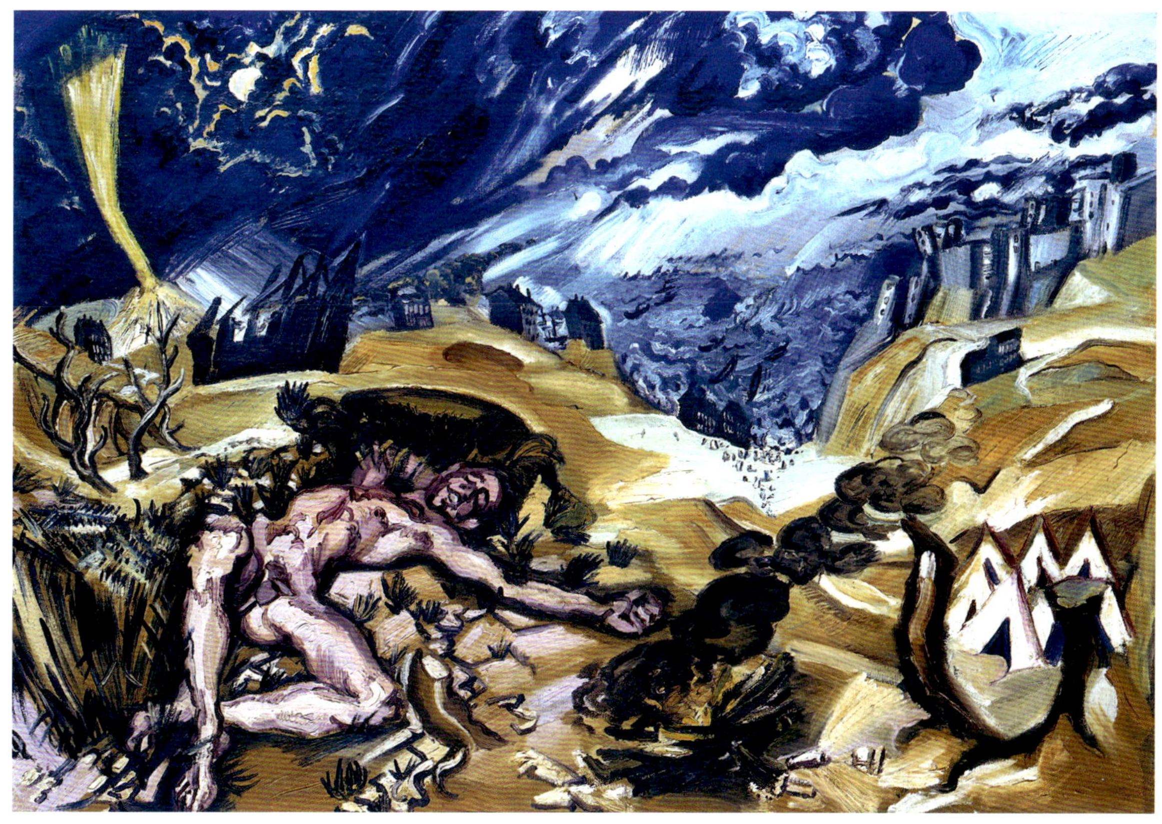

Women Artists at the Sturm Gallery

Displaying an unusual openness for the times, Herwarth Walden offered many women artists an opportunity to present their work in his magazine *Der Sturm* (published since 1910) and his exhibition programme for the same-named gallery opened two years later.

The first woman in the history of Der Sturm was the poet Else Lasker-Schüler, whose drawings were published in the magazine. She was married to Walden (1903–12), who at that time was still using his given name, Georg Lewin. Lasker-Schüler invented the pseudonym Herwarth Walden and the programmatic Sturm title, which expressed a desire for radical change in society and culture.

Through the years, works by nearly forty women artists were shown at the Sturm gallery. Three women painters were represented in its first exhibition: Gabriele Münter, Natalia Goncharova and Elisabeth Epstein. The fact that this development was just beginning and the moment of recognition for women's contributions to art seemed to be rapidly approaching is perhaps the message behind Goncharova's painting *Die Uhr* (The Clock), made in 1910, the same year the Sturm magazine was founded. The mechanics of the clock seem to accelerate as its numbers and hands whirl around.

In the spring of 1913, Gabriele Münter was the first woman artist to receive a solo exhibition at the Sturm gallery. Like her partner Wassily Kandinsky, she was a member of the artist group

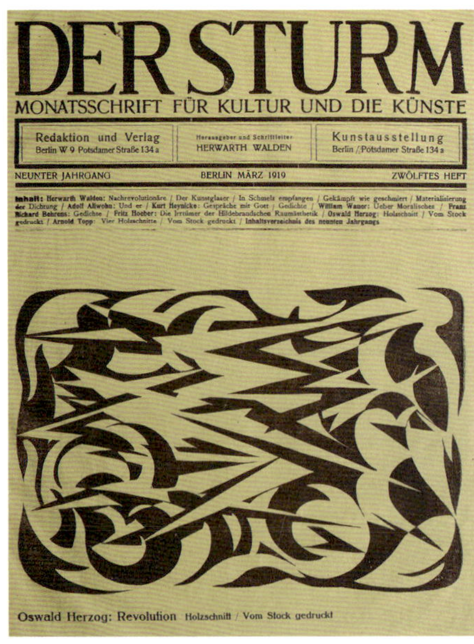

DER STURM

MONATSSCHRIFT FÜR KULTUR UND DIE KÜNSTE

Redaktion und Verlag Berlin W 9 Potsdamer Straße 134 a | Herausgeber und Schriftleiter HERWARTH WALDEN | Kunstausstellung Berlin / Potsdamer Straße 134 a

NEUNTER JAHRGANG BERLIN MÄRZ 1919 ZWÖLFTES HEFT

Inhalt: Herwarth Walden: Nachrevolutionäre / Der Kunstglaser / In Schmelz empfangen / Gekämpft wie geschmiert / Materialisierung der Dichtung / **Adolf Allwohn:** Und er / **Kurt Heynicke:** Gespräche mit Gott / Gedichte / **William Wauer:** Ueber Moralisches / **Franz Richard Behrens:** Gedichte / **Fritz Hoeber:** Die Irrtümer der Hildebrandschen Raumästhetik / **Oswald Herzog:** Holzschnitt / Vom Stock gedruckt / **Arnold Topp:** Vier Holzschnitte / Vom Stock gedruckt / **Inhaltsverzeichnis des neunten Jahrgangs**

Oswald Herzog: Revolution Holzschnitt / Vom Stock gedruckt

↗ Herwarth Walden with his second wife Nell in the dining room of their apartment in Potsdamer Straße, Berlin, 1916

→ Oswald Herzog, *Revolution*, cover page, *Der Sturm*, vol. 9, no. 12, March 1919

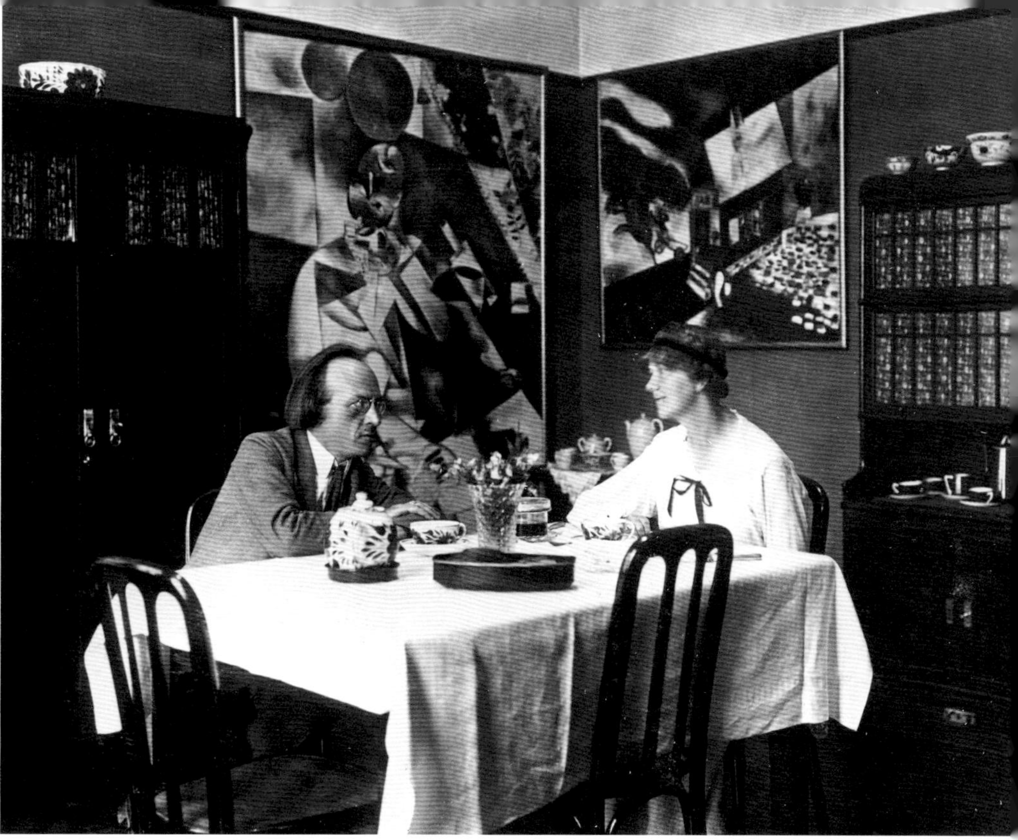

Der Blaue Reiter (The Blue Rider). Marianne von Werefkin and Alexej von Jawlensky, Werefkin's partner for many years, were also closely tied to the Blaue Reiter, as were Natalia Goncharova and Mikhail Larionov. These women were part of a network and artists' partners, yet still independent.

Walden maintained a particularly close relationship with Jacoba van Heemskerck, whose works he became familiar with in 1913 while organizing an exhibition with Franz Marc in The Hague. She became the most frequently represented woman artist in Sturm exhibitions, with the number of her woodcuts published in the magazine only being surpassed by Oskar Kokoschka's works. Heemskerck gave Walden exclusive rights to exhibit her works. After she died in 1923, Walden organized a commemorative exhibition the following year and published a Sturm-Bilderbuch artist's catalogue dedicated to her.

Heemskerck was also friends with Swedish organist Nell Roslund, who became Walden's second wife in 1912. Nell Walden began to paint in 1915, during the First World War, while Heemskerck busied herself with translating Dutch texts for the wartime news office established at the Sturm. In 1916 Nell Walden attended the Sturm art school, and in 1917 her works were shown for the first time at the Sturm gallery. In her memoirs, she wrote that Herwarth Walden considered women to be "more finely differentiated" and "more sensitive and artistically receptive than men". Men still predominated at Der Sturm, but Walden, unlike many of his contemporaries, had already considered the presence of women artists quite natural.

Dieter Scholz

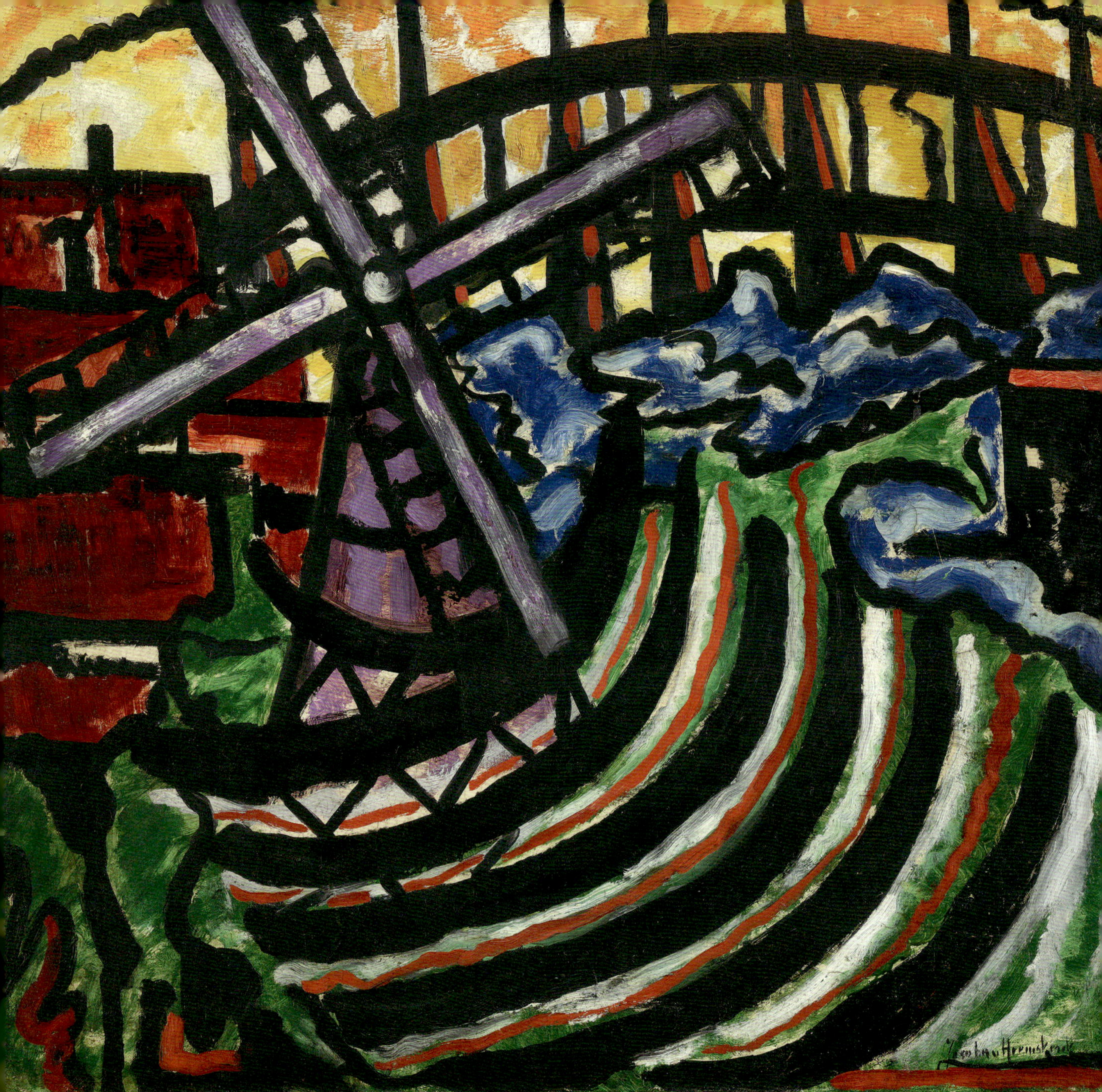

↑ Jacoba Heemskerck van Beest, *Picture 56 (Dutch Mill)*, 1916
Oil on canvas, 56 × 60 cm
Acquired in 1960 from the Galerie Nierendorf, Berlin, for the Nationalgalerie, Berlin (West)

→ Natalia Goncharova, *The Clock*, 1910
Oil on canvas, 105 × 79 cm
Acquired in 1961 from the Galerie Beyeler, Basel, for the Nationalgalerie, Berlin (West)

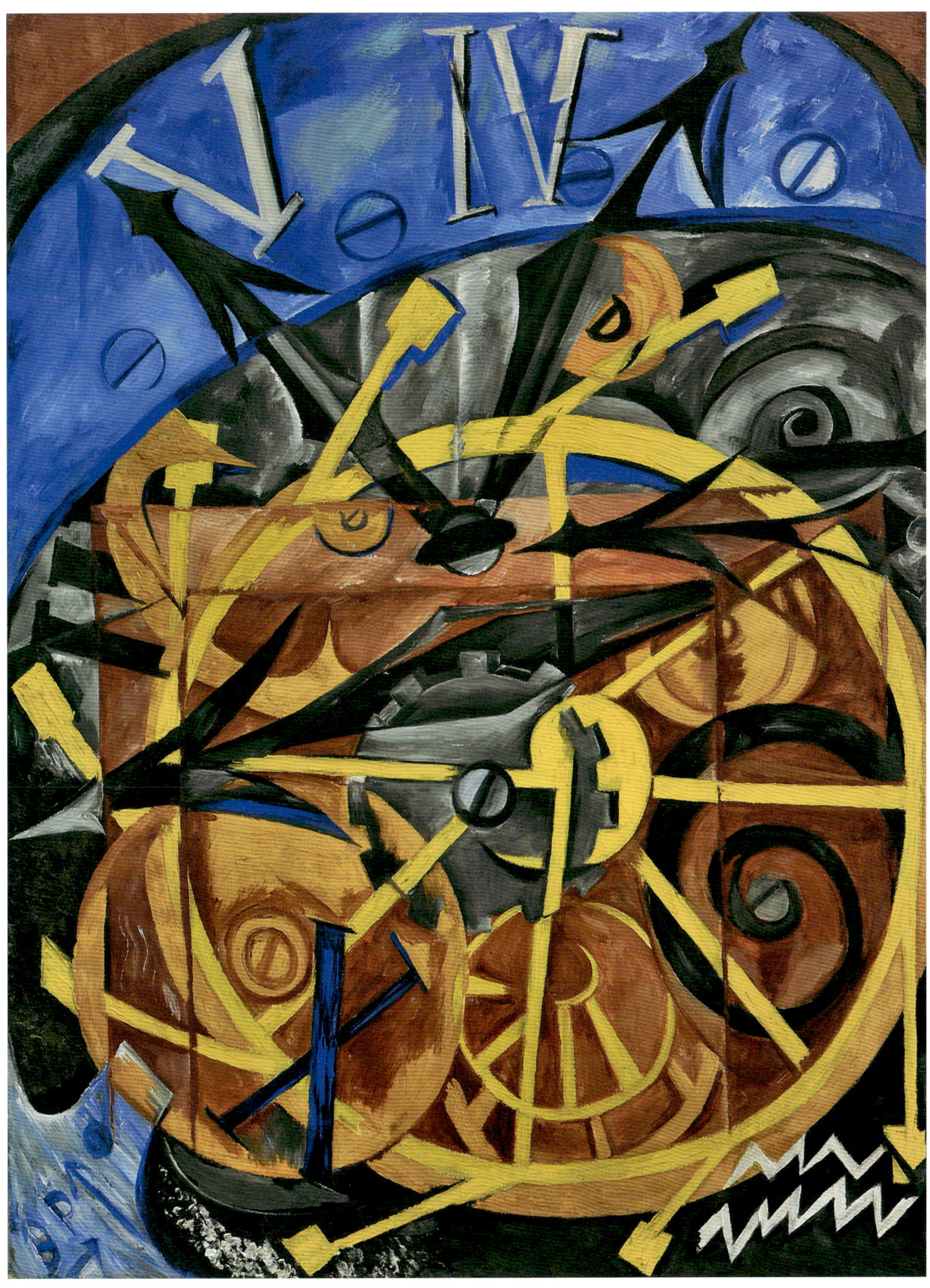

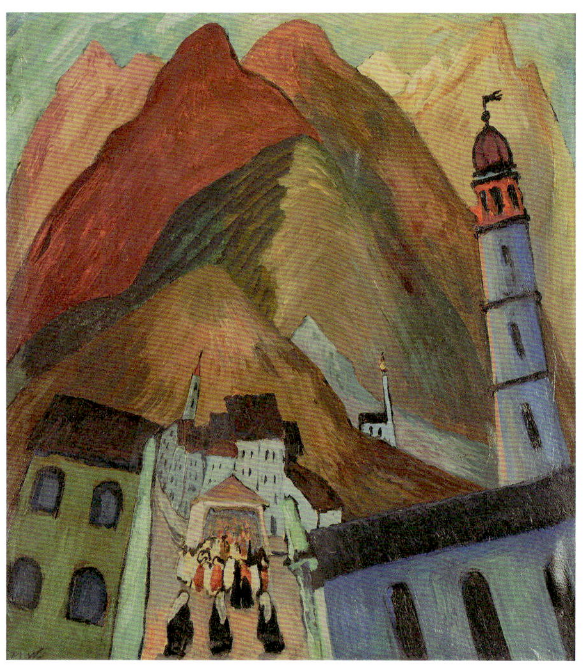

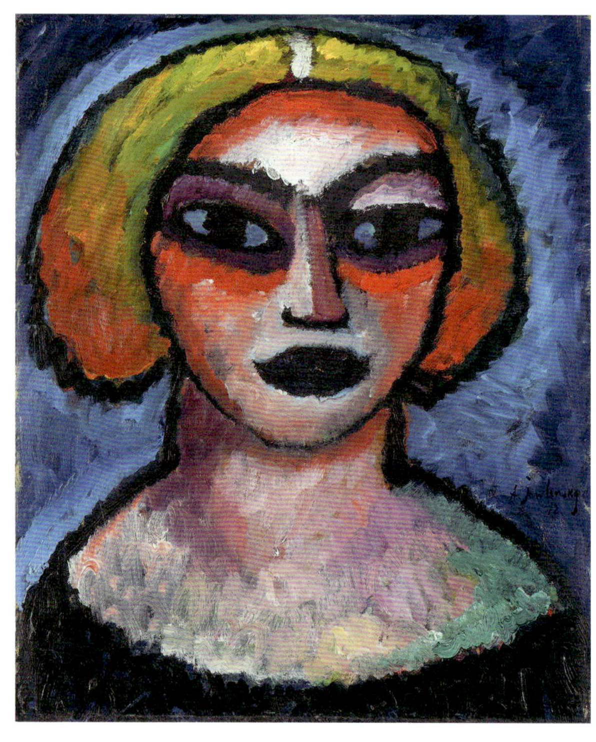

↑ Marianne von Werefkin, *Procession Near Ascona*, c. 1924
Oil on cardboard, 46.2 × 42.2 cm
Acquired in 1962 from the Lou Scheper-Berkenkamp Collection, Berlin (West), by the Land Berlin for the Galerie des 20. Jahrhunderts, Berlin (West)

→ Alexej von Jawlensky, *Head of a Woman*, 1912
Oil on cardboard, 61 × 51 cm
Acquired in 1959 by the Land Berlin for the Galerie des 20. Jahrhunderts, Berlin (West)

↗ Franz Marc, *Three Horses II (Smaller Version)*, 1913
Oil on canvas, 59 × 80.5 cm
Loan from a private collection since 1994

→ Wassily Kandinsky, *Sketch (Rider)*, 1909
Oil on canvas, 67 × 100 cm
Loan from a private collection since 1994

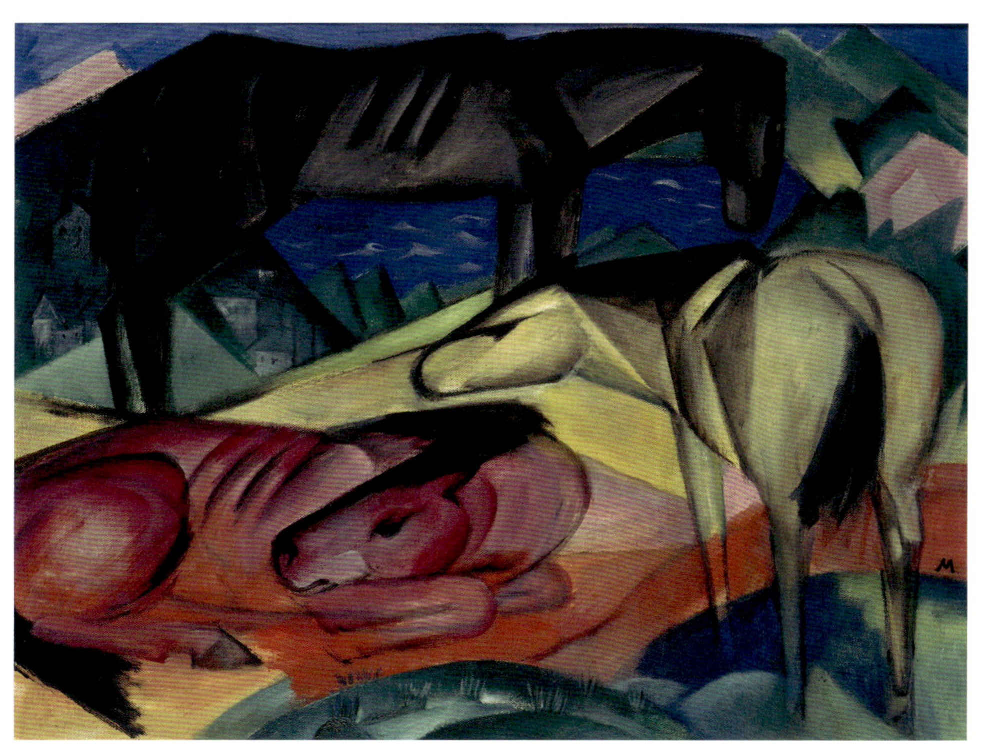

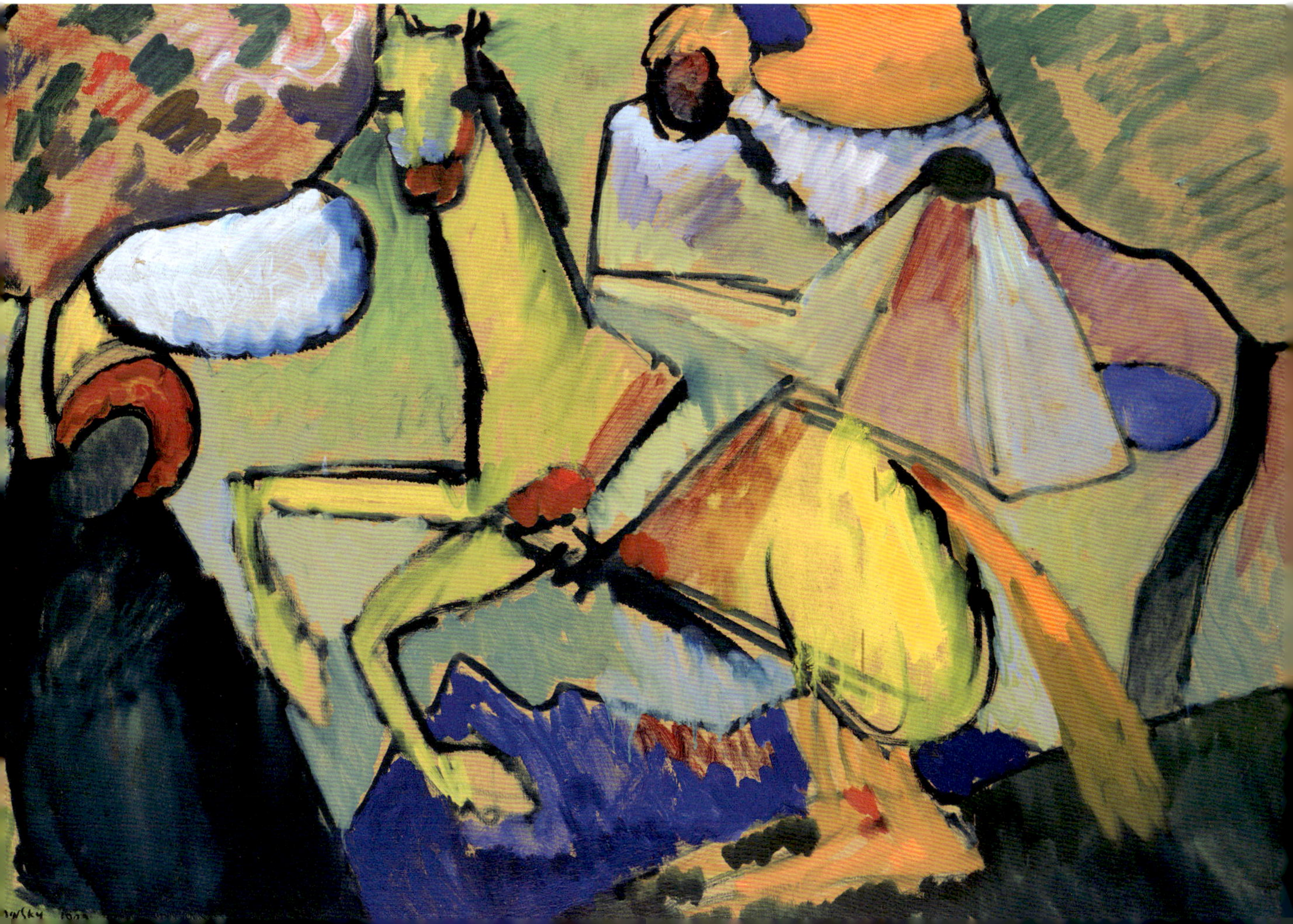

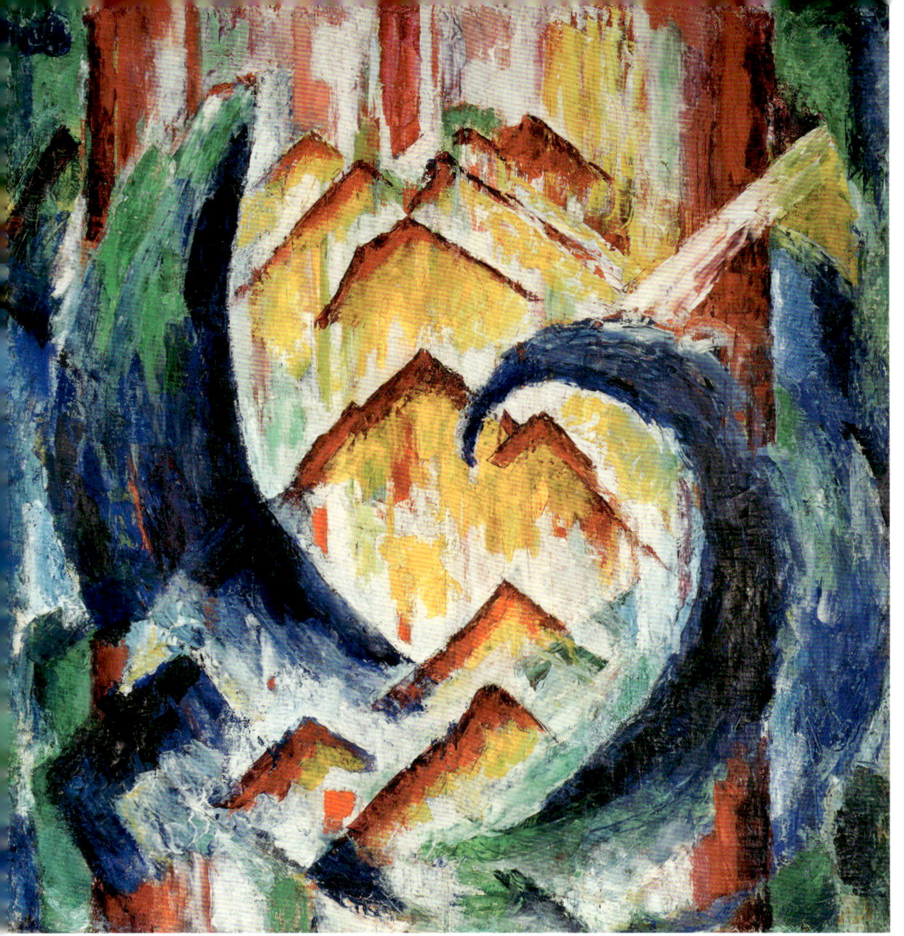

↑ Erich Buchholz, *Blood Song*, 1920
Oil on canvas, 148 × 148 cm
Acquired in 1959 from the artist with funds from Theodor Heuss for the Nationalgalerie, Berlin (West)

→ Fernand Léger, *Composition*, 1920
Oil on cardboard, 38.5 × 31.5 cm
Acquired in 1958 from the Kunsthandlung Walter Feilchenfeldt, Zurich, by the Land Berlin for the Galerie des 20. Jahrhunderts, Berlin (West)

↗ Edmund Kesting, *Red Sickle*, 1927
Oil on paper on wood, 38 × 38 cm
Acquired in 1972 from the widow of the artist, Gerda Kesting, Rostock, for the Nationalgalerie, Berlin (East)

↗ Laszlo Peri, *Water between Houses*, 1920/1921 (Artist's variation c. 1950, with posthumous alterations)
Oil on concrete, 57.2 × 42.5 × 1.3 cm
Gift from Susanne and Michael Liebelt, Hamburg, 2019

→ Sándor Bortnyik, *Still Life with Jug*, 1923
Oil on cardboard, 35 × 44.5 cm
Acquired in 1960 from the Galerie Nierendorf, Berlin, for the Nationalgalerie, Berlin (West)

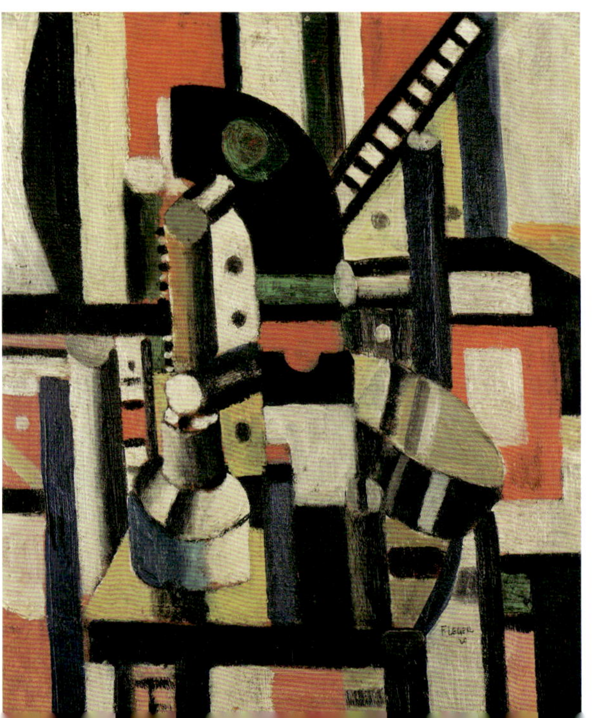

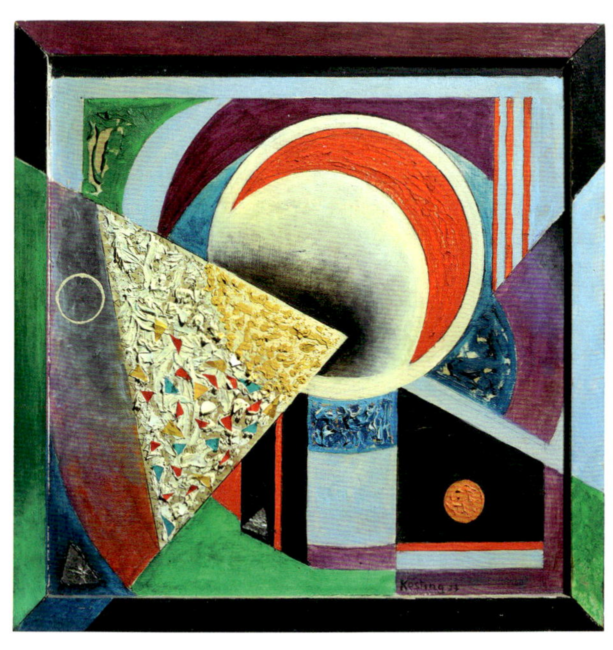

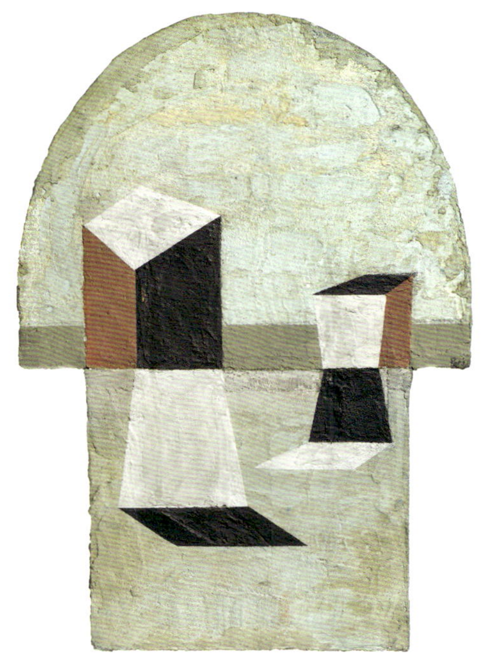

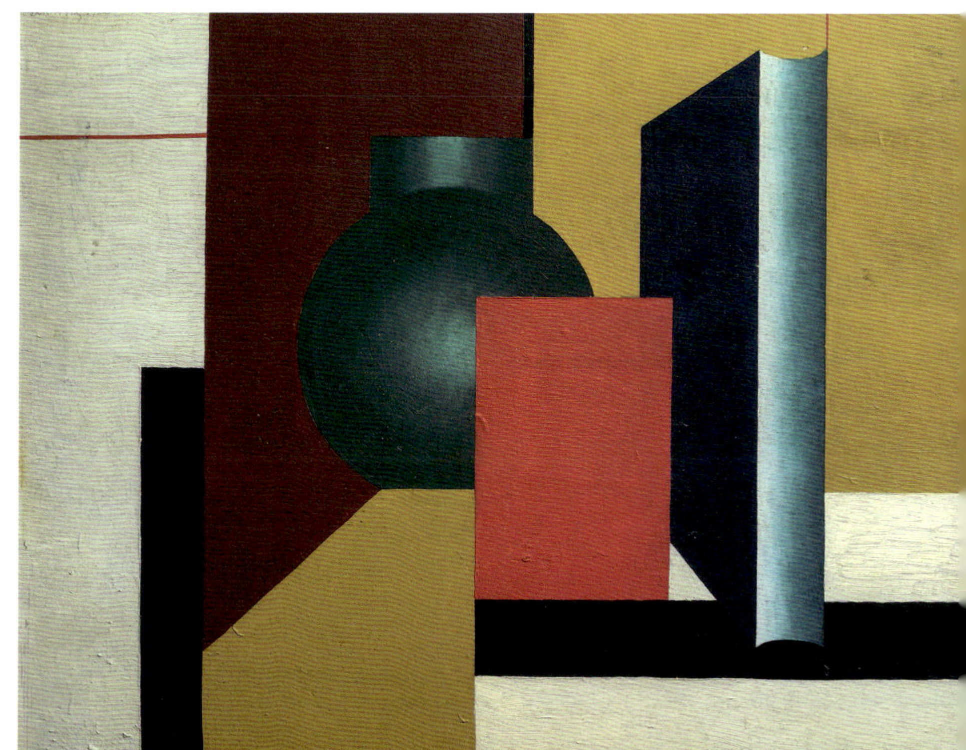

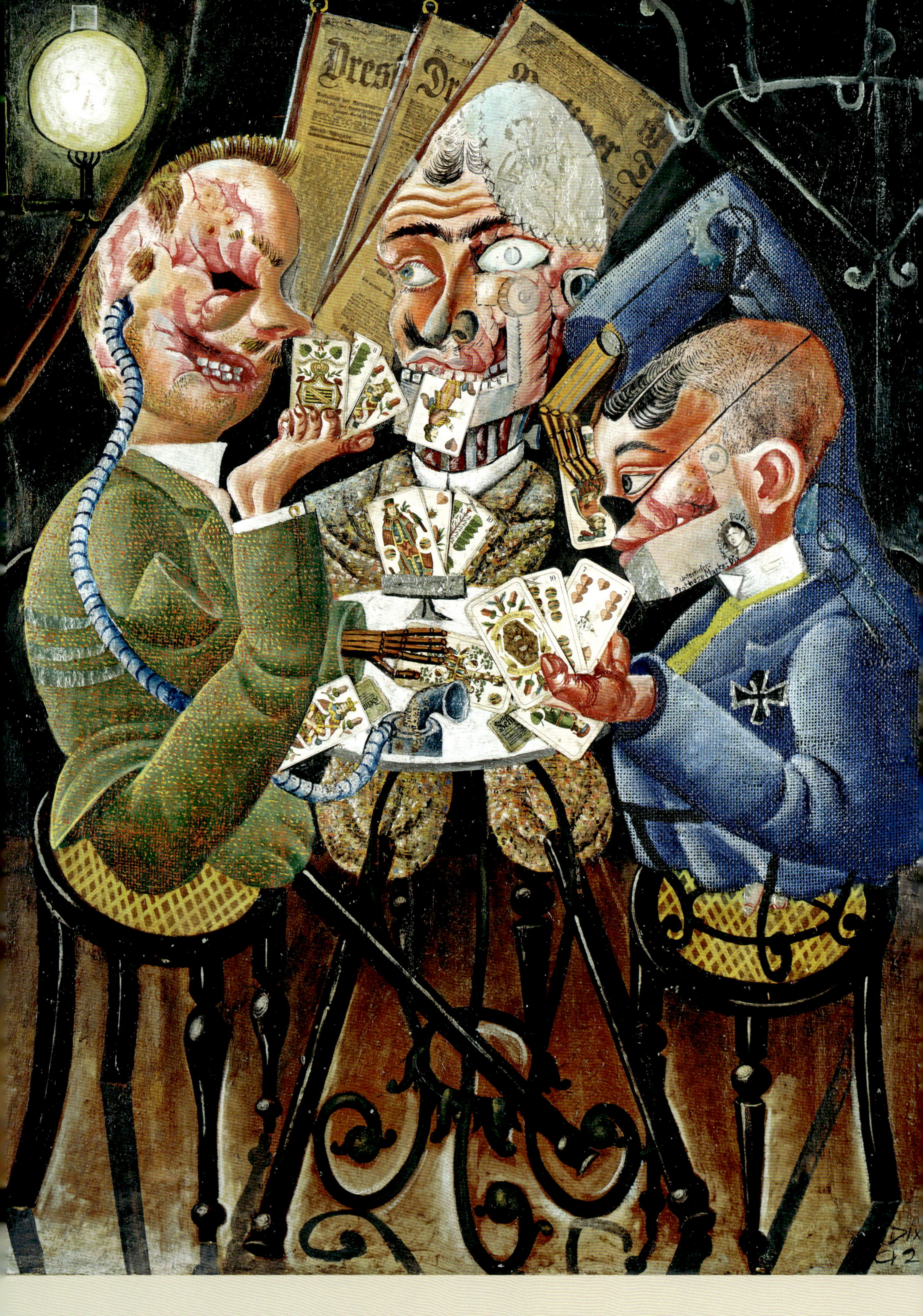

Trauma and Destruction

What lingering aspects of the First World War continued to affect society during the Weimar Republic? The sheer number of mutilated and disabled war veterans on the streets, who often had to beg for alms, was much more visible than the millions of corpses that had remained on the battlefields. In a café in Dresden, Otto Dix watched three maimed veterans playing cards and captured the grotesque scene in a painting. Josef Scharl's *Ecce homo* portrays a man with a disfigured face, traumatically marked by the war injury he suffered.

Violent conflicts and crises also characterized post-war order in Germany. There were attempted coups, politically motivated murders and dramatic inflation. George Grosz depicted the great social disparities that would escalate into a crucial test for the social fabric. Workers and the educated middle-class, war cripples and office menials no longer shared common perspectives within the faceless world of industry. After the brief "Golden Twenties" between 1924 and 1929, mass unemployment began with the world economic crisis in 1929. The large coalition of democratic parties in parliament broke down and the National Socialist German Workers' Party (NSDAP) takeover of the government in 1933 ultimately sealed the demise of the first German Republic.

Otto Dix, *The Skat Players*, 1920
Oil on canvas, 110 × 87 cm
Acquired in 1995 by the Freunde der Nationalgalerie
and the Land Berlin for the Nationalgalerie, Berlin (West)

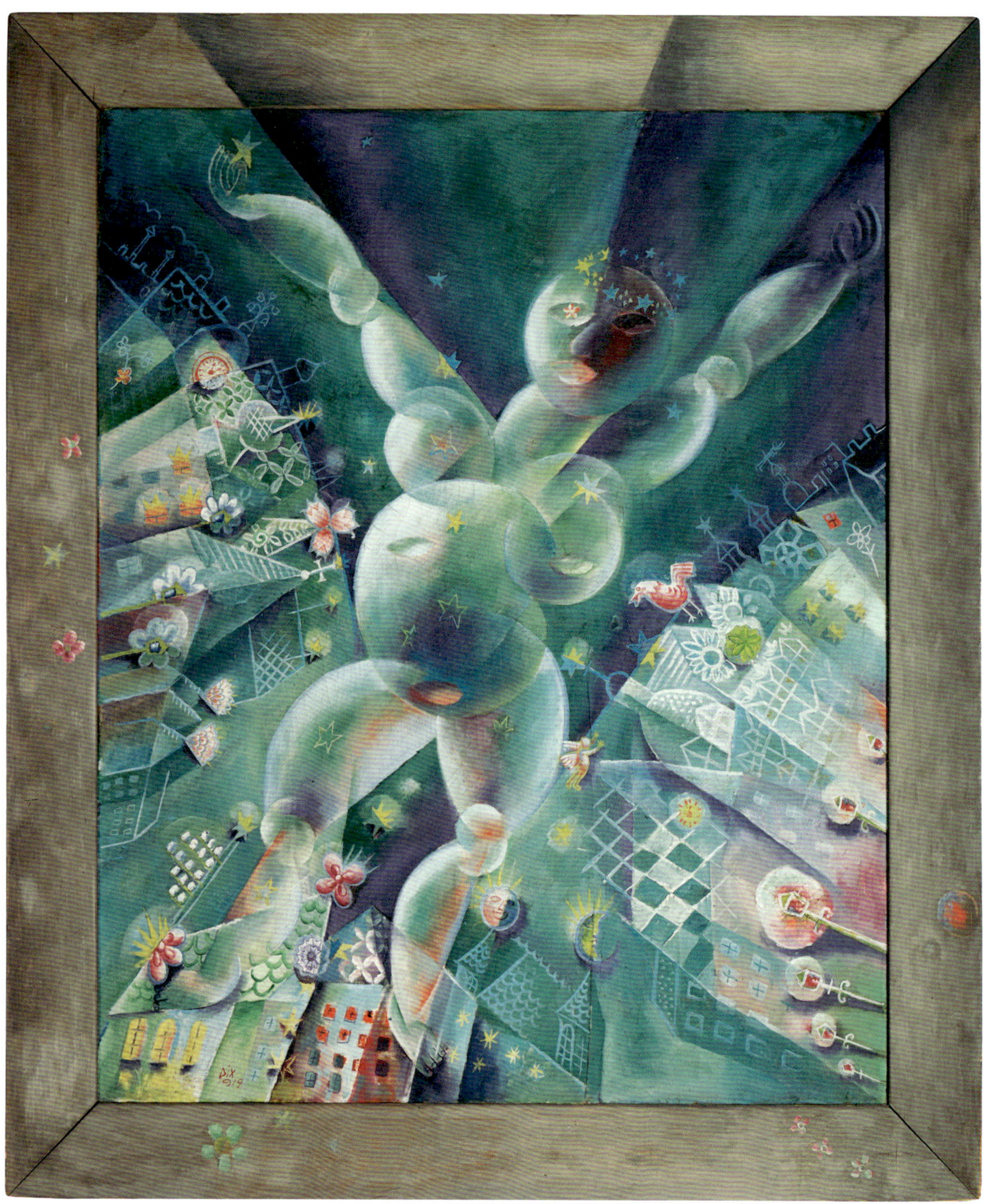

↑ Otto Dix, *Moon Woman*, 1919
Oil on canvas, 120.5 × 100.5 cm
Acquired in 1982 with funds from the Kulturfonds
der DDR for the Nationalgalerie, Berlin (East)

→ Otto Dix, *The Family of the Painter Adalbert Trillhaase*, 1923
Oil on canvas, 119 × 95 cm
Acquired in 1953 by the Land Berlin for the Galerie des
20. Jahrhunderts, Berlin (West)

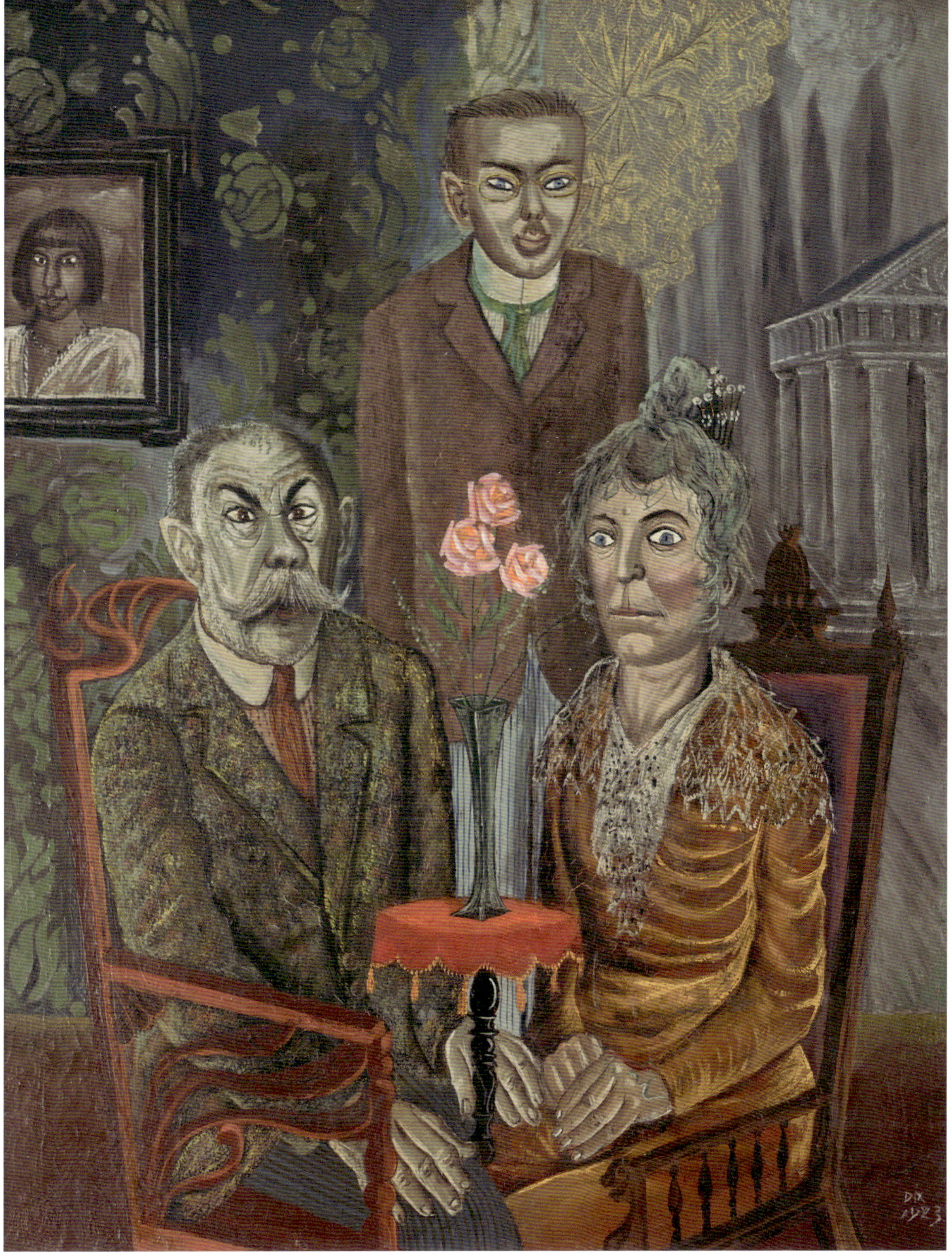
DIX
1923

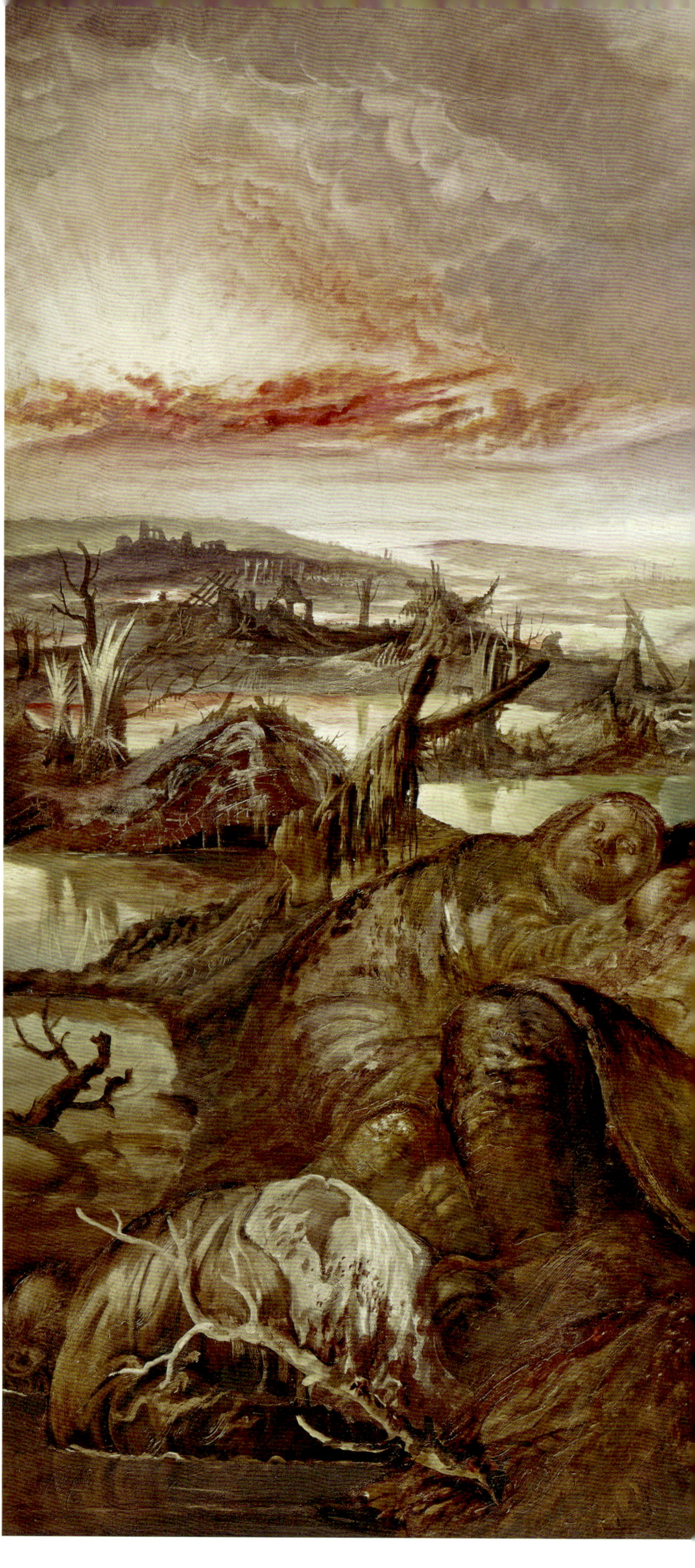

Otto Dix, *Flanders*, 1934–36
Oil and tempera on canvas, 200 × 250 cm
Acquired in 1963 from the artist with funds from the Deutsche Klassen-lotterie by the Land Berlin for the Galerie des 20. Jahrhunderts, Berlin (West)

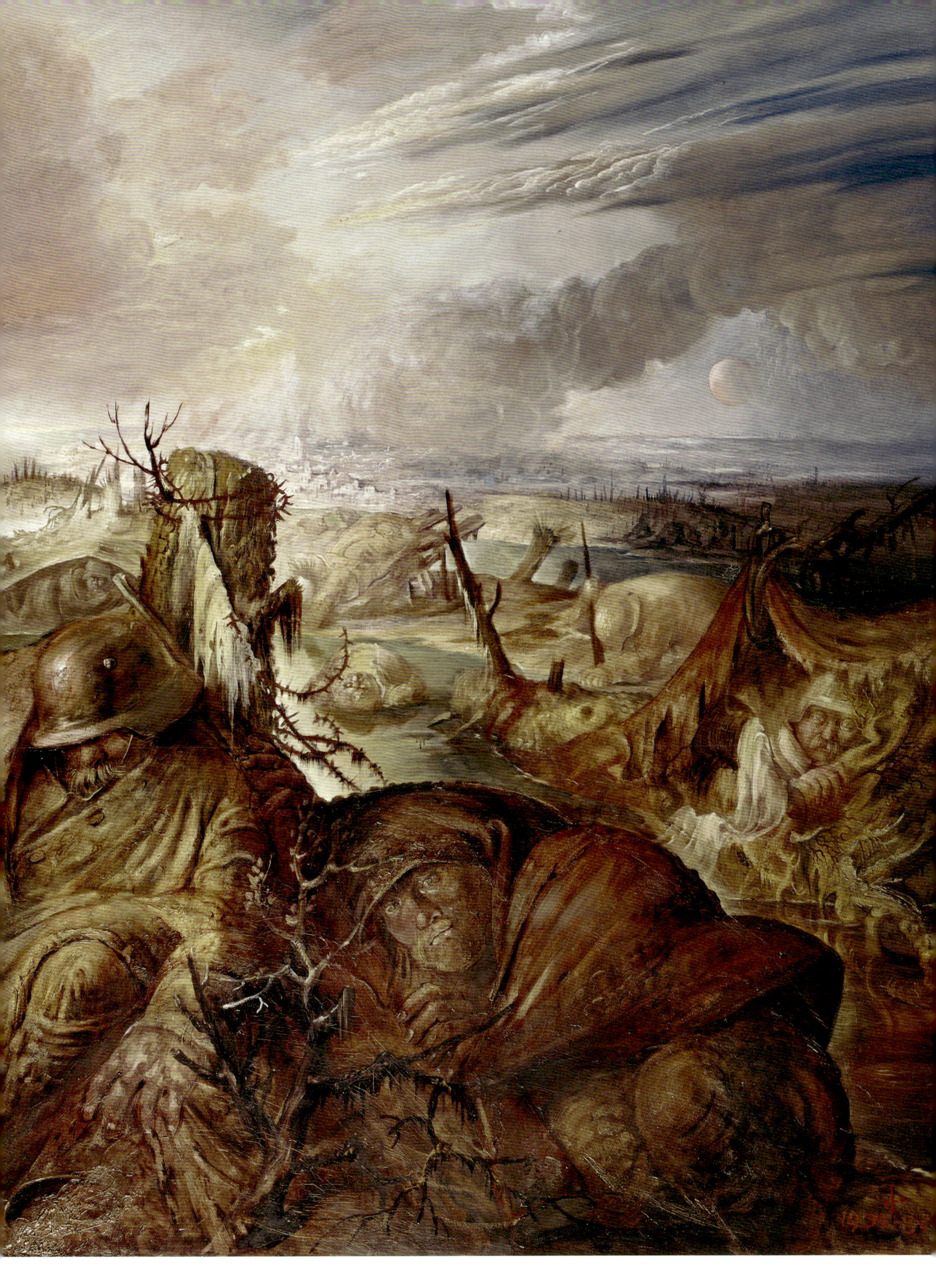

Where Did the First World War Take Place?

Relying on the painter's own war experiences, Otto Dix's painting *Flandern* (Flanders) shows a ravaged battlefield. As a German soldier in the First World War, Dix was deployed to the Western Front in Belgian and French territory. He fought in Flanders in 1917, where several months of trench warfare caused enormous loss of human lives but yielded little territorial gain.

The war began in Europe in 1914 but its reach did not remain limited to this continent. In Flanders as well, the troops involved in the war came not only from France and Great Britain, but also from several self-governing British "dominions", including Australia, New Zealand, Canada and Newfoundland. Many of the major powers had colonies and protectorates where military actions also took place, which is how Japanese troops came to occupy German territories in the South Pacific.

Altogether 40 nations were involved in the most extensive war to date. The United States of America also entered the war when the German Empire began engaging in unrestricted submarine warfare in February 1917. However, the war not only took place on land and by sea but increasingly in the air. It began with airborne zeppelins dropping bombs, but these were soon replaced by fighter planes.

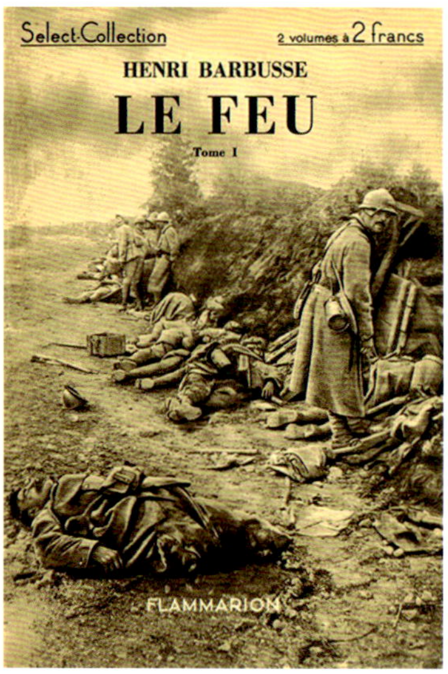

Henri Barbusse
Le feu

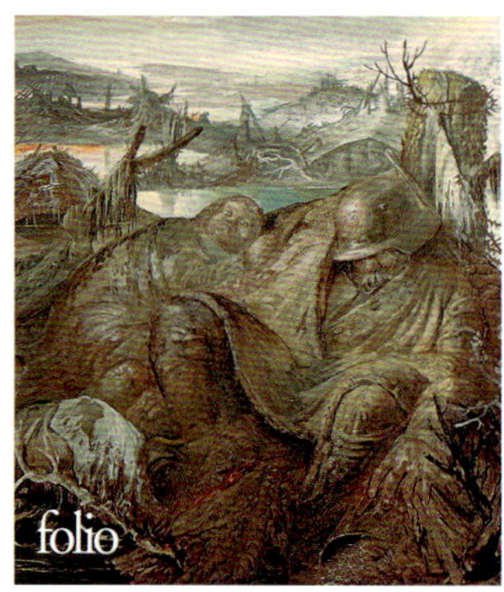

↗ The World in the First World War
→ Henri Barbusse, *Le Feu*, covers of the 1935 and 2013 issues

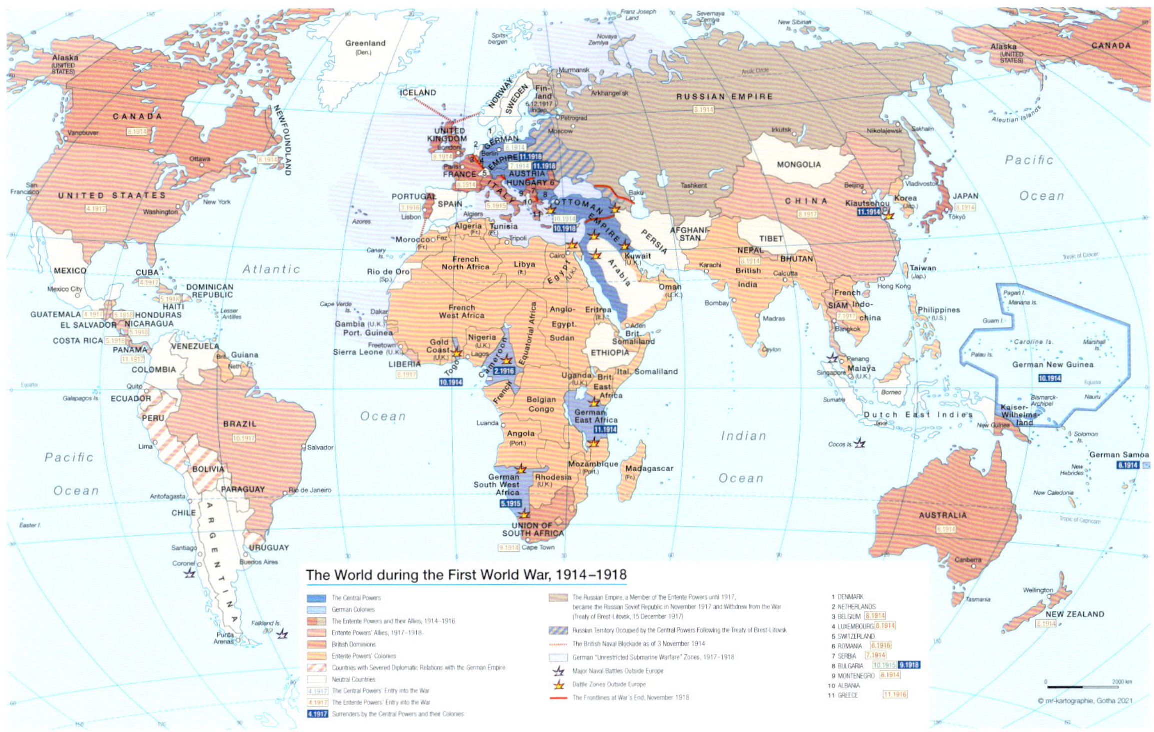

The First World War is often designated as a "battle of materials", yet war equipment cannot be seen in the work *Flandern*. Dix dedicated his painting to the French writer Henri Barbusse, whose anti-war novel *Le Feu* (Under Fire) – a diary-like eyewitness account of his squad – was published in French in 1916. It contains a passage, which reads like a visual description of *Flandern*: "We are waiting for daylight in the place where we sank to the ground. […] The leaden plain and its mirrors of sullied water seem to issue not only from the night but from the sea. […] There are no more trenches; those canals are the trenches enshrouded. […] And what is this silence, too, this prodigious silence? […] Ah, the men! Where are the men? – We see them gradually. Not far from us, there are some stranded and sleeping hulks so molded in mud from head to foot that they are almost transformed into inanimate objects. […] 'Are they really not dead?'"

Hopes that this would be humankind's last war remained unfulfilled. While Dix was working on the painting *Flandern* from 1934 to 1936 – dedicating it not coincidentally to a member of a once enemy nation – the image seemed not only to look back at the First World War but also to foreshadow the coming Second World War, which would soon leave behind a shattered world landscape once again.

Dieter Scholz

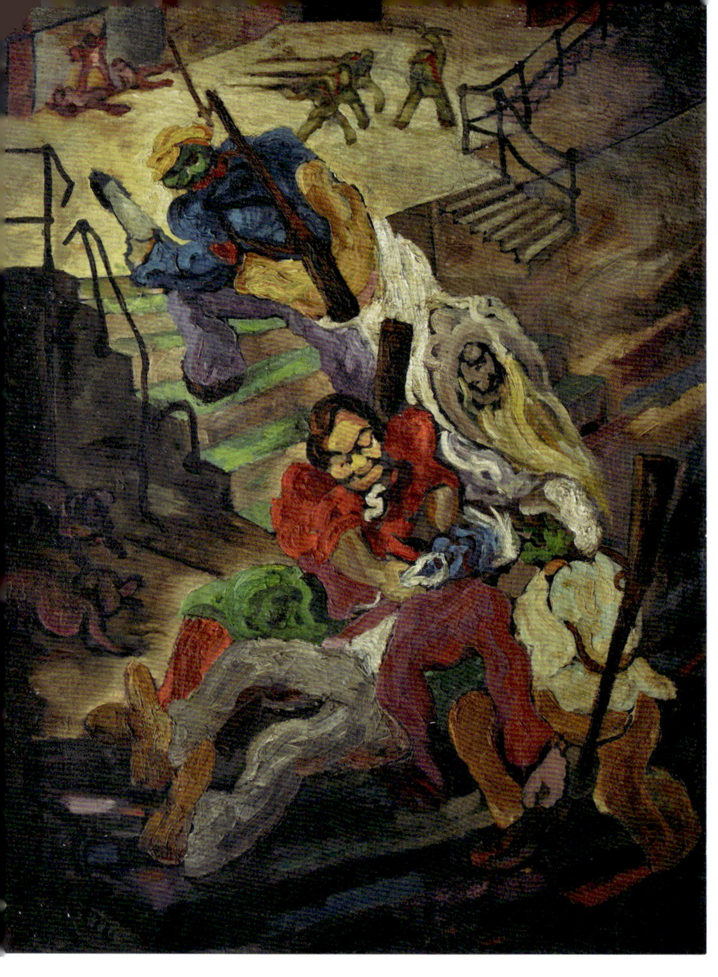

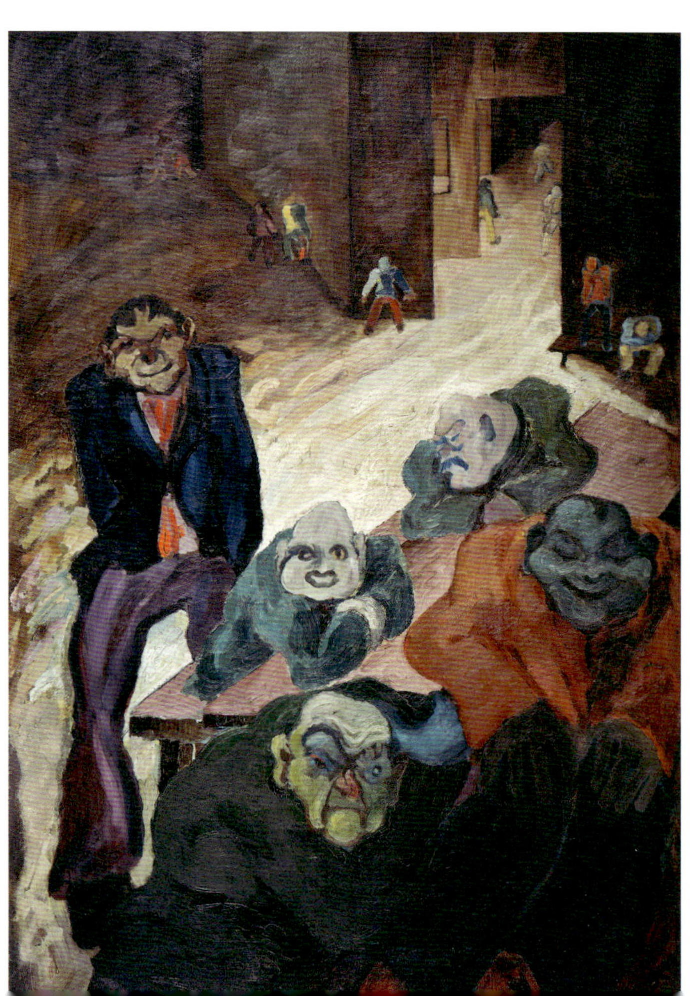

↑ Heinrich Ehmsen, *Execution of Hostages (Revolution I)*, 1924
Oil on canvas, 135 × 105.5 cm
Transferred in 1984 by the Kulturfonds der DDR to the Nationalgalerie, Berlin (East)

→ Heinrich Ehmsen, *In the Asylum*, 1925
Oil on canvas, 133 × 93 cm
Acquired in 1969 from the widow of the artist, Lis Bertram-Ehmsen, Berlin, for the Nationalgalerie, Berlin (East)

↗ Josef Scharl, *Ecce Homo*, 1931
Oil on canvas, 47 × 37 cm
Acquired in 2009 by the Freunde der Nationalgalerie

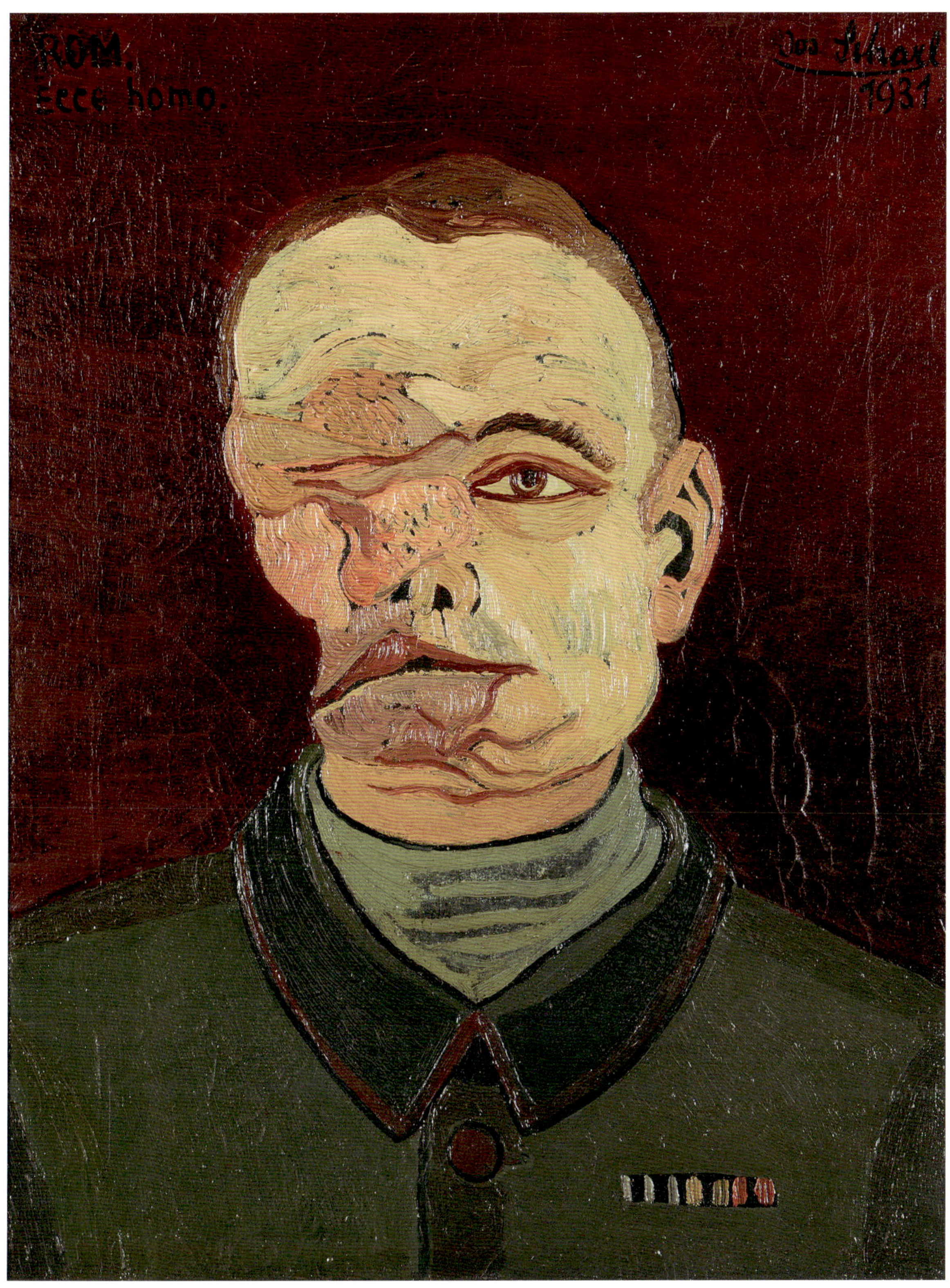
ROM.
Ecce homo.
1931.

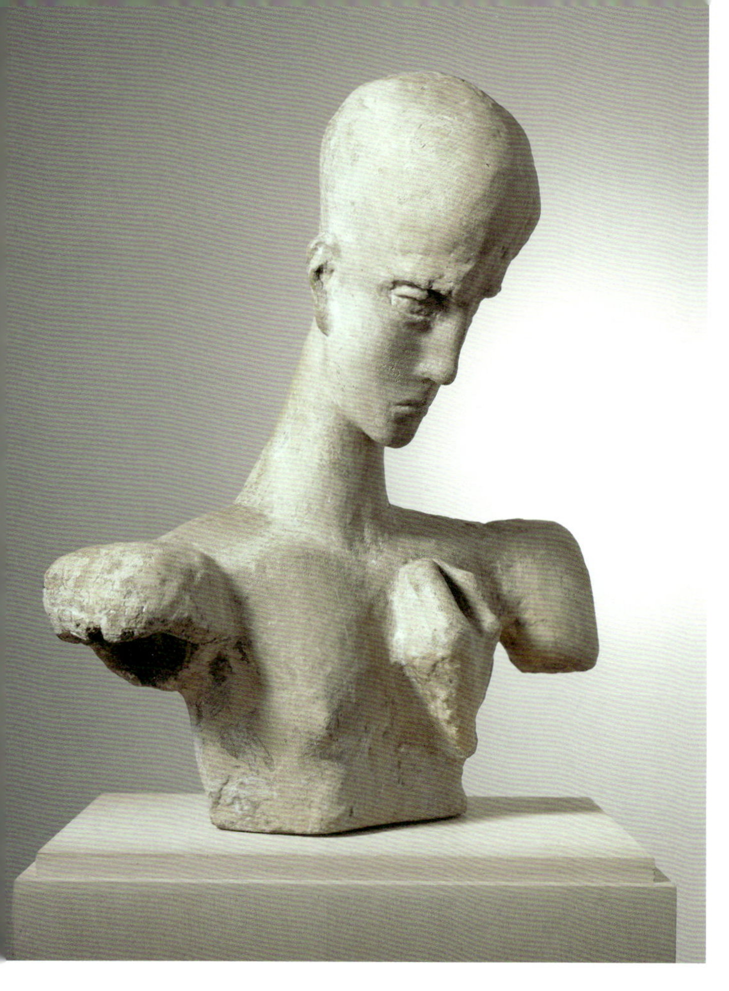

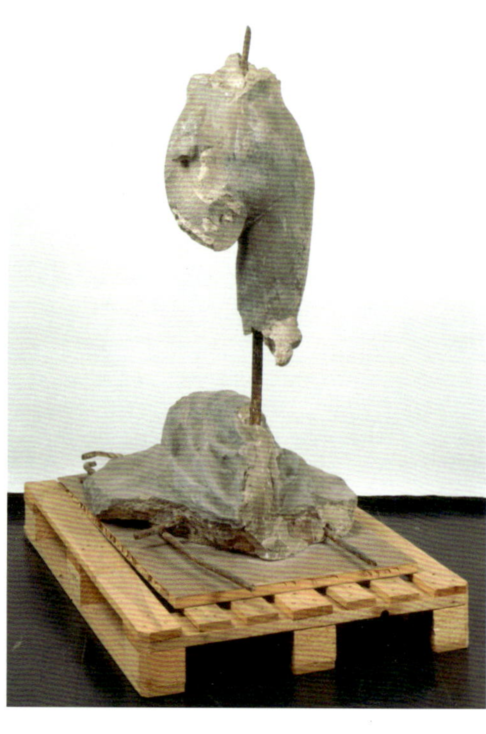

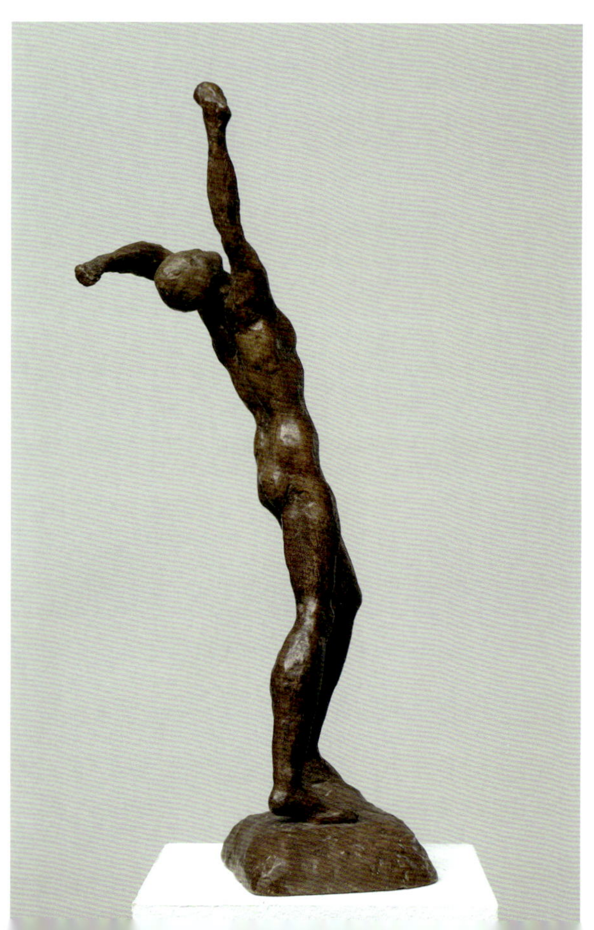

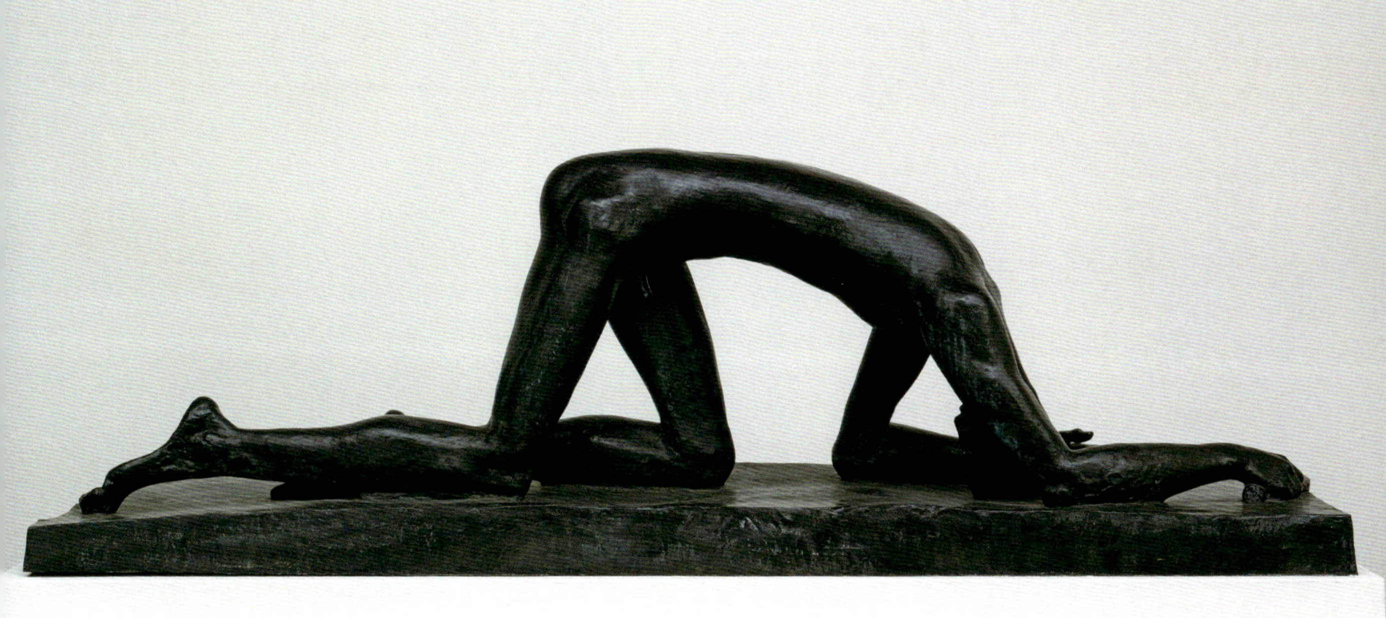

↖ Wilhelm Lehmbruck, *Head of a Thinker (with Hand)*, 1918
Cast stone, 64 × 59 × 32 cm
Acquired in 1985 via Staatlicher Kunsthandel der DDR for the Nationalgalerie, Berlin (East)

↖ Wilhelm Lehmbruck, *Kneeling Woman (Fragment)*, 1911
Cast stone, 124.5 × 64 × 124 cm
Acquired in 1919 from the artist's widow; destroyed in the war, 1945

← Wilhelm Lehmbruck, *The Storming One (Struck)*, 1914–15
Cement, 45 × 14 × 12 cm
Acquired in 1961 from Edgar Wedepohl, Berlin, with funds from the Stiftung der Victoria-Versicherungs-AG, Berlin, for the Nationalgalerie, Berlin (West)

↑ Wilhelm Lehmbruck, *Fallen Man*, 1915–16 (cast posthumously)
Bronze, 77 × 239 × 83 cm
Acquired in 1979 from the artist's son, Guido Lehmbruck, Leinfelden-Oberaichen, for the Nationalgalerie, Berlin (West)

→ Wilhelm Lehmbruck, *Torso of the Kneeling Woman*, 1911–13
Plaster on cement, 156 × 71 × 23 cm
Acquired in 1919–20 from the estate of the artist

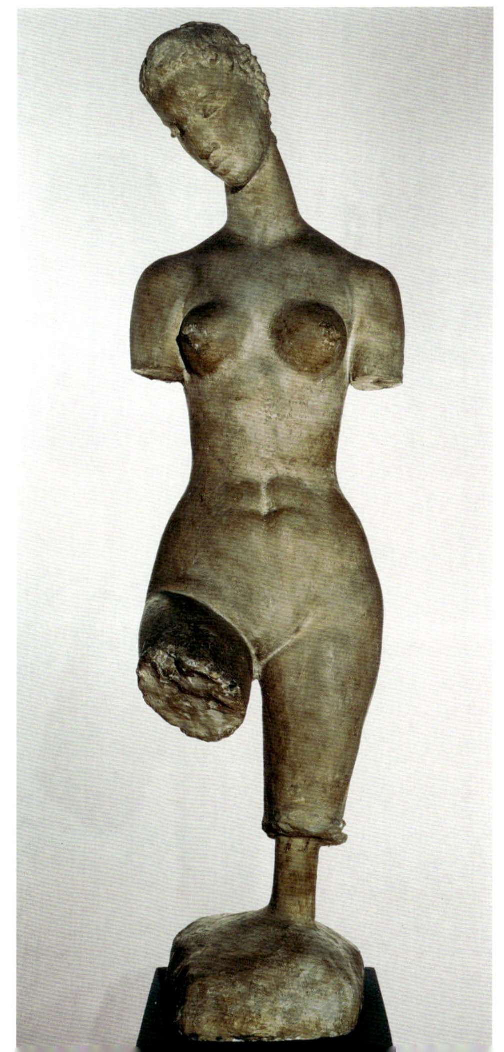

Who Were the *Pillars of Society?*

The title of George Grosz's 1926 painting *Stützen der Gesellschaft* (Pillars of Society) cites Henrik Ibsen's theatre play of the same name from 1877. The Norwegian author's drama indicts the ruling class of the time for its immorality. Grosz also took aim at *Das Gesicht der herrschenden Klasse* (The Face of the Ruling Class) – printing two drawings in a book by this title published in 1921 that would serve as preliminary designs for the painting.

Grosz wanted to create "modern history paintings". He placed his modern pillars, the *Stützen der Gesellschaft*, above one another in portrait format. The political figure at the bottom of the image is characterized as a right-wing extremist jurist. The beer glass identifies him as a fellow "regular customer" at this table, the sabre as a member of a fighting student association. The black armband on his jacket signifies he was a cavalry officer in the First World War, and the swastika on his tie shows he is a member of the NSDAP, the Nazi Party. The legal paragraph symbols (§) and the tiny horseman emerging from his head expose this member of the legal profession as a "paragraph stickler". And the blades of straw imply he is as "dumb as straw". Grosz's illustration of proverbs and sayings recalls an Old Master's painting that the artist knew from Berlin's Gemäldegalerie: Pieter Brueghel (the Elder)'s *Netherlandish Proverbs* from 1559 had been in the collection since 1914.

Behind the lawyer is a representative of the press, who resembles the right-wing publisher Alfred Hugenberg. Hugenberg owned the newspapers *Deutsche Zeitung* and the *Berliner Lokal-Anzeiger* and was a founding member of the Deutschnationale Volkspartei (DNVP, German National People's Party),

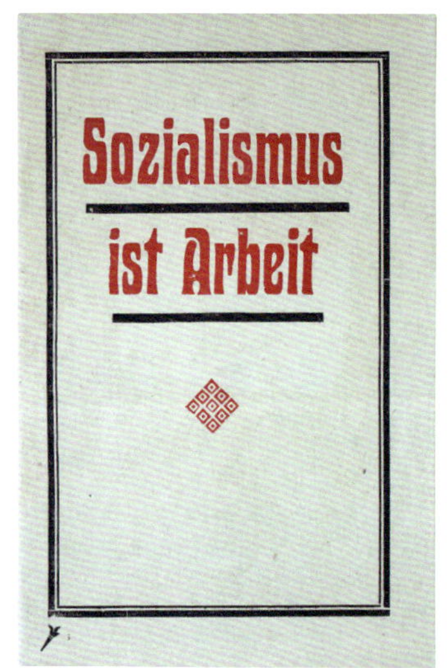

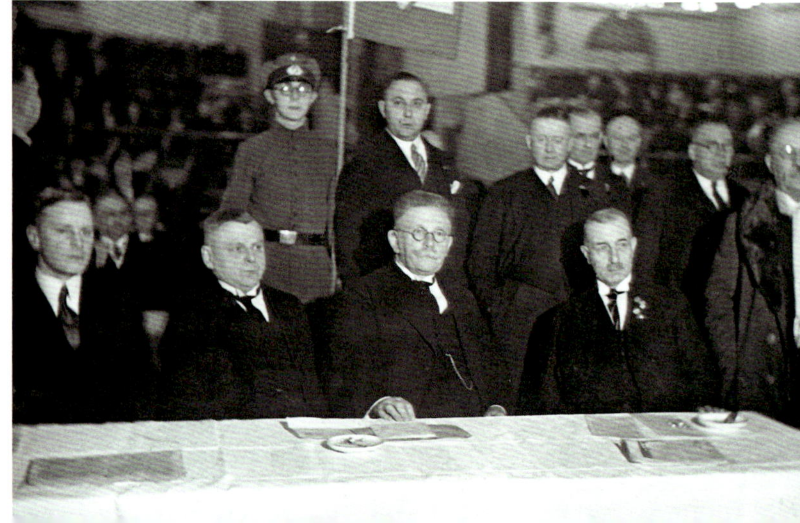

↗ *Sozialismus ist Arbeit* (Socialism Is Work), cover page, Berlin, 1918
→ Bruno Doehring and Alfred Hugenberg at a celebration for the 60th anniversary of the founding of the German Empire, 18 January 1931
→ George Grosz, *Das Gesicht der herrschenden Klasse: 57 politische Zeichnungen* (The Face of the Ruling Class: 57 Political Drawings), 3rd, expanded edition, Malik-Verlag, Berlin, 1921, p. 6 and p. 50.

which became the second strongest party in 1924. His pencil is sharp, and blood clings to his quill. He wears a chamber pot turned upside down on his head. This stands for the military group "Stahlhelm" (Steel Helmet), the "League of Front Soldiers".

A drastic figure of speech is illustrated further up in the composition, where a parliamentarian has "shit for brains". He carries a small flag that at first seems harmless. However, it turns out to be a political statement in the Weimar flag controversy. The year the painting was made, 1926, the new Reich President Paul von Hindenburg, elected the year before, allowed German representatives in European and overseas trading ports to again hoist the flag of the old German Empire (black-white-red) in addition to the flag of the Weimar Republic (in the colours black-red-gold). The small flag demonstrates this bias towards imperial restoration. The parliamentarian also holds a booklet with the inscription *Sozialismus ist Arbeit* (Socialism Is Work). It is an actual pamphlet of the Social Democratic government from 1919, which asked people to go back to work and not take part in the communist calls for strikes.

At the top of the painting, the official is a judge or a clergyman in a black gown, a warmonger loyal to the former Kaiser (Emperor), like the court and cathedral preacher Bruno Doehring, who was still at his post in 1926. In the painting, he covers for monarchist soldiers who commit acts of carnage behind him. The House of the Republic is in flames, also figuratively.

Dieter Scholz

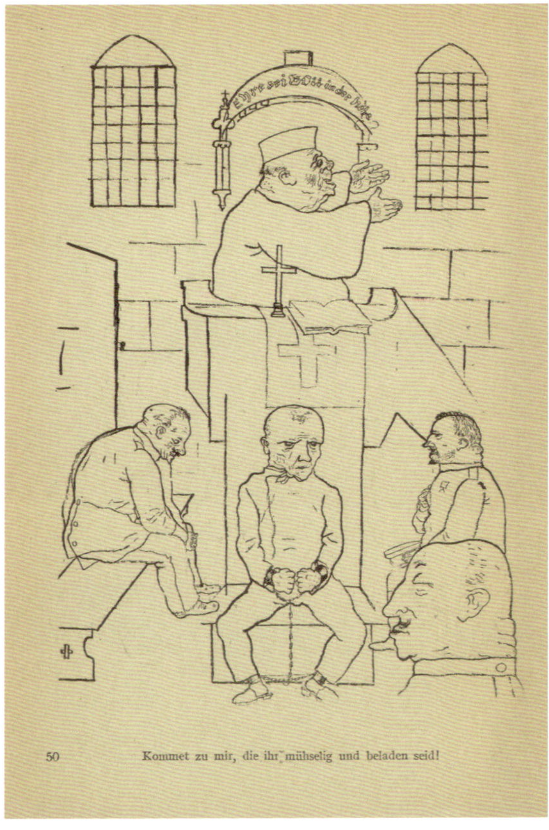

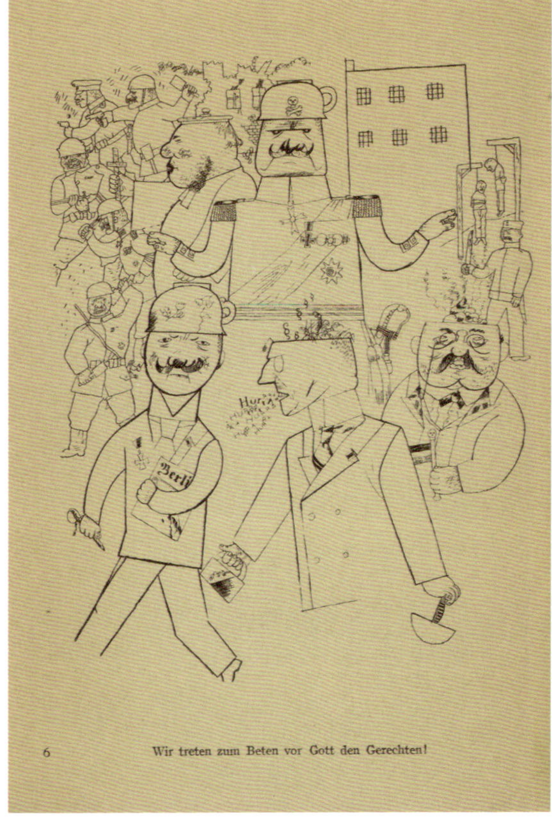

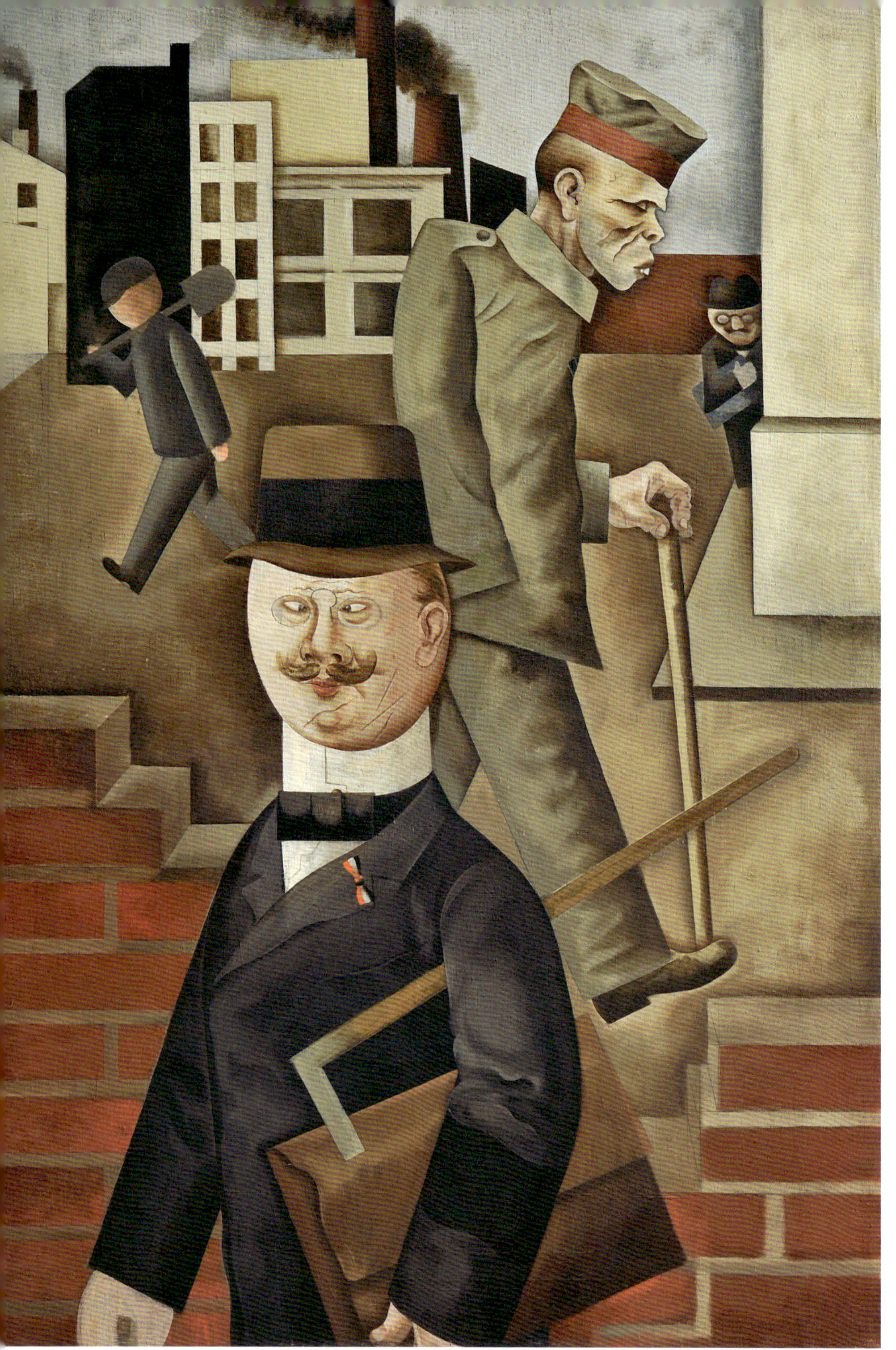

↑ George Grosz, *Grey Day*, 1921
Oil on canvas, 115 × 80 cm
Acquired in 1954 from the artist by the Land Berlin
for the Galerie des 20. Jahrhunderts, Berlin (West)

→ George Grosz, *Pillars of Society*, 1926
Oil on canvas, 200 × 108 cm
Acquired in 1958 from the Galerie Meta Nierendorf,
Berlin, for the Nationalgalerie, Berlin (West)

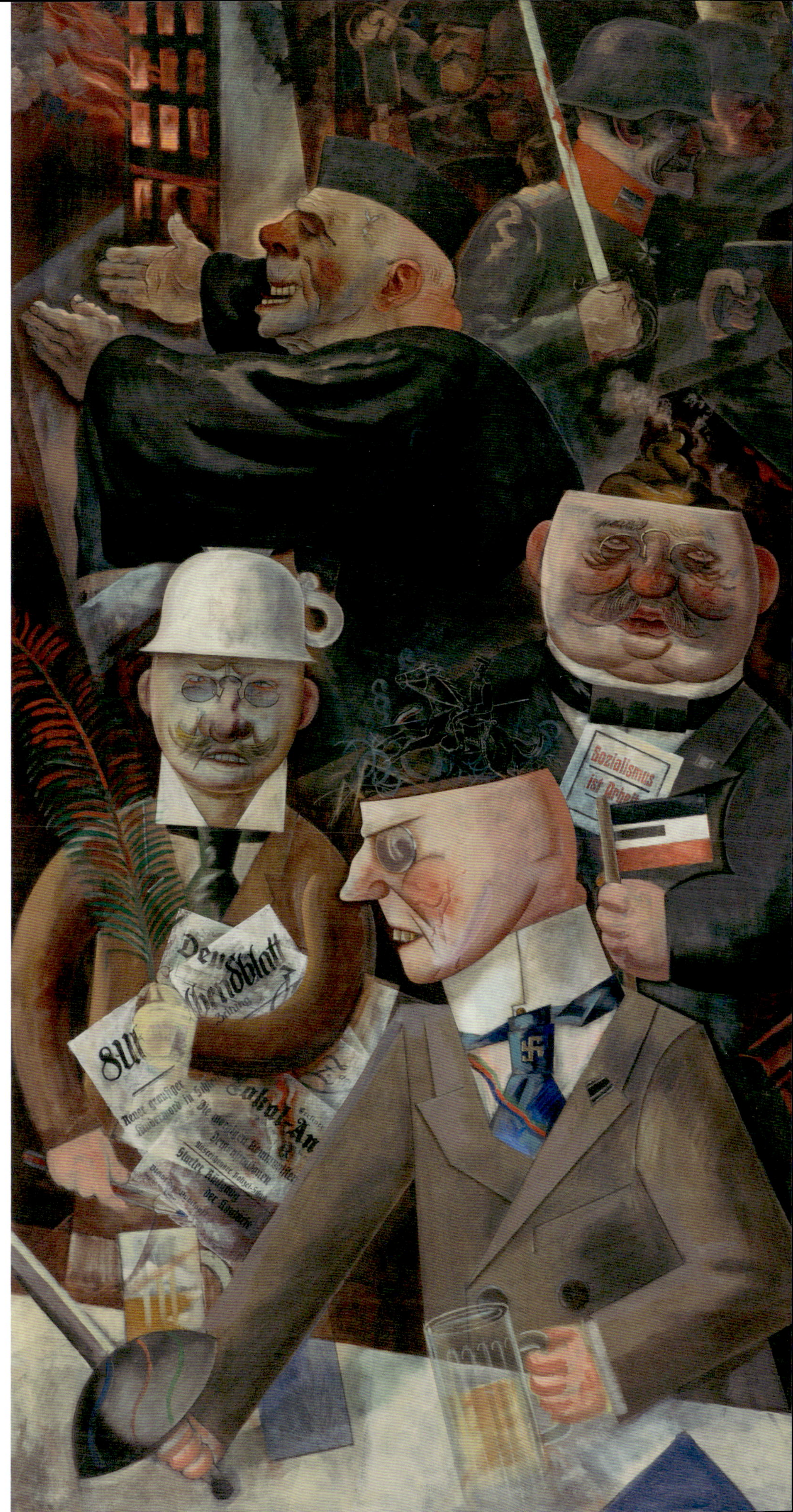
Sozialismus

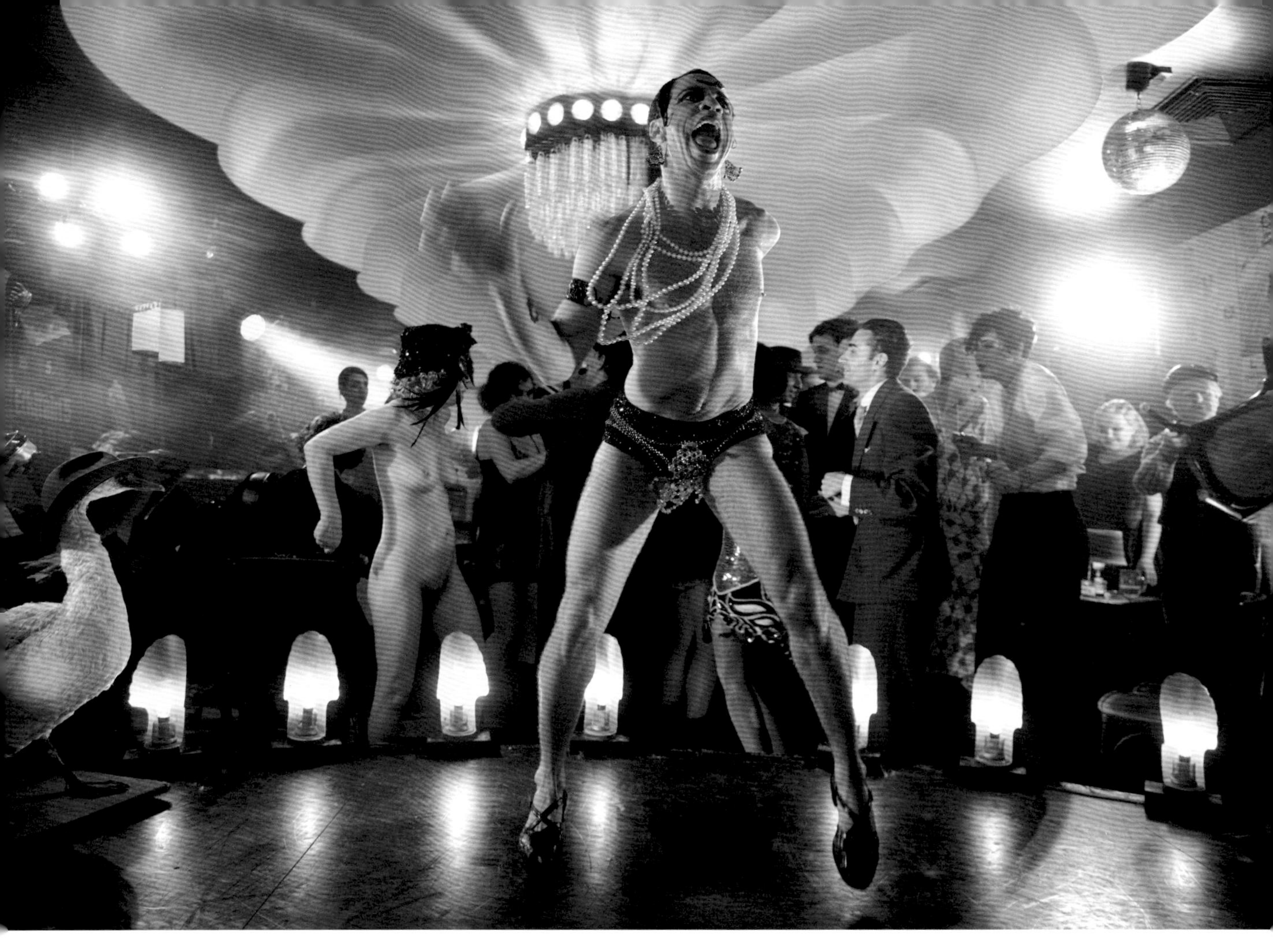

Julian Rosefeldt, *Deep Gold*, 2013–14
One-channel film installation, HD, 18:12 min.
Loan from the artist

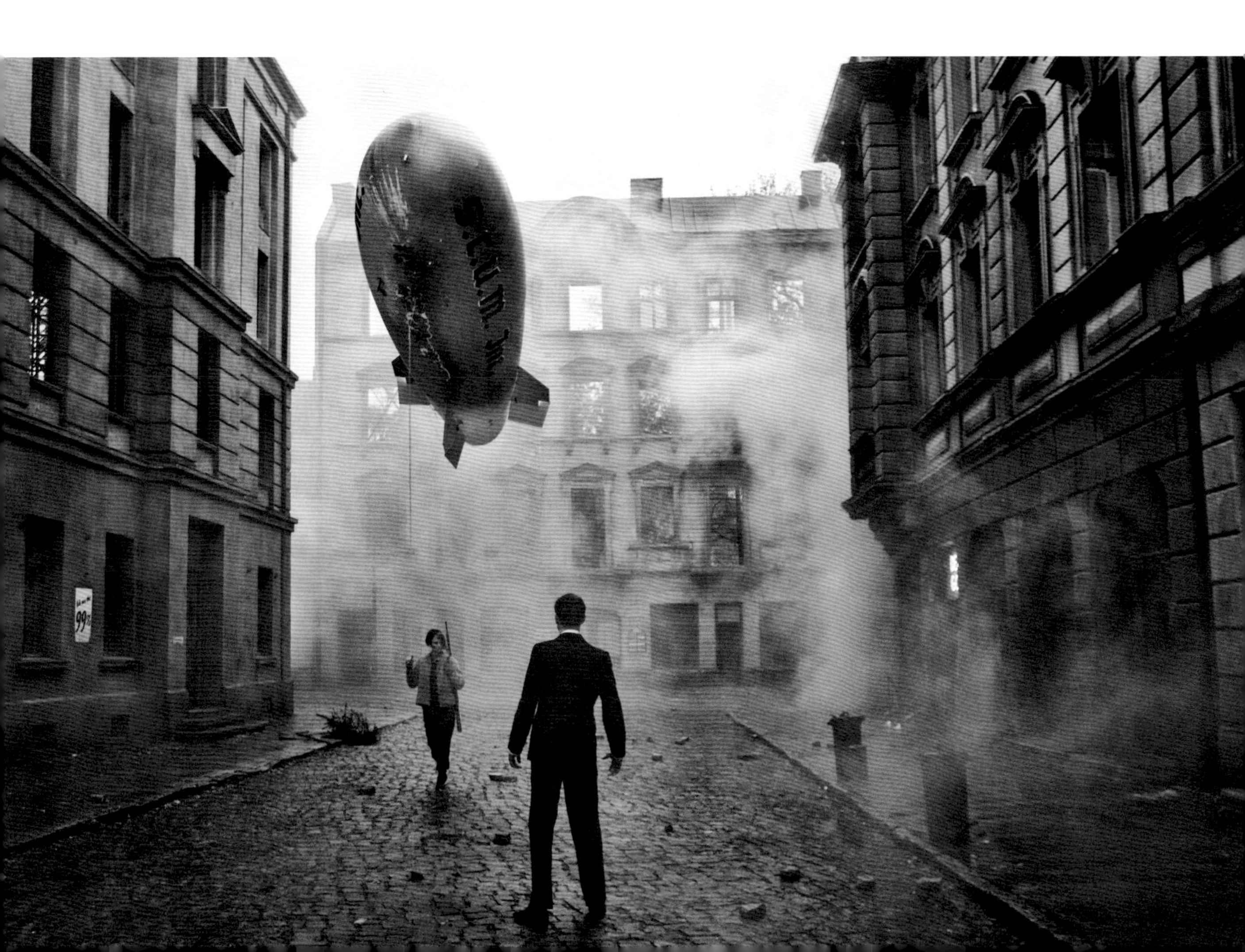

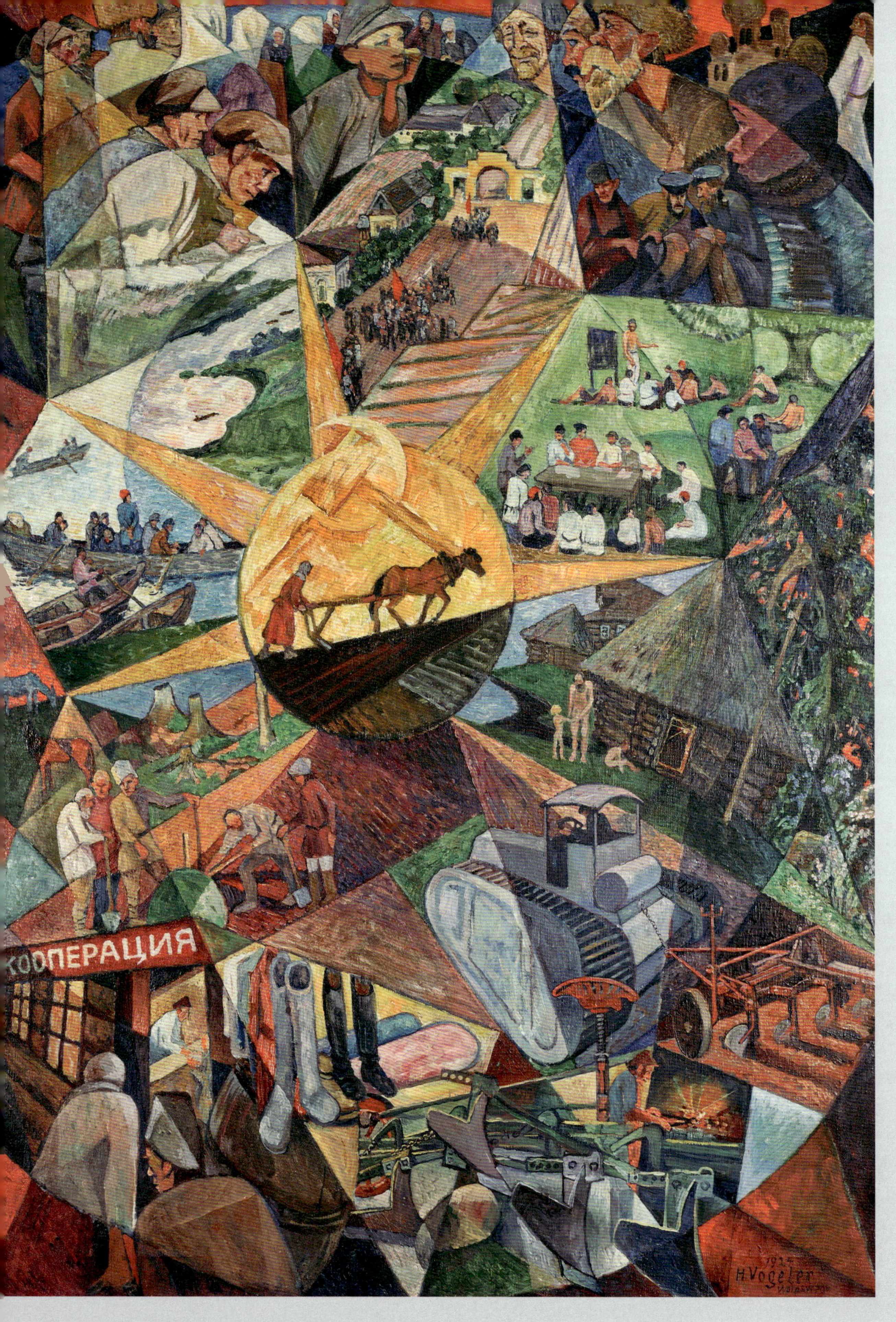
КООПЕРАЦИЯ
H.Vogeler

Politics and Propaganda

How is the political notion of communism reflected in visual art? Conrad Felixmüller chose to show a man in action when he painted Otto Rühle addressing the Communist Workers' Party of Germany (KAPD) at an event in Dresden in April/May of 1920. The straightforward reference remained easily identifiable, even years later, which is why Felixmüller cut up the image and hid the central fragment in 1933 for fear of being persecuted by the National Socialists. He repainted the entire work from a photograph in 1946.

Between 1924 and 1927, Heinrich Vogeler developed his *Komplexbilder* (Complex Images) to convey political statements visually. Working with a Cubist aesthetic, he divided the image's surface into crystalline planes, which he filled in with realistically painted scenes of daily life in Soviet society. Symbolic shapes, such as the Soviet star or the hammer and sickle, constitute a painting's unifying structure. Although avant-garde approaches to form were being rejected as too individualistic in the Soviet Union, Vogeler managed to unify what was increasingly considered irreconcilable. At the same time his *Komplexbilder* remain a valuable educational resource on the subject of communist agitation.

Heinrich Vogeler, *Students' Work Effort During the Summer*, 1924
Oil on canvas, 126 × 90 cm
Gift from the USSR government to the GDR in 1952, from the Moscow estate of Heinrich Vogeler; transferred to the Nationalgalerie, Berlin (East) in 1953

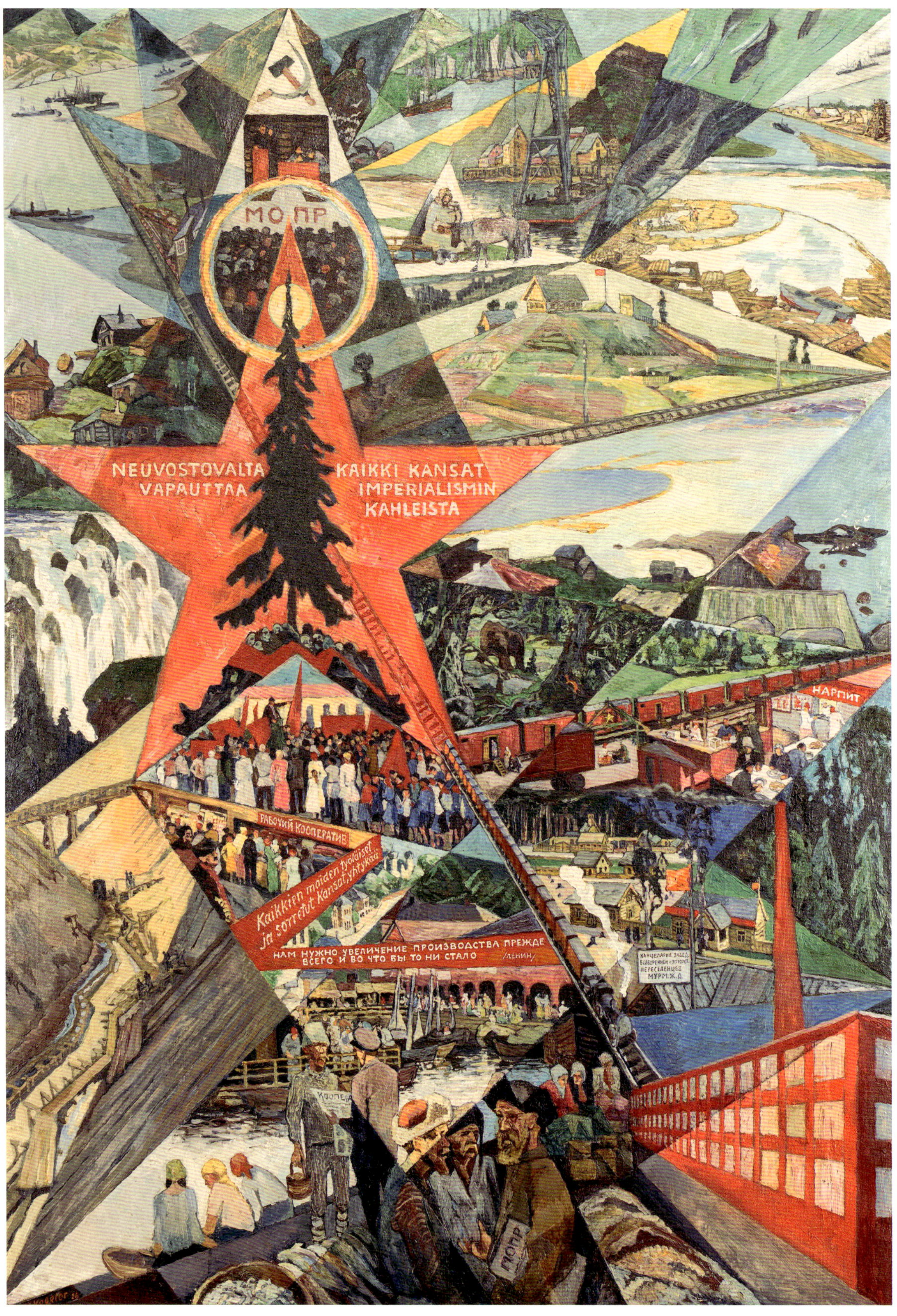
МОПР
NEUVOSTOVALTA VAPAUTTAA
KAIKKI KANSAT IMPERIALISMIN KAHLEISTA
НАРПИТ
РАБОЧИЙ КООПЕРАТИВ
Kaikkien maiden työläiset ja sorretut kansat, yhtykää
НАМ НУЖНО УВЕЛИЧЕНИЕ ПРОИЗВОДСТВА ПРЕЖДЕ ВСЕГО И ВО ЧТО БЫ ТО НИ СТАЛО /ЛЕНИН/
КАНЦЕЛЯРИЯ ЗАВЕД.
ПЕРЕСЕЛЕНЦЕВ
МУРМ.Ж.Д
МОПР

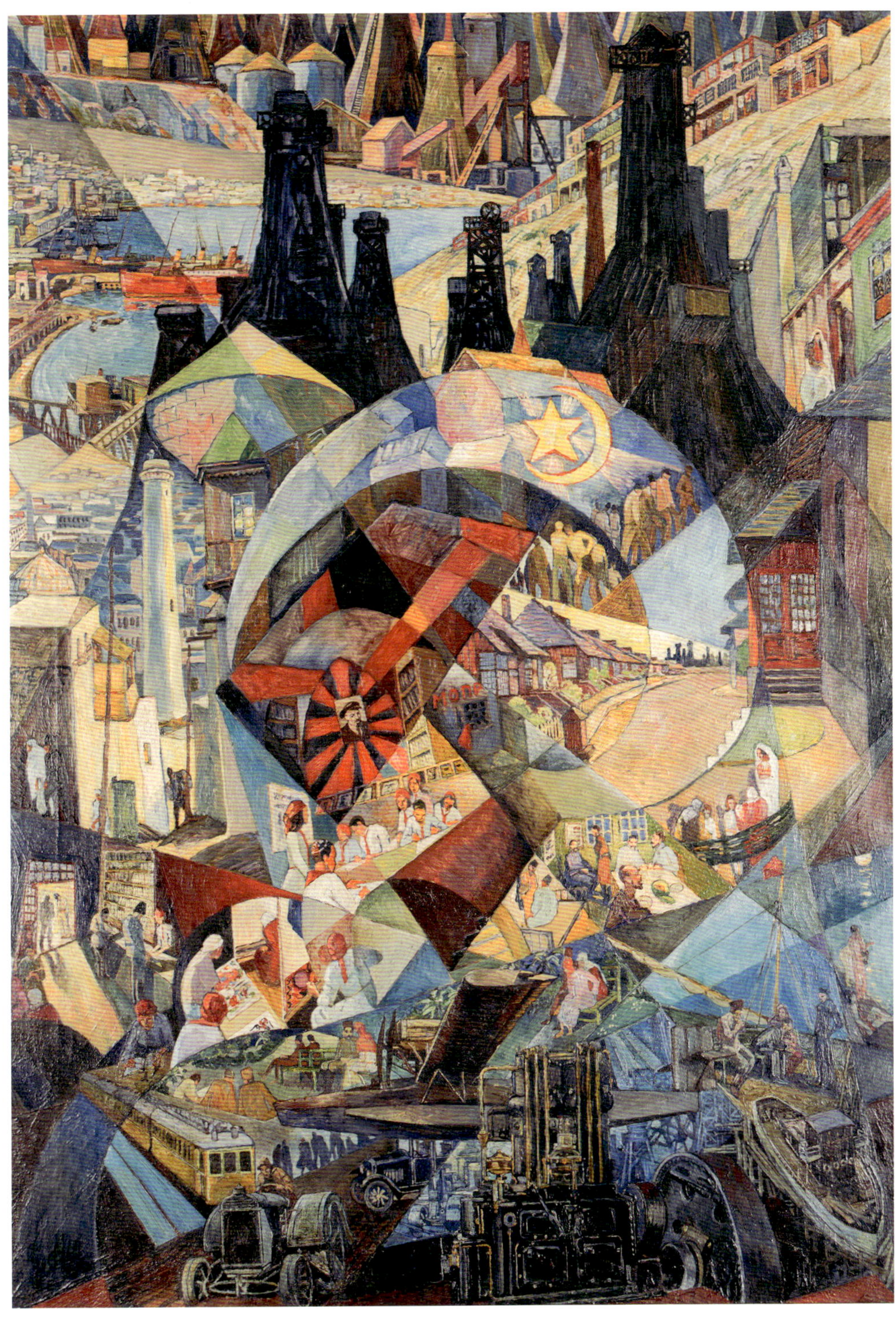

↗ Heinrich Vogeler, *Baku*, 1927
Oil on canvas, 125 × 90 cm
Gift from the USSR government to the GDR in 1952, from the Moscow estate of Heinrich Vogeler; transferred to the Nationalgalerie, Berlin (East) in 1953

← Heinrich Vogeler, *Karelia and Murmansk*, 1926
Oil on canvas, 125 × 90 cm
Gift from the USSR government to the GDR in 1952, from the Moscow estate of Heinrich Vogeler; transferred to the Nationalgalerie, Berlin (East) in 1953

Heinrich Vogeler Produced a New Form: The *Komplexbild*

Heinrich Vogeler had lived at the Barkenhoff in Worpswede since 1895 and was best known for his works in the Jugendstil or Art Nouveau style. The fact that he had begun developing communist leanings a year after the Russian Revolution in 1917 is less known. His social inclinations also allowed the charitable organization Rote Hilfe (Red Aid) to host children from working-class families at the Barkenhoff for several weeks of holidays from 1923 onwards.

In 1923–24 Vogeler travelled to the Soviet Union for the first time. He started by painting individual pictures of daily life, which he interlocked into a new avant-garde pictorial composition that ultimately produced a new form: The *Komplexbild* (Complex Image). Much like a school teacher at a chalkboard, Vogeler would use a wooden pointer when presenting his work to indicate the different steps in constructing a socialist society, as illustrated in the separate sections of his paintings.

In the summer of 1925, Vogeler travelled to Soviet Karelia near the Finnish border on an assignment for the Rote Hilfe. His impressions of the journey were published in the magazine *Das Neue Russland* in 1926. They include a detailed explanation of the painting titled *Karelien* (Karelia). The Finnish inscription at the centre reads, "The Soviet power frees all peoples from the chains of imperialism," and below that, "Workers and oppressed people of all nations unite." Lower still, Lenin is quoted in Russian: "Above all else, we must increase production at all costs." The painting's various subsections can be further deciphered:

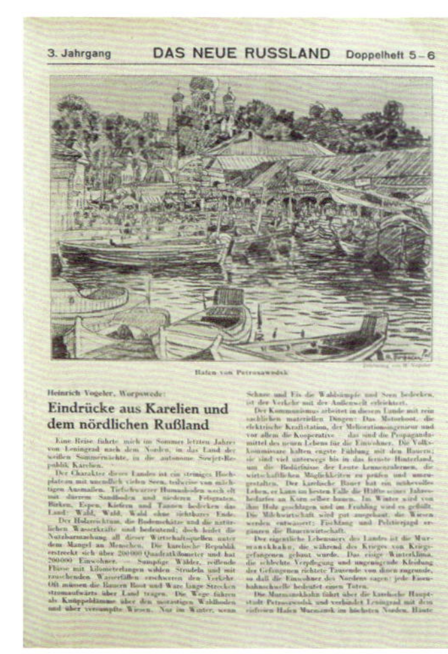

3. Jahrgang DAS NEUE RUSSLAND Doppelheft 5–6

Hafen von Petrosawodsk

Heinrich Vogeler, Worpswede:

Eindrücke aus Karelien und dem nördlichen Rußland

↗ Map of Karelia showing the railway connection between Leningrad (today St Petersburg) and Murmansk
→ Heinrich Vogeler, *Eindrücke aus Karelien und dem nördlichen Rußland* (Impressions of Karelia and Northern Russia), *Das Neue Russland*, vol. 3, no. 5/6, 1926, pp. 1–9, here p. 1

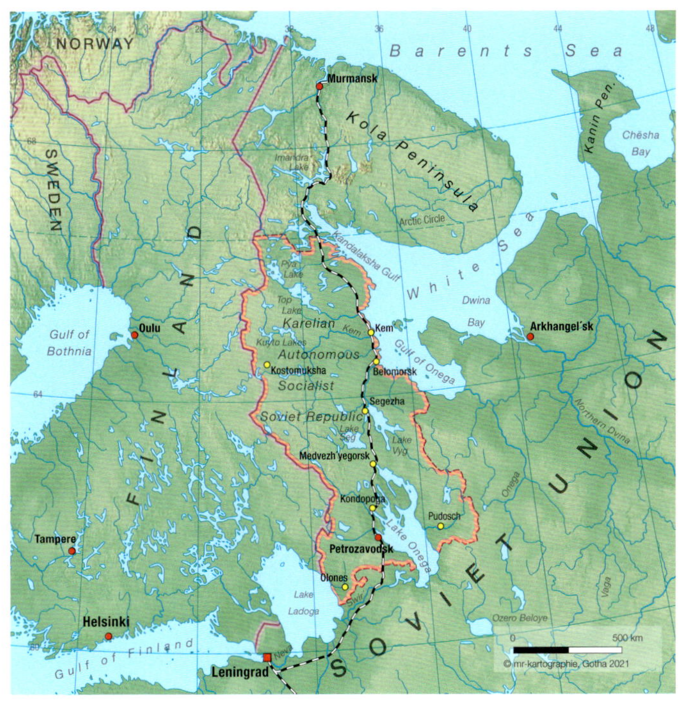

"Tilted left across the painting, the central axis bisects the red Soviet star with a pine tree at its centre that is haloed by the circling midnight sun. This axis around which everything gathers represents revolutionary life, the life of the political party. Below the pine tree, dead revolutionaries from the woodland marshes lie. Above the star party members gather in an assembly under the 'Rote Hilfe' slogan [Russian: МОПР or MOPR], below it, scenes from the Revolutionary Council in Petrozavodsk play out next to images of economic activity. The main line of energy leading diagonally down the painting across the Soviet star is the Murmansk Railway, beginning at Murmansk's port and coming to an end at a textile factory in central Russia. [Correction: the factory building was recently identified as part of the aluminium smelting facility in Kandalaksha.] From here, the painting breaks up into various images of colonization: from below, a modern, organized colony with a workers' club and a cafeteria for 'feeding the people', etc. Next, a primitive settlement of train cars and finally an old fishing colony at the White Sea. The northernmost experimental agricultural testing site, Chibine, is painted along an indistinct railroad track. – The left portion of the painting is dedicated to various manifestations of water: It is shown as a form of transportation at the Murmansk port, as a force of nature in the Kivach Falls, and beneath as a source of electrical power in the form of a feed duct for the construction of an industrial plant. – The painting's upper planes show the Arctic Ocean ports connecting to the Dvina at Archangelsk – here, fish are shown as an economic link, similar to the fur-bearing animals at the centre of the image."

Dieter Scholz

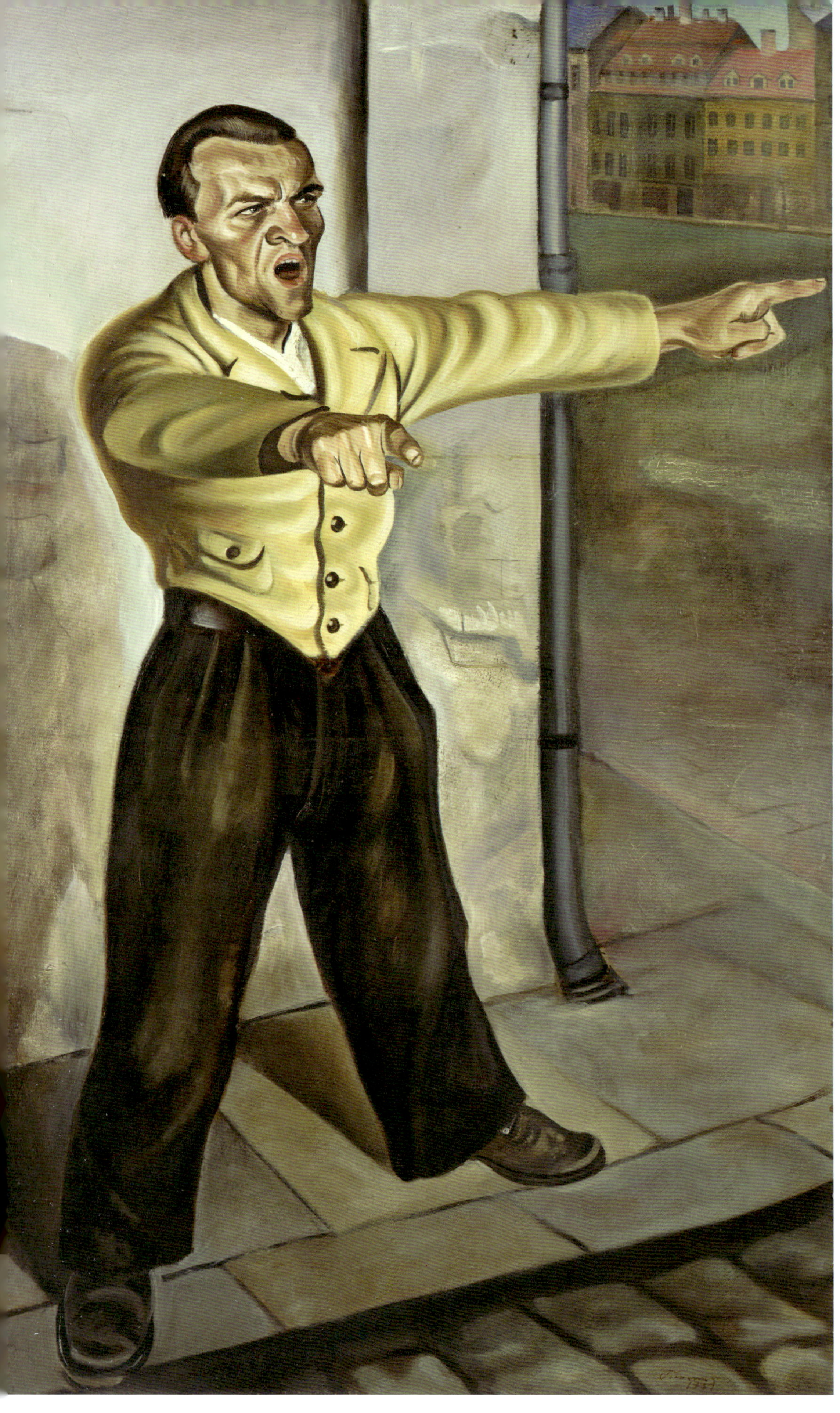

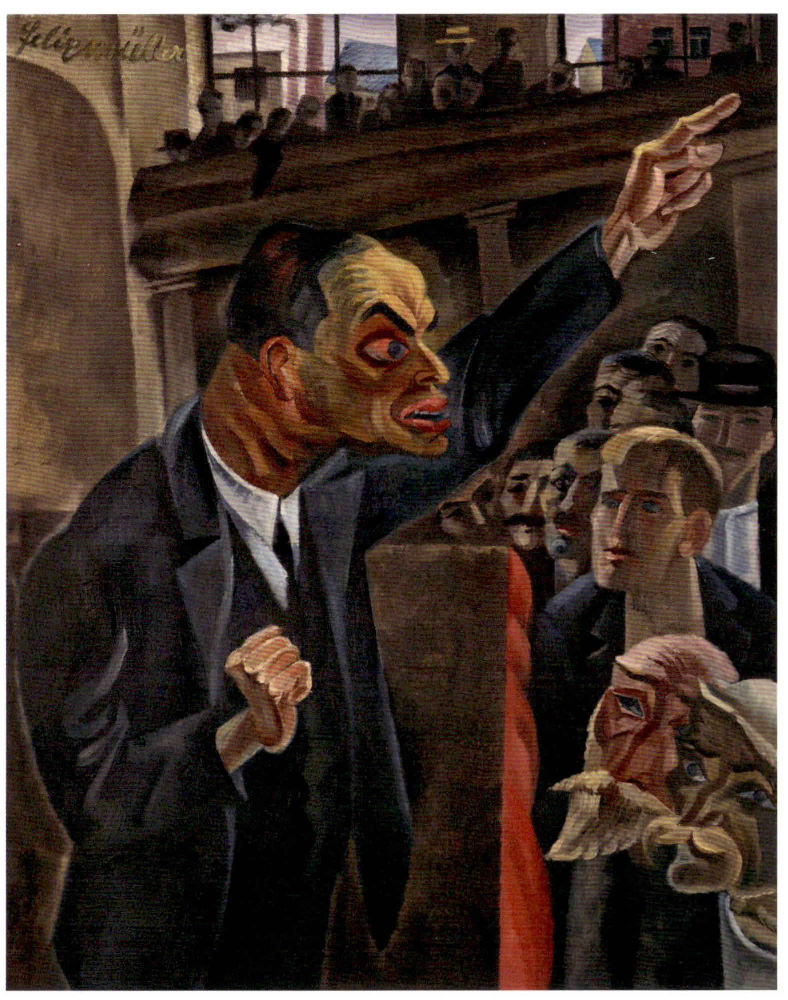

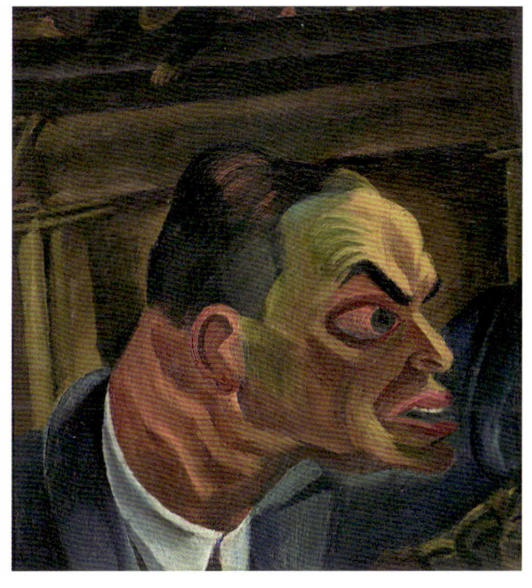

↑ Conrad Felixmüller, *The Speaker No. I Otto Rühle*, 1920
(Replica by the artist from 1946)
Oil on canvas, 125 × 93 cm
Gift from the artist's son, Titus Felixmüller
to the Nationalgalerie, Berlin (East), 1977

→ Conrad Felixmüller, *The Speaker No. I Otto Rühle*
(fragment), 1920
Oil on canvas, 54 × 40 cm
Gift from the heirs of Conrad Felixmüller, 2019

← Curt Querner, *Agitator*, 1931
Oil on canvas, 160 × 100 cm
Acquired in 1966 from the artist with funds from the
Kulturfonds der DDR for the Nationalgalerie, Berlin (East)

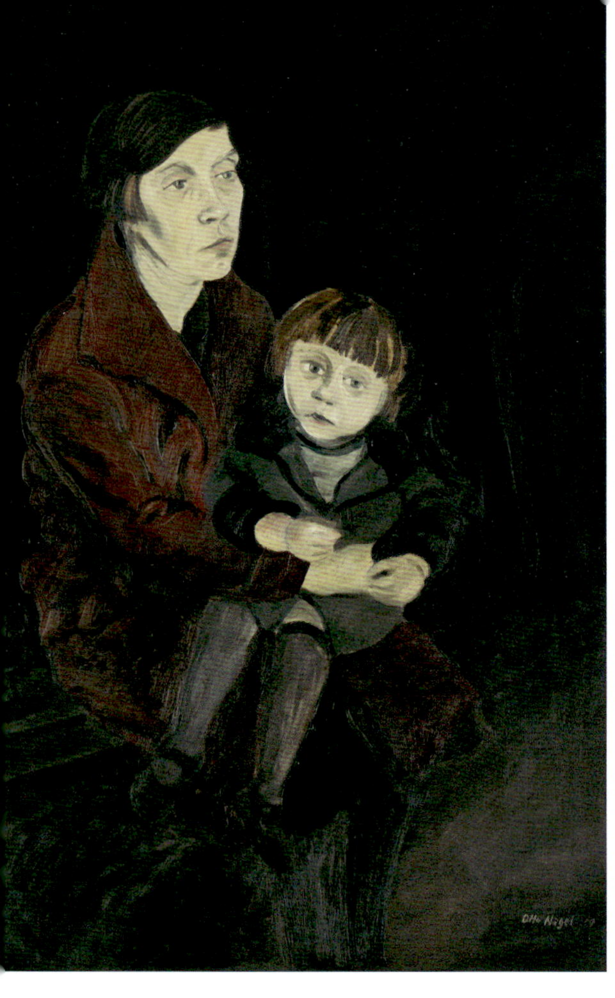
Otto Nagel

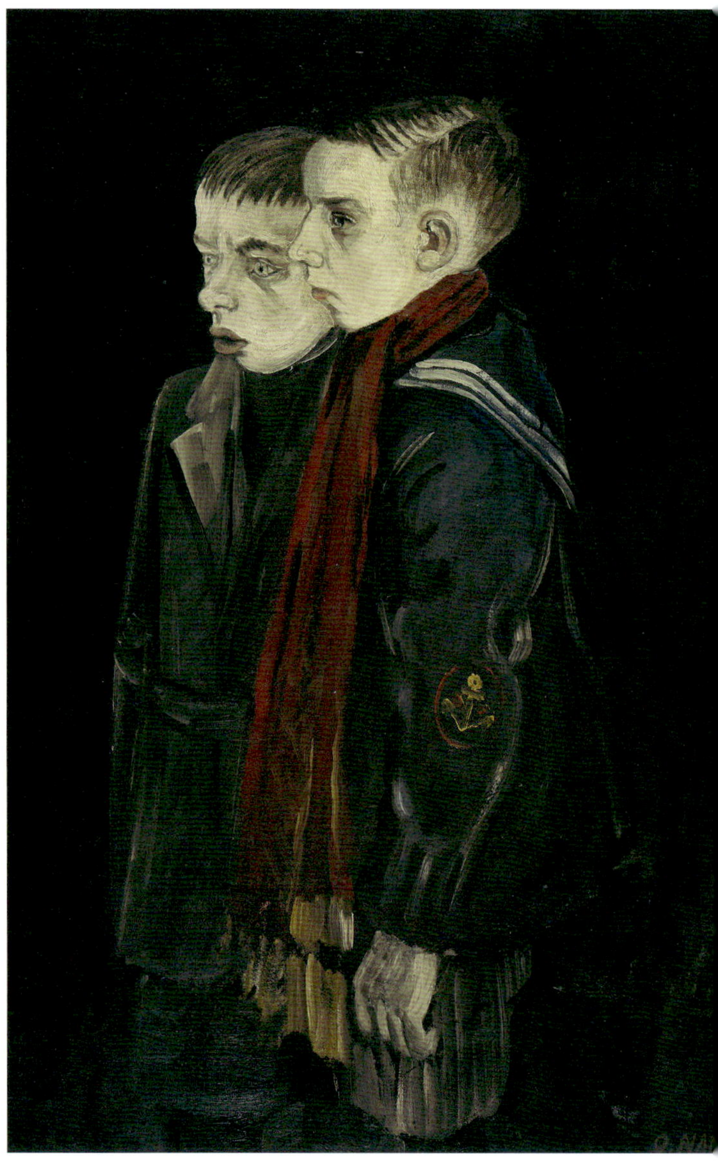

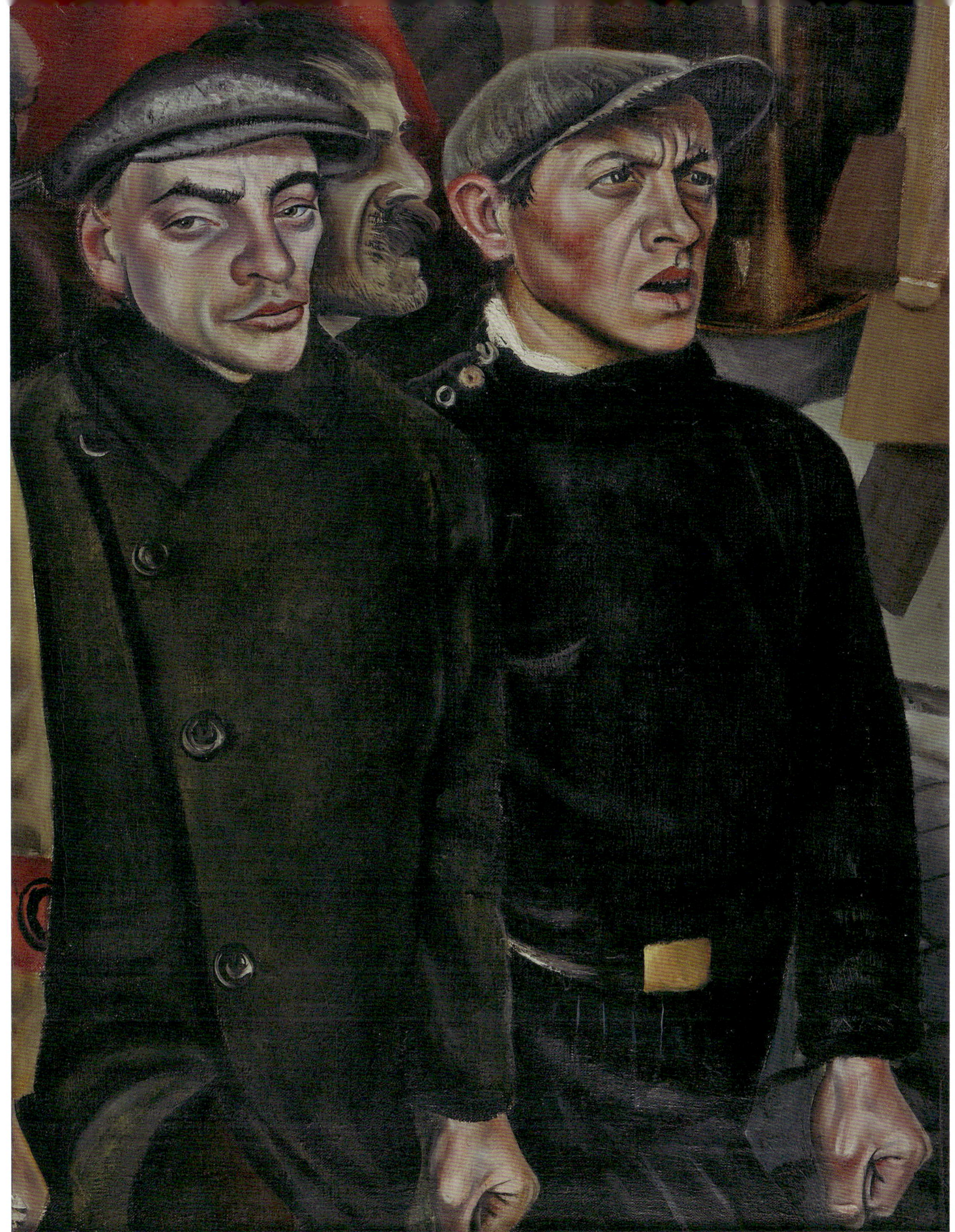

↑ Curt Querner, *Demonstration*, 1930
Oil on canvas, 87 × 66 cm
Acquired in 1965 from the artist with funds from the Kulturfonds der DDR for the Nationalgalerie, Berlin (East)

↖ Otto Nagel, *Mother with Child*, 1929
Oil on canvas, 120.5 × 81 cm
Acquired in 1963 from the artist by the Ministerium für Kultur with funds from the Kulturfonds der DDR for the Nationalgalerie, Berlin (East)

← Otto Nagel, *Boys from Wedding*, 1928
Oil on canvas, 91 × 62 cm
Acquired in 1963 from the artist by the Ministerium für Kultur with funds from the Kulturfonds der DDR for the Nationalgalerie, Berlin (East)

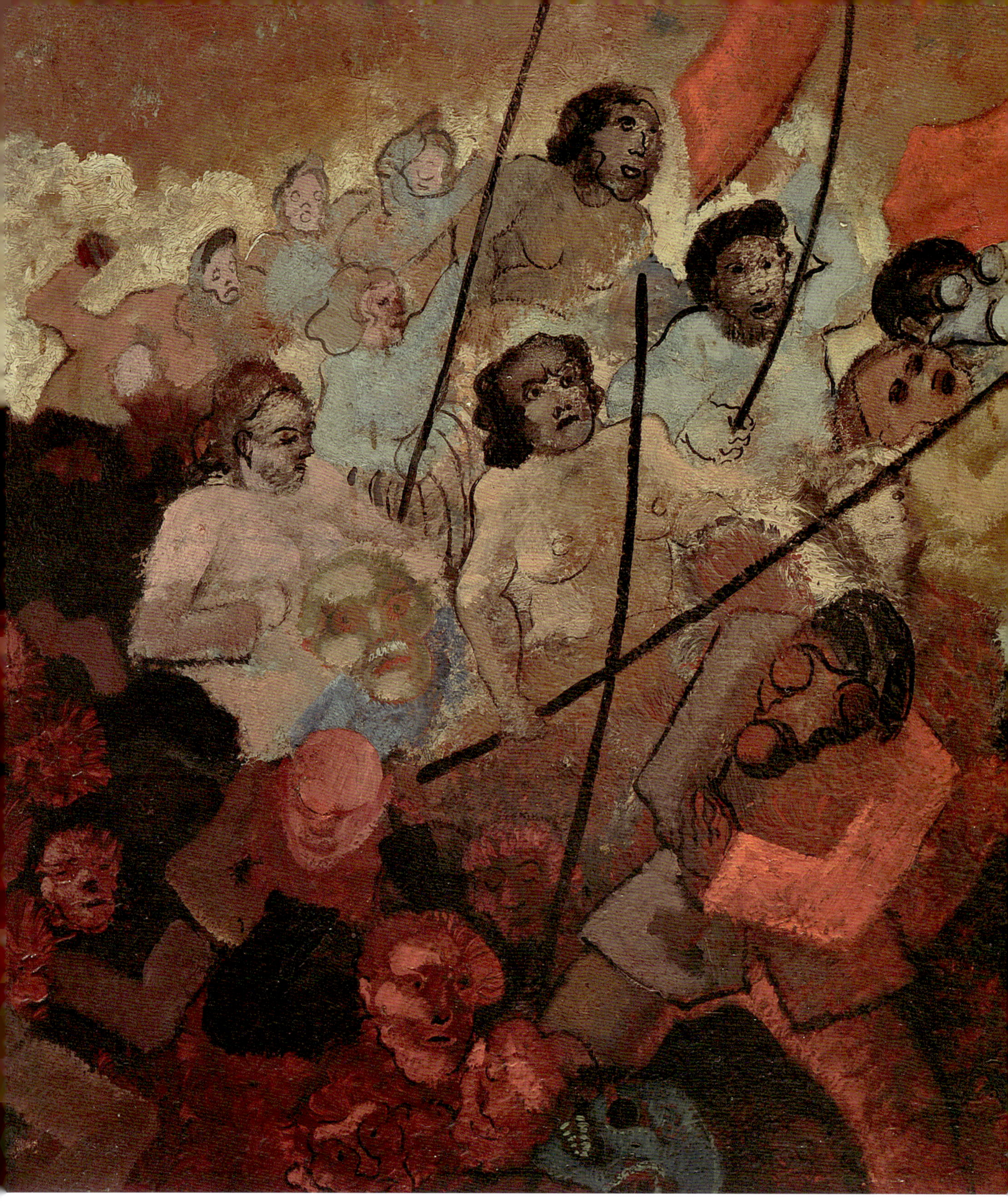

Heinrich Ehmsen, *Women in Need I*, 1932
Oil on cardboard, 38 × 54.5 cm
Transfer in 1982 from the Kulturfonds der DDR to the Nationalgalerie, Berlin (East)

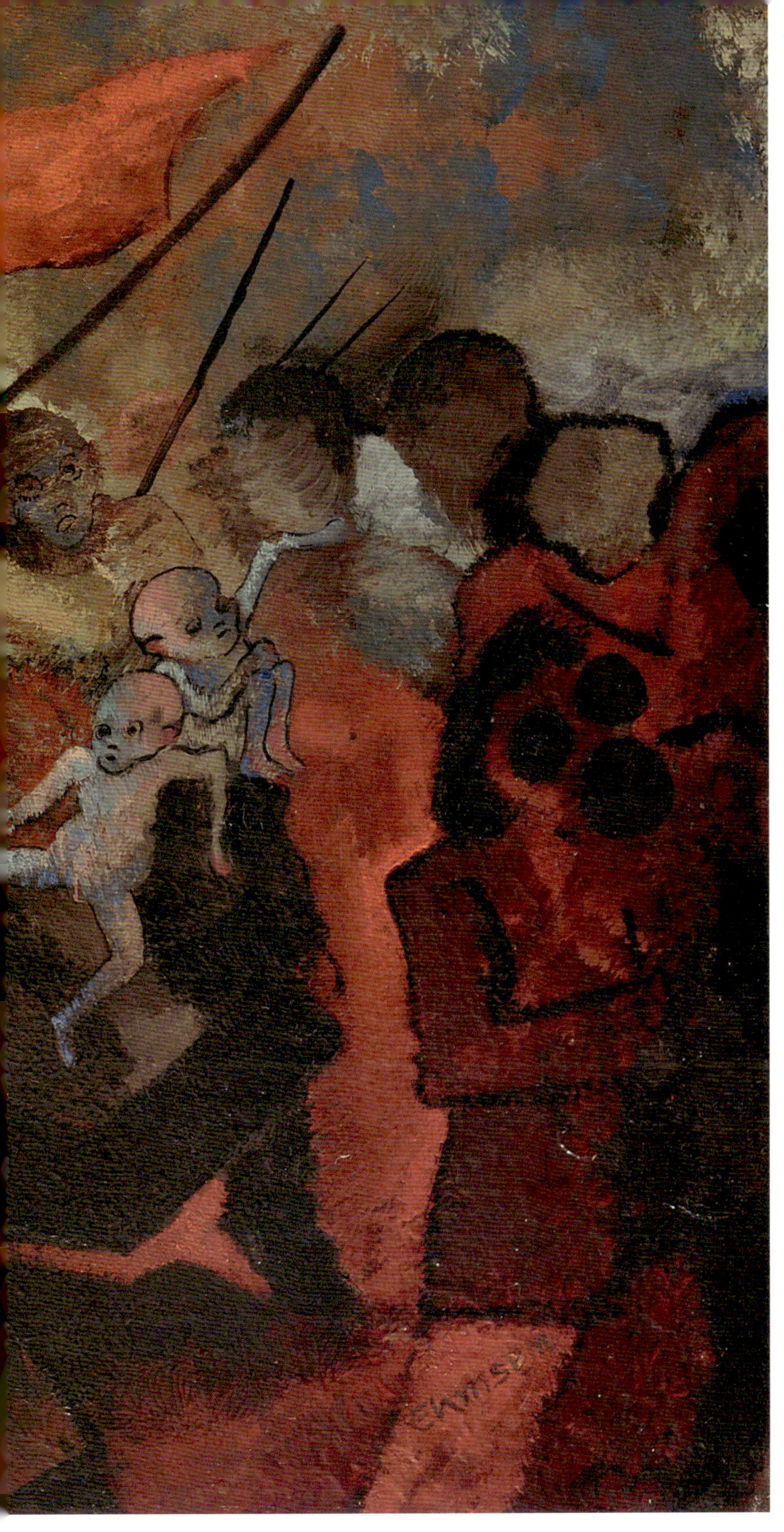

Women in Need. The Struggle to Legalize Abortion

Paragraph (§) 218 triggered a widespread debate in Weimar Republic society. It had been incorporated into the penal code in 1871 to prohibit the termination of a pregnancy and make infringements on this prohibition punishable by up to five years in prison. While the Christian church and conservative and nationalist political parties defended the abortion ban, women's groups, Germany's Social Democratic Party (SPD) and the Communist Party of Germany (KPD) advocated for its abolition. They were most concerned with the plight of working-class families whose poverty would only be further exacerbated by each new birth.

Many artists joined the struggle to legalize abortion. Käthe Kollwitz pointed out the connection between women bearing many children and economic deprivation in the 1924 poster she designed for the KPD, entitled *Nieder mit den Abtreibungsparagraphen!* (Down with the Abortion Paragraphs!). The poster shows a pregnant, prematurely aged working-class woman with two young children wearing an expression of hopelessness. Alice Lex-Nerlinger used a spray technique to create a painting of a group of women struggling to push over a monumental cross bearing the inscription *§ 218*, while the silhouette of a pregnant woman towers over them. In 1931 Lex-Nerlinger's work was shown in the Berlin exhibition *Frauen in Not* (Women in Need), which included many artists both from Germany and abroad.

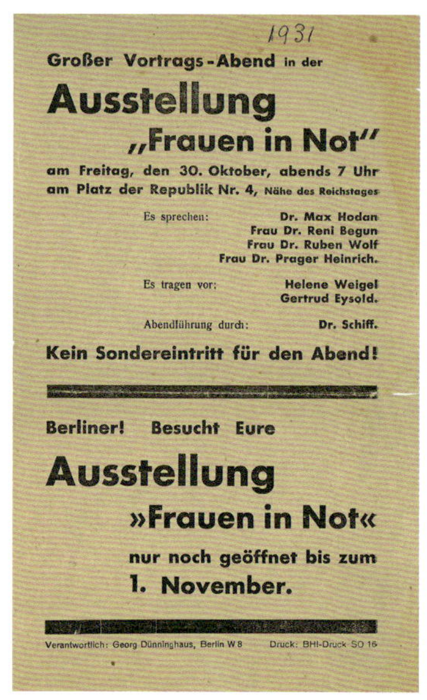
1931
Großer Vortrags-Abend in der
Ausstellung
„Frauen in Not"
am Freitag, den 30. Oktober, abends 7 Uhr
am Platz der Republik Nr. 4, Nähe des Reichstages
Es sprechen: Dr. Max Hodan, Frau Dr. Reni Begun, Frau Dr. Ruben Wolf, Frau Dr. Prager Heinrich.
Es tragen vor: Helene Weigel, Gertrud Eysold.
Abendführung durch: Dr. Schiff.
Kein Sondereintritt für den Abend!

Berliner! Besucht Eure
Ausstellung
»Frauen in Not«
nur noch geöffnet bis zum
1. November.

Verantwortlich: Georg Dünninghaus, Berlin W 8 Druck: BHI-Druck SO 16

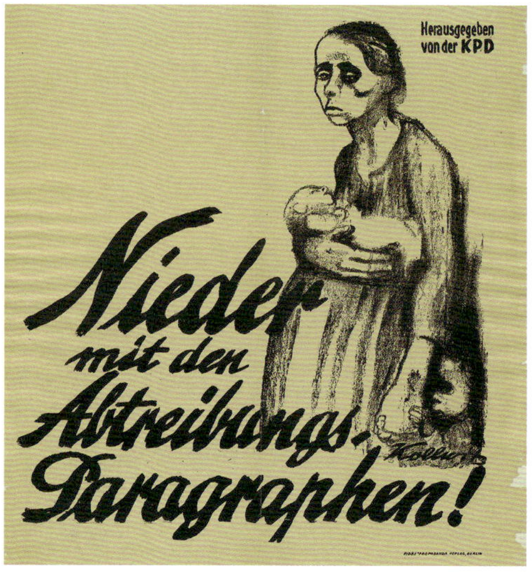

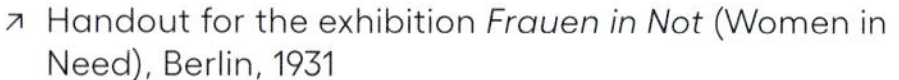

↗ Handout for the exhibition *Frauen in Not* (Women in Need), Berlin, 1931
→ Käthe Kollwitz, *Nieder mit den Abtreibungs-Paragraphen!* (Down with the Abortion Paragraphs!), poster of the Communist Party of Germany, 1924
→ Alice Lex-Nerlinger, *Paragraph 218*, 1931

Heinrich Ehmsen's 1932 painting *Frauen in Not I* was undoubtedly produced in connection with the exhibition, as he was on its artists' committee. However, Ehmsen himself was not represented because this work was completed after the show opened. His painting, now in the Nationalgalerie, shows a protest march under red flags consisting of men and women, some of whom bear their maternal breasts. Two malnourished infants stand out from the crowd. Some of the protesters' faces are distorted into grotesque grimaces or skulls. The gas masks worn by others were intended to point out the anti-abortionists' true intentions – children were also needed as "cannon fodder" for the war.

Efforts to abolish the abortion law during the Weimar Republic all failed. National Socialist ideology glorified the role of mothers and even increased the punishment for terminating a pregnancy. After the end of the Second World War, § 218 was incorporated into the Federal Republic of Germany's penal code nearly unchanged. It was not until the 1970s that the women's movement drummed up a renewed zeal to abolish the abortion ban with their slogan, "My belly belongs to me!", triggering intense public and parliamentary debates. But not even the social-liberal coalition in power at the time succeeded in changing the law. Today's law still technically prohibits terminating a pregnancy. However, a termination is not punishable if it is preceded by a consultation and carried out within the first trimester of pregnancy.

Irina Hiebert Grun

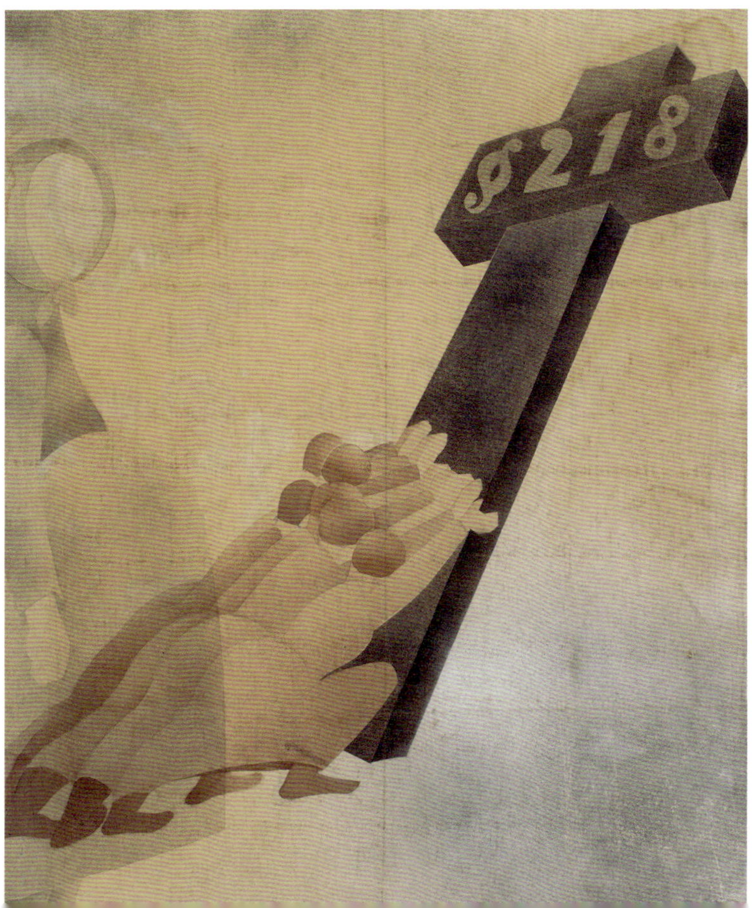

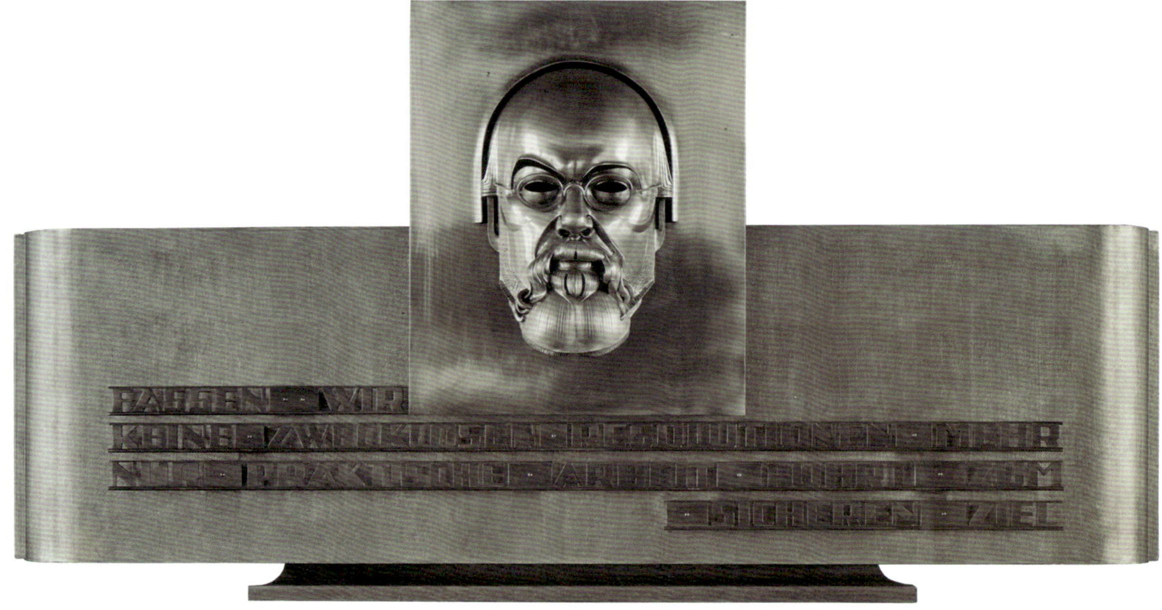

The silver-plated bronze relief depicts Richard Härtel, founder of the Verband der Deutschen Buchdrucker (Union of German Book Printers). The portrait mask was made in 1926 when the workers' association opened its headquarters in Berlin-Kreuzberg. Max Taut designed the building in the New Objectivity style. It still exists in Dudenstraße 10. Rudolf Belling was commissioned to create a wall relief, a drinking fountain and the portrait. The latter is the only work not destroyed under the National Socialists, having survived because it was hidden in a wall. The plea Härtel made at the founding of the Union of German Book Printers in 1866 can be read under the portrait (in German): "Let's not pass any more pointless resolutions: Only practical work leads to an assured goal."

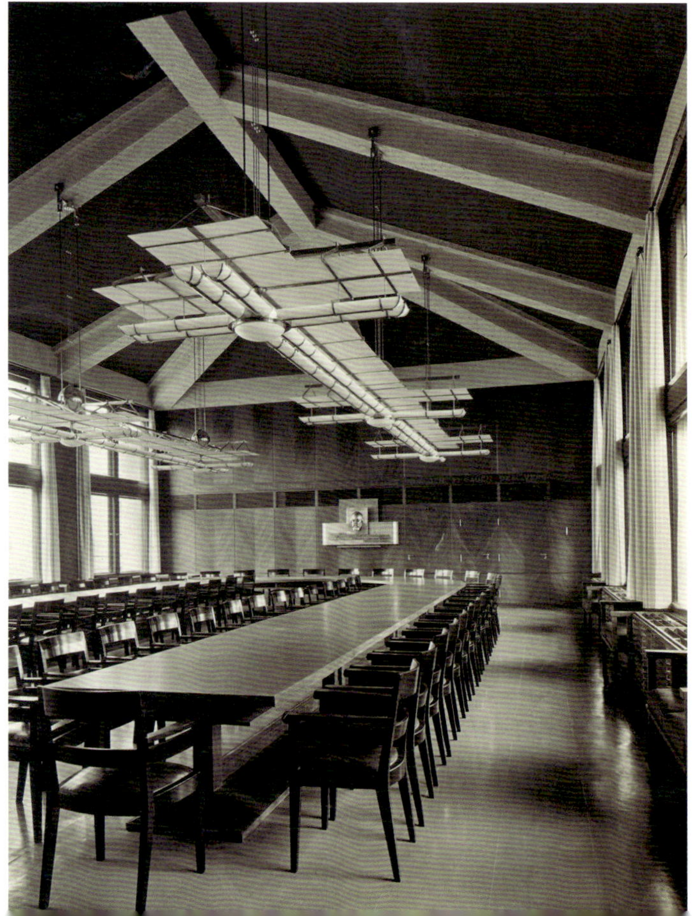

↑ *Portrait of Richard Härtel* in the meeting room of the Buchdruckerhaus, Berlin-Kreuzberg, 1926
→ Max Taut and Franz Hoffmann, Meeting room in the Verbandshaus der Buchdrucker, Berlin-Kreuzberg, 1926, with Rudolf Belling's *Portrait of Richard Härtel* on the wall
↗ Rudolf Belling, *Portrait of Richard Härtel*, 1926 silver-plated, 62 × 51 × 22 cm. Loan from the Karl-Richter-Verein, Berlin, since 2017

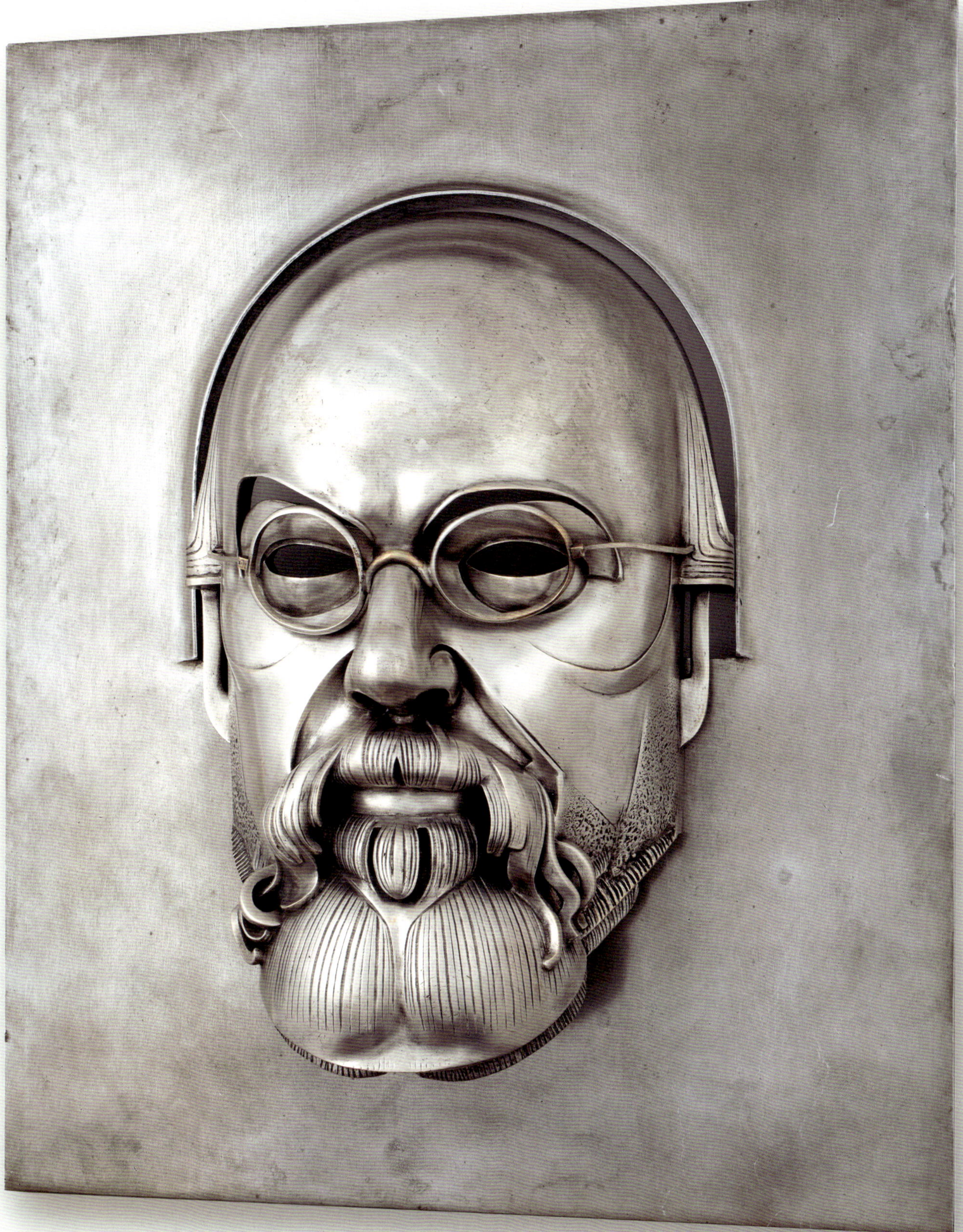

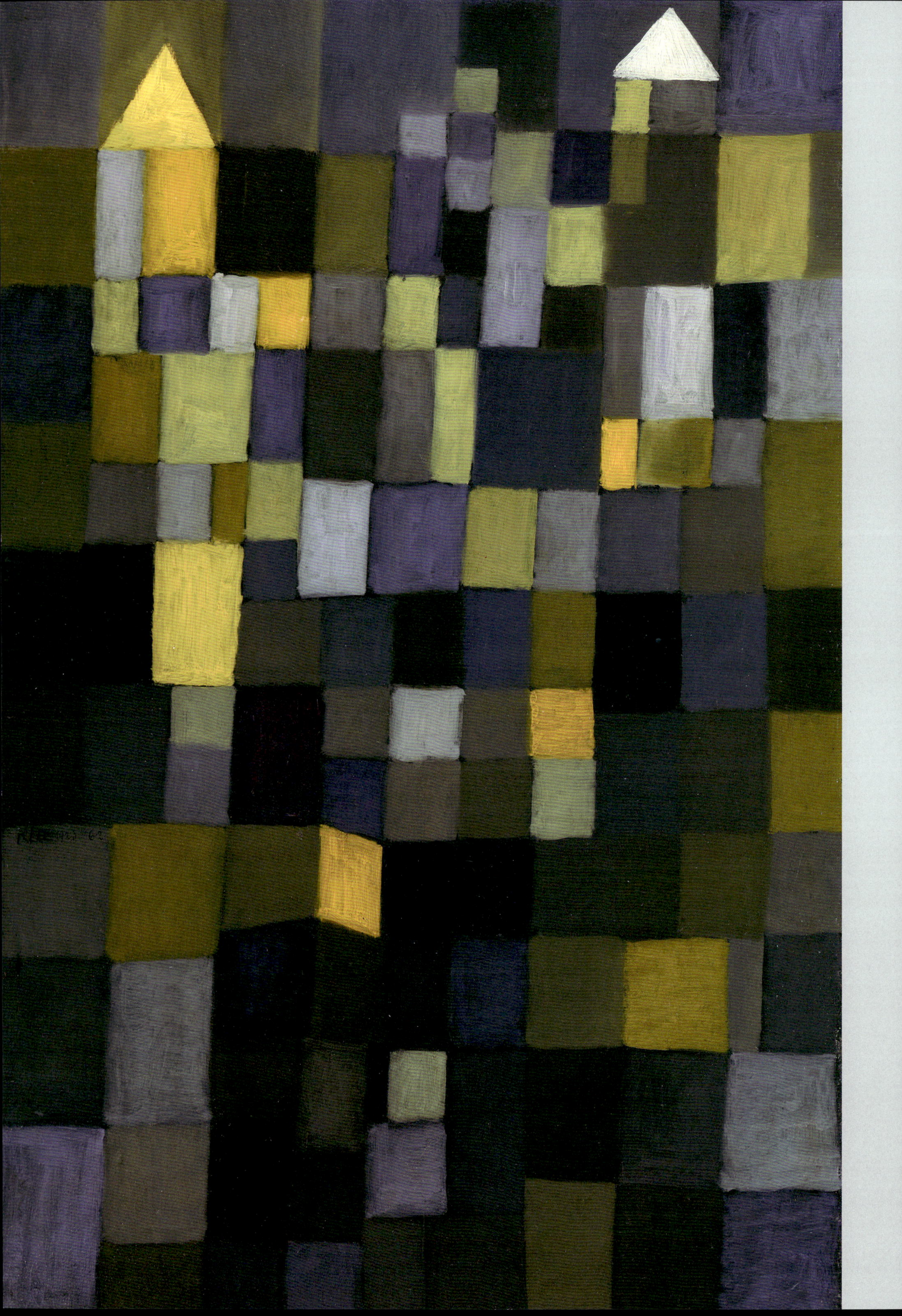

Modes of Abstraction

Abstraction is considered Classical Modernism's greatest achievement in the visual arts. At its most fundamental level, to "abstract" means to disregard the tangible, representational or concrete form and focus on the essence. The process only becomes truly radical when the object disappears entirely, and colour and form are applied completely independent from it. Only then can we speak of "non-representational art" as one of the variations of abstraction.

Western art history traces a series of increasingly daring experiments that led to the emergence of abstraction. It was connected to a social vision of modernism that reached far beyond the realm of visual art. Abstract art was understood as an entirely new language that appeared to be universal. Nevertheless, abstraction can be found much earlier in non-Western cultures and decorative ornamentation. The Bauhaus was one of the most significant laboratories for abstraction, where fine and applied arts were considered equal and taught side by side. Like Wassily Kandinsky, Paul Klee was a "master" instructor at the Bauhaus. His interpretation of abstract art retained certain representational echoes, and in 1915 he referred to himself as being "abstract with memories".

Paul Klee, *Architecture*, 1923
Oil on hardboard, 58 × 39 cm
Acquired in 1968 from the Galerie Renée Ziegler, Zürich/Zollikon, for the Nationalgalerie, Berlin (West)

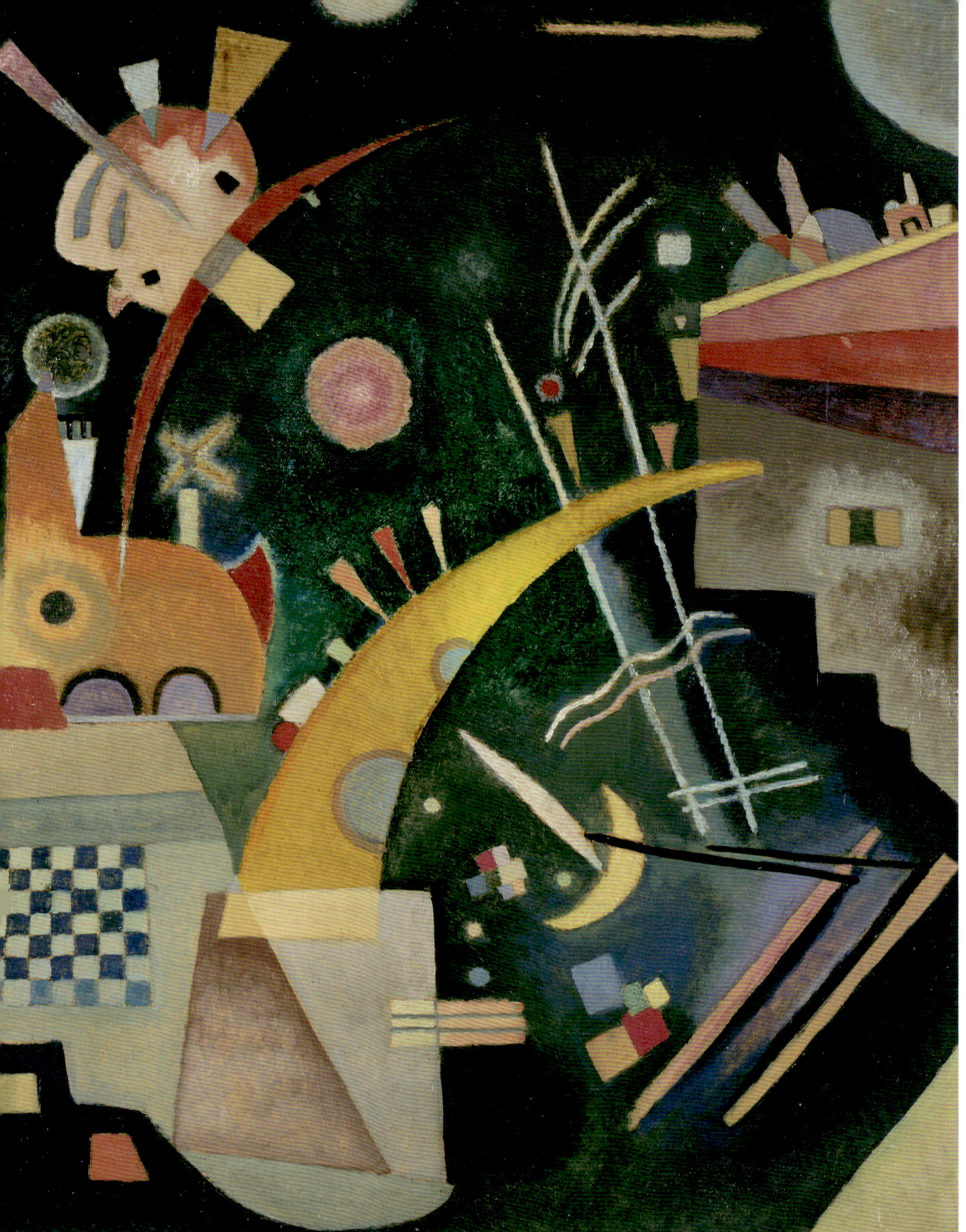

↑ Wassily Kandinsky, *Hornform*, 1924
Oil on cardboard, 57.5 × 49.5 cm
Acquired in 1953 by the Land Berlin for the Galerie des 20. Jahrhunderts, Berlin (West)

↗ Paul Klee, *Palace in Passing*, 1928
Oil on nettle on cardboard, 30.4 × 45.2 cm
Acquired in 2000 from Heinz Berggruen with funds from the Bundesregierung and the Land Berlin

→ Paul Klee, *Ships Departing*, 1927
Oil and ink on canvas, 50.2 × 64.4 cm
Acquired in 1967 from the Galerie Michael Hertz, Bremen, for the Nationalgalerie, Berlin (West)

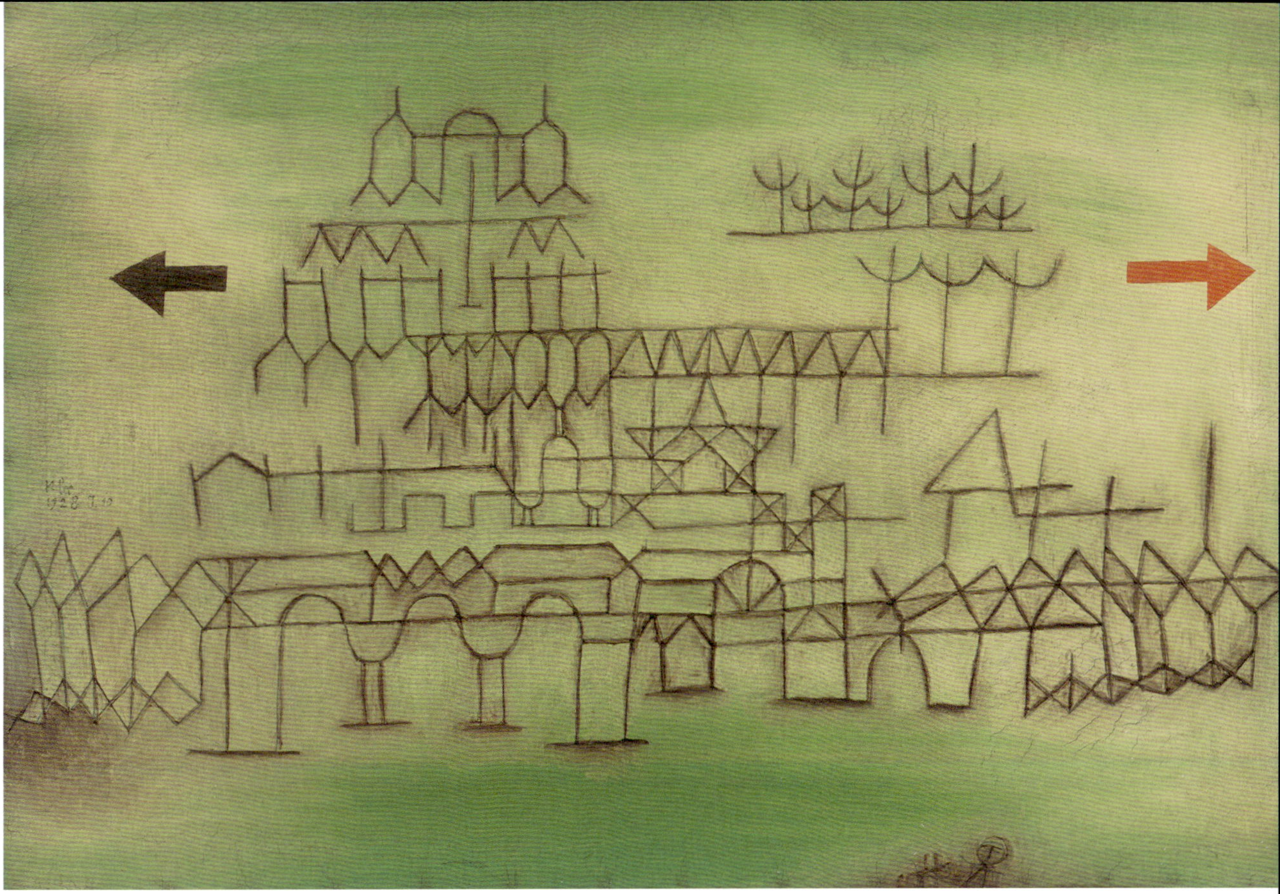

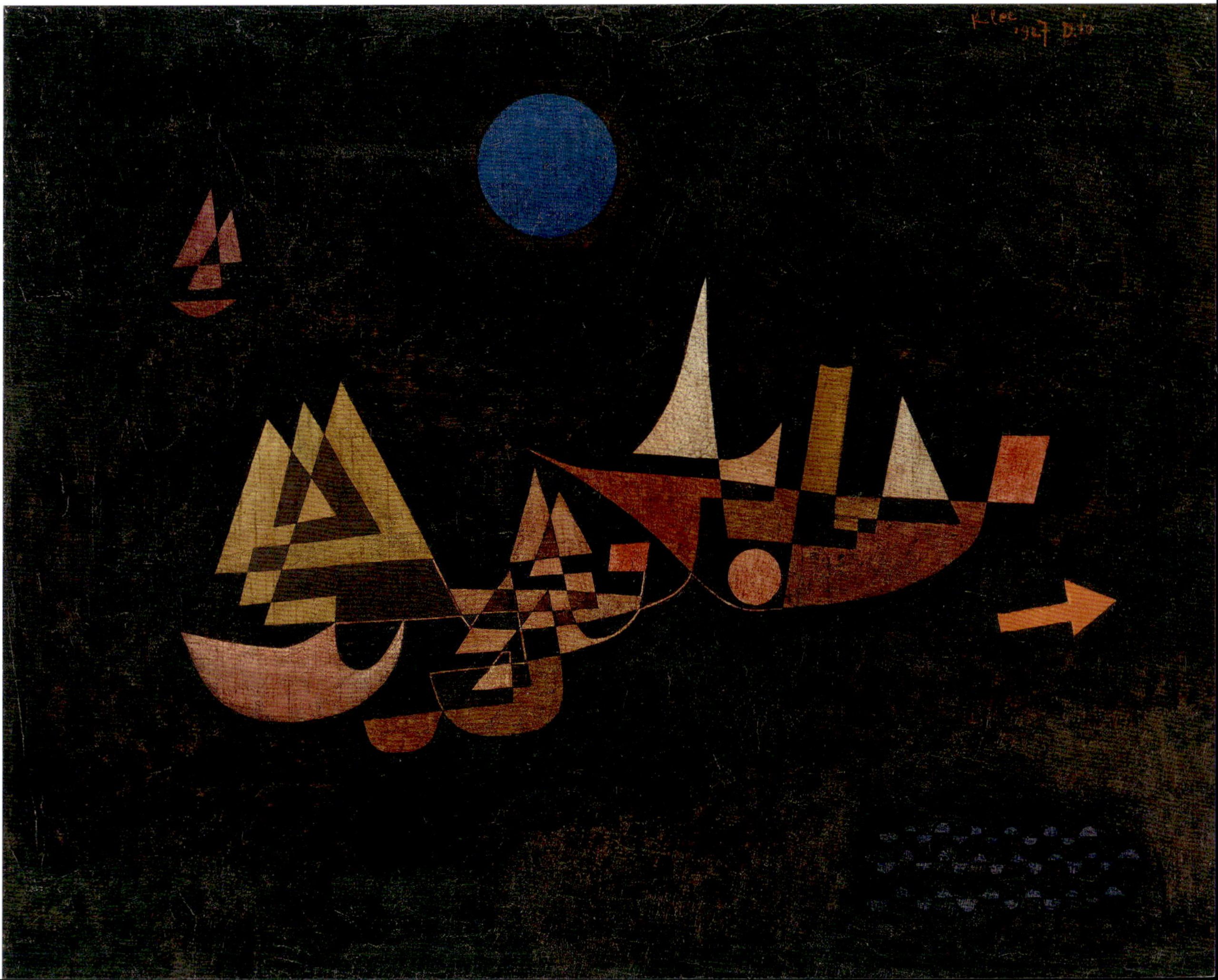

Creativity and Child's Play at the Bauhaus

Although the Bauhaus was to become European Modernism's most prominent centre for experimentation and abstraction, at its founding in 1919 the public art academy was actually named after medieval masons' guilds and their lodges. To underscore this, the manifesto of founding director Walter Gropius and the school's syllabus each bore the motif of a gothic cathedral. Gropius wanted to connect art with craft and see "architects, sculptors, painters [...] erect the new building of the future together". Nothing less than a new society was at stake after the end of the First World War. The painter Oskar Schlemmer, who designed the Bauhaus signet in 1922, spoke of a "cathedral of socialism". Wassily Kandinsky referenced Schlemmer's striking and jagged vertical profile in his 1924 painting *Hornform*.

The painting is a playful commentary on the Musterhaus Am Horn, a model house created by Georg Muche for the first Bauhaus exhibition in Weimar in 1923. Various Bauhaus workshops were involved in furnishing the house: the carpentry, weaving, sculpture and painting workshops, as well as the metal and ceramics workshops. Gropius coined a new motto at its opening: "Art and technology – a new unity." The Bauhaus focus was no longer just about craftsmanship, it now included developing prototypes for industrial production. The objective was to create functional, elegantly designed yet inexpensive objects that enriched and simplified daily life.

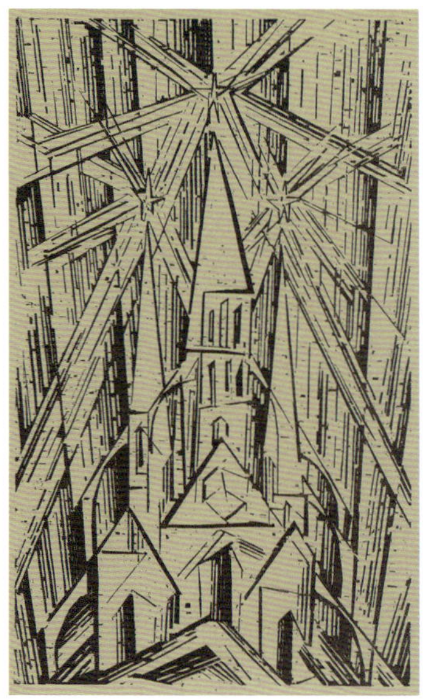

→ Lyonel Feininger, Cover woodcut for the programme of the State Bauhaus in Weimar, 1919
↗ Alma Siedhoff-Buscher, Ship-building Game, 1923
→ Oskar Schlemmer, Bauhaus signet, 1922

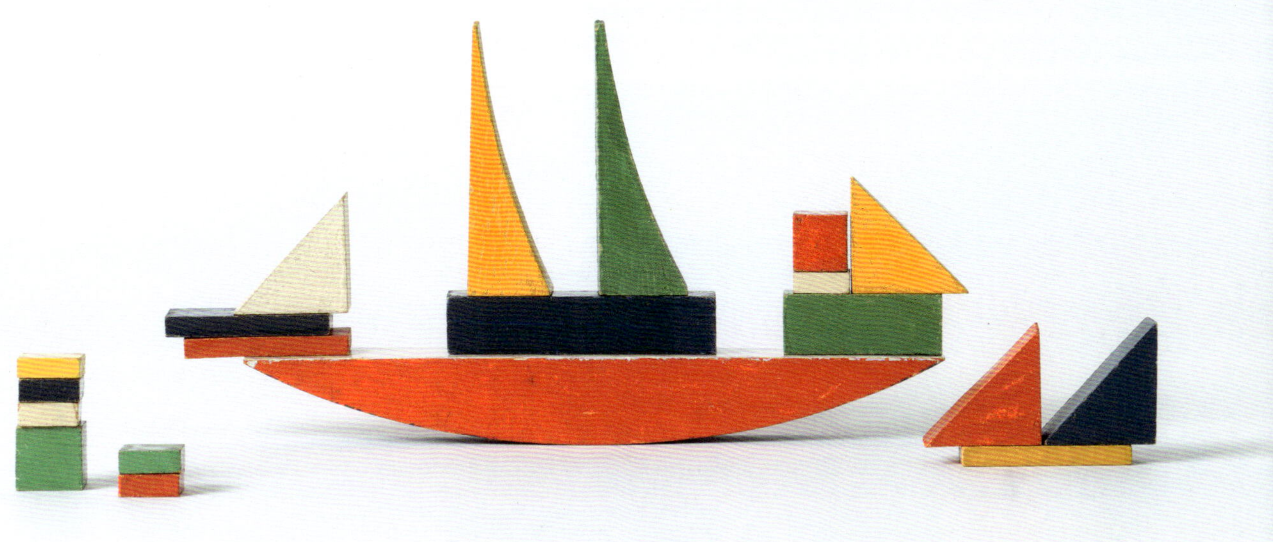

Thus the Haus Am Horn included a nursery for which Alma Buscher had made designs such as the *Bauspiel: Ein Schiff*. The building block game consists of wooden blocks in the primary colours red, yellow and blue, as well as green and white. They can be combined to form a rocking sailboat, among other objects. The toy's design – of modular components – is in keeping with the new pedagogical concepts that inspired it.

Both creativity and child's play are born from experimentation, from trying things out in order to discover new forms. This is true of architecture and the design of utilitarian objects, and also of painting, a field as male-dominated at the Bauhaus as elsewhere at the time. Lyonel Feininger, Wassily Kandinsky, Paul Klee, László Moholy-Nagy, Georg Muche and Oskar Schlemmer taught at the Bauhaus as "masters", a term Gropius had adopted from medieval mason's guilds. Each of these artists stood for a different type of abstraction.

Their experiments with abstraction often still hint at objects, as can be seen in Kandinsky's *Hornform*. The large yellow horn refers to the musical instrument; below that, the small yellow sickle with a taut sail surrounded by colourful squares makes reference to a female Bauhaus student's influential work. Just like the chessboard at the painting's lower left edge, it is a highly successful Bauhaus product that continues to be serially produced to this day: Alma Buscher's building block sailboat.

Dieter Scholz

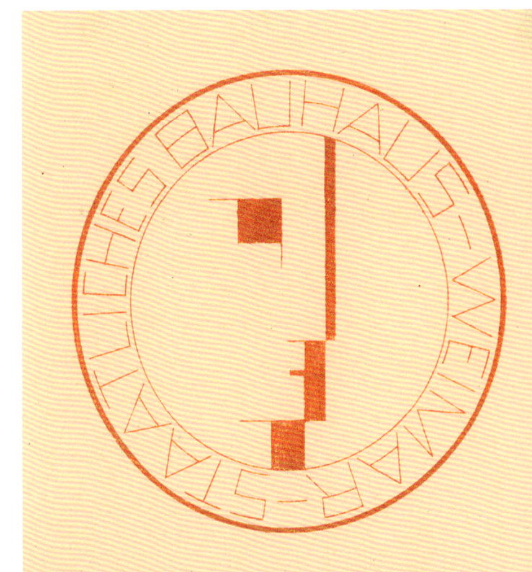

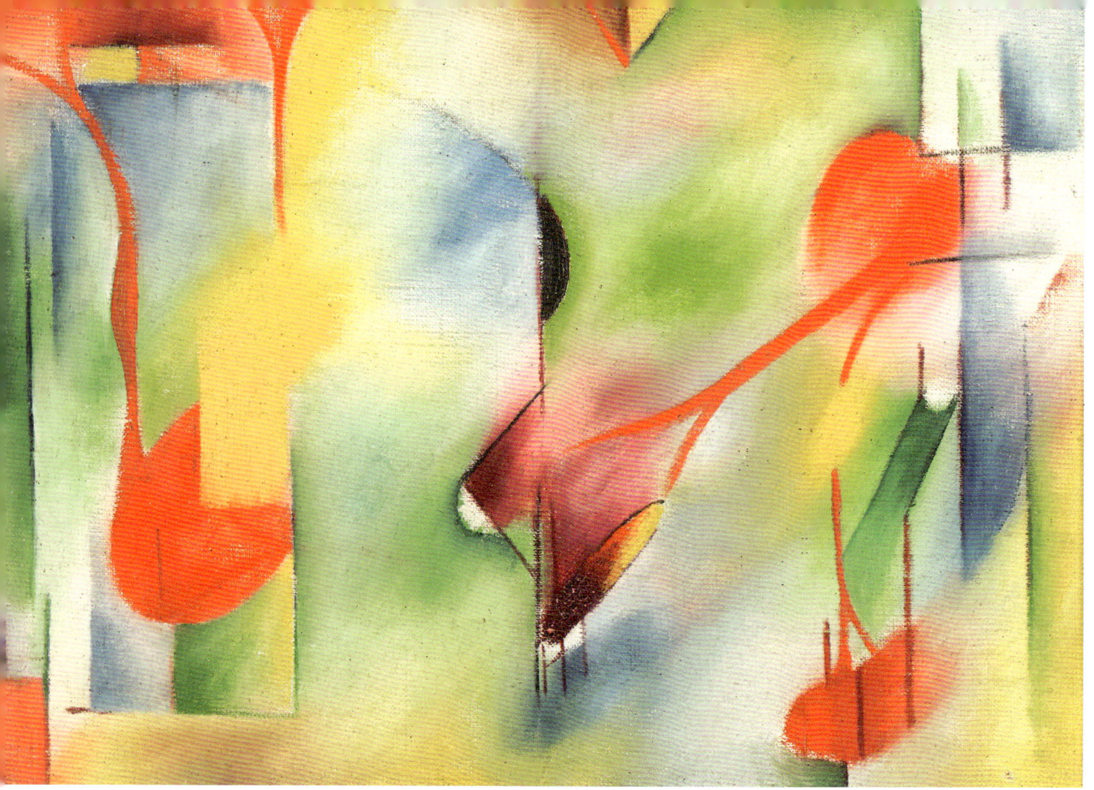

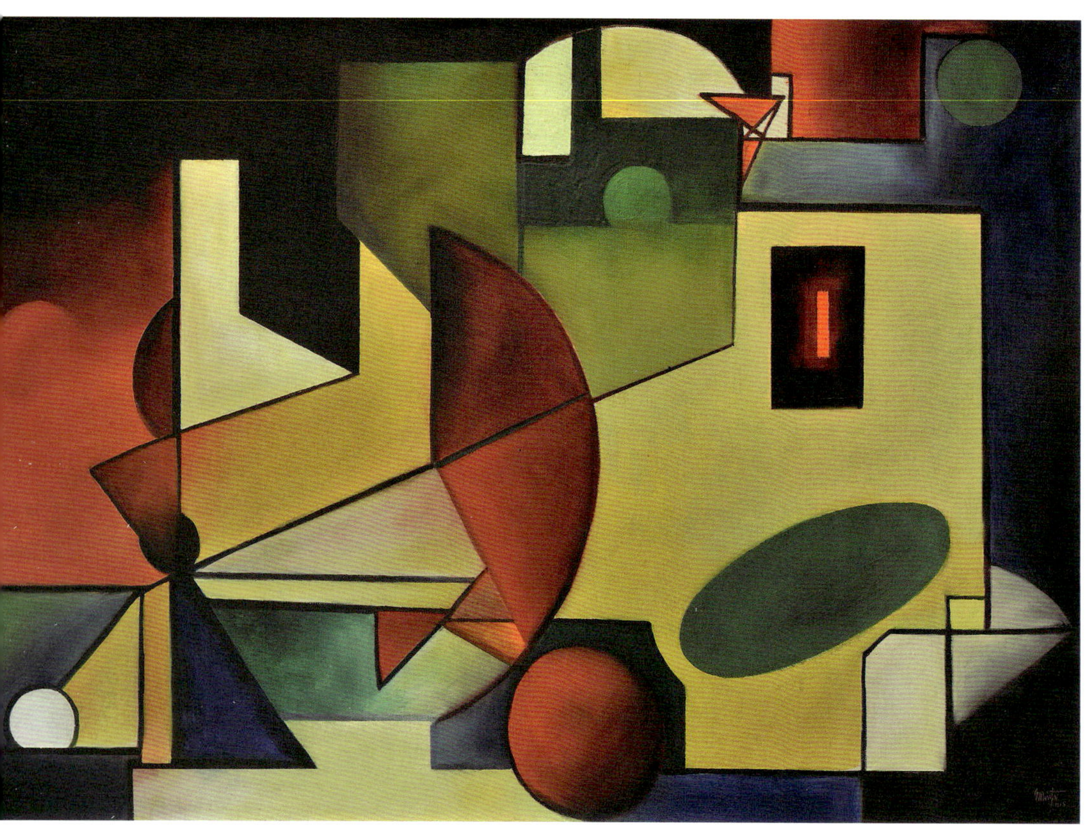

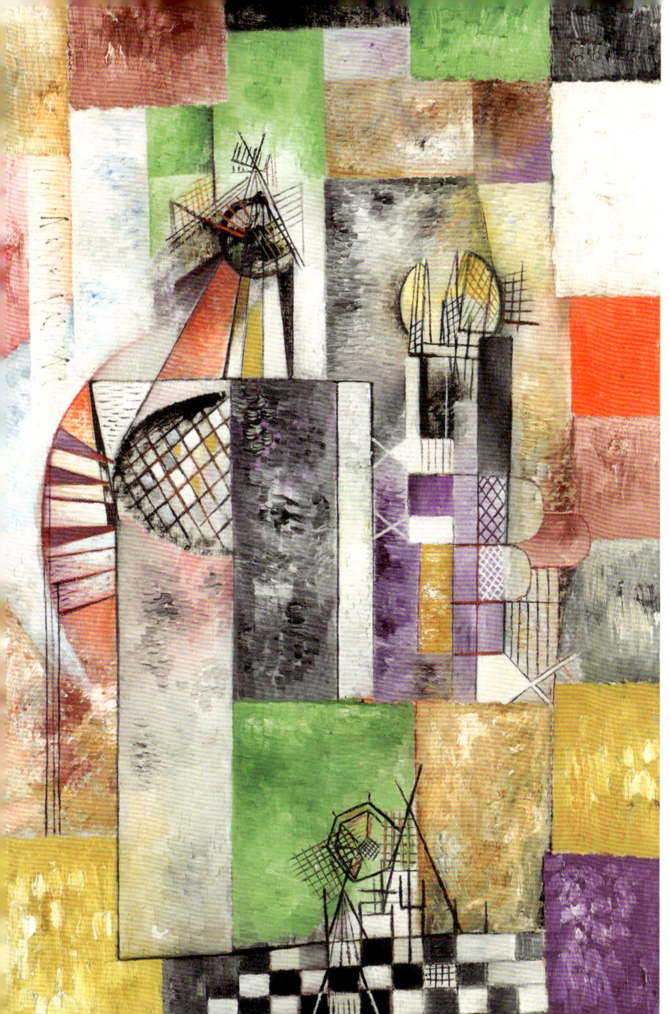

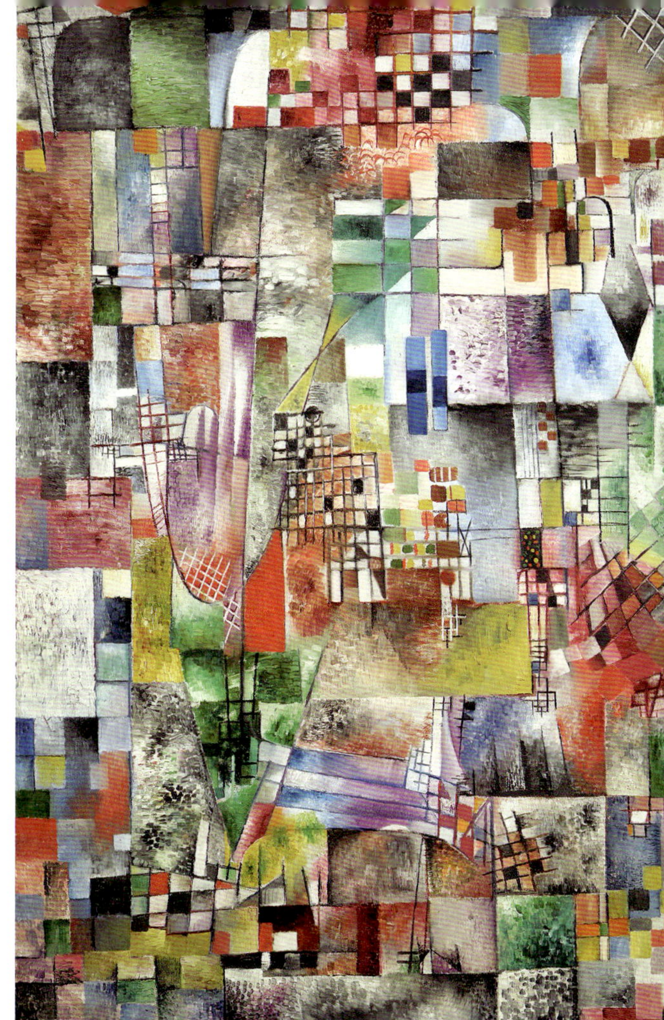

↖ Georg Muche, *Summer*, 1916
Oil on canvas, 44 × 63 cm
Acquired in 1951 from Werner Kampmann, Berlin, by the Land Berlin for the Galerie des 20. Jahrhunderts, Berlin (West)

← Georg Muche, *Painting XVIII. Dedicated to Nell Walden*, 1915
Oil on canvas, 69 × 100 cm
Gift from the artist to the Nationalgalerie, Berlin (East), 1973

↑ Georg Muche, *Triad*, 1919–20
Oil on canvas, 75 × 53 cm
Acquired in 1965 from the estate Dr Fritz Salo Glaser, Dresden, for the Nationalgalerie, Berlin (East)

↗ Georg Muche, *Picture with the Grid Motif in the Middle*, 1919
Oil on canvas, 138.5 × 95 cm
Gift from the Heinrich Evert Collection, Berlin, for the Galerie des 20. Jahrhunderts, Berlin (West), 1966

→ Georg Muche, *The Small Picture with the Grid Motif*, 1917
Oil on canvas on cardboard, 61 × 68.5 cm
Gift from the artist to the Nationalgalerie, Berlin (East), 1973

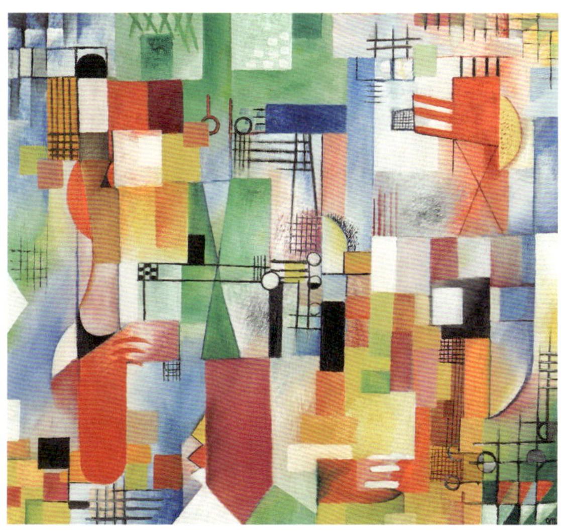

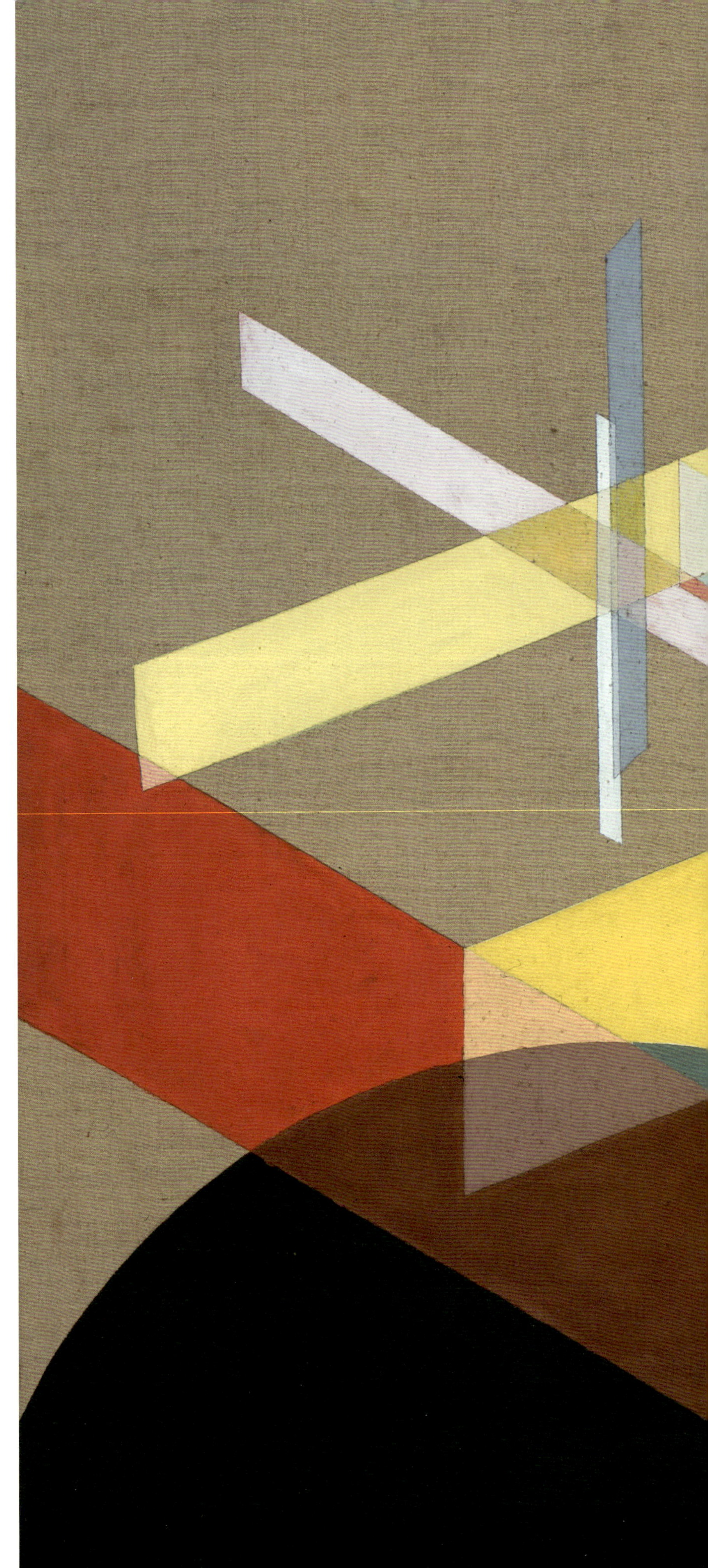

Lázló Moholy-Nagy, *Z VIII*, 1924
Distemper on canvas, 114 × 132 cm
Acquired in 1959 for the
Nationalgalerie, Berlin (West)

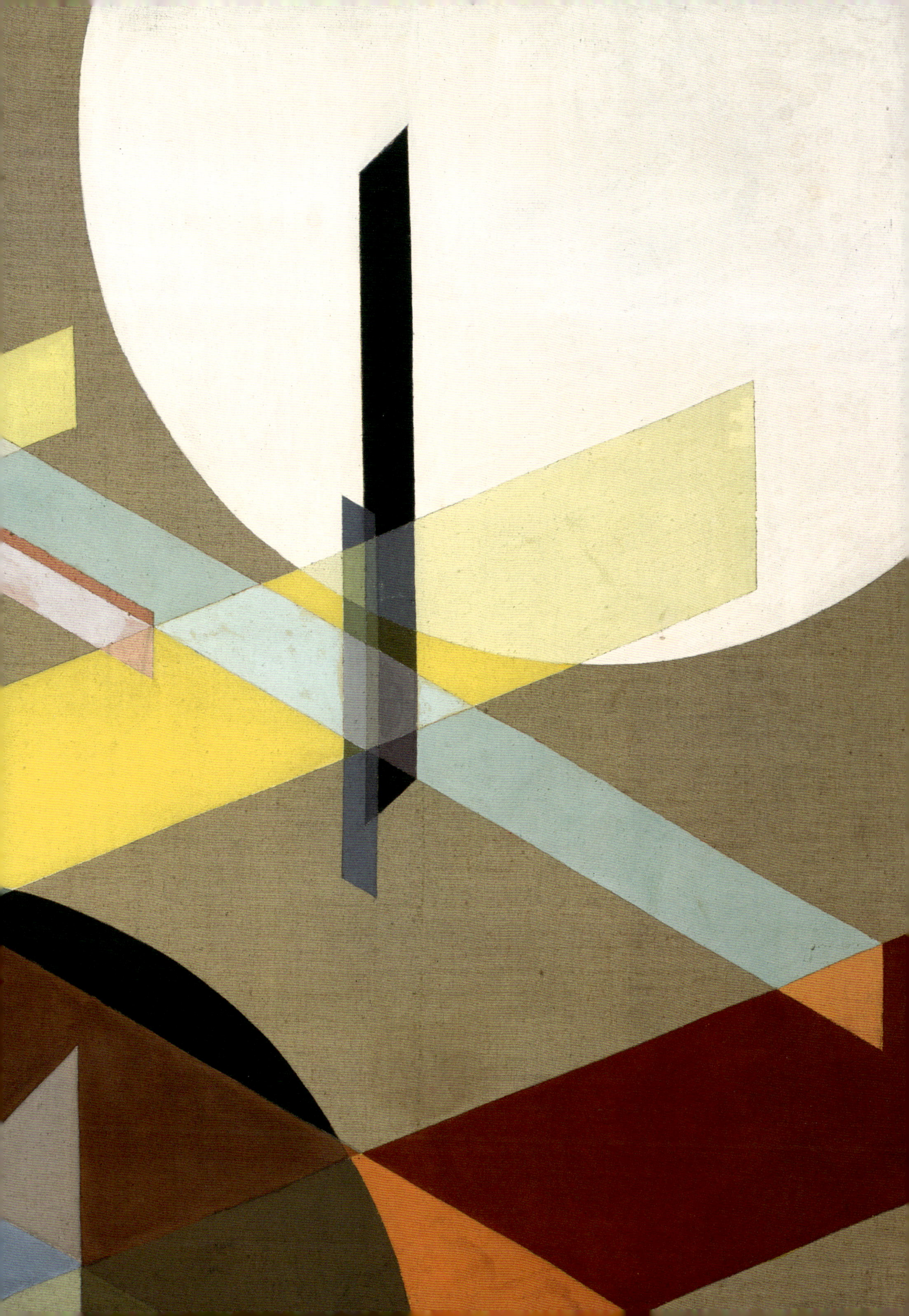

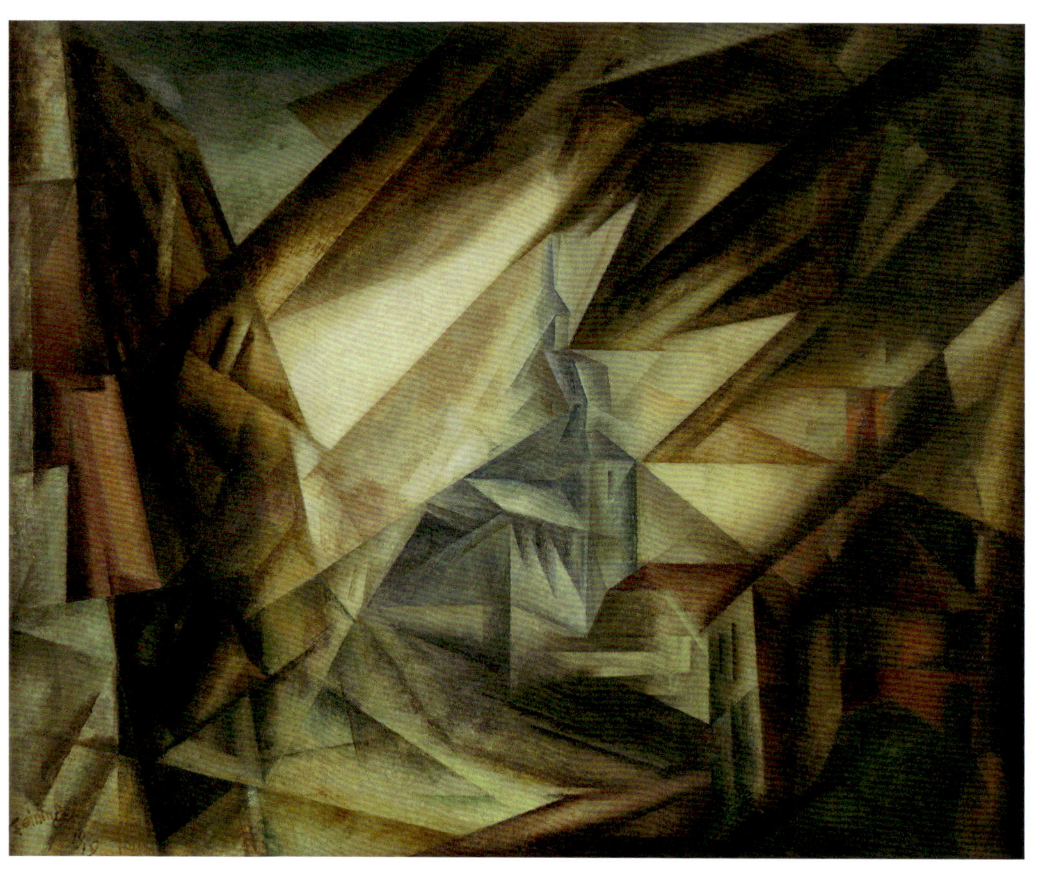

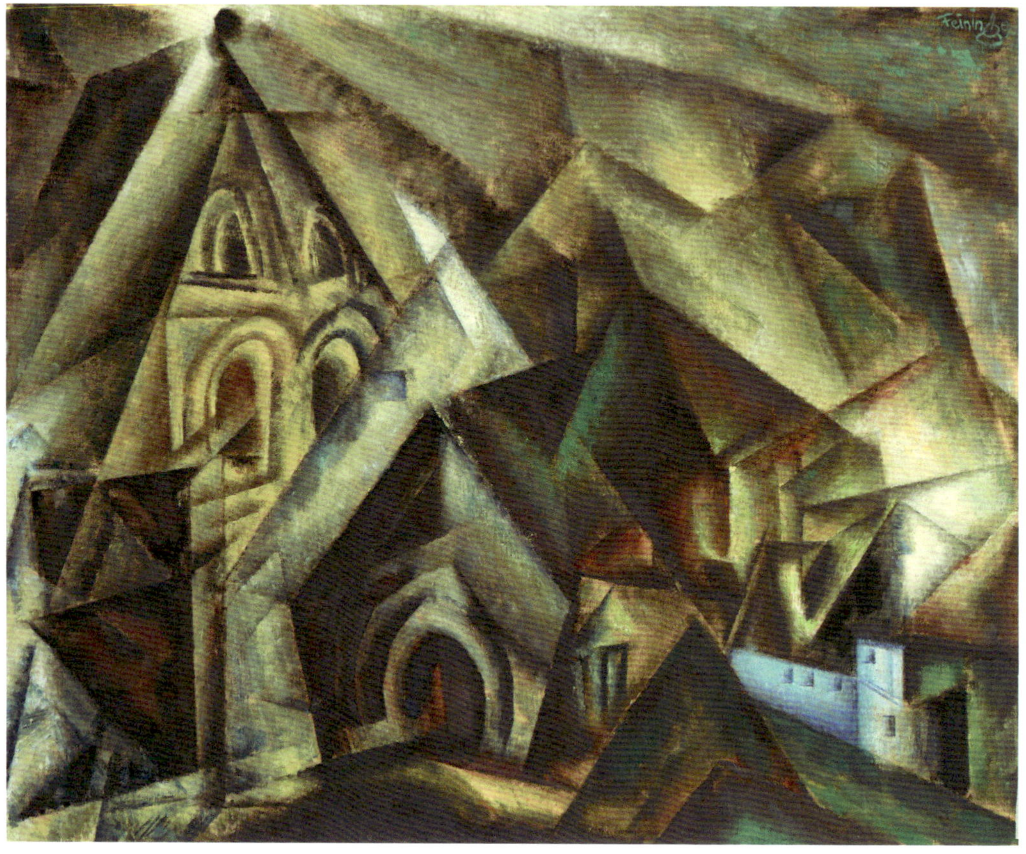

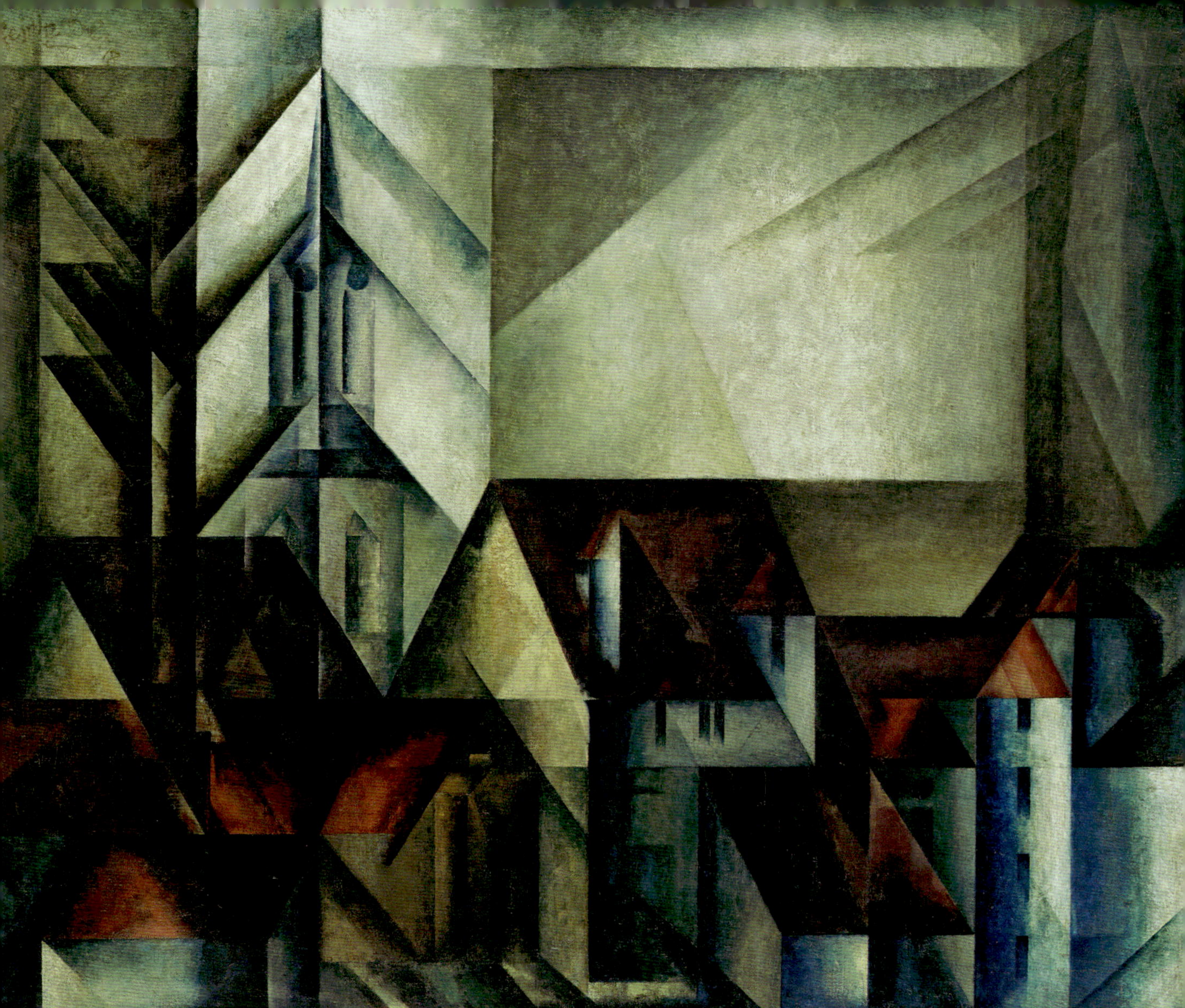

↑ Lyonel Feininger, *Teltow II*, 1918
Oil on canvas, 101 × 126 cm
Acquired in 1921 from the artist in exchange for *Vollersroda III*; confiscated as "degenerate" in 1937; seized after 1945 on the premises of the art dealer Bernhard A. Böhmer and given to the Nationalgalerie, Berlin (East) in 1949

↖ Lyonel Feininger, *Church of Niedergrunstedt*, 1919
Oil on canvas, 101 × 125 cm
Acquired in 1949 from the Galerie Franz, Berlin, by the Land Berlin for the Galerie des 20. Jahrhunderts, Berlin (West)

← Lyonel Feininger, *Eichelborn*, 1920
Oil on canvas, 80 × 103 cm
Acquired in 1964 from the Paul Drey Gallery, New York for the Nationalgalerie, Berlin (West)

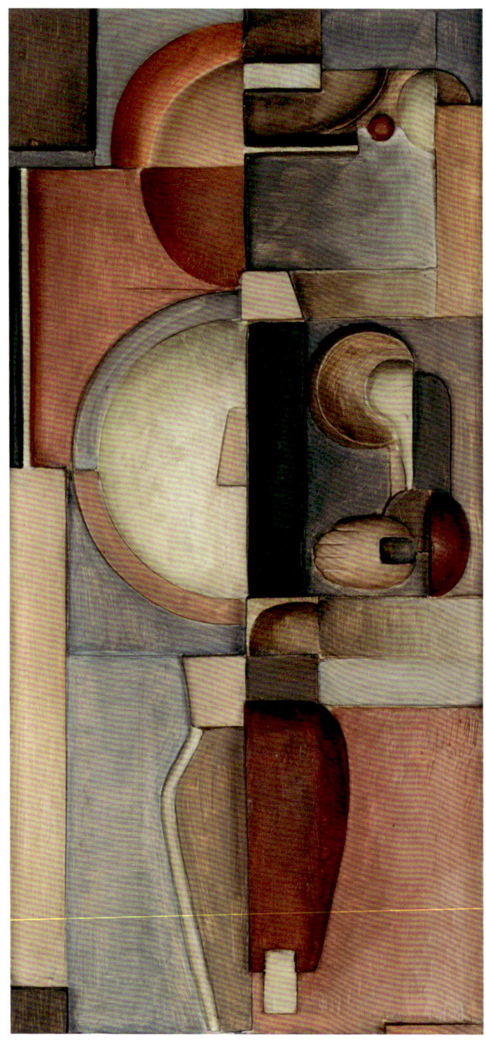

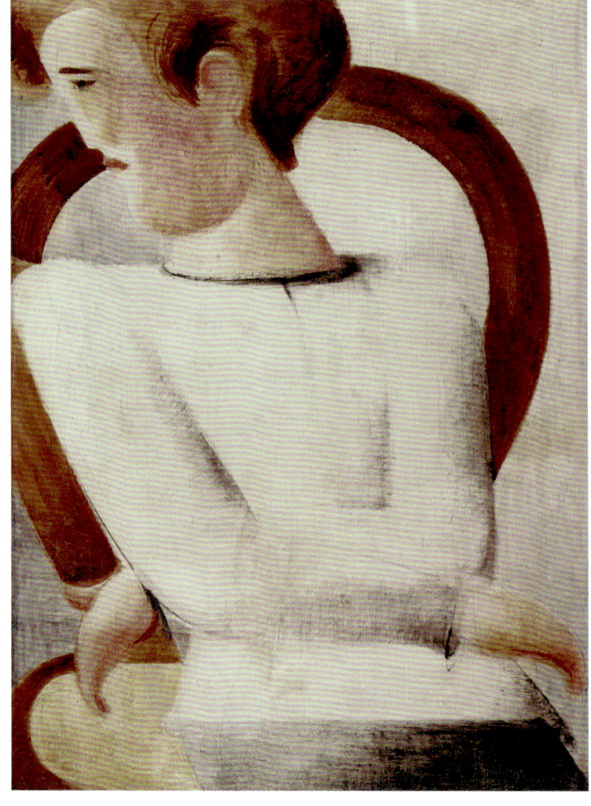

↑ Oskar Schlemmer, *Relief JG I*, 1919–21
Oil on plaster, 67.5 × 33 cm
Acquired in 1960 for the Nationalgalerie, Berlin (East)

→ Oskar Schlemmer, *White Youth*, 1930
Oil on canvas, 60 × 45.5 cm
Owned by the city of Breslau (now Wrocław) in 1932; confiscated by the Reichskammer der bildenden Künste in 1937, brought to Güstrow by Bernhard A. Böhmer; transferred to Rostock in 1945, to Berlin (East) in 1949; gift from the Magistrat von Groß-Berlin to the Nationalgalerie, Berlin (East) in 1951

↗ Oskar Schlemmer, *Grotesque I*, 1923
Walnut, ivory and metal, 55 × 26.5 × 10 cm
Acquired in 1957 from the Galerie Meta Nierendorf, Berlin, for the Nationalgalerie, Berlin (West)

↗ Oskar Schlemmer, *Nude, Woman and Approaching Figure*, 1925, oil on canvas, 128 × 64.2 cm
Acquired in 1956 from the Richard Merz Collection, Stuttgart, by the Land Berlin for the Galerie des 20. Jahrhunderts, Berlin (West)

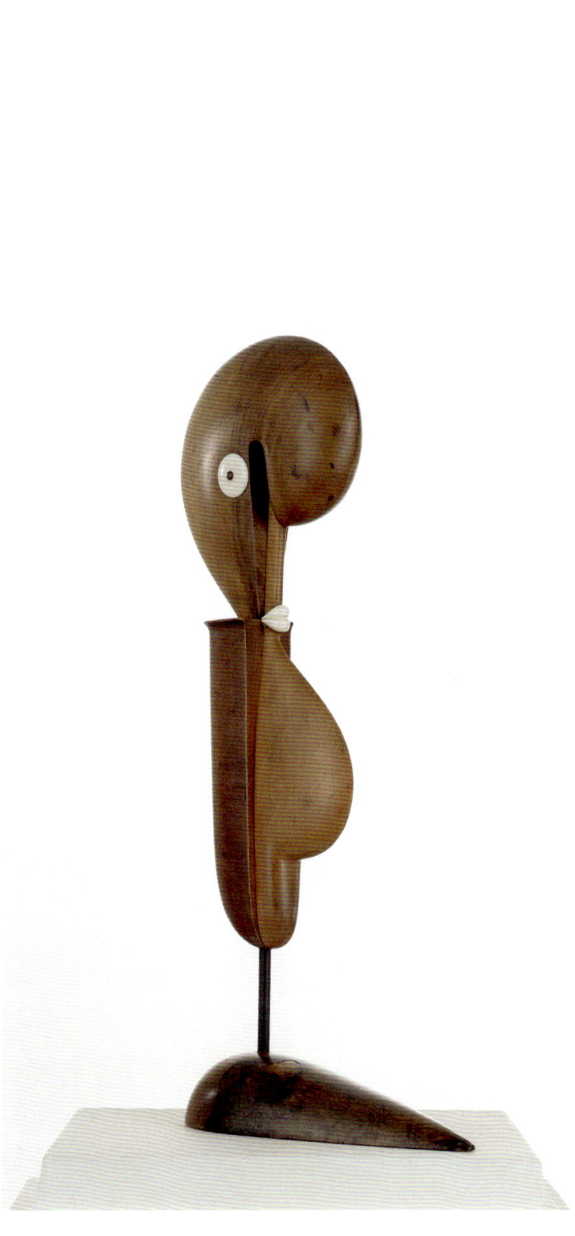

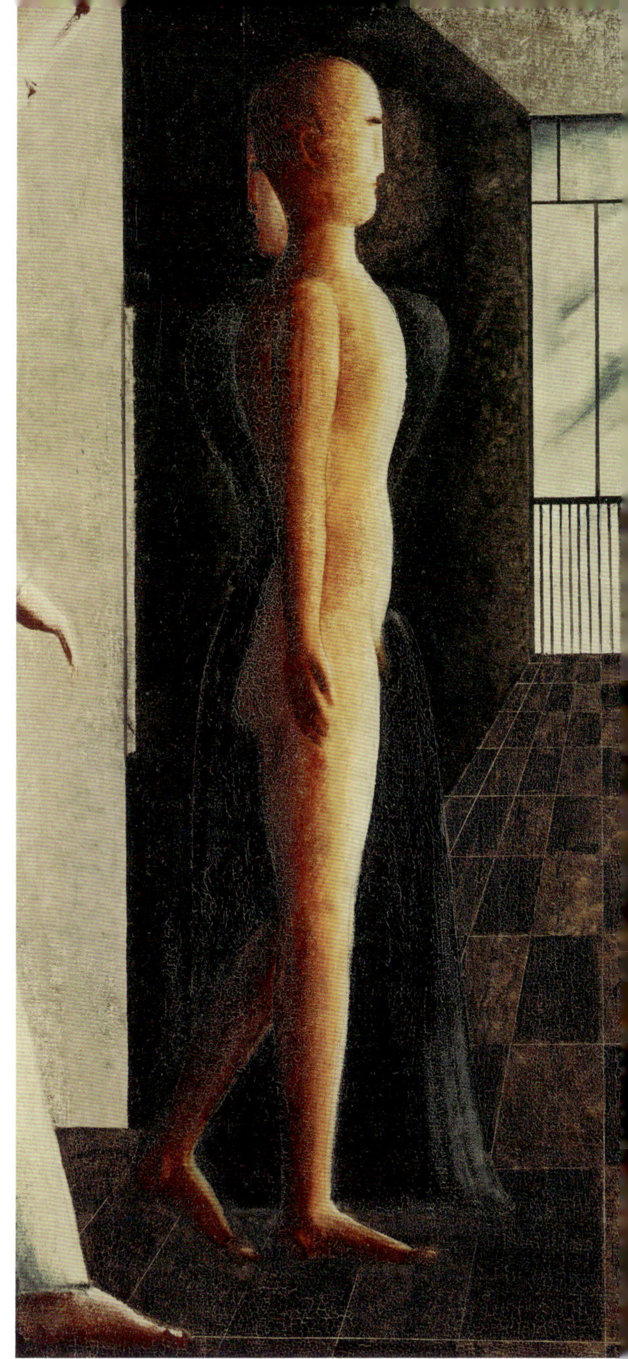

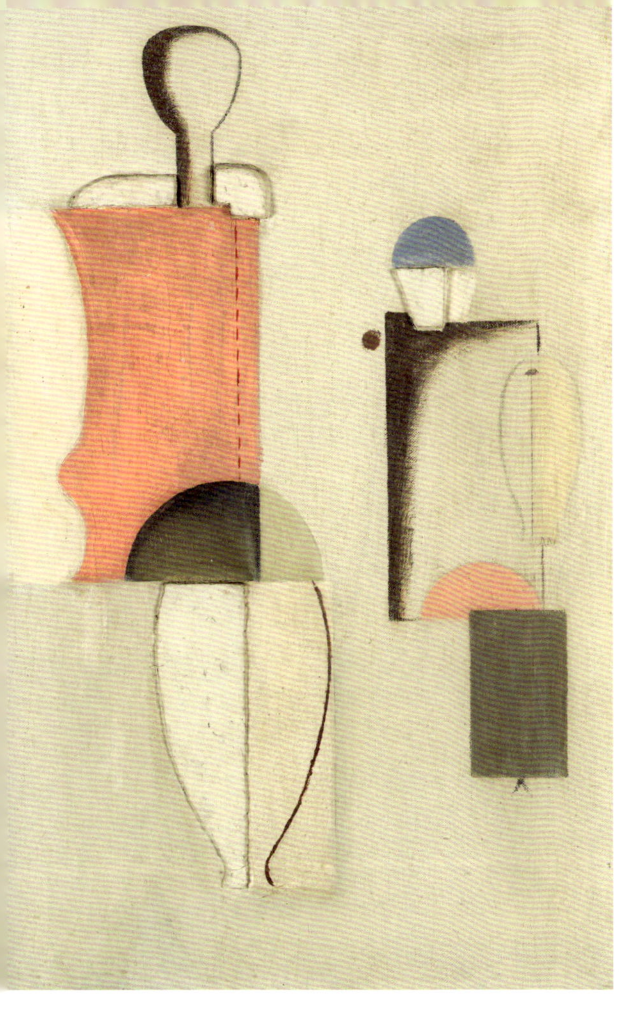

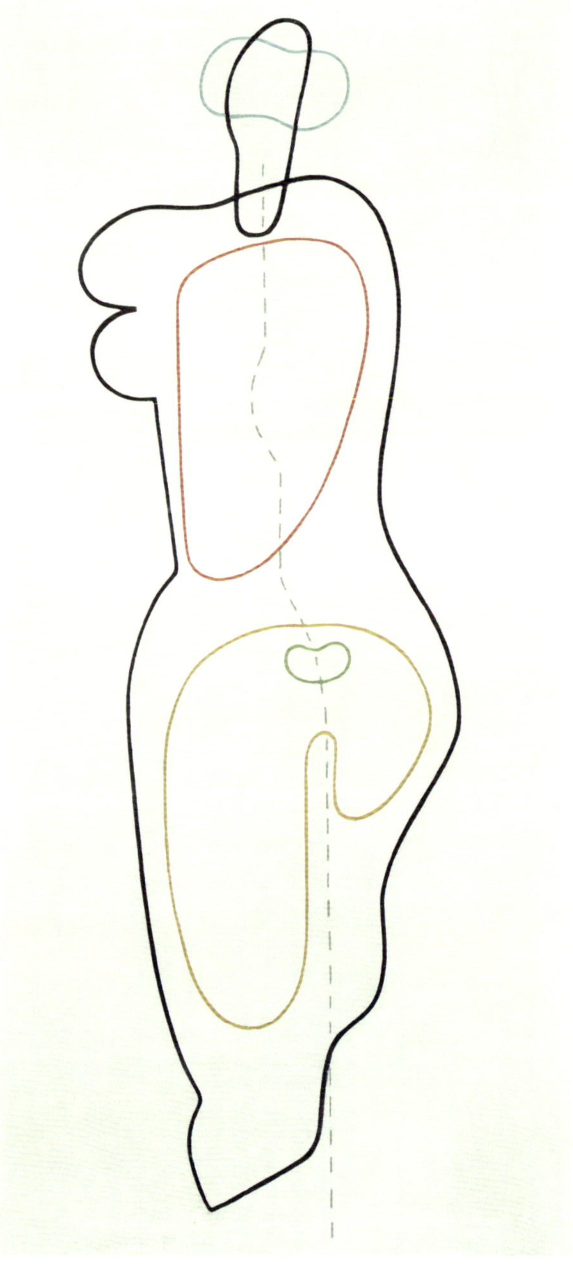

↑ Willi Baumeister, *Two Figures with Blue and Pink. Wall Painting*, 1920
Oil, pencil, plaster and papier mâché on canvas, 60.3 × 39.5 cm
Gift to the Galerie des 20. Jahrhunderts, Berlin (West), 1951

→ Willi Baumeister, *Woman*, 1930
Oil on canvas, 120 × 58 cm
Acquired in 1951 from the Galerie Gerd Rosen, Berlin, by the Land Berlin for the Galerie des 20. Jahrhunderts, Berlin (West)

↗ Willi Baumeister, *Three Staggered Figures with Black*, 1920
Oil and papier mâché on canvas, 57.5 × 45 cm
Acquired in 1968 for the Nationalgalerie, Berlin (East)

→ Willi Baumeister, *Figure with Stripes*, 1920
Oil, plaster, papier mâché and filler on canvas, 72.5 × 52.5 cm
Acquired in 1966 for the Nationalgalerie, Berlin (East)

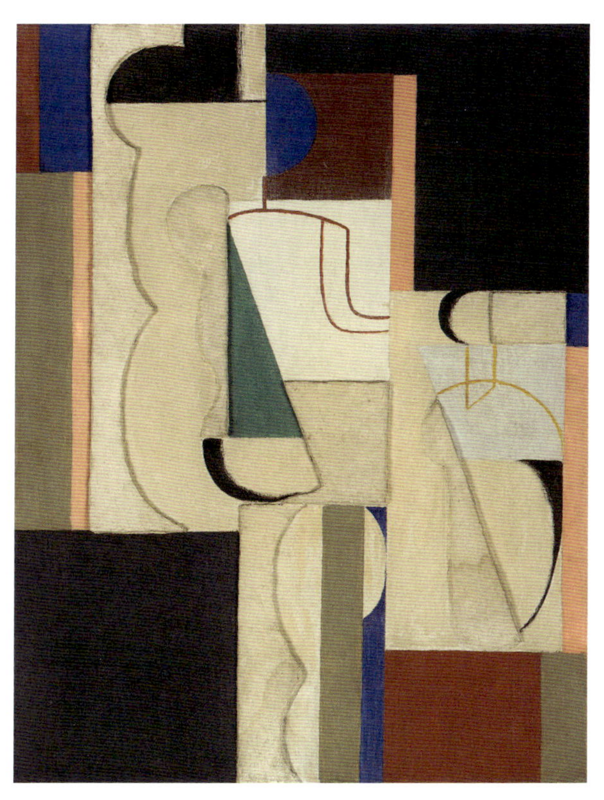

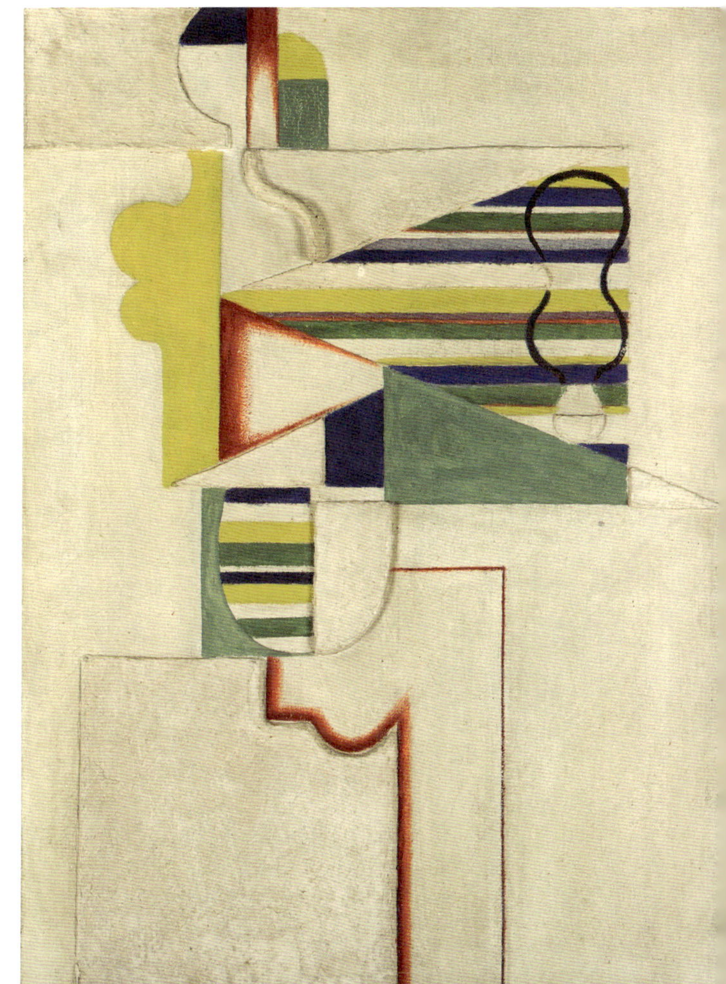

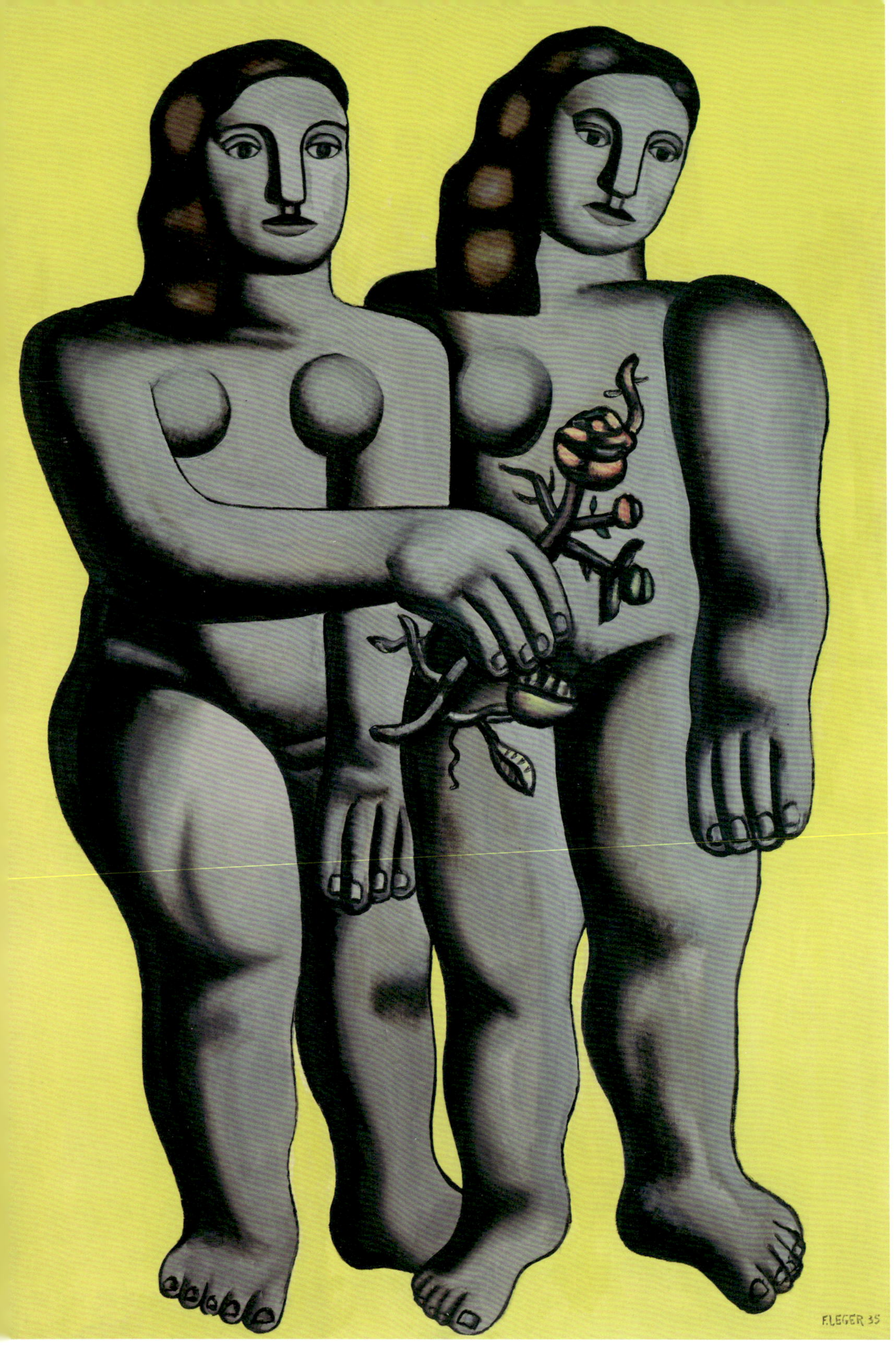
F.LEGER 35

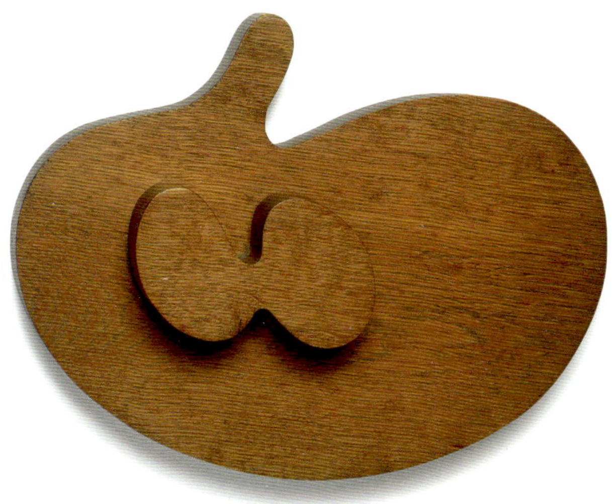

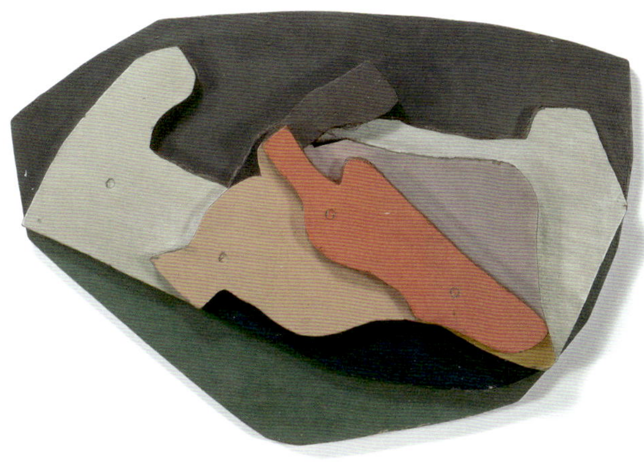

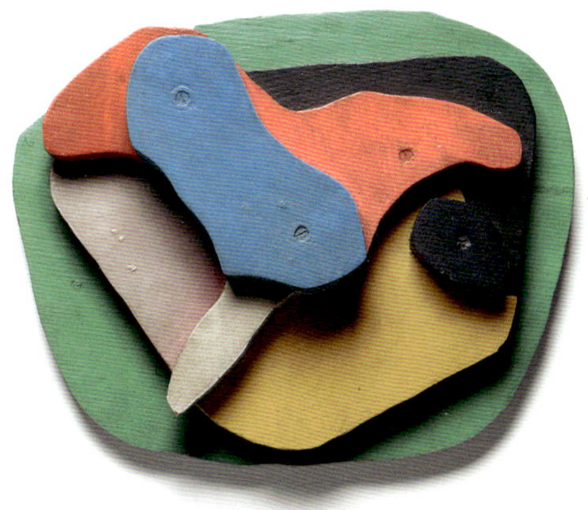

↗ Hans Arp, *Constellation (Shell Head and Tie)*, 1928
Wood, 25.1 × 33.9 × 6 cm
Gift from the Ulla and Heiner Pietzsch Collection to the Land Berlin, 2010

↑ Hans Arp, *Concrete Relief*, 1916–17
Wood, 41.2 × 60.6 × 12 cm
Acquired in 1979 from the estate of Hannah Höch, Berlin, by the Freunde der Nationalgalerie for the Nationalgalerie, Berlin (West)

→ Hans Arp, *Concrete Relief*, 1916/1923
Wood, 21.4 × 27.7 × 7 cm
Acquired in 1979 from the estate of Hannah Höch, Berlin, by the Freunde der Nationalgalerie for the Nationalgalerie, Berlin (West)

← Fernand Léger, *Two Sisters*, 1935
Oil on canvas, 162 × 114 cm
Acquired in 1979 for the Nationalgalerie, Berlin (West)

Envoy of the Metaphysical: Hilma af Klint

Many paths lead to abstraction. One of them is rooted in the mystical-philosophical discipline of theosophy and involves the belief that thoughts take specific shapes; that there is something called *Gedankenformen* (Thought Forms). The painter Hilma af Klint's pursuit of these phenomena beyond the physical realm took on a highly unique form.

Born the daughter of a Swedish naval officer in 1862, af Klint studied at the Royal Swedish Academy of Fine Art in Stockholm and subsequently worked as a portrait and landscape painter in the naturalist style. At the same time, she began participating in spiritist séances. In 1896 she and four female friends formed the circle De Fem (The Five) with the intent of establishing contact with higher entities. The members of De Fem understood themselves as passive vehicles whose drawing pencils were not guided by their own hands. In this capacity as an envoy of the metaphysical, Hilma af Klint generated hundreds of automatic drawings before entering into the service of a spirit being named Amaliel to paint *Die Gemälde zum Tempel* (Paintings for the Temple).

She produced 111 of these paintings from 1906 to 1908, including her expressive-abstract depictions of the *Urchaos* (Primordial Chaos). The series was completed with another 82 paintings between 1912 and 1915, including the geometric-abstract *Altarbilder* (Altarpieces). Afterwards, she painted eight more series of smaller geometric works, the last of which was finished in March 1920. The *Utgångsbild* (Source Image) for this final series reflects on the relationship between the external and the internal, and the struggle to reach the essence of one's own being. The colours blue and yellow represent the duality of

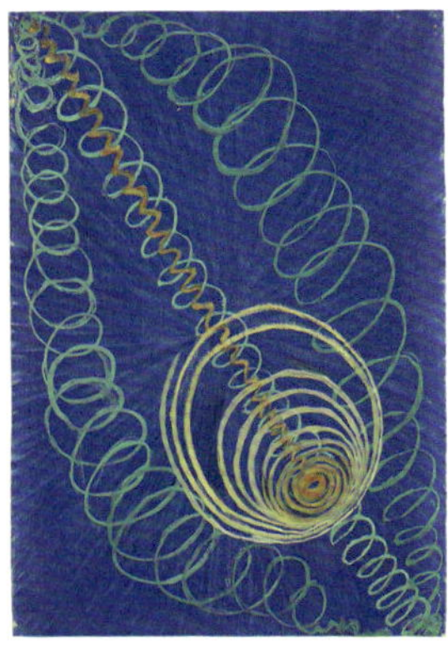

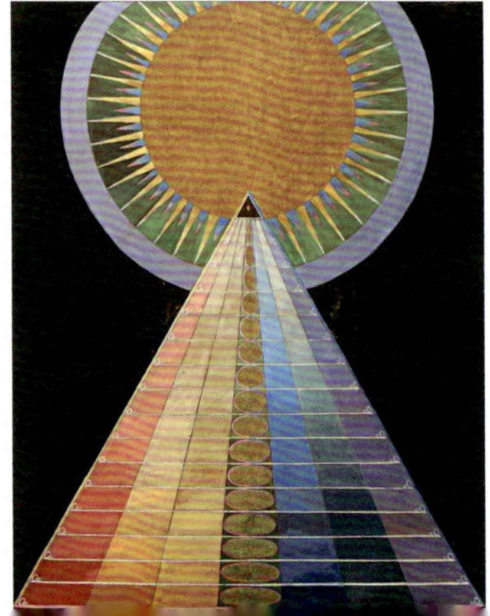

female and male. The earthly battle of these polarities should be overcome by a harmonious unity on the astral plane. The "temple" for her paintings is intended to be crowned with a spiral.

In 1920 af Klint became a member of the Anthroposophical Society and visited its founder Rudolf Steiner, whom she had known for years, in Dornach, Switzerland. Steiner was dedicated to a "scientific investigation of the spiritual world," which required the development of the "inquiring soul's [...] latent powers." He rejected both the reproduction of nature and the spiritual world's representation via symbols or allegories in art. Instead, he propagated "painting from the essence of colour." The visit provoked a change in af Klint's style. Leaving behind her radically autonomous geometric abstractions, she now chose to let water-colours flow softly into one another.

The painter left behind more than 1.000 works and over 125 notebooks when she died in 1944. A selection was first shown in the 1986 Los Angeles exhibition *The Spiritual in Art: Abstract Painting, 1890–1985*. The title refers to Wassily Kandinsky's book *Das Geistige in der Kunst*. Kandinsky was already writing himself into art history by publishing this treatise to coincide with the first exhibition of work by the artist group Der Blaue Reiter (The Blue Rider) in 1911 and by continuing to produce his own style of abstract work. By contrast, af Klint's work remained unseen for many years and has only recently come to the public's attention.

Dieter Scholz

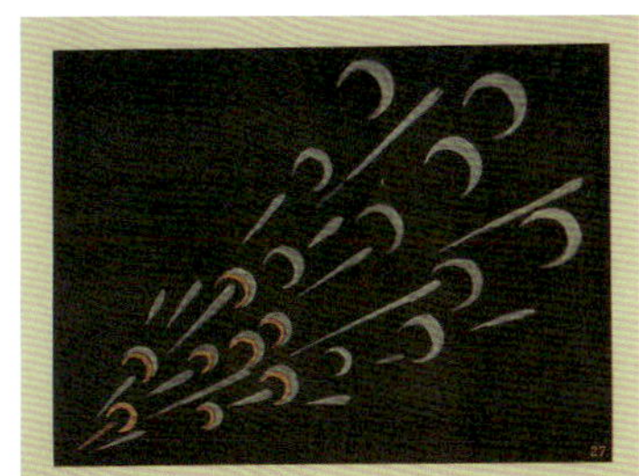

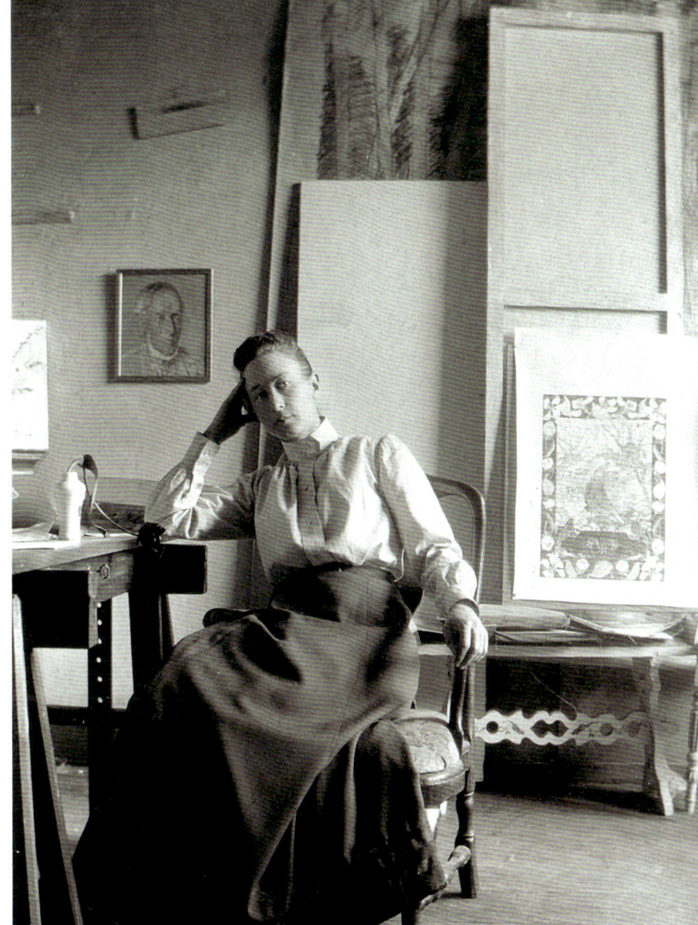

↗ *Sudden Fright*, published in Annie Besant and Charles W. Leadbeater, *Thought Forms*, London, 1905, p. 54, fig. 27
→ Hilma af Klint in her studio at Hamngatan 5 in Stockholm, c. 1895
← Hilma af Klint, *Primordial Chaos, No. 16*. From the *WU/ROSEN series, Group I*, 1906–07
← Hilma af Klint, *Altarpiece, No. 1, Group X, Altarpieces*, 1907

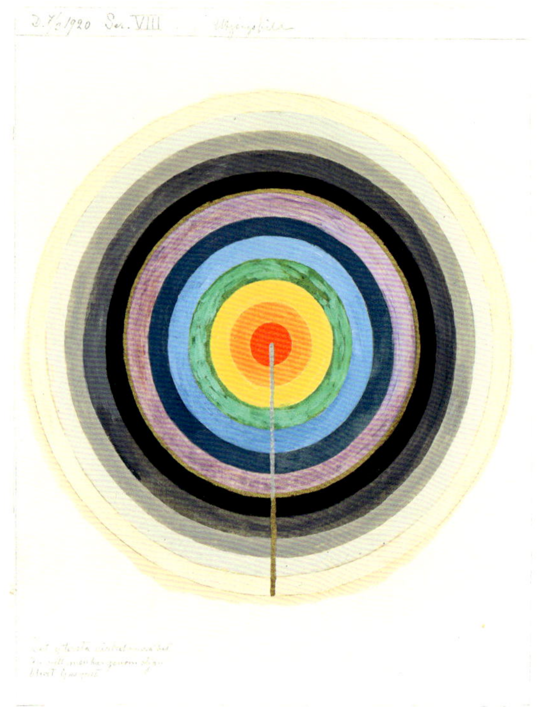

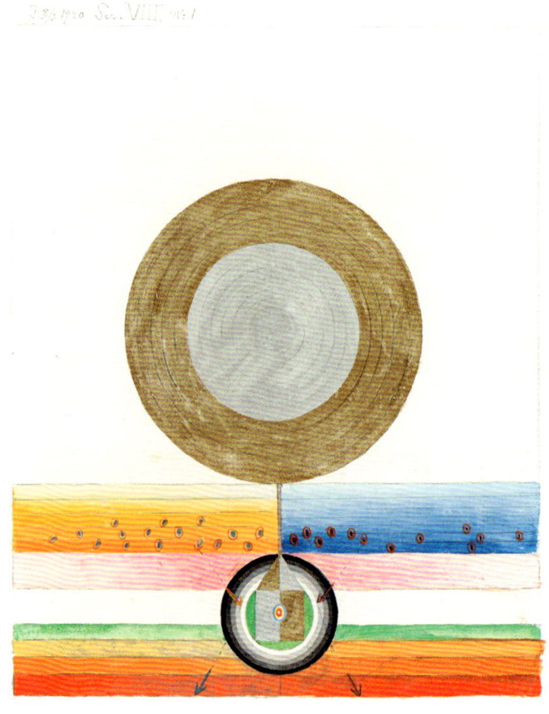

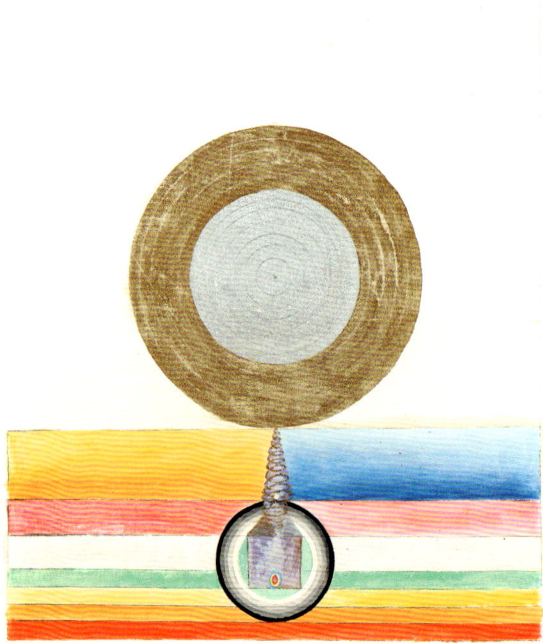

Hilma af Klint, *Source Image, No. 1–5, Series VIII*, 1920
Oil on canvas, each 50 × 30 cm
By courtesy of The Hilma af Klint Foundation

↑ *Source Image*, 1920
↗ *No. 1, Series VIII*, 1920
→ *No. 4, Series VIII*, 1920

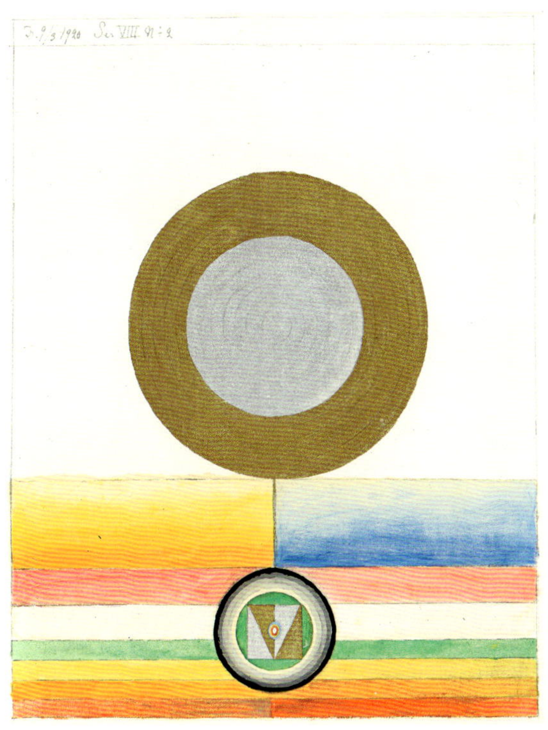

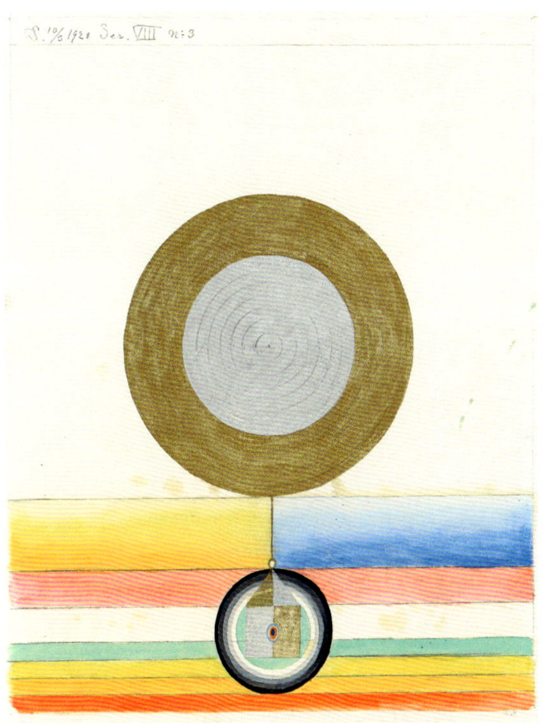

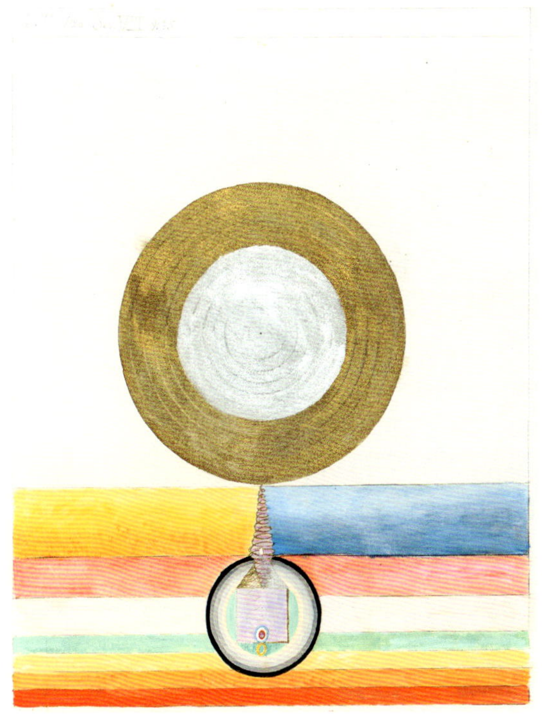

↑ *No. 2, Series VIII*, 1920
↗ *No. 3, Series VIII*, 1920
→ *No. 5, Series VIII*, 1920

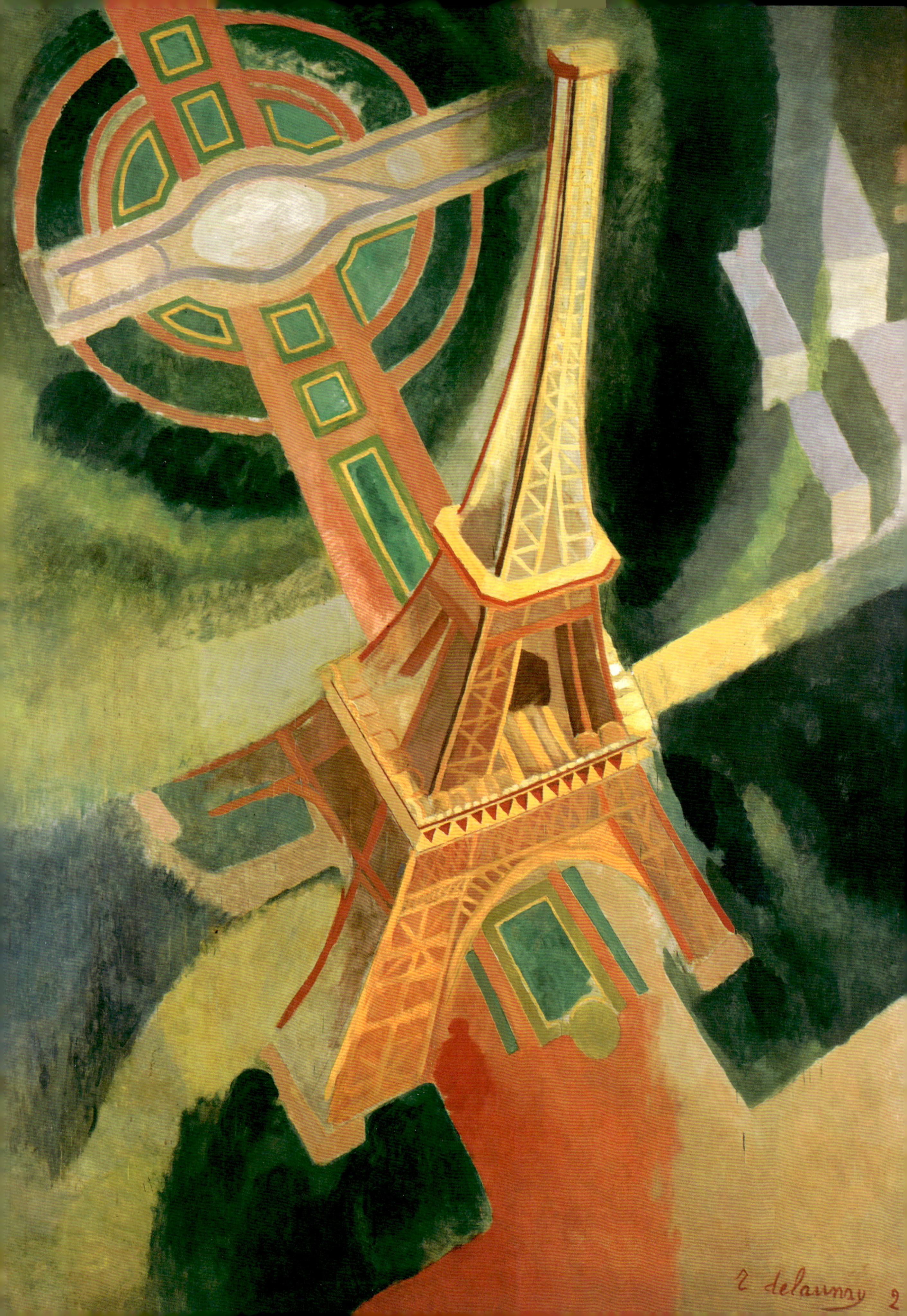
r delaunay 2

The Architecture of Progress

Radio towers, train stations and factories are all structures of industrial Modernism. The engineer Gustave Eiffel's lookout tower for the 1889 World's Fair in Paris showcased the aesthetic value technological structures were beginning to take on in architecture. When Robert Delaunay drew the Eiffel Tower from a bird's eye or aeroplane view in 1928, he was also referencing technology, aviation, and the transitional.

In a break with the past, Western Modernism displayed constructions openly instead of hiding them behind façades. A strict constructivism of pure geometrical forms also developed in visual art. While Lou Loeber combined colour planes to form an image of a factory, Friedrich Vordemberge-Gildewart composed a point, square and rectangles into an abstract painting, free of representational objects, which he enhanced by integrating an architects' straightedge ruler. Construction itself entered the composition using its own tools and vocabulary. Kurt Schwitters also referenced architecture in his small-scale Dada assemblage *Kathedrale* (Cathedral), which he nailed together out of found wood scraps.

Robert Delaunay, *The Eiffel Tower*, 1928
Oil on canvas, 364 × 266.5 cm
Acquired in 1982 from the Galerie Gmurzynska, Cologne, for the Nationalgalerie, Berlin (West)

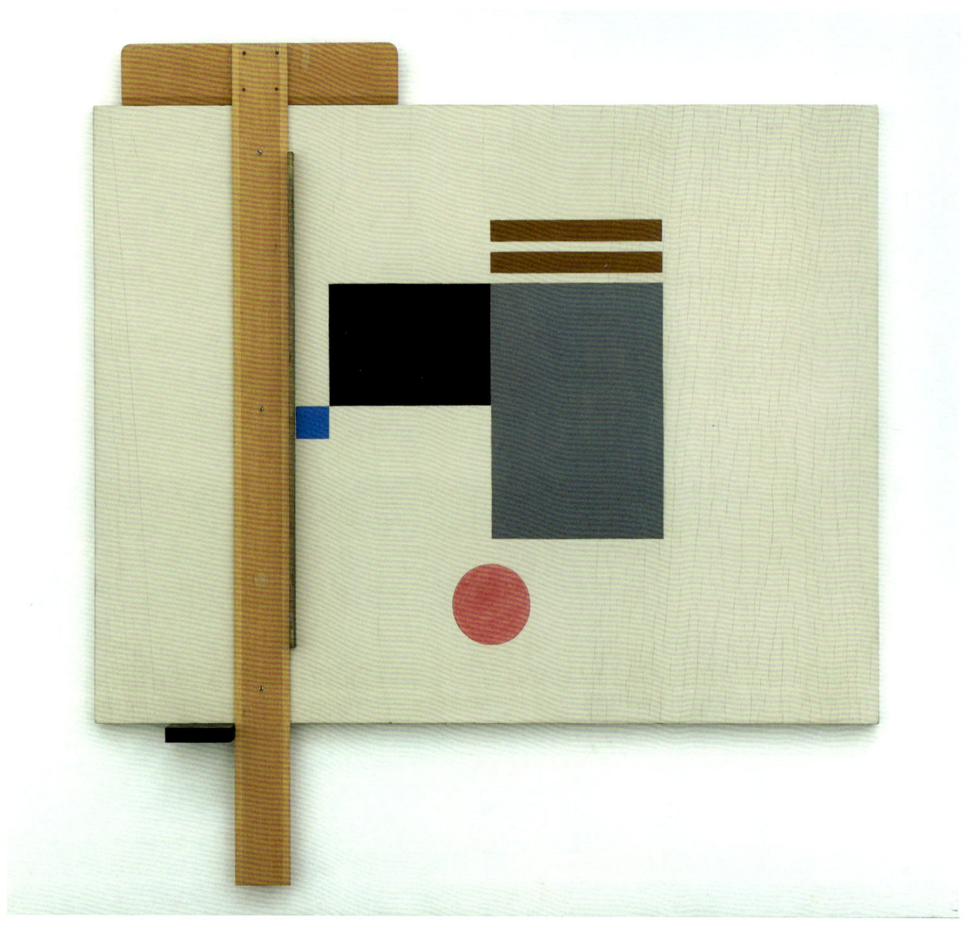

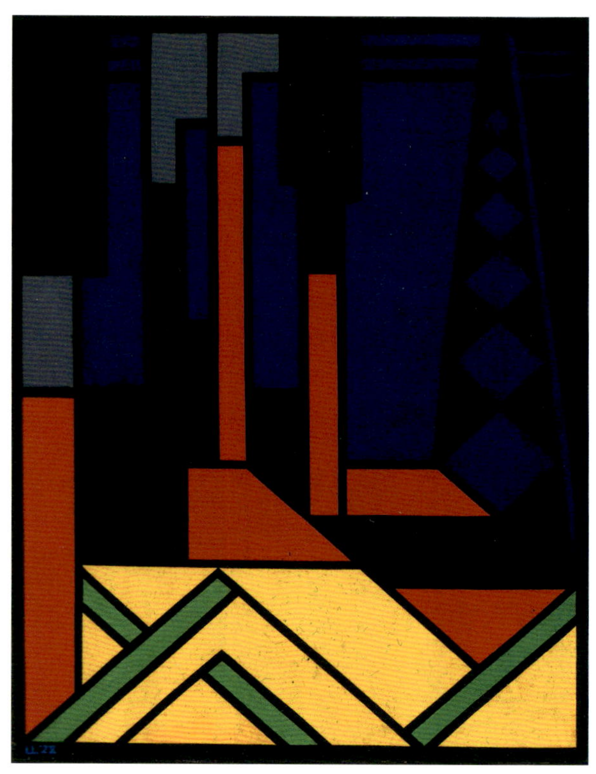

↑ Friedrich Vordemberge-Gildewart, *Construction No. 8*, 1924
Oil on wood, 96.5 × 106 cm
Acquired in 1978 with funds from the Stiftung Deutsche Klassenlotterie Berlin for the Nationalgalerie, Berlin (West)

→ Lou Loeber, *Seintoestellen Fabriek II*, 1928
Oil on cardboard, 78.5 × 61.5 cm
Loan from a private collection

↗ Constantin Brancusi, *Bird in Space*, 1926 (cast 1972)
Bronze, marble, sandstone, 258 × 46.5 × 40 cm
Acquired for the Nationalgalerie, Berlin (West) in 1973 from the artist's heir, Alexandre Istrati, Paris, with support from the Dresdner Bank AG

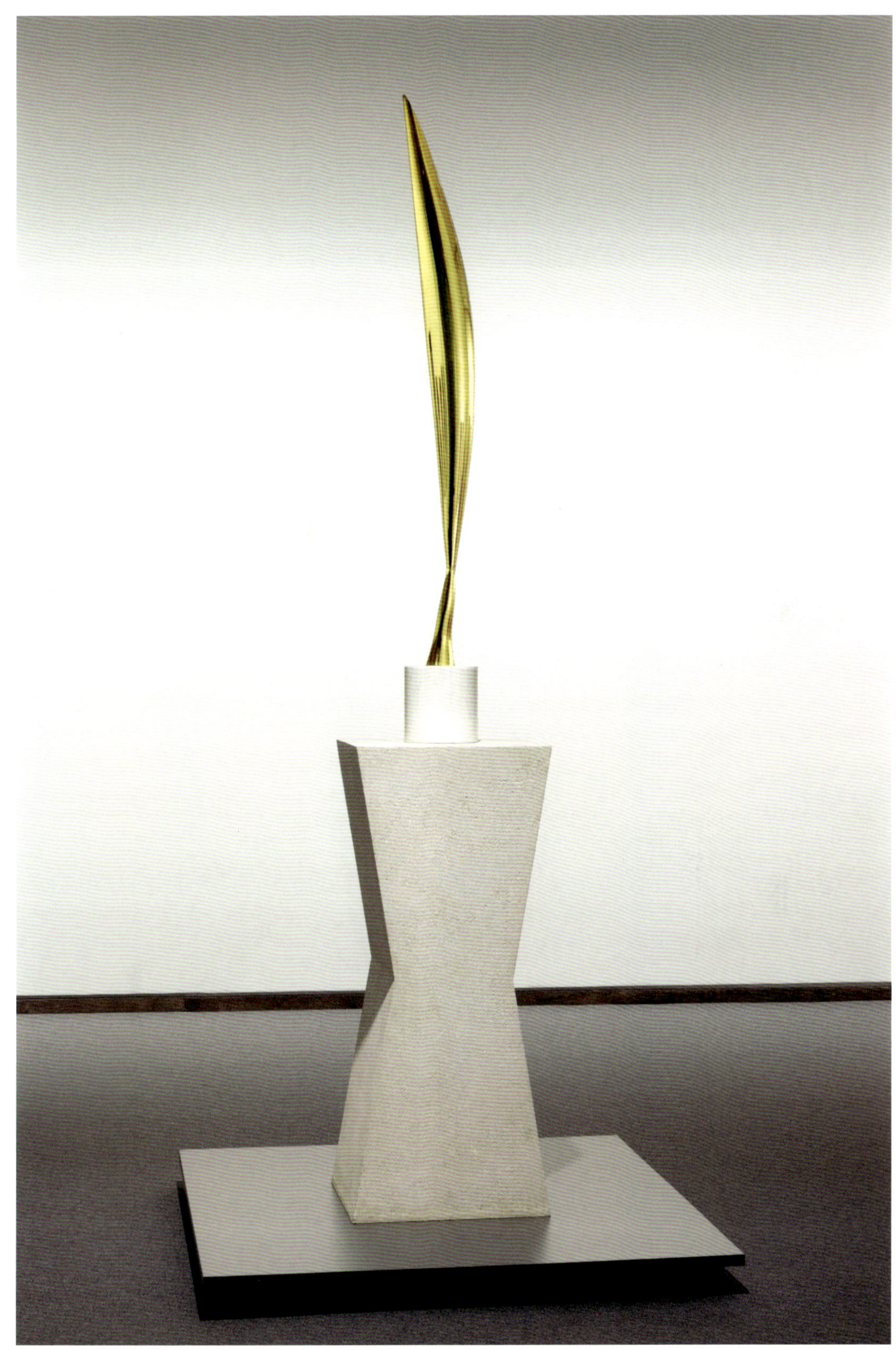

A Railway Station with Three Bridges: Social Analysis in Painting

Paul Fuhrmann painted his urban architectural scene titled *Am Bahnhof* (At the Train Station) in 1930 and exhibited it at the *Große Berliner Kunstausstellung* (Great Berlin Art Exhibition) the same year. After decades in museum storage, this work is in focus again as part of the *The Art of Society* exhibition. Inviting viewers to immerse themselves in the site, it shows a railway station with three bridges. Do the station and the bridges actually exist?

Fuhrmann was born in Berlin's Spandau district in 1893 and spent his entire life in the city, making it the most obvious place to search for the painting's setting. The Bellevue station near the River Spree stands out on a map of the city. At this juncture we find a bridge for Berlin's metropolitan rail line, which has travelled between the eastern Ostbahnhof (then known as Schlesischer Bahnhof) and Bahnhof Charlottenburg at Stuttgarter Platz in the west since 1882. In 1915, an arched pedestrian bridge made of steel with solid concrete abutments was added. It was called Bellevuesteg but renamed Gerickesteg in 1920. Two hundred metres downriver, a stone-built bridge, Moabiter Brücke, connects the city centre to the district of Moabit. It is also called Bärenbrücke because of the bear sculptures embellishing its bridgeheads.

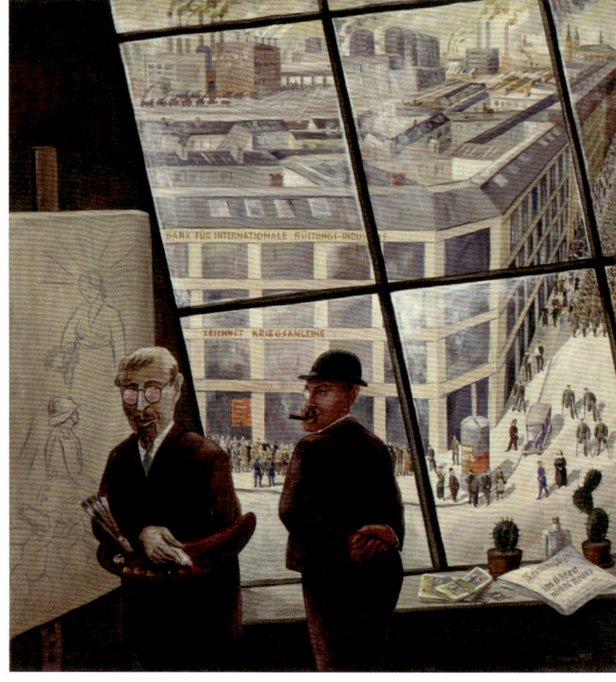

→ Paul Fuhrmann, *War Profiteer*, 1932
↗ Map of Berlin, 1936, detail showing the S-Bahn bridge, Gerickesteg and Moabiter Brücke, as well as Thomasiusstraße and the area of Meierei Bolle (dairy) at the upper left edge
↗ Gerickesteg, Moabiter Brücke and Meierei Bolle in the background, 1947

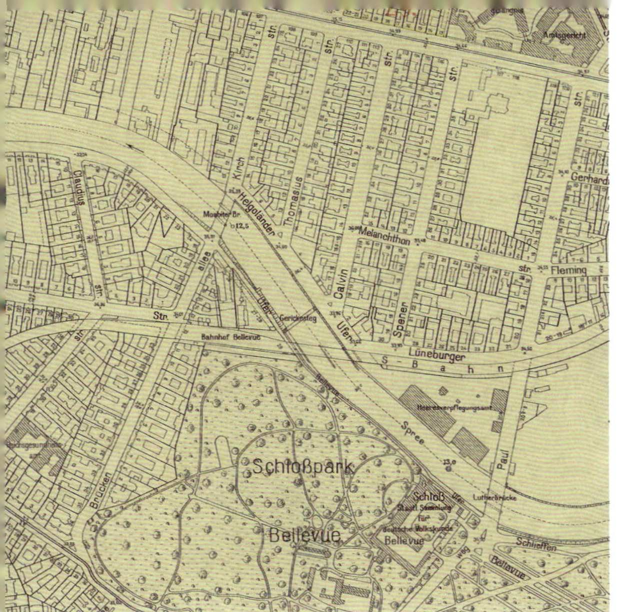

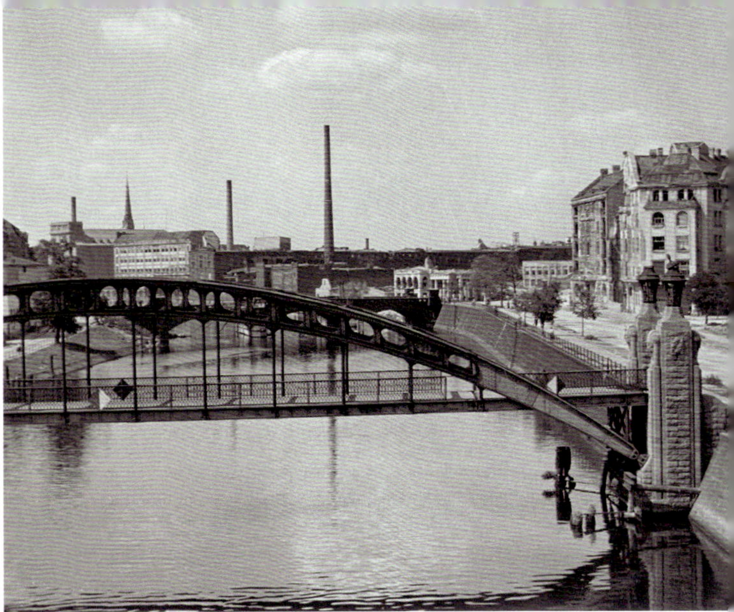

Fuhrmann's painting guides the viewer's gaze northwest from the Bellevue bank across the Spree to where the well-known Bolle dairy has been located since 1887. In 1911 it became a stock corporation with 2.500 employees. Its grounds included a boiler system, smokestacks, workshops and vehicles for transporting milk, as well as a company chapel, a banquet hall and the Welt-Kino cinema. In fact, Fuhrmann's painting resembles a cinema poster. But in his case, the clear outlines separating various planes, the constructive organization of his composition, and the elegant Art Deco colour combinations typical of the period are all part of an effort to create socially reflective art.

The male figure with the milk jug makes reference to the labour force while another carrying a briefcase represents an office worker; both appear to be leaving the Bolle company. A pair of lovers and an athletic lady stroll along the riverbank while a beggar with a bandage around his head asks for charity, the news vendor waits for customers, a mariner toils with his barge, and people crowd together in overfilled train cars. The relationship between the individual and the collective is as prevalent in the painting as the correlation between work and leisure. Class affiliations are clearly demarcated. Behind the manmade traffic structures, factory smokestacks signify industrial production. At the time, Berlin was one of the most advanced industrial hubs in the world.

Fuhrmann's membership in the Communist Party of Germany (KPD) and the Association of Revolutionary Visual Artists (ASSO) further contextualize his social analysis in painting. The artist lived at Thomasiusstraße 26 in the working-class district of Moabit. His street led directly to the Spree, where the bourgeois Tiergarten district lay just across the Gerickesteg. The river is a social boundary here, but nevertheless, there are bridges.

Dieter Scholz

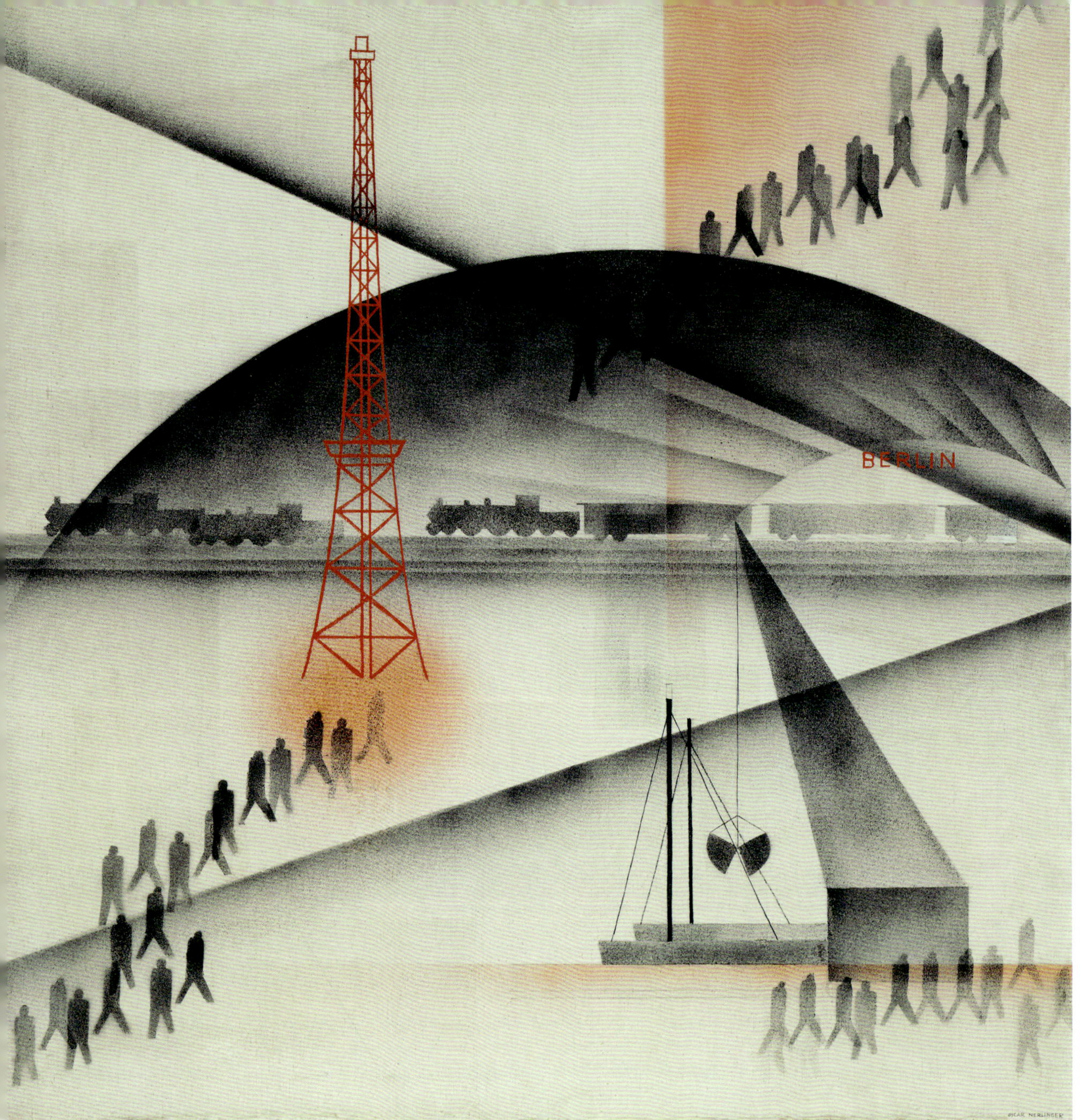

↑ Oskar Nerlinger, *The Early Train*, 1928
Casein tempera on canvas, 100 × 100 cm
Acquired in 1963 from the artist for the Nationalgalerie, Berlin (East)

→ Paul Fuhrmann, *At the Train Station*, 1930
Oil on canvas, 111 × 86 cm
Acquired in 1966 from the estate of the artist for the Nationalgalerie, Berlin (East)

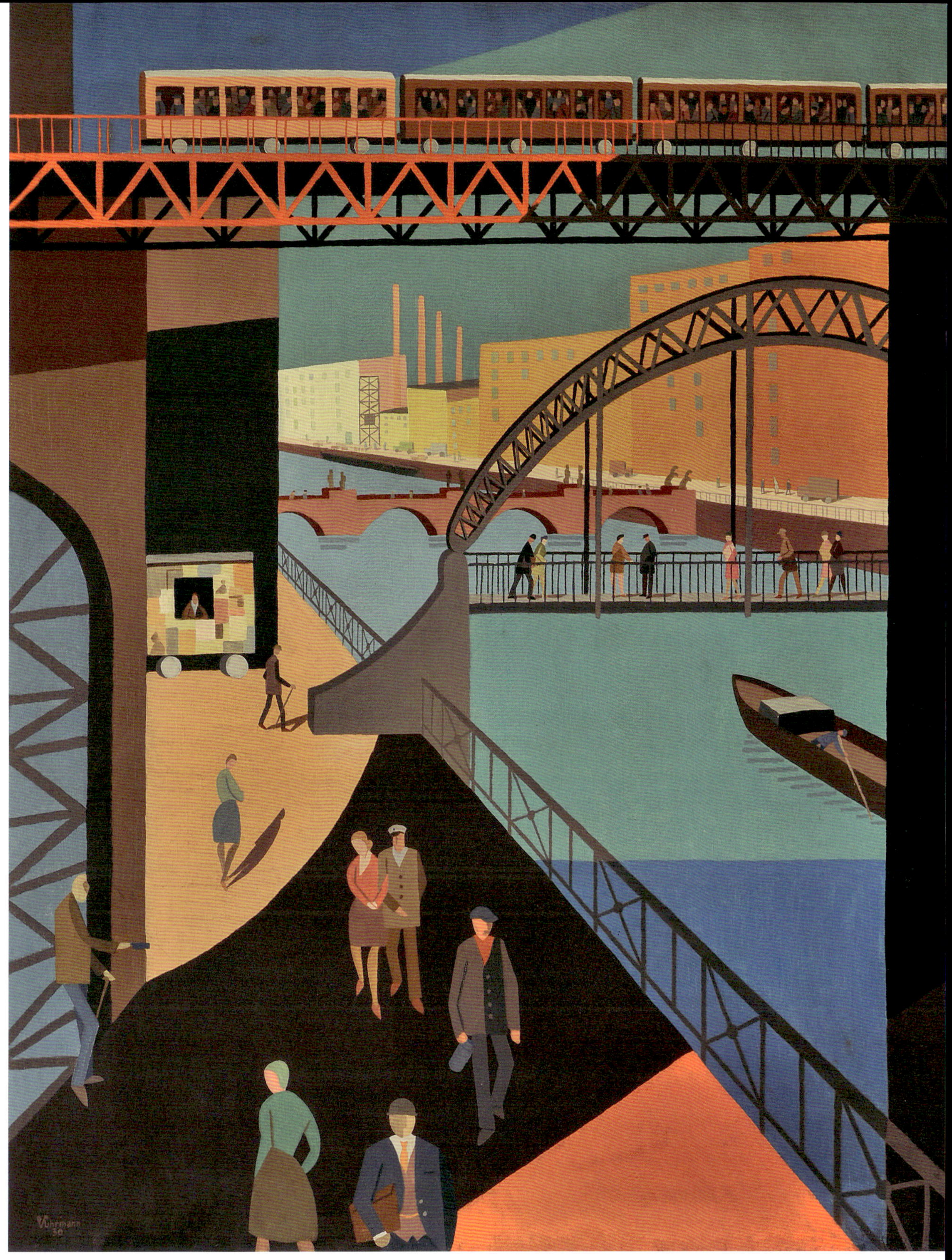

The Great Metaphysician – What's Wrong with It?

Giorgio de Chirico's painting *Der Große Metaphysiker* (The Great Metaphysician) was acquired in 1965 and has been on view at the Neue Nationalgalerie since 1968. In 1970 the artist visited his work and declared it "falso, falso, falsissimo!" But what's wrong with it?

De Chirico's early work produced from 1909 to 1919 is considered to be particularly innovative and valuable. The paintings from this period show broad town squares encircled by archways casting long shadows in the afternoon sun. Monumental mannequins emerge from the scenes like memorial statues encased in geometric wooden wedges, boxes, frames, and cloths. These works are emblems of a puzzling existence in a world of artifice and automation where people no longer experience a relationship with the spiritual. In contrast, metaphysics contemplates life's "final questions". What lies behind or beyond physics and nature? Does the spiritual exist?

Only a few of these melancholy compositions in the *Pittura metafisica* (Metaphysical Painting) style were made. But they were in high demand, which is why de Chirico painted many variations over several decades and backdated them to increase their value. In addition, the Surrealist Oscar Domínguez produced an estimated three dozen "de Chiricos" in the 1940s that are undoubtedly forgeries. The Nationalgalerie's painting is, however, by the artist himself. But was it actually painted in 1916, as purported by the date below the signature?

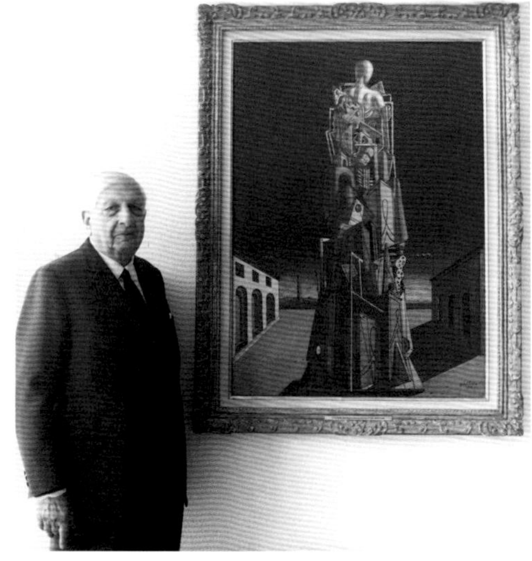

→ Giorgio de Chirico at the Neue Nationalgalerie standing next to his painting *The Great Metaphysician*, 1970
↗ X-ray of the painting *The Great Metaphysician*, 1974

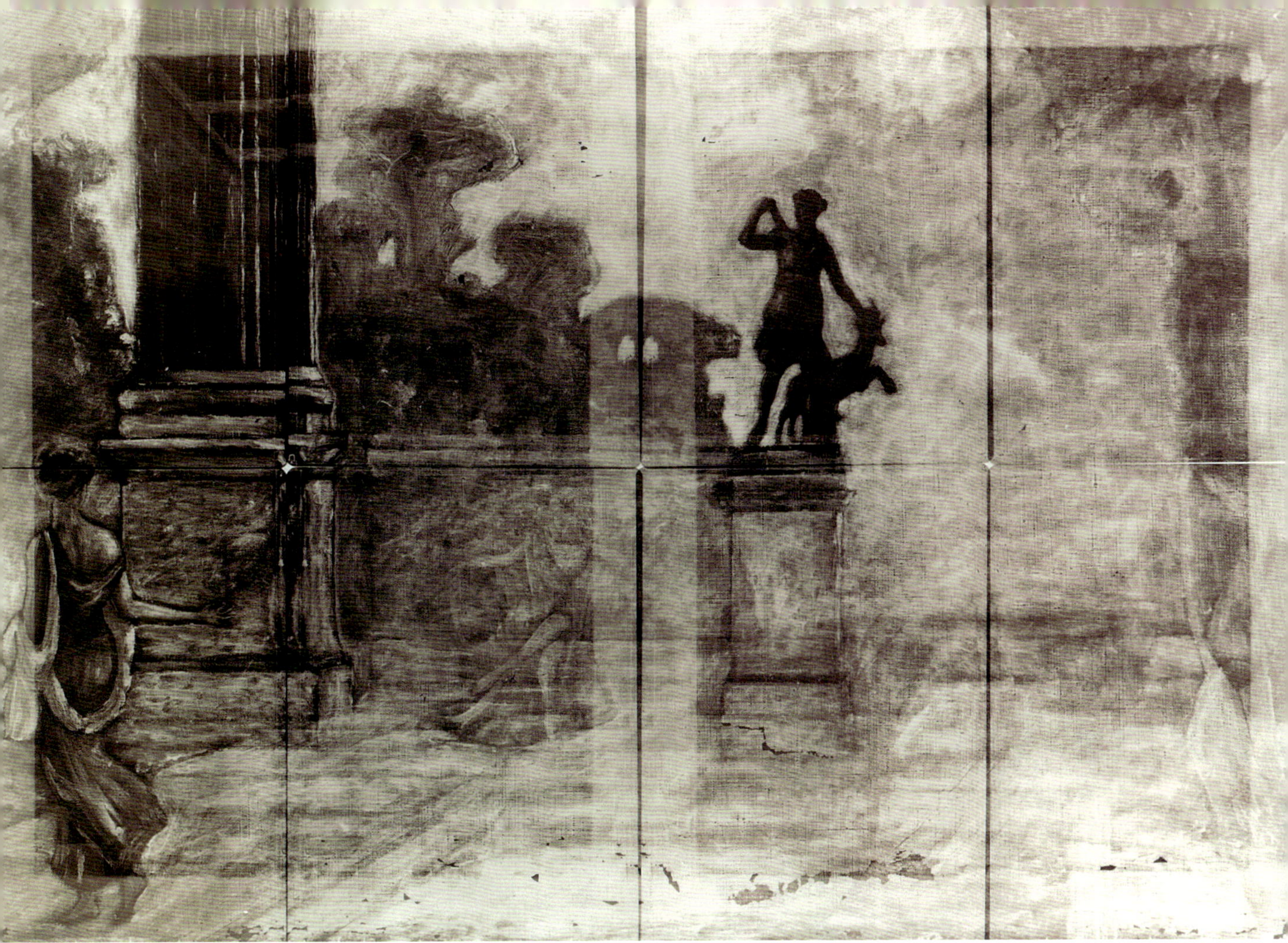

The painting's existence was first documented when a men's tailor from Milan lent it to an exhibition in 1950. When the work was resold, de Chirico further authenticated it with an additional signature on the back of the canvas and even went so far as to have his signature notarized. The painting was inventoried accordingly upon its acquisition in Berlin – with 1916 as its date of origin. But a New York museum expert who compared it to a version of *The Great Metaphysician* verifiably painted in 1917 concluded that the latter version is the historical original. Based on stylistic choices, he judged Berlin's painting to have been made later and connected it to a third variation from 1925.

In 1974 the painting was x-rayed to reach a consensus about its period of creation. A Roman villa motif emerged from beneath the visible top layer of the image and was first assumed to be a work from de Chirico's youth that he had painted over. However, this theory was recently disproved by art historian Gerd Roos. He also used x-rays to determine that between 1944 and 1947–48 de Chirico repeatedly painted over old canvasses he had purchased from Roman flea markets, indicating that the Berlin painting was likely produced during this period. In the end, it is definitely not a forgery, but the year 1916 is false.

Dieter Scholz

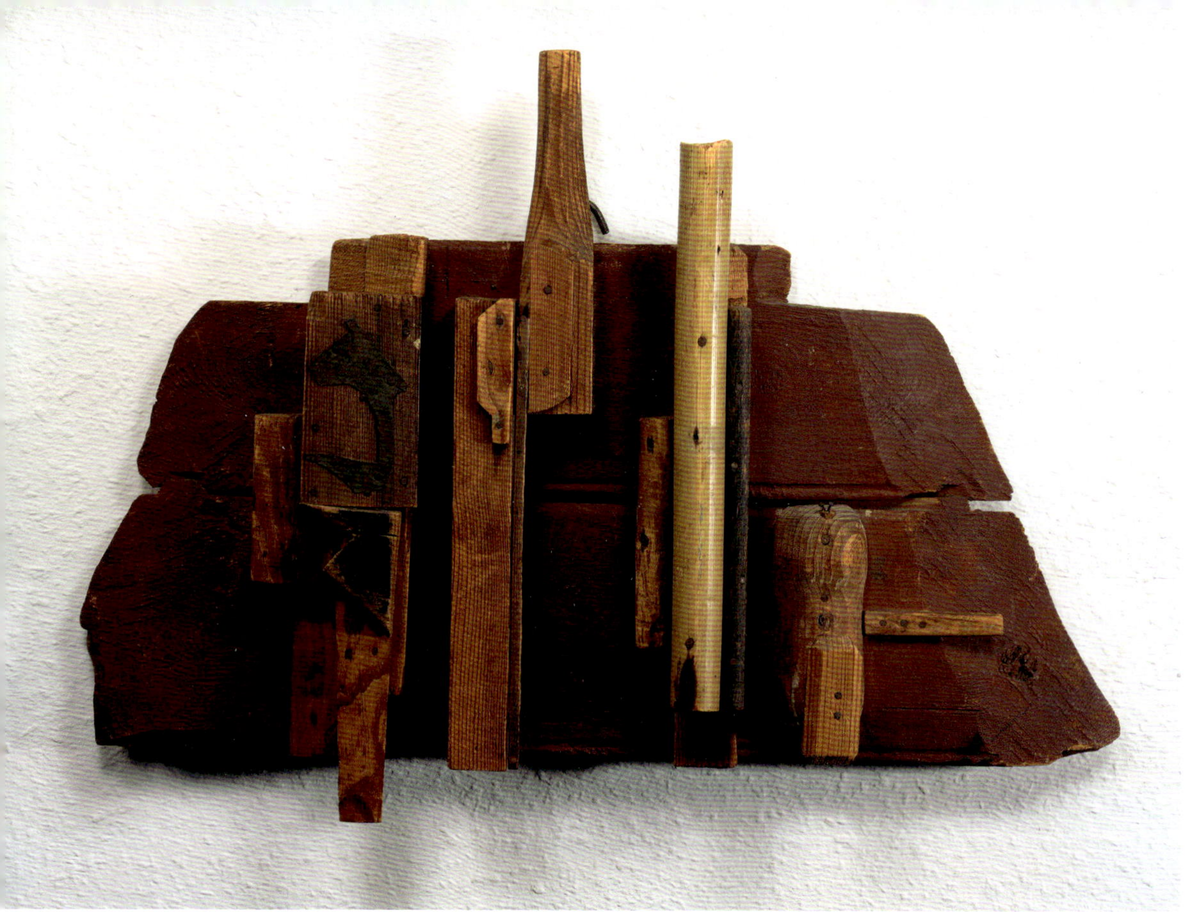

↑ Kurt Schwitters, *Broad Schmurchel*, 1923
Oil on wood and metal on wood, 39 × 55 × 9 cm
Acquired in 1979 from the estate of Hannah Höch, Berlin, by the Freunde der Nationalgalerie for the Nationalgalerie, Berlin (West)

→ Kurt Schwitters, *Cathedral*, 1923–26
Wood, 39 × 17 × 7 cm
Acquired in 1979 from the estate of Hannah Höch, Berlin, by the Freunde der Nationalgalerie for the Nationalgalerie, Berlin (West)

↗ Giorgio de Chirico, *The Great Metaphysician*, c. 1945
Oil on canvas, 110 × 80 cm
Acquired in 1965 by the Land Berlin for the Galerie des 20. Jahrhunderts, Berlin (West)

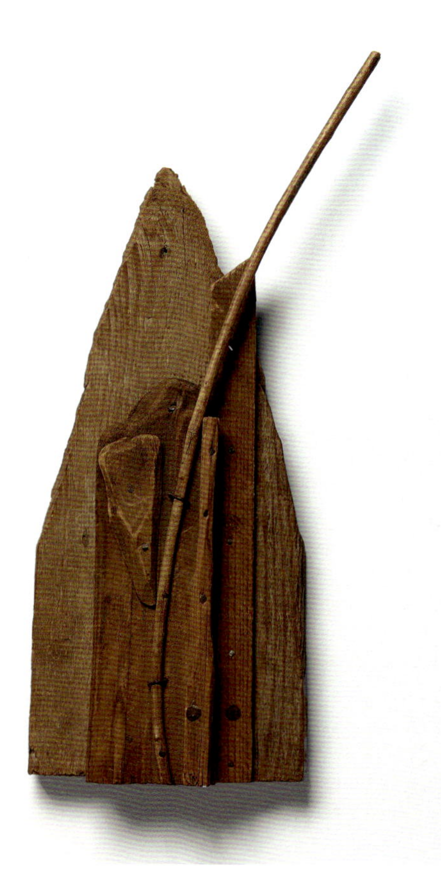

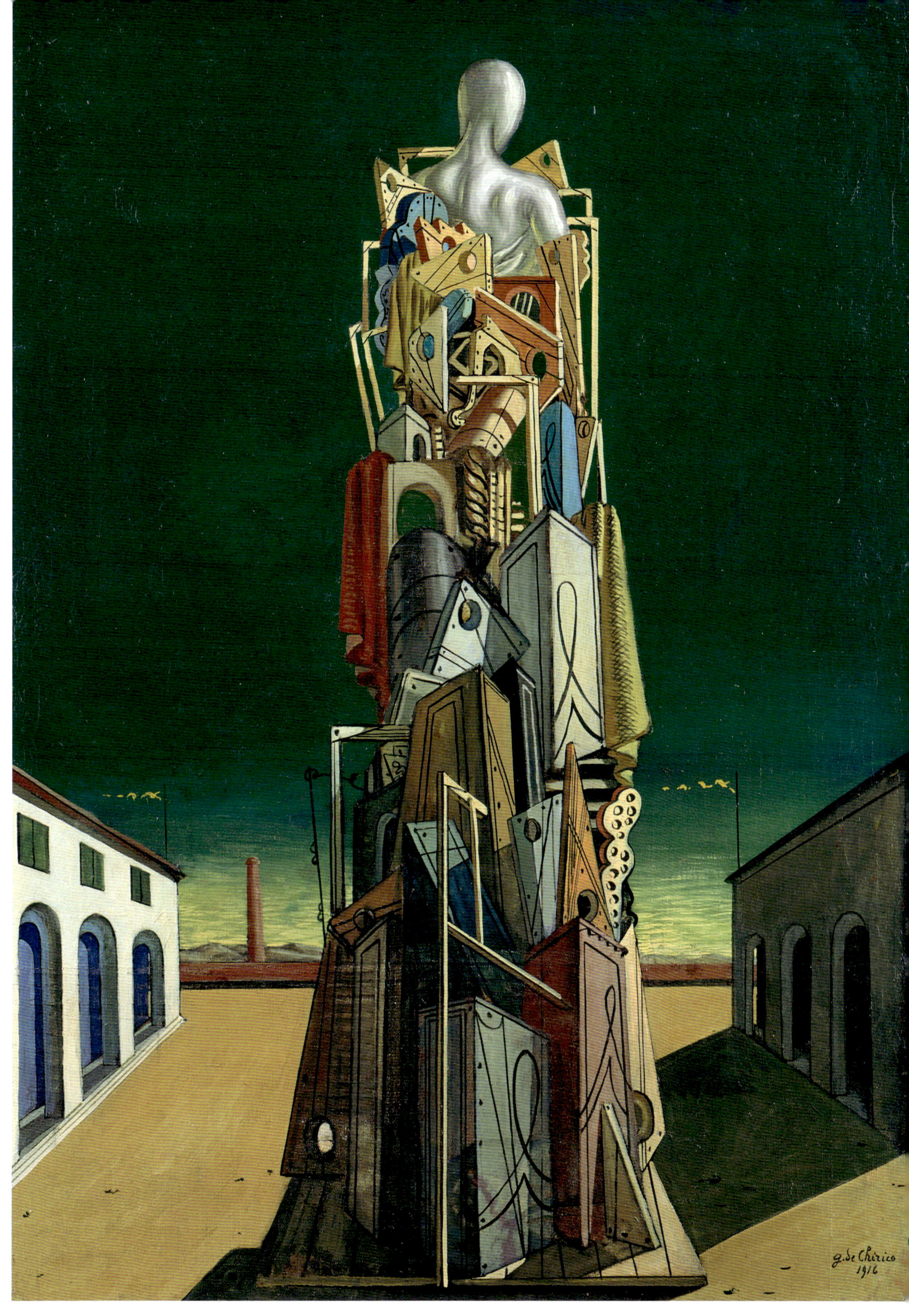
g. De Chirico
1916

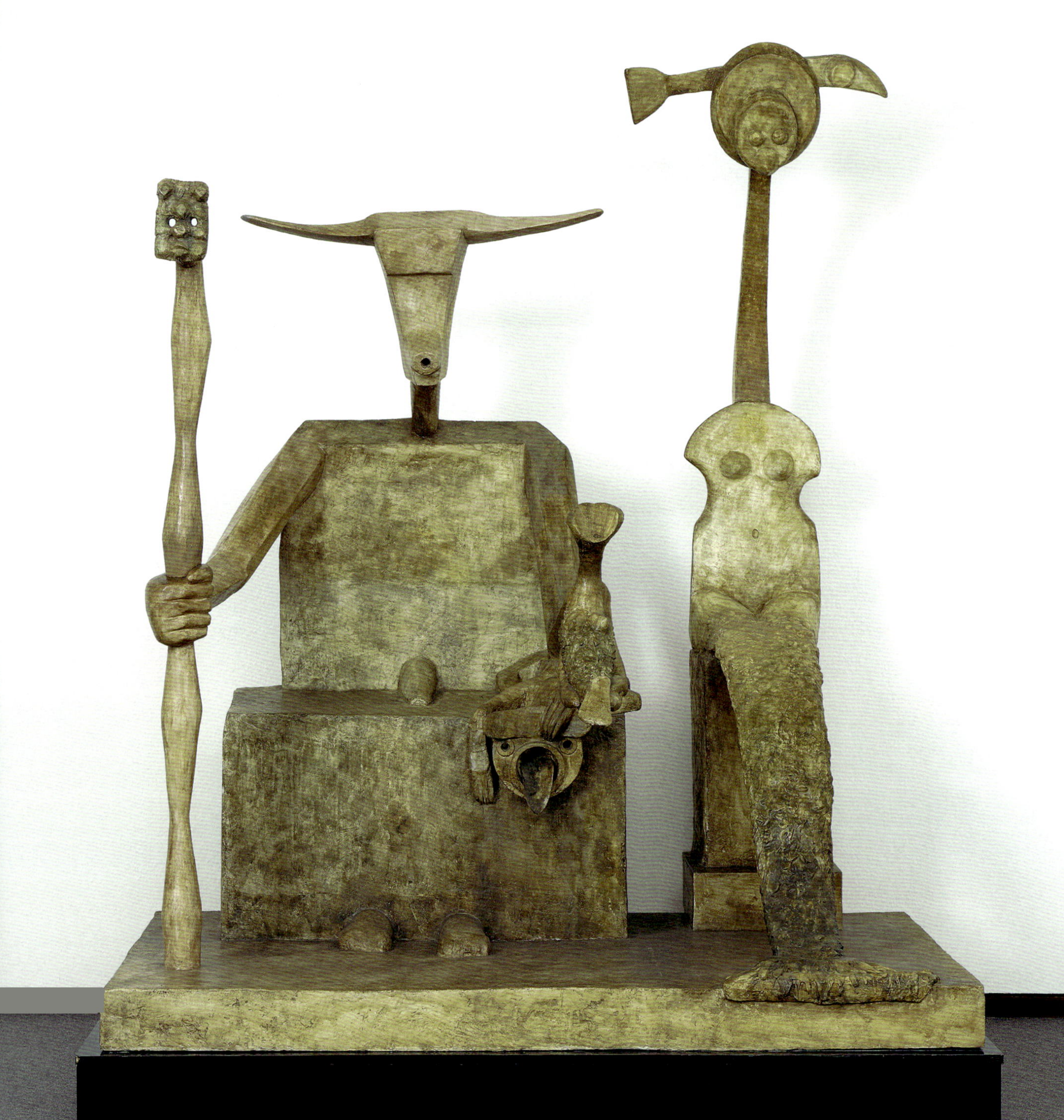

Dream Worlds

What does reality mean when compared to the world of dreams? For the Surrealists, the importance of dreams was decisive, with this conviction being justified by Sigmund Freud's book *Traumdeutung* (The Interpretation of Dreams), published in 1900. Dreams provide us with information in coded images, similar to picture puzzles, about all that remains unconscious while we are awake. Surrealism viewed its practical objective in eliminating logic and reason – using diverse approaches in order to create visionary imagery of another truth.

In his *Manifeste du surréalisme* (Surrealist Manifesto), published in 1924, the poet André Breton recommended a fast, spontaneous and "automatic" form of writing and painting. Max Ernst experimented with chance, let paint drip freely onto his works and used various counterproof and rubbing techniques. Salvador Dalí, whose fine arts style schooled by the Old Masters juxtaposed reality and imaginary visions, worked quite differently. René Magritte also deliberately combined visual motifs to create new contexts. The literary poet, the Comte de Lautréamont, set the stage for the Surrealists with his famed comparative remark: "as beautiful as the chance encounter of a sewing machine and an umbrella on a dissecting table".

Max Ernst, *Capricorne*, 1948/1964
Tinted plaster, 247 × 210 × 155 cm
Acquired in 1973 from the artist for the Nationalgalerie, Berlin (West)

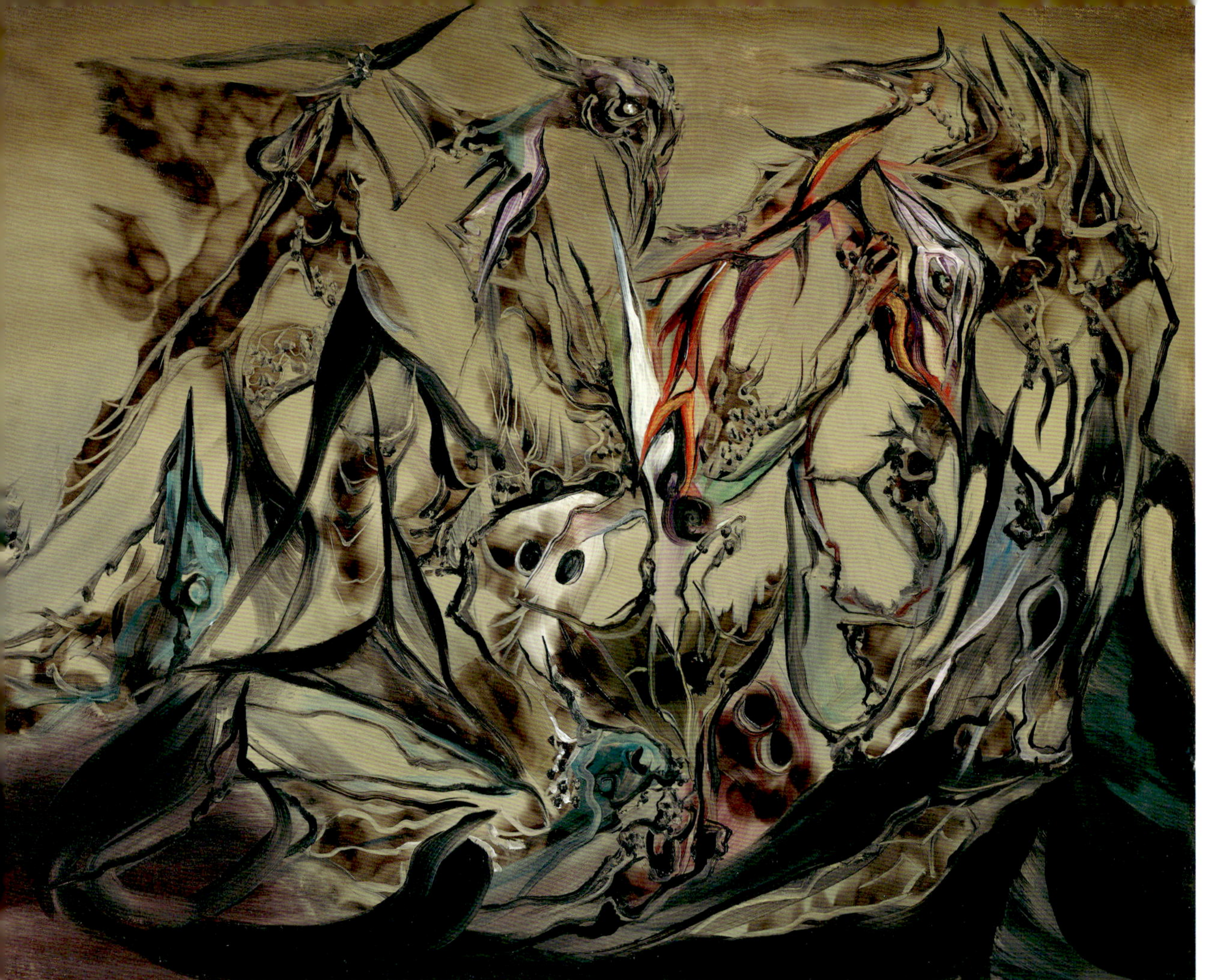

↑ Wolfgang Paalen, *Plumage*, 1938
Fumage and oil on canvas, 73 × 92 cm
Gift from the Ulla and Heiner Pietzsch
Collection to the Land Berlin, 2010

↗ André Masson, *Massacre*, 1931
Oil on canvas, 120 × 160 cm
Gift from the Ulla and Heiner Pietzsch
Collection to the Land Berlin, 2010

→ Julio González, *Mask of Montserrat Screaming*, 1936–37
Bronze, 23 × 15 × 12.5 cm
Acquired in 1959 from the Galerie Czwiklitzer, Cologne, by the
Land Berlin for the Galerie des 20. Jahrhunderts, Berlin (West)

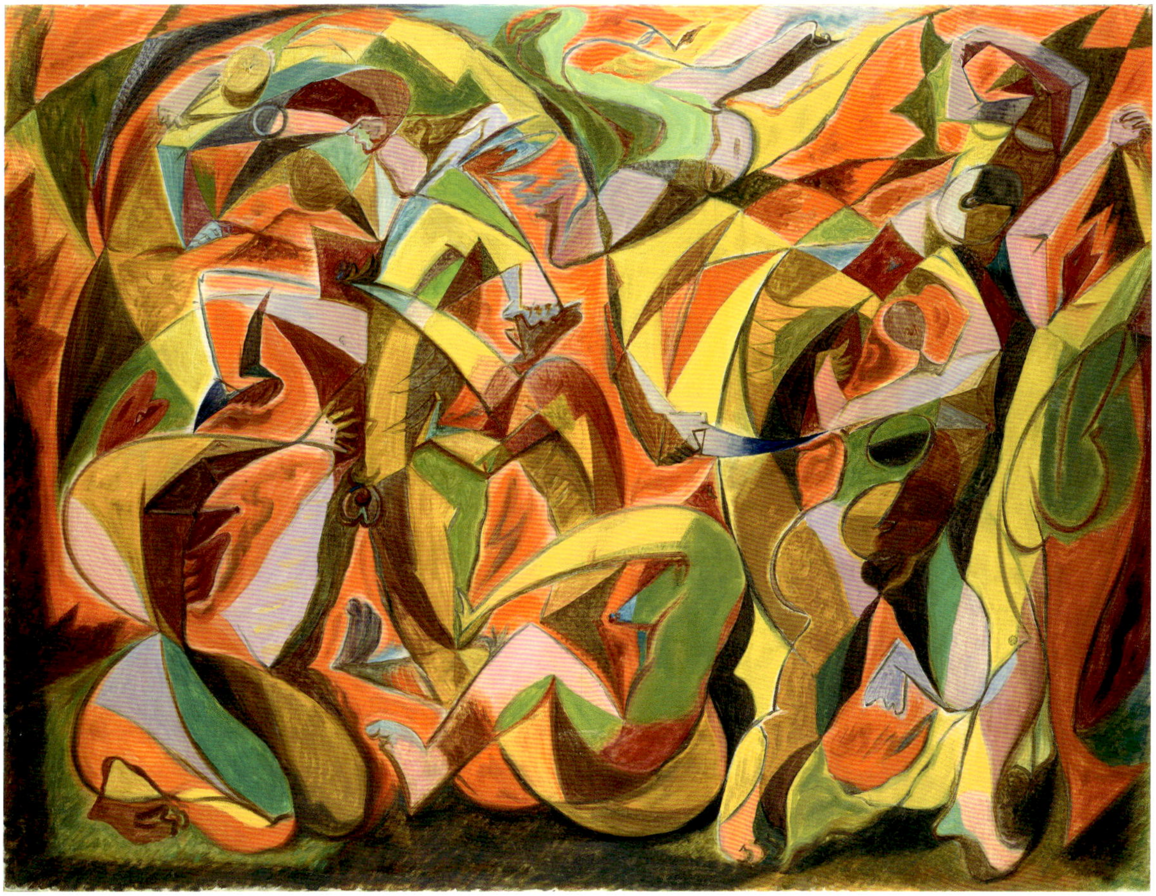

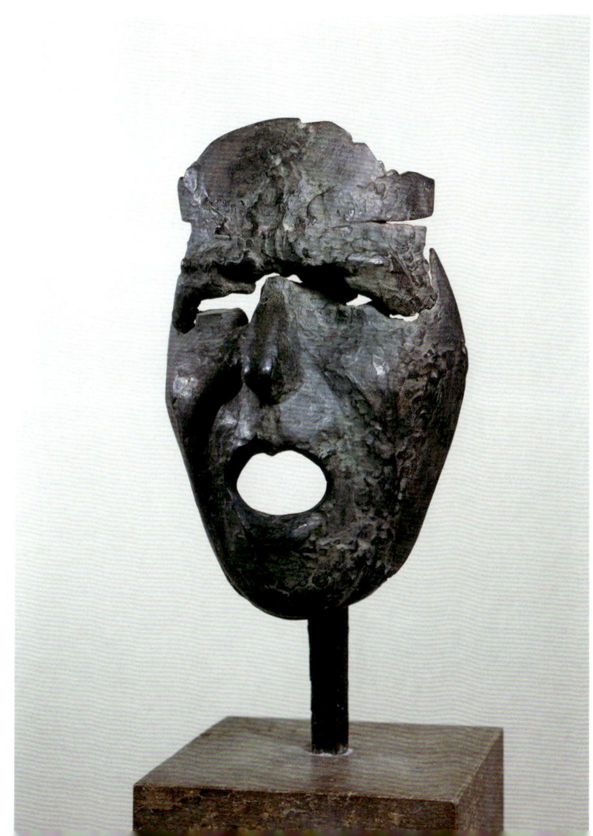

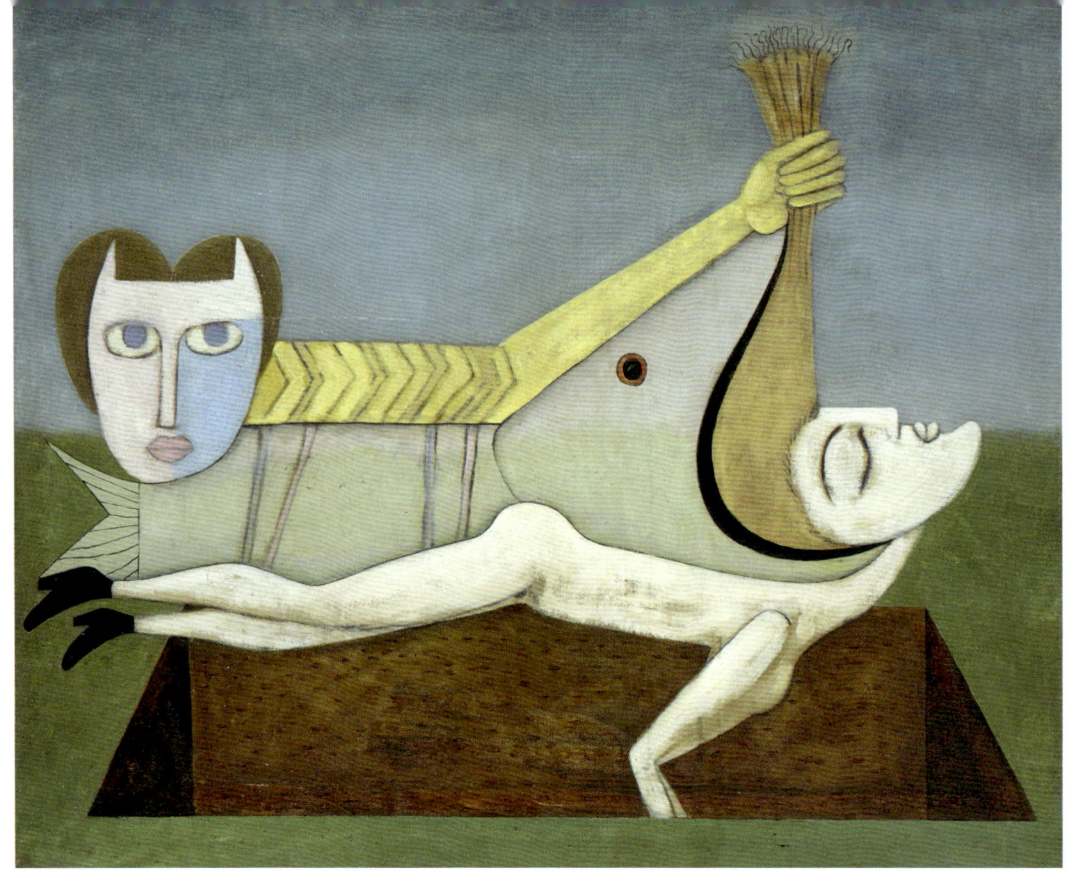

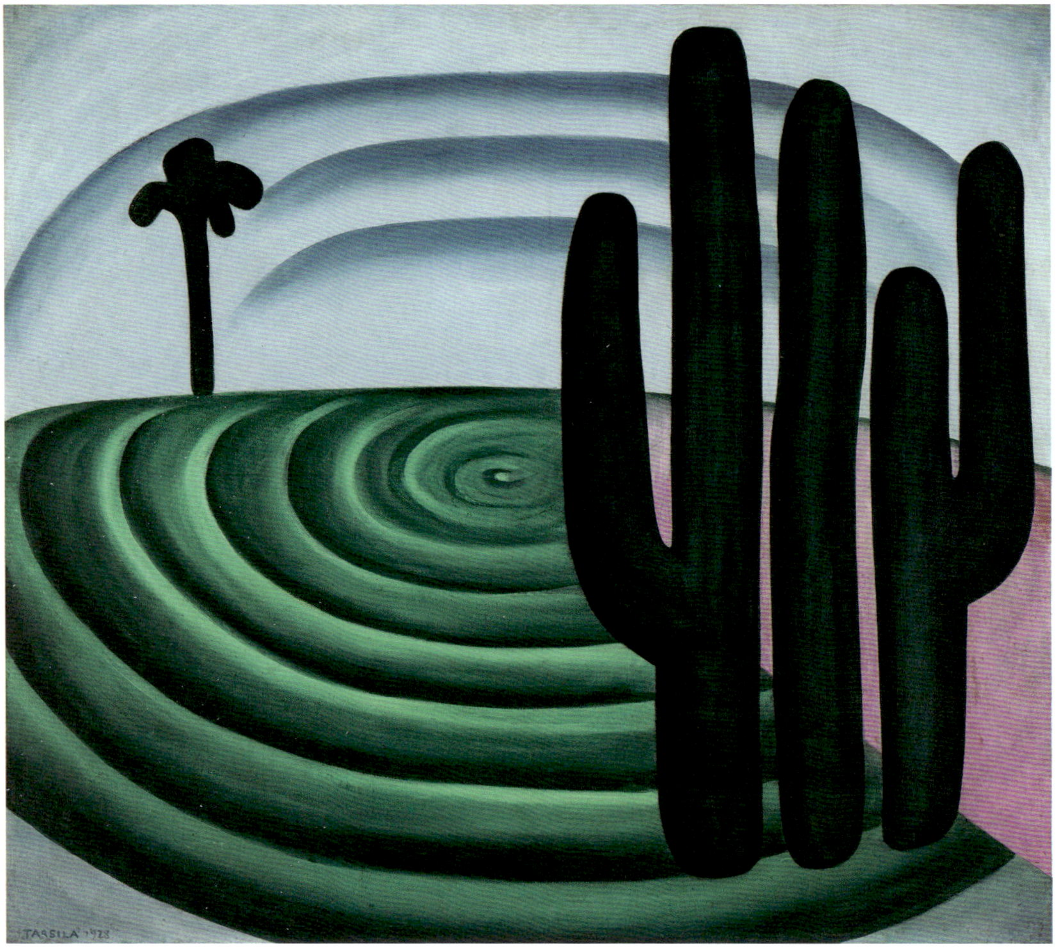

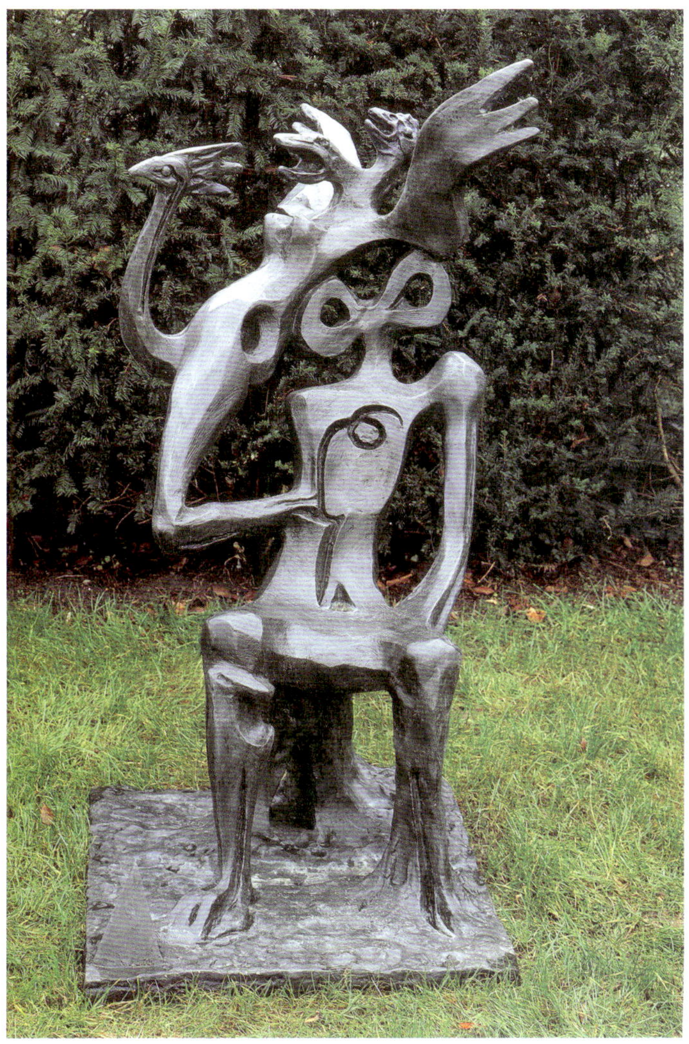

↗ André Masson, *Desert Monument*, 1941 (cast 1986–87)
Bronze, 146.4 × 91.4 × 121.2 cm
Gift from the Ulla and Heiner Pietzsch
Collection to the Land Berlin, 2010

↖ Victor Brauner, *The Manual Animal*, 1943
Oil on canvas, 54 × 65 cm
Gift from the Ulla and Heiner Pietzsch
Collection to the Land Berlin, 2010

← Tarsila do Amaral, *Distance*, 1928
Oil on canvas, 65 × 74.5 cm
Long-term loan from the Fundação José e Paulina
Nemirovsky to the Pinacoteca do Estado de São Paulo

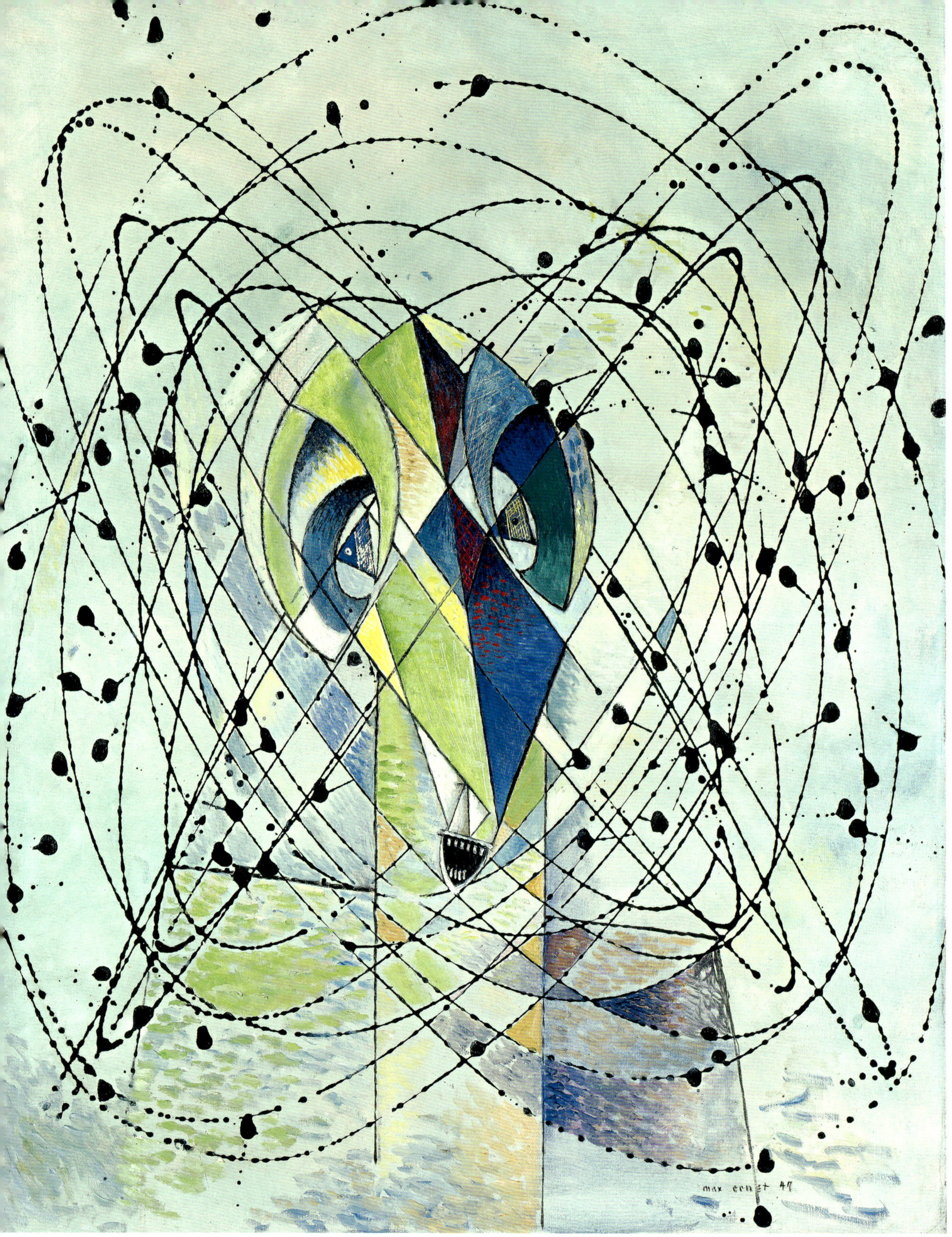
max ernst 47

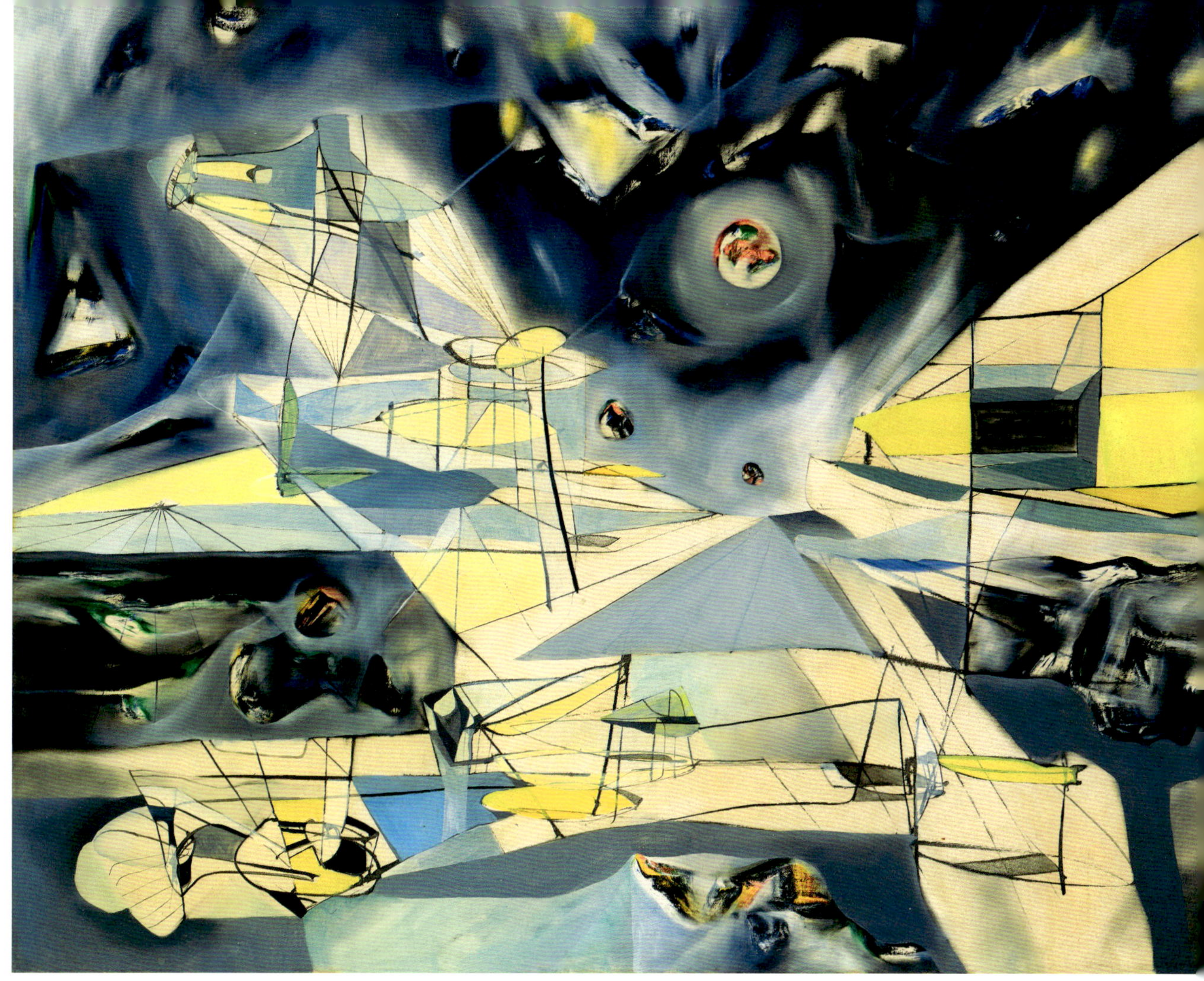

↑ Roberto Matta, *Locus Solus*, 1941–42
Oil on canvas, 74.5 × 95.5 cm
Gift from the Ulla and Heiner Pietzsch
Collection to the Land Berlin, 2010

↖ Max Ernst, *Young Man, Intrigued by the Flight of a Non-Euclidean Fly*, 1942/1947
Oil and enamel paint on canvas, 82 × 66 cm
Gift from the Ulla and Heiner Pietzsch
Collection to the Land Berlin, 2010

“Oscillation” and “Action Painting”

Did European Surrealism influence post-war art in the USA? A painting by Max Ernst does, in fact, seem to suggest this. He gave it the unusual title *Junger Mann, beunruhigt durch den Flug einer nicht-euklidischen Fliege* (Young Man Intrigued by the Flight of a Non-Euclidean Fly). It depicts a geometrically abstracted head, surrounded by many curved lines and blotches painted in black.

How did this painting come about? In the summer of 1941, Ernst, who had lived in France for some time, fled from the National Socialist occupation forces there to the USA, where he spent the next twelve years in exile. The Surrealist journal *VVV* was first published in New York in June 1942. Ernst designed the cover of its inaugural issue using scientific diagrams taken from the three-volume publication *Design in Nature*. The diagrams trace the course of movement involved in the flapping of birds' wings. In parallel, the artist experimented with a semiautomatic painting method. He drilled a hole into a paint can hung on a cord that he swung back and forth over a canvas. The paint trickled down in droplets and created overlapping ellipses.

Max Ernst gave this work, which originally only showed the drip marks, the provisional title *Abstrakte Kunst, konkrete Kunst* (Abstract Art, Concrete Art). He exhibited it in 1942 at the Wakefield bookshop in New York, where Betty Parsons, who would later become a successful gallerist, also showed art. A young American painter took particular interest in Ernst's work. Ernst told him how

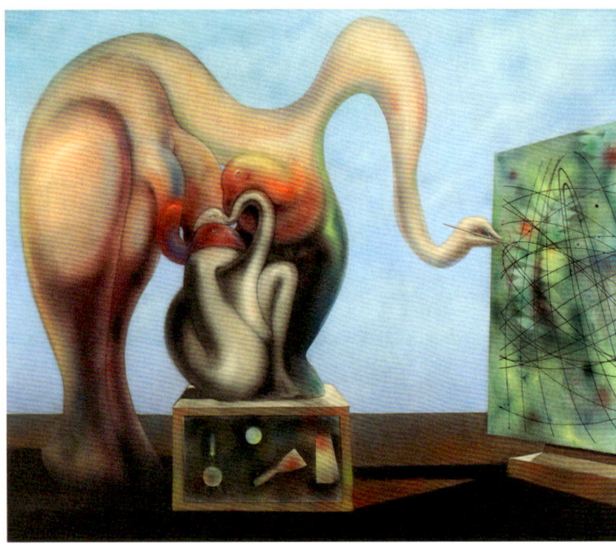

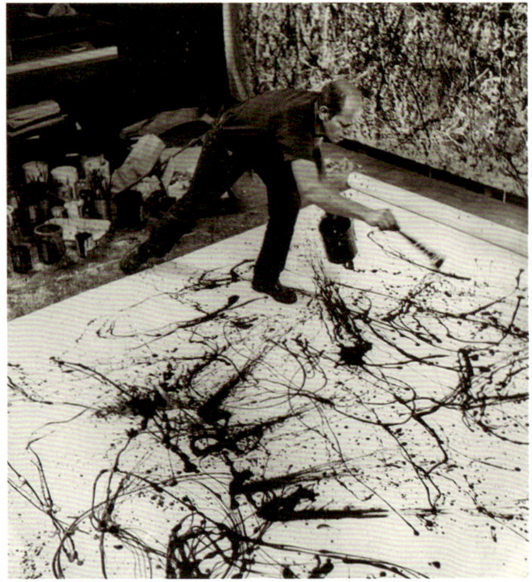

the painting was made, using the term "oscillation" from the field of physics to describe the process he had used. The young man was Jackson Pollock. Pouring enamel paints or letting them drip was already known to Pollock from the Mexican muralist David Alfaro Siqueiros' workshop. But there such painting experiments were used for the production of flags, banners and posters. It was not until after Pollock's encounter with Max Ernst that he began to splatter oil paints on his canvasses without using a paintbrush in 1943. It earned him the nickname "Jack the Dripper" – an allusion to the infamous serial killer. Pollock's painting method became famous as "action painting" because he used his body's entire gestural range when working on his immense canvasses. "Oscillation" and "action painting" are indeed directly related.

Max Ernst renewed work on his painting in 1947, rendering a head within the lines. As a basis, he relied on photographs of objects from the Institut Henri Poincaré in Paris meant to depict mathematical formulas in three dimensions. Ernst added a mouth and eyes and transformed the triangles into a stylized fish and a bird's head. The universal vision consequently extends from the deep sea up to the sky. The title of Ernst's painting initially varied and did not become definitive until 1959. Art historian Jürgen Pech asserts the image is an imaginary portrait of Jackson Pollock, whose head literally started spinning when confronted with a demonstration of Max Ernst's invention.

Dieter Scholz

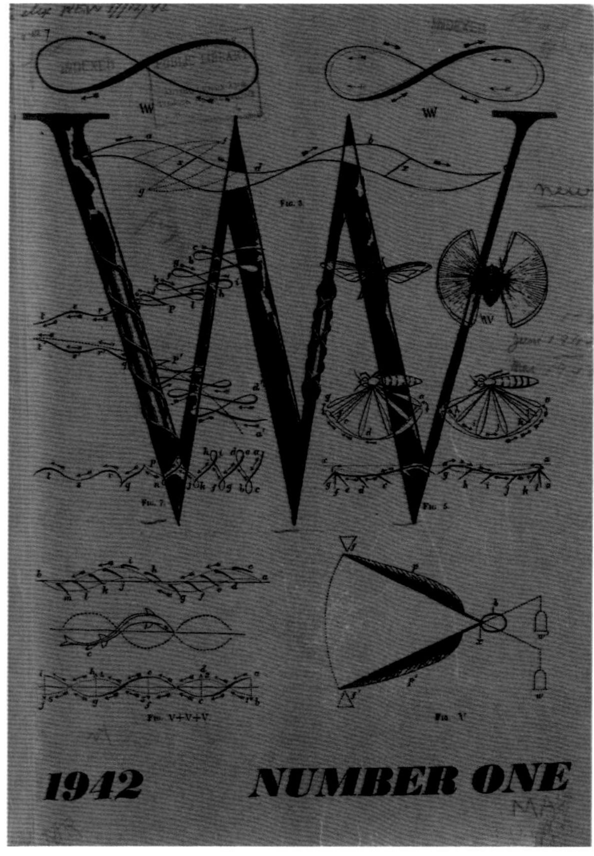

→ Max Ernst, cover page of the magazine *VVV*, no. 1, June 1942
← Max Ernst, *Surrealism and Painting*, 1942
← Jackson Pollock, 1950

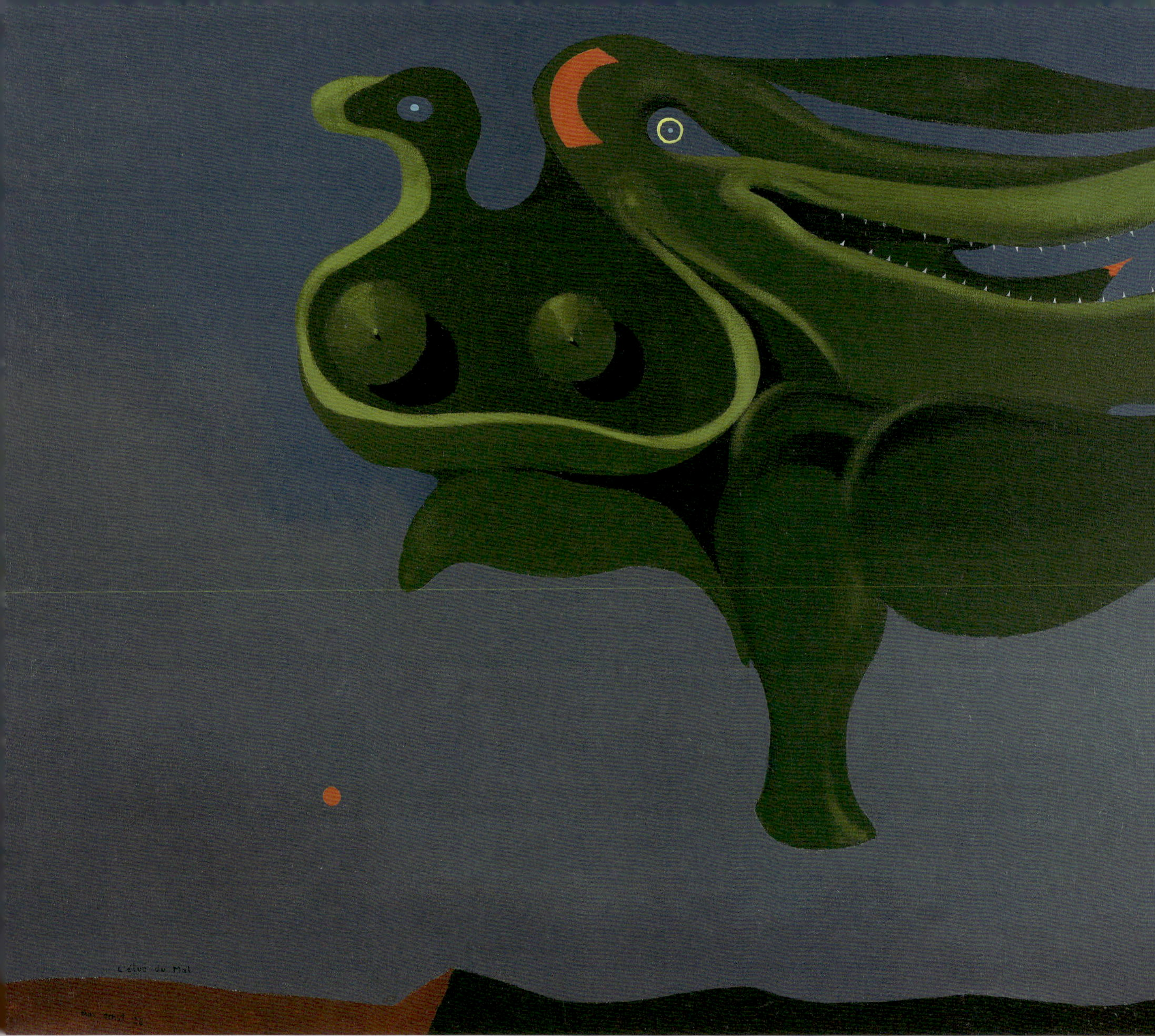

↑ Max Ernst, *The Evil Elect*, 1928
Oil on canvas, 197.5 × 301 cm
Acquired in 1967 by the Land Berlin for the Galerie des 20. Jahrhunderts, Berlin (West)

→ Joan Miró, *Painting*, 1925
Oil on canvas, 130 × 97 cm
Gift from the Ulla and Heiner Pietzsch Collection to the Land Berlin, 2010

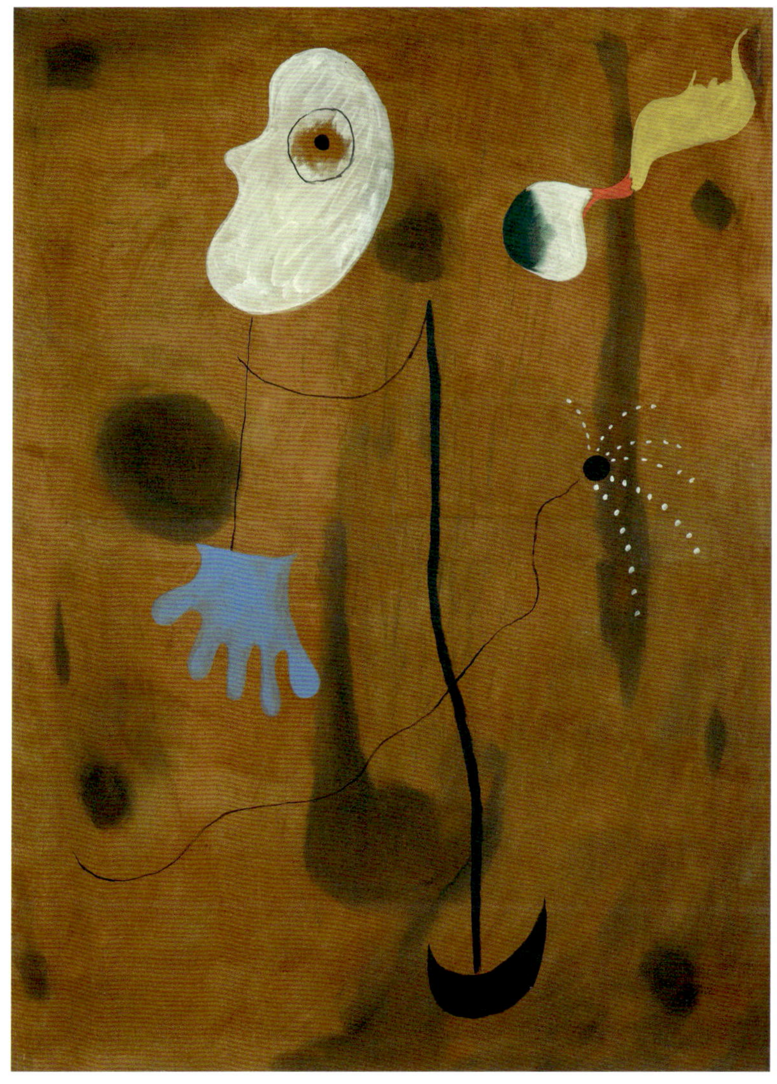

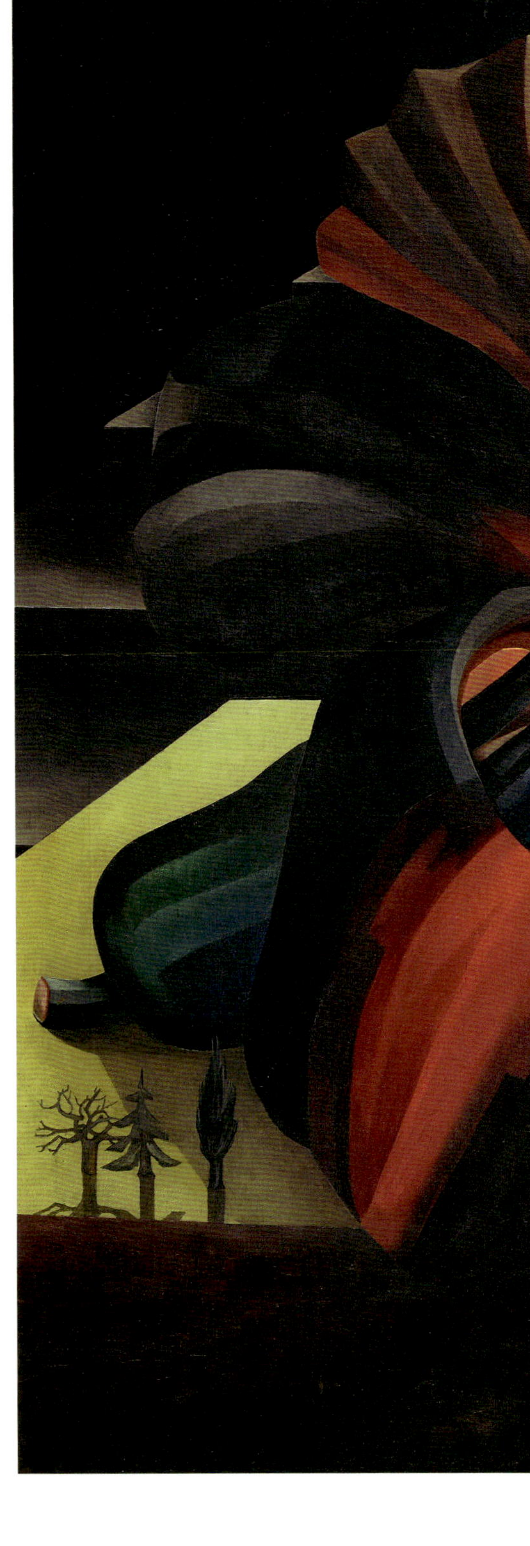

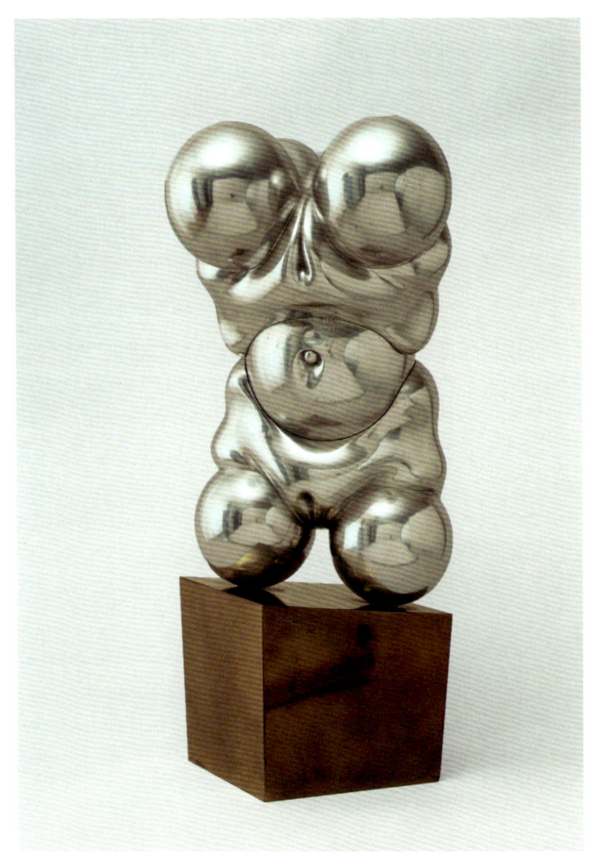

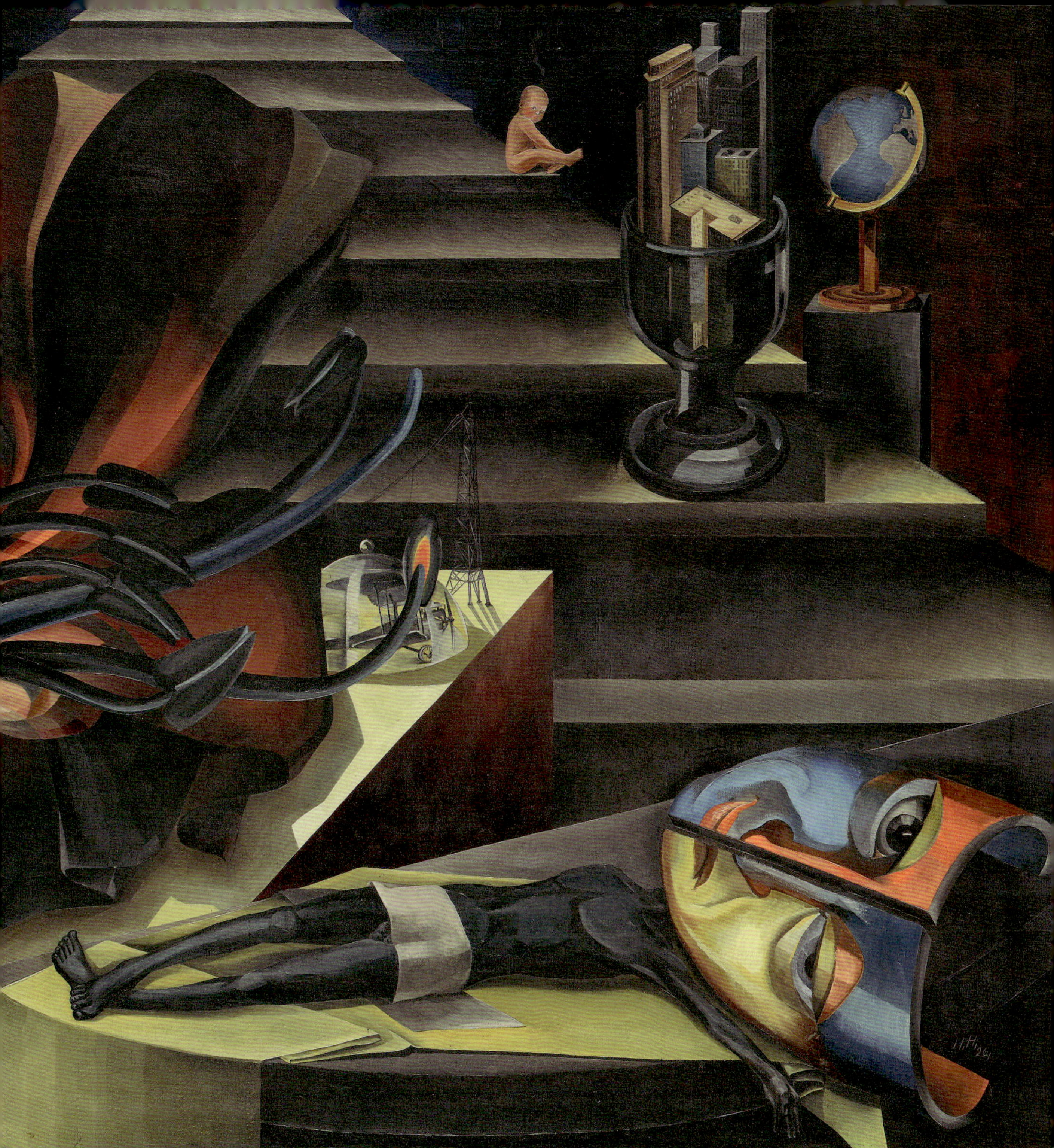

↑ Hannah Höch, *The Staircase*, 1923–26
Oil on canvas, 77 × 106 cm
Gift to the Nationalgalerie, Berlin (West) from the estate of the artist
by the heirs of Hannah Höch, 1978

← Hans Bellmer, *The Puppet*, 1936 (cast 1965)
Aluminium on a gold-patinated bronze pedestal, 50 × 27 × 25 cm
Gift from the Ulla and Heiner Pietzsch Collection to the Land Berlin, 2010

The Nonconformist Surrealist Leonor Fini

In the painting *Zwei Frauen* (Two Women), an androgynous, tall woman strides gracefully through a barren landscape of melting ice floes. She wears men's clothing in a Renaissance style, consisting of tights and a tunic that resembles a doublet. Burning candles are aglow in her extravagant coiffure. A second woman with long straight hair, dressed in a blue skirt, watches her. This figure is shown kneeling in front of a freestanding door, peering at the other woman through the keyhole. The work is signed with the name *Leonor Fini*.

Born in Argentina and raised in Italy, Fini had been associated with the Surrealists' circle in Paris since the mid-1930s. However, she never became an official member of this artist group founded exclusively by men. Fini repeatedly criticized André Breton's dogmatic understanding of art and his misogynistic worldview. Other women artists were also connected with the Surrealist movement in addition to Fini. These women appeared to be caught in a conflict between participating in what was happening and maintaining their distance. Leonora Carrington, Meret Oppenheim, Dora Maar and Dorothea Tanning also took up aspects of the unconscious, the dream and chance in their works but found their own, independent means of expression to expand the canon of Surrealist imagery.

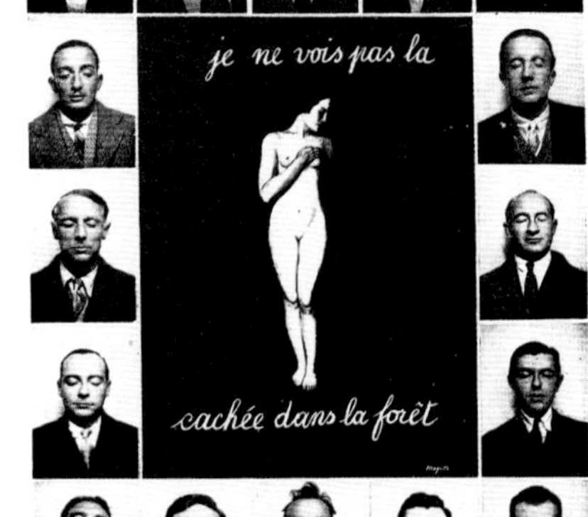

↗ Dora Maar, *Portrait of Leonor Fini, Lying on the Floor*, c. 1934
→ René Magritte, *Je ne vois pas la (femme) cachée dans la forêt*, surrounded by portraits of the Surrealists, in: *La Révolution Surréaliste*, no. 12, 1929

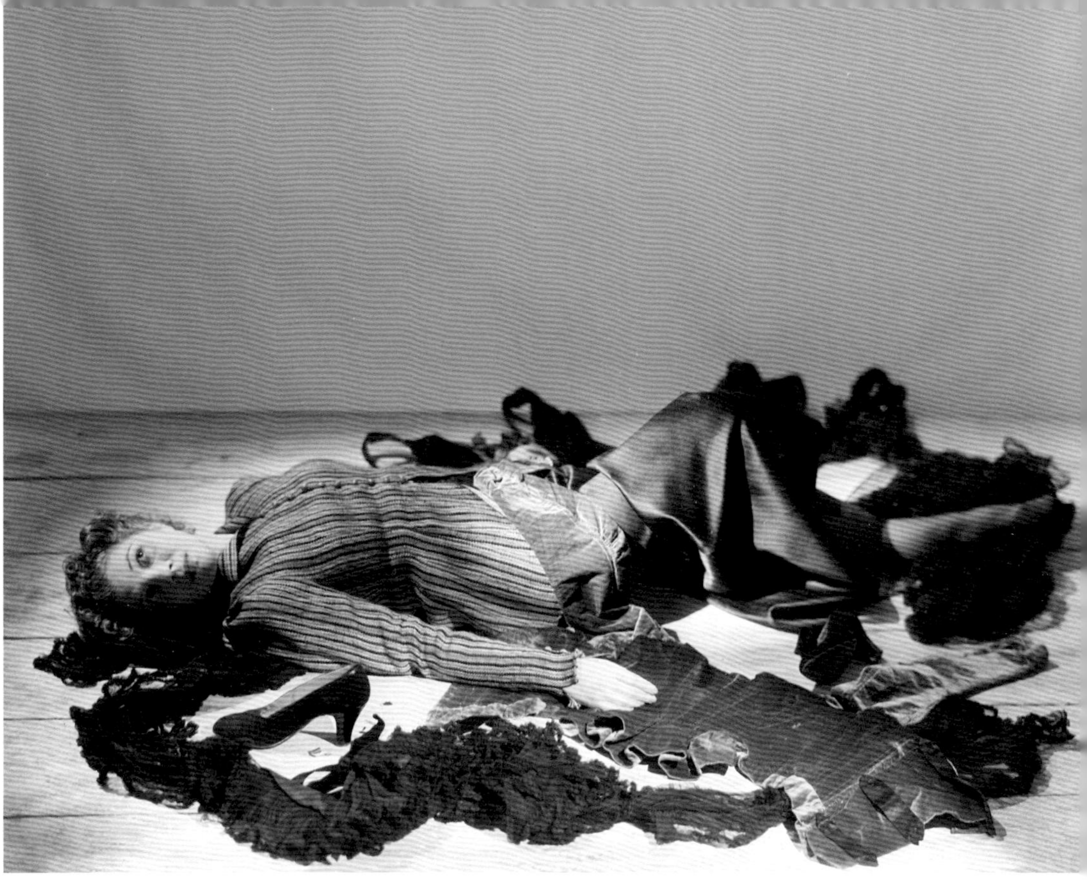

The nonconformist Surrealist Leonor Fini developed an alternative model for feminine identity in her works. The women she depicted appear to be sensual and omnipotent beings, whether portrayed as nymphs, priestesses or sphinxes. The artist often staged an interaction between a dominant woman and a passive man, turning traditional gender roles on their heads. Repeatedly, Fini also depicted two opposite types of women, usually in an ambivalent relationship that oscillates between rivalry and eroticism. In *Zwei Frauen*, Fini is possibly portrayed as the striding woman, suggested by the upswept, feline hairstyle familiar from several of her self-portraits. In this scene, the figure is shown as literally "inflamed" with passion yet fully autonomous. The second woman, on the other hand, has been assigned the role of the adoring voyeur.

The painting fits well into Fini's oeuvre. Helena Rubinstein in New York was the work's first documented owner. Following her death, it was sold at auction in 1966, after which the painting changed hands several times and went to England, returned to the USA, then to Italy and Austria. Ulla and Heiner Pietzsch purchased the work for their collection in 1997, which they gave to Berlin in 2010. It is now on permanent loan to the Nationalgalerie. For decades the painting was attributed to Fini. Late in her life, however, the artist claimed that this work was not by her hand. As a result, the painting is not listed in the new catalogue raisonné on Leonor Fini, published in 2021 by Richard Overstreet and Neil Zukerman. The question of attribution remains open. Extensive conservation studies may provide clarification.

Irina Hiebert Grun

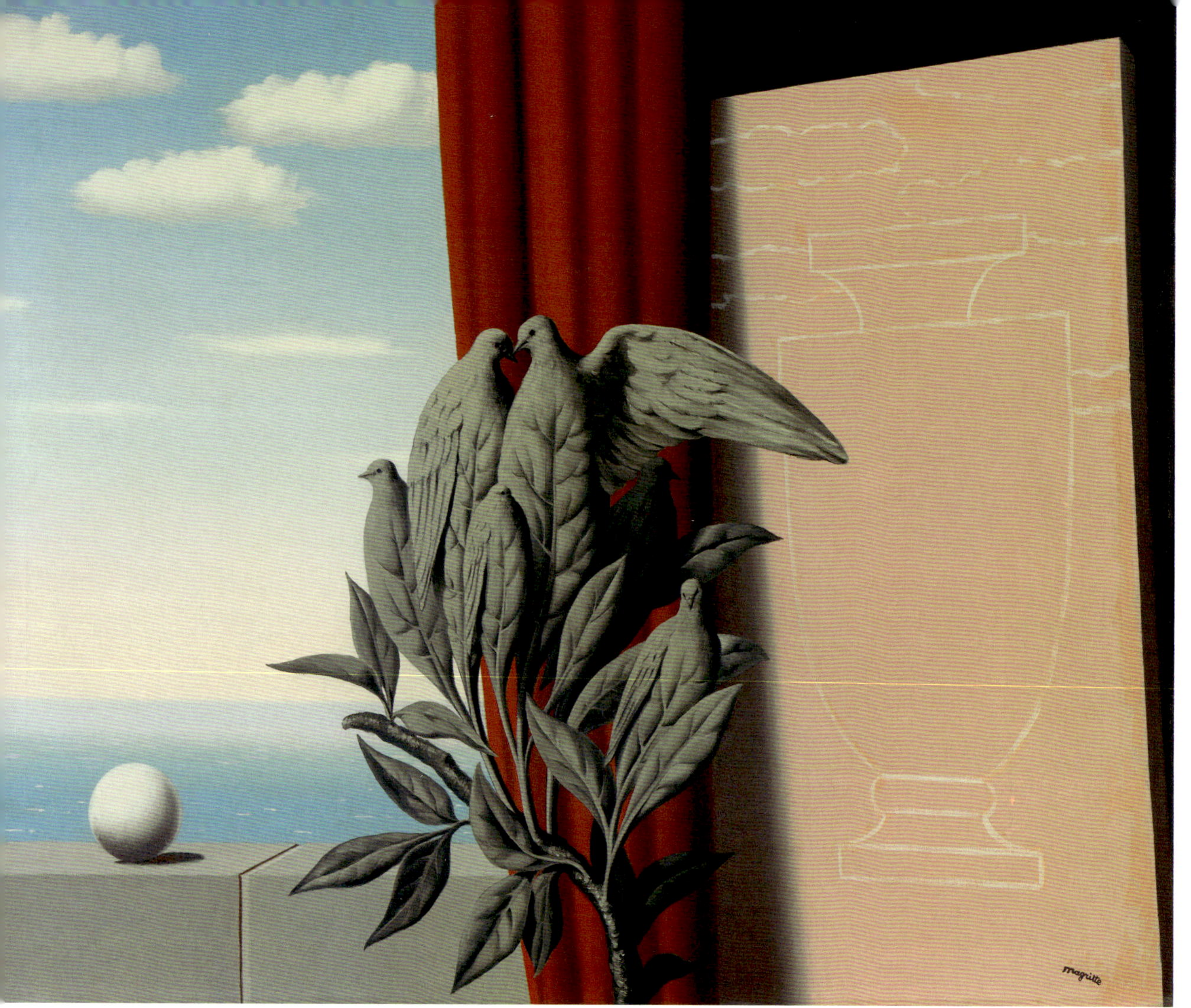

↑ René Magritte, *The Equator*, 1942
Oil on canvas, 59.5 × 73 cm
Gift from the Ulla and Heiner Pietzsch
Collection to the Land Berlin, 2010

→ Attribution in dispute (formerly Leonor Fini), *Two Women*, 1939
Oil on canvas, 34 × 24.5 cm
Gift from the Ulla and Heiner Pietzsch
Collection to the Land Berlin, 2010

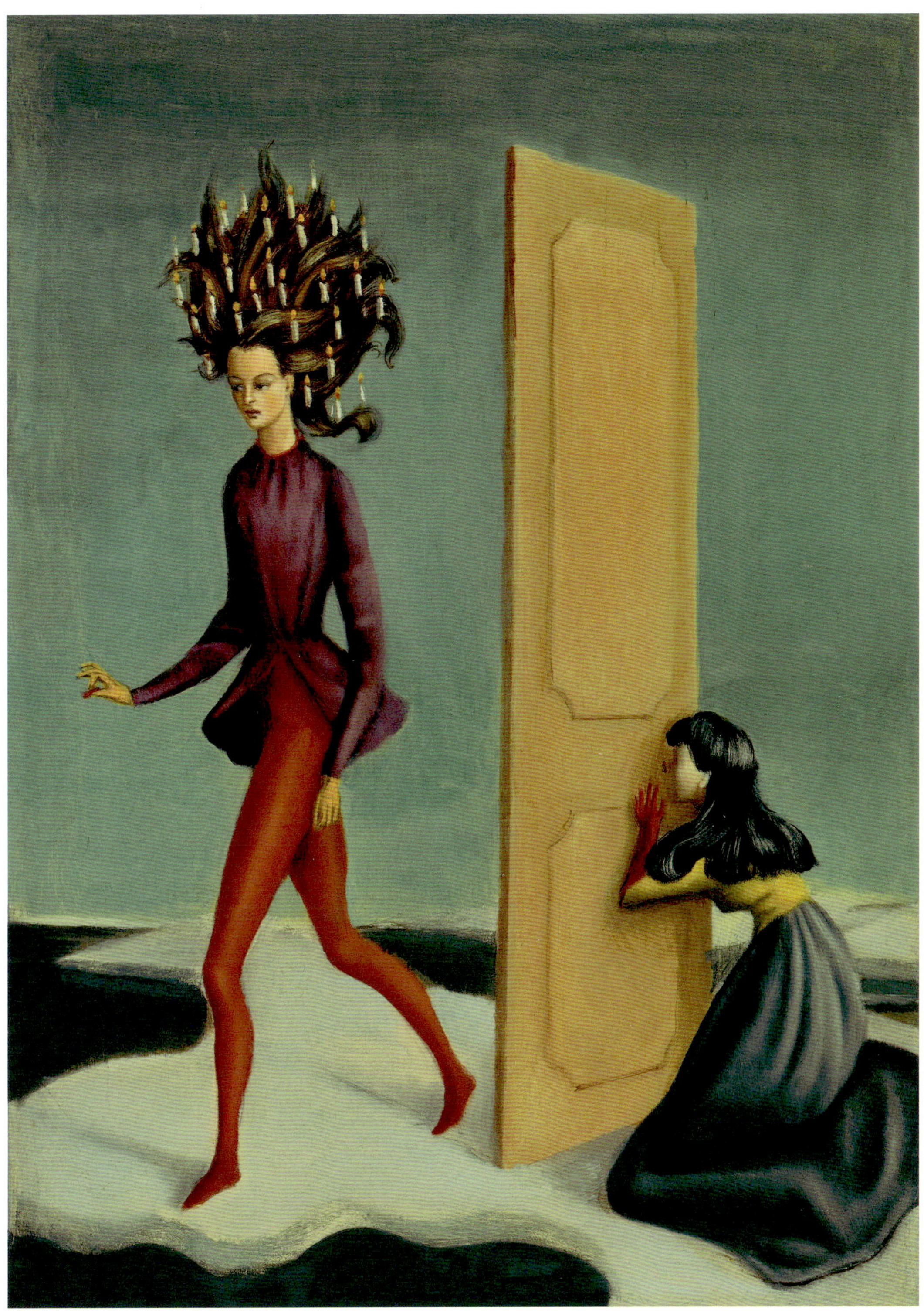

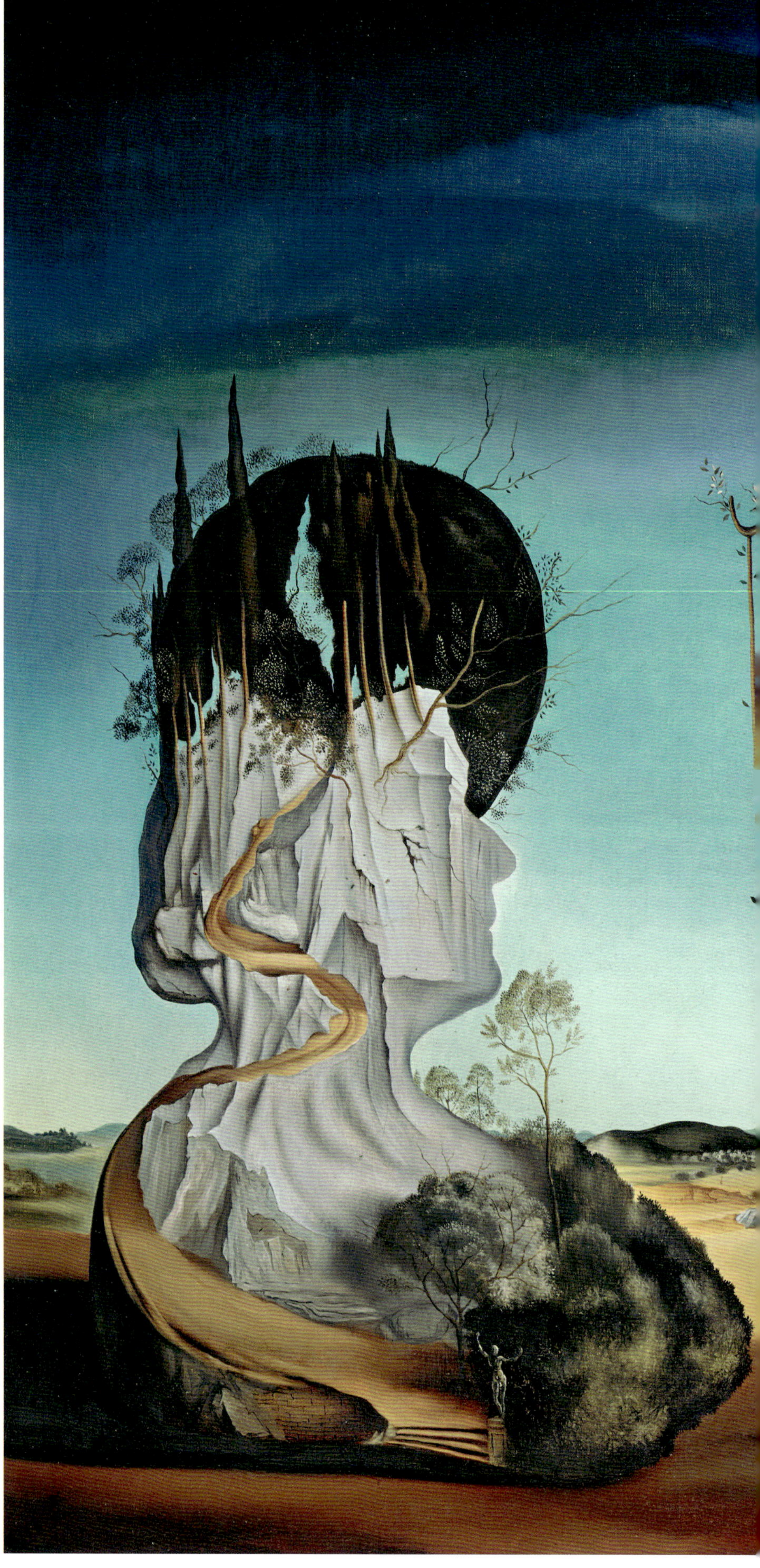

Salvador Dalí, *Portrait of Mrs Isabel Styler-Tas (Melancolía)*, 1945
Oil on canvas, 65.5 × 86 cm
Acquired in 1958 by the Land Berlin with funds from the Deutsche Klassenlotterie for the Galerie des 20. Jahrhunderts, Berlin (West)

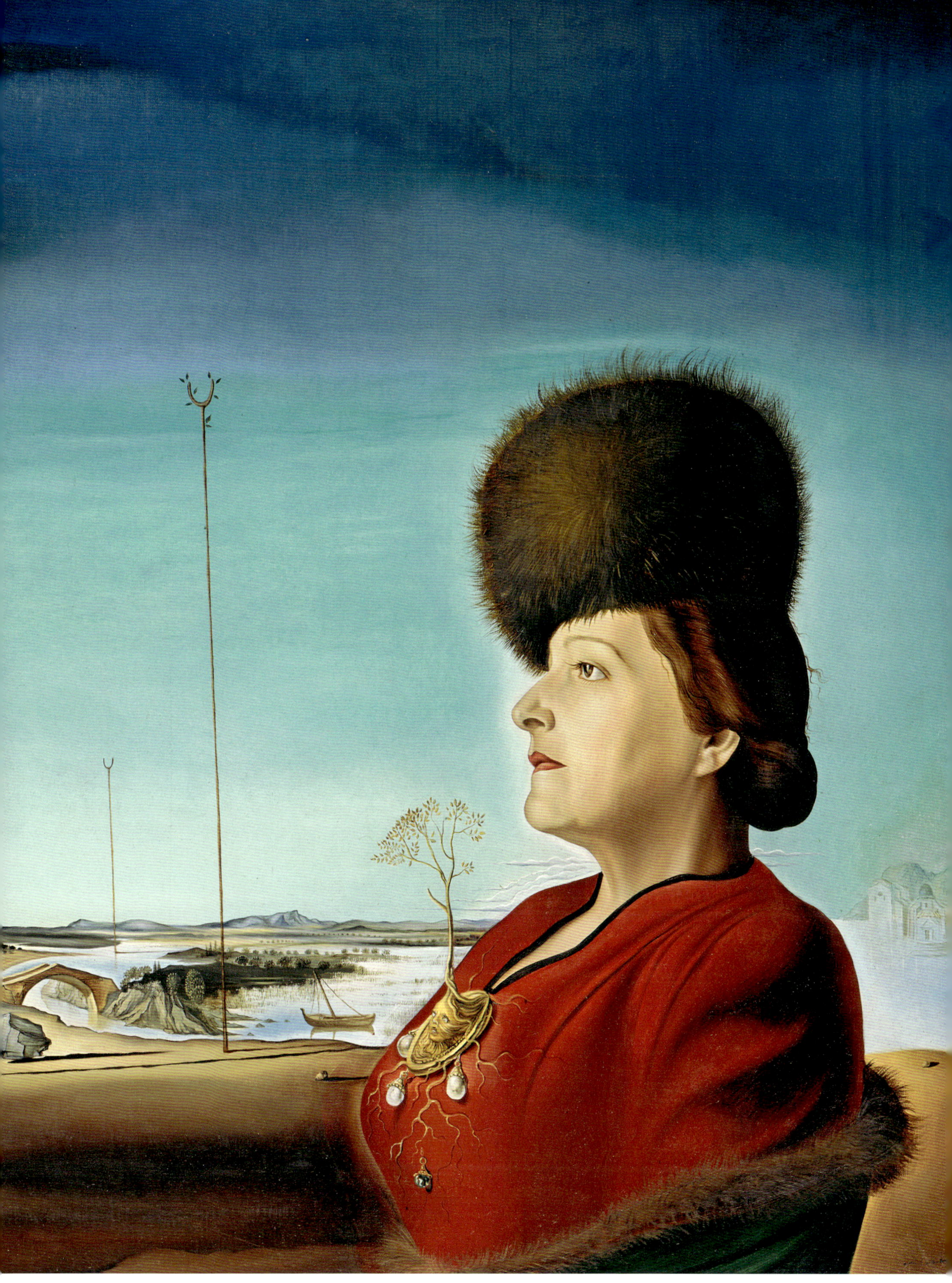

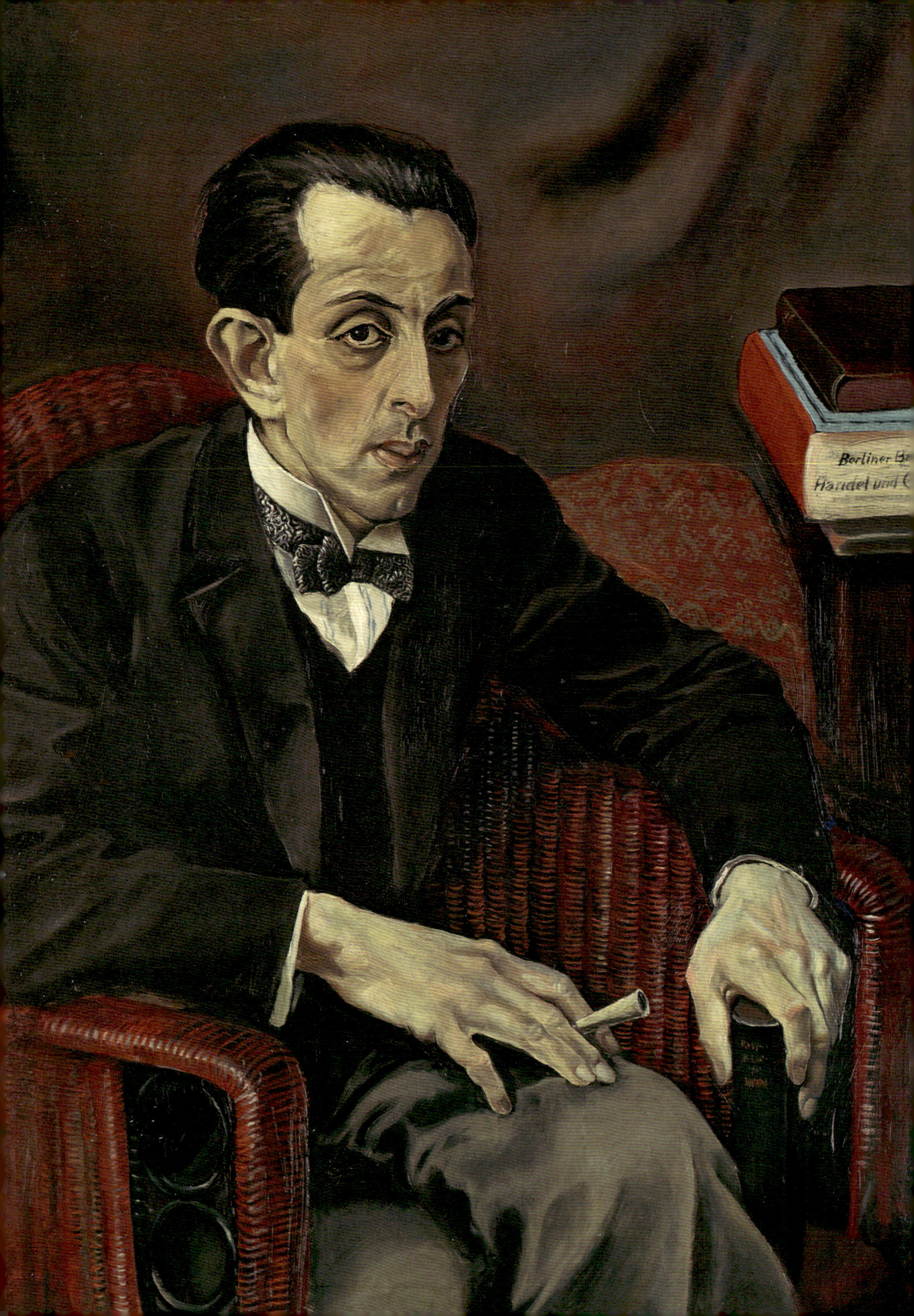
Berliner
Handel und

Sharp Looks

The New Objectivity movement established a painting style in the Weimar Republic that brought its subject matter into razor-sharp focus. Embodying a new sobriety, its artists produced sober portraits, still lifes and landscapes precisely reflecting social developments of the times. With his portrait of an emancipated woman sitting in a Berlin café, Christian Schad summarized a modern attitude towards life in the 1920s. The integration of new technologies into the world of work and daily life also found expression, for example, when Kurt Günther showed the radio listener at home (*Der Radionist*) and when Georg Schrimpf captured radio transmission towers in the landscape.

Alongside explicit references to technological progress, visual elements appear whose hidden political or melancholy statements first have to be decoded. In 1933, for instance, Curt Querner painted a self-portrait holding a (stinging) nettle in his hand as a symbol of resistance to the National Socialists, who had just come to power. In another work from 1933, Wilhelm Lachnit painted an allegory of spring, traditionally associated with youth and beauty, but here it appears personified as an ageing, withering woman. *Der traurige Frühling* (The Melancholy Spring) is a symbol for the arts at the beginning of the National Socialist dictatorship.

Rudolf Schlichter, *Portrait of Géza von Cziffra*, 1926–27
Oil on cardboard, 100 × 74 cm
Acquired in 1948 from the Galerie Meta Nierendorf, Berlin, for the Galerie des 20. Jahrhunderts. Gift from the Magistrat von Groß-Berlin to the Nationalgalerie, Berlin (East), 1951

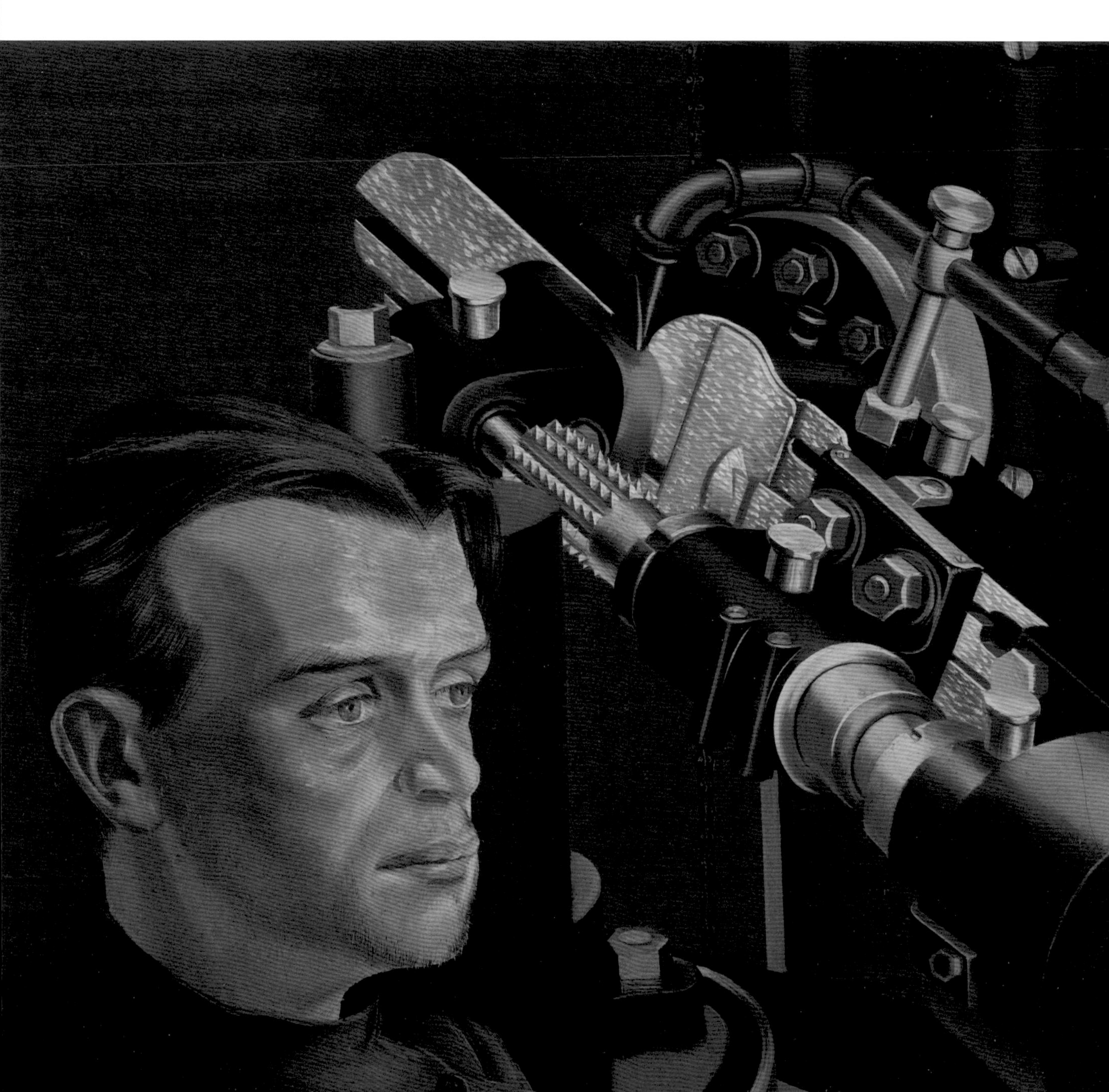

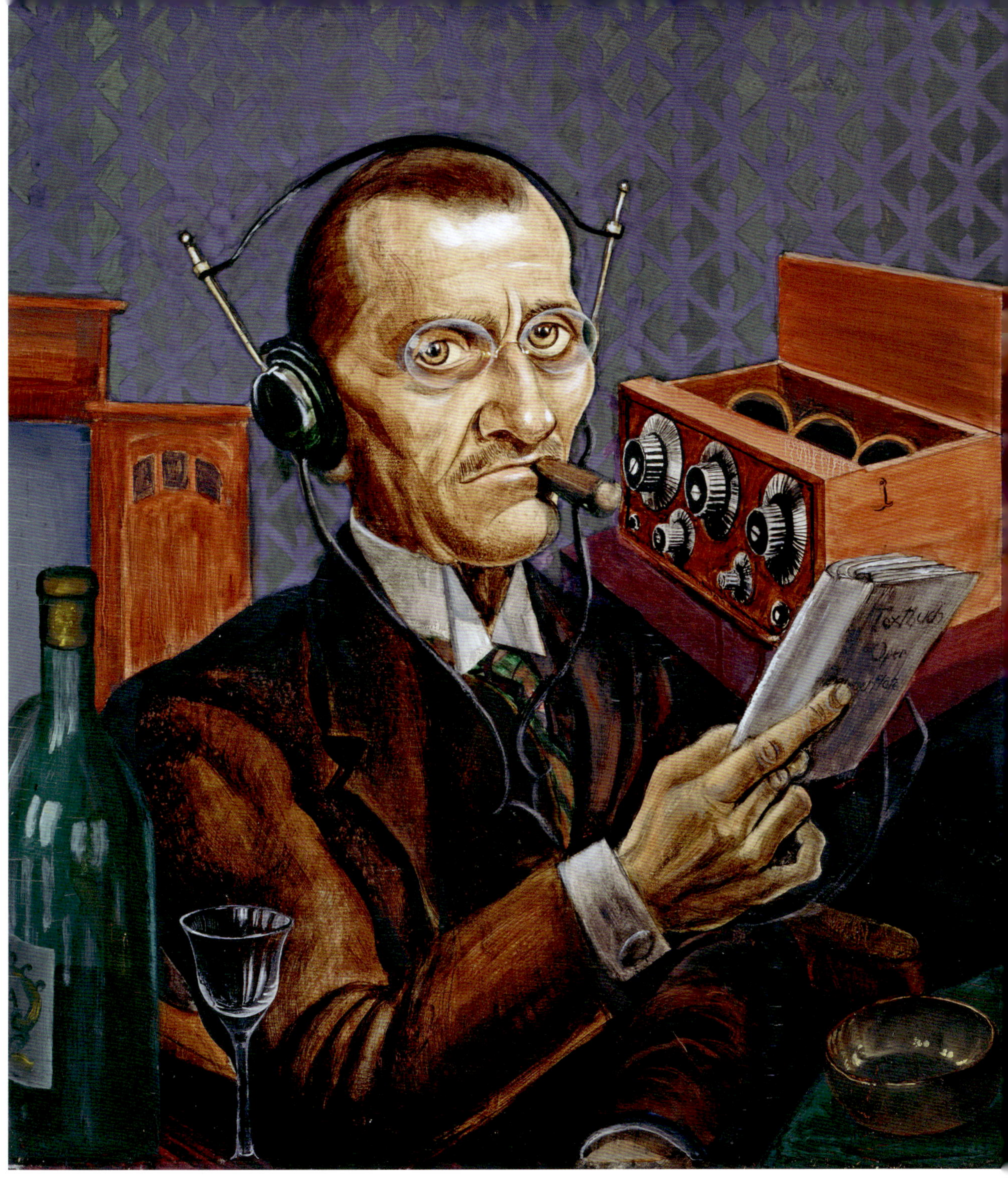

↑ Kurt Günther, *The Radionist*, 1927
Tempera on wood, 55 × 49 cm
Acquired in 1967 from the artist's widow, Maria Günther, Gera, for the Nationalgalerie, Berlin (East)

← Wilhelm Lachnit, *Worker With Machine*, 1924–28
Oil on wood, 50 × 52 cm
Acquired in 1964 from Max Lachnit, the artist's brother, Dresden, for the Nationalgalerie, Berlin (East)

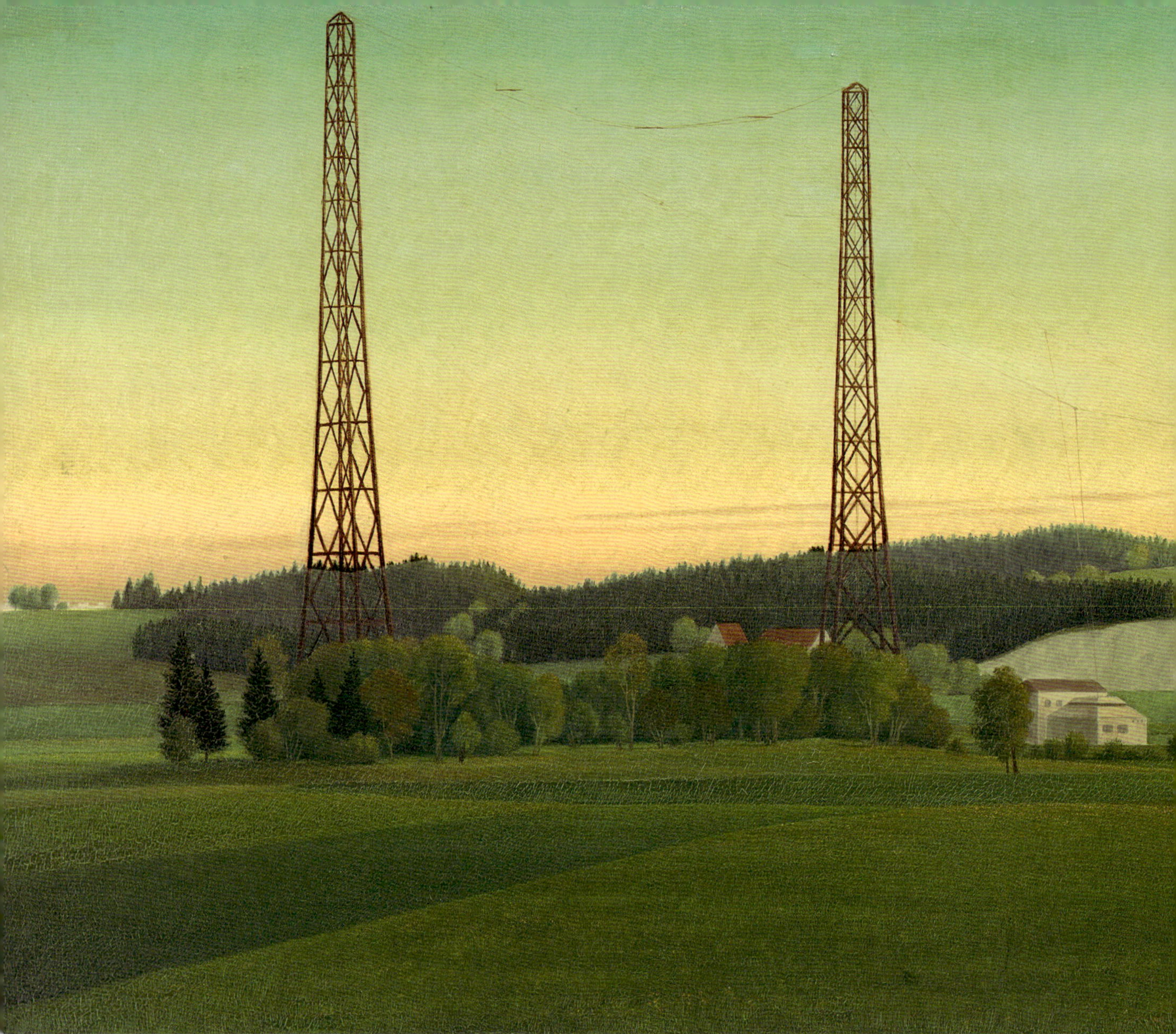

↑ Georg Schrimpf, *Radio Transmitters (Fürstenfeldbruck)*, 1933
Oil on canvas, 57 × 90.5 cm
Transferred in 1935 from the Ministerium für Wissenschaft, Kunst und Volksbildung

→ Georg Schrimpf, *Two Girls by the Window*, 1937
Oil on canvas, 78.5 × 73 cm
Acquired in 1966 from the artist's widow, Hedwig Schrimpf, Berlin (East), for the Nationalgalerie, Berlin (East)

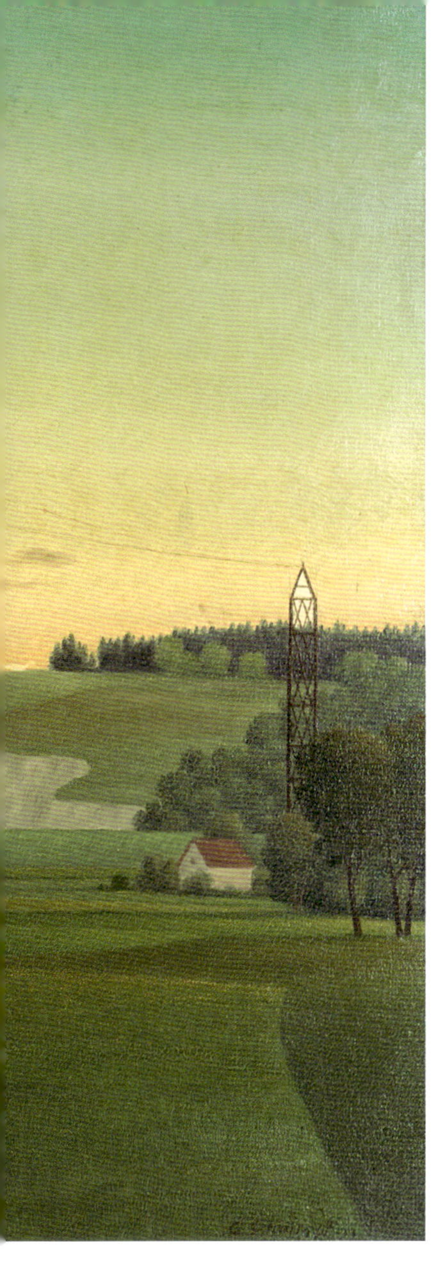

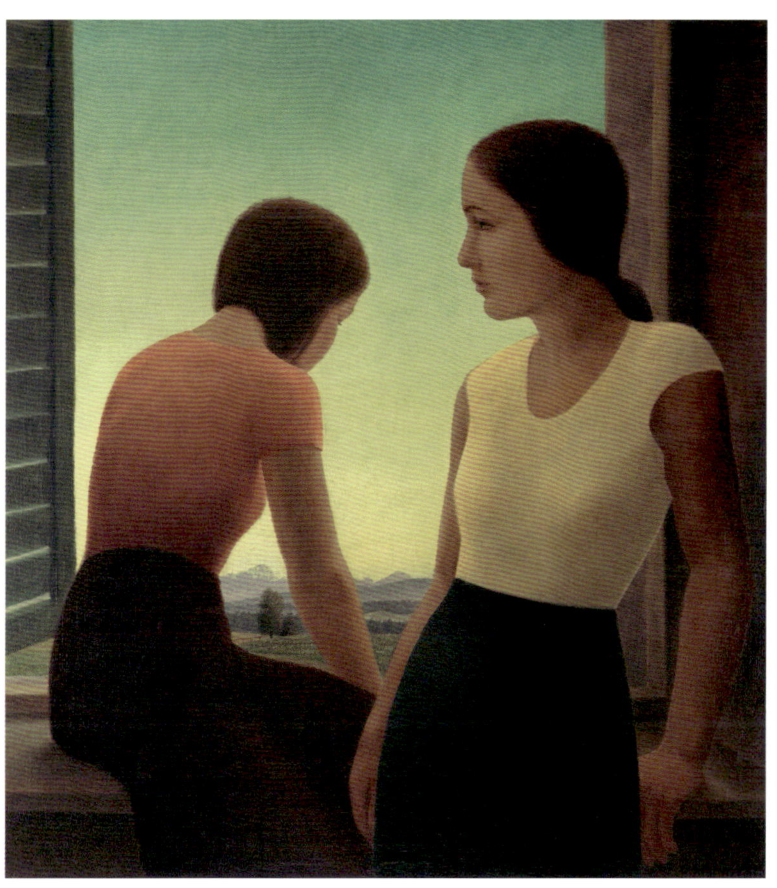

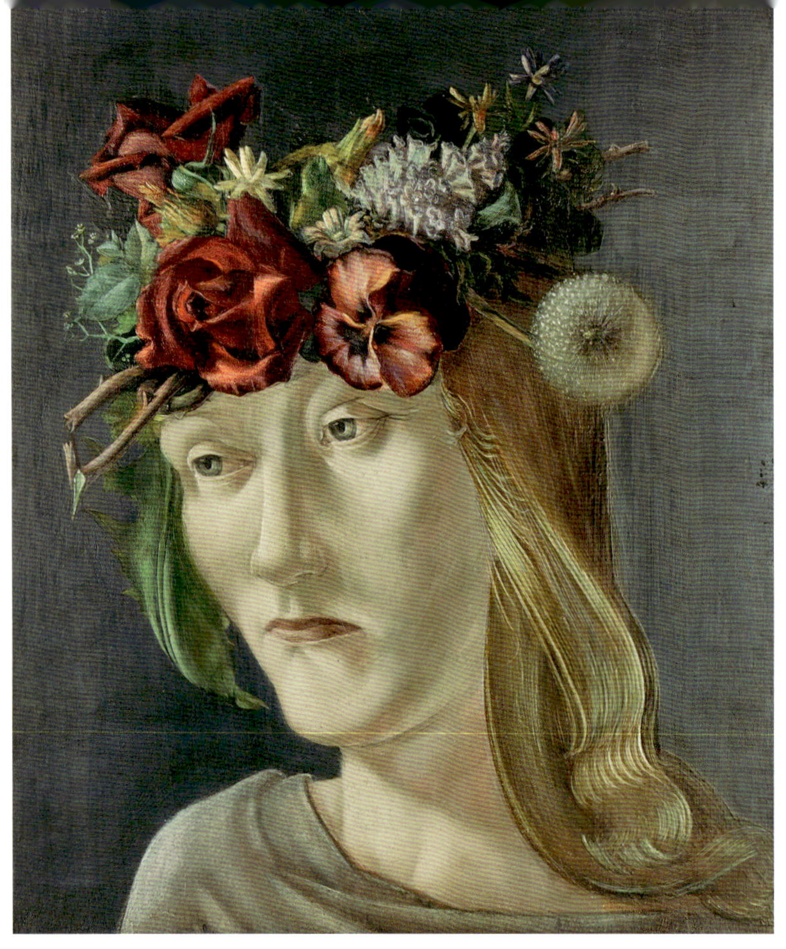

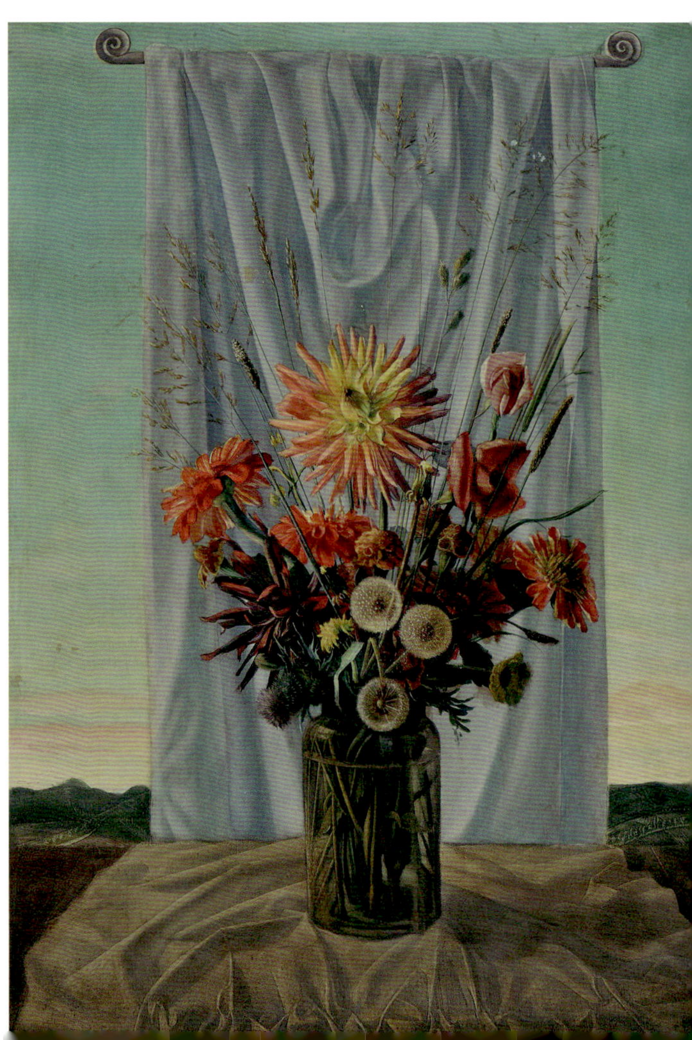

↑ Wilhelm Lachnit, *The Melancholy Spring*, 1933
Oil on wood, 35 × 29 cm
Acquired in 1969 from the artist's brother, Max Lachnit, Dresden, for the Nationalgalerie, Berlin (East)

→ Wilhelm Lachnit, *Bouquet of Flowers in Front of Curtain and Landscape*, c. 1933
Oil on canvas on wood, 75 × 54.5 cm
Acquired in 1973 from the sister-in-law of the artist, Helene Lachnit, born Tischer, Dresden via Kunsthandlung Kühl, Dresden, for the Nationalgalerie, Berlin (East)

↗ Kurt Günther, *Portrait of a Boy*, 1928
Tempera on wood, 48 × 37 cm
Acquired in 1967 from the artist's widow, Maria Günther, Gera, for the Nationalgalerie, Berlin (East)

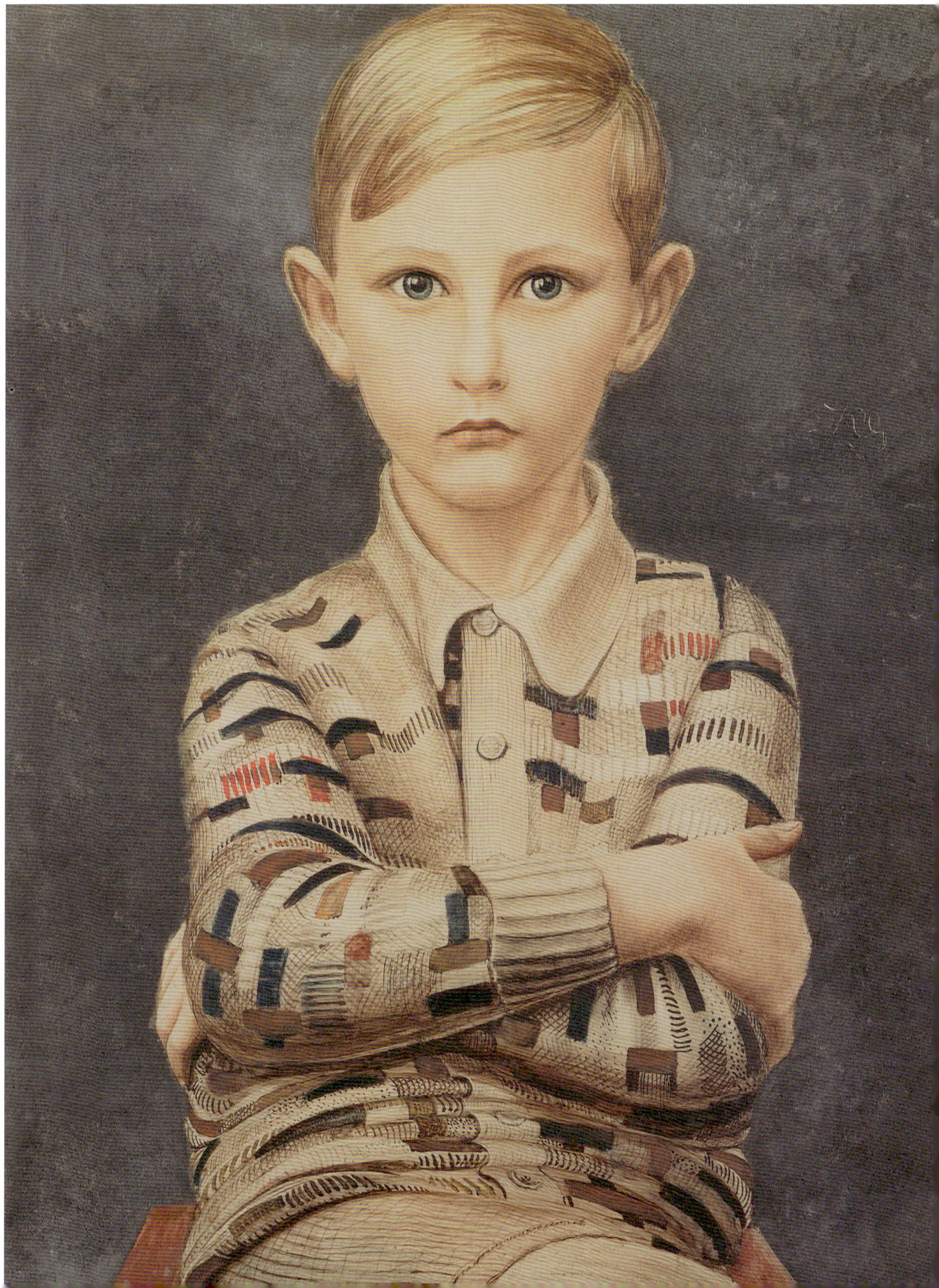

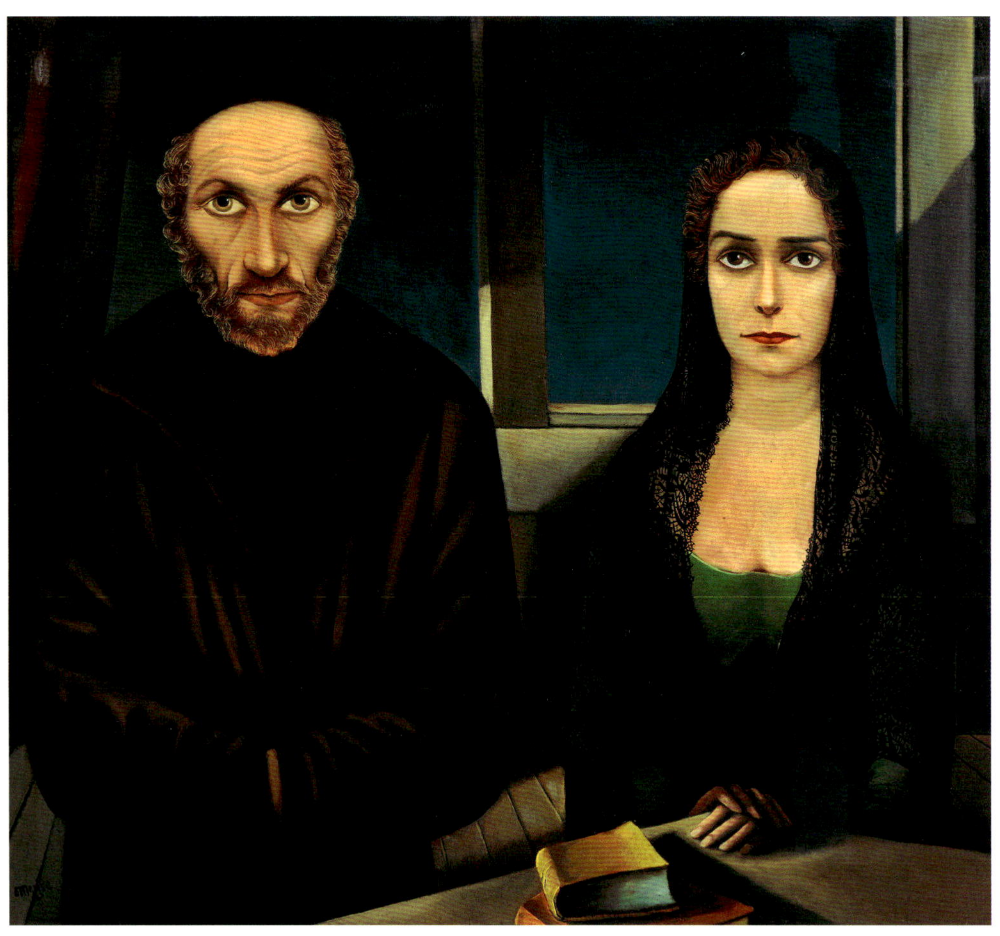

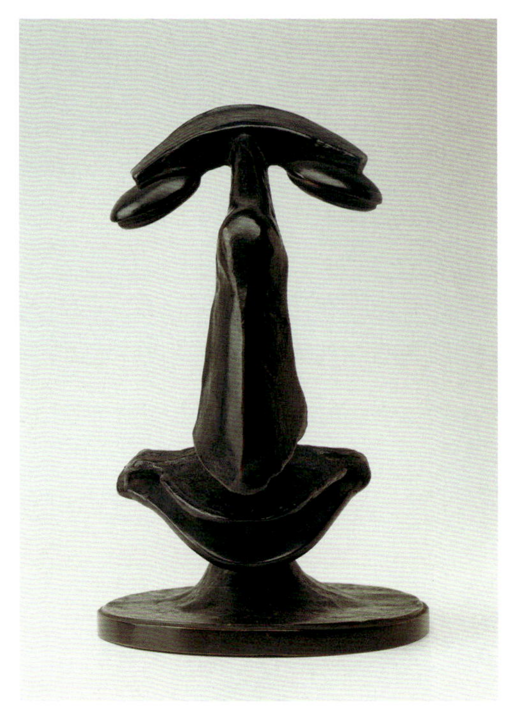

↑ Carlo Mense, *Double-Portrait (Rabbi S. and Daughter)*, c. 1925–26
Oil on canvas, 90 × 100.5 cm
Acquired by Ismar Littmann, Breslau (now Wrocław); transfer of ownership to the Dresdner Bank in Breslau after 1929; purchased from the Dresdner Bank's art holdings by the Prussian state and transferred to the Staatliche Museen zu Berlin in 1935; previous owner Schwedenberg

→ Rudolf Belling, *Portrait of Alfred Flechtheim*, 1927 (cast 1920s)
Bronze, 18.7 × 12 × 13 cm
Gift from Wolfgang Werner, Bremen, to the Freunde der Nationalgalerie, 2005

↗ Otto Dix, *The Art Dealer Alfred Flechtheim*, 1926
Oil on wood, 120 × 80 cm
Acquired in 1961 from the artist by the Land Berlin with funds from the Deutsche Klassenlotterie for the Nationalgalerie, Berlin (West)

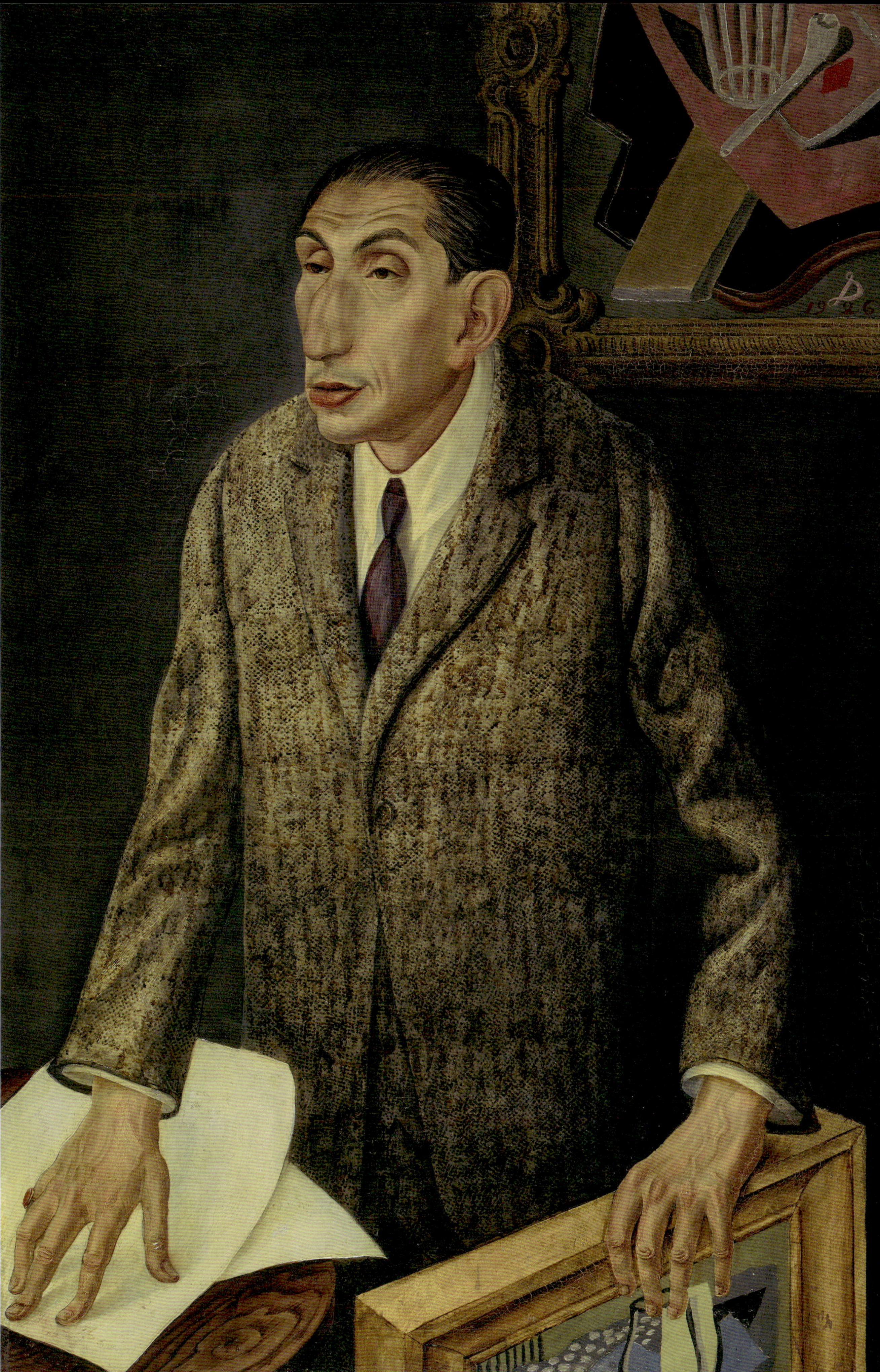
1926

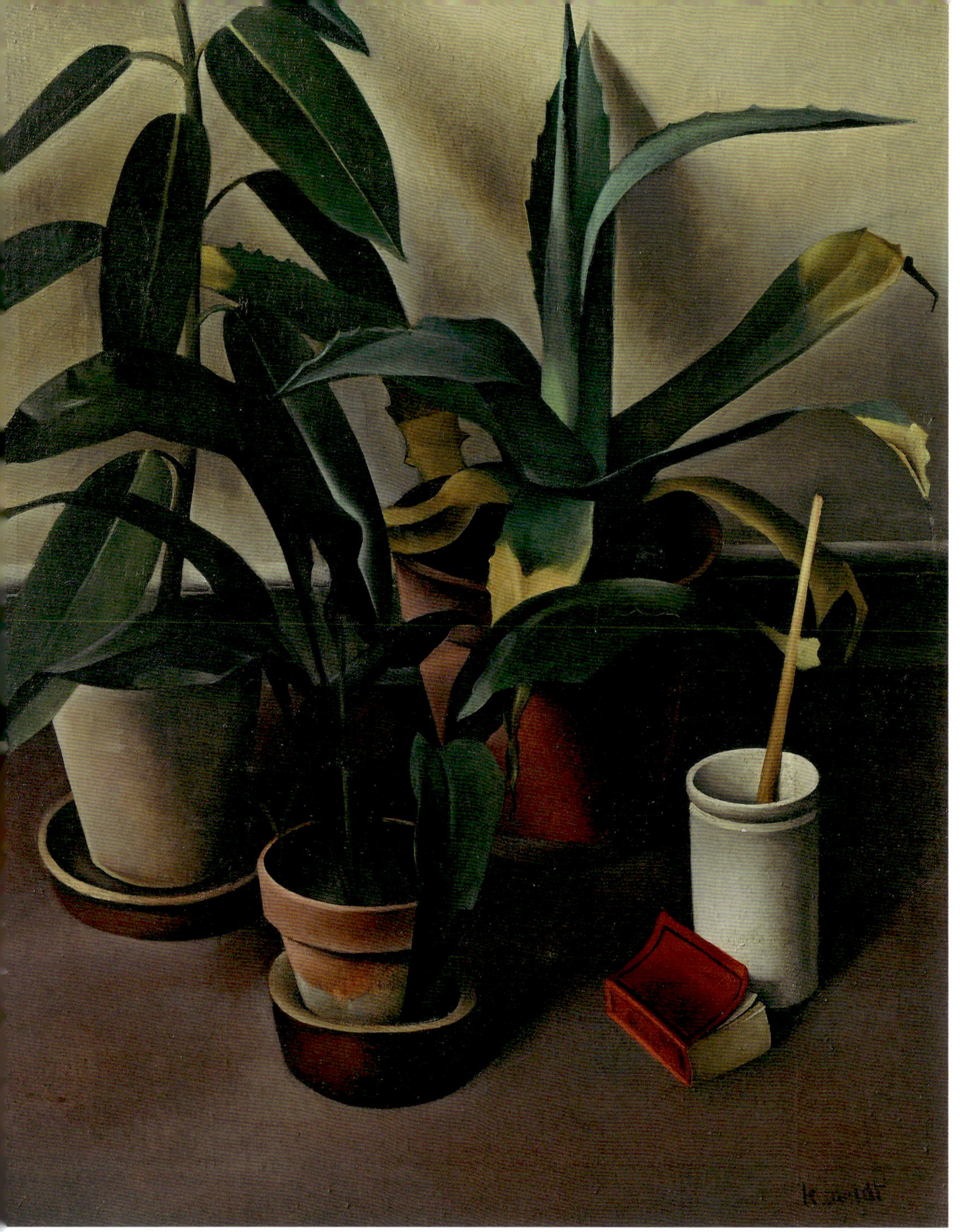

↑ Alexander Kanoldt, *Still Life I*, 1926
Oil on canvas, 78.5 × 64 cm
Acquired in 1928 from the Ministerium für Wissenschaft, Kunst und Volksbildung and transferred to the Nationalgalerie

→ Franz Lenk, *Amaryllis*, 1930
Egg tempera on canvas on wood, 66 × 44 cm
Acquired in 1930 by Eduard Freiherr von der Heydt for the Freunde der Nationalgalerie

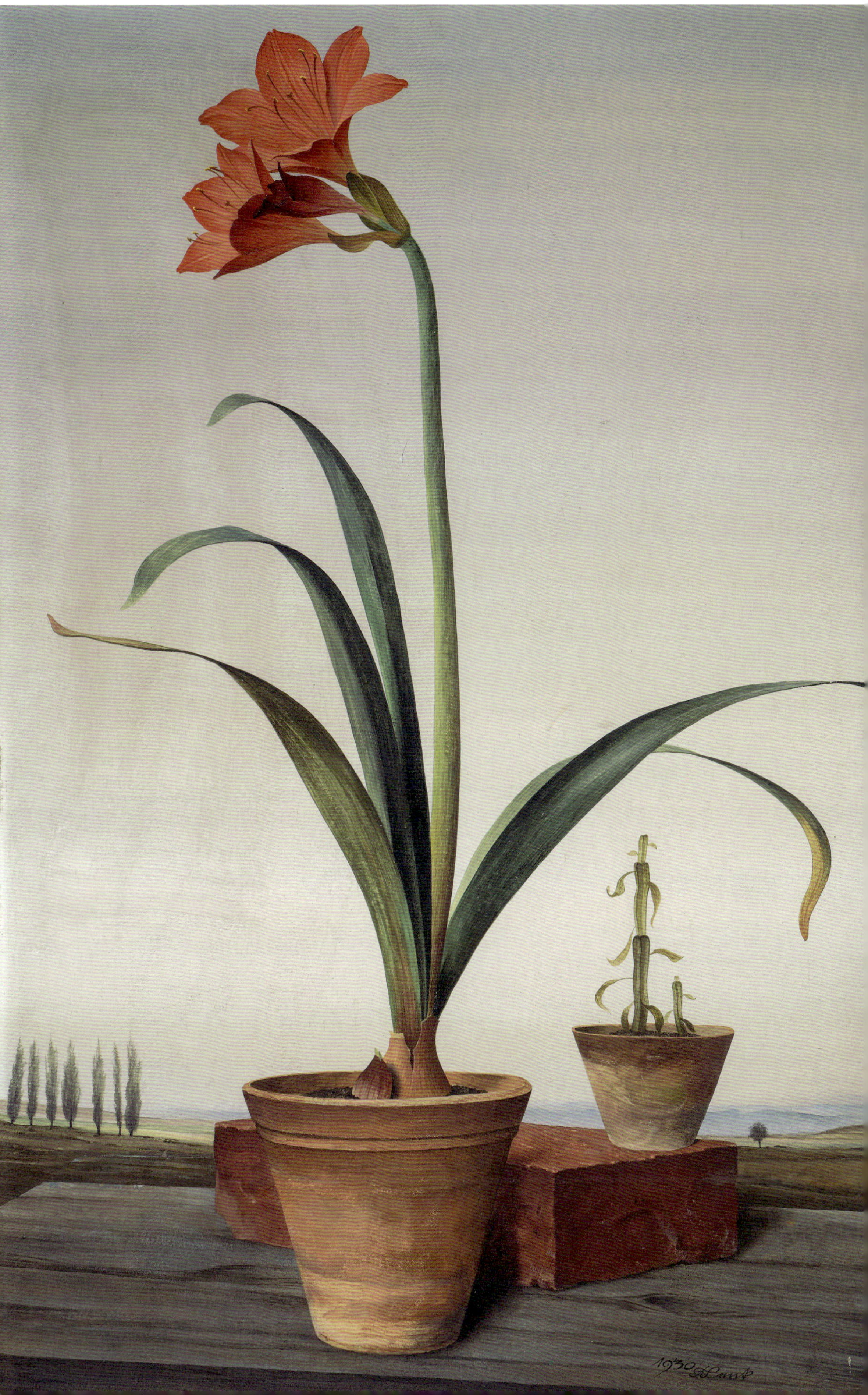

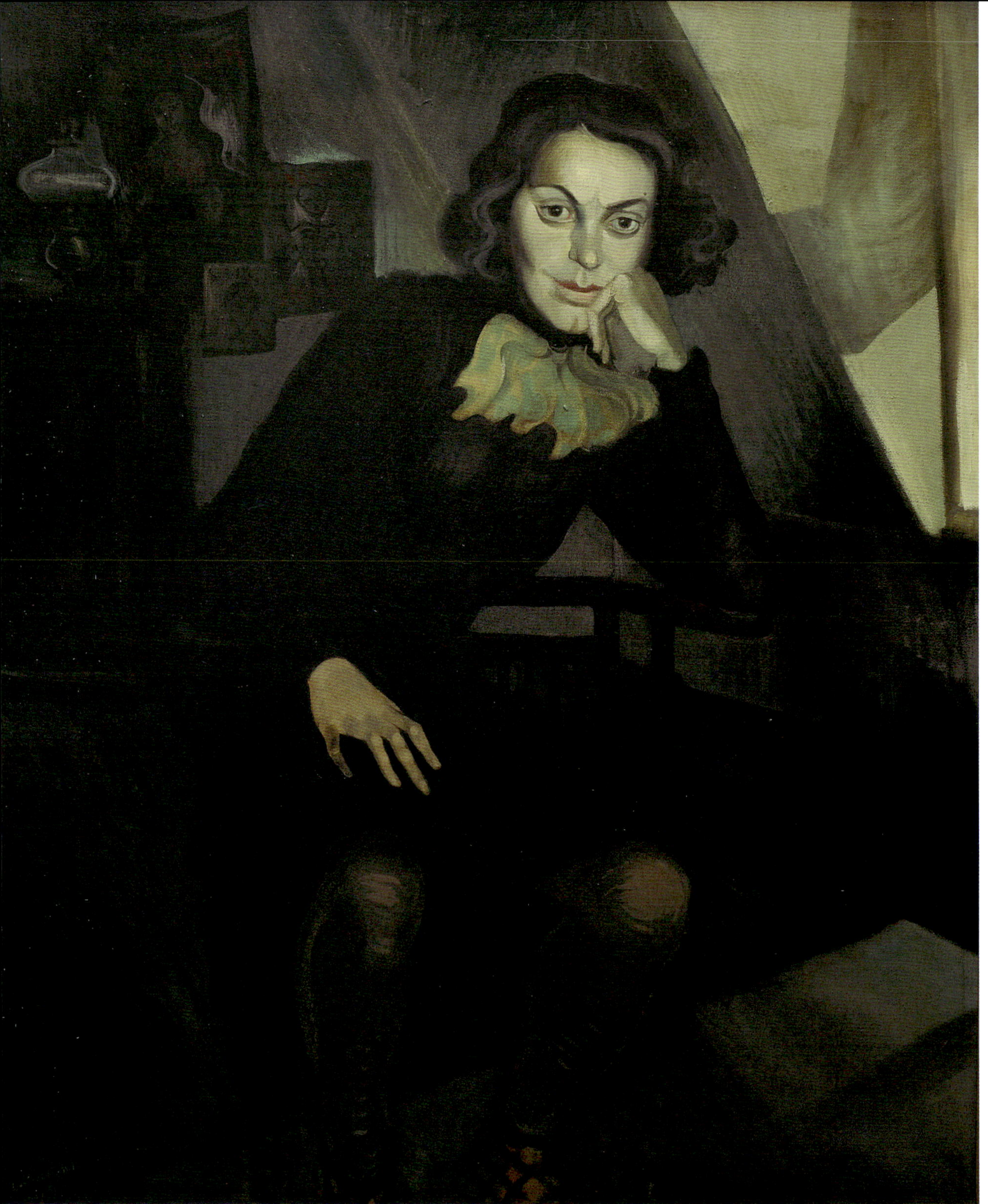

↑ Hans Grundig, *Portrait of my Wife*, 1929
Oil on canvas, 120 × 100 cm
Acquired in 1965 from the estate of the artist with funds from the Kulturfonds der DDR for the Nationalgalerie, Berlin (East)

→ Curt Querner, *Self-Portrait with Stinging Nettle*, 1933
Oil on cardboard, 102 × 68 cm
Acquired in 1983 from the artist's widow, Regina Querner, with funds from the Kulturfonds der DDR for the Nationalgalerie, Berlin (East)

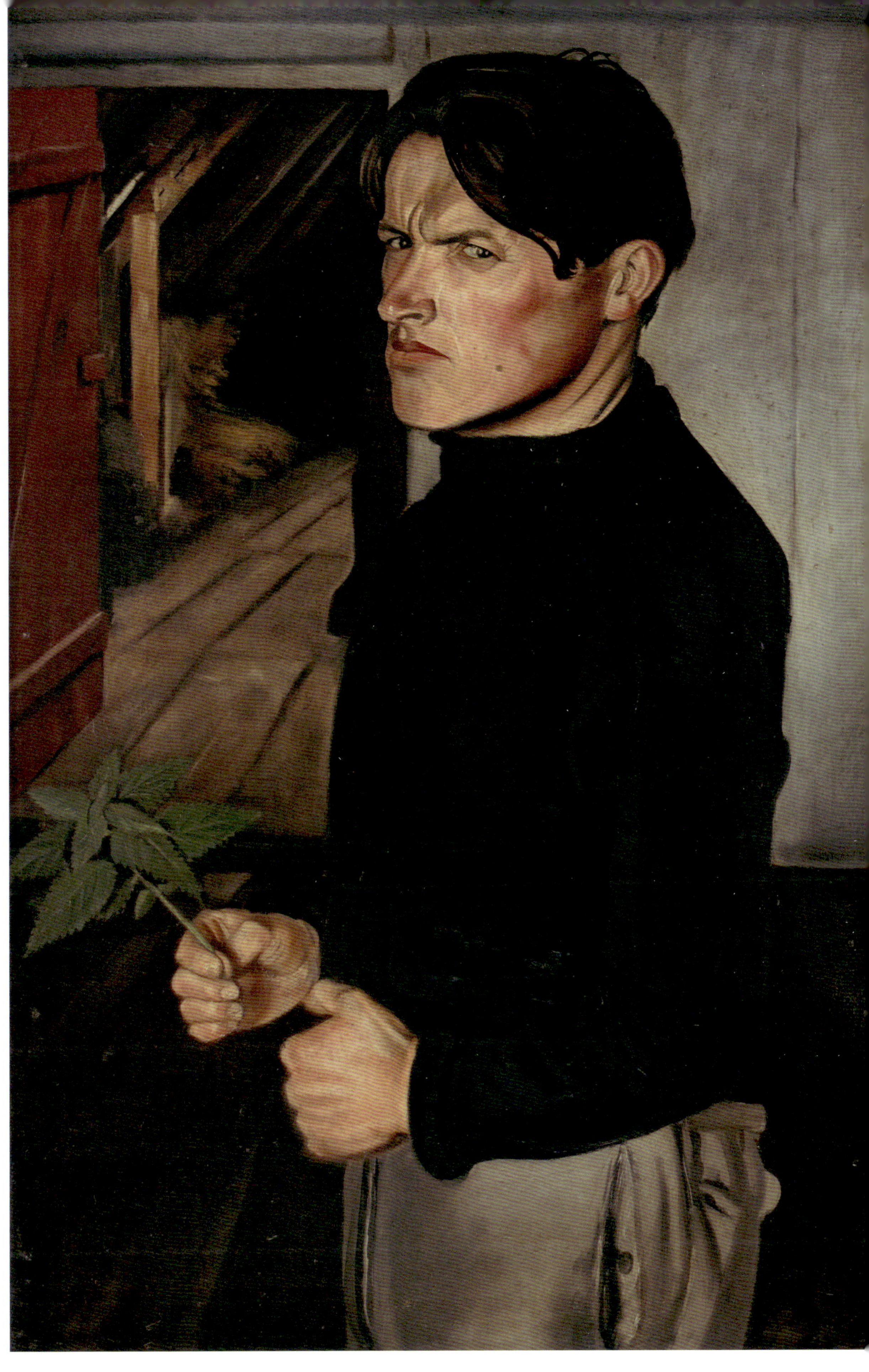

The New Feminine Self-Image

At the start of the 20th century, a process of social modernization began, which went hand in hand with a new understanding of gender roles. During the First World War, women took over new, independent tasks in society and the working world, brought about by the absence of the men, who were at the front. At war's end, many young women did not want to be forced back into their traditional roles and broke with the conventional lifestyles expected of them. The introduction of the right to vote in 1918 was another decisive step for the emancipation of women.

Increasing urbanization gave rise to modern mass society, and the increasing demand for employees opened new opportunities for women from lower social classes to earn a living. This new feminine self-image led to the appearance of the "New Woman" in everyday urban life, much like Christian Schad had staged her in his painting *Sonja*. Novels, magazines, film and advertising shaped and communicated the image of this new woman.

The typical modern woman took a job as an employee, working as a saleswoman, shorthand typist or telephone operator. She also frequented cafés and nightclubs alone, without a male companion, and chose her own lovers – whether her choice was male or female. The game with gender boundaries played itself out especially through clothes and fashions, because women rid themselves of their corsets, choosing instead to wear pantsuits, ties and men's hats, as well as knee-length skirts and dresses. Kate Diehn-Bitt depicted herself in this way in her self-portraits, sporting a stylish, short

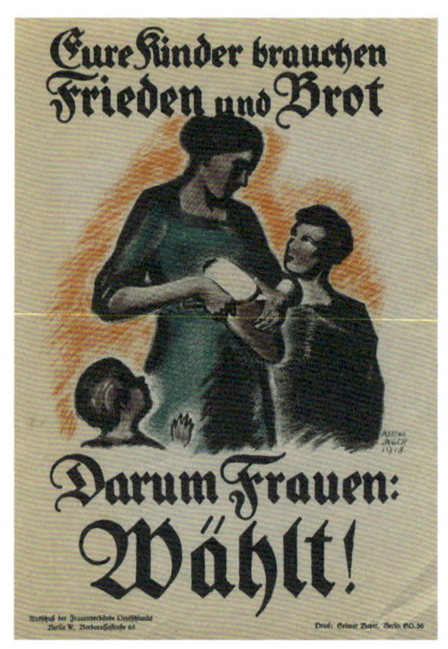

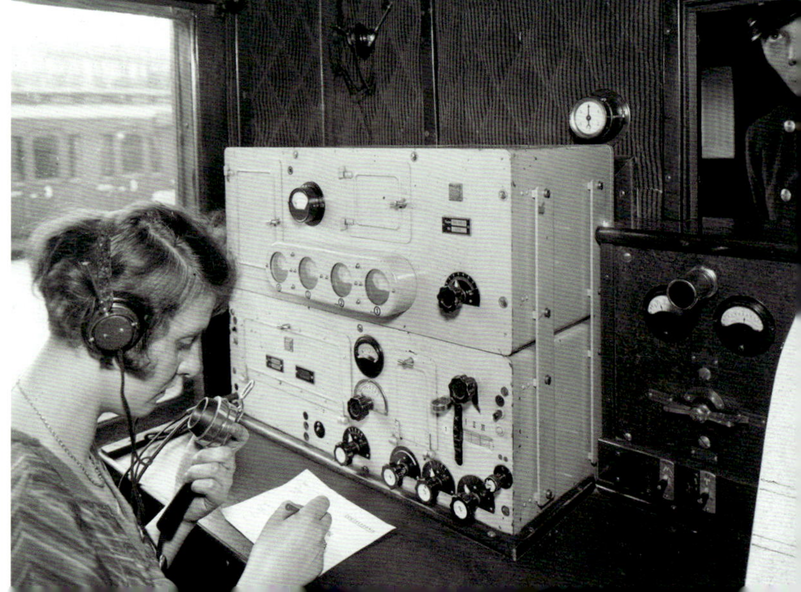

↗ Call to vote by the Committee of Women's Associations in Germany, poster with a motif by Matha Jäger, Berlin, 1918
→ Telephone operator, 1926
↗ Tamara de Lempicka, cover page, *Die Dame*, vol. 56, no. 21, 1929

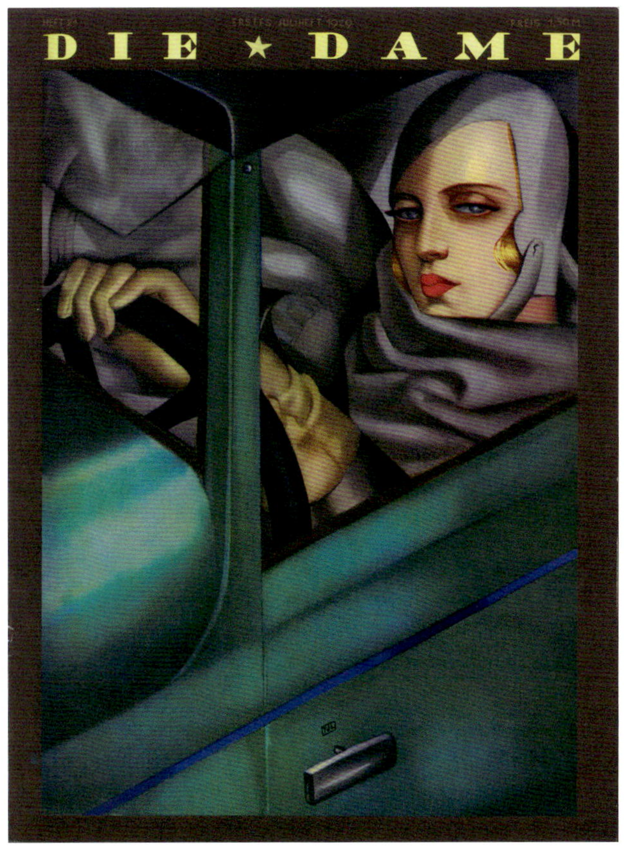

haircut and looking androgynous. At the end of the 1920s, Tamara de Lempicka achieved great popularity in Paris with works visualizing a new, emancipated image of women. Her female models exude a melancholy elegance or pride, occasionally in masculine poses, while self-confidently exhibiting their sensuality.

Lempicka's art optimally incorporated itself into the entertainment culture of the times. The artist designed several title pages for *Die Dame*, a chic women's magazine in Berlin. However, the consumer-oriented image of the New Woman it promoted could usually only be realized by women with adequate financial resources. Even if the current fashion style was intended for women of all social classes, unrestricted participation in education, fashion, sports and culture was generally reserved for women from upper and upper middle-class circles. In contrast, a night at the cinema or a new coat often remained hard-earned exceptions for ordinary employees.

With the onset of the world economic crisis in 1929 and its repercussions for society, the social phenomenon surrounding the New Woman increasingly disappeared from daily life. The National Socialists, who rose to power in 1933, fought against this role model of a self-reliant and independent woman. They instead propagated a return to an image of women limited to the conventional roles of wife and mother.

Irina Hiebert Grun

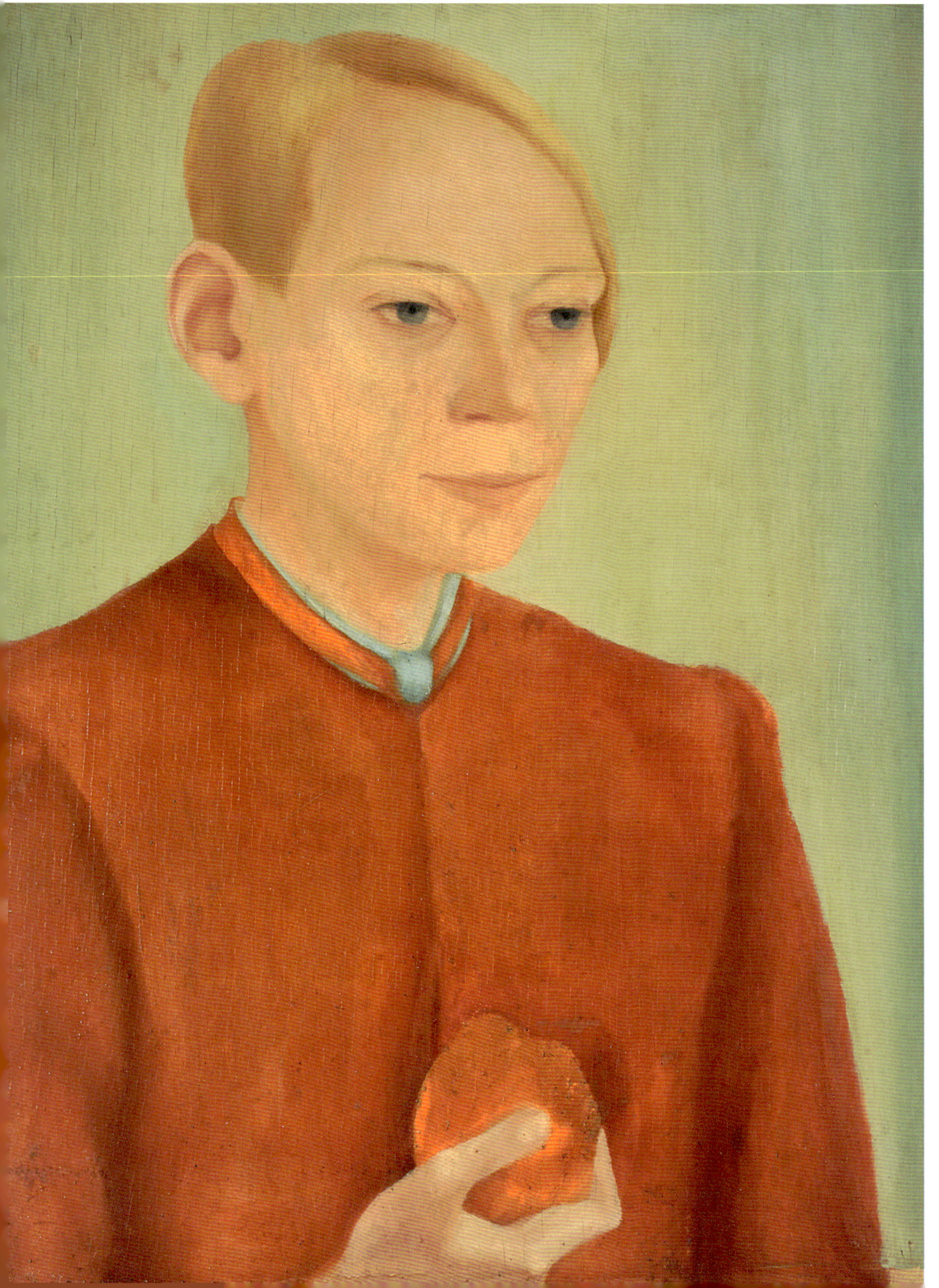

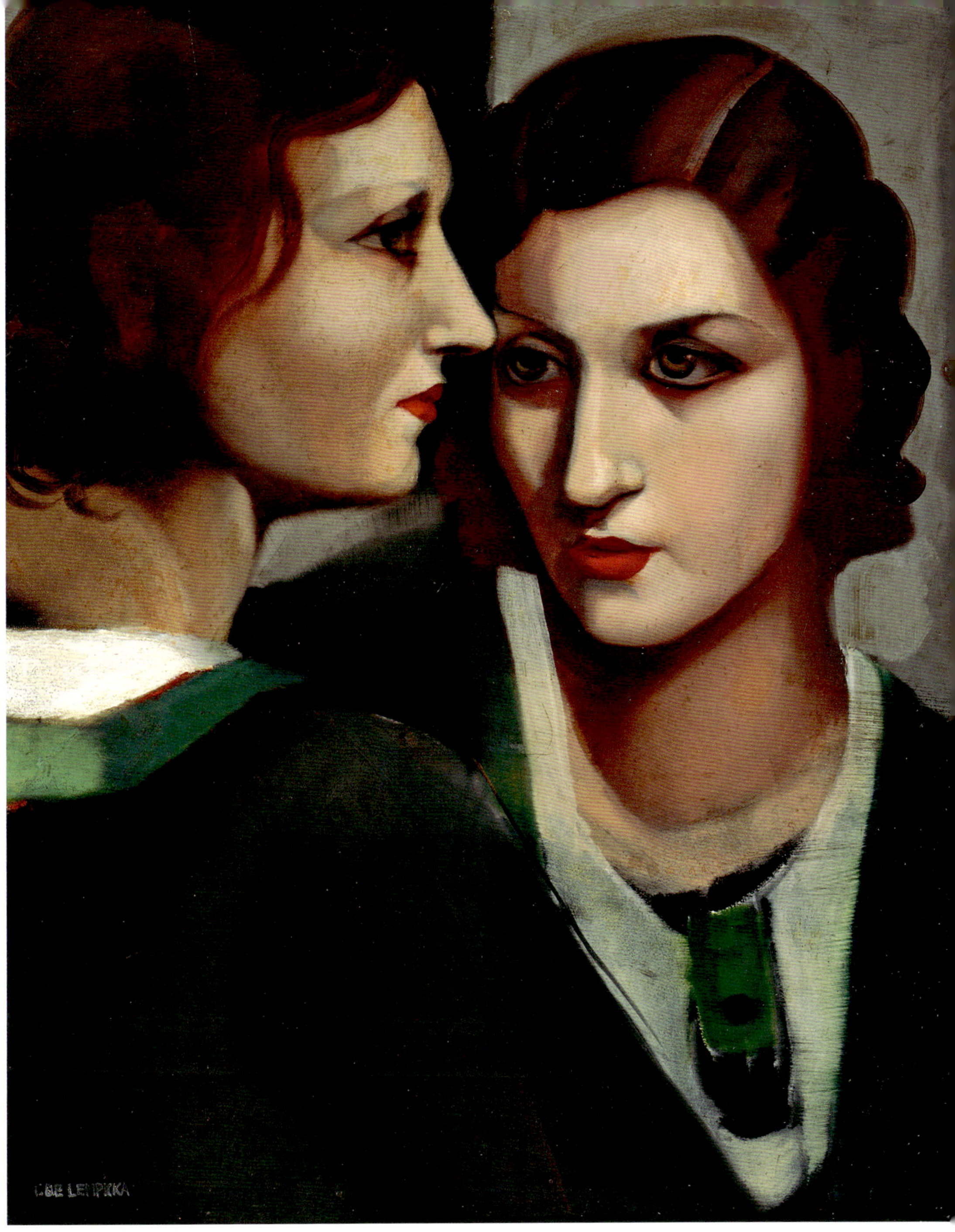

↗ Tamara De Lempicka, *Portrait (Face and Profile)*, c. 1931
Oil on wood, 45 × 37 cm
Gift from the Ulla and Heiner Pietzsch Collection
to the Land Berlin, 2010

← Kate Diehn-Bitt, *Self-Portrait with an Orange*, 1930–31
Oil on wood, 64.3 × 48.8 cm
Acquired in 1968 from the artist for the Nationalgalerie,
Berlin (East)

Who Is *Sonja*?

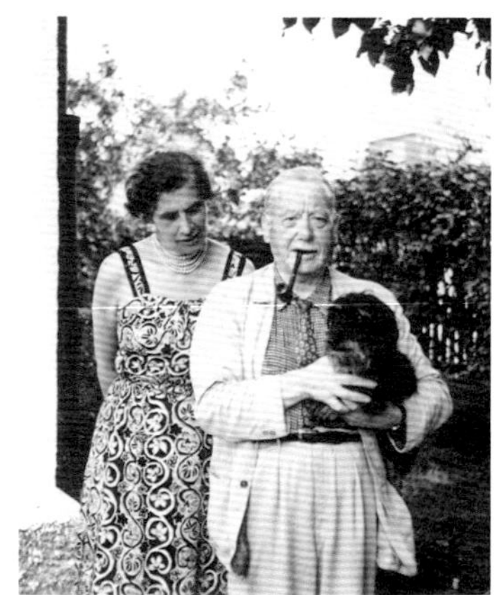

Christian Schad's portrait of a young woman ensconced in the setting of a Berlin café, painted in 1928, is considered an icon of the New Objectivity movement. The sitter, named Sonja, epitomizes the self-confident, emancipated woman of the Weimar Republic. She sits upright between two tables with her legs crossed casually. Her gaze is cool and somewhat melancholy. A curly lock of her fashionably short, bobbed haircut falls across her forehead. Shown with a cigarette holder between her fingers and a packet of Camel cigarettes, a powder compact and lipstick on the table, she exudes independence.

Sonja's chiffon outfit recalls a creation by fashion designer Coco Chanel that the American fashion magazine *Vogue* had debuted as the "Little Black Dress" in 1926. The cloth's partial translucency and the silk camellia on her shoulder lend the painting an erotic overtone, which, however, is subverted by her reserved posture and serious facial expression. A pianist and the writer Max Herrmann-Neisse – widely recognized at the time and identifiable by his distinctive head – can be seen in the background. This marks the locale as an establishment of Berlin's literary bohemia.

But who is *Sonja*? The young woman's real name was Albertine Gimpel. She was born in Schwerin in 1896 and worked as a correspondent at the Olex Petroleum company in Berlin. As a modern woman, she replaced her first name – a feminine derivative of a man's name – with "Sonja", which was especially popular in Russia and Scandinavia. The nickname can likely be traced to Felix Bryk, an entomologist and friend of Schad's, who was in Berlin in 1928, following extended stays in Sweden and East Africa. He was responsible for the initial meeting between Albertine and Schad in the latter's studio at Hardenbergstraße 1. Albertine, called Sonja, was 32 years old at the time.

↗ Albertine and Franz Herda in the USA in the early 1950s
→ Albertine Gimpel, Passport photo, Berlin, 1926

The later life of the young woman has been documented by the Holocaust researcher Susanna Schrafstetter and a family descendant, Christoph von Weitzel. In 1933 Albertine Gimpel, who was Jewish, was dismissed from her job without notice. She moved from Berlin to Munich, where she met and became friends with the painter Franz Herda. Born in Brooklyn in 1887, the son of German emigrants, he would become her salvation. Herda's American passport and his incredibly fearless demeanour repeatedly managed to keep her safe from deportation to Auschwitz. He also helped other Jews, some of whom he did not even know, saving lives in this way. In 2015 the Yad Vashem World Holocaust Remembrance Center in Jerusalem recognized Herda with the honorific "Righteous Among the Nations".

Herda initially hid Albertine in his studio, then later with friends. She survived, and they married in 1948. "Sonja" became Albertine Herda. The couple lived in New York until 1962 when they returned to Germany. Franz Herda died in 1965, Albertine in 1973. The painting *Sonja* was first exhibited in 1964. It was part of a private collection until the Nationalgalerie acquired it in 1995.

Dieter Scholz

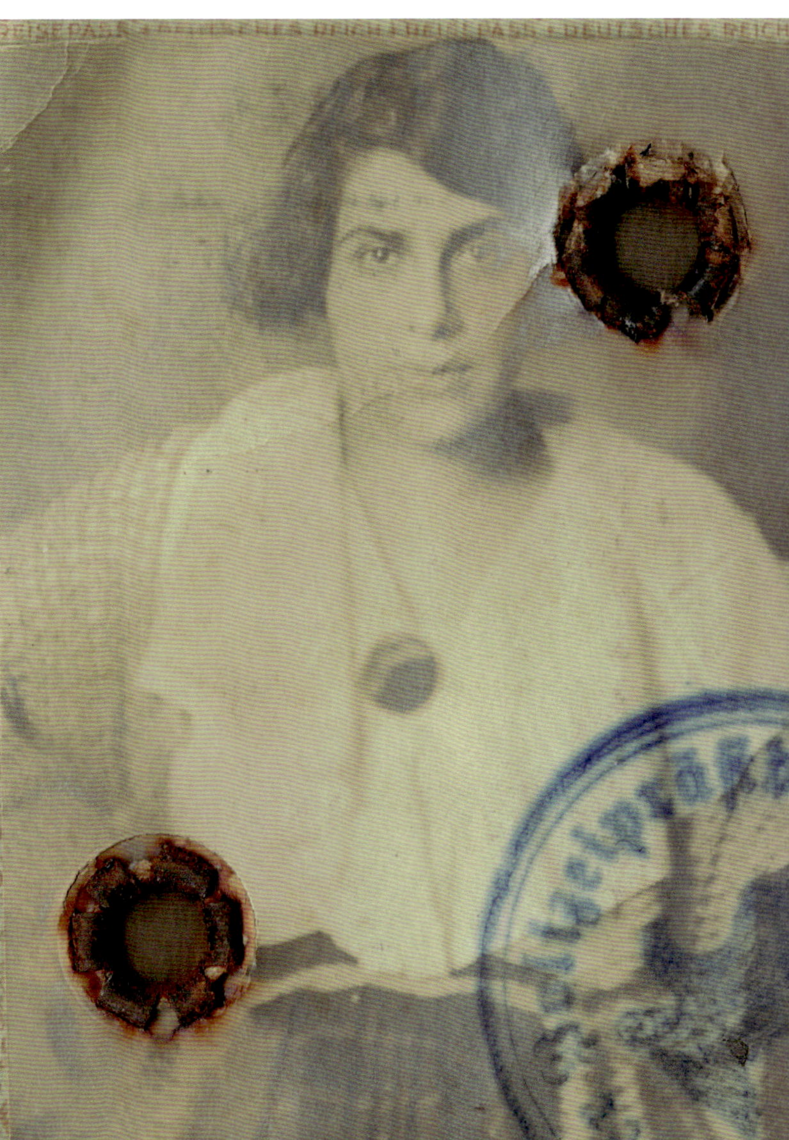

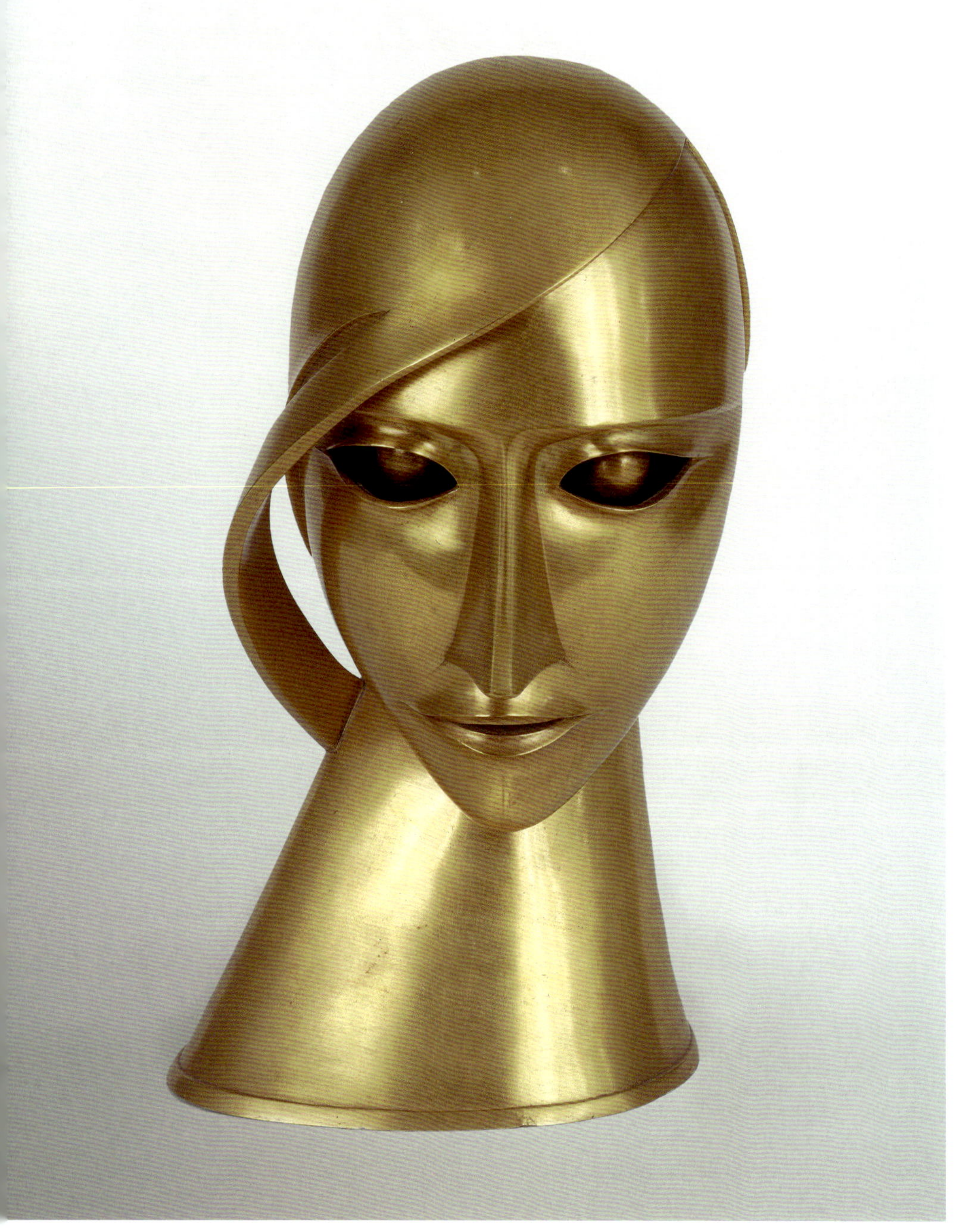

↑ Rudolf Belling, *Head in Brass*, 1925
Brass, 38.3 × 22.5 × 19 cm
Acquired in 1928; exhibited in the Kronprinzen-Palais until 1933; confiscated as "degenerate" in 1937 and brought to Munich; on consignment to Bernhard A. Böhmer, Güstrow in 1939, where it was seized in 1947 and returned to the Nationalgalerie, Berlin (East) in 1949

→ Christian Schad, *Sonja*, 1928
Oil on canvas, 90 × 60 cm
Acquired in 1997 from the Galerie Brockstedt, Hamburg, by the Freunde der Nationalgalerie with funds from the Stiftung Ingeborg und Günter Milich, Berlin

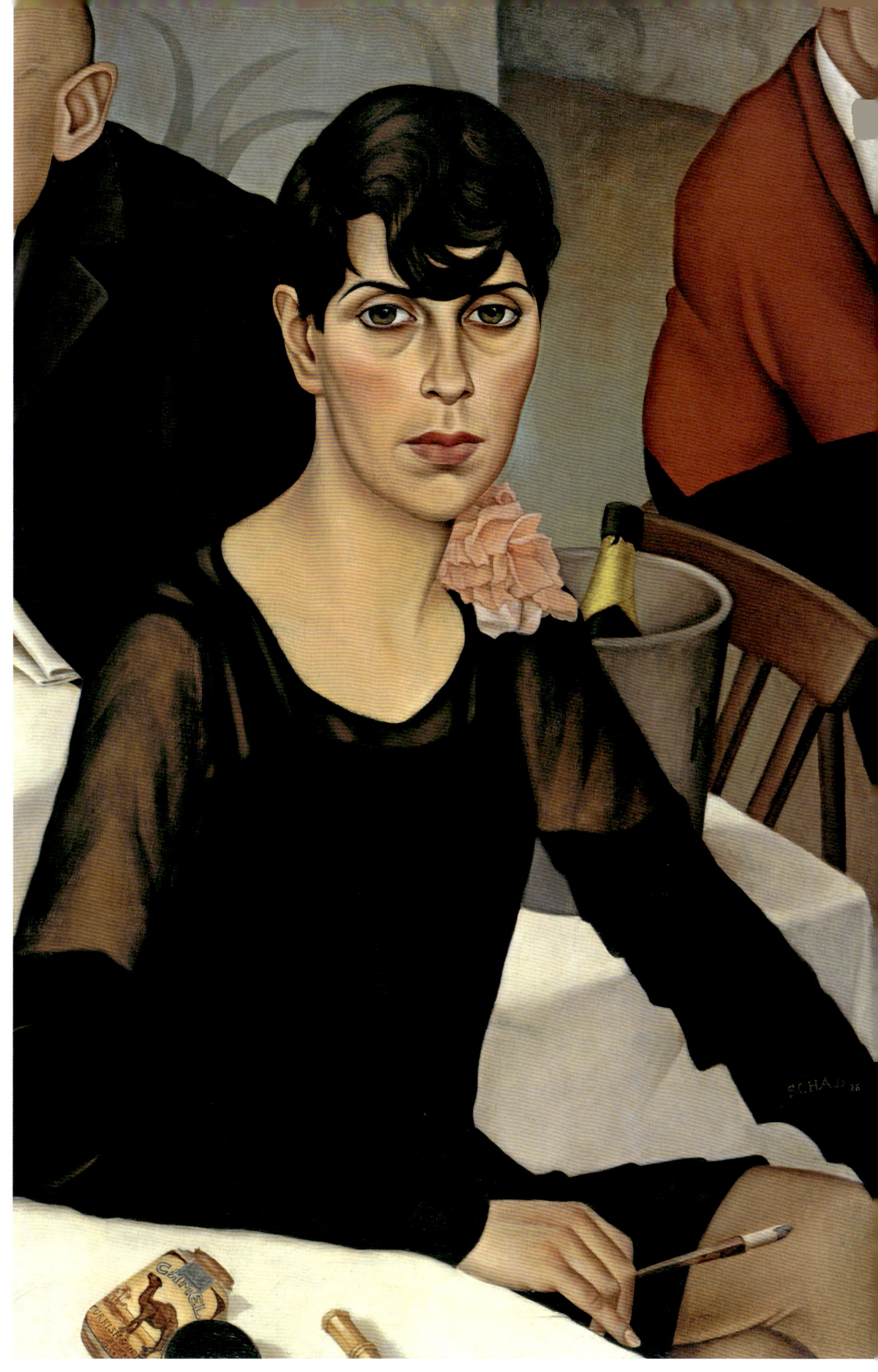

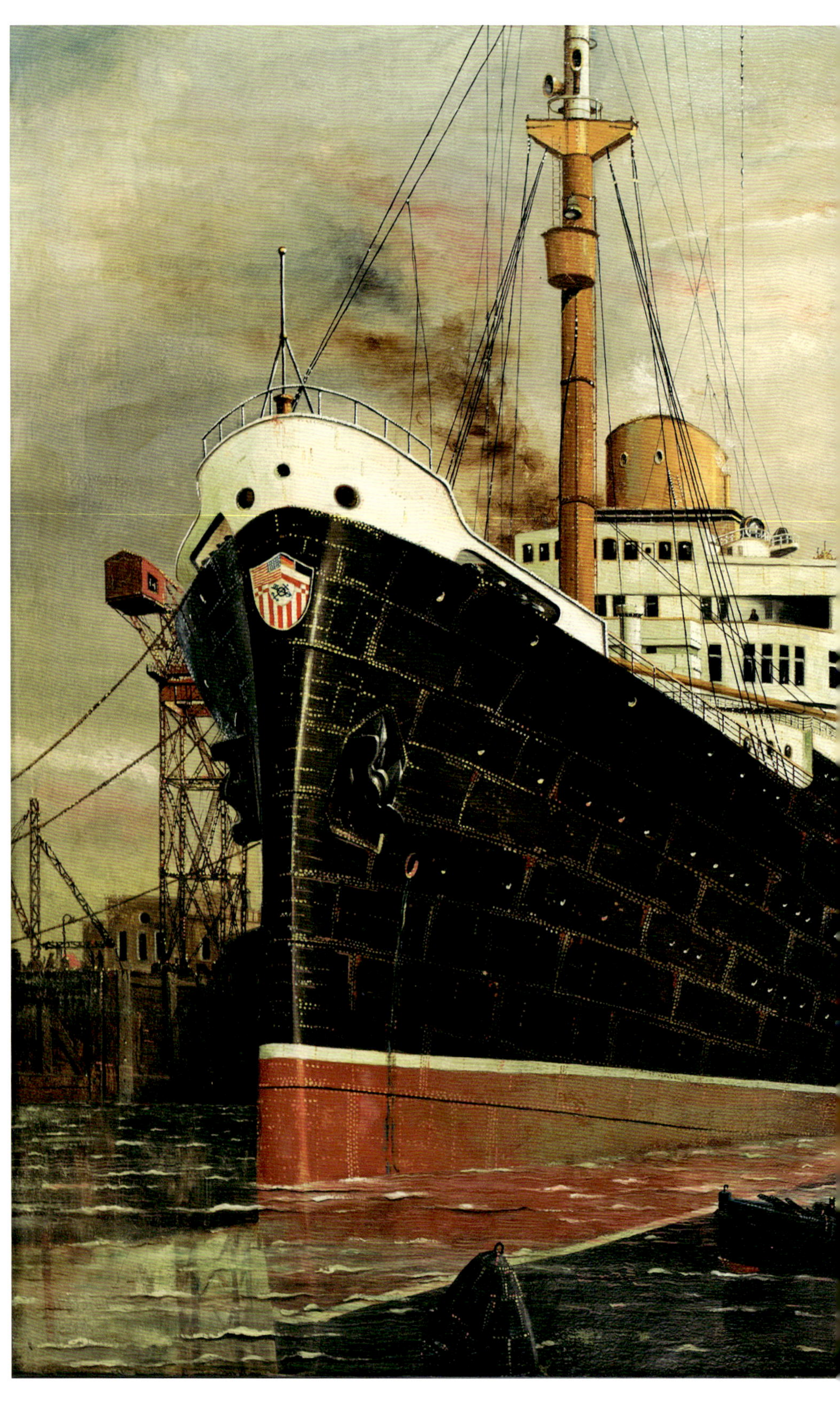

Franz Radziwill, *The Harbour II*, 1930
Oil on canvas, 76 × 99.5 cm
Acquired in 1932 from the artist

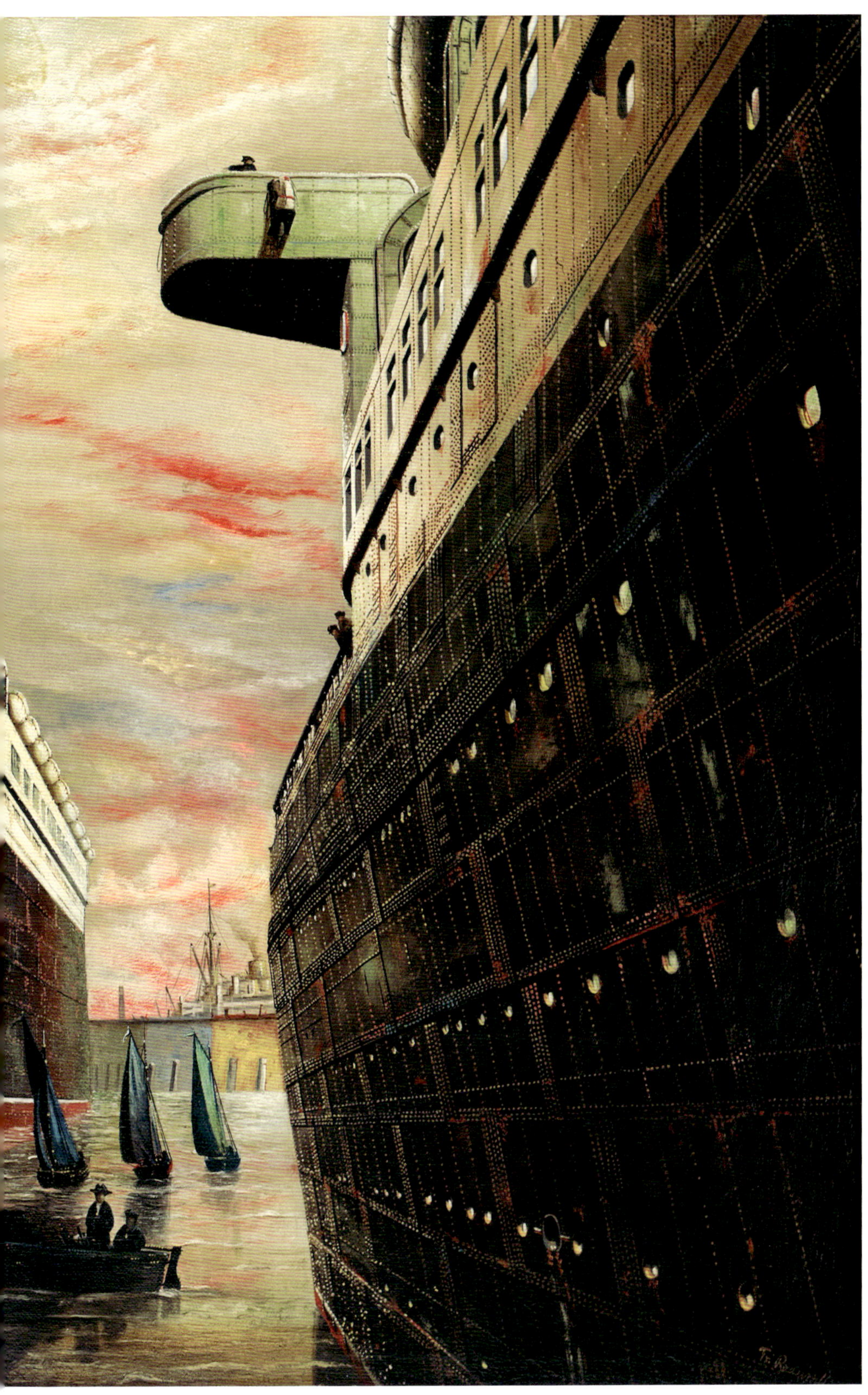

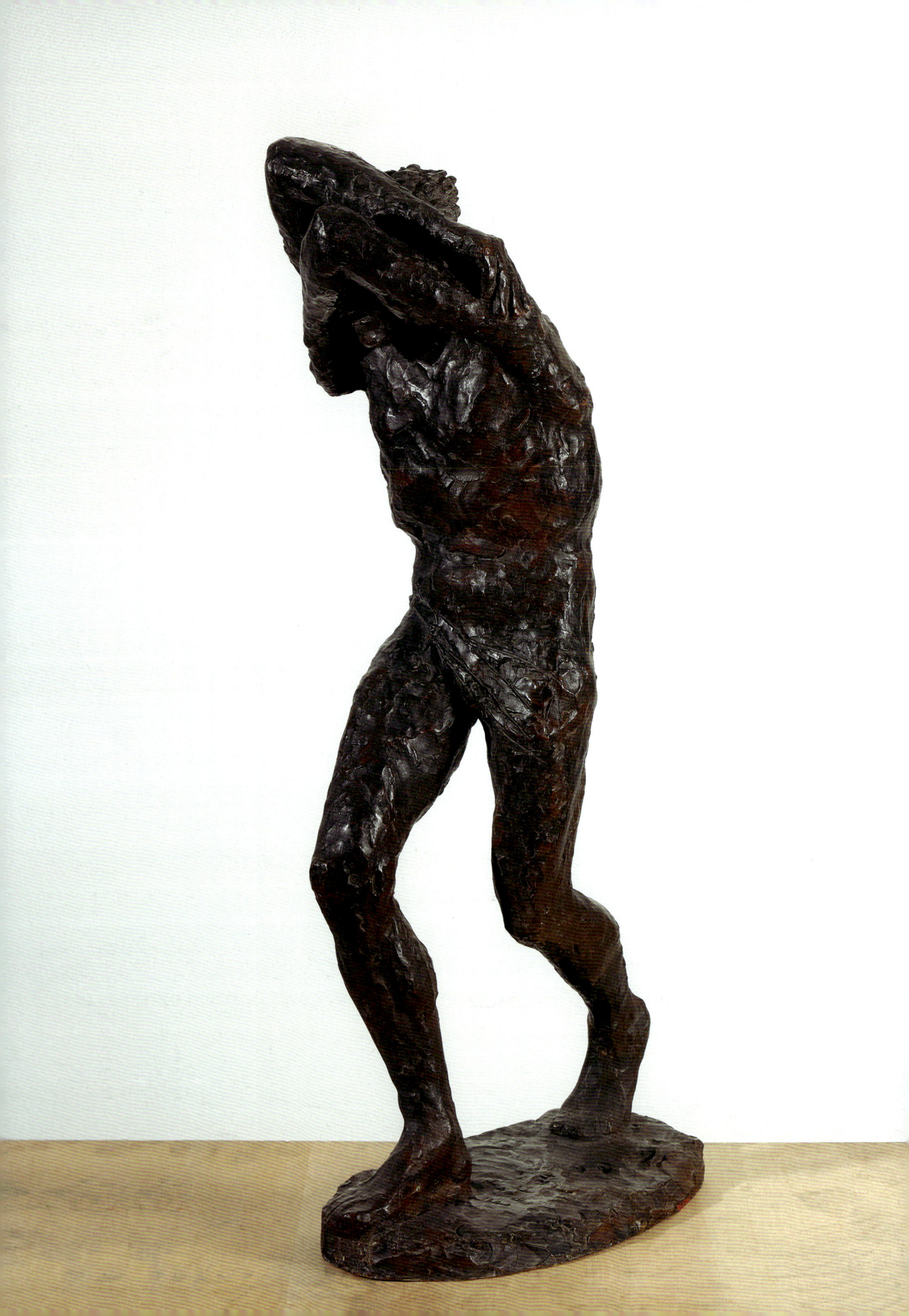

Exile

From 1933 to 1945, the National Socialist regime forced countless artists into exile. Efforts to bring museum and art academy staffs into line with the National Socialist Party began in 1933. Anyone considered undesirable politically or in terms of the regime's race ideology was forced out of office. Those belonging to the artistic avant-garde were banned from exhibiting or even from practising their professions.

Ernesto de Fiori's bronze figure *Fliehender* (Fugitive) was made in 1934, after his Jewish gallerist Alfred Flechtheim had already emigrated. Two years later, the artist would also leave Germany for Brazil. Max Beckmann was dismissed from his position as professor at the Städelschule in Frankfurt in 1933. After hearing the radio broadcast of Adolf Hitler's speech condemning modern art at the opening of the *Große Deutsche Kunstausstellung* (Great German Art Exhibition) in 1937, he left for Amsterdam as soon as he could. After the Netherlands was occupied in 1940, Beckmann tried in vain to obtain a visa for the USA. Josef Scharl, on the other hand, managed to flee to New York in 1938, where he renewed contact with Albert Einstein, who supported the artist financially and helped him take part in exhibitions. Johannes Molzahn had also been living in exile in the United States since 1938, where he met Piet Mondrian, Marcel Duchamp and Fernand Léger and was able to gain a university teaching position.

Ernesto de Fiori, *The Fugitive (The Desperate Man)*, 1934
Bronze, 104 × 30 × 52 cm
Found in 1948 in Berlin's Osthafen and given to the Nationalgalerie for safekeeping; donated by the Magistrat von Groß-Berlin to the Galerie des 20. Jahrhunderts, Berlin (East) in 1951

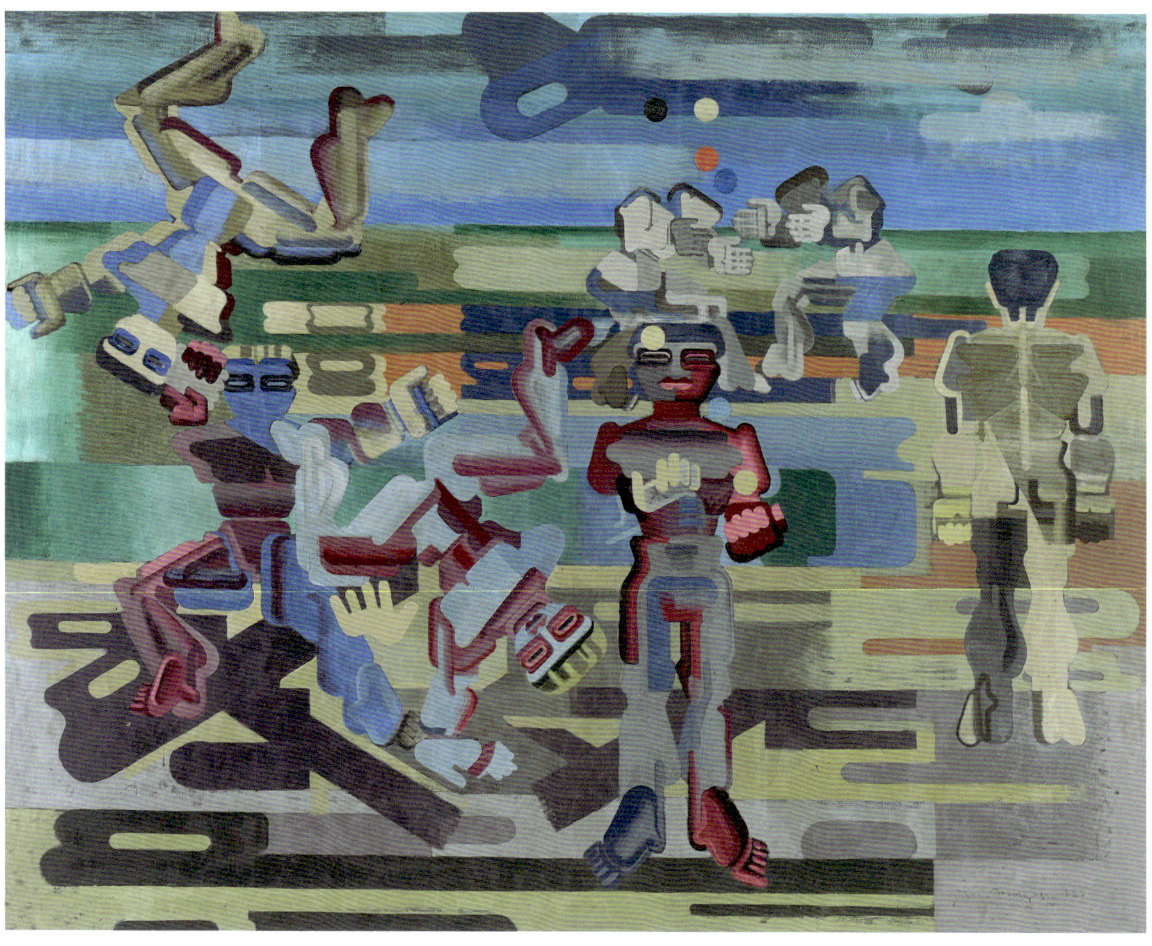

↑ Johannes Molzahn, *The Small World Theater I*, 1935
Oil on canvas, 113 × 142 cm
Loan from the Johannes-Molzahn-Centrum®, Kassel

→ Johannes Molzahn, *Heroic Perspective*, 1935
Oil on canvas, 130 × 96 cm
Loan from the Johannes-Molzahn-Centrum®, Kassel

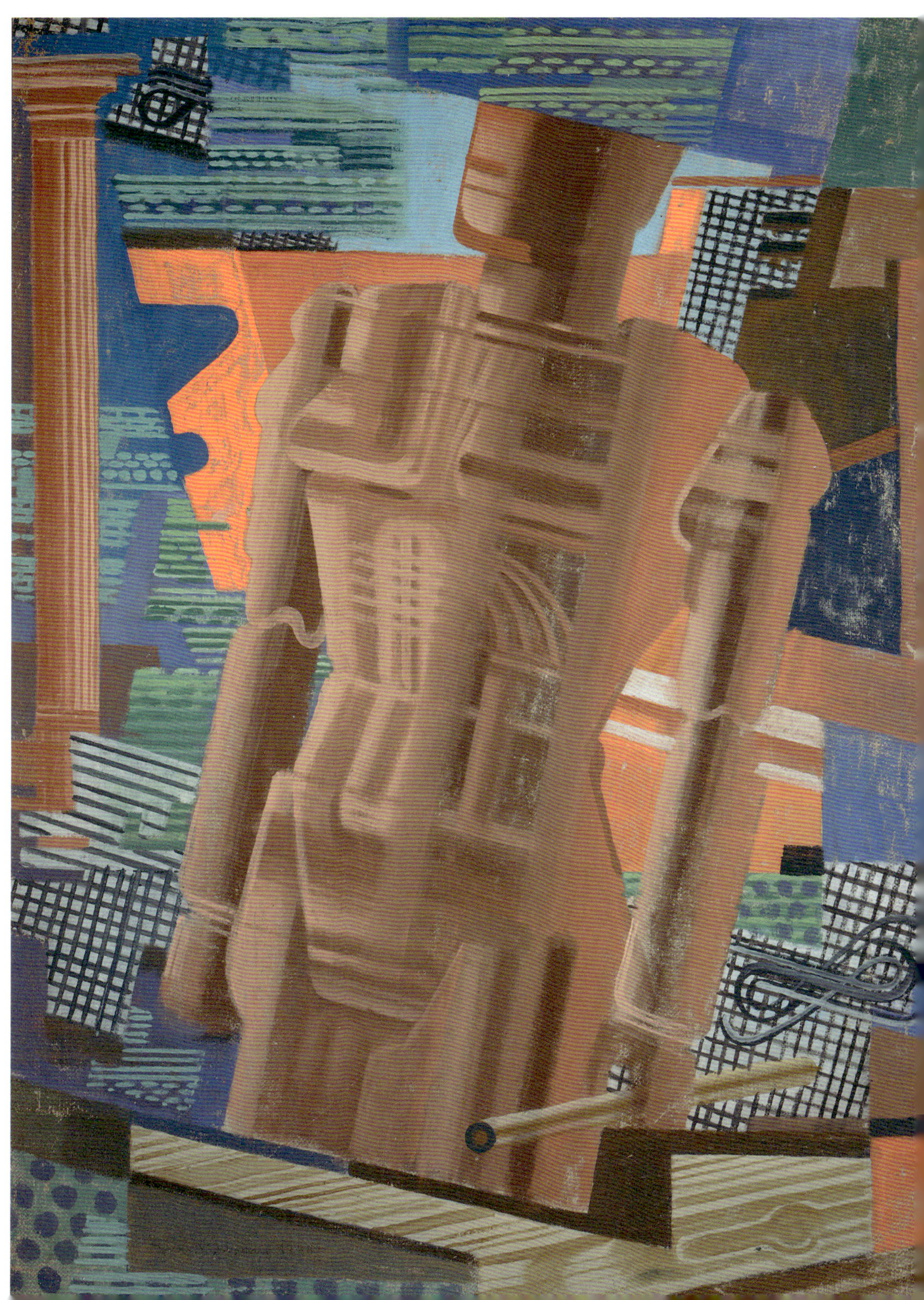

What Is "Degenerate Art"?

The National Socialist dictatorship defamed works of art it viewed as incompatible with its ideology by branding them "degenerate". Adolf Hitler was fundamentally opposed to "modernity", resulting in the persecution of all avant-garde tendencies in art. Moreover, work and exhibition bans were placed on Jewish and communist artists.

An exhibition under the title *Entartete Kunst* (Degenerate Art) had been shown in Dresden as early as 1933. The derogatory label was taken up again in July 1937, when numerous works of art were seized from German museums. Only a short time later, some of these objects were put on display and denounced as an "expression of the decline of art" at the *Entartete Kunst* exhibition in Munich. The show travelled to other German cities until 1941 and was viewed by more than three million people.

The criteria used for defining "degenerate art" were hazy at best, and the commissions entrusted with the confiscations made arbitrary decisions. For example, a bronze sculpture by Wilhelm Lehmbruck was confiscated in one museum, but an identical figure was spared in another. And the sculptor Rudolf Belling was represented in both the *Entartete Kunst* exhibition and the *Große Deutsche Kunstausstellung*, which were shown simultaneously in Munich. These antithetical presentations aimed to clearly define the National Socialist artistic ideal.

Approximately 20.000 works of art were removed from more than 100 German museums in further purges after August 1937. Many of the confiscated objects were sold to other countries or exchanged for older works of art. By contrast, works not classified

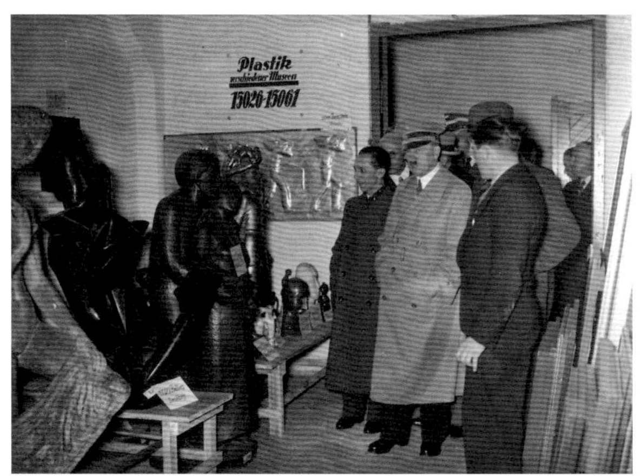

→ Rudolf Belling's *Triad* and *Head in Brass* in the collection depot for *Entartete Kunst* (Degenerate Art) at Köpenicker Straße 24a in Berlin. Viewed by Adolf Hitler and Joseph Goebbels on 13 January 1938
↗ *Triad* and *Head in Brass* by Rudolf Belling at the *Entartete Kunst* (Degenerate Art) exhibition in Munich, 1937
→ Max Beckmann, *Self-Portrait in Tuxedo*, 1927

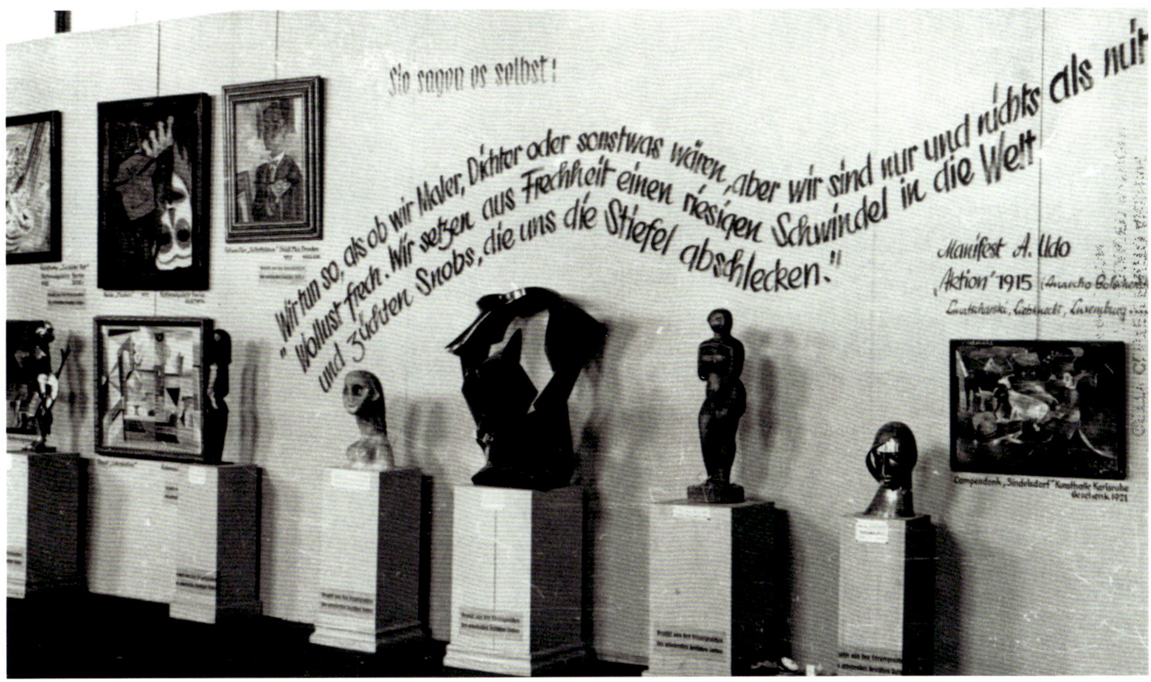

as having "international worth" were destroyed on a massive scale. It is believed the National Socialist regime burned some 5.000 artworks in the courtyard of Berlin's main fire station in 1939.

The confiscations left gaps in museum collections that still remain. The Nationalgalerie lost more than 500 works, nearly half of which ended up abroad. Attempts have been ongoing since after the war to compensate for these losses in modern art through acquisitions of equivalent pieces. For instance, ten works by Max Beckmann could be purchased between 1949 and 1988. A Beckmann self-portrait head, made of plaster, entered the collection in 1993, to stand in, at least for the time being, for the artist's *Selbstbildnis im Smoking* (Self-Portrait in Tuxedo) – a painting confiscated by the National Socialists that has been at the Busch-Reisinger Museum of Germanic Culture in Cambridge, Massachusetts (USA) since 1941.

However, it was not until 2018 that the lost work could be more adequately replaced by the painting *Selbstbildnis in der Bar* (Self-Portrait at a Bar). It arrived, together with Beckmann's *Bildnis Erhard Göpel* (Portrait of Erhard Göpel), as a gift to the Nationalgalerie. Created during the war in 1942, during Beckmann's exile in Amsterdam, the artist depicts himself in a melancholy thinker's pose. Sandwiched into the space by a dark scrollwork element at the left of the composition and before a black area to the right, his body seems cramped and constricted, almost locked in. Influenced by the circumstances, it shows a very different Beckmann than the self-portrait he painted in 1927 wearing an elegant tuxedo.

Irina Hiebert Grun

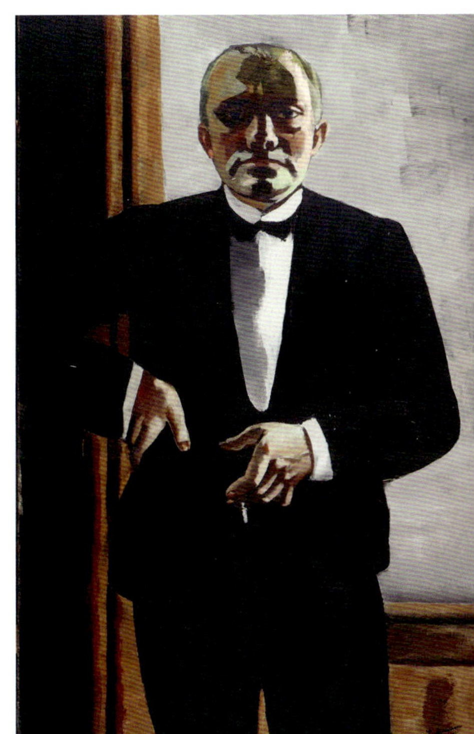

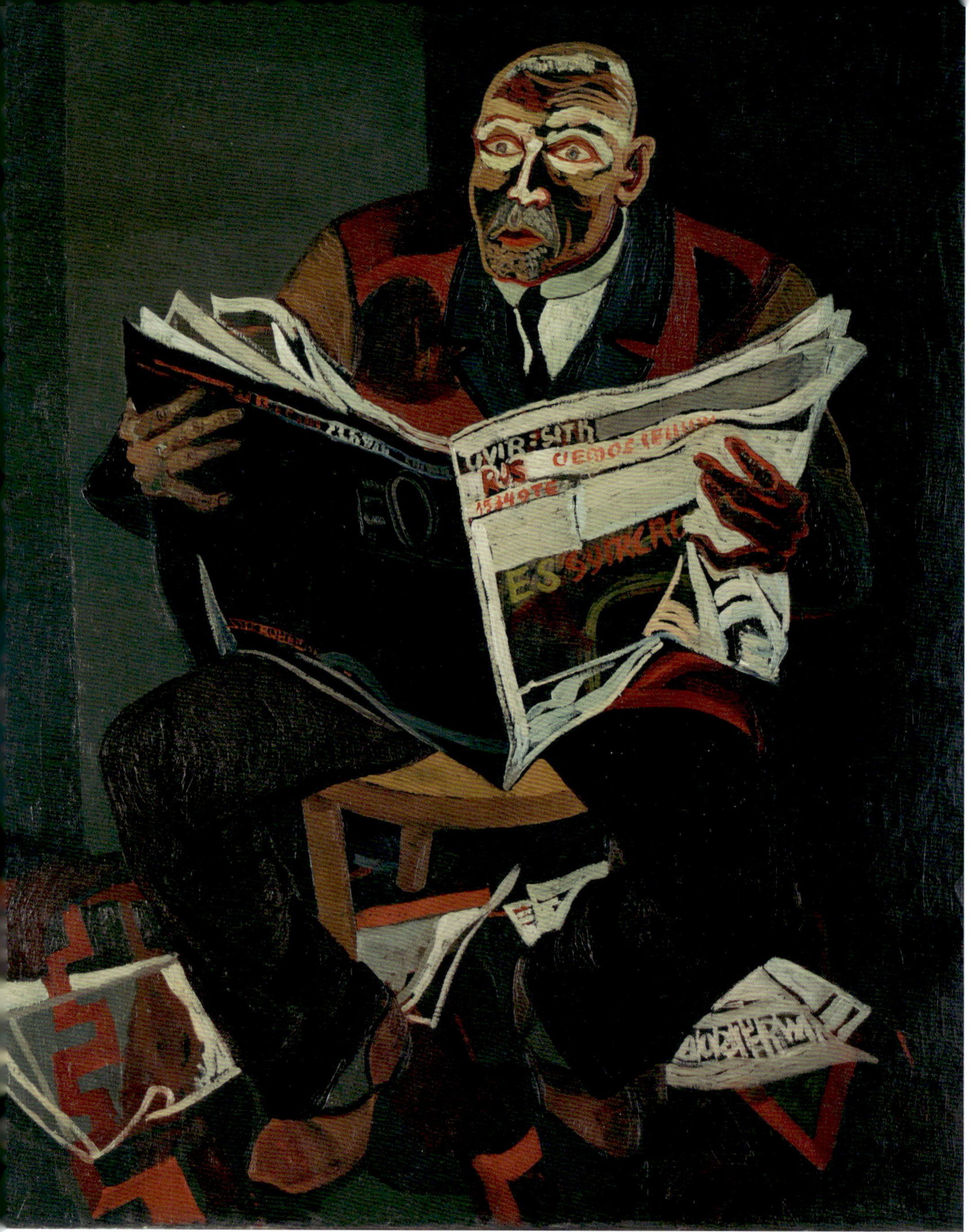

↑ Josef Scharl, *The Newspaper Reader*, 1935
Oil on canvas, 115 × 96 cm
Acquired in 1964 from the Galerie Nierendorf, Berlin, for the Nationalgalerie, Berlin (West)

→ Max Beckmann, *Family Portrait of Heinrich George*, 1935
Oil on canvas, 215 × 100 cm
Acquired in 1954 from Berta Drews-George, Berlin, by the Land Berlin with funds from the Deutsche Klassenlotterie for the Galerie des 20. Jahrhunderts, Berlin (West)

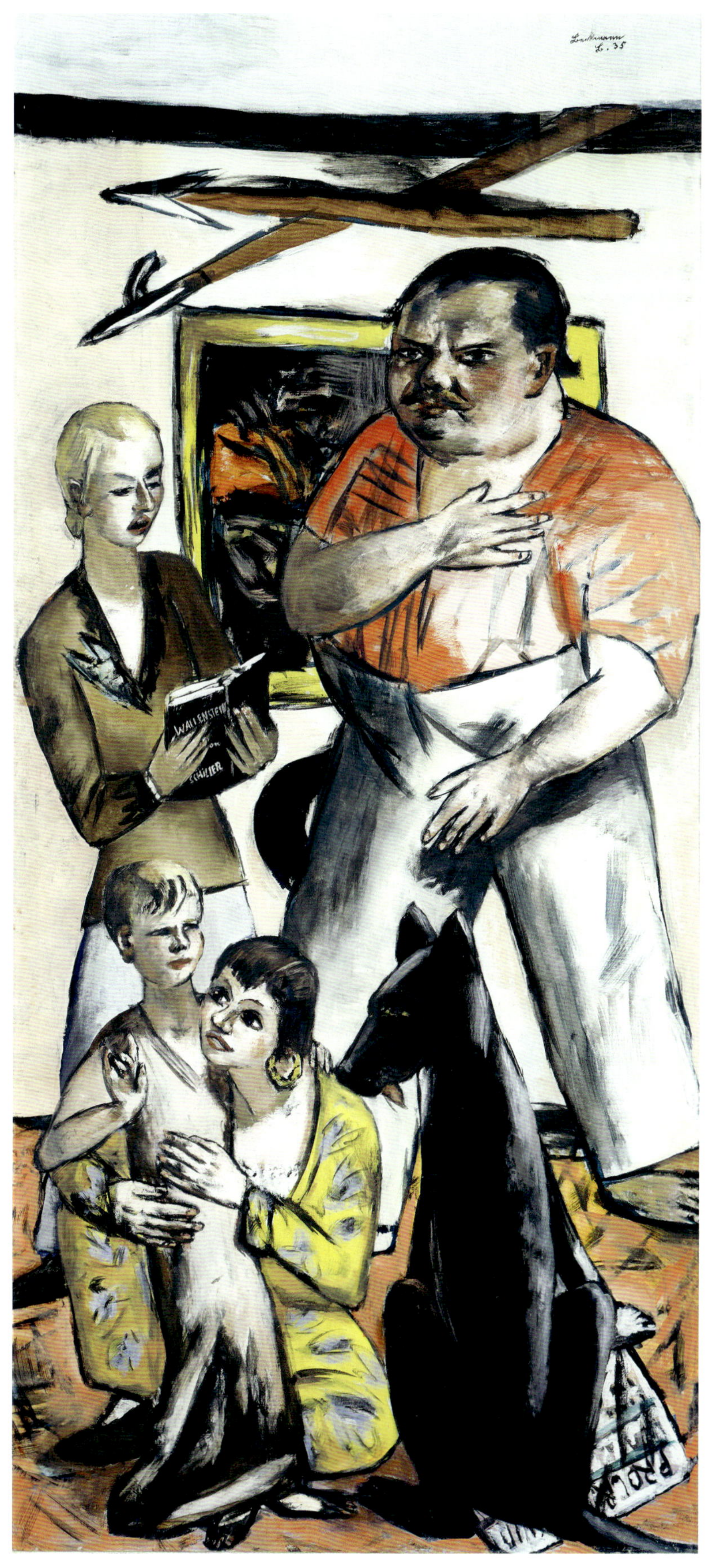
WALLENSTEIN
von
SCHILLER

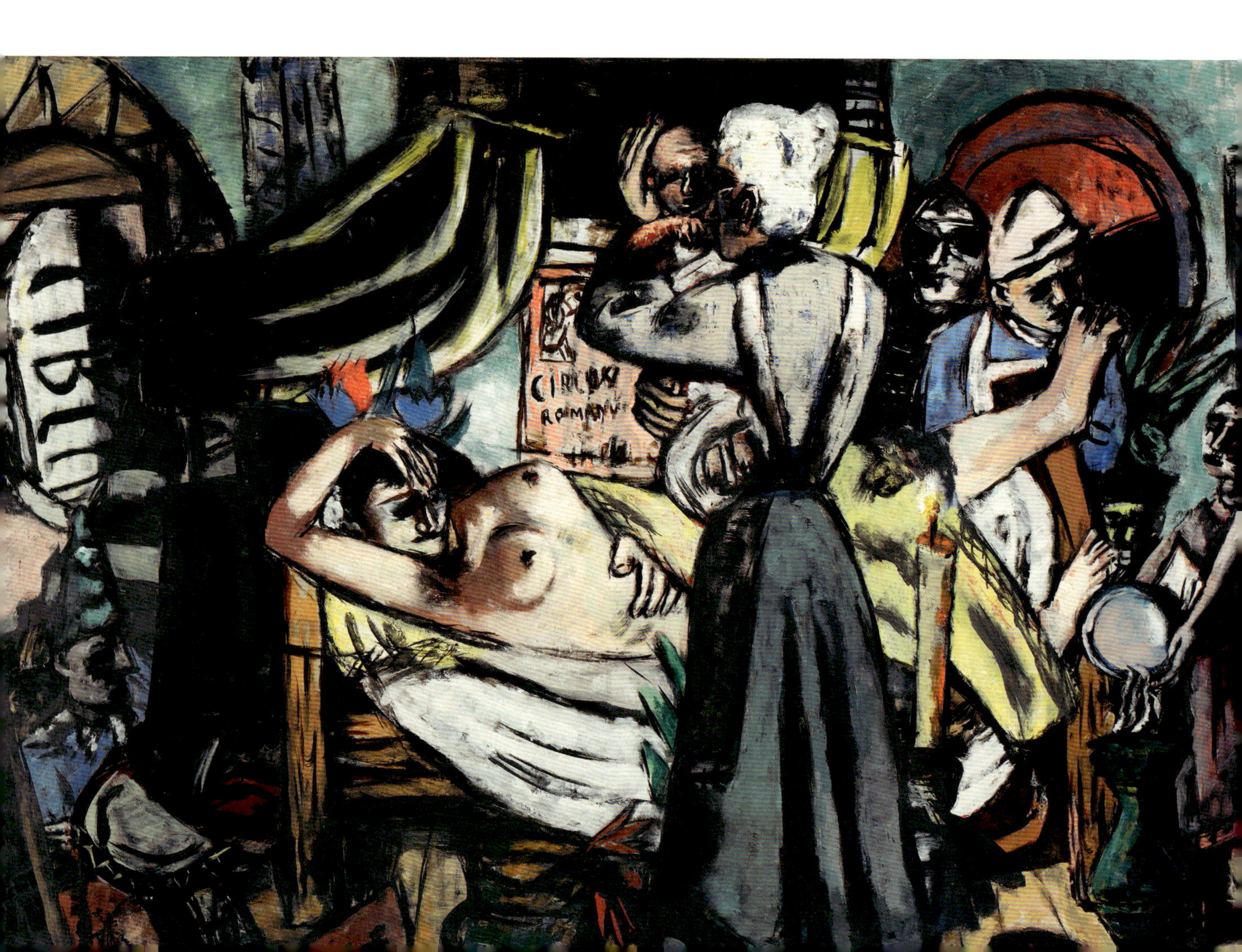

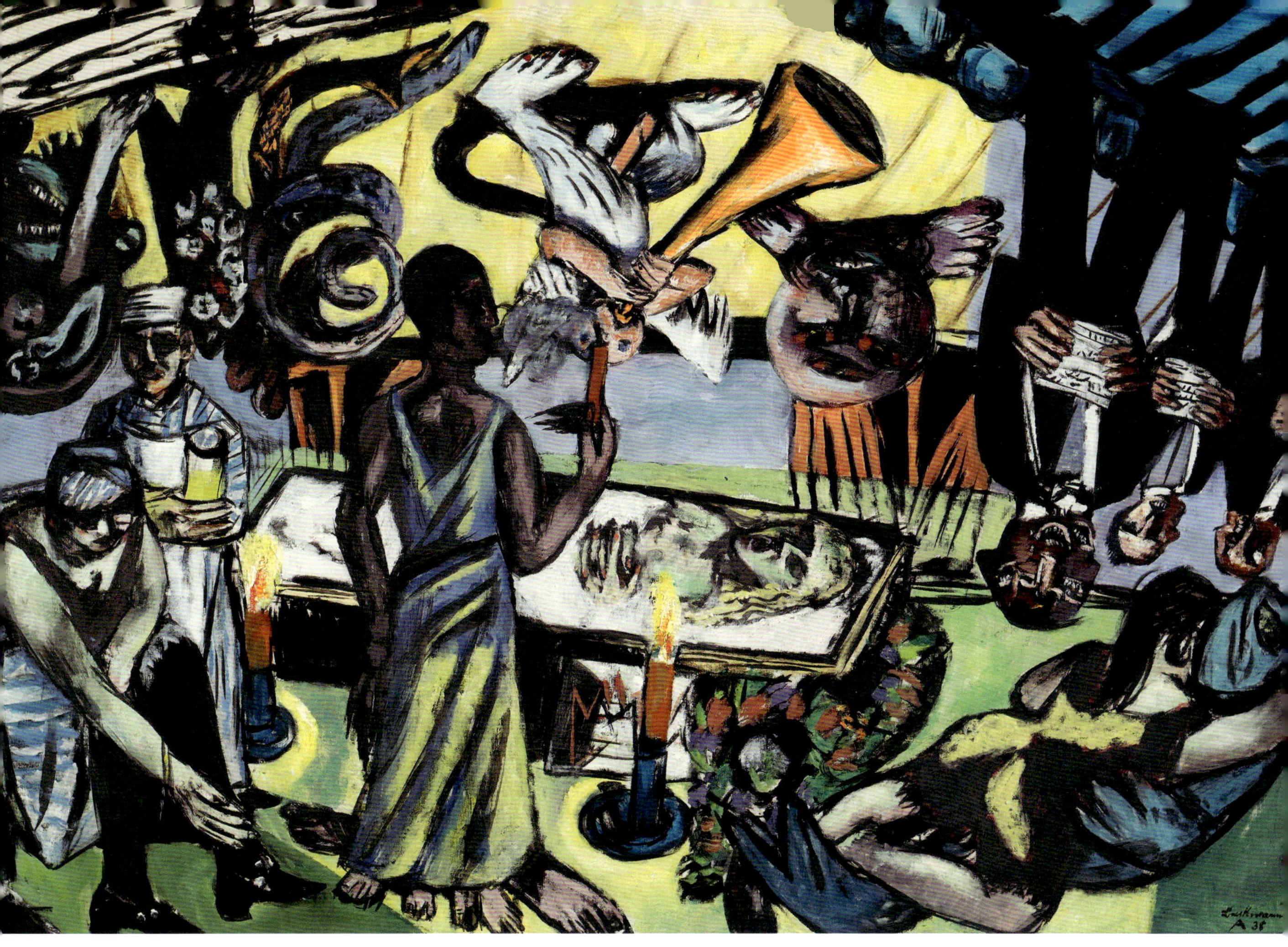

↑ Max Beckmann, *Death*, 1938
Oil on canvas, 121 × 176.5 cm
Acquired in 1952 from the Galerie Curt Valentin, New York, by the Land Berlin for the Galerie des 20. Jahrhunderts, Berlin (West)

← Max Beckmann, *Birth*, 1937
Oil on canvas, 121 × 176.5 cm
Acquired in 1951 from the Galerie Curt Valentin, New York, by the Land Berlin for the Galerie des 20. Jahrhunderts, Berlin (West)

A Discomforting Portrait by Max Beckmann

It is a discomforting portrait that Max Beckmann painted in Amsterdam in 1944 – discomforting because it was made during the war, because the painter lived in exile, and because the professional activities of the sitter were highly ambiguous. The art historian Erhard Göpel, whom Max Beckmann portrayed, was 38 years old at the time. The two men had known each other since 1932. Göpel was an expert in the field of Dutch Old Masters, with many years of professional experience. Due to his specialist knowledge, he was discharged from the Wehrmacht in 1942 and assigned to the "Sonderauftrag Linz" (Linz Special Commission), concerned with assembling an art collection for a museum planned by Adolf Hitler.

As a "representative of the Special Commission", Göpel worked in The Hague for the National Socialist Reich Commissioner for the occupied Dutch regions, also responsible for France and Belgium. He was tasked with finding exceptional works of art and recommending their purchase. The focus was also on Jewish property that could be acquired below value or expropriated. Göpel actively participated in National Socialist acquisitions of looted art. Apparently, he also protected Jews at the same time. He employed about 90 Jews on his staff, declaring them indispensable because of their skills in building frames or restoration, which led to his having to defend himself before the Reich Commissioner in October 1943. He also saved art experts from deportation, either temporarily or outright. By doing so, he secured their cooperation at the very least. After the war, various art dealers and antiquarians acknowledged that they owed their survival to Göpel.

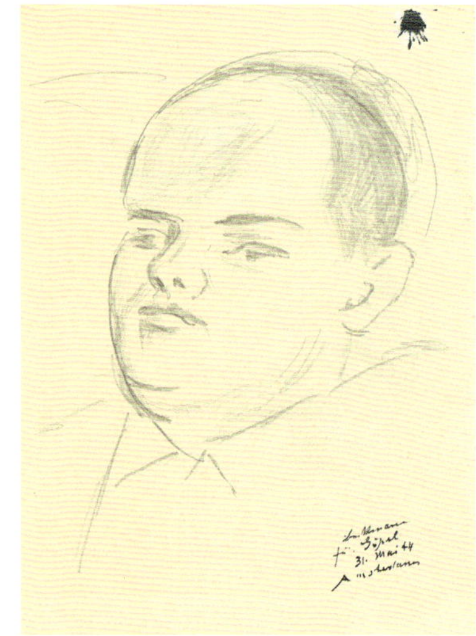

→ Max Beckmann, *Head Study for the Portrait of Erhard Göpel*, 1944
↗ Max Beckmann, *The Burning House*, pencil sketch for Johann Wolfgang von Goethe. *Faust II*, Act 5, 1925
↗ Max Beckmann, *The Three Mighty Accomplices*, pen and ink drawing for Johann Wolfgang von Goethe. *Faust II*, Act 5, 1943–44

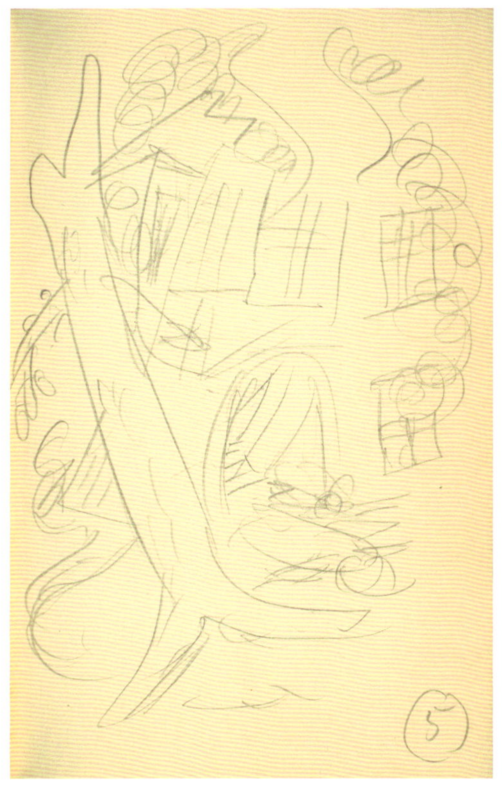

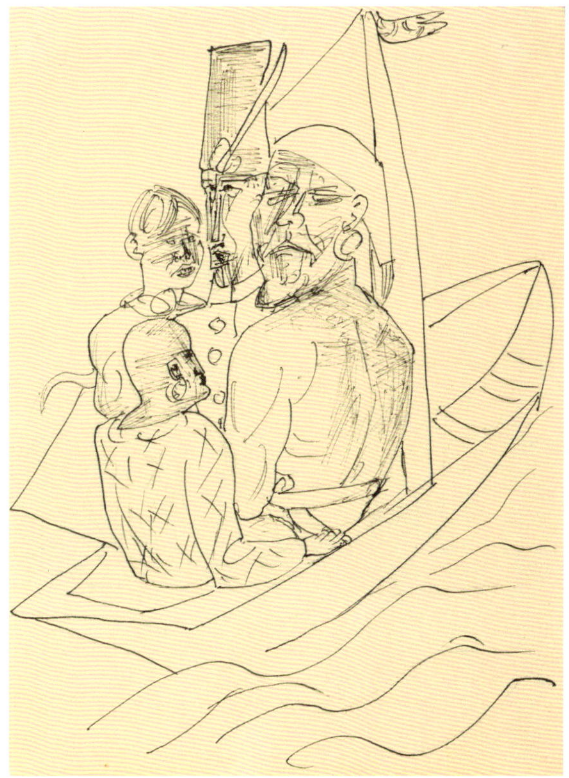

Göpel repeatedly used business trips to visit Beckmann during the artist's exile in Amsterdam. He smuggled the artist's paintings, drawings and prints into Germany. And he accompanied and supported Beckmann when the 60-year-old painter was called up again for military service in May 1944 despite his age.

Work on the portrait is noted in Beckmann's diary from 23 January to 20 May 1944. The head and hands were drawn during one of Göpel's visits. Afterwards, Beckmann fleshed out the composition alone in his studio. After the artist was definitively declared unfit for service on 31 May 1944, he gave Göpel the drawings as a gift.

Before Beckmann began working on the portrait, he showed Göpel some other sketches. They were his own illustration designs for the fifth act of Johann Wolfgang von Goethe's *Faust. Der Tragödie zweiter Teil* (Faust: A Tragedy, Part II), drawn into a copy of the play. In the finished oil painting, art historian Eugen Blume sees a representation of the moment in which Göpel holds this book in his hands and uneasily averts his gaze. Because Beckmann's sketches also include the devilish Mephisto, who upon his return from a looting raid with his trio of accomplices "War, Trade and Piracy" tells Faust: "You have the might, and so the right." The message that Beckmann conceals in the painting can only be ascertained from Goethe's text, but it is obvious: Göpel has made a pact with the devil.

Dieter Scholz

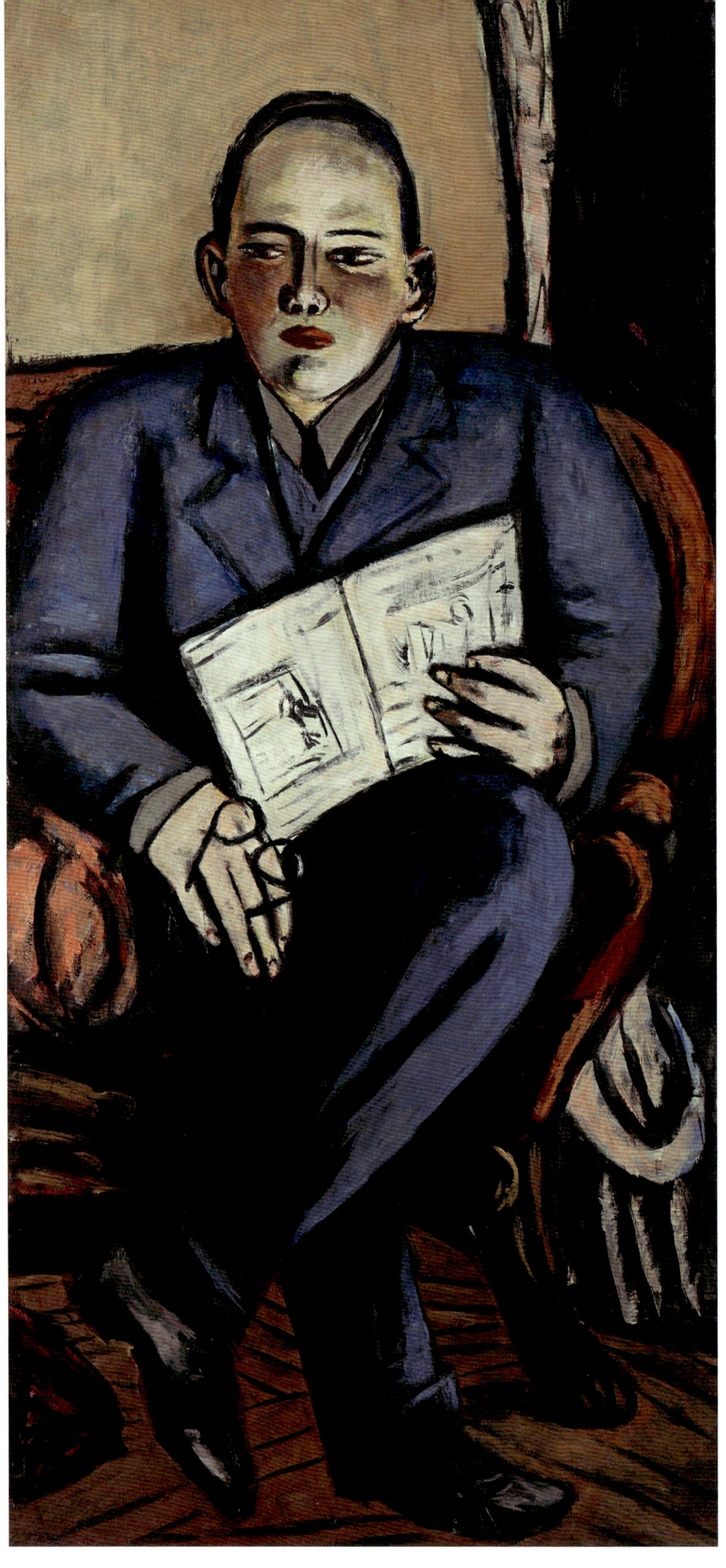

← Max Beckmann, *Portrait of Erhard Göpel*, 1944
Oil on canvas, 178 × 84 cm
Gift from Barbara and Erhard Göpel, Munich, 2018

↘ Max Beckmann, *Self-Portrait at a Bar*, 1942
Oil on canvas, 90 × 70 cm
Gift from Barbara and Erhard Göpel, Munich, 2018

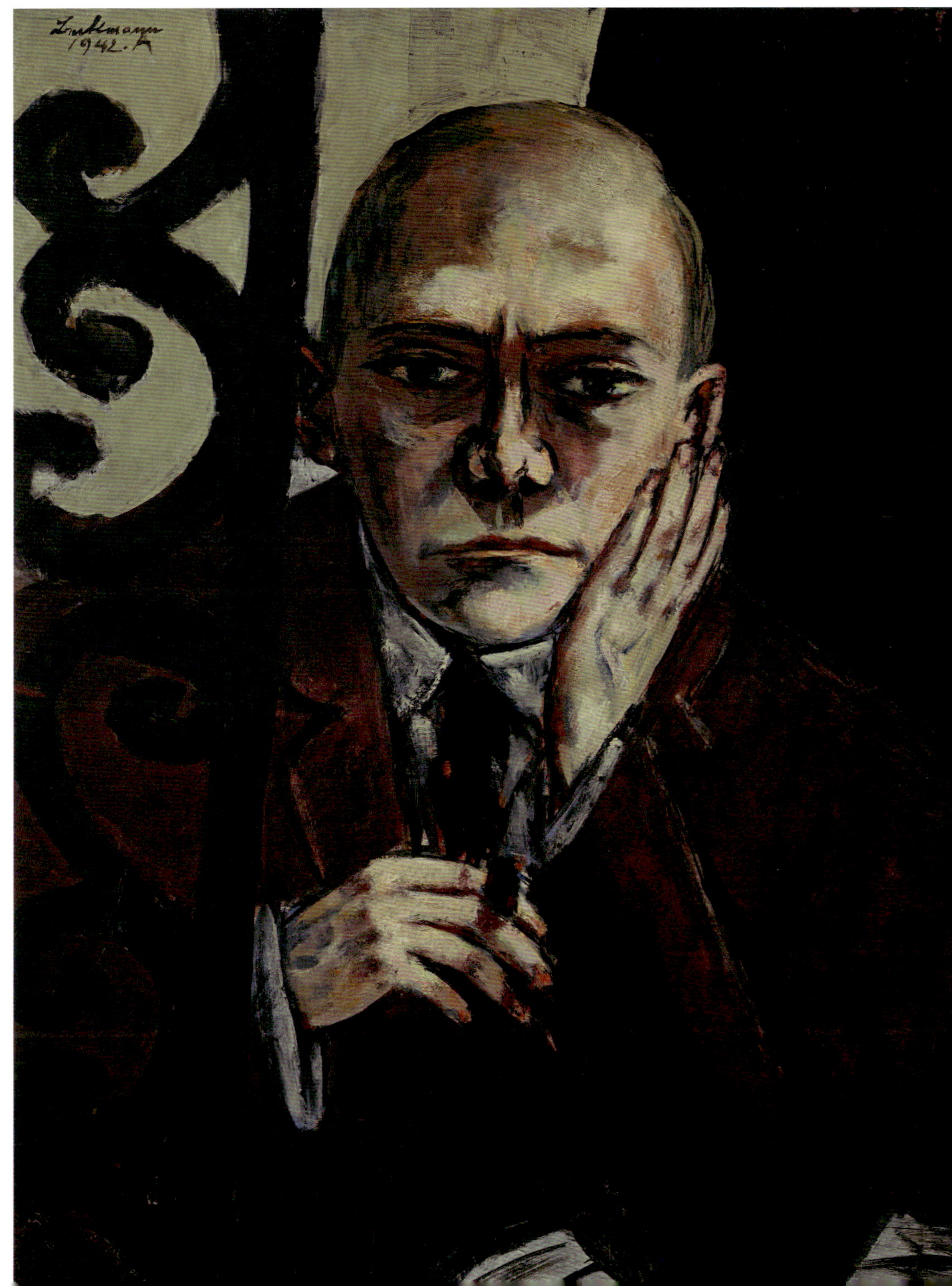

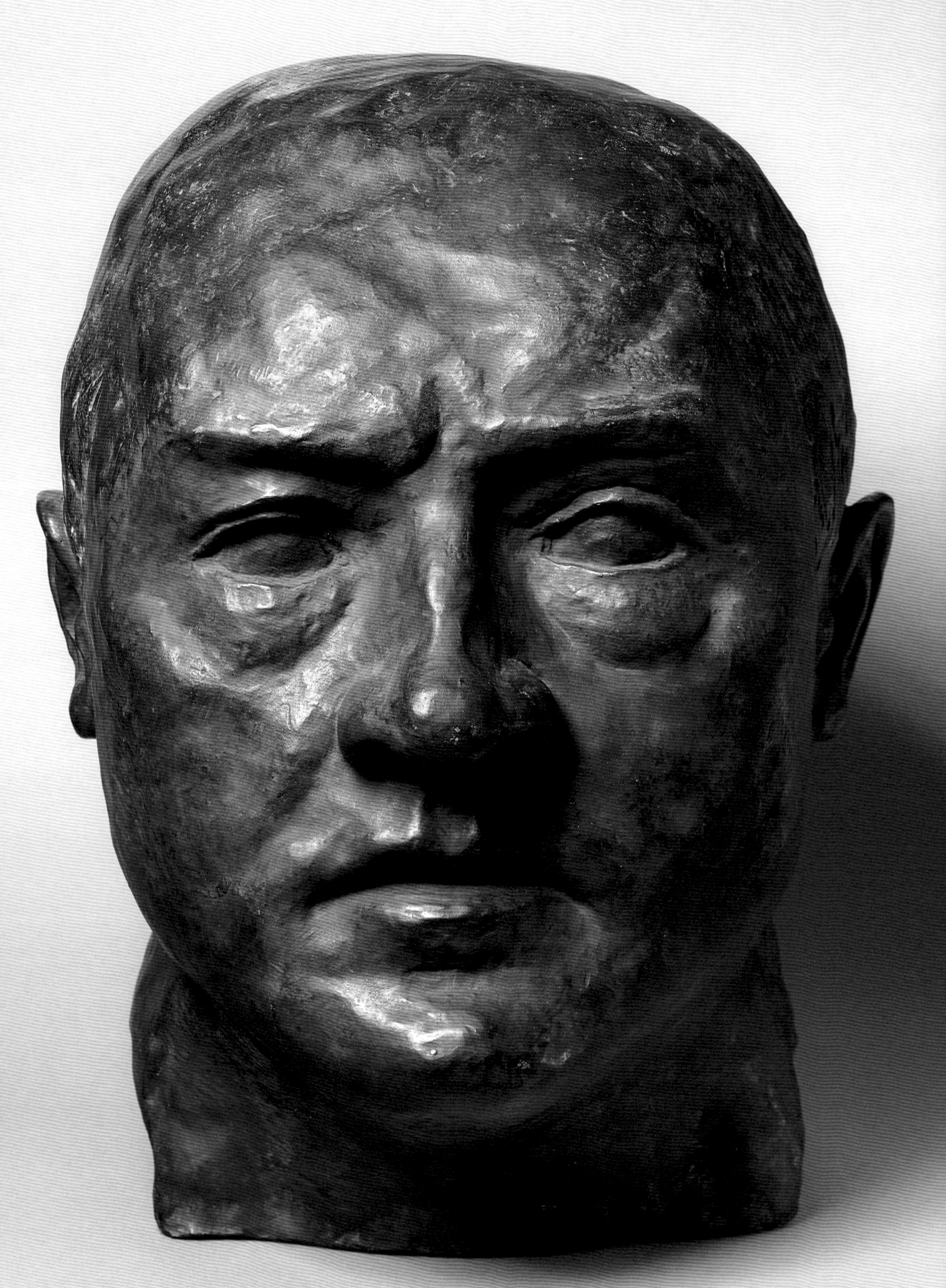

Faces of the Day

Over the course of many years, the sculptor Renée Sintenis chronicled her image in self-portraits. The busts reflect her development into a mature artist, visibly affected by the historical events from 1933 onwards. Artists including Käthe Kollwitz and Max Beckmann also documented their psychic states in self-portraits. Portraits are also invariably a means of representation. They frequently depict personalities or social types, such as the worker or the soldier.

Figurative and abstract tendencies existed parallel to one another in 1920s and 1930s sculpture. But while abstract sculpture was judged "degenerate" under National Socialism, figurative sculpture could maintain its public function as long as it corresponded to the National Socialist worldview about the human being. Some sculptors, such as Josef Thorak or Arno Breker, provided the National Socialists with heroic imagery in line with their racist ideology. Others, like Gerhard Marcks, struggled with the restrictions but were able to continue working.

Max Beckmann, *Self-Portrait*, 1936
Plaster, 37.5 × 30 × 33 cm
Acquired in 1993 from the Galerie Pels-Leusden, Berlin, by the Freunde der Nationalgalerie

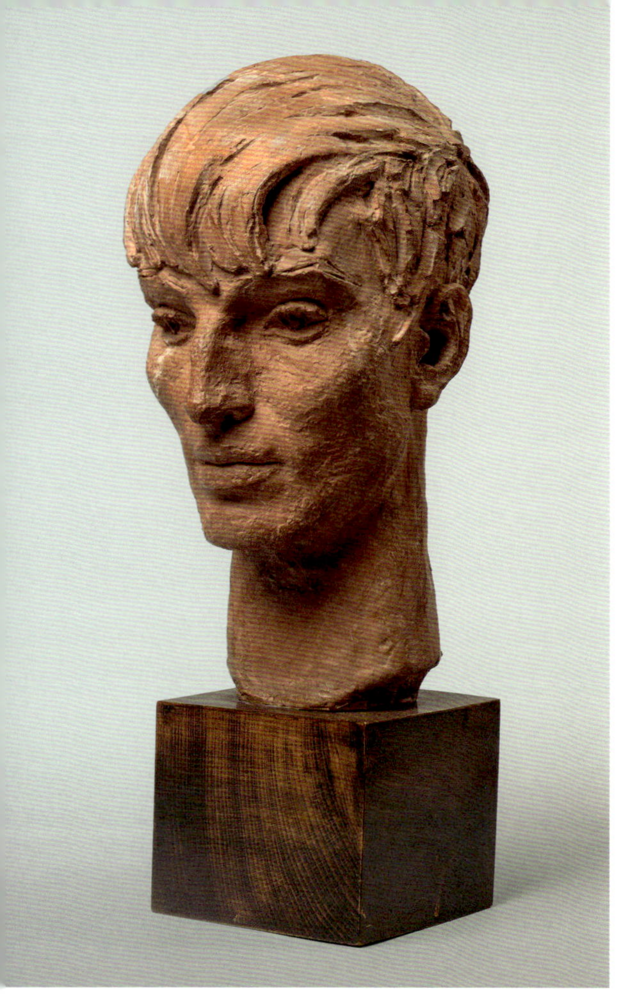

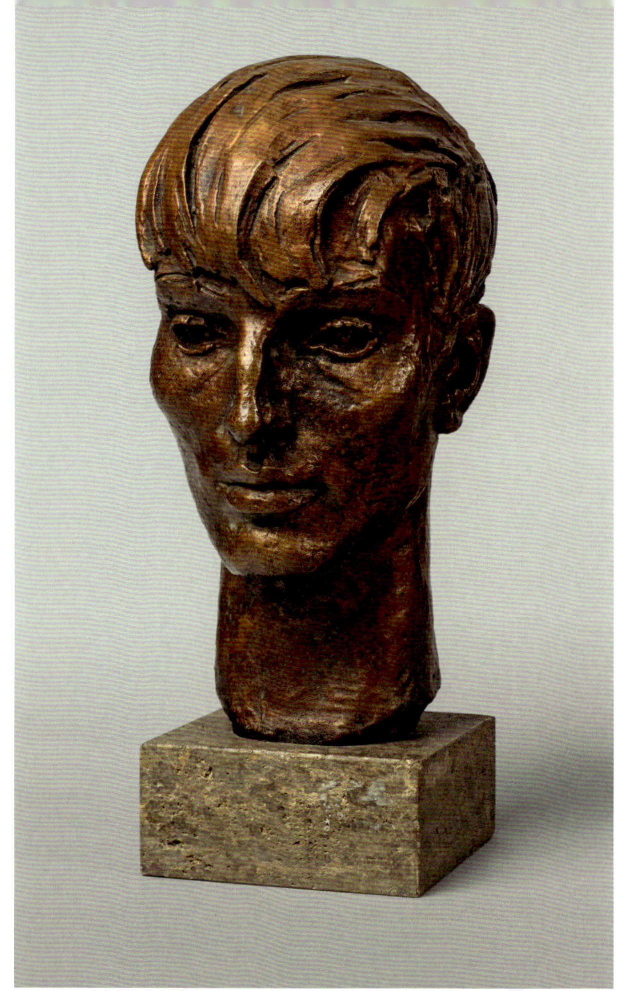

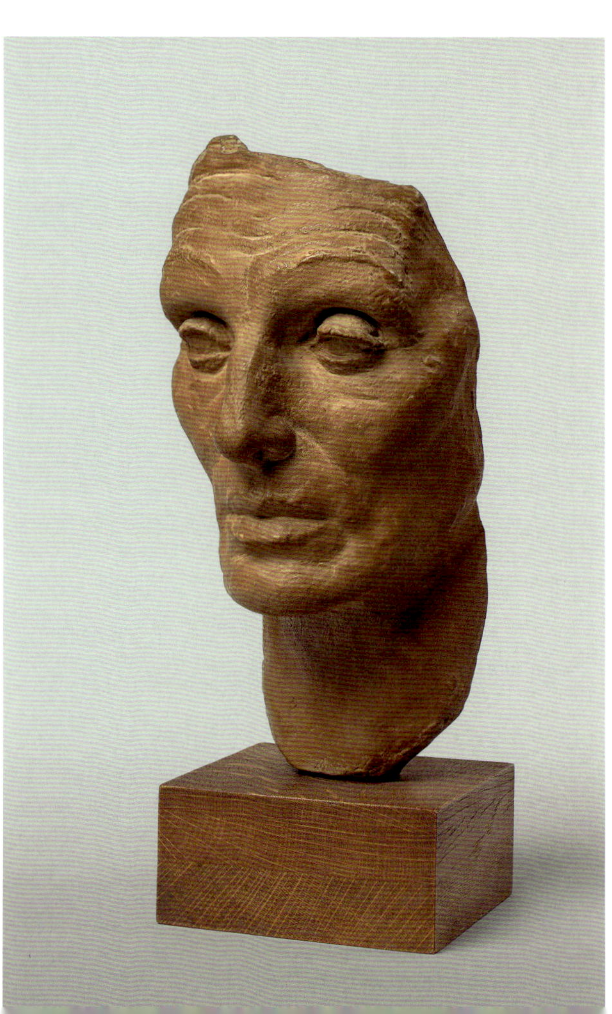

↑ Renée Sintenis, *Self-Portrait*, 1926
Stucco, 32.9 × 17.5 × 21.5 cm
Bequest of Magdalena Goldmann, Berlin, from the estate of Renée Sintenis, to the Nationalgalerie, Berlin (West), 1981

↗ Renée Sintenis, *Self-Portrait*, 1926
Bronze, 31 × 17 × 21 cm
Bequest of Magdalena Goldmann, Berlin, from the estate of Renée Sintenis, to the Nationalgalerie, Berlin (West), 1981

→ Renée Sintenis, *Self-Portrait*, 1944
Clay, 28 × 13.7 × 15 cm
Bequest of Magdalena Goldmann, Berlin, from the estate of Renée Sintenis, to the Nationalgalerie, Berlin (West), 1981

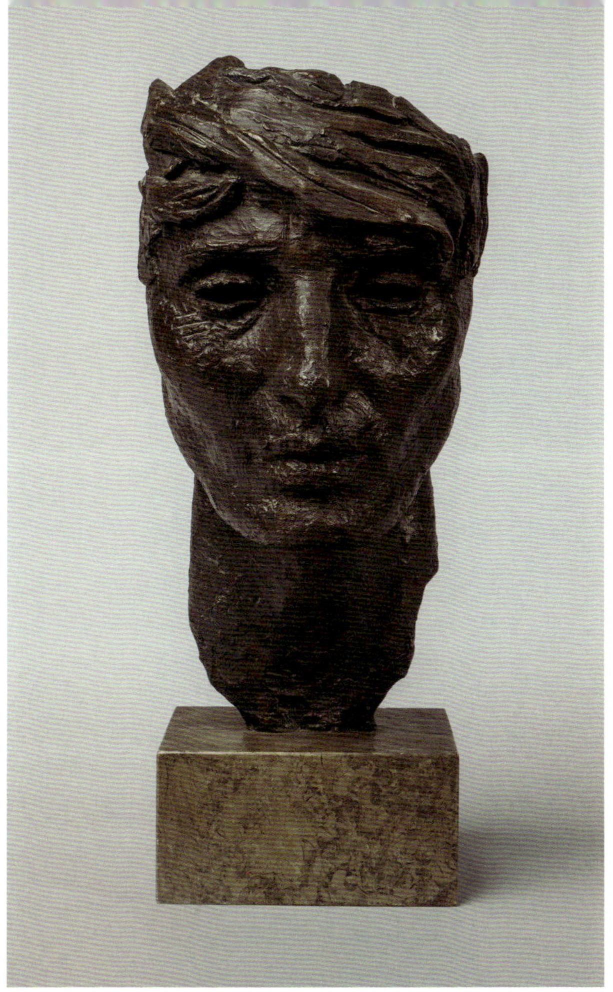

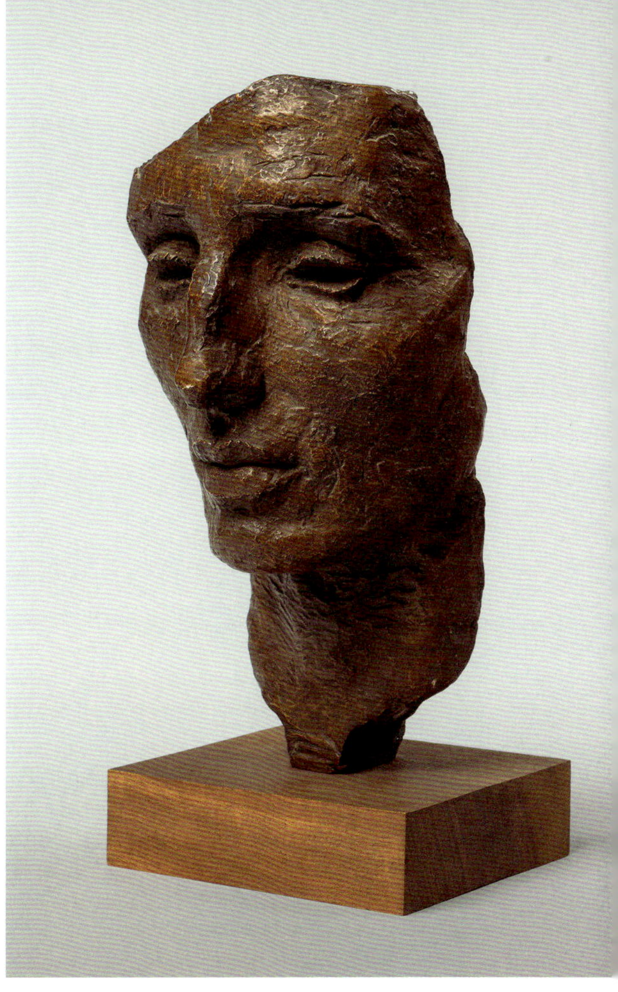

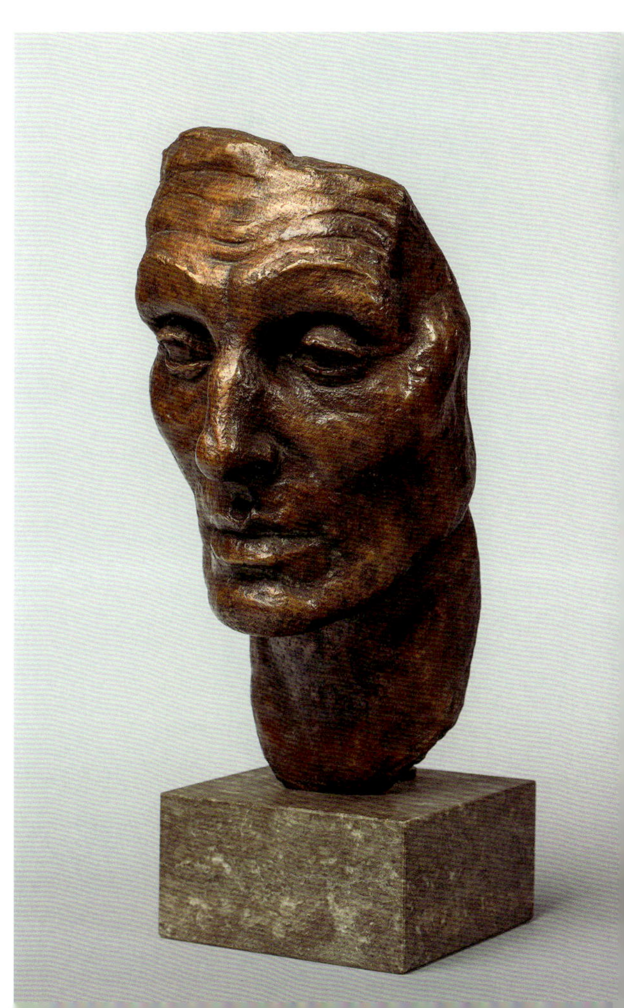

↑ Renée Sintenis, *Self-Portrait (Mask)*, 1931
Bronze, 32.5 × 16.5 × 22 cm
Transfer in 1932 from the Ministerium für Wissenschaft, Kunst und Volksbildung

↗ Renée Sintenis, *Self-Portrait*, 1933
Plaster, 26.5 × 14.2 × 15 cm
Bequest of Magdalena Goldmann, Berlin, from the estate of Renée Sintenis, to the Nationalgalerie, Berlin (West), 1981

→ Renée Sintenis, *Self-Portrait*, 1944
Bronze, 28 × 14 × 15.5 cm
Bequest of Magdalena Goldmann, Berlin, from the estate of Renée Sintenis, to the Nationalgalerie, Berlin (West), 1981

The Sculptor Renée Sintenis

Sleeping deer, leaping gazelles, horses rearing up on their hind legs, overconfident foals and frolicking dogs and bears are all part of sculptor Renée (Renate Alice) Sintenis' repertoire. Born in Silesian Glatz in 1888 and raised in Neuruppin, Stuttgart and Berlin, as a young woman she began studying sculpture at the institute associated with Berlin's Kunstgewerbemuseum (Museum of Decorative Arts) in 1907. Family disputes prevented her from completing her studies. But rather than yielding to her father's wish that she become a typist, Sintenis began modelling for the sculptor Georg Kolbe in 1910 and creating her own art in 1913. Two years later, she produced her first animal figurines, which would become her signature pieces. In these small-format, usually bronze cast sculptures, the artist sought to capture each animal's distinctive characteristics. She did so in momentary, ephemeral depictions that give expression to the animals' reflexes and innate instincts, their joyful greetings, their fearful eyes, how they rear up in fright or hone in with undivided focus, sniff out information or retreat into contented states of rest.

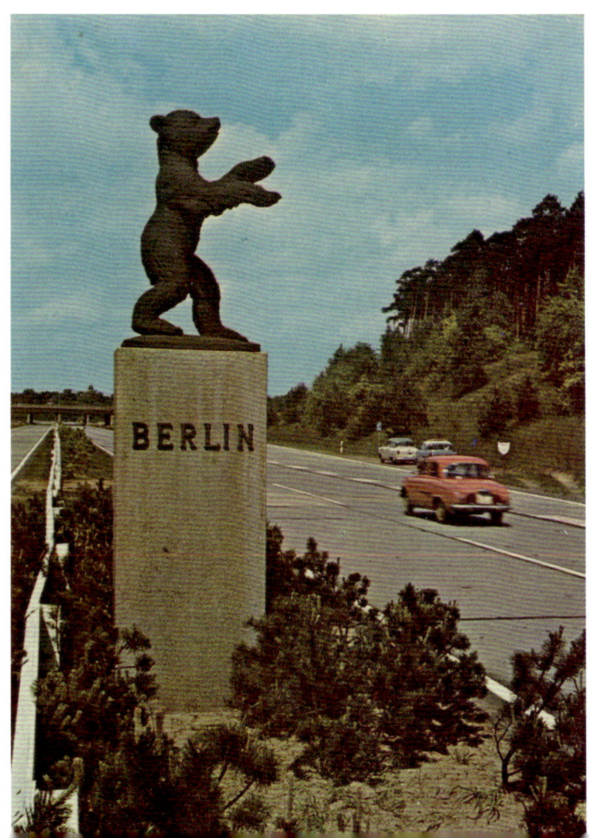

→ Renée Sintenis' *Large Berlin Bear* seen in the median strip of the A115 federal motorway, shortly before the interchange to Zehlendorf, c. 1980
→ Renée Sintenis (dressed in a fur coat) with Magdalena Goldmann and Sintenis' fox terrier Philipp in front of the book dealers Schneider & Amelang at the corner of Königin-Augusta-Straße 33 (now Reichpietschufer) and Bendlerstraße (now Stauffenbergstraße), Berlin, 1931
→ Renée Sintenis photographed with *Little Goat*, c. 1927

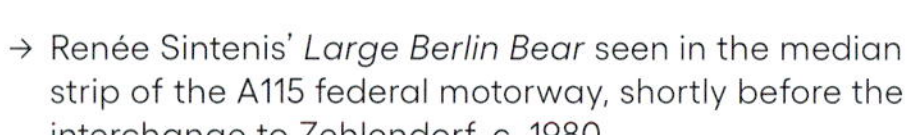

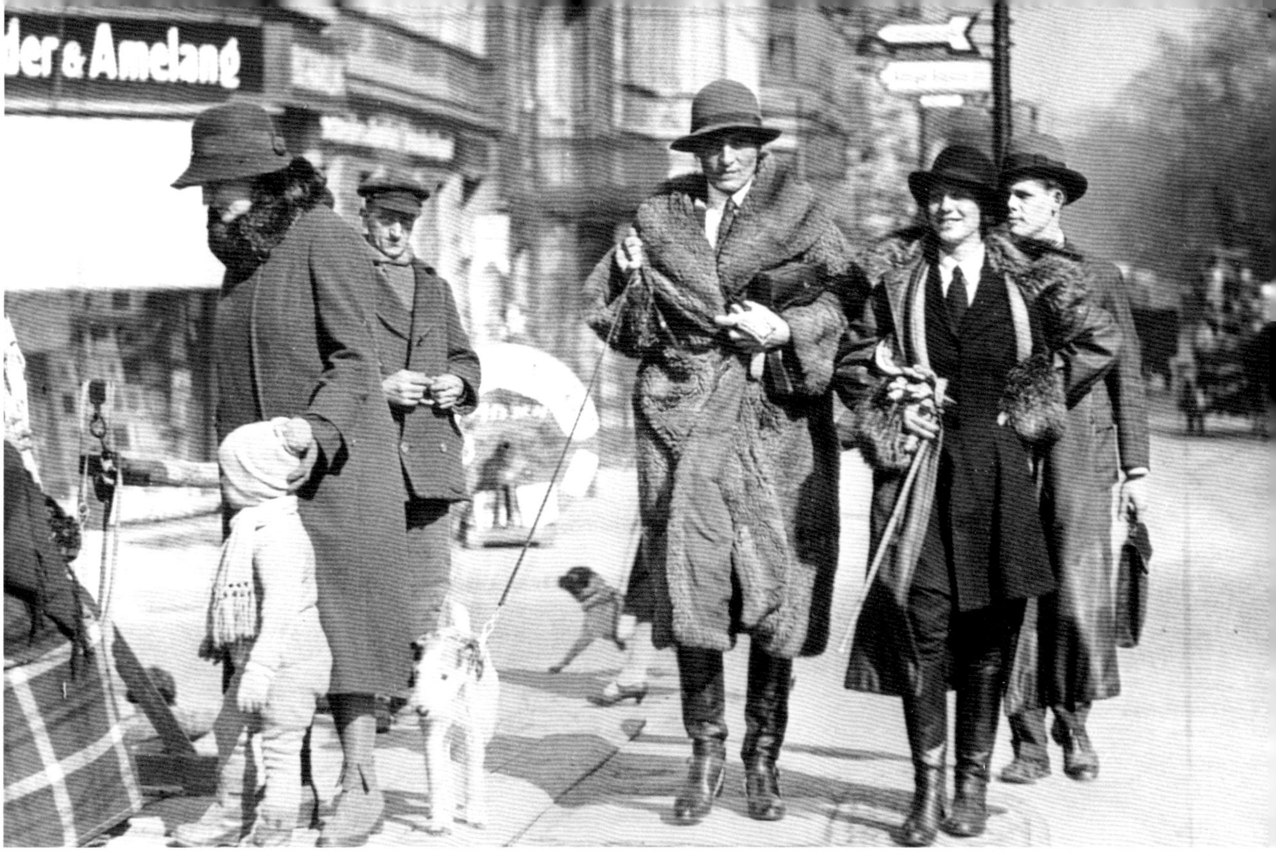

The sculptor soon celebrated her first successes and was well-established in Berlin society by the mid-1920s. Represented by the gallerist Alfred Flechtheim, her works sold well and Sintenis was a welcome guest at a wide variety of the city's events and festivities. She spent her days horseback riding in Berlin's Tiergarten, strolling down Kurfürstendamm in elegant suits with her terrier by her side or driving her sports car to the Noack foundry. Sporting a fashionably short haircut, androgynous looks and a confident demeanour, the artist personified the Weimar Republic's prototypical modern woman. The numerous self-portraits Sintenis created between 1916 and 1944 are a poignant testament to her self-perception and sensibility. Following Käthe Kollwitz, she became the second woman sculptor to teach at the male-dominated Preußische Akademie der Künste (Prussian Academy of Arts), placing her at the height of her career in 1931. Although Sintenis was not directly affected by work prohibitions or the "degenerate art" campaign, the National Socialist takeover in January 1933 increasingly restricted her artistic practice.

After the Second World War, Renée Sintenis was able to build on her earlier artistic successes. The *Berliner Bär* (Berlin Bear) undoubtedly remains her most popular sculpture. In 1956 she completed the first design of the *Großer Berliner Bär* (Large Berlin Bear), which was installed on an autobahn median strip in 1957, near what was then the border checkpoint Dreilinden between West Berlin and the German Democratic Republic (GDR). A miniature cast of the upright bear has served as the prize for the Berlinale, the Berlin International Film Festival, since 1960.

Maike Steinkamp

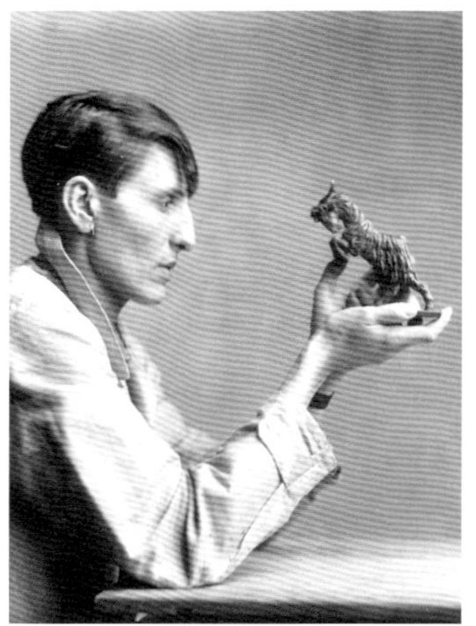

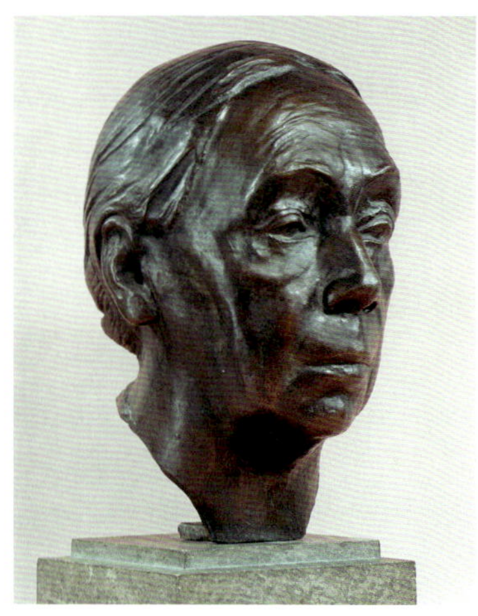

Käthe Kollwitz, *Self-Portrait,* 1926–36
Bronze, 37 × 23 × 28 cm. Acquired in 1960 from the Galerie Alex Vömel, Düsseldorf, by the Land Berlin for the Galerie des 20. Jahrhunderts, Berlin (West)

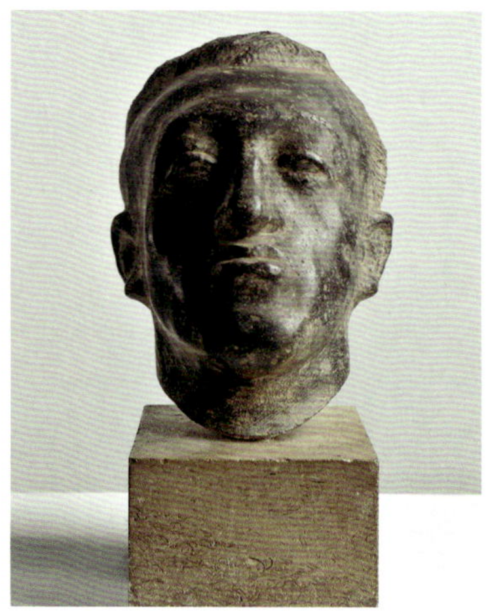

Joseph Wackerle, *Male Head*, c. 1933
Granite, 20 × 14 × 19 cm
Loan from the Ministerium für Wissenschaft, Kunst und Volksbildung since 1935

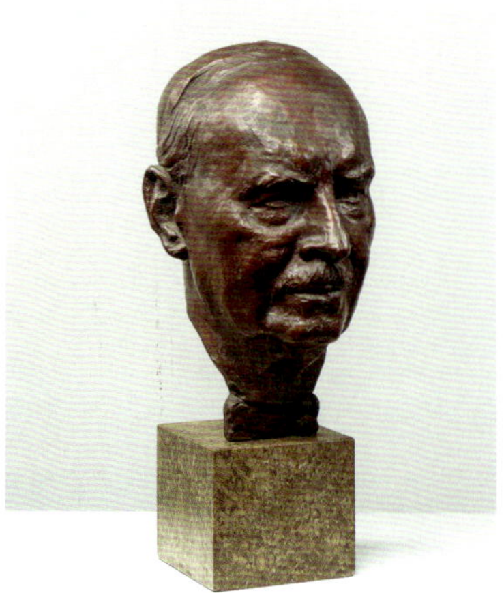

Fritz Klimsch, *Theodor Wiegand*, 1933–34
Bronze, 31.5 × 18.5 × 25.5 cm
Gift from friends of Privy Councillor Theodor Wiegand, 1936

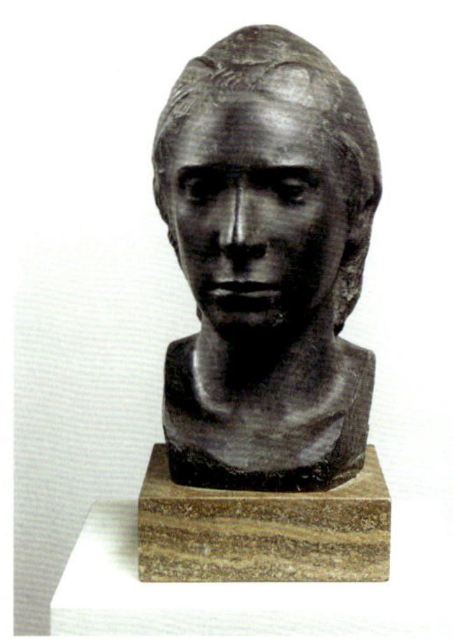

Richard Scheibe, *Bust of a Woman*, 1934
Bronze, 46 × 26 × 28.5 cm
Acquired in 1967 from a private owner, Zwickau, for the Nationalgalerie, Berlin (East)

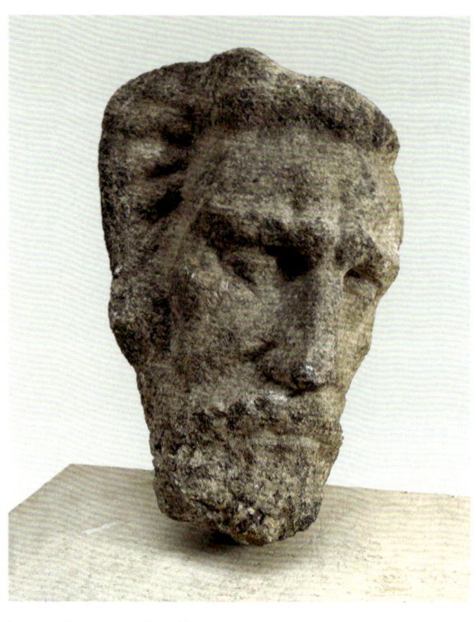

Joachim Utech, *On the Sea*, 1934
Granite, 38 × 26 × 23 cm
Acquired in 1938 from the artist in exchange

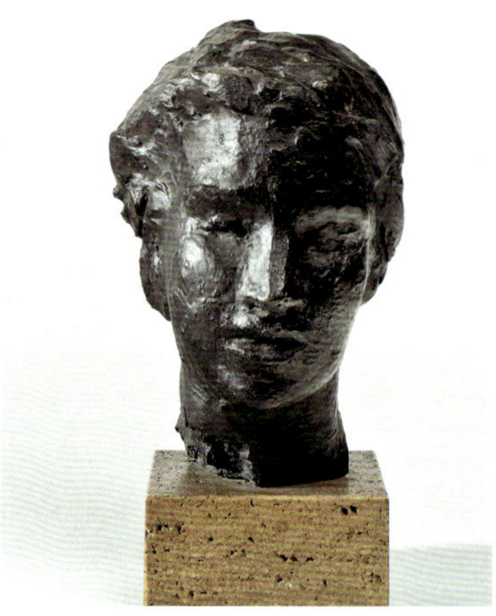

Hilde Plate, *Head of a Girl*, c. 1934
Bronze, 17.5 × 11 × 13.5 cm
Acquired in 1936 from the artist

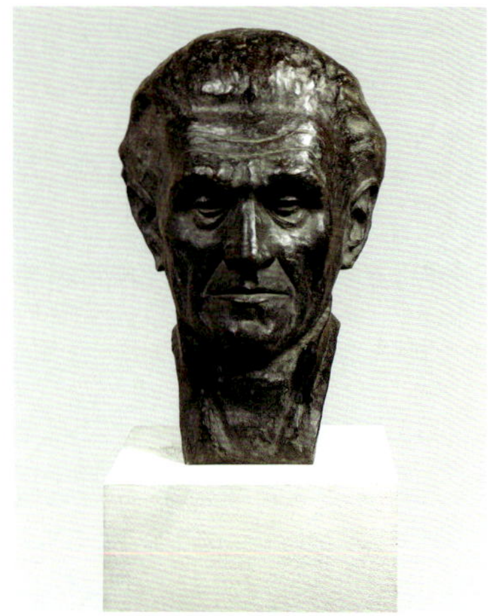

Max Nienhaus, *Stefan George*, 1934
Bronze, 72 × 39 × 46 cm
Transferred in 1966 from the Ermeler-Haus, Berlin, to the Nationalgalerie, Berlin (East)

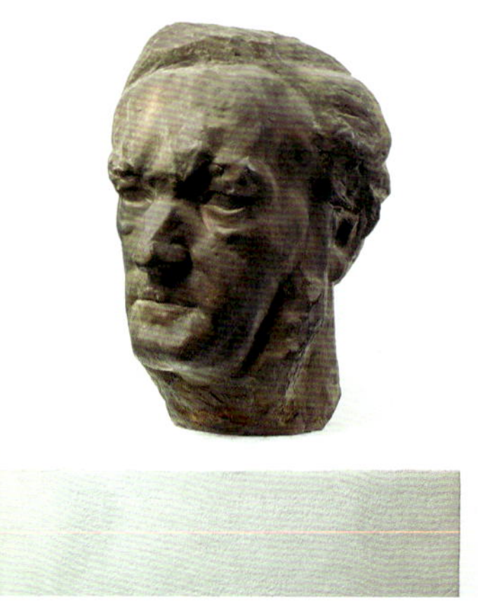

Adolf Wamper, *Portrait of Richard Wagner*, 1935, Bronze, 36 × 28 × 33 cm
Loan from the Bundesrepublik Deutschland since 2011

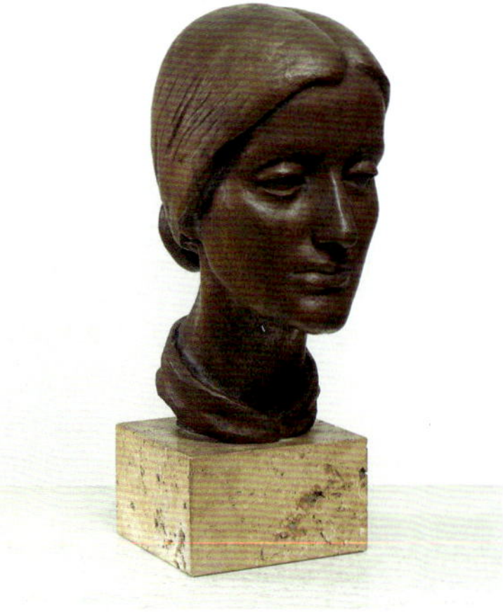

Hermann Blumenthal, *Ursula Niemöller*, 1935 (cast 1936)
Bronze, 34 × 20 × 26.6 cm
Acquired in 1936 from the artist

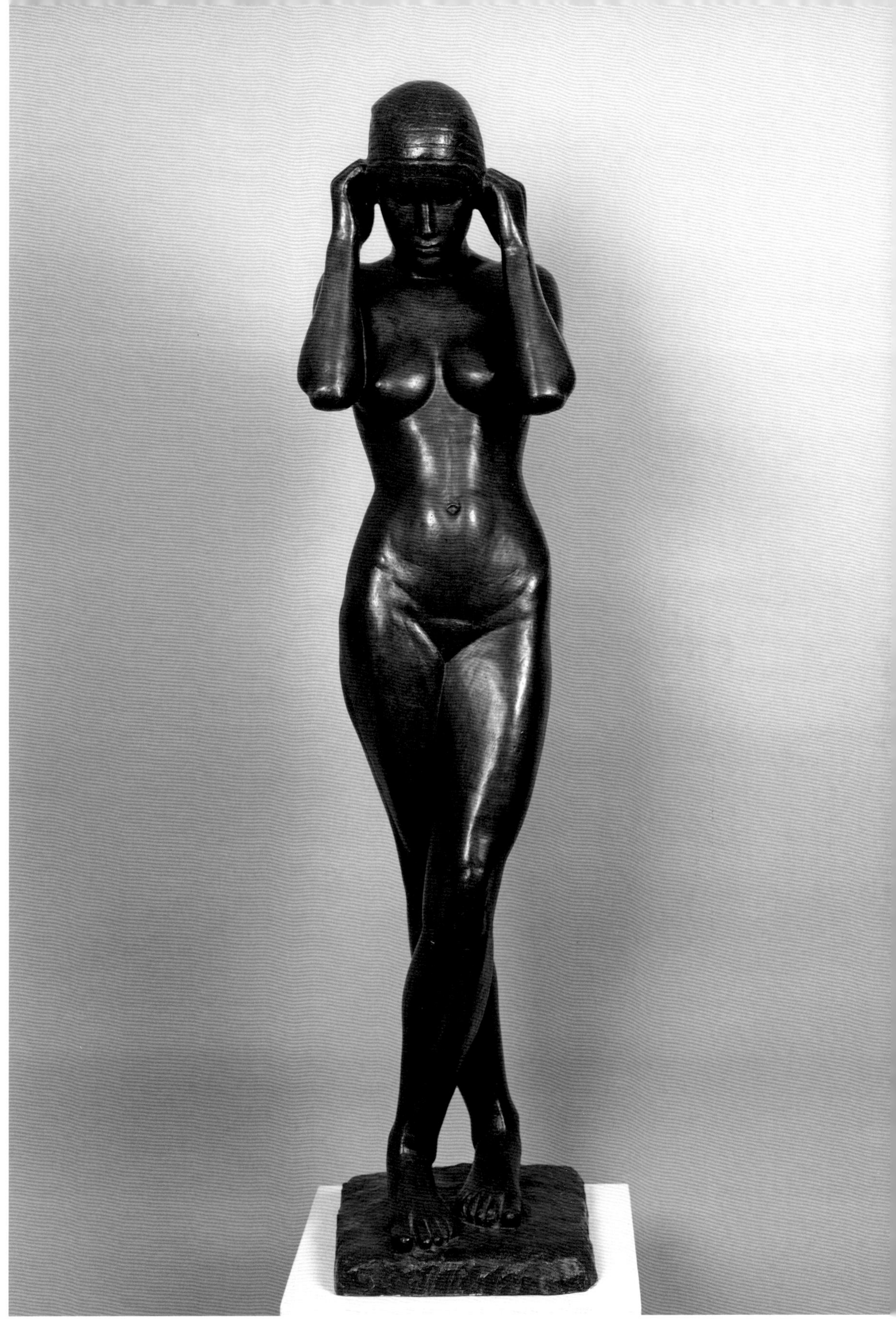

Gerhard Marcks, *Swimmer II*, 1938 (cast 1940)
Bronze, 169 × 41 × 47 cm
Acquired in 1964 from the Felix Weise Collection, Halle (Saale), for the Nationalgalerie, Berlin (East)

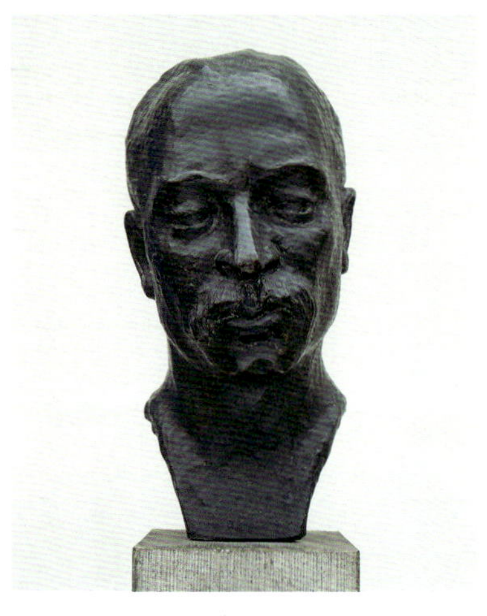

Clara Rilke-Westhoff, *Rainer Maria Rilke*, 1936
Bronze, 37.5 × 18 × 26 cm
Acquired in 1938 from the artist from the *Große Deutsche Kunstausstellung*, Munich

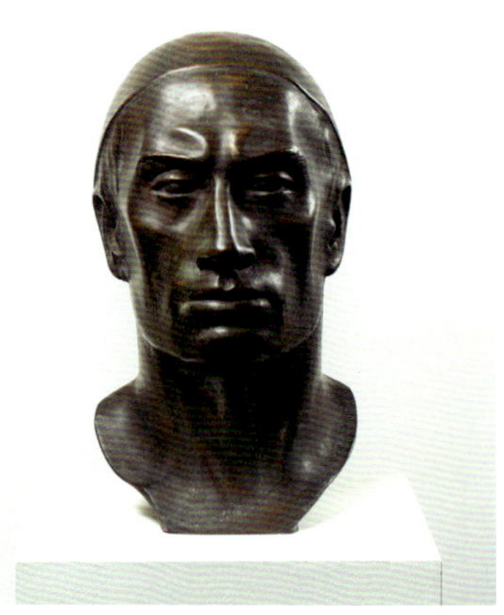

Fritz Koelle, *Head Of A Miner*, 1936
Bronze, 42 × 23 × 27 cm. Found in 1948 in Berlin's Osthafen; donated by the Magistrat von Groß-Berlin to the Galerie des 20. Jahrhunderts, Berlin (East) in 1951

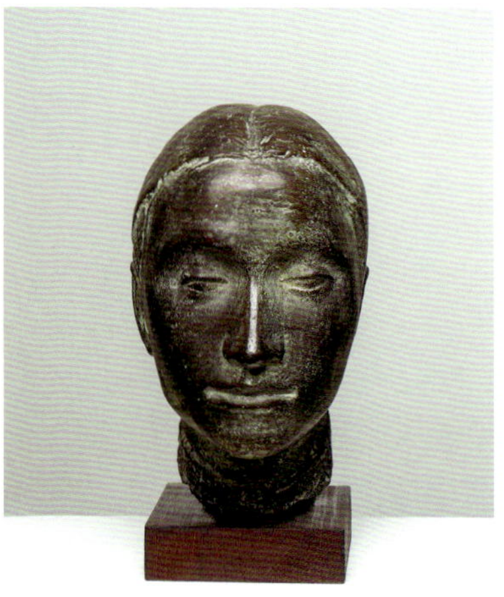

Gerhard Geyer, *Head Gerda*, 1936
Bronze, 28 × 16 × 22 cm
Acquired in 1966 from the artist, Halle (Saale), for the Nationalgalerie, Berlin (East)

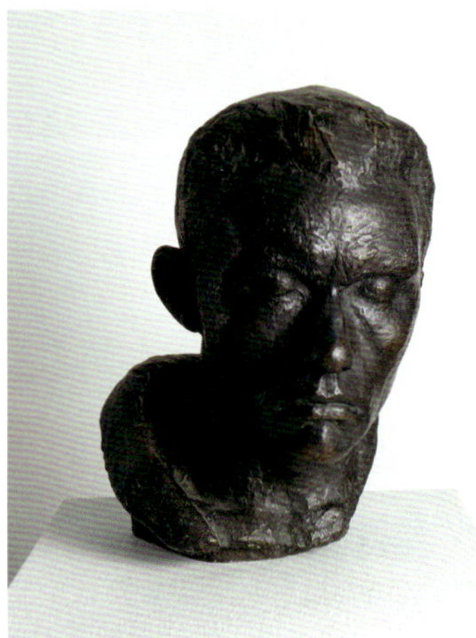

Fritz Cremer, *Head of a Dying Soldier (Self-Portrait)*, 1937
Bronze, 36.5 × 26 × 32 cm
Acquired in 1956 from the artist for the Nationalgalerie, Berlin (East)

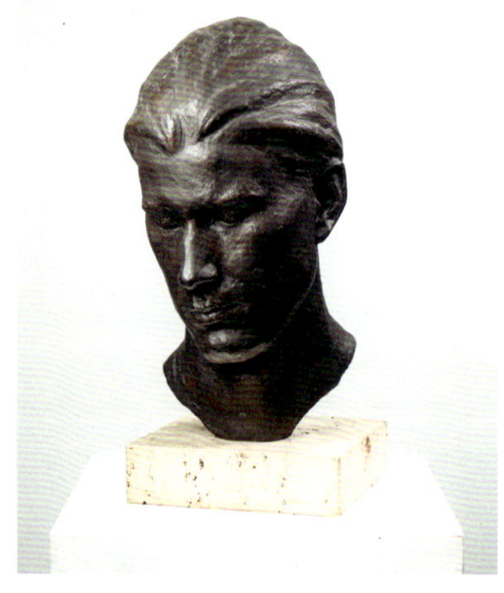

Ruthild Hahne, *Portrait of Hans Bertram*, 1939 (cast 1979–80)
Bronze, 49 × 23 × 34 cm
Acquired in 1979 from the artist for the Nationalgalerie, Berlin (East)

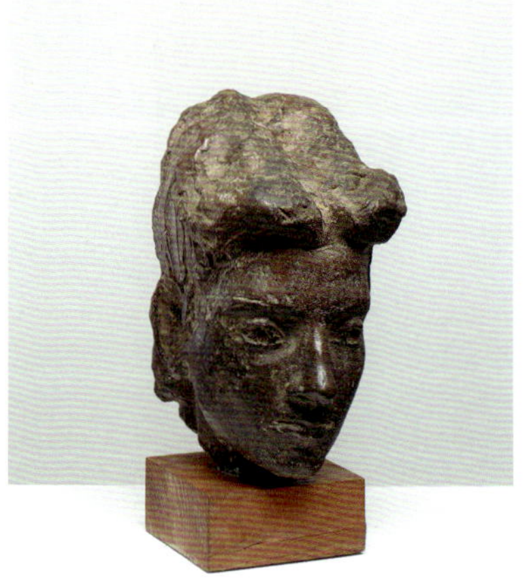

Jenny Wiegmann Mucchi, *Head of a Girl (Portrait Pucci)*, 1942
Bronze, 26 × 15.5 × 23.5 cm
Acquired in 1963 from the artist for the Nationalgalerie, Berlin (East)

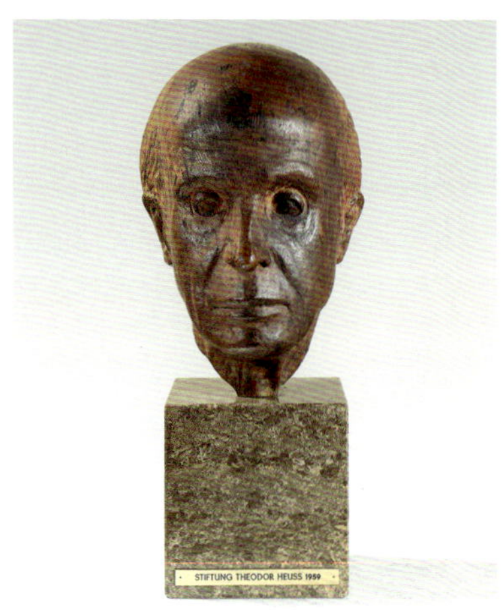

Gerhard Marcks, *Portrait Leo von König*, 1942
Bronze, 26.3 × 18.5 × 22 cm
Acquired in 1959 from the Galerie Stangl, Munich, with funds from Theodor Heuss for the Nationalgalerie, Berlin (West)

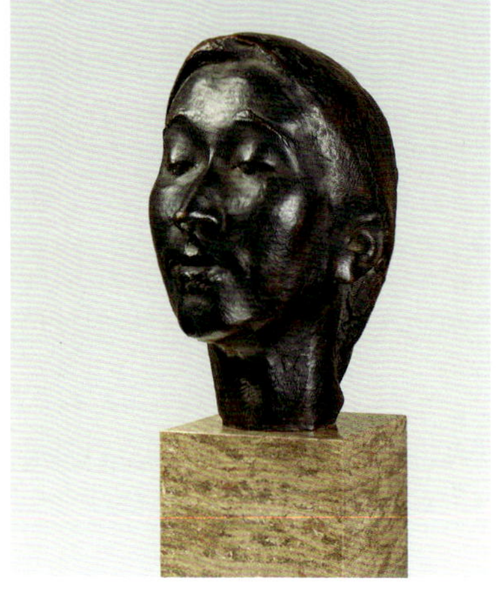

Bernhard Heiliger, *Head Gardener*, 1943
Bronze, 29.5 × 19 × 27 cm
Acquired in 1964 from the Linde family by the Land Berlin for the Galerie des 20. Jahrhunderts, Berlin (West)

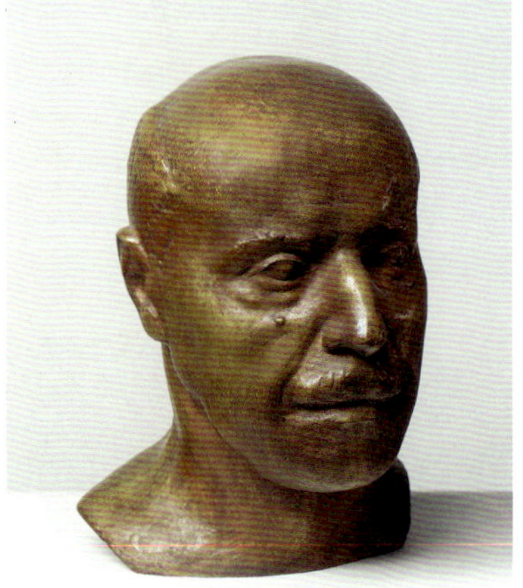

Gustav Weidanz, *Portrait Head Wilhelm Waetzoldt*, 1945
Bronze, 29 × 23 × 25 cm
Gift from H. J. Wilms, Hamburg, to the Nationalgalerie, Berlin (West), 1966

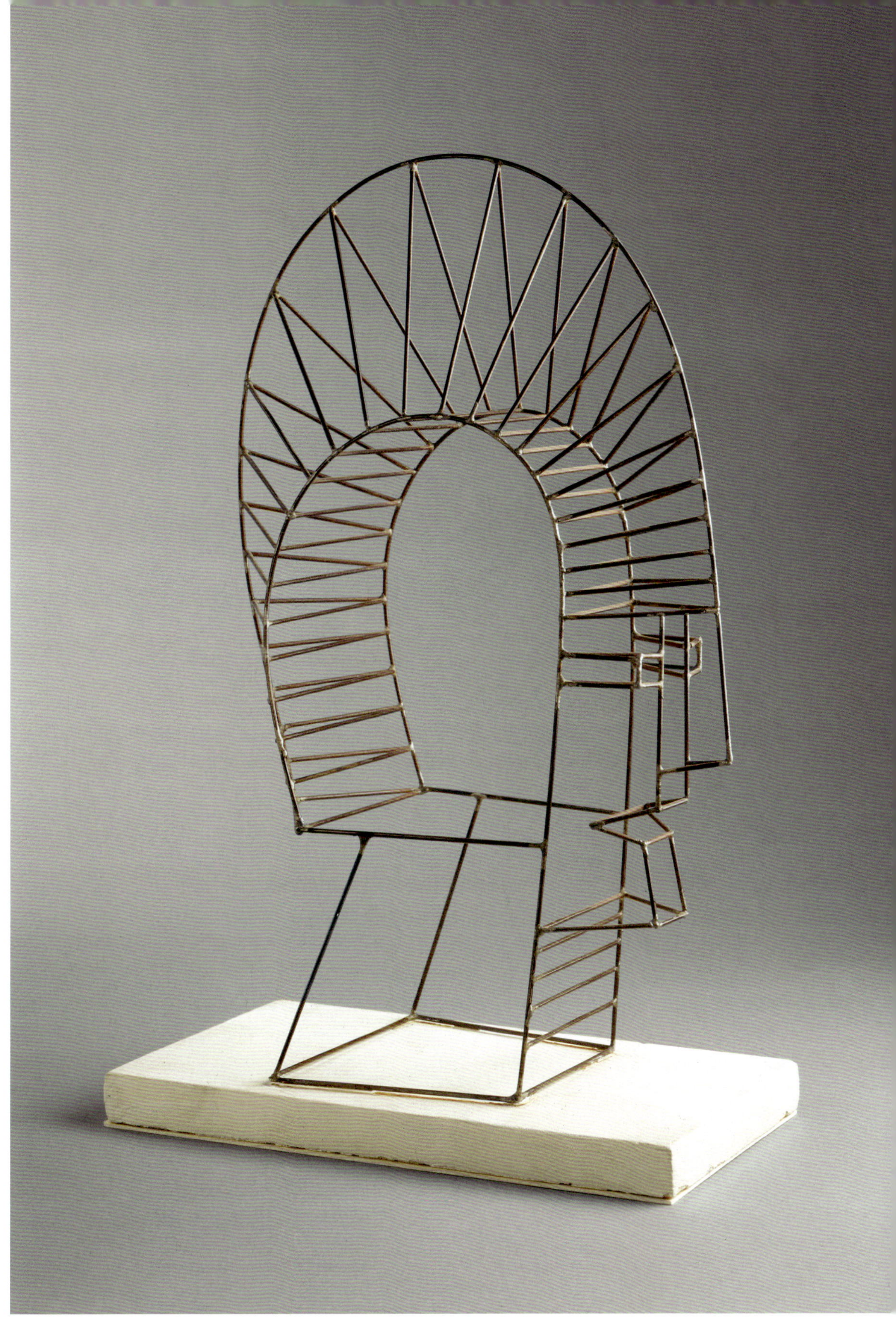

Hans Uhlmann, *Head,* 1935
Iron wire, 37 × 12 × 23 cm
Gift to the Nationalgalerie, Berlin (West) from Hildegard Uhlmann, Berlin, as part of the "Haftmann Gift", 1976

Sculpture and the Human Being: *Prometheus* and *Zwitter*

The origins of Javier Téllez' work can be found in his interest in the world of the mentally ill. The contemporary artist is invested in creating visibility for those who society has cast out. They are captured in photographic portraits; they play protagonists in his films and are often active participants in his artistic process. Téllez' interest in so-called outsider art also stems from this context.

In the early 20th century, avant-garde art movements discovered a source of inspiration in the visual art created by patients at psychiatric hospitals. Paul Klee, Emil Nolde and Ernst Ludwig Kirchner all saw an anti-academic, authentic form of expression manifested in the "art of the insane". André Breton's Surrealist circle also believed the work of the mentally ill revealed the subconscious in its natural state. Thus doctors were ardent collectors of visual resources for outsider art, although they were initially focused on the images' diagnostic usefulness. Hans Prinzhorn, an art historian and psychiatrist from Heidelberg, became a pioneer in both fields when he attributed aesthetic value to these works. He compiled a collection of close to 5000 pieces from 1919 to 1921 and publicized his influential study *Bildnerei der Geisteskranken* (Artistry of the Mentally Ill) the following year.

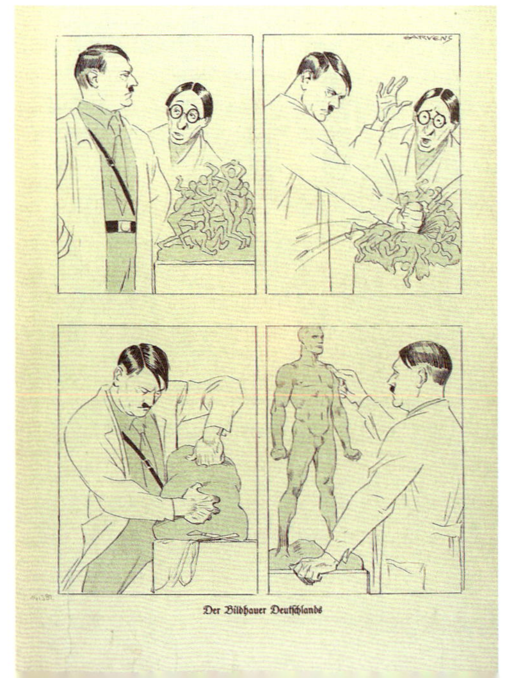

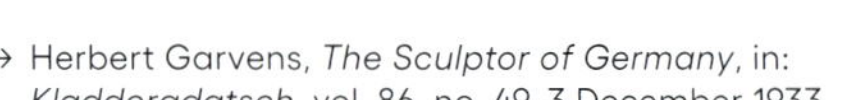

→ Herbert Garvens, *The Sculptor of Germany*, in: *Kladderadatsch*, vol. 86, no. 49, 3 December 1933
↗ Guide to the exhibition *Entartete Kunst*, Berlin, 1937
↗ Arno Breker working on *Prometheus*, 1935

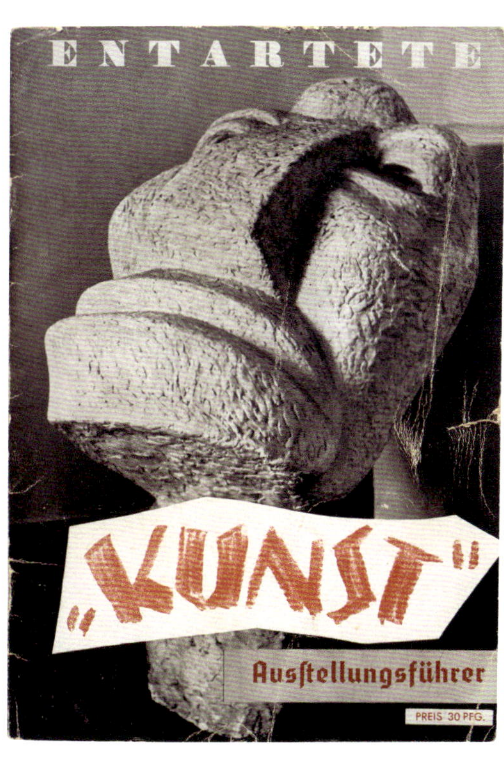

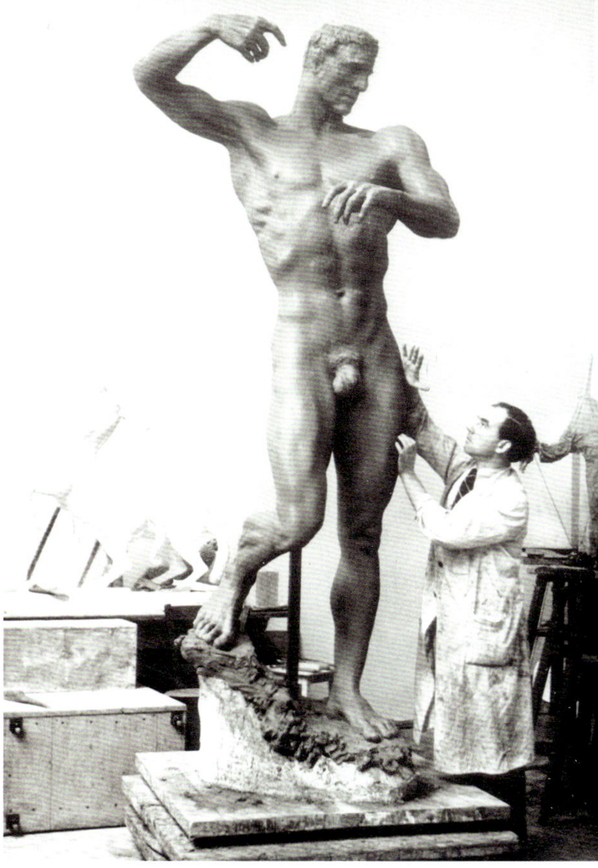

Prinzhorn's intention was soon perverted by National Socialist propaganda, which would refer to outsider art to defame modern art as pathological. From 1938 onwards, many works from Prinzhorn's collection were shown in the travelling exhibition *Entartete Kunst* (Degenerate Art), which emphasized their similarities in form or content to modern art. The presentation included the sculpture *Zwitter* (Hermaphrodite) by Karl Genzel, a diagnosed schizophrenic. The abstracted hermaphroditic figure stood in opposition to the aesthetic ideals promoted by National Socialist teachings on race, which the National Socialists found instead to be embodied in the work of Arno Breker, one of Hitler's favourite sculptors. Breker's sculpture of a heroic, muscular youth entitled *Prometheus* was designed for the National Socialist Ministry of Propaganda in Berlin and exhibited at the *Große Deutsche Kunstausstellung* (Great German Art Exhibition) immediately after its completion in 1937.

For his 2011 film work *Rotations (Prometheus and Zwitter)*, Javier Téllez had both sculptures brought to his studio, where he placed each one onto a rotating base and filmed it at extremely close range. The double projection of simultaneous films dissolves their real-life proportions: Breker's monumental bronze figure now appears as small as Genzel's wooden sculpture, which is only about 30 cm high. In a surprisingly simple gesture, Téllez composed a powerful encounter between two fundamentally different views of the human being that invalidates both the exaltation of state-sanctioned art and the National Socialists' denigration of outsider art.

Irina Hiebert Grun

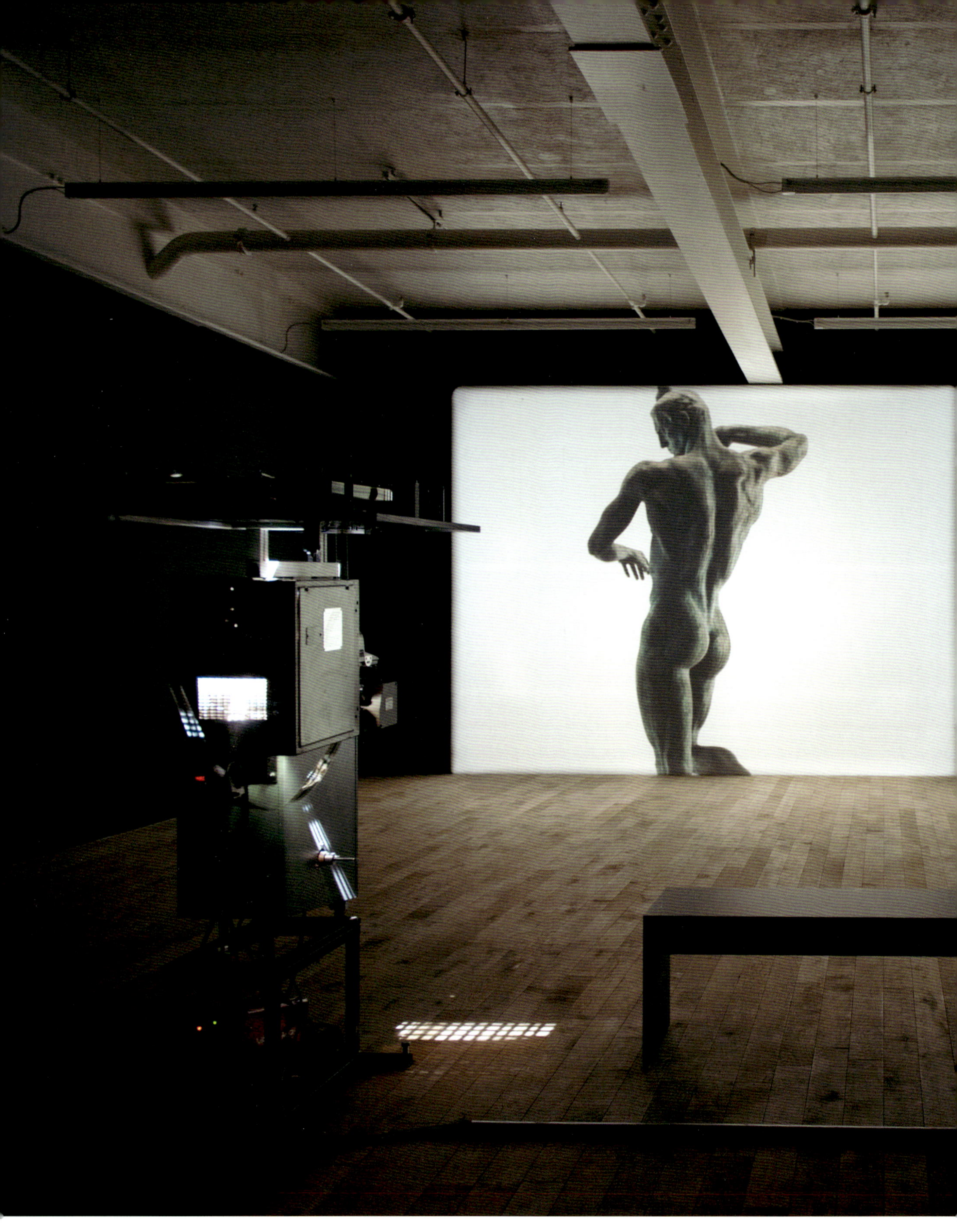

Javier Téllez, *Rotations (Prometheus and Zwitter)*, 2011
Two-channel projection, 35 mm film, colour, silent, 7 min. and archival documents
Acquired in 2013 by the Freunde der Nationalgalerie

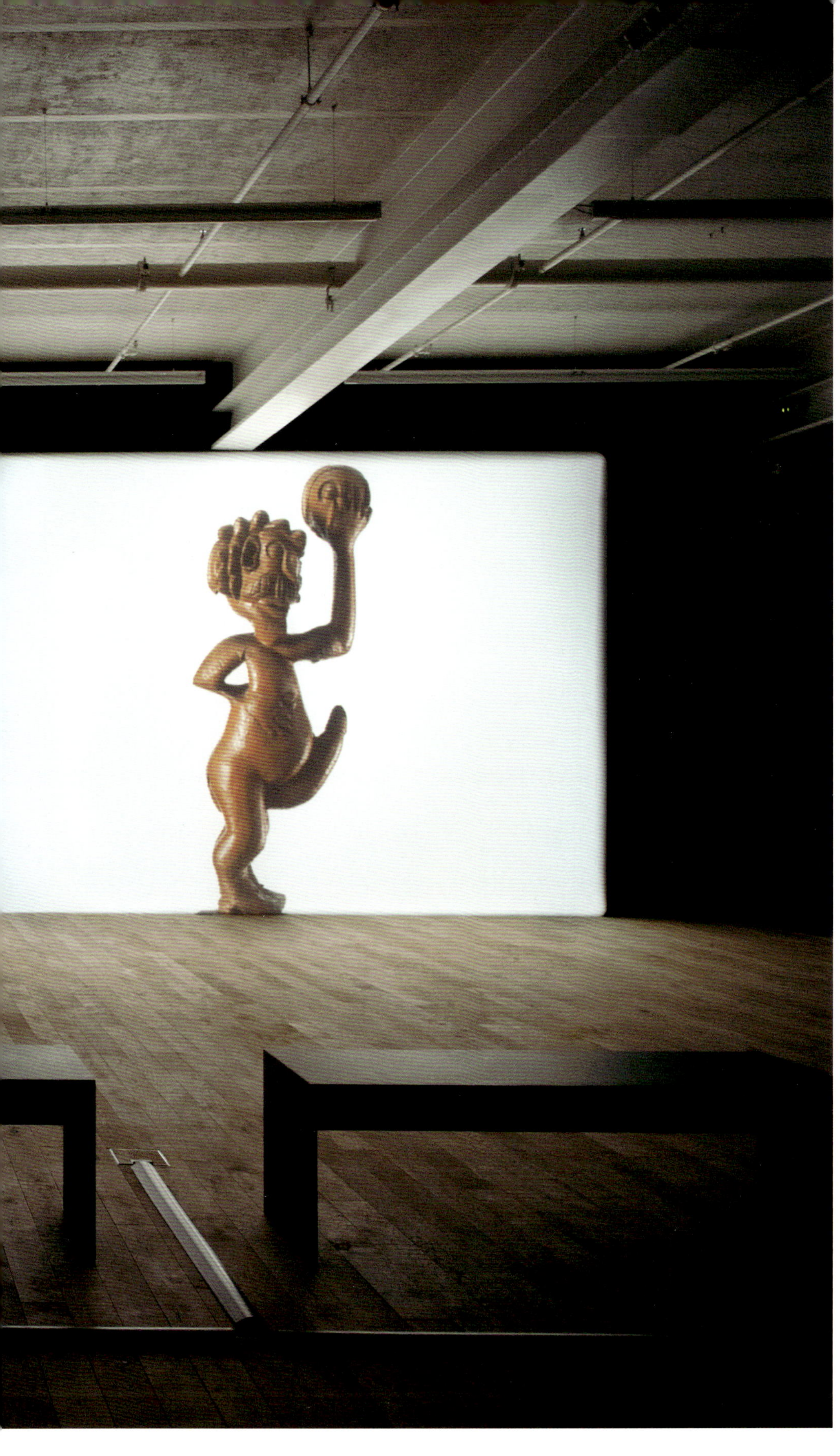

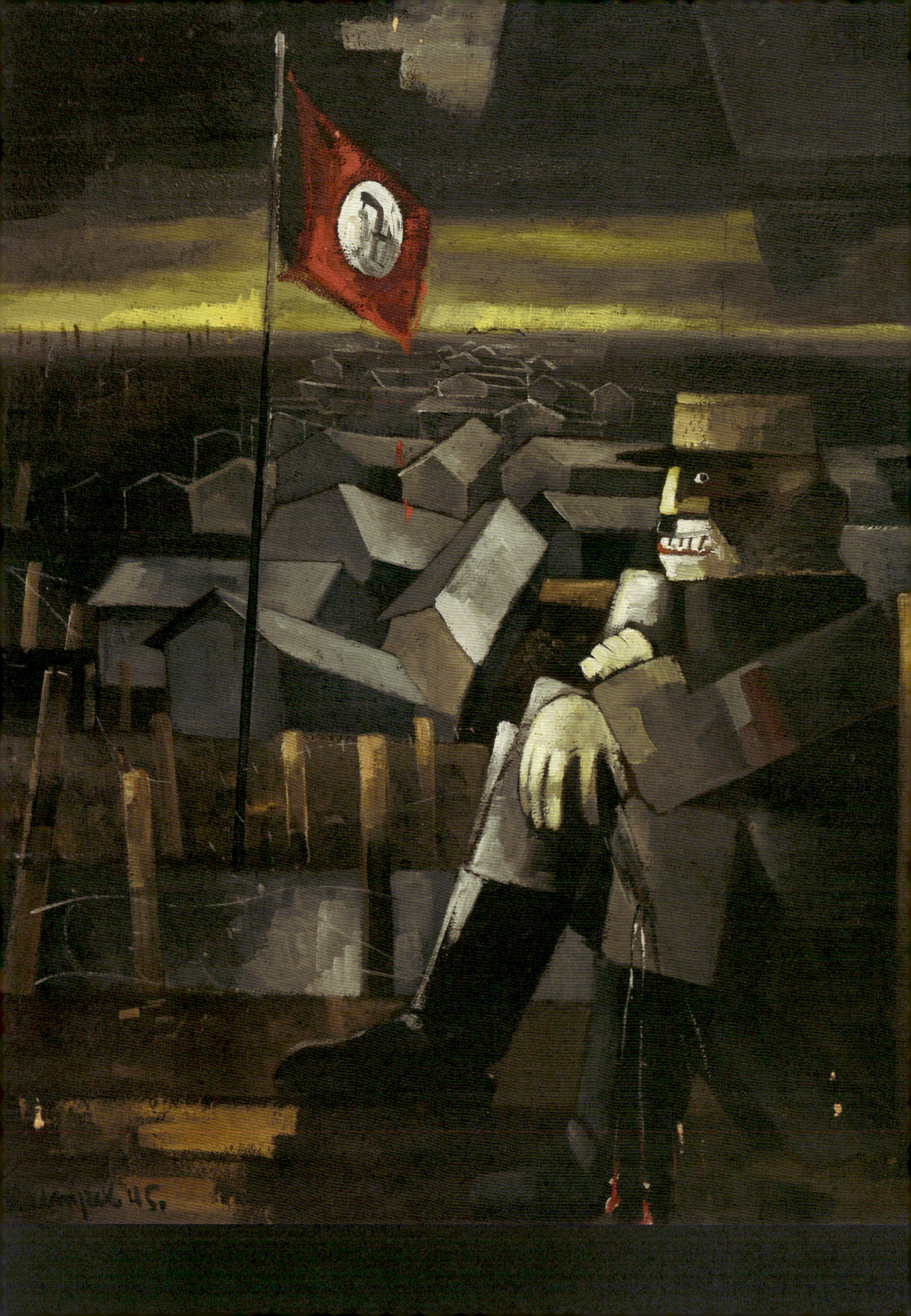

War and Annihilation

Creating modern art under the National Socialist dictatorship required courage long before the outbreak of the Second World War in 1939. And yet, individual cases of artists doing just that have been documented. Four days after Karl Hofer's studio in Berlin was bombed in 1943, he set to work defiantly repainting the works lost, such as *Die schwarzen Zimmer* (The Black Rooms). In Augsburg, Karl Kunz worked under cover of his father's wood and veneer workshop. He used the plywood available there as "canvasses" for his paintings. If danger arose, the planks could simply be turned around to blend into the workshop.

Kunz was inspired to paint *Deutschland erwache!* (Germany, Awaken!) by an image of Pablo Picasso's *Guernica* he had acquired in an under-the-counter purchase in 1942. Picasso himself was already world-famous and working undeterred in German-occupied Paris at the time. His unflinching approach undoubtedly placed him in danger, but he was left unscathed. Meanwhile, Horst Strempel had been processing his own experiences of internment through painting since 1941. Immediately after the end of the war, he completed *Nacht über Deutschland* (Night Over Germany), his triptych addressing the Jewish population's annihilation in National Socialist concentration camps.

Horst Strempel, *Night Over Germany (1st Sketch)*, 1945
Oil on chipboard, 60 × 48.5 cm
Acquired in 1985 via the Staatlicher Kunsthandel der DDR with funds from the Kulturfonds der DDR from the estate of the artist; transferred in 1986 to the Nationalgalerie, Berlin (East)

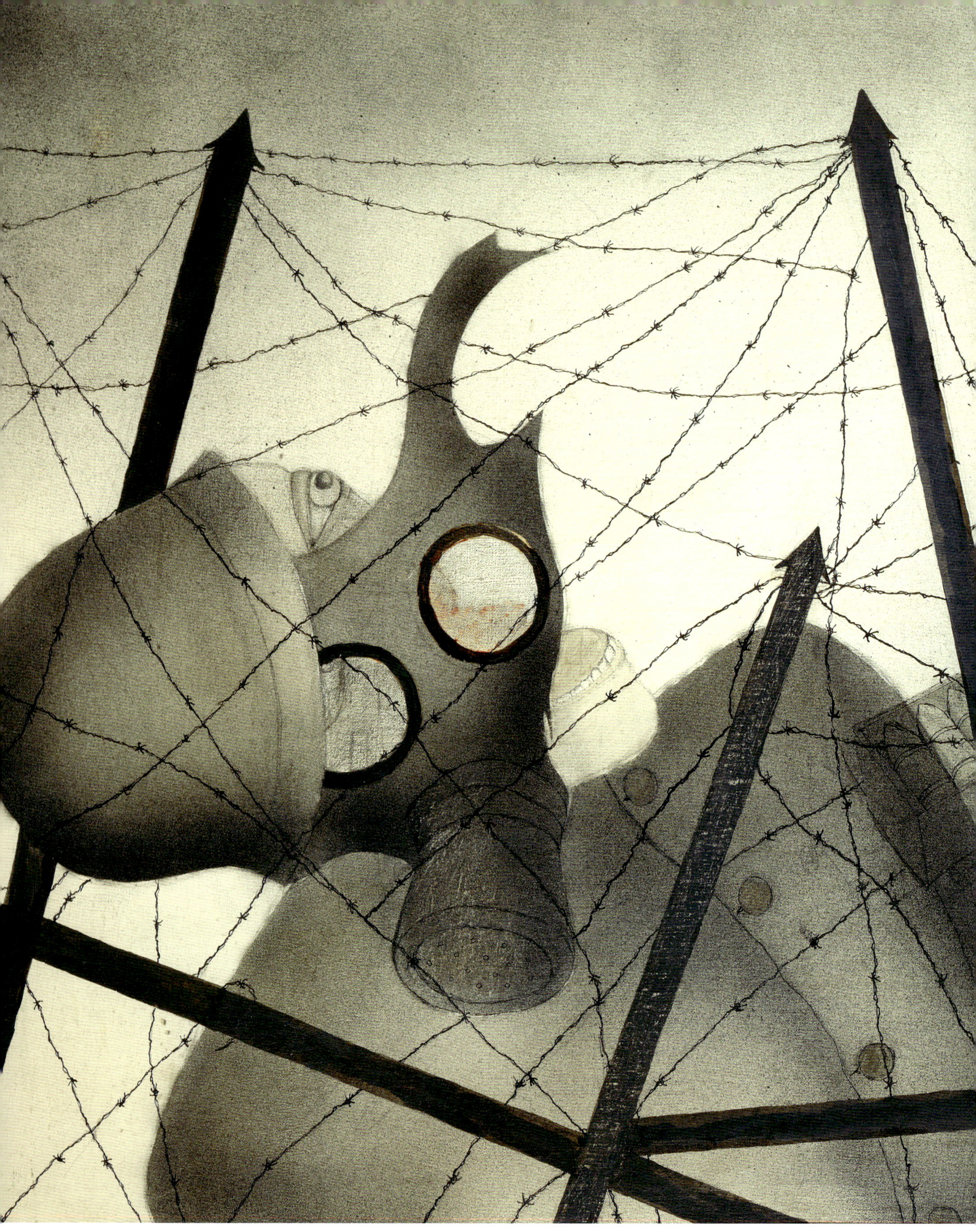

Alice Lex-Nerlinger, *Field-Grey Yields Dividends*, 1931
(Replica by the artist from 1961)
Casein tempera on canvas, 70 × 101 cm
Acquired in 1967 from the artist with funds from the
Kulturfonds der DDR for the Nationalgalerie, Berlin (East)

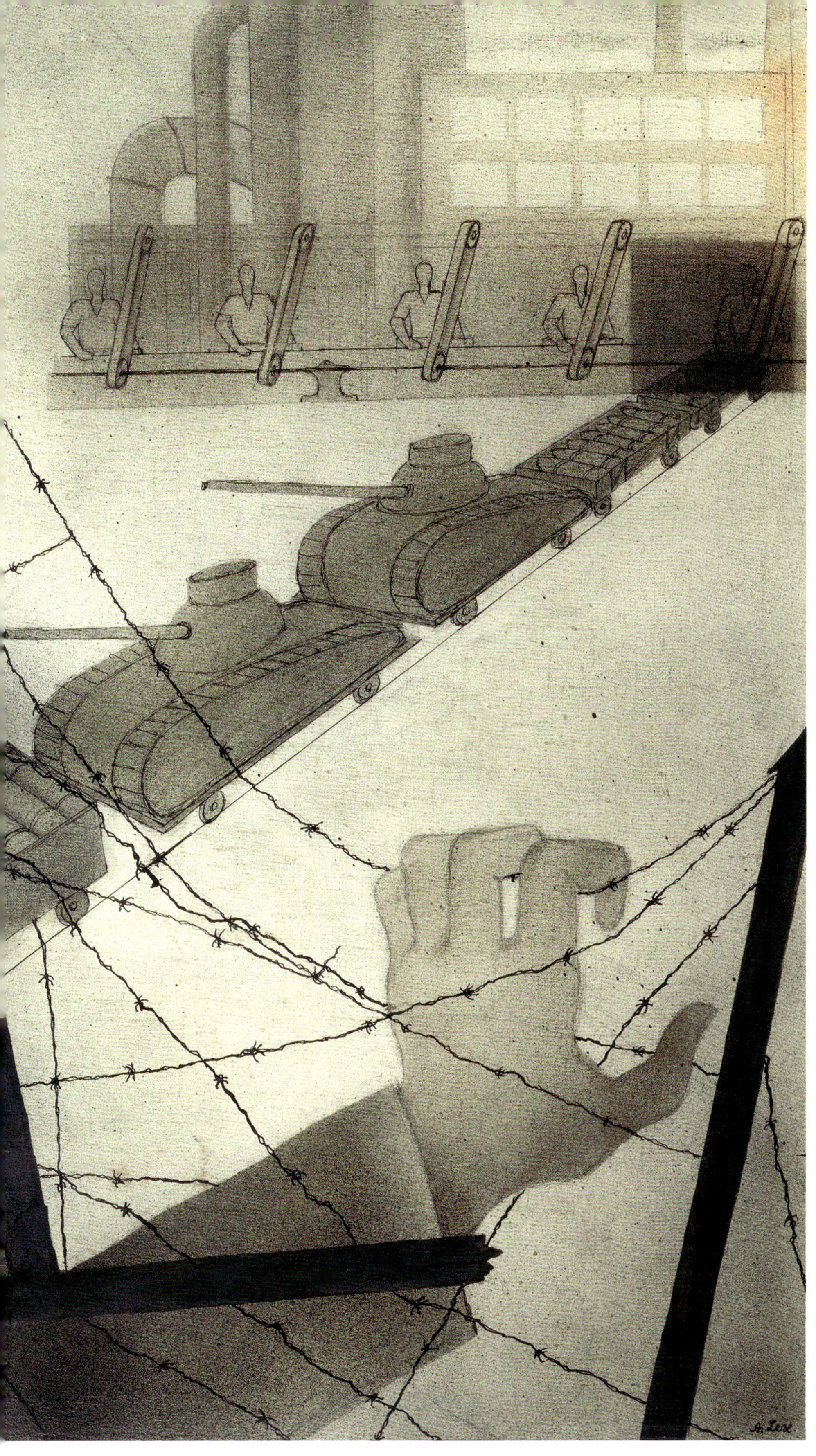

Alice Lex-Nerlinger: *Field-Grey Yields Dividends*

Who was Alice Lex-Nerlinger? The Berlin artist was among those of the Weimar Republic's avant-garde who embraced proletarian-revolutionary political leanings. Soviet Constructivism was one of her earliest influences. Together with her husband Oskar Nerlinger and other artists from the Sturm circle, she formed the artist group known as Die Abstrakten in 1926. She wanted to find a way to use abstraction for socially critical art. But Lex-Nerlinger soon concluded that the broader public did not understand this rather intellectual art form.

Combining photomontage and a spray technique she developed herself, the artist eventually found a suitable format for articulating class differences, women's struggles and militarism while retaining certain abstract stylistic elements. In 1928 she joined the Communist Party of Germany (KPD) and the Association of Revolutionary Visual Artists of Germany (ASSO). Her now overtly political artwork was created in direct support of the working-class struggle.

Lex-Nerlinger's work *Feldgrau schafft Dividende* (Field-Grey Yields Dividends) is both a condemnation of war and a scathing denunciation of capitalism, specifically its exploitation of the working class. She used her spray technique and stencils to show a fallen soldier wearing a gas mask caught in a barbed-wire fence. An armament factory and a line of faceless workers in the background emphasize the anonymity of industrial production. A freight train transporting tanks and ammunition crosses the image at a diagonal, connecting the two scenes. The title refers to the weapons industry profiting from the countless casualties of battle and the dividends its investors receive. The fallen soldier in the "field-grey" uniform from the First World War embodies this connection.

This "anti-war work" was exhibited at the *Große Berliner Kunstausstellung* (Great Berlin Art Exhibition) in 1932 and it met with heavy criticism in the National Socialist press. The piece was destroyed soon afterwards. It wasn't until 1961 that the artist created the replica that eventually came into the National-galerie. By early April 1933 the National Socialists had already banned Lex-Nerlinger from working. She destroyed a portion of

↗ Alice Lex-Nerlinger, *1931–1933*, 1933

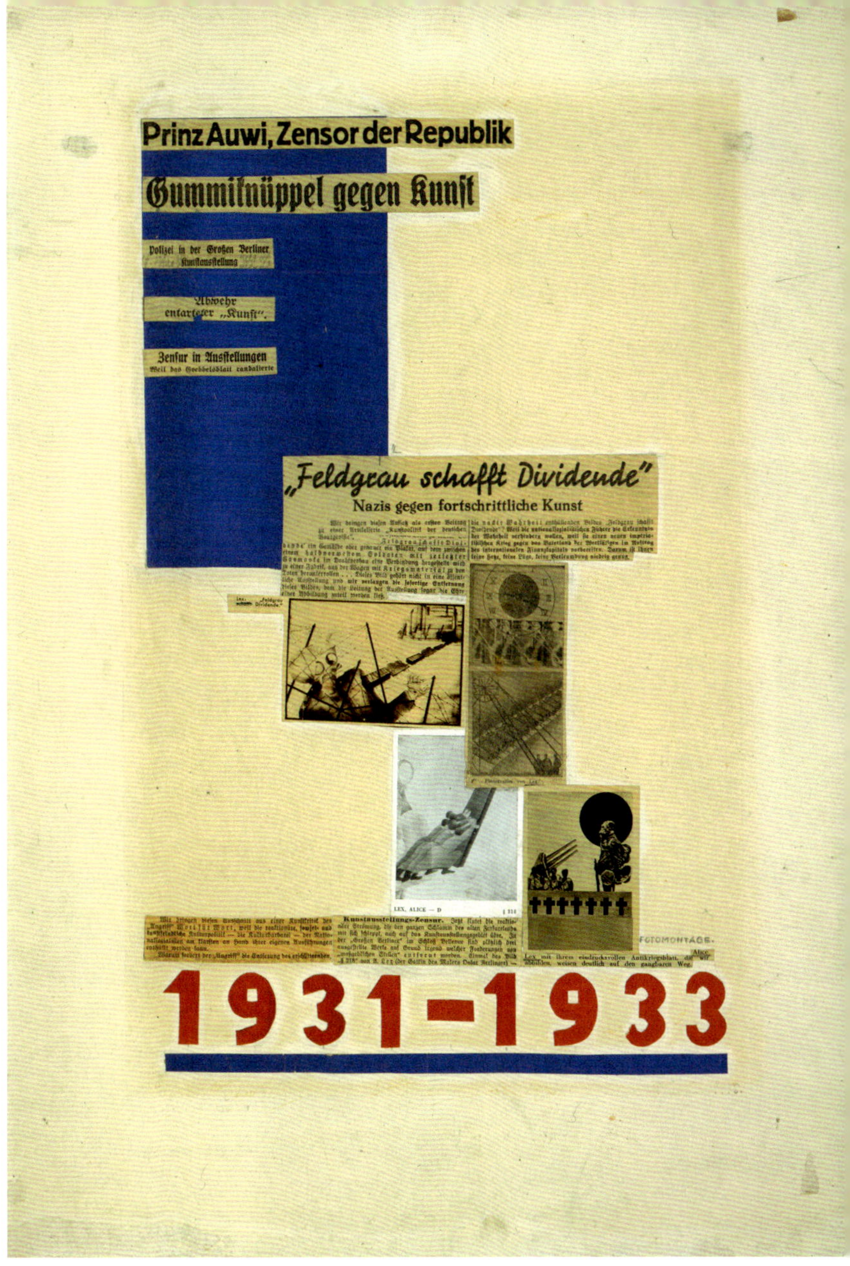

her oeuvre and suspended all her public activities but continued creating political work in secret. After the war ended, the staunch socialist returned to advocating for “art in service of the struggle for communism” in the German Democratic Republic (GDR). She created commissioned portraits of factory workers for the Socialist Unity Party of Germany (SED). Many of them were female, enabling her to emphasize the significance of women in society. The subject of war also remains present in her later work. The artist’s experiences of both World Wars and the tensions of the Cold War continuously moved her to express her categorical rejection of militarism.

Irina Hiebert Grun

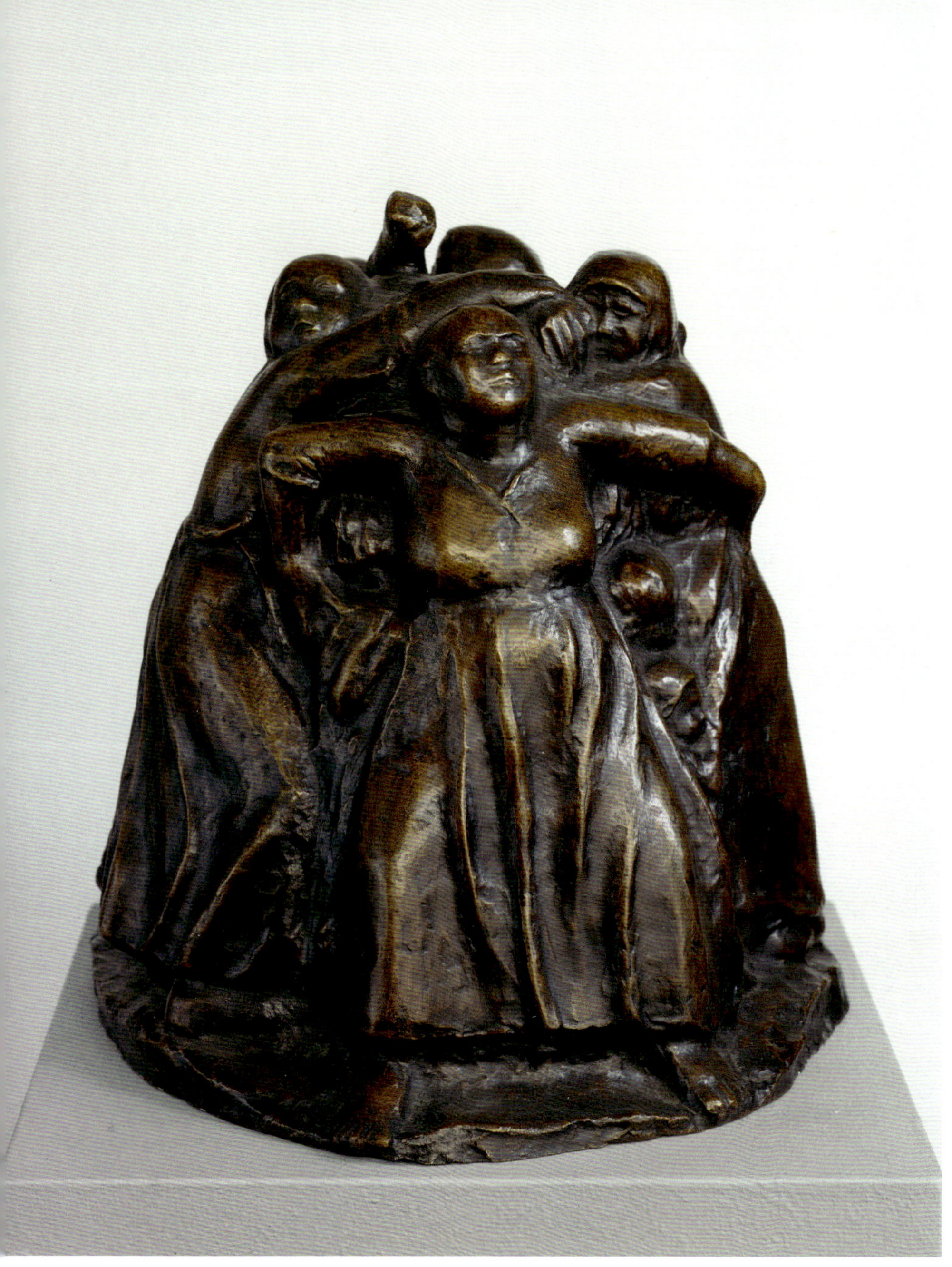

↑ Käthe Kollwitz, *Tower of Mothers*, 1937–38 (cast after 1958)
Bronze, 27 × 27.5 × 28 cm
Acquired in 1984 from a private collection, Berlin, with funds from the Kulturfonds der DDR, for the Nationalgalerie, Berlin (East)

→ Theo Balden, *Head of a Beaten Jew*, 1943
Lead and bronze, 44 × 25 × 32 cm
Acquired in 1976 from the artist for the Nationalgalerie, Berlin (East)

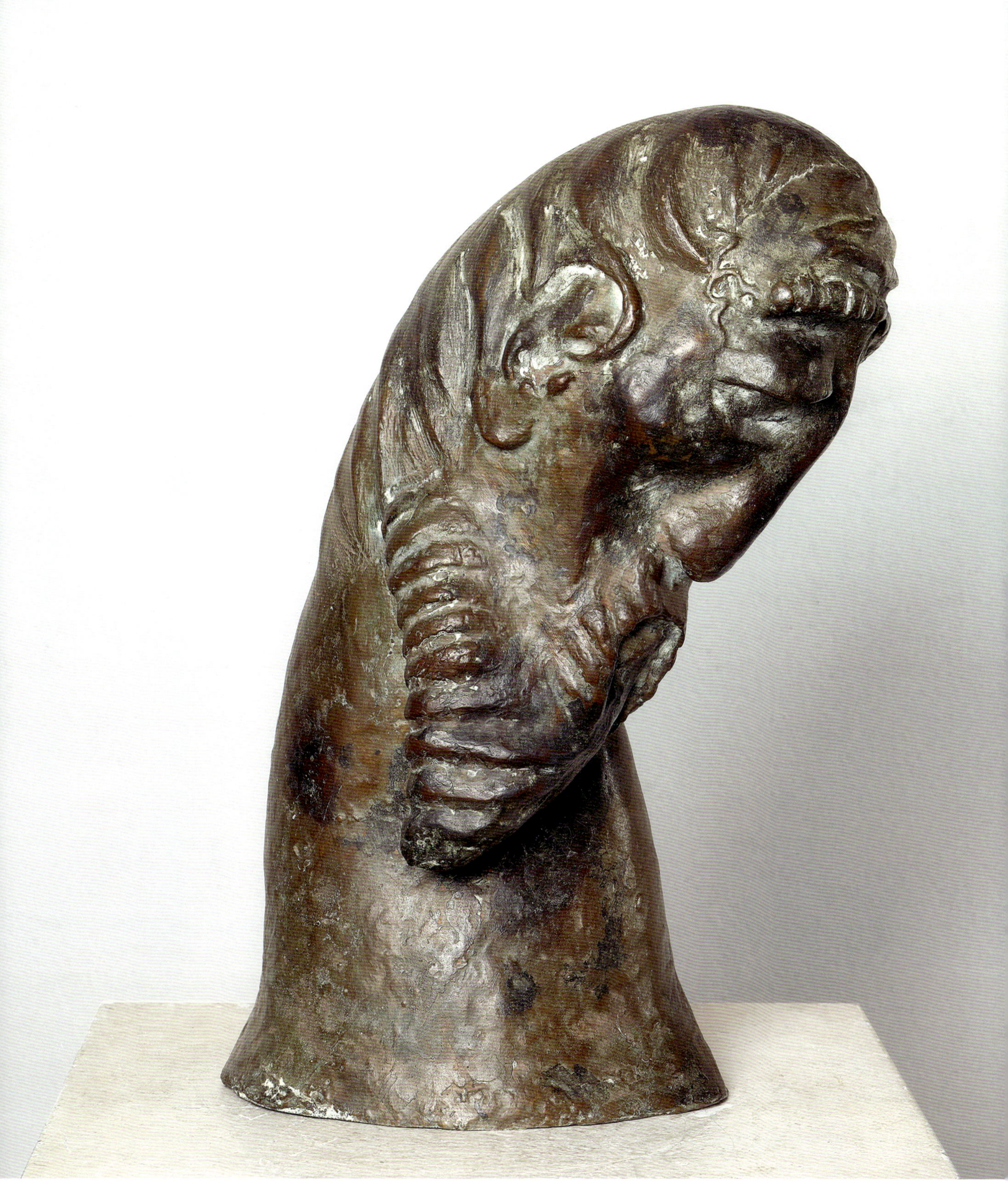

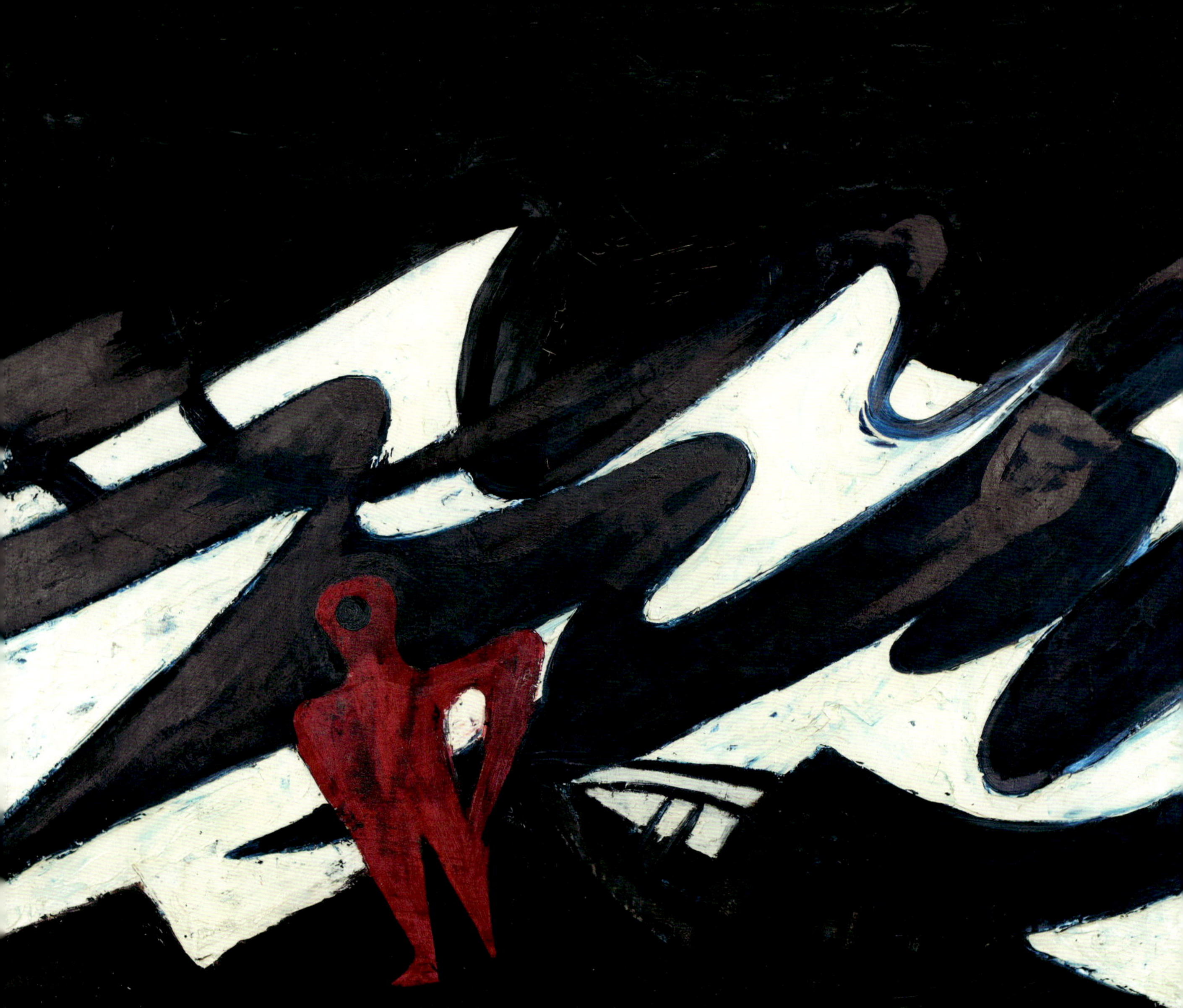

↑ Ernst Wilhelm Nay, *Stormy Waves*, 1935
Oil on canvas, 80.5 × 100.5 cm
Acquired in 1949 by the Land Berlin for the
Galerie des 20. Jahrhunderts, Berlin (West)

→ Karl Hofer, *The Black Rooms (Version II)*, 1943
Oil on canvas, 149 × 110 cm
Acquired in 1953 from the artist by the Land Berlin
for the Galerie des 20. Jahrhunderts, Berlin (West)

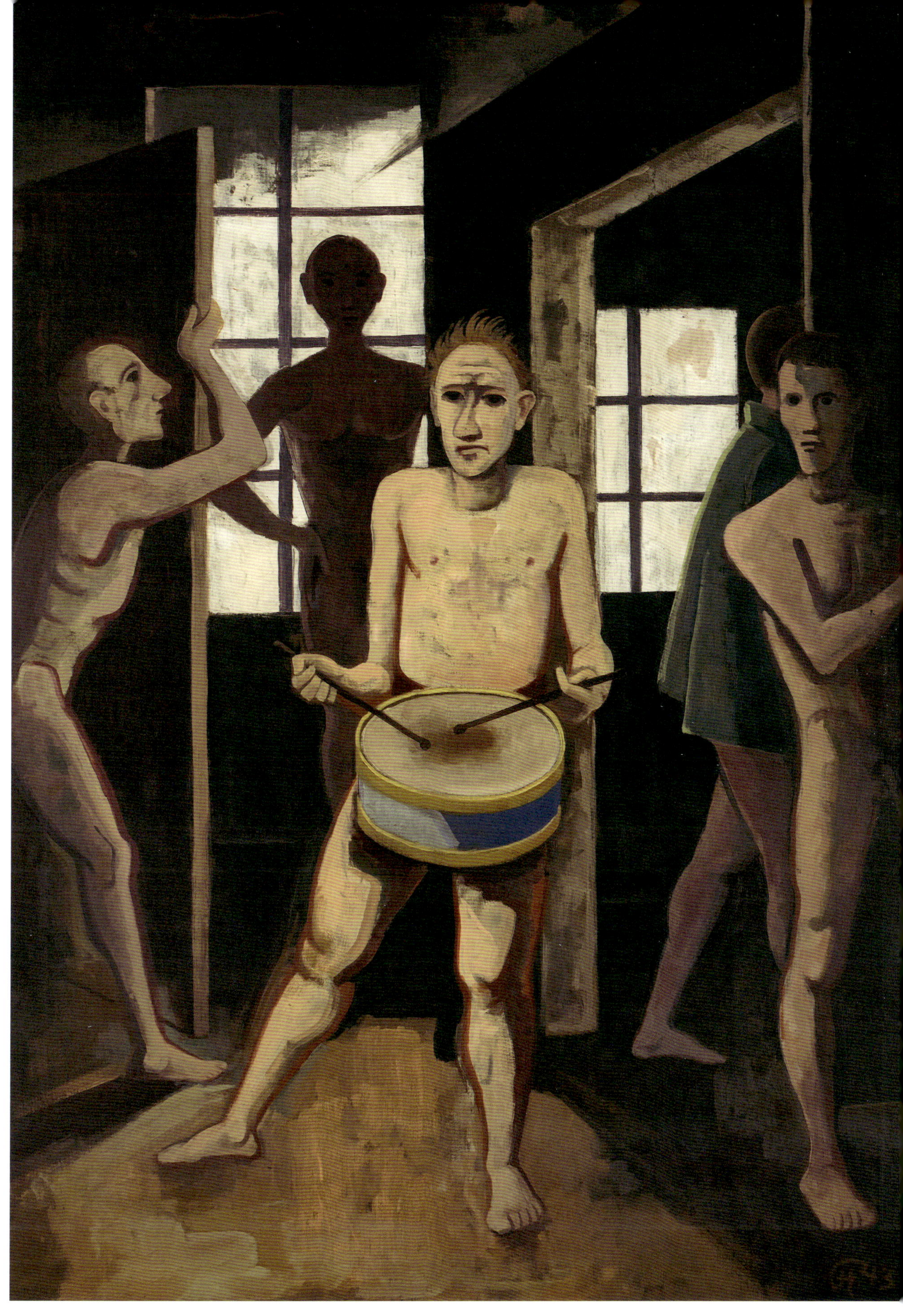

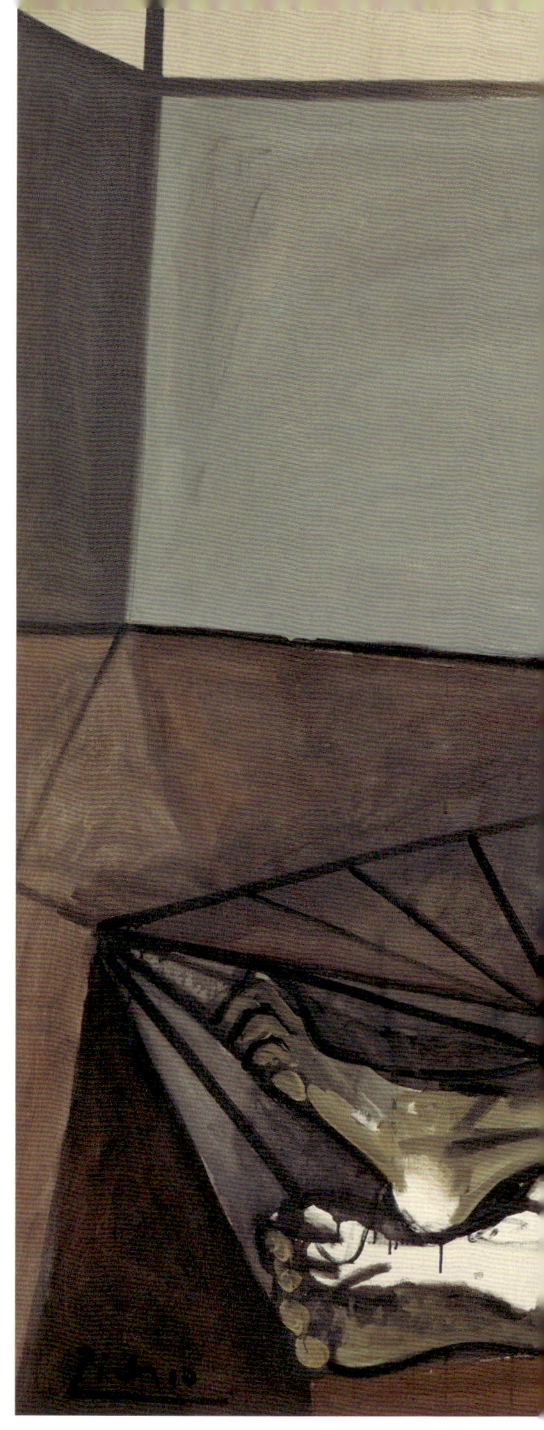

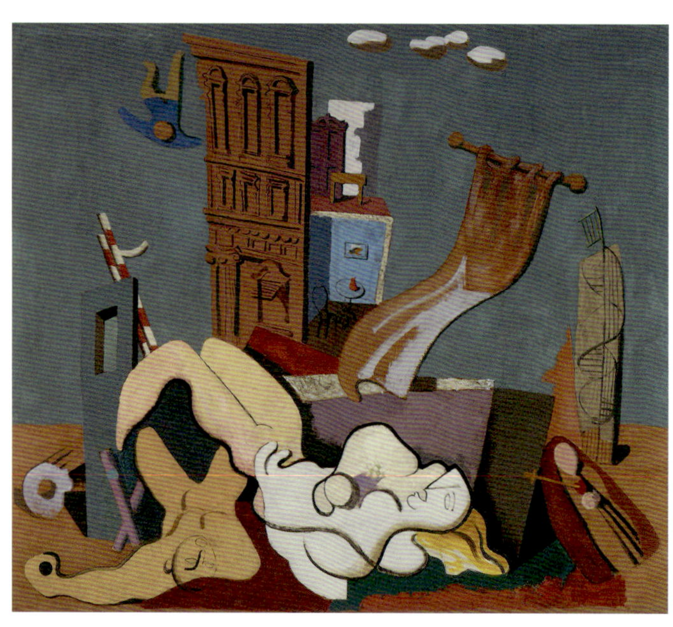

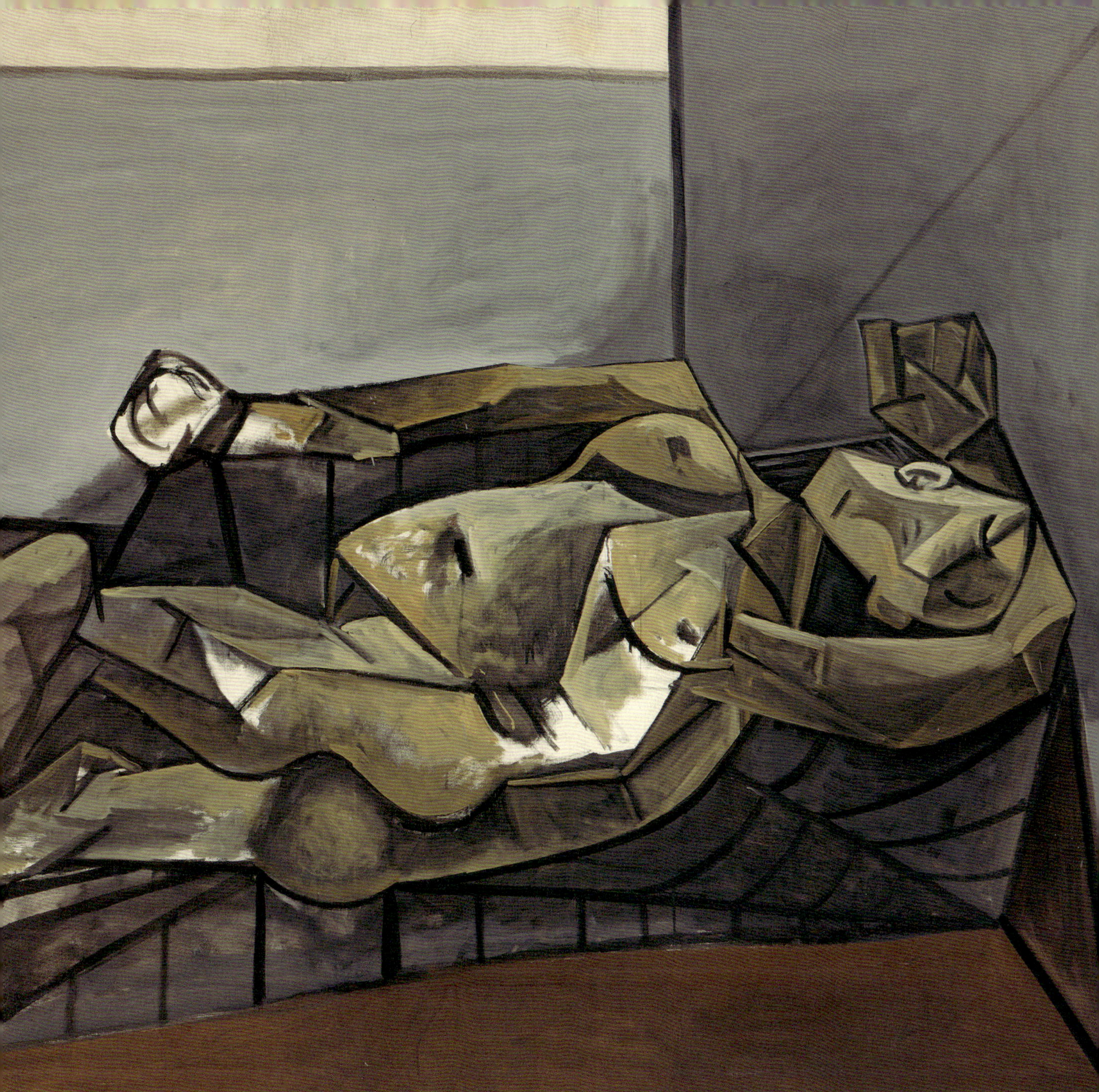

↑ Pablo Picasso, *Sleeping Nude*, 1942
Oil on canvas, 129.5 × 195 cm
Acquired in 2000 from Heinz Berggruen with support from the Bundesregierung and the Land Berlin

← Karl Kunz, *Germany, Awaken!*, 1942
Oil on plywood, 120 × 142 cm
Gift from the son of the artist, Wolfgang Kunz, Berlin, 2015

Why Are Paintings Altered Retroactively?

The works by Franz Radziwill, Horst Strempel and Hans Richter no longer appear the way they did originally. Why are paintings altered retroactively? A comparison of their histories reveals a different story behind each case.

As a soldier in the German Wehrmacht, Franz Radziwill participated in the attack on Belgium in 1940. Soon after, he began work on the painting *Flandern* (Flanders). The first version was a realistic depiction of war, showing dive bombers over a farm in ruins, soldiers' helmets hanging on burial crosses, frightened horses, and refugees. It is on their behalf that the original title asks, *Wohin in dieser Welt?* (Where To in This World?). Radziwill, a member of the National Socialist German Workers' Party (NSDAP), the Nazi party, added several more fighter planes to the painting over the course of the war. But between 1945 and 1950, he added a floral ornament, preternatural beings floating in the air and a crack splitting earth and sky in two. These surreal elements may have been Radziwill's reaction to the new state of politics; the war's most recent events now appear consciously removed from reality.

Horst Strempel painted *Nacht über Deutschland* (Night Over Germany) in the winter of 1945–46. Its form alludes to a Christian winged altarpiece. The central panel portrays survivors of a National Socialist concentration camp, including children raising their arms tattooed with serial numbers. In the right panel, a father holding his wife and son looks fearfully up at the sky. A preliminary sketch of the work shows the family bearing the yellow Stars of David that the National Socialist regime required Jews to wear as of 1941. Initially, these stars were clearly visible in the painting. But in the spring of 1947, the acquisition committee for Berlin's municipal art collection, the Galerie des 20. Jahrhunderts, ostensibly found that "the right-hand panel was too weak." Strempel's decision to refashion the yellow stars and serial numbers into undefined blurs of colour suggests that direct references to the Holocaust were not desirable in art at the time. Once the historical references had literally been smudged out beyond recognition, the gallery acquired the altered painting in April 1948.

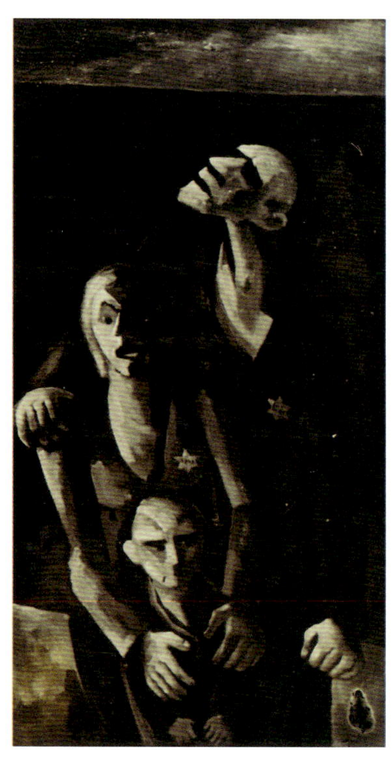

Hans Richter's scroll painting *Invasion* shows events of the war, beginning with the landing of Allied troops in Normandy in June 1944 and concluding with the Germans' capitulation in May 1945. Richter produced the painting while in exile in New York, where it was first exhibited in October 1946. At the time, it was still a non-representational colour composition. Similar in form

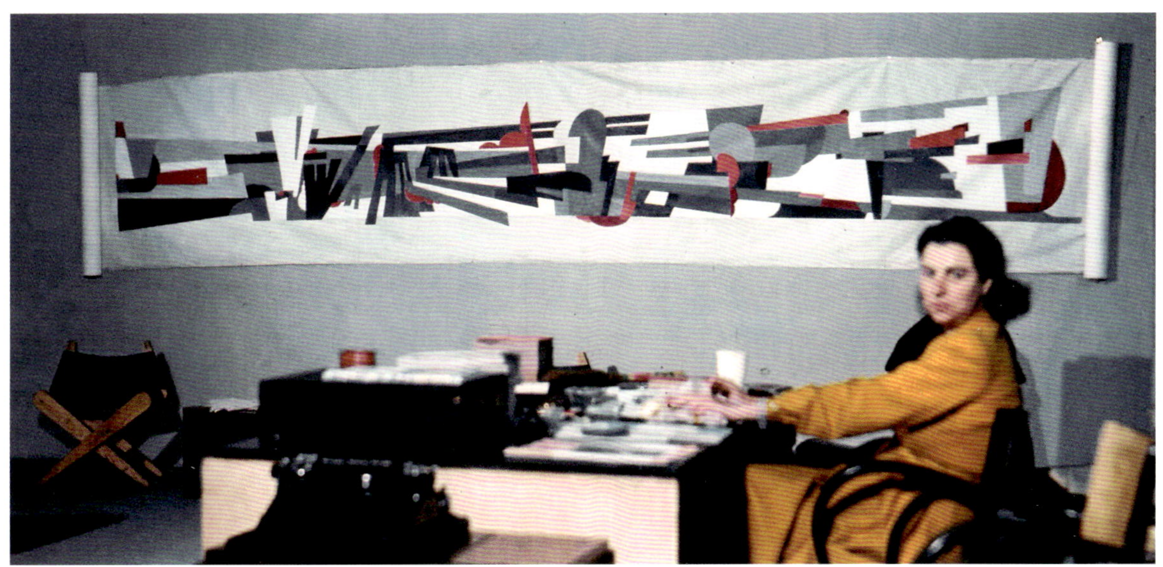

to *Invasion*, the paintings *Stalingrad (Sieg im Osten)* [Stalingrad (Victory in the East)] and *Befreiung von Paris* (The Liberation of Paris), in the same exhibition, included newspaper clippings from the times glued into place on the canvas. The *New York Times* criticized the collages while praising the non-representational work. The prevailing taste was changing; the term "Abstract Expressionism" had been used in the *NYT* as early as May 1946 to define a new trend that would soon come to dominate the art world. This may have motivated Richter's initial decision not to transform his abstract work *Invasion*, even though he had already selected the newspaper clippings with which to do so. Richter would not paste them to the canvas until the 1960s, finally completing this work as a political and historical document.

Dieter Scholz

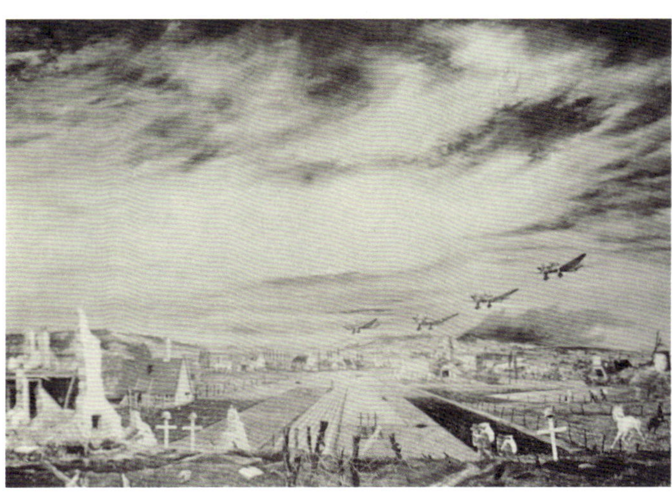

↑ Peggy Guggenheim seated in front of Hans Richter's *Momentum of Invasion* (later titled *Invasion*) at the Art of This Century gallery in New York, 1946
→ Franz Radziwill, *Flanders (Where To in This World?)*, first version, 1940
← Horst Strempel, *Jewish Family*, first version of the triptych *Night Over Germany* (right wing), illustrated in a catalogue of the Galerie Franz, Berlin, 1947

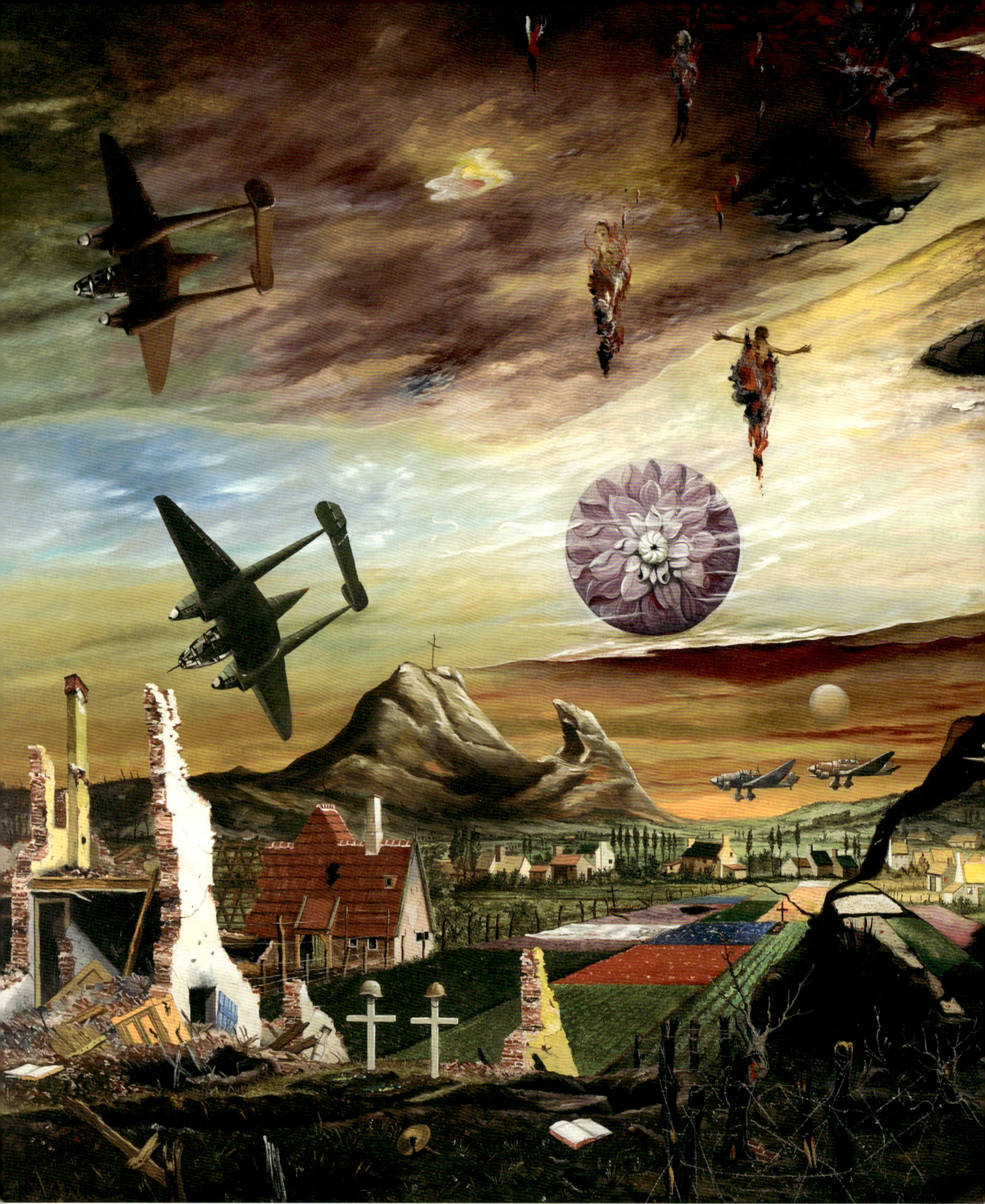

Franz Radziwill, *Flanders (Where To in This World?)*, 1940–50
Oil on canvas on plywood, 119 × 170 cm
Acquired in 2012 with support from the Freunde der Nationalgalerie, the Bundesrepublik Deutschland and the Kulturstiftung der Länder

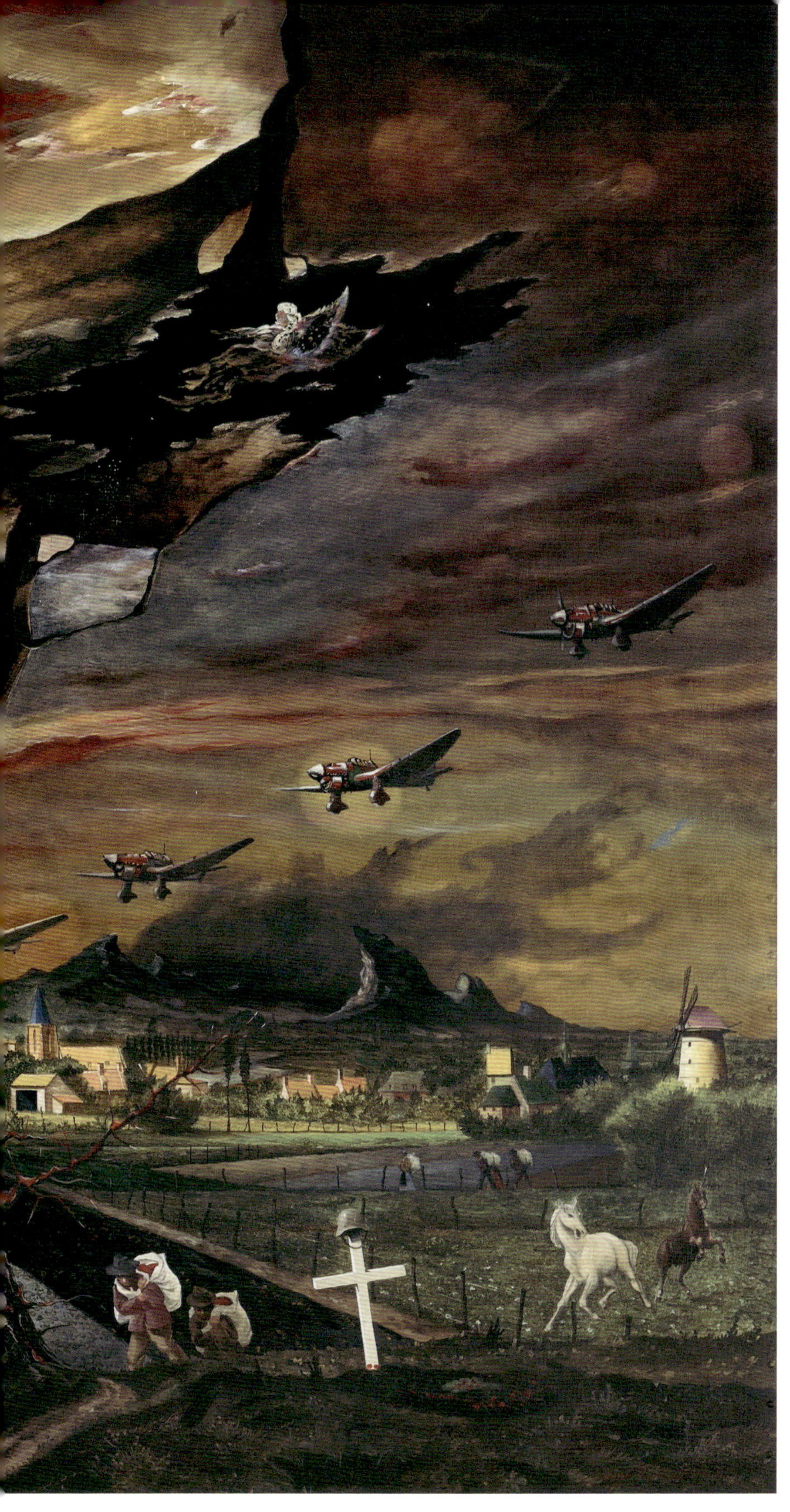

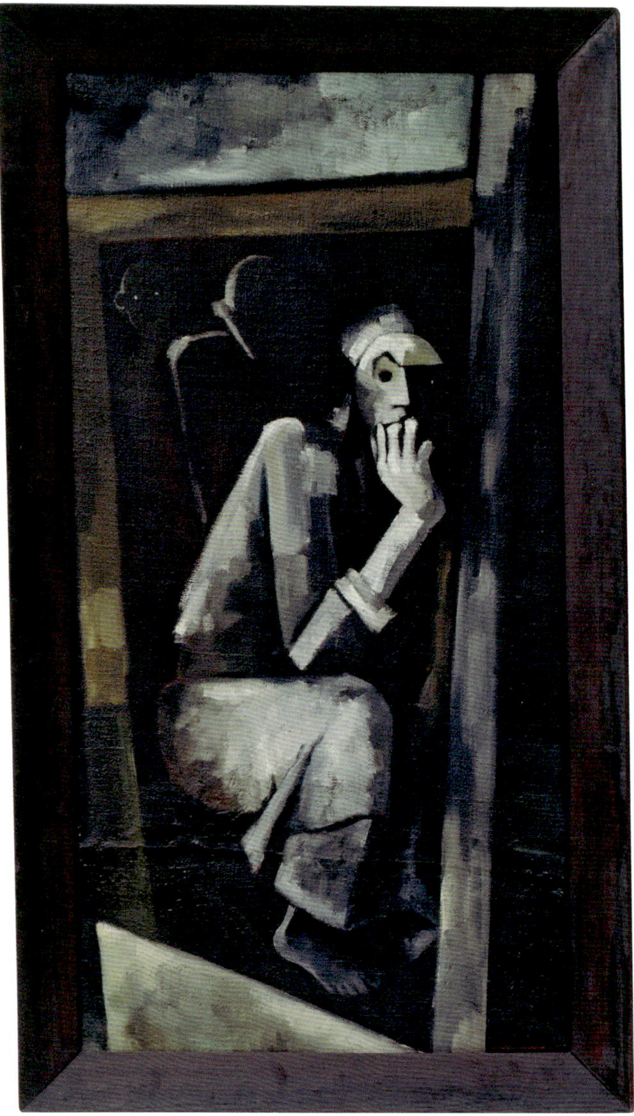
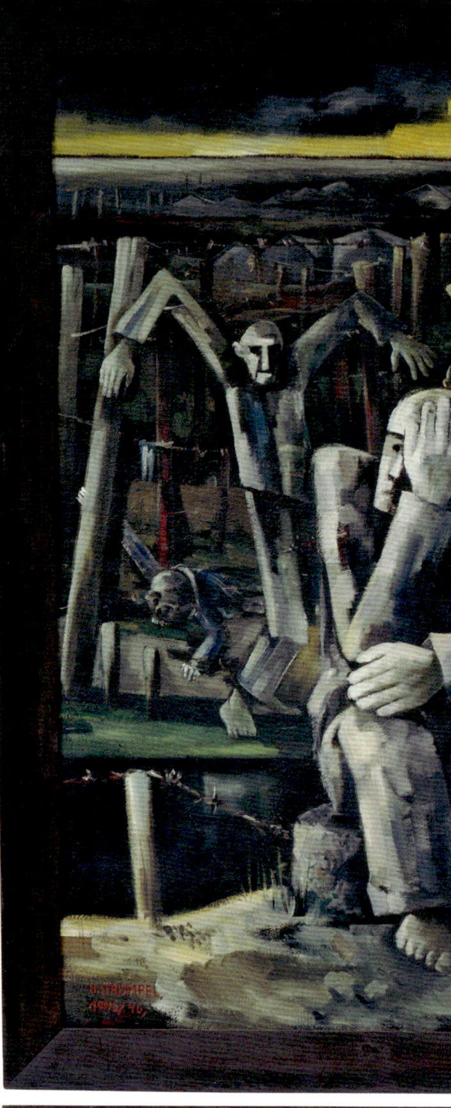
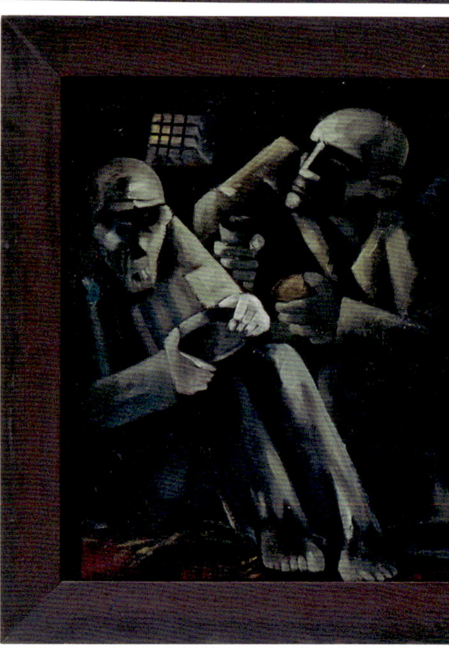

Horst Strempel, *Night Over Germany*, 1945–46
Oil on canvas, 229 × 324 cm
Acquired in 1948 from the artist for the Galerie des 20. Jahrhunderts. Gift from the Magistrat von Groß-Berlin to the Nationalgalerie, Berlin (East), 1951

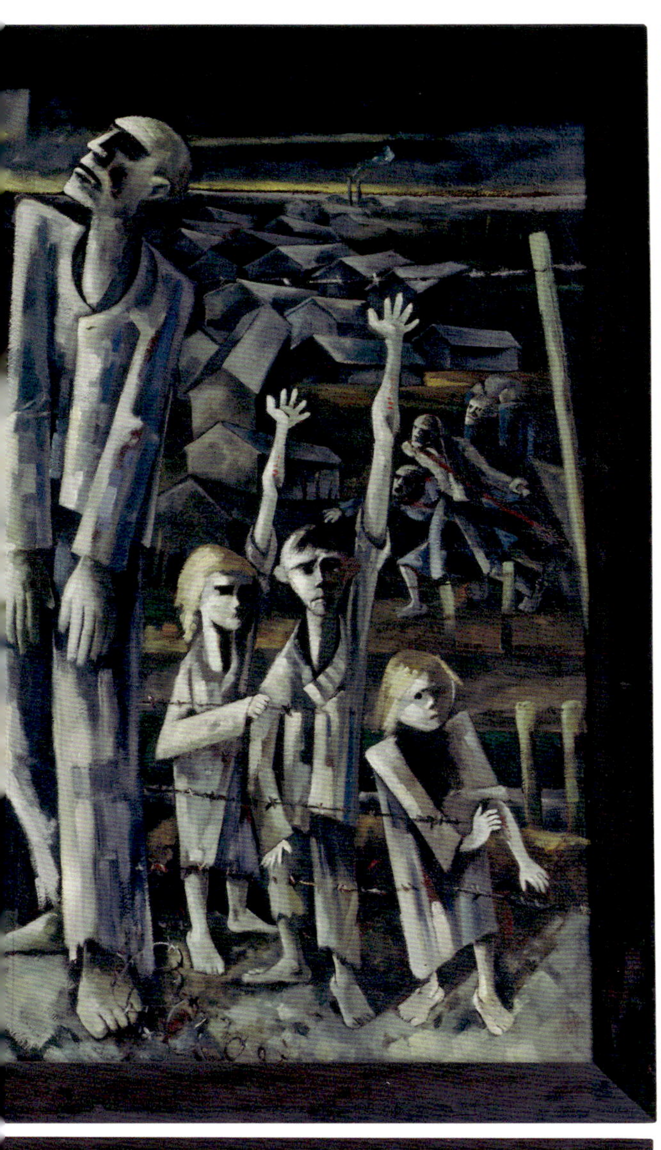

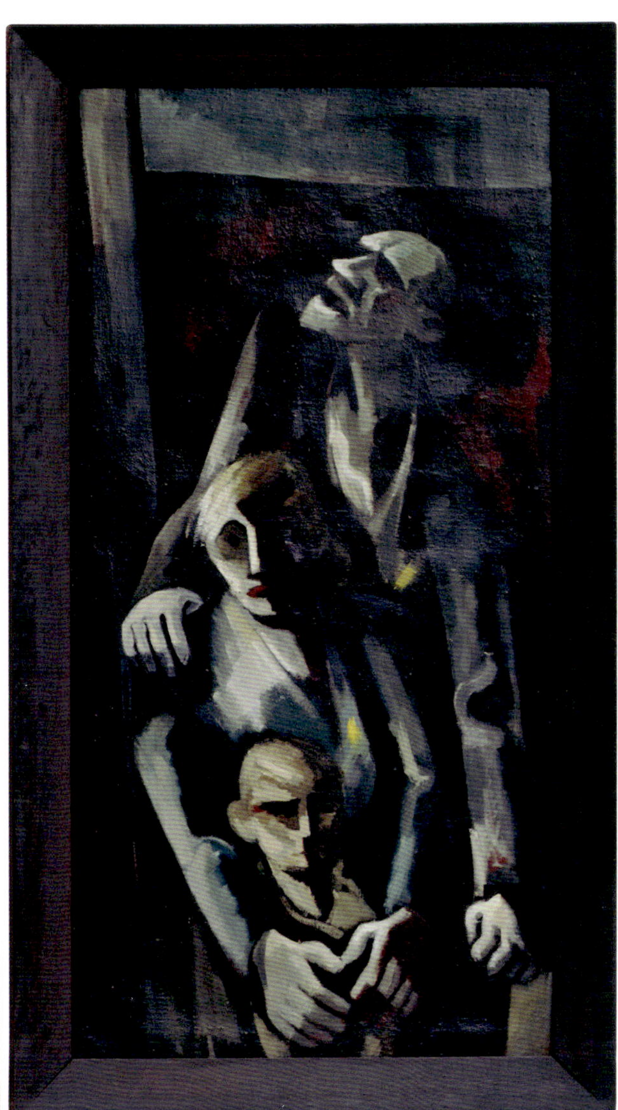

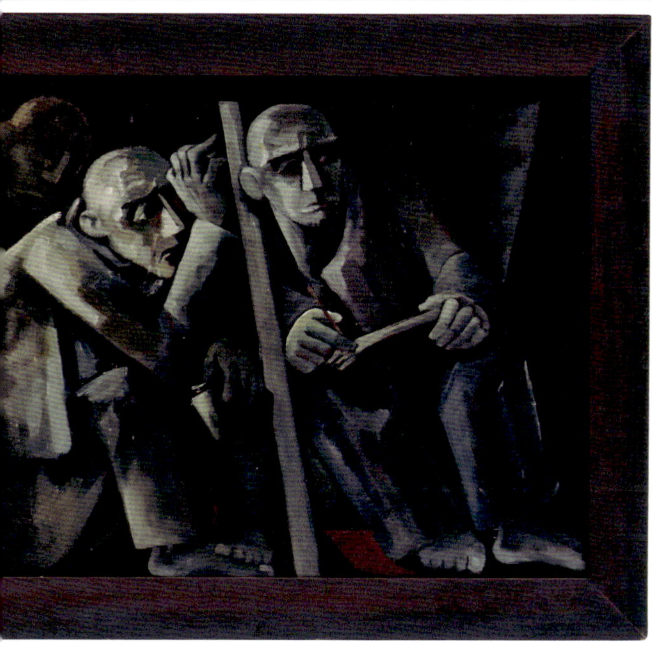

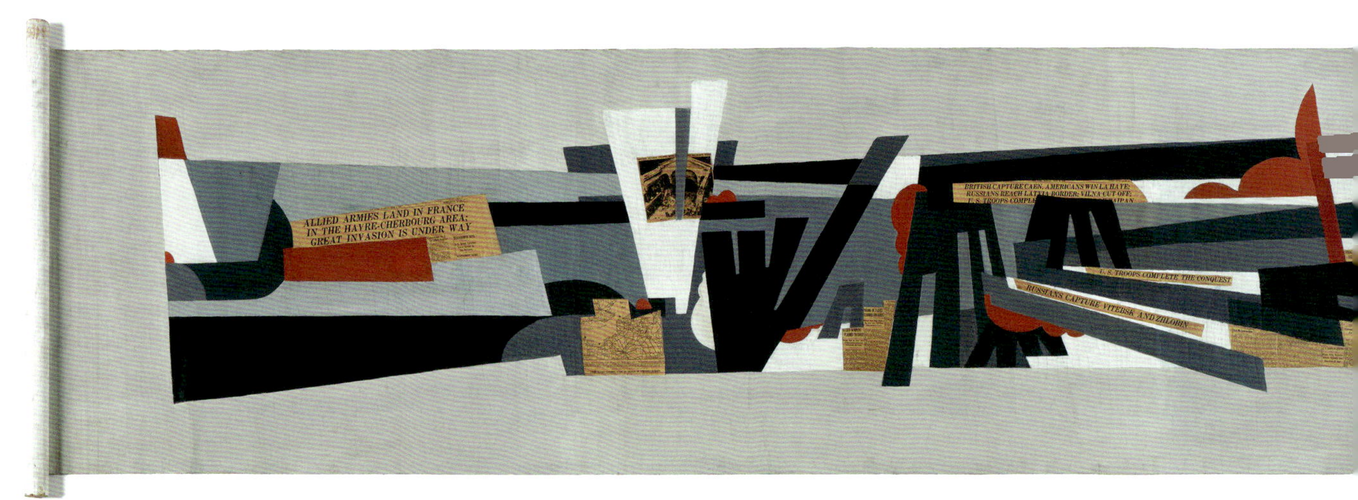

Hans Richter, *Invasion*, 1944–45 / before 1976
Oil on canvas, 82 × 516 cm
Gift from the Pressestiftung Tagesspiegel, Berlin, from the estate of the artist to the Nationalgalerie, Berlin (West), 1982

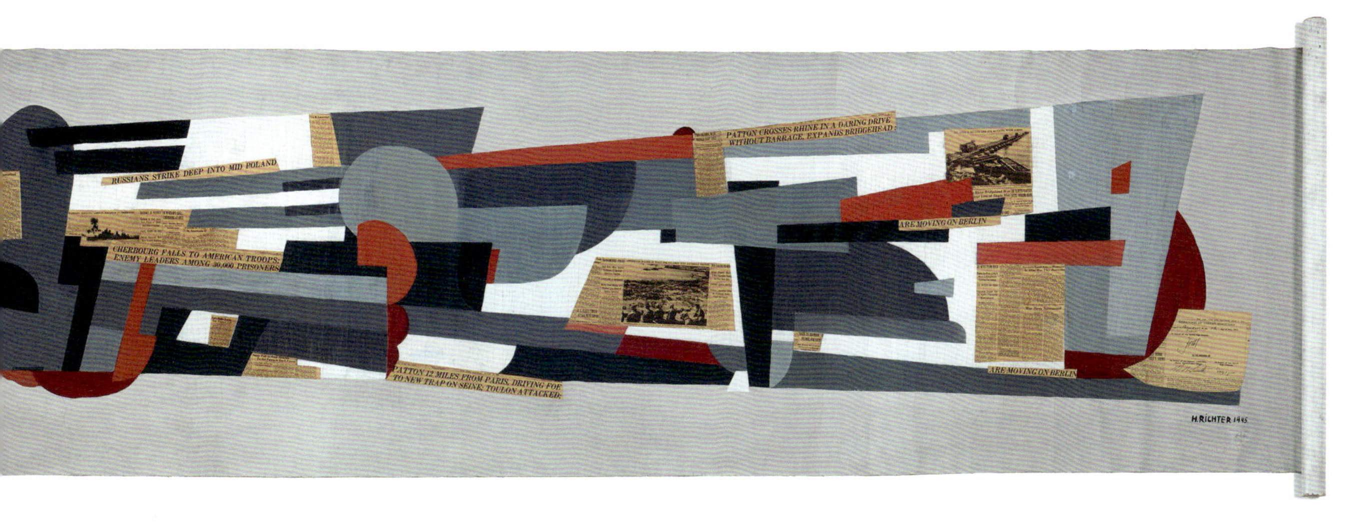
RUSSIANS STRIKE DEEP INTO MID POLAND
CHERBOURG FALLS TO AMERICAN TROOPS; ENEMY LEADERS AMONG 30,000 PRISONERS
PATTON CROSSES RHINE IN A DARING DRIVE WITHOUT BARRAGE, EXPANDS BRIDGEHEAD
ARE MOVING ON BERLIN
ARE MOVING ON BERLIN
PATTON 12 MILES FROM PARIS, DRIVING FOE TO NEW TRAP ON SEINE; TOULON ATTACKED;
H. RICHTER 1945

Selected Bibliography

Longing for What?

Wenzel Hablik. Expressionistische Utopien. Malerei, Zeichnung, Architektur, Katrin Maibaum and Katharina Gräber (eds.), for the Wenzel-Hablik-Museum, Itzehoe, exh. cat., Martin-Gropius-Bau, Berlin, Munich/London/New York, 2017.

Georg Kolbe 1877–1947, Ursel Berger (ed.), exh. cat., Georg-Kolbe-Museum, Berlin, and the Gerhard Marcks-Haus, Bremen, Munich/New York, 1997.

Images from the Modern Psyche: Edvard Munch's Frieze

Nikolaus Bernau, "Wo hing Edvard Munchs Lebensfries? Zu dem Bau der Kammerspiele und ihrem berühmtesten Schmuck", in: *Max Reinhardt und das Deutsche Theater. Texte und Bilder aus Anlass des 100-jährigen Jubiläums seiner Direktion*, Roland Koberg, Bernd Stegemann and Henrike Thomsen (eds.), (Blätter des Deutschen Theaters), Berlin, 2005, pp. 65–78.

Roland März, "Edvard Munch und Max Reinhardt", in: *Edward Munch. Melancholie. Aus dem Reinhardt-Fries 1906/07*, published by the Kulturstiftung der Länder in association with the Nationalgalerie, Staatliche Museen – Preußischer Kulturbesitz, Berlin, 1998, pp. 9–47.

Edvard Munch. Der Lebensfries für Max Reinhardts Kammerspiele, exh. cat., Nationalgalerie, Staatliche Museen – Preußischer Kulturbesitz, Berlin, 1978.

Who Were the Female Models for the *Brücke* Artists?

Fränzi und Marzella, Magdalena M. Moeller (ed.), exh. cat., Brücke-Museum, Berlin, Heidelberg, 2014.

Der Blick auf Fränzi und Marcella. Zwei Modelle der Brücke-Künstler Heckel, Kirchner und Pechstein, Norbert Nobis (ed.), exh. cat., Sprengel-Museum Hannover and the Stiftung Moritzburg, Kunstmuseum des Landes Sachsen-Anhalt, Halle (Saale), Hanover, et al., 2010.

Rosa Shapire, More Than a "Passive" *Brücke* Member

Rosa und Anna Schapire. Sozialwissenschaft, Kunstgeschichte und Feminismus um 1900, Burcu Dogramaci and Günther Sandner (eds.), Berlin, 2017.

Rosa. Eigenartig Grün. Rosa Schapire und die Expressionisten, Sabine Schulze (ed.), Leonie Beiersdorf (catalogue), exh. cat., Museum für Kunst und Gewerbe Hamburg and the Kunstsammlungen Chemnitz, Ostfildern, 2009.

How Is the *Brücke* Connected to Germany's Colonial History?

Kirchner and Nolde: Expressionism. Colonialism, exh. cat., SMK – Statens Museum for Kunst, Copenhagen, Stedelijk Museum, Amsterdam, and the Brücke-Museum, Berlin, Munich, 2021.

Aya Soika, "'Ein wahrer Atlas der schwarzen Rasse in unseren Kolonien'. Emil Noldes Südsee-Aquarelle im kolonialen Kontext", in: *Sønderjylland-Schleswig Kolonial: Eine Spurenlese*, Marco Petersen (ed.), Odense, 2017, pp. 277–304.

Jill Lloyd, *German Expressionism: Primitivism and Modernity*, New Haven, 1991.

At the Centre of the Metropolis: Potsdamer Platz

Roland März, "Die Stützen der Gesellschaft. George Grosz und die Physiognomie der Weimarer Republik", in: *Kunst der Weimarer Republik. Meisterwerke der Nationalgalerie Berlin*, Moritz Wullen (ed.), in collaboration with Maren Eichhorn, exh. cat., Neues Museum Weimar, Berlin/Cologne, 2004, pp. 21–36.

Der Potsdamer Platz. Ernst Ludwig Kirchner und der Untergang Preußens, Katharina Henkel and Roland März (eds.), exh. cat., Neue Nationalgalerie, Staatliche Museen zu Berlin – Preußischer Kulturbesitz, Berlin, 2001.

Ernst Ludwig Kirchner and Max Liebermann

Anke Daemgen and Peter-Klaus Schuster, *Kirchner malt Liebermann*, exh. cat., Stiftung Brandenburger Tor, Max Liebermann Haus, Berlin, (Liebermanns Welt), Berlin, 2015.

Hanna Strzoda, “*Ernst Ludwig Kirchners Berlin-Aufenthalt im März 1926*”, in: *Ernst Ludwig Kirchner. Die Deutschlandreise 1925/1926 von Davos nach Frankfurt am Main, Chemnitz, Dresden, Berlin*, Ingrid Mössinger and Beate Ritter (eds.), exh. cat., Kunstsammlungen Chemnitz, Cologne, 2007, pp. 218–261.

What Is “Modernity”?

Hello World. Revising a Collection, Udo Kittelmann and Gabriele Knapstein (eds.), exh. cat., Hamburger Bahnhof – Museum für Gegenwart – Berlin, Munich, 2018.

museum global. Microhistories of an Ex-centric Modernism, Susanne Gaensheimer, Kathrin Beßen, Doris Krystof, Isabelle Malz and Maria Müller-Schareck (eds.), exh. cat., Kunstsammlung Nordrhein-Westfalen, Düsseldorf, Cologne, 2018.

Multiple Modernities, 1905–1970, Catherine Grenier (ed.), exh. cat., Centre Pompidou, Paris, 2014.

Hannah Höch’s Epochal Image of the Weimar Republic

Hanne Bergius, *Montage und Metamechanik. Dada Berlin – Artistik von Polaritäten*, Berlin, 2000.

Jula Dech, *Hannah Höch. Schnitt mit dem Küchenmesser. DADA – Spiegel einer Bierbauchkultur*, Frankfurt am Main, 1989.

Women Artists at the Sturm Gallery

Storm Women: Artists from the Avant-Garde in Berlin 1910–1932, Ingrid Pfeiffer and Max Hollein (eds.), exh. cat., Schirn Kunsthalle Frankfurt, Cologne, 2015.

Der Sturm. Zentrum der Avantgarde, Antje Birthälmer and Gerhard Finckh (eds.), exh. cat., Von der Heydt-Museum Wuppertal, Wuppertal, 2012, vol. I, pp. 152–171, 192–209, vol. II, pp. 343–376.

Rediscovered Identity: Erich Mühsam

Peter Kropmanns, “Auguste Herbin, Porträt Erich Kurt Mühsam, 1907”, in: *Weltkunst*, vol. 83, no. 73, May 2013, p. 120–121.

Christian Schröder, *Fackeln im Sturm. Das Leben der Boheme: Herwarth Walden und Erich Mühsam*, in: *Merkur*, vol. 67, no. 1, January 2013, pp. 58–63.

Where Did the First World War Take Place?

Oliver Janz, “Einführung: Der Erste Weltkrieg in globaler Perspektive”, in: *Geschichte und Gesellschaft*, vol. 40., no. 2, April–June 2014, pp. 147–159.

Die letzten Tage der Menschheit. Bilder des Ersten Weltkrieges, Rainer Rother (ed.), exh. cat., Deutsches Historisches Museum, Berlin, et al., Berlin, 1994.

Britta Schmitz, “Otto Dix’ Flandern 1934–36”, in: *DIX. Otto Dix zum 100. Geburtstag 1891–1991*, exh. cat., Galerie der Stadt Stuttgart and the Neue Nationalgalerie, Staatliche Museen – Preußischer Kulturbesitz, Berlin, Stuttgart, 1991, pp. 268–271.

Who Were the *Pillars of Society*?

Roland März, “Die Stützen der Gesellschaft. George Grosz und die Physiognomie der Weimarer Republik”, in: *Kunst der Weimarer Republik. Meisterwerke der Nationalgalerie Berlin*, Moritz Wullen (ed.), in collaboration with Maren Eichhorn, exh. cat., Neues Museum Weimar, Berlin/Cologne, 2004, pp. 21–32.

George Grosz. Berlin – New York, Peter-Klaus Schuster (ed.), exh. cat., Neue Nationalgalerie, Staatliche Museen – Preußischer Kulturbesitz, Berlin, and the Kunstsammlung Nordrhein-Westfalen, Düsseldorf, Berlin, 1994.

Heinrich Vogeler Produced a New Form: The *Komplexbild*

Rena Noltenius, *Heinrich Vogeler 1872–1942. Ein Leben in Bildern. Mit einem aktuellen Werkkatalog der Gemälde*, Fischerhude, 2013.

Heinrich Vogeler in Karelien 1925–1936. Aquarelle und Zeichnungen, Christine Hoffmeister (catalogue), exh. cat., Stadtmuseum Tübingen, Barkenhoff-Stiftung Worpswede and the Kunstsammlung Neubrandenburg, Lilienthal, 1992.

Christine Hoffmeister, *Heinrich Vogeler. Die Komplexbilder*, Lilienthal, 1980.

Women in Need. The Struggle to Legalize Abortion

Cornelie Usborne, *Cultures of Abortion in Weimar Germany*, New York, 2011.

Gisela Schirmer, *Käthe Kollwitz und die Kunst ihrer Zeit. Positionen zur Geburtenpolitik*, Weimar, 1998.

Creativity and Child's Play at the Bauhaus

Bauhaus 1919–1933: Workshops for Modernity, Barry Bergdoll and Leah Dickerman (eds.), exh. cat., The Museum of Modern Art, New York, 2009.

Alma Siedhoff-Buscher. Eine neue Welt für Kinder, exh. cat., Stiftung Weimarer Klassik und Kunstsammlungen, Bauhaus-Museum, Michael Siebenbrodt (catalogue and exhibition), Weimar, 2004.

Envoy of the Metaphysical: Hilma af Klint

Julia Voss, *"Die Menschheit in Erstaunen versetzen". Hilma af Klint. Biographie*, Frankfurt am Main, 2020.

Hilma af Klint – A Pioneer of Abstraction, Iris Müller-Westermann and Jo Widoff (eds.), exh. cat., Moderna Museet, Stockholm, Hamburger Bahnhof – Museum für Gegenwart – Berlin, and the Museo Picasso, Málaga, Ostfildern, 2013.

Åke Fant, "The case of the artist Hilma af Klint", in: *The Spiritual in Art: Abstract Painting 1890–1985*, Maurice Tuchman and Judi Freeman (eds.), exh. cat., Los Angeles County Museum of Art, New York, 1986, pp. 154–163.

A Railway Station with Three Bridges: Social Analysis in Painting

Paul Fuhrmann. Malerei, Aquarelle, Druckgrafik und Zeichnungen aus der "Sturm-Zeit", exh. cat., Galerie am Sachsenplatz, Leipzig, 1976.

The Great Metaphysician – What's Wrong with It?

Gerd Roos, "Fälschung oder Falschdatierung? Eine Fallstudie zu Giorgio de Chiricos 'Il grande metafisico'", in: *Jahrbuch der Berliner Museen*, formerly the *Jahrbuch der Preußischen Kunstsammlungen*, new series, vol. 58, 2016, Berlin, 2019, pp. 117–140.

The Nonconformist Surrealist Leonor Fini

Fantastic Women: Surreal Worlds from Meret Oppenheim to Frida Kahlo, Ingrid Pfeiffer (ed.), exh. cat., Schirn Kunsthalle Frankfurt, Munich, 2020.

Laufen Sie, meine Damen, ein Mann ist im Rosengarten. Künstlerinnen | Die Sammlung Ulla Pietzsch, Ulla and Heiner Pietzsch (eds.), Munich/Berlin/London/New York, 2009, p. 14–15.

"Oscillation" and "Action Painting"

Irene Herter, "Siqueiros and Surrealism?", in: *Journal of Surrealism and the Americas*, vol. 3, no. 1, 2009, pp. 107–127.

Jürgen Pech, *Max Ernst. Jeune homme intrigué par le vol d'une mouche non-euclidienne* (private printing), Bonn, 2007.

Ellen G. Landau, "Jackson Pollock und die Mexikaner", in: *Siqueiros/Pollock, Pollock/Siqueiros*, Jürgen Harten (ed.), exh. cat., Kunsthalle Düsseldorf, 1995, vol. II, pp. 38–54.

The New Feminine Self-Image

Damenwahl! 100 Jahre Frauenwahlrecht, Dorothee Linnemann (ed.), exh. cat., Historisches Museum Frankfurt, Frankfurt am Main, 2018.

Who Is _Sonja_?

Susanna Schrafstetter, *Flucht und Versteck. Untergetauchte Juden in München – Verfolgungserfahrung und Nachkriegsalltag*, Göttingen, 2015, pp. 91–95.

Thomas Ratzka, *Christian Schad 1894–1982, Werkverzeichnis, Band 1: Malerei*, published by the Christian Schad Stiftung Aschaffenburg, Cologne, 2008, p. 155.

What Is "Degenerate Art"?

Andreas Hüneke, "What Is 'Degenerate Art' and How Do We Recognize It?", in: *Unmastered Past? Modernism in Nazi Germany: Art, Art Trade, Curatorial Practice*, Meike Hoffmann and Dieter Scholz (eds.), Berlin, 2020, pp. 52–61.

Christoph Zuschlag, *"Entartete Kunst". Ausstellungsstrategien im Nazi-Deutschland*, Worms, 1995.

"Degenerate Art": The Fate of the Avant-Garde in Nazi Germany, Stephanie Barron (ed.), exh. cat., Los Angeles County Museum of Art, New York, 1991.

A Discomforting Portrait by Max Beckmann

Eugen Blume, "'Then Commerce, War, and Piracy are Three in One and Can't be Parted': Some Thoughts on Erhard Göpel", in: *Unmastered Past? Modernism in Nazi Germany: Art, Art Trade, Curatorial Practice*, Meike Hoffmann and Dieter Scholz (eds.), Berlin, 2020, pp. 148–157.

Max Beckmann. Das Vermächtnis Barbara Göpel, Andreas Schalhorn and Petra Winter (eds.), with assistance from Corinna Alexandra Rader, exh. cat., Staatliche Museen zu Berlin, Kupferstichkabinett, Berlin, 2018.

The Sculptor Renée Sintenis

Zwischen Freiheit und Moderne – die Bildhauerin Renée Sintenis, Alexandra Demberger (catalogue), exh. cat., Kunstforum Ostdeutsche Galerie Regensburg, Berlin, 2019.

Renée Sintenis. Das plastische Werk, Ursel Berger and Günter Ladwig (eds.), on behalf of Karl H. Knauf, Berlin, 2013.

Silke Kettelhake, *Renée Sintenis. Berlin, Boheme und Ringelnatz*, Berlin, 2010.

Sculpture and the Human Being: *Prometheus* and *Zwitter*

Mirjam Varadinis, "Prometheus and Zwitter – An Encounter Between Equals", in: *Prometheus's Torches: Henry Fuseli, Javier Téllez*, exh. cat., Kunsthaus Zürich, Zurich, 2014, pp. 6–27.

Alice Lex-Nerlinger: *Field-Grey Yields Dividends*

Alice Lex-Nerlinger 1893–1975. Fotomonteurin und Malerin, Marion Beckers (ed.), Rachel Epp Buller (catalogue), exh. cat., Das verborgene Museum, Berlin, 2016.

Why Are Paintings Altered Retroactively?

Die schwarzen Jahre. Geschichten einer Sammlung. 1933–1945, Dieter Scholz and Maria Obenaus (eds.), exh. cat., Neue Galerie im Hamburger Bahnhof – Museum für Gegenwart – Berlin, Berlin, 2015.

Kathrin Hoffmann-Curtius, *Judenmord – Art and the Holocaust in Post-War Germany*, London, 2018.

Doris Berger, "The Moving Canvas: Hans Richter's Artistic Practice in the 1940s", in: *Hans Richter. Encounters*, Timothy O. Benson (ed.), exh. cat., Los Angeles County Museum of Art and Martin-Gropius-Bau, Berlin, Munich/London/New York, 2013, pp. 138–153.

Der Maler Franz Radziwill in der Zeit des Nationalsozialismus, Birgit Neumann-Dietzsch and Viola Weigel (eds.), exh. cat., Franz Radziwill Haus, Dangast, and the Kunsthalle Wilhelmshaven, Bielefeld, 2011.

Gabriele Saure, *"Nacht über Deutschland". Horst Stempel – Leben und Werk 1904–1975*, Hamburg, 1992.

List of Names

Amaral, Tarsila do – **190**
Archipenko, Alexander – **78**
Arp, Hans – 14, 18, **98,** 107, **169**
Baader, Johannes – 95
Balden, Theo – **265**
Barbusse, Henri – 124–25.
Baumeister, Willi – **166–67**
Beckmann, Max – 231, 235, **237–39,** 240, **242–44,** 245
Belling, Rudolf – 13–14, 19, **73, 75–77, 79–81, 151, 214, 226,** 234
Bellmer, Hans – **198**
Bleyl, Fritz – 46
Blumenthal, Hermann – **250**
Böcklin, Arnold – 28
Bortnyik, Sándor – **117**
Brancusi, Constantin – **177**
Braque, Georges – **93**
Brauner, Victor – **190**
Breker, Arno – 245–55
Breton, André – 187
Bryk, Felix – 224
Buscher, Alma – 157
Buchholz, Erich – **116**
Čapek, Karel – 13
Carrington, Leonora – 200
Cézanne, Paul – 89
Chanel, Coco – 224
Cremer, Fritz – **252**
Dalí, Salvador – 187, **204–05**
De Chirico, Giorgio – 182, 183, **185**
De Fiori, Ernesto – **230**, 231
Degas, Edgar – 89
Delaunay, Robert – 19, **103**, 107, **174**, 175
Diehn-Bitt, Kate – 220, **222**
Dix, Otto – **118,** 119, **120–23**, 124, **215**
Döblin, Alfred – 83
Domínguez, Oscar – 182
Duchamp, Marcel – 231
Ehmsen, Heinrich – **126, 146–47,** 149
Eiffel, Gustav – 175
Einstein, Albert – 94, 231
Epstein, Elisabeth – 110
Ernst, Max – **97, 186,** 187, **192,** 194, **196**
Feininger, Lyonel – 157, **162–63**
Fehrmann, Lina Franziska (Fränzi) 46–47
Felixmüller, Conrad – 14–16, 19, **143,** 137
Fini, Leonor – 200–01
Flechtheim, Alfred – 214–15, 231, 249
Freud, Sigmund – 187
Freundlich, Otto – 107
Fuhrmann, Paul – 178, **181**
Genzel, Karl – 255
Geyer, Gerhard – **252**
Giacometti, Alberto – **79**
Gimpel, Albertine – 224–25
Göpel, Erhard – 234, 240–43
Goncharova, Natalia – 110, 111, **113**
González, Julio – **189**
Gramatté, Walter and Sonia – 56, **59**
Gris, Juan – **90**
Gropius, Walter – 156
Große, Doris (Dodo) 46
Grosz, George – **68,** 95, 119, 130–31, **132–33**
Grundig, Hans – **218**
Guggenheim, Peggy – 271
Günther, Kurt – 207, **209, 213**
Hablik, Wenzel – 28, **32–33**
Hahne, Ruthild – **252**
Hanfstaengl, Eberhard – 15
Hausmann, Raoul – 94–95
Heartfield, John – 95
Heckel, Erich – 46, **48,** 56, 61
Heckel, Manfred – 61
Heemskerck van Beest, Jacoba – 111, **112**
Heiliger, Bernhard – **252**
Herbin, Auguste – **105,** 106–07
Herda, Franz – 225
Hermann-Neiße, Max – 224
Herzog, Oswald – **74**
Höch, Hannah – 67, **92,** 94–95, **199**
Hodler, Ferdinand – **26–27**
Hofer, Karl – 259, **267**
Holzmann, Johannes – 106
Horn, Richard – **96**
Ibsen, Henrik – 34–35, 130
Jäger, Martha – 220
Jakimov, Igor von – **80**
Jawlensky, Alexej von – 111, **114**
Justi, Ludwig – 15, 17
Kandinsky, Wassily – 12, 110, **115,** 153, **154**, 156–57, 171
Kanoldt, Alexander – **216**
Kaprolat, Charlotte (Lotte) 47
Kessler, Harry Graf – 30, 34
Kesting, Edmund – 101, **117**
Kirchner, Ernst Ludwig – **44–45,** 46–47, **48, 54–55,** 56, 82–83, **84–87,** 88–89, 101, 254
Klee, Paul – **152,** 153, **155**, 157, 254
Klein, Cesar – 11
Klimsch, Fritz – **250**

Klint, Hilma af – 6–7, 170–71, **172–73**
Kokoschka, Oskar – 101, **102, 104**, 111
Kolbe, Georg – **22, 24,** 28, **31,** 47, **72,** 248
Kölle, Fritz – **252**
Kollwitz, Käthe – 148, 245, 249, **250, 264**
Kunz, Karl – 259, **268**
Lachnit, Wilhelm – 207, **208, 212**
Lammert, Will – **80**
Landauer, Gustav – 107
Lautréamont – 187
Larionov, Mikhail – 111
Laserstein, Lotte – **8**, 9–10, 13, 19
Lasker-Schüler, Else – 106, 110
Laurens, Henri – **96, 98–99**
Léger, Fernand – **116, 168**, 231
Lehmbruck, Wilhelm – 7, **128–29**, 234
Lempicka, Tamara de – 220–21, **223**
Lenk, Franz – **217**
Lex-Nerlinger, Alice – 148, **260–61**, 262–63
Liebermann, Max – 86, 88–89
Lipchitz, Jacques – **99**
Lissitzky, El – 14
Loeber, Lou – 175, **176**
Maar, Dora – 200
Macke, August – 101
Magritte, René – 187, 200, **202**
M'Ahesa, Sent – 94
Manet, Éduard – 89
Marc, Franz – 101, 111, **115**
Marcks, Gerhard – 245, **251–52**
Masson, André – **189, 191**
Mataré, Ewald – **80**
Matta, Roberto – **193**
Mayerhofer, Maria (Maschka) 47
Mehring, Walter – 95
Meidner, Ludwig – **108–09**
Melzer, Moriz – **2**
Mense, Carlo – **214**
Miró, Joan – **197**
Modersohn-Becker, Paula – 23, **25**
Moholy-Nagy, László – 157, **160–61**
Moll, Marg – **76**
Möller, Otto – **66**
Molzahn, Johannes – 231, **232–33**
Mondrian, Piet – 231
Mosse, Rudolf – 9, 11
Muche, Georg – 156–57, **158–59**
Mueller, Otto – **42, 43, 45**, 47, **53**
Münter, Gabriele – 101, 110
Munch, Edward – 23, **30,** 34–35, **36–39**
Nagel, Otto – **144**
Nay, Ernst Wilhelm – **266**
Nerlinger, Oskar – **180**
Nienhaus, Max – **250**
Nolde, Ada – 61
Nolde, Emil – 35, 60–61, **62–63**, 254
Oppenheim, Meret – 200
Paalen, Wolfgang – **188**
Parsons, Betty – 194
Pechstein, Max – **44,** 46–47, **50–51**, 56, 61, 101
Picasso, Pablo – 13, 67, **91, 93,** 259, **269**
Plate, Hilde – **250**
Pollock, Jackson – 195
Prinzhorn, Hans – 254–55
Querner, Curt – **142, 145,** 207, **219**
Radziwill, Franz – **228–29,** 270–71, **272–73**
Reinhardt, Max – 34
Richter, Hans – 270–71, **276–77**
Rilke-Westhoff, Clara – **252**
Rosefeldt, Julian – 7, **134–35**
Roslund, Nell – 111
Rubinstein, Helena – 201
Rühle, Otto – 15–16, 137, 142
Schad, Christian – 207, 220, 224, **227**
Scharl, Josef – 119, **127,** 231, **236**
Scheibe, Richard – **250**
Schilling, Erna and Gerda – 47, 83
Schlemmer, Oskar – 13, 156–57, **164–65**
Schlichter, Rudolf – **206**
Schlingensief, Christoph – 18
Schmidt-Rottluff, Karl – **40,** 46, **49, 52,** 56–57
Schrimpf, Georg – 207, **210–11**
Schwitters, Kurt – 175, **184**
Sintenis, Renée – 77, 81, 245, **246–47**, 248–49
Siqueiros, David Alfaro – 195
Spies, Walter – **65, 69**
Steiner, Rudolf – 171
Steinhardt, Jakob – **68**
Stern, Irma – 6, **58, 64**
Strempel, Horst – **258,** 259, 270–71, **274–75**
Tanning, Dorothea – 200
Téllez, Javier – 7, 254–55, **256–57**
Thorak, Josef – 245
Trotz, Adolf – **71**
Udaltsova, Nadezhda – 6
Uhde, Wilhelm – 106
Uhlmann, Hans – **253**
Utech, Joachim – **250**
Vogeler, Heinrich – **136**, 137, **138–39**, 140
Vordemberge-Gildewart, Friedrich – 175, **176**
Wackerle, Joseph – **250**
Walden, Herwarth – 12, 101–02, 106, 110–11
Walden, Nell – 110, 159
Wamper, Adolf – **250**
Wauer, William – **77, 100**
Weidanz, Gustav – **252**
Werefkin, Marianne von – 111, **114**
Werner, Anton von – 9–11
Wiederhold, Sascha – 7, 9, 11–13, 19, **20–21**
Wiegmann Mucchi, Jenny – **252**

Photo Credits and Copyrights

If there is more than one image per page, the position is noted for clear attribution. The following abbreviations appear after a page number: t (top), b (bottom), l (left), m (middle) and r (right).

We sincerely thank all individuals, institutions and archives involved for their permission to reprint images and their support in producing the catalogue. The Nationalgalerie – Staatliche Museen zu Berlin has endeavored to identify copyright holders for all images. Copyright holders are requested to contact us in cases that remain unidentified, or if the information is incorrect or incomplete.

The works of the Nationalgalerie – Staatlichen Museen zu Berlin were photographed by:

Jörg P. Anders, pp. 25, 26, 30, 36 t, 36 b, 37 t, 37 b, 38 t, 38 bl, 38 br, 39 t, 39 b, 42, 44, 48 t, 49, 50, 52 t, 62–63, 68 l, 84 t, 85, 86 t, 91, 92, 102, 108-09, 115 t, 115 b, 118, 122-23, 154, 164 b, 165 r, 166 r, 169 m, 169 b, 174, 176 t, 184 t, 184 b, 185, 204–05, 208, 227, 237
Kai-Annett Becker, pp. 2, 133
S. Bethke, p. 233
Thomas Bruns, pp. 48 b, 151
Reinhard Friedrich, pp. 81, 186, 189 b, 250 tm
Klaus Göken, pp. 51, 75, 126 b, 143 t, 163, 180, 209, 251
Andres Kilger, pp. 22, 59, 76 t, 78 t, 78 b, 79 b, 80 tl, 80 tr, 96 t, 112, 113, 114 b, 117 t, 117 m, 117 b, 132, 143 b, 144 r, 145, 146–47, 152, 155 b, 158 b, 159 tr, 162 b, 181, 196, 199, 212 b, 214 t, 215, 216, 217, 218, 222, 230, 232, 242, 243, 250 tl, 250 tr, 250 ml/m/r and bl/m/r, 252 tm/r, 252 m/r, and bl/m/r, 260–61, 265, 268
Bernd Kuhnert, p. 142
André van Linn, pp. 40, 45, 52 b, 53, 66, 68 r, 84 b, 86 b, 114 t, 116 t, 116 b, 120, 121, 126 t, 127, 136, 138, 139, 144 l, 158 t, 159 tl, 159 b, 164 t, 166 l, 167 t, 167 b, 168, 206, 210, 211, 212 t, 213, 219, 228–29, 236, 238, 239, 258, 267, 266, 272–73.
Jochen Littkemann, pp. 79 t, 96 b, 97, 98 t, 99 b, 169 t, 188, 189 t, 190 t, 191, 192, 193, 197, 198, 202, 203, 223
Roman März, pp. 8, 24, 73, 76 b, 77 t, 77 b, 80 bl, 87, 99 t, 100, 104, 128 mr, 128 b, 129 t, 162 t, 177, 214 b, 252 tl, 252 ml, 253, 264, 276–77
Photographer unknown, pp. 226, 129 b.
Rolf Sachsse, p. 43
Reinhard Saczewski, pp. 31, 103
Volker-H. Schneider, pp. 26-27, 90
Bernd Sinterhauf, pp. 246 tl, 246 tr, 246 b, 247 tl, 247 tr, 247 b
Thomas Strub, pp. 256-257
Jens Ziehe, pp. 16, 65, 69, 72, 74, 80 br, 93 t, 93 b, 98 b, 128 t, 155 t, 160–61, 165 l, 244, 269, 274–75.

Lenders and corresponding images:

p. 11, © Jüdisches Museum Berlin, inv. no. GEM 90/28/0 / Roman März
p. 12, © KHM – Museumsverband, Theatermuseum Wien
p. 18 Filmgalerie 451
pp. 20-21, Galerie Brockstedt, © Sebastian Schobbert
p. 28, © Kunstmuseum Basel
p. 29 t, © bpk / Nationalgalerie, Staatliche Museen zu Berlin / Andres Kilger
p. 29 b, © Bildarchiv Foto Marburg / Franz Stoedtner
p. 32, Wenzel-Hablik-Stiftung, Itzehoe
p. 33, Wenzel-Hablik-Stiftung, Itzehoe
p. 34 l, © TU Berlin Architekturmuseum, inv. no. TBS 024,10
p. 34 r, © Munchmuseet, Oslo / VG Bild-Kunst, Bonn, 2021
p. 35, © Kunstbibliothek, Staatliche Museen zu Berlin / Dietmar Katz
p. 46, © Kirchner Museum Davos
p. 47, © Kirchner Museum Davos
p. 56, © Museum für Kunst und Gewerbe Hamburg / VG Bild Kunst, Bonn, 2021
p. 57 t, © Museum für Kunst und Gewerbe Hamburg / VG Bild Kunst, Bonn, 2021
p. 57 b, © Hermann Gerlinger, Würzburg
p. 58, The Irma Stern Trust Collection
p. 60, © mr-Kartographie
p. 61 t, © mr-Kartographie
p. 61 b, © Nolde Stiftung Seebüll
p. 64 The Irma Stern Trust Collection
p. 71 t, m, b, © absolut Medien
p. 82, © bpk / Kupferstichkabinett, Staatliche Museen zu Berlin / Dietmar Katz
p. 83 t, © Stiftung Stadtmuseum Berlin
p. 83 b, © Brücke-Museum, Berlin / Roman März
p. 88, © ullstein bild archiv / Felix H. Man
p. 89, l, © Galerie Neher, Essen
p. 89 r, © Kirchner Museum Davos
p. 94 t, © bpk / Staatsbibliothek zu Berlin / Dietmar Katz
p. 94 b, © Berlinische Galerie / Anja Elisabeth Witte / VG Bild-Kunst, Bonn, 2021
p. 95 t, © Berlinische Galerie / Kai-Annett Becker
p. 95 b, © VG Bild-Kunst, Bonn, 2021
p. 105, Galerie Lahumière, Paris
p. 106, © Deutsches Literaturarchiv Marbach
p. 107 l and r, © Deutsches Literaturarchiv Marbach
p. 111, © bpk
p. 110, © Deutsches Literaturarchiv Marbach
p. 124 m, r, © Collection Folio, Gallimard
p. 125, © mr-Kartographie
p. 130 t, Nationalgalerie, Staatliche Museen zu Berlin
p. 130 b, © Suddeutsche Zeitung / Scherl
p. 134, Julian Rosefeldt, © VG Bild-Kunst, Bonn, 2021
p. 135, Julian Rosefeldt, © VG Bild-Kunst, Bonn, 2021
p. 140, © SLUB Dresden
p. 141, © mr- Kartographie
p. 148 t, © Berlinische Galerie / Anja Elisabeth Witte
p. 148 b, © bpk / Deutsches Historisches Museum / Arne Psille
p. 149, © Sigrid Nerlinger / Stiftung Stadtmuseum Berlin / Michael Setzpfandt
p. 150 t, © Akademie der Künste, Berlin, Max Taut Photo Collection, no. 53, photo 22
p. 150 b, © Akademie der Künste, Berlin, Max Taut Photo Collection, no. 53, photo 20
p. 156, © Bauhaus-Archiv Berlin / VG Bild-Kunst, Bonn, 2021
p. 157 t, © Die Neue Sammlung – The Design Museum at the Pinakothek der Moderne / A. Laurenzo
p. 157 b, © Bauhaus-Archiv Berlin
p. 170 l, © Stiftelsen Hilma af Klints Verk / Albin Dahlstrom / Moderna Museet
p. 170 r, © Stiftelsen Hilma af Klints Verk
p. 171 t, © Universitatsbibliothek Heidelberg
p. 171 b, © Hilma af Klint Archives / Stiftelsen Hilma af Klints Verk
p. 172 tl, tr, b, © Stiftelsen Hilma af Klints Verk / Moderna Museet, Stockholm
p. 173 tl, tr, b, © Stiftelsen Hilma af Klints Verk / Moderna Museet, Stockholm
p. 176 b, © Galerie Brockstedt
p. 178, © bpk / Deutsches Historisches Museum
p. 179 l, © Landesarchiv Berlin, Histomap Berlin
p. 179 r, © Stiftung Stadtmuseum Berlin / Harry Croner
p. 182, © Erika Schmied / VG Bild-Kunst, Bonn, 2021
p. 190 b, © Isabella Matheus
p. 194 l, © Menil Collection Houston / VG Bild-Kunst, Bonn, 2021
p. 194 r, © Hans Namuth Ltd.
p. 195, © VG Bild-Kunst, Bonn, 2021
p. 200, © VG Bild-Kunst, Bonn, 2021
p. 201, © bpk / CNAC-MNAM / Dora Maar
p. 220 t, © AddF – Archiv der deutschen Frauenbewegung, Kassel, Sign.: A-F2-00066
284 285

p. 220 b, © bpk
p. 221, © Tamara de Lempicka Estate, LLC / VG Bild-Kunst, Bonn, 2021
p. 224, © Archiv Christoph von Weitzel
p. 225, © Archiv Christoph von Weitzel
p. 234, © National Archives (Still Picture Records, College Park, MD), Identifier 242-HB-32016-2
p. 235 t, © bpk / Zentralarchiv, Staatliche Museen zu Berlin
p. 235 b, © bpk / Busch-Reisinger Museum – Harvard Art Museums/ Art Resource, NY / Katya Kallsen
p. 240, © bpk / Kupferstichkabinett, Staatliche Museen zu Berlin / Dietmar Katz
p. 241 l, © National Gallery of Art, Washington, DC
p. 245 r, © Freies Deutsches Hochstift / Frankfurter Goethe-Museum * Mayen Beckmann
p. 248, © Stiftung Stadtmuseum Berlin / Sammlung H. Schneider
p. 249 t, © Ullstein Bild
p. 249 b, © Ullstein Bild / Hans Robertson / VG Bild-Kunst, Bonn, 2021
p. 254, © Universitätsbibliothek Heidelberg
p. 255, © picture-alliance / akg-images
p. 263, © Sigrid Nerlinger/ Akademie der Künste
p. 270, © Zentralarchiv, Staatliche Museen zu Berlin / VG Bild-Kunst, Bonn, 2021
p. 271 t, © HR Productions
p. 271 b, © Franz Radziwill Haus, Dangast / VG Bild-Kunst, Bonn, 2021
p. 287 © Markus Heltschl, 2021
© ZKM | Zentrum für Kunst und Medien Karlsruhe, 2021

Acknowledgements

Our special thanks to all the lenders to this exhibition:
Ulla and Heiner Pietzsch, Berlin
Julian Rosefeldt, Berlin
Deutsche Kinemathek – Museum für Film und Fernsehen, Berlin
Staatliche Museen zu Berlin, Alte Nationalgalerie
Staatliche Museen zu Berlin, Museum Berggruen
Staatliche Museen zu Berlin, Hamburger Bahnhof – Museum für Gegenwart – Berlin
absolut MEDIEN, Fridolfing
The Irma Stern Trust Collection, Cape Town
Wenzel-Hablik-Stiftung, Itzehoe
Markus Heltschl and the ZKM | Zentrum für Kunst und Medien Karlsruhe
Johannes-Molzahn-Centrum® für Documentation & Publikation, Kassel
State Tretyakov Gallery, Moscow
Indivision Lahumière, Paris
Pinacoteca do Estado de São Paulo
Stiftelsen Hilma af Klints Verk, Stockholm

Sincerest thanks go to everyone mentioned in the imprint, as well as all the individuals and institutions who assisted us in the making of the exhibition and catalogue, in particular:
Hanne Bergius, Harald Brommer, Francisca Cruz, Nadja Daehnke, Catarina Felixmüller, Bernhard Fulda, Anna-Catharina Gebbers, Hermann Gerlinger, Katharina Gräber, Tatyana Gubanova, Markus Heltschl, Martin Hoernes, Jessica Höglund, Horst Jordt, Andres Kilger, Peter Kropmanns, Babette Küster, Ove Kvavik, Aino Laberenz, Diane Lahumière, Susanne and Michael Liebelt, Wolfgang Maßmann, Molto Menz, Andres Pardey, Jürgen Pech, Hans Peter Reisse, Frieder Schlaich, Lisa-Marei Schmidt, Aya Soika, Javier Téllez, Zelfira Tregulova, Jochen Volz, Alexis von Poser, Christoph von Weitzel, Ulf Wagner, Nina Wegel, Kathy Wheeler, Wolfgang Wittrock, Isabel Wünsche, Kyllikki Zacharias, Christoph Zuschlag

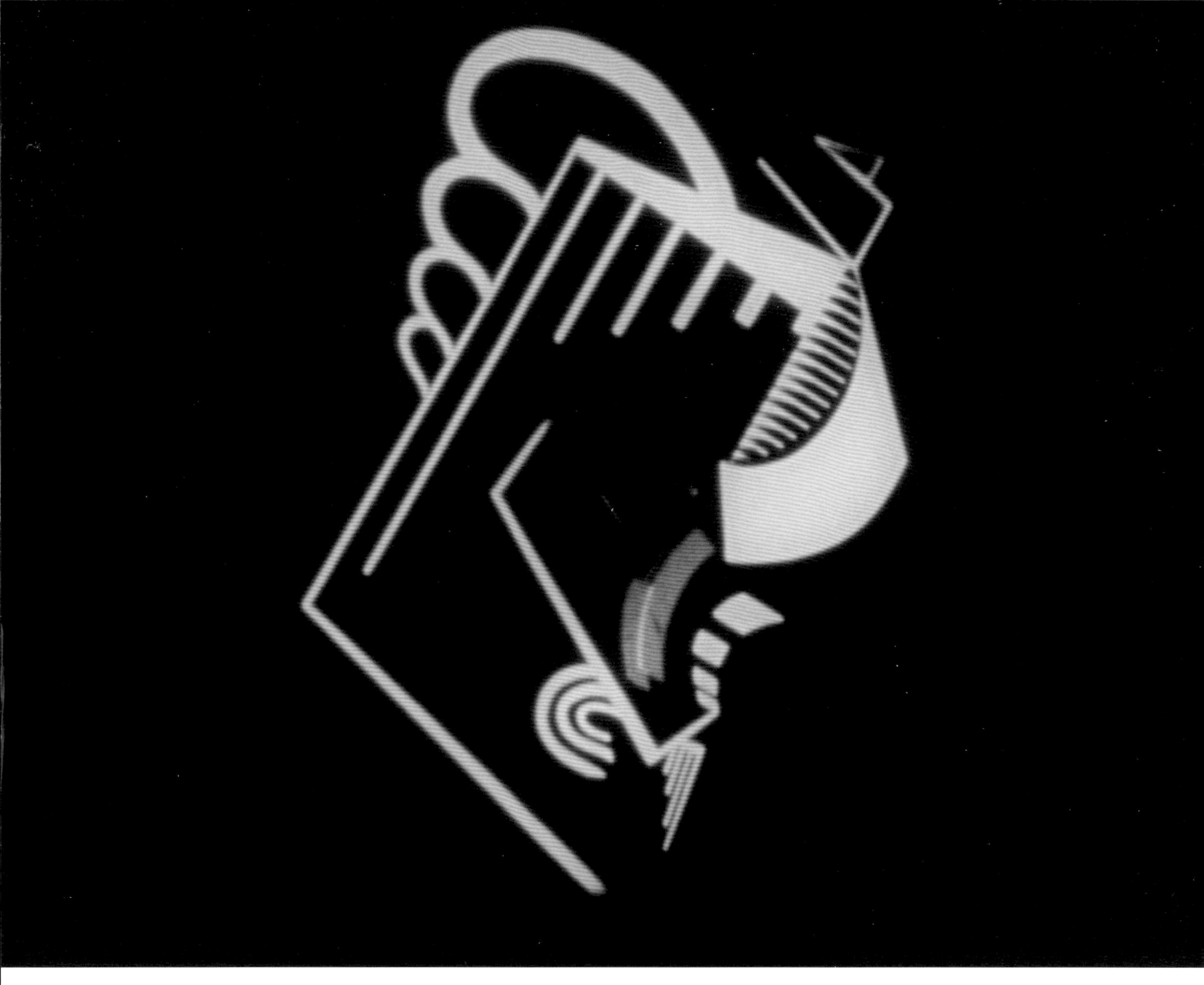

Viking Eggeling, *Symphonie Diagonale*, 1925
Film (Still), b/w, 7 Min.
Reconstruction: Markus Heltschl
On behalf of the ZKM | Zentrum für Kunst und Medien Karlsruhe
Digitisation supported by the "Förderprogramm Filmerbe" (FFE),
a film heritage funding programme

Imprint

This publication accompanies the presentation of the collection:
The Art of Society, 1900–1945: The Nationalgalerie Collection
22 August 2021 – 2 July 2023
Staatliche Museen zu Berlin, Neue Nationalgalerie

Catalogue
For the Nationalgalerie – Staatliche Museen zu Berlin, Dieter Scholz, Irina Hiebert Grun and Joachim Jäger (eds.)
Editor-in-chief: Dieter Scholz
Publication management for the museums: Sigrid Wollmeiner, Marika Mäder
Photo editing: Johanna Yeats
Translations: Moira Barrett, James Bell and Wendy Wallis
Graphic design and layout: Book Book, Berlin
Lithography: dpi-factory, Krefeld
Production management: DCV
Printing and binding: Gutenberg Beuys Feindruckerei, Langenhagen
Sales and marketing: DCV, sales@dcv-books.com

Audioguide
Production: Acoustiguide GmbH
Media consulting for the Museums: Wolfgang Davis
Coordination: Janet Röder
Copy editing: Veronika Deinzel, Irina Hiebert Grun, Janet Röder
Photo editing: Johanna Yeats

Exhibition
Curators: Dieter Scholz, Irina Hiebert Grun, Joachim Jäger
Exhibition coordination: Katharina Wippermann
Conservation: Hana Streicher, Ina Hausmann, Ella Dudew
Storage managers: Torsten Neitzel, Paul Markus
Communication: Fiona Geuß
Education and Outreach: Veronika Deinzel, Judith Boegner
Research assistance: Stefanie Meisgeier, Laila Borlak
Exhibition design: Holzer Kobler Architekturen in collaboration with David Chipperfield Architects
Exhibition graphics: 2xGoldstein
Exhibition construction: Körling Interiors
Audiovisual equipment: EIDOTECH
Installation: Lutz Bertram – Ausstellungstechnik und Objektbetreuung, Berlin (Lutz Bertram, Christoph Bannat, Tamon Imai, Oliver Lehmann, Ralph Müller, Thomas Ravens, Markus Wirthmann, Andre Zickert)
Lighting: 50 Lux / Victor Kegli

Bibliographic information published by the Deutsche Nationalbibliothek
The Deutsche Nationalbibliothek (German National Library) lists this publication in the Deutsche Nationalbibliographie; detailed bibliographic data is available online: http://www.dnb.de

ISBN 978-3-96912-034-7
Printed in Germany

www.smb.museum
www.dcv-books.com
Published by DCV

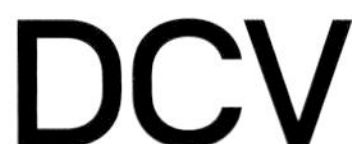